D1614647

SPECULUM DUORUM

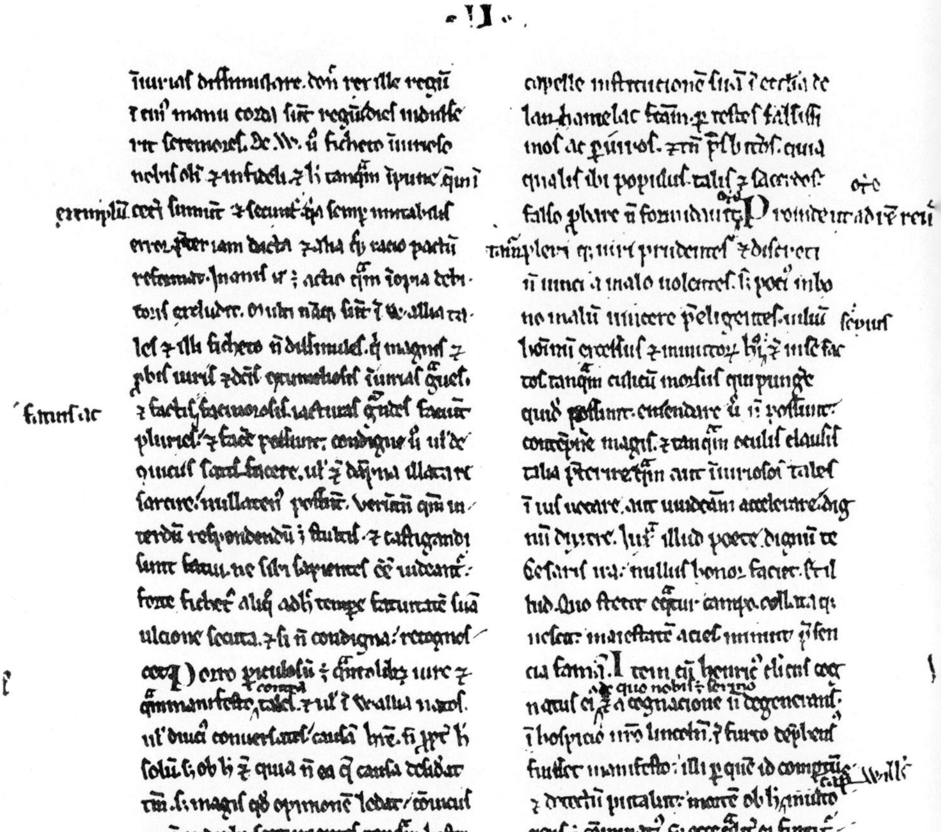

FIG. 1. Folio 66 verso

GIRALDUS CAMBRENSIS
SPECULUM DUORUM

OR

A MIRROR OF TWO MEN

Preserved in the Vatican Library in Rome
Cod. Reg. Lat. 470

Edited by YVES LEFÈVRE and R. B. C. HUYGENS
English translation by BRIAN DAWSON
General editor MICHAEL RICHTER

BOARD OF CELTIC STUDIES, UNIVERSITY OF WALES
HISTORY AND LAW SERIES, NO. 27

CARDIFF
UNIVERSITY OF WALES PRESS
1974

ISBN 0 7083 0544 X

Printed in Great Britain
at the University Press, Oxford
by Vivian Ridler
Printer to the University

PREFACE

IN 1861 the first volume of the complete works of Giraldus Cambrensis appeared in the *Rolls Series*; thirty years later seven more volumes were available. In 1920 a new edition, this time from the original manuscript, was prepared of the *De Invectionibus* by W. S. Davies and published as volume xxx of *Y Cymmrodor*. The present volume completes the edition of the works of Giraldus Cambrensis.

This volume is the result of research carried out, independently for the greater part, by R. B. C. Huygens, Yves Lefèvre, and myself, and combined for this edition at a late stage. In the present volume, the responsibilities have been divided: Yves Lefèvre is responsible for the textual edition and notes of Parts I and II, R. B. C. Huygens for the same of the Letters, while I have written the Introduction. Yet all three editors have contributed substantially to every section of the volume, and it is hoped that the advantages achieved by this effort outweigh any shortcomings which might occur in a joint scheme. An English translation, by Brian Dawson, was included at the request of the Board of Celtic Studies.

I myself am responsible for co-ordinating the text and notes at the final stage, while profiting at the same time from suggestions and advice which were generously given by my co-editors: any faults which remain must be my responsibility. Both my co-editors normally publish in French, and it was left to me to present the notes to the text in English.

As is always the case when a volume is ready for the press, the number of people who have helped at various stages with the work is great, and the debt to them remains to be acknowledged. Firstly, we enjoyed the hospitality and working facilities of the Vatican Library in Rome where the manuscript of the *Speculum Duorum* has been preserved. A microfilm of the manuscript has been purchased by the National Library of Wales, Aberystwyth, and is available there for inspection. My thanks are due to the Librarian and staff of the National Library for much help with my work. The same also applies to my colleagues in the Department of Welsh History at the University College of Wales, Aberystwyth. The list would not be complete without naming specifically six people who have done more than their share in helping with the work: Professor C. N. L. Brooke, who kindly

consented to read the complete typescript and whose valuable suggestions have greatly improved it, Dr. Susan Davies and Mrs. N. M. Fryde, who have given generously of their time and expertise in the subject, and Professor Glanmor Williams, who suggested that the work should be published in the *History and Law Series* of the *Board of Celtic Studies*. My debt to him is particularly great. Mr. Edward James, by kindly offering his assistance in proof-reading, has saved me from numerous mistakes, rough passages, and inconsistencies. It is a great pleasure also to record Dr. R. Brinley Jones's unfailing energy and encouragement to promote the publication of this book, which now appears in the year following the 750th anniversary of the author's death.

Finally, I should like to thank the authorities of the University of Wales for the honour of electing me a Senior Fellow. Without this substantial support I should never have been able to complete the work.

MICHAEL RICHTER

CONTENTS

LIST OF FIGURES

(BY PERMISSION OF THE BIBLIOTHECA
APOSTOLICA VATICANA, ROME)

ABBREVIATIONS

BBCS   *Bulletin of the Board of Celtic Studies*

CC   *Corpus Christianorum*, Series Latina

CSEL   *Corpus Scriptorum Ecclesiasticorum Latinorum*

Decret. Greg. IX: *Corpus Iuris Canonici*, vol. 2 (as below under Gratian)

Dig.   Digesta, *Corpus Iuris Civilis*, ed. T. Mommsen, P. Krüger, R. Schoell, 3 vols. (Berlin, 1954)

Dugdale, *Mon. Angl.*:   *Monasticon Anglicanum*, ed. R. Dodsworth and W. Dugdale, new edn. J. Caley, H. Ellis, B. Bandinel, 6 vols. in 8 (London, 1817–30)

Ep. Acts   J. C. Davies, *Episcopal Acts relating to Welsh Dioceses, 1066–1272*, 2 vols. (Historical Society of the Church in Wales Publications, nos. 1, 3, 4, 1946–8)

Gratian   *Corpus Iuris Canonici*, ed. Aemilius Friedberg, 2 vols. (Lipsiae, 1879–81)

Inst.   Institutiones (as above under Dig.)

JL   *Regesta Pontificum Romanorum ab condita ecclesia ad a. 1198*, 2nd edn. by S. Löwenfeld, F. Kaltenbrunner, P. Ewald, 2 vols. (Berlin, 1885–8, repr. Graz, 1958)

MGH AA   Monumenta Germaniae Historica, Auctores Antiquissimi

Migne, *P.L.*   J. P. Migne, *Patrologia Latina*, 217+4 index vols. (Paris, 1841–64)

NLWJ   *National Library of Wales Journal*

NMT   Nelson's Medieval Texts

Op.   Unless otherwise specified, Giraldus Cambrensis, *Opera*, 8 vols. (R.S., 1861–91)

R.S.   *Rerum Britannicarum Medii Aevi Scriptores*, 99 vols. (London, 1858–1911), Rolls Series

H. Walther, *Lateinische Sprichwörter*:   Hans Walther, *Lateinische Sprichwörter und Sentenzen des Mittelalters in alphabetischer Anordnung*, 5 vols. (Göttingen, 1963–7)

INTRODUCTION

THE *Speculum Duorum* is one of the last works of Giraldus Cambrensis (whose real name was Giraldus de Barri), *c.* 1146–*c.* 1223; it is printed here for the first time in full.[1] It has been preserved in a single manuscript (referred to in the present edition as *V*) and forms part of the *Codices Reginenses Latini*, MS. 470 in the Vatican Library in Rome.[2] The codex, deriving from the first quarter of the thirteenth century, contains two works by Giraldus, both written in Latin. The other work is his *De Invectionibus*,[3] of which the copy in the Vatican manuscript is also the only one known to exist.

Hardly anything is known of the provenance of this manuscript. It would appear to have been written at Lincoln but has left no trace in the old catalogues there. It was part of the library of Queen Christina of Sweden, whose collection was bought by Pope Alexander VIII in 1690.[4] It seems to have come to Queen Christina from the antiquarian Paul Petau of Orleans (died 1614), whose Greek motto is written on f. 3ʳ of our manuscript. Petau also annotated the codex in various places (e.g. ff. 2ᵛ, 13ᵛ, 15ʳ, 23ʳ, 78ʳ). The longest note of his is written on f. 1ᵛ; it lists several manuscripts containing works by Giraldus at Cambridge and refers to Thomas James, *Ecloga Oxonio-Cantabrigiensis* (London 1600).[5] The codex also has other annotations by an English hand of the fifteenth century which the editors were unable to identify.

[1] Small portions have been edited by Yves Lefèvre, 'Un brouillon du XIIIᵉ siècle: le manuscrit 470 du fonds de la reine Christine. Étude sur quelques inédits de Giraud de Barri', *Mélanges d'archéologie et d'histoire*, 58, 1941–6, pp. 145–77. Letter No. 3 in *Epistolarum Pars*, below, pp. 168–75, has been edited by R. B. C. Huygens, 'Une lettre de Giraud le Cambrien à propos de ses ouvrages historiques', *Latomus*, 26, 1965, pp. 90–100. This letter has also been transcribed by Hugh MacKinnon, 'The Life and Works of William de Montibus' (unpublished D.Phil. thesis Oxford, 1959), Appendix I, pp. 1–4; also Letter No. 4 has been edited by R. B. C. **Huygens**, 'Deux sermonnaires médiévaux: Tétère de Nevers et Giraud de Barri. Textes inédits', *Studi medievali*, x, 3, 1969, pp. 271–96.

[2] Andreas Wilmart, *Bibliothecae Apostolicae Vaticanae codices manuscripti recensiti iussu Pii XII Pontificis Maximi, Codices Reginenses Latini*, Tomus ii, nos. 251–500 (Rome, 1945), pp. 631–4.

[3] W. S. Davies, ed., 'Giraldus Cambrensis: De Invectionibus', *Y Cymmrodor*, xxx, 1920.

[4] J. Bignami Odier, 'Le fonds de la reine à la Bibliothèque Vaticane', *Collectanea Vaticana in honorem Anselmi M. Card. Albareda a Bibliotheca Apostolica edita*, Studi e Testi 219 (Città del Vaticano, 1962), pp. 159–89, here p. 174.

[5] 'In catal. lib. Bibl. Cantabrigie p. 69 ponitur Giraldi Cambrensis de topographia Hibernie. Item Itinerarium Giraldi et tam Cambrie quam Britannie descriptio. Et p. 78

Bale's sixteenth-century catalogue of British historians[6] lists: 'Speculum commonitorium lib. 1, Speculum consolatorium lib. 1, Remordentes epistolae lib. 1, Querulum carmen lib. 1.' This obviously refers to the *Speculum Duorum*, yet this entry would appear to stem not from any knowledge of the manuscript itself, but of Giraldus' own *Catalogus Brevior Librorum Suorum*.[7]

The codex, bound in dark red leather, consists of 104 folios of vellum measuring on average 230–3 × 165 mm. and is written, for the most part, in double columns of 29 to 52 lines. The *De Invectionibus* covers folios 1–50[ra],[8] the *Speculum Duorum* starts on the same folio in the second column (f. 50[rb]) and comes to an end on f. 104[va]. The text of both works was written by a number of scribes. Chapter headings are generally rubricated, initials are for the most part executed in plain red or blue (alternating), while some initials in the letters appended to the *Speculum Duorum* show more elaborate details.

Editorial methods

With only one copy of the text available for editing, it has been thought desirable to retain the spelling in the manuscript as far as possible. Uniformity has been introduced with regard to capital letters, which have been given to all personal names and place-names. Abbreviations have been expanded, except for personal and place-names where the correct expansion is doubtful. In these instances the full names are given in brackets, e.g. R(irid). All punctuation is the editors', and while the division into paragraphs in general follows the rubrics in the manuscript, some long paragraphs have been subdivided where it seemed advisable. Place-names in the translation and index are given in a standardized version;[9] most places are marked on the Ordnance Survey of Great Britain one inch to one mile map (7th series, 1952).

The manuscript of the *Speculum Duorum* is very close to the author, although it is certainly not a holograph. It falls into two distinct sections

descriptio Britannie per Giraldum Sylvestrem cum mappa Britannie et Hibernie. Item Itinerarium Cambrie per eundem. Et dialogus eiusdem de Ecclesia Menevensi. Et Giraldi de Barri vel Giraldi dicti Cambrensis de Vitiis quorundam Episcoporum Lincoln et aliorum.' For the information about Thomas James's catalogue the author is indebted to Professor C. R. Cheney.

[6] John Bale, *Scriptorum Illustrium maioris Brytannie . . . catalogus* (Basileae, 1559), pp. 250–2.

[7] *Op.* i (*Rolls Series, no.* 21), p. 422.

[8] A full analysis is given by Wilmart, loc. cit.

[9] In the spelling of place-names we follow *A Gazetteer of Welsh Place Names, Rhestr o Enwau Lleoedd*, ed. Elwyn Davies, (UWP, Cardiff, 1957), or Melville Richards, *Welsh Administrative and Territorial Units* (UWP, Cardiff, 1969).

which we call (*a*) the primitive text, and (*b*) the additions. The primitive text is an early complete version of the *Speculum Duorum* which was later enlarged. It has been thought advisable to distinguish in the printed version between primitive text and additions and thus all material falling into category (*b*) has been marked by brackets. Longer additions are marked by half brackets ⌐ ¬. A further distinction has been made for all additions and corrections within the additions. These are marked by double half brackets ⌐⌐ ¬¬. The reader will see the purpose of this policy by consulting the accompanying plates. At times these short additions merely correct the scribe, who had left out a letter, a syllable, or a word. It is possible that such correcting was done by the author himself, but since we do not possess any authentic specimen of Giraldus' hand which would make a comparison of handwriting possible, this cannot be ascertained. Occasionally, words which are essential to the understanding of the text are missing. These instances have been marked, and wherever the missing word can be established beyond reasonable doubt, it has been added to the text in angle brackets ⟨ ⟩. The same also applies to all other emendations by the editors, of which there are very few.

The complexity of the manuscript made it necessary to distinguish not only between the recto and verso of the folios (r, v), but also between the two columns on each folio, by referring to them as a and b.

Analysis of the manuscript

The gatherings of the manuscript consist on average of four sheets of parchment, which produce eight folios.[10] The sequence of gatherings is as follows:

1. Folios o (glued to the cover), a, b, I. Folio oᵛ gives the old classmark of the manuscript: 1390.[11] Folio Iᵛ has the note quoted above.[12] a and b are of modern origin. They are blank apart from giving the modern class-mark on f. aᵛ: 470, and they were added, so it seems, when the codex received its present binding.
2. Folios 1, 2.
3. Folios 3–10 (regular); the single folios are marked on the bottom right-hand corner by the letters *a–h* (*b* cut off).

---

[10] The description is based on Wilmart, but supplemented and corrected whenever necessary.

[11] From the catalogue of Montfaucon, *Bibliotheca Bibliothecarum Manuscriptorum* (1793).

[12] Above, n. 5.

4. Folios 11–18 (regular), marked likewise by letters *a–h*.

5. Folios 19–26 (regular).

6. Folios 27–33 (irregular). The gathering consists of six leaves, f. 31 being inserted after the middle sheet.

7. Folios 34–40 (irregular). This gathering also consists of six leaves, f. 36 being inserted before the middle sheet.

8. Folios 41–54 (irregular). The primitive text is written on ten leaves, ff. 41/54, 42/52, 44/50, 45/49, and 47/48, folios 43, 46, 51, and 53 having additional text.

9. Folios 55–63 (irregular). The gathering consists of eight leaves, f. 57 being inserted between the second and the third sheet.

10. Folios 64–77 (irregular). The primitive text is written on eight leaves, ff. 64/77, 65/74, 66/73, and 68/72, folios 67, 69, 70, 71, 75, and 76 having additional text.

11. Folios 78–85 (regular).

12. Folios 86–92 (irregular). The gathering consists of six leaves, f. 86 having additional text.

From f. 93 to the end, the original composition of the manuscript can no longer be safely established. Folios 93/94 form one bifolium, folio 95 is a single leaf. The folio which should follow this is at present misplaced as f. 103. Folios numbered 96/99 and 97/98 form one sheet each, as did, presumably, folios 100/101. Folios 102 and 104 were possibly single leaves from the beginning.

The transition from one gathering to the following one is occasionally indicated by a catchword, e.g. ff. 26/27: *G credere*; ff. 33/34: *Thome*; ff. 40/41: *denotare*; ff. 63/64: *sigillo nostro*; ff. 85/86: *sua*. Between f. 3ʳ (*Incipit Liber Invectionum*) and f. 92ᵛ (*et in commune ec-*[clesiam]) the leaves within the gatherings are ordered either by letters written on the recto of each folio, as in gatherings 3 and 4, or by catchword, as in 2 and 5–9, with the exception of 10, which is the end of *Speculum Duorum, Secunda Pars*, and the beginning of the later *Epistolarum Pars*.

The text is, for the greatest part, rubricated in a simple way, in red and blue. The chapter headings of the *De Invectionibus* and the *Speculum Duorum* are executed in red. The beginning of a new paragraph in the latter is marked by capital letters, alternately in red and blue. In addition, ff. 3–94 have a rubric at the head of the folio, consisting of *I PARS*, *II PARS*, etc., in the *De Invectionibus* and the *Speculum Duorum*, and of *EPL' PARS* on ff. 79–94 (on f. 26ᵛ we read *II PARS* instead of *IIII PARS*, a mistake which has not been corrected). The rubric was made after the primitive text was written. It can be seen, however, in various

places (e.g. ff. 54, 58, 59, 60, 64, 65, 73, 75, 77) that it was made after
only part of the additions had been written. There is no rubric at the top
of folios 95–104, and it would thus appear that the last two letters of
Epistolarum Pars were added to the manuscript after the rubrication of
the preceding pages.

The manuscript was written by a number of contemporary scribes,
and the text shows a variety of fairly good book-hands which (as will
be shown from other evidence) all belong to the first quarter of the
thirteenth century. The work of the different scribes is, however,
extremely difficult to disentangle, and this is a task which has to be left
for special study.[13] For a better understanding of the composition of
the manuscript in this edition a rough and schematic classification of
hands, applied to the primitive text alone, will have to suffice.

> Hand I, ff. 3–10
> Hand II, ff. 11–17
> Hand III, ff. 18–40
> Hand IV, ff. 1–2; 41–50 (except for f. 46)
> Hand V, ff. 50–77^r
> Hand VI, ff. 78–92^r (?f. 46)
> Hand VII, ff. 92^v–95^v, 103
> Hand VIII, ff. 96–7,
> Hand IX, ff. 98–102; 104.

Date of the De Invectionibus

The text of the *Speculum Duorum* starts on the second column of f. 50^r.
This folio forms part of gathering 8, and so another gathering was
not started for the new work. If this does not explain much, at least it
suggests that the primitive text of the *Speculum Duorum* was copied
into the *Reginensis* MS. after the *De Invectionibus* had been written.
The composition of the latter work has not been discussed in the edition
by W. S. Davies, nor can it be fully done here. Only if a firm *terminus
a quo* for the writing of the *Speculum Duorum* in the present codex is
found can the composition of the work itself be profitably discussed.
The text of the *Speculum Duorum* as we have it has been described by
Yves Lefèvre as a working copy of the author's,[14] which shows that the
Speculum Duorum is the first full version of the work, a version, moreover,
not in a final stage, but subject to numerous enlargements. It is enough

---

[13] Further studies on the *Speculum Duorum* have been announced by Yves Lefèvre.
[14] Loc. cit. (above ,n. 1). For a more detailed discussion see below, pp. lvii ff.

to cite evidence from the contents of the *De Invectionibus* which will put all discussion of the *Speculum Duorum* on a new basis.

Giraldus himself speaks about the dates of the writing of his works only in the most general terms and is notoriously imprecise. So he states that the *De Invectionibus* was written 'anno quasi quinquagesimo'.[15] The date of his birth has been fixed as approximately 1146, so his own statement would bring us to the year 1196. This is obviously too early, because the *De Invectionibus* deals with Giraldus' fight over his election to the see of St. David's in 1199, and the dispute concerning his election lasted for four years. While the whole work thus cannot have been written before 1203, Giraldus says specifically that he wrote the first book of it, to which alone the title *De Invectionibus*[16] really applies, in the first year of his suit in Rome, which brings us to the year 1200.[17] When therefore he refers to the *De Invectionibus* as having been written in his fifties Giraldus may have had only the first part in mind.[18] Furthermore, it is not necessary to assume that he wrote the rest of the book very early after his defeat. Two other works of his deal with the same controversy. Of these the *De Rebus a se Gestis* is the earlier one, dating from *c.* 1208. When compared with the *De Invectionibus*, it appears that the *De Rebus* already contained the great bulk of the material.[19] Also Giraldus himself says[20] that he copied part vi of the *De Invectionibus* from the *De Rebus*. This part vi is the last part of that work. Out of its twenty-six chapters no fewer than twenty-one have the same heading as those in the *De Rebus*; these chapters therefore appear to have gone straight from the earlier work into the later one. Moreover, it is possible that more chapters of the *De Rebus* appear in the *De Invectionibus*, but under different headings.[21]

The third work of Giraldus which covers the same ground is the *De Iure et Statu Menevensis Ecclesiae*. It is the latest of the three. It provides information on issues which are still open in the *Speculum Duorum*, which, we have seen, was copied after the completion of the *De*

---

[15] *Op.* iii, p. 373.

[16] Ed. W. S. Davies, p. 130: 'Expliciunt invectiones et responsiones. Incipiunt quedam ad invectiones.'

[17] Cf. below, p. 164, ll. 65–7: 'anno laboris nostri primo . . . editus in curia libellus hic erat.'

[18] Cf. below, p. 162, ll. 45–8: 'Sciant etiam illi, qui in librum De Invectionibus tituli intuitu solum tam acriter invehuntur, quod licet due vel tres epistole prime invective videantur, . . . Sed mos est in scripturis a principiis libros denominari.'

[19] This was in the third part, which is now lost, apart from a small fraction, but the content of this book of the *De Rebus* can be estimated from the still extant table of contents.

[20] *De Invectionibus*, vi, 1, p. 204; he also copied one chapter from the *De Rebus* into the late *Speculum Ecclesie*, cf. *Op.* iv, pp. 340 f.

[21] *De Invect.* chapters 3–24 correspond to *De Rebus* chapters 218–38.

Invectionibus. This trilogy on Giraldus' fight for St. David's is not simply a mechanical repetition of identical material. The *De Rebus* gives the chronological account, the *De Invectionibus* digests it systematically, and the *De Iure* departs from the source-book method altogether and gives instead a discussion, based on the available material, of the respective rights and wrongs in the St. David's election and the twin issue of the archbishopric for Wales.

Part vi of the *De Invectionibus* could have been copied into our manuscript at any time after the completion of the *De Rebus*. On the other hand, the chapters which now form part v, which do not seem to have been preserved anywhere else, refer to specific events which make it possible to place this part of the *De Invectionibus* into a firmer chronological framework. Giraldus here mentions the election of Stephen Langton to the archbishopric of Canterbury, which took place in 1206.[22] Then he speaks of Meiler fitzHenry as 'tunc Hibernie justiciarius',[23] which points to a date after 1208, in which year Meiler lost the justiciarship of Ireland. Finally, Giraldus refers to Pope Innocent III (1198–1216) in terms which strongly suggest that the pope was already dead.[24] This particular passage of part v of *De Invectionibus* cannot therefore have been written before late in 1216 at the earliest, and thus the year 1216 becomes the earliest possible date for the copying of the *Speculum Duorum* into the *Reginensis* MS. That the *Speculum Duorum* in its present form is the product of a long process of work will be shown later. Contrary to traditional opinion we have to assume that this work kept Giraldus' attention to the last years of his life. The core of the *Speculum* is a letter which Giraldus wrote to his nephew Giraldus de Barri *c.* 1208. Ten years later the author felt strongly enough about the dispute to prepare a book on it for publication.

The Speculum Duorum *among the works of Giraldus*

The *Speculum Duorum* is, in some respects, unique in the ranks of Giraldus' works.[25] It deals more than any other with a personal controversy of the author's, a rather trivial subject in itself. Not that Giraldus saw it in such light; on the contrary, he had been betrayed and deserted by so many people in the past that the ingratitude of his nephew Giraldus

[22] *De Invect.* v, 22, p. 202. [23] Ibid. v, 14, p. 194.
[24] Ibid. v, 12, p. 192: '. . . hospitalis Sancti Spiritus, qui locus scola Anglicana dici solet, ab Innocentio Tercio, qui tunc prefuit, egregie constitutus . . .'
[25] All previous editions and a fairly full account of secondary material on Giraldus are contained in E. A. Williams, 'A Bibliography of Giraldus Cambrensis, *c.* 1147–*c.* 1223', *NLWJ*, xii, 1962–2, pp. 97–140. This has been brought up to date below, p. lxix.

de Barri (fitzPhilip) and William de Capella towards their common benefactor may well have been the straw that broke the camel's back. Giraldus had suffered many set-backs in his life, but he found it impossible to accept that one of his most bitter disappointments should have been engineered by his nephew whom he had raised to a comfortable position. The world was against him, there was no faith even in closest relatives: this had to be shown to posterity, as an example of evil and a warning not to be generous light-heartedly. Thus the subject of the book is not only trivial, but its treatment pompous, sadly lacking in a sense of proportion.

The *Speculum Duorum* is the least finished of Giraldus' writings which have been preserved. It shows the author still at work, enlarging the original version—he never shortened any of his works on revision!— and finally adding to it material which is helpful to a better understanding of the *Speculum*, in a third part: letters and a prologue to a sermon. The constant revision of his texts is one of the basic features of Giraldus' working method; yet the extent of the changes and amplifications in most cases cannot now be estimated, and will probably never be fully evaluated. A new critical edition of his works might improve our knowledge in this field.[26] The *Speculum Duorum*, however, is a special case. In the first instance, what is preserved is the working copy only, and secondly the core of the work is a letter, not a treatise. In the form in which it is now extant it does not even share the basic elements of treatises by Giraldus, since it has no preface nor a table of contents. These are always written and added after a work has been completed, something for which the *De Invectionibus* of the Vatican manuscript gives clear palaeographical evidence. The same manuscript does not even leave room for either a preface or a table of contents for the *Speculum Duorum*. Thus it would seem that initially this work was intended as little more than an appendix to the *De Invectionibus*.

The *Speculum* is based on a letter by Master Giraldus, the former archdeacon of Brecon, to his nephew and successor. The uncle was an ambitious man, but perhaps not sufficiently realistic in his ambitions. He failed in a number of cases to get where he wanted to go, but seldom did failure discourage him; he never questioned whether he was attempting the impossible, but readily shifted blame to other persons or institutions. Yet Giraldus was not insensitive to failure. This comes out best in the small fraction of his correspondence which has been pre-

---

[26] With the exception of the Irish works, which are at present being re-edited, and apart from the uncritical edition of *De Invectionibus*, all of Giraldus' works are available only in editions from the last century in the Rolls Series, no. 21.

served. If more had survived, one would be able to grasp even better
the complex and sensitive personality of this great individualist. His
Symbolum Electorum[27] gives a good foretaste. It contains in its first
part one sermon and thirty-one letters which throw valuable light on an
otherwise obscure period of his life, the decade before his election to the
bishopric of St. David's in 1199. The letters vary both in quality and
interest, but there are a few of a high standard. Closest to the spirit of
the *Speculum Duorum* come the letters to Peter de Leia, bishop of St.
David's (1176–98),[28] and to Hugh of Avalon, bishop of Lincoln (1186–
1200).[29] Not all of them are written in a spirit of complaint. There are
sober instructions by Giraldus to his officials in the archdeaconry of
Brecon[30] and rather touching letters to Adam, abbot of Evesham,[31] and
to William Foliot, precentor of Hereford.[32] Others, like the letter to
Walter Map, archdeacon of Oxford (died *c.* 1210–12),[33] are in typical
Giraldine style, advising on matters of intellectual activity, a field in
which he felt thoroughly competent. On the whole, however, the impression conveyed by the *Symbolum Electorum* is one of a man who
has been wronged and is ready to defend himself. The work starts
appropriately with a bitter complaint by Giraldus to William, abbot of
Garendon, about William Wibert,[34] a treacherous monk and at one time
abbot of the Cistercian house of Biddlesden (Bucks.), whose deposition
in 1198 resulted from an inquiry started by Giraldus,[35] and it comes to
a grandiose climax in a letter to the chapter of St. David's.[36]

Nor is this all. We know from a letter by Giraldus to William de
Vere, bishop of Hereford (1186–98), of the existence of a long account
in which he discussed the injustice he had suffered from Bishop Peter
of St. David's.[37] The latter unfortunately has not survived. It was
perhaps written in a language which made it unsuitable to be included
in a florilegium such as the *Symbolum Electorum*; it must have been of
considerable length since Bishop Peter complained to Giraldus about
that letter 'which people call a libel'.[38]

Yet the *Speculum Duorum* would not fit happily in the *Symbolum
Electorum*, for although it was originally a letter, in the course of revision
it assumed features which made it more like a treatise, in particular its

---

[27] *Op.* i, pp. 197–395.   [28] Nos. vii, xix.   [29] No. xxii.
[30] No. xx.   [31] No. ix.   [32] No. xxiii.   [33] No. xxiv.   [34] No. i.
[35] D. David Knowles, 'Some Enemies of Gerald of Wales', *Studia Monastica*, i, 1959,
pp. 137–41; on Biddlesden cf. Leopold Janauschek, *Originum Cisterciensium Tomus* i
(Vindobonae, 1877), p. 94; also D. Knowles, C. N. L. Brooke, V. London, *The Heads
of Religious Houses, England and Wales, 940–1216* (Cambridge, 1972), p. 126.
[36] No. xxxi.   [37] No. xxix.
[38] 'quas vestri, ut dicitur, famosum libellum appellant', no. viii, *Op.* i, p. 228; see
Corpus Iuris Civilis, Cod. 9. 36. 1 'De famosis libellis'.

subdivision into two parts. Its most interesting feature, however, is the fact that it is based on a genuine letter, that it was meant ultimately to be a treatise, but that the transformation was not completed. The initial letter to the nephew was already very long,[39] but, whereas from a treatise one expects at least a full coverage of the ground, a story complete in itself, the study of the *Speculum Duorum* shows that a number of issues remain obscure to the reader. There are many allusions, especially to the central point of controversy, namely the appeal launched by the nephew and his tutor against Master Giraldus at Hereford, but there is no associated narrative. Private letters tend to be incomplete to the outside reader in this way because they are based on some situation known only to the persons involved. Thus in giving supplementary illustration to a well-known background, the letter behind the *Speculum Duorum* would have been satisfactory in information both to the sender and to the recipient.[40]

It would appear that Giraldus himself was left with the impression that the *Speculum Duorum*, once it had passed beyond the stage of private correspondence, was not satisfactory in its two parts. In the first place, he added information to the reader which was superfluous for the nephew but essential to a better understanding of the dispute, and then he added the body of letters to the book in a third part. Without these letters it would be more difficult to understand the story behind the *Speculum Duorum*. Yet there is no clear design behind the selection of these particular letters. Apart from Epp. 3 and 8 they bear directly on the issue between uncle and nephew, but Ep. 7, which gives the clearest account of the quarrel, has been added very late, after the rubrication of the main text. It is significant that this relatively full account is written to the prior of Lanthony, a friend of Giraldus', who was not directly involved as were the nephew, William de Capella, or Bishop Geoffrey, and who therefore had to be informed more fully.

The career of Giraldus

The career of Giraldus Cambrensis, as far as it is relevant to an understanding of the *Speculum Duorum*, can be briefly told.[41] He was born, of

[39] Below, p. 160, ll. 27–9 (Ep. 2): 'epistolam nostram nepoti nostro transmissam et exuberante materia in libellum conversam famosum, ut fertur, libellum vocant.'

[40] An interesting illustration of this is given below, p. 250, l. 163. In this letter to Prior Gilbert of Lanthony by Gloucester Giraldus covers the story fairly fully, but still reminds Gilbert of information which he has provided by word of mouth: 'satis viva voce vobis indicavimus.'

[41] The best single study is F. M. Powicke, 'Gerald of Wales', *Bulletin of the John Rylands Library*, xii, 1928, pp. 389–410; the latest study, M. Richter, *Giraldus Cambrensis* (Aberystwyth, 1972), deals with the integration of the Welsh Church into the

Norman-Welsh parents, at Manorbier in Pembrokeshire *c.* 1146.
During his long life—he died *c.*1223—he became the greatest writer
in Latin whom Wales has ever produced. It is typical of his style that he
wrote not from a position of detachment, as an observer of events, but
in an attractive, subjective way inspired by his experience in the political
and ecclesiastical events of his time. His career was remarkable, but
certainly not smooth. Failure and disappointment by far outweighed
success. Twice he was a candidate for the bishopric of his home diocese
of St. David's in the south-west of Wales, first in 1176 at the death of
his uncle, Bishop David fitzGerald (bp. 1148–76), and again in 1198.
The first bid for the bishropic was brushed aside quickly by the secular
and ecclesiastical authorities in England. His second election in 1199,
however, caused a prolonged dispute at the papal court between Canterbury and St. David's, and it was declared invalid by Pope Innocent
III in 1203 only, after four years of negotiation. It was not Giraldus
as a person who was objectionable to Canterbury but rather the idea
he stood for and of which he became one of the principal champions:
to separate the Welsh Church from the jurisdiction of Canterbury. It
has often been misunderstood that Giraldus did not only want an archbishopric for Wales under the primacy of Canterbury, but that initially
he wanted to have the Welsh province subject to Rome alone.[42] He
wanted to become archbishop *and* primate of Wales. He thus wished
to secure the privileges which had been granted to the Scottish and the
Irish Church in the second half of the twelfth century. If Giraldus
was not the first person to attempt this,[43] however, he was the last one
seriously to do so.[44] Thus since Giraldus was the leading personality in

province of Canterbury during the twelfth century and with Giraldus' view of the
Welsh. The general reader should also consult H. E. Butler, *The Autobiography of
Giraldus Cambrensis* (London, 1937).

[42] As a concession to Hubert Walter, Giraldus proposed the following terms in 1202:
'iterum si placet [ecclesia Menevensis] metropolitica fiat, sed ecclesie Cantuariensi
subiecta, sicut una ecclesia metropolis alii metropoli *iure primacie* subici solet', *De
Invect.* iv, 1, p. 162.

[43] It is not quite clear whether Bishop Bernard (1115–48) worked towards an archbishopric of Wales *within* the primatial jurisdiction of Canterbury or towards a position
of archbishop and primate of Wales. On him see M. Richter, 'Canterbury's Primacy in
Wales and the First Stage of Bishop Bernard's Opposition', *Journal of Ecclesiastical
History*, xxii, 1971, pp. 177–89.

[44] The combined effort of the English kings and the archbishops of Canterbury had,
in the twelfth century, effected the welding of the four Welsh dioceses to the province
of Canterbury. After Giraldus was defeated in 1203, the issue was raised only once
again, by Bishop Thomas Bek of St. David's (bp. 1280–93), on the occasion of the first
metropolitan visitation by an archbishop of Canterbury in Wales, that of John Pecham
in 1284, cf. Haddan and Stubbs, *Councils and Ecclesiastical Documents relating to
Great Britain and Ireland* (Oxford, 1869), i, pp. 577–9; also William Greenway,
'Archbishop Pecham, Thomas Bek and St. David's', *Journal of Ecclesiastical History*,
xi, 1960, pp. 152–63.

the affair, he assumes a very important place in describing the dispute, although from an an extremely partisan point of view.

The highest position Giraldus ever held in the hierarchy of the Church was the office of archdeacon of Brecon in the diocese of St. David's. He was one of many relatives advanced by Bishop David fitzGerald, and was made archdeacon *c.* 1174.[45] Giraldus later secured the archdeaconry for his own nephew. From the circumstances of this transaction, and the behaviour of the new archdeacon of Brecon, stems the material of the *Speculum Duorum.*

This work sheds some light on otherwise rather obscure years in the life of Giraldus: in the late autumn of 1203 he gave up his long struggle for the bishopric of St. David's, six months after the pope had annulled his election of 1199. This new move also involved his abandonment of the metropolitan controversy which Giraldus had fought for four years against Canterbury and the skilful and powerful archbishop, Hubert Walter. Now that Giraldus had changed his mind, a reconciliation with the archbishop was possible. Hubert Walter seems to have been surprised that Giraldus should abandon the metropolitan claim, and he was mistrustful at first. Giraldus not only proposed to withdraw from the battlefield, but also agreed to resign the archdeaconry in favour of his nephew. The first part of his plan was highly pleasing to the archbishop, who promised to assign to him an annual income of the value of 60 marks. Giraldus actually received a third of this before the death of Hubert Walter in 1205.[46] As to the second part of his proposal, the resignation of the archdeaconry in favour of his nephew, Giraldus says that Hubert Walter tried to dissuade him from doing so, for he knew the character of the nephew, and was not favourably impressed.[47]

This is how Giraldus tells the story, but there is reason to believe that his resignation from the archdeaconry was not completely voluntary. When complaining to the nephew that he had not kept the terms of the agreement, namely that he should hold the archdeaconry only in name as long as his uncle lived, not enjoying its income until after the latter's death, Master Giraldus used a suggestive phrase from the *Digest*: if

[45] The de Barri family then held a strong position in south-west Wales. In 1175, Bishop David granted the stewardship of the bishopric to his brother Maurice fitz-Gerald, an act which was attested by the new archdeacon of Brecon, Master Giraldus, J. C. Davies, *Episcopal Acts relating to Welsh Dioceses 1066–1272* (Historical Society of the Church in Wales Publ. 1, 1946), p. 280, D. 193, also D. 263, 411. The stewardship of the bishopric remained in the same family for at least three generations; nor were these the only cases where David fitzGerald preferred members of his family. Other acts of nepotism by that bishop were strongly criticized in *De successione episcoporum*, ed. M. Richter, *BBCS*, xxii, 1967, p. 248.

[46] Below, pp. 194–6, ll. 97–101.

[47] Below, p. 194, ll. 90–2.

sailors in a storm are forced to throw their goods from the ship into the
stormy sea in order to improve their chance of survival, they do not
thereby lose the ownership of these goods.[48] Likewise Giraldus implied
later that his nephew had already cherished the notion of supplanting
him before the final defeat.[49] Thus it appears that Giraldus was forced
to resign the archdeaconry of Brecon, although for what precise reasons
we do not know.

Giraldus' reconciliation with Hubert Walter and the quashing of his
election to St. David's brought a speedy conclusion to the prolonged
struggle over the bishopric. After a vacancy of five and a half years,
the prior of Lanthony by Gloucester, Geoffrey, was elected, and he was
consecrated on 7 November 1203.[50] The bishop was acceptable to
Giraldus mainly because, while prior of Lanthony, he had maintained
an impartial attitude towards Giraldus' metropolitan claim, unlike
many others who had deserted and betrayed him as bishop-elect.[51]
Four or five days after Geoffrey's consecration,[52] Giraldus resigned his
position. The archbishop recommended the nephew, Giraldus de Barri,
to the bishop as the successor in the archdeaconry. Bishop Geoffrey

[48] Below, p. 74, ll. 1243–7. Giraldus does not seem to quote verbatim, but perhaps
alludes to Dig. 14. 2. 8 (De lege Rodia de Iactu): 'Qui levandae navis gratia res aliquas
proiciunt, non hanc mentem habent, ut eas pro derelicto habeant . . . ' An interesting
parallel of the division of an archdeaconry, although in that case not among relatives, is
recorded by Roger of Howden. Peter of Dinan is installed as archdeacon of the West
Riding, but he leaves the administration and revenues to Adam de Thornover in return
for an annual pension of 60 marks, 'Praeterea inter illos statutum est, quod quandocum-
que simul fuerint in Eboraco, unus illorum una die tenebit stallum in choro nomine
archidiaconi, et alter illorum altera die similiter, et sic mutabunt vices suas de die in
diem quamdiu moram simul fecerint in Eboraco', Chronica, ed. William Stubbs, iv,
pp. 8 f.; cf. D. L. Douie, Archbishop Geoffrey Plantagenet and the Chapter of York, St.
Anthony's Hall Publications no. 18 (York, 1960), pp. 10 f.

[49] Below, p. 134, ll. 983–90.

[50] Geoffrey de Henlaw, seventh prior of Lanthony c. 1189–1203 (cf. D. Knowles,
C. Brooke, V. London, The Heads of Religious Houses, England and Wales, 940–1216
[Cambridge, 1972], p. 172). Geoffrey, having some reputation as a doctor (History of
the Priory of Lanthony, British Museum, Cotton MS. Julius D x, ff. 52ᵛ–53ᵛ; W. Dugdale, Monasticon Anglicanum, vi [London, 1849], prints on pp. 128–34 only ff. 32ᵛ–50ʳ
of the History, but the MS. extends from ff. 31ʳ–53ᵛ), was called to Lanthony when
Prior Roger had suffered a stroke c. 1189. On the latter's death Geoffrey was elected
prior. The date of his consecration as bishop of St. David's is usually given as 7 Dec.
1203 (e.g. Giraldus, Op. iii, p. 321). Yet a contemporary account from Canterbury gives
7 Nov. as the date of the consecration (the endorsement of Geoffrey's profession of
obedience to Canterbury, Canterbury Chapter Archives, Chart, Ant. C 115 no. 70;
'vii idus Novembris'). According to Giraldus, who wrote his account ten years later,
7 Nov. was the day when the electors first met, while Geoffrey was nominated three
days later (Op. iii, pp. 318–21).

[51] Op. iii, p. 322: 'considerans quoque personam electi, quod nunquam, sicut alii,
palam sibi presumpserat adversari . . . ' While Bishop Geoffrey is mentioned only in
passing in the primitive text of the Speculum Duorum, a very late addition on one of the
schedules censures him severely, although without naming him; cf. below, p. 16, ll. 280–
1. Also M. Richter, Giraldus Cambrensis, pp. 99–124.

[52] Below, p. 216, ll. 147–51.

then made the nephew a canon of St. David's, assigning to him the prebend of Mathry, and conferred the archdeaconry of Brecon to him. Still in line with the earlier agreement between Hubert Walter and Giraldus, the nephew then presented his uncle to the bishop as the actual administrator of his office. All this took place at Newbury.[53] Up to that stage not very much had been changed. Giraldus had consented to the election of Geoffrey as bishop, and the bishop and archbishop had agreed to a highly irregular transaction concerning a major ecclesiastical office.

But the deal did not stop there. A document[54] of Giraldus' has been preserved in which he solemnly promised never to raise again the question of the metropolitan status for St. David's. It gives the terms of the final agreement which had been reached after prolonged negotiations. Two arbiters seem to have worked out the terms of a compromise. They were Eustace, bishop of Ely, whom Giraldus had chosen, and William, bishop of London, Hubert's choice.[55] The agreement seems to have been reached the day before Bishop Geoffrey's consecration. The document mentions a number of bishops involved in the settlement: William of Sainte-Mère-Église of London, Gilbert Glanvill of Rochester, Herbert Poore of Salisbury, Eustace of Ely, Savaric fitzGeldewin of Bath and Glastonbury, John de Gray of Norwich, and Mauger of Worcester. Some of these bishops assisted in Geoffrey's consecration, namely William of London, Gilbert of Rochester, William of Blois of Lincoln, Henry Marshal of Exeter, Mauger of Worcester, and Murchad Ó hAodha of Cork.[56]

Giraldus issued his charter after his resignation from the archdeaconry. He is styled *Geroldus quondam archidiaconus de Breghen'*. His nephew attested the document as (*testibus*) *Geraldo filio Philippi archidiacono de Breghen'*. These documents taken together enable us to reconstruct the various stages of the reconciliation between Hubert Walter and Giraldus. A complicated package-deal came to an end with the charter; both sides had guarded their position most carefully and gave in over only one item at a time: (1) Giraldus withdrew his opposition to Geoffrey's election; (2) Hubert promised to recommend the nephew's promotion to the archdeaconry and agreed that this appointment should have only a nominal character; (3) Geoffrey promised to appoint the nephew on these terms; after Geoffrey's consecration the archdeaconry was duly conferred upon the nephew; (4) Giraldus resigned by a charter

[53] Below, p. 214, ll. 128 ff.
[54] Printed from an undated copy from Canterbury Chapter Archives, Reg. A, f. 73ᵛ, no. 215, in M. Richter, *Giraldus Cambrensis*, pp. 135–6.
[55] *Op.* iii, pp. 323 f.　　　　　　　[56] M. Richter, *Giraldus Cambrensis*, p. 135.

any future metropolitan ambitions. Thus even though Giraldus was forced to abandon both the metropolitan issue and the archdeaconry of Brecon, he proved to be a most skilful opponent in obtaining from the archbishop of Canterbury the greatest concessions possible.

In some respects he was able to negotiate with Hubert from a position of strength, knowing that the archbishop had acted against the strict command of the pope when forcing Giraldus to abandon the metropolitan claim.[57] Such an impression is strengthened when it is noted that Giraldus' charter, although prepared with the assistance of a number of suffragan bishops of Canterbury, is not attested by any of them, while members of the *familia* of the archbishop figure prominently in it;[58] the majority of them were outstanding canonists.[59] This is ironical when one recalls that the pope had explicitly forbidden their master to take any steps which would prevent a resumption of the metropolitan claim of St. David's. Giraldus later blamed Bishop Geoffrey for acting against the pope's commands and promising on his consecration never to raise the metropolitan issue.[60] But Giraldus, long champion of an independent archbishopric in Wales, had done the same thing.

The issue of the metropolitan dignity of St. David's was closed with Giraldus' promise of good behaviour in future. He kept his promise. It is interesting, however, to read in the *De Invectionibus*[61] that the controversy was well remembered in England. Giraldus there implied that King John, enraged by the appointment of Stephen Langton to the archbishopric of Canterbury in 1206 in Rome, declared publicly at Oxford in February 1207 that he should have supported Giraldus in his fight,[62] if only to annoy the new archbishop. When Giraldus returned from Rome—he had gone there in 1206 on a pilgrimage—the king suggested to him that he should again take up the metropolitan issue. Giraldus refused, and pointed instead to the man who was competent to undertake such a task, the bishop of St. David's. There is no evidence whether or not John approached Geoffrey also, and one would expect

---

[57] *De Invect.* iv, 4, p. 172.

[58] The list runs in full: 'Hiis testibus, magistro Simoni de Siwell thesaurario Lychesfeldensi, magistro Johanne de Tynemue, magistro Roberto de Balbo, Geraldo filio Philippi archidiacono de Breghen', magistro Michaele de Ryngefeld, Rogero de Basyngham, Roberto de Bristoll. et aliis multis.'

[59] On the *familia* of the archbishop cf. C. R. Cheney, *Hubert Walter* (London, 1967), pp. 158–71; *magister Robertus de Balbo* may be identical with the canon of Rouen of the same name. He does not attest for Hubert Walter after early 1204 at the latest. This information was kindly supplied to the author by Professor C. R. Cheney.

[60] Below, Ep. 7, p. 252, ll. 205–10. Such a promise had first been extracted from Giraldus' uncle, Bishop David fitzGerald, in 1148, and it was repeated by his successor, Bishop Peter de Leia, in 1176; cf. M. Richter, 'Professions of Obedience and the Metropolitan Claim of St. David's', *NLWJ*, xv, 1967, pp. 197–214, at 210f.

[61] v, 22, pp. 202 f.   [62] M. Richter, *Giraldus Cambrensis*, pp. 123–4.

Giraldus to have mentioned such a thing. The only instance in which he later touched upon the matter was in a letter to Bishop Geoffrey, deploring the fact that whereas the bishop had announced his intention of going to Rome in 1207 or 1208 to revive the metropolitan controversy, and had received money from the cathedral chapter for this purpose, he had not carried out his intention. Full of indignation Giraldus declared this to be an aspersion on the good intentions of the community of St. David's.[63] It is evident that the issue remained alive in the diocese at least for a few years after Giraldus' defeat in 1203.

Giraldus' quarrel with his nephew

We now have to look in some detail at the background of Giraldus' quarrel with his nephew. The quarrel was made possible by the very terms of the arrangements under which the archdeaconry of Brecon was conferred on the young Giraldus. A hereditary succession to a major ecclesiastical office was certainly an abuse in the framework of Church administration. Archbishop Hubert Walter was aware of this, and yet he agreed to the transaction. He would appear to have agreed to it despite its uncanonical nature for a very good reason: Giraldus had become, by his suit in Rome, a key figure in the relations between the archbishop of Canterbury and his Welsh suffragan bishops. The first concern of Hubert Walter was to remove him from the focus of attention, while at the same time making sure that Giraldus would submit to his wishes. We have already seen that Hubert Walter's measures to eliminate Giraldus as a future metropolitan candidate of St. David's went against the explicit papal commands. So he—as everybody else concerned— found a formula for a dignified retirement of Giraldus. By the compromise of 1203 Giraldus was treated kindly and rather generously, while at the same time he was effectively kept out of Wales and far removed from further metropolitan adventures.

This formula guaranteed fairly good chances of success as long as everybody involved kept the terms of the arrangement. With the compromise of 1203 Giraldus stepped down from his prominent place in public life. He was then almost sixty years old, and perhaps looked forward to ending his days in retirement, to writing further books, and to continuing his studies in theology. If these were his plans, however, events pushed him in a different direction when his nephew started to upset the arrangements which had been painfully drawn up. Now Giraldus was forced to defend in public the highly irregular transactions

[63] Below, Ep. 8, p. 270, ll. 130–6.

concerning the archdeaconry of Brecon, and to do this, furthermore when his well-meaning partner, Hubert Walter, was dead and no successor installed at Canterbury, and when he had apparently lost the sympathetic tolerance of the new bishop of St. David's. Unshielded by either Canterbury or St. David's, his position was extremely vulnerable.

In the course of his lawsuit, Giraldus had lost part of his income. The greatest material loss was perhaps the payments which he is known to have received from the Exchequer between 1193 and 1202.[64] This money was assigned to two other people in 1203.[65] Furthermore, Archbishop Hubert Walter had promised to assign to Giraldus income in England to the value of 60 marks by way of compensation, and he actually gave a portion of it to Giraldus before 1205. Once Giraldus had given up his official position, his expenses would be smaller in any case, and he could have lived quite comfortably from the money he still received from the archdeaconry.[66] This was upset by the viciousness of his nephew. Master Giraldus had committed himself to the education and promotion of his nephew, the younger son of his brother Philip de Barri, lord of Manorbier. He had taken him to Lincoln when he himself studied there after 1194, before his election to St. David's in 1199. Giraldus implies that his nephew, then in his early twenties,[67] enjoyed the time when his uncle was away from Lincoln and busy with greater issues, and that he did not study as diligently as was expected. The archdeaconry remained entrusted to officials in the absence of the new archdeacon. A tutor was appointed for the nephew, now nominally in possession of the archdeaconry, when Giraldus left England early in 1204 to spend two years with his relatives in Ireland.[68] It would appear that on his return he found the situation much worse than he could have feared. His nephew had sadly neglected his studies and syllabus. A new start was attempted then: Giraldus appointed Master William de Capella as a new tutor, and Thomas of Hay as official for the archdeaconry. Both betrayed him after being in his service for two years.[69]

It is possible that after his return from Ireland Giraldus made some

[64] *Pipe Roll*, 5 Rich. I to 4 John, £15. 8s. 2d. for 1193, £7. 12s. 1d. for the other years.
[65] *Charter Rolls*, 5 John, printed Giraldus, *Op.* i, p. 435, also *Rotuli Chartarum*, 1, i, ed. T. D. Hardy (London, 1837), p. 105.
[66] The prebend of the archdeacon of Brecon was assessed at £5. 0s. 0d. in the *Taxatio Ecclesiastica Anglie et Wallie Auctoritate P. Nicholai IV*, c. 1291 (ed. 1802, *Record Commission*), p. 274, and was the richest archidiaconal prebend in the diocese of St. David's. Giraldus also had a considerable income from various livings which had not been conferred on his nephew. He specifically mentions one (unnamed) in Wales; cf. below, p. 26, ll. 431–6.
[67] His elder brother William de Barri, who inherited Manorbier, was in 1188 a boy of about 12 years, below, p. 52, ll. 863–71.
[68] Below, p. 44, ll. 736–46.   [69] Below, p. 90, ll. 238–43; p. 98, ll. 356–8.

attempt to introduce his nephew into the practical side of his office
as archdeacon, since two undated charters are attested, among others,
by Master Giraldus de Barri and Giraldus, archdeacon of Brecon.[70]
That in both charters Master Giraldus precedes Giraldus the nephew
reflects the real distribution of power. Otherwise, there is little indication
how much either uncle or nephew worked in the archdeaconry or was
involved in other affairs in the diocese of St. David's.

The dispute between uncle and nephew apparently broke out early in
1208. The only reliable dates upon which to reconstruct the events are
the years of the Interdict which lay over England between 1208 and 1214.
In the last item of the *Speculum Duorum*, the letter to Bishop Geoffrey,
Giraldus speaks of the quarrel as then lasting over five years, and implies
that the Interdict had not been lifted. The dispute started with a journey
of the nephew with his tutor William de Capella from Lincoln to Wales.
As became apparent later, their intrigues had already assumed a definite
shape by that time, probably with the consent of the bishop of St.
David's. While Giraldus had been away in Rome, the bishop took a sum
of five or six marks which belonged to the income of the archdeaconry
of Brecon, to use it for himself. Giraldus was informed about it by the
rural chapters of Elfael, Maelienydd, and Buellt. When he complained
to the bishop, he was told to send the archdeacon to clear this alleged
misunderstanding, although Giraldus pointed out that more money
would have to be spent on the actual journey than the quarrel involved.
But the archdeacon and the tutor were eager to go, and so Giraldus
finally consented.[71] Both had promised to return to Lincoln by Michaelmas (29 September). On their way to Wales they met Bishop Geoffrey
at Hereford. There, in the presence of the dean and chapter, the
nephew appealed against his uncle to the pope. The terms of the
appeal are nowhere stated but it is implied that he complained to
the pope that his uncle unlawfully withheld from him money which
came from the archdeaconry of Brecon and various benefices attached
to it, and that this should be changed in his favour. The legal position
of his appeal is not crucial here. On his last visit to Rome in 1206,
Giraldus had resigned all his benefices into the hands of the pope,
imitating a similar move by Thomas Becket.[72] It also appears that he

---

[70] *Cartularium Prioratus S. Johannis Evangelistae de Brecon*, ed. R. W. Banks (London, 1884), pp. 32 f., J. C. Davies, *Ep. Acts*, D 393. Dr. Davies assigns both charters
to *c.* 1207–8.

[71] Below, Ep. 7, p. 246, l. 101–p. 248, l. 129.

[72] On Becket, *De Invect.* v, 16, pp. 195 f.; on Giraldus, ibid. v, 13, p. 193. On the
occasion of that visit Giraldus became a brother of the English hospital in Rome, ibid.
v, 12, p. 192. This house had been established by Pope Innocent III in 1201, cf. *The
English Hospice in Rome*, Sexcentenary Issue (May 1962, vol. xvi), p. 17.

informed the pope about the compromise concerning the archdeaconry, and Innocent III, if not quite enthusiastic about it, at least tolerated this arrangement.[73] It was of some consequence that the Interdict over England and Wales[74] delayed a settlement of the issue, and Giraldus was at a serious disadvantage, because Bishop Geoffrey clearly favoured the nephew. Since the new archbishop of Canterbury was still in exile, Giraldus appealed to Rome. He received a favourable reply, and the nephew and de Capella were cited to appear, but it seems that owing to the hostile reaction of the diocesan bishop nothing was settled.[75]

The bishop of St. David's, who was present when the nephew appealed, did nothing to prevent this, although it was clearly against the spirit of the arrangement of 1203. For this he was later severely reproached by Giraldus. The archdeacon and his tutor, William de Capella, hurried from Hereford to Brecon where they repeated their appeal, and then went to St. David's to do the same. Between the stages of their journey they stopped at several places which belonged to Master Giraldus and were there received as his relatives and friends with great hospitality, because their treason against him was not yet widely known. But when they came to Lincoln again, they learned that Giraldus in the meantime had been informed about their appeal. He did not care to see them and refused to have any contact with them. So the nephew and his tutor went back to Wales to strengthen their position.

This was the state of affairs when Giraldus wrote a long letter of complaint to his nephew, the letter which forms the basis of the *Speculum Duorum*, parts i and ii. As we have it now it is not a straight copy of the original, but a greatly enlarged, later version. It is the only account of the dispute, and a deeply emotional one at that. In retrospect when writing his letter, Master Giraldus explained the development of his nephew's treason, but little is known about the evolution of the dispute after this letter had been written.

---

[73] Below, Ep. 7, p. 256, l. 252.

[74] The way in which Giraldus speaks about the Interdict deserves closer attention, p. 98, l. 367: 'dum etenim *ut* nunc laborat *Anglicana* ecclesia miserie nostre condolentes'... The two words in italics are not in the primitive text but added in the margin, perhaps by the author himself. This emendation probably refers to the fact that Pope Innocent III lifted the Interdict from Wales in 1212, earlier than from England, where it lasted from 24 March 1208 to 2 July 1214; cf. J. E. Lloyd, *A History of Wales* (London, 1911), ii, p. 638 and n. 128; also *Brut y Tywysogion* (RBH), ed. Thomas Jones (Cardiff, 1955), p. 195, and 'Cronica de Wallia', ed. Thomas Jones, *BBCS* xii, 1948, pp. 27–44, *s.a.* (1211, *recte*) 1212. For a general discussion of the Interdict see C. R. Cheney, 'The Alleged Deposition of King John', *Essays presented to F. M. Powicke* (Oxford, 1948), pp. 100–16.

[75] Below, Ep. 7, p. 250, ll. 156–63.

The letter is written in a spirit of bitterness. Giraldus tells how he took his nephew into his care, and how he tried to educate him (in which he had apparently failed as became evident by the appeal). Learning and work had never attracted the nephew, ingratitude was the only characteristic which he constantly exhibited.[76] He had been given a tutor, but the only thing the tutor taught his pupil was to become malicious and mischievous. The second part of the letter is devoted to elucidating the deeds of William de Capella. The main responsibility for the nephew's behaviour is ascribed to him. Not only did he boast that he had more influence in the archdeaconry than the archdeacon himself, but Giraldus believed that he was the instigator of the appeal. Master Giraldus was very proud of his family, and he found it impossible to accept that one of its members could be as malicious as his nephew had been. What was bad in him he had certainly inherited from his mother's side, from the Baskervilles. King Henry II had said that if only one Baskerville was alive, this would be sufficient to contaminate the whole world.[77] Giraldus seems to have shared this view. Yet even the descent from the Baskervilles alone would not be enough to outdo the qualities of the de Barris. His nephew's elder brother William, also from the Baskerville mother, was an example of goodness, but he had taken after his father. In the nephew Giraldus, the bad disposition of the Baskervilles had to be set free by a scoundrel like William de Capella to produce these disastrous results. Giraldus' letter became a mirror (*speculum*) of two bad characters. 'Therefore we offer you a wide and large mirror [in this letter], in which both tutor and pupil can contemplate the features of their nature.'[78] In the form in which it is preserved, however, the *Speculum Duorum* became more than a letter of complaint: it became a song which was intended to comfort the composer himself,[79] Giraldus added later. Not only would the content of the *Speculum* serve as a warning to anybody who might think of giving a benefice to his relatives, but from the composition of the song the author drew a consolation.

Giraldus' use of *Speculum* in the title of his work is obvious in its intention: he tried to depict reality, and by setting it against a whole catalogue of moral instructions taken from the Scriptures, the Church Fathers, and other authors, he showed the degree by which his nephew

---

[76] Elaborating on the theme of ingratitude, Giraldus drew heavily on Petrus Cantor, *Verbum Abbreviatum*, especially chapter 139, 'De ingratitudine'. Migne, *P.L.* ccv, 335–7.

[77] Below, p. 58, ll. 975–8.

[78] Below, p. 152, ll. 1316–18, cf. R. Bradley, 'Backgrounds of the Title *Speculum* in Medieval Literature', *Speculum* 29, 1954, pp. 100–15.

[79] 'nos quasi querulo carmine consolari', below, p. 152, l. 1326.

had left the path prescribed to the faithful in a Christian society. Both title and content of the book classify it as belonging to the last phase of Giraldus' writings, which was, broadly speaking, moral and ethical. Four works belong to that phase: the *Speculum Duorum*, the *Speculum Ecclesie*, the *De Principis Instructione* (a *Mirror of Princes*), and the *Dialogus de Iure et Statu Menevensis Ecclesie*. In his last years, the author had arrived at the final stage of his development where he advised, condemned, and evaluated.

The charges which Giraldus raised against his nephew and William de Capella respectively are quite different ones, and therefore treated in separate parts. The nephew had broken the compromise of 1203 which had been designed to last until Giraldus' death. He had pretended that the income of the archdeaconry and the related benefices should have gone to his uncle only temporarily. He was therefore charged with breach of contract. He also had behaved immorally: this was graver. Nothing could justify ingratitude towards a relative who had shown great kindness without being obliged to do so. Although his behaviour could be partly explained by the bad company which he had always chosen, he had still broken natural law.[80] Giraldus was especially annoyed that one of his relatives should behave in such a way, because it brought discredit to the name of the de Barri family throughout England, Wales, and Ireland. Time and again he pointed out that it was not so much the material loss which he was concerned about but rather the moral and ethical side of such behaviour. In this way, the *Speculum Duorum* is an evaluation of education in the broader, humanistic sense, going far beyond the actual starting-point. We should perhaps assume that Giraldus at this age was too self-centred to see the disproportion between the rather trivial cause of the quarrel and the global way in which he treated it.

Education had always been a major concern of Giraldus'.[81] Especially at times when he had faced disappointment in his own career, he had found consolation in his renewed search for knowledge. He found comfort and reassurance in classical literature, in the writings of the Church Fathers, and in the Holy Scriptures. The *Speculum Duorum* bristles with quotations from such works, becoming at times merely an artistic display of knowledge, in an abundance, furthermore, which might appear to be wasted on the nephew who had refused to learn

[80] Below, p. 148, ll. 1241–55. Also in this section, Giraldus follows largely the *Verbum Abbreviatum* of Petrus Cantor, especially chapters 69–71, Migne *P.L.* ccv, cols. 205–13.

[81] His stern methods of education (significantly, Giraldus quotes frequently from the Old Testament!) should be compared with those of St. Anselm, as told by Eadmer, *Vita Sancti Anselmi*, ed. R. W. Southern (London 1962, NMT), ch. xxii, pp. 37–9.

even simple things. The vast mass of quotations makes more sense once the letter assumes the character of an open letter directed to posterity rather than the nephew.

In the second part of the *Speculum Duorum*, which is concerned mainly with William de Capella, the tone changes. William also had been ungrateful to Giraldus, and could find no means to justify himself, but the different kind of treatment derives from the nature of his dependence on Master Giraldus. Capella had been employed by Giraldus, and his dismissal would sever any bond that might have existed between the two men. Nevertheless, this was easier said than done, since only part of Capella's services was paid in cash, the rest being supplied by his acquisition of benefices.[82] He had thus gradually assumed a position of semi-independence from his employer. To make his ungrateful attitude clear, Giraldus gave a detailed list of what he had given to him.

William had spent a whole summer with his relatives at Llanddew where his brother held a vicarage,[83] and lived off the income which, under normal circumstances, Giraldus would have received from a grange he had there. The grange yielded, on average, up to 20 marks a year, but in that year, despite a good harvest, Giraldus could expect only 5 to 6 marks' value. Capella spent the rest of the income for himself, a fact which could be easily obscured and hardly proved. He also received other money directly from Giraldus. Furthermore, Giraldus later found out by what doubtful means William had acquired the church of Llanhamlach from his father, who was a priest there. William produced a schedule authenticated with the seal of W. de Oildebof the elder[84] in which his father allegedly resigned the church in favour of William de Capella.[85] Giraldus, in good faith, wrote to the pope and the bishop of St. David's recommending the new appointment.[86] The truth became apparent only when Capella's father, then on his death-bed, confessed to Giraldus that the letters which his son had produced at Lincoln were forged, and that he had never intended to confer the church upon his son. William had managed to obtain, by fraud,

---

[82] e.g. Llanhamlach and Llangan, cf. the subsequent notes.

[83] Below, p. 78, l. 27–p. 80, l. 38.

[84] According to the text, W. de Oildebof had the advowson of the church of Llanhamlach. He may be identical with William de Weldeboef who issued a charter to the monks of Brecon Priory at the end of the twelfth century, *Brecon Cartulary*, p. 100. This charter lists among the witnesses a 'William de Weldeboef *juvenis*', which may explain the *'vetus* W. de Oildebof' of our text. The family appears to have come to Brecon with Bernard of Neufmarché; cf. *A History of the County of Brecknock*, by Theophilus Jones, 3 vols. (Glanusk edition), (Brecknock, 1909–11), ii, p. 61: (Gifts of manors to Normans) 'to Sir John Walbieffe or Walbeoff the manor of Llanhamlach and Llanfihangel tal y llyn'. [85] Below, p. 88, l. 207–p. 90, l. 213. [86] Below, p. 92, ll. 255–61.

empty schedules of his father's, and only after they had been sealed did he fill in the content, so that in the end they looked, to the unknowing observer, thoroughly genuine.[87] William had also received the church of Llangan[88] from Giraldus and had undertaken to resign this benefice to his employer in the event of the nephew misbehaving. He had broken this promise.

William de Capella should have been faithful to Giraldus for other reasons as well. His master had saved his life when he was attacked by a group of bandits at Kinnersley (Herefordshire); instead of being grateful, William had stolen from Giraldus a precious Lombard sword. He always believed that attack was his best way of defence. So he spread a rumour that Giraldus owed the sum of 50 marks to the Exchequer and refused to pay.

What was probably graver, William had done everything to prevent a reconciliation between Master Giraldus and his nephew, fearing that, if that came about, he would lose all his influence in Wales and his family would be deprived of their rich financial resources. The worst Capella ever did was an attempt to discredit Giraldus by his own works. While the nephew and his tutor were still at Lincoln, they searched Master Giraldus' works in his library for compromising passages, wrote them down, and compiled in this way a dubious list of quotations from Giraldus which they passed on to those people who were depicted most unfavourably therein. By this means they won Bishop Geoffrey in particular over to their side, a most valuable supporter if they wanted to hold out against Giraldus.

While Giraldus explained neither in the *Speculum Duorum* nor in the *De Iure* how the quarrel with his nephew ended, it is known that at least part of the controversy with the bishop of St. David's ended well for our author. He received the church of Tenby after the Interdict had been lifted.[89] At about that time the archdeacon of Brecon, the young Giraldus, apparently took over the administration of his office as his

---

[87] The abuse of the empty but signed schedules produced some scandal in the thirteenth century, cf. Matthew Paris, *Chronica Majora*, ed. H. R. Luard, *Rolls Series*, iv, p. 368: 'Unde fuerunt qui dicerent ipsum (i.e. the papal legate Martin) habere multas schedulas non scriptas tamen bullatas, ut in eis quicquid ei placeret scriberet; quod absit.' Similarly an injunction issued by Bishop Godfrey Giffard of Worcester after a visitation of Lantony by Gloucester in 1276: 'Item prohibemus quod decetero nulle cedule vacue signentur sigillo conventus', Reg. Godfrey Giffard, Worcester Diocesan Registry, f. 66ᵛ. This information was very kindly supplied by Dr. Susan Davies; for a twelfth-century case of empty schedules see E. O. Blake, ed., *Liber Eliensis* (Camden Third Series 92, 1962), p. 345; cf. also Donald E. Queller, 'Diplomatic "Blanks" in the Thirteenth Century', *English Historical Review*, 80, 1965, pp. 476–91.

[88] Below, p. 108, ll. 560–1). Presumably Giraldus acted as patron of the benefices in his capacity as acting archdeacon. [89] *Op.* iii, p. 353.

own responsibility; already before the death of his uncle (*c.* 1223) he appears repeatedly in contemporary documents, occasionally together with William de Capella. As archdeacon he can be traced in the records down to 1246/7,[90] by which time he would have been about 65 years old. Giraldus fitzPhilip appears more often in the records than his uncle, and in the end he would appear to have regarded his office more as a full-time occupation than as merely a source of income, as his uncle and predecessor had done. Of Master William de Capella hardly anything is known outside the *Speculum Duorum*. The next bishop of St. David's, Gervase (Iorwerth, 1215–29) mediated *c.* 1219–22 in a dispute between the monks of Brecon and a certain Hothelen. As a result, Master William de Capella received an income of 20 shillings annually for the rest of his life.[91] Thus his connection with the archdeaconry of Brecon, which had started with his appointment by Master Giraldus as a private tutor to his nephew, continued even after the break between the two men.

In showing the ungrateful behaviour of his nephew, Giraldus put a great emphasis on the environmental influence. In the narrow sense, it had been the company of Master William de Capella and perhaps Geoffrey, the bishop of St. David's, which brought about such a bad effect. In a wider sense, however, the blame fell heavily on the Welsh in general. The nephew took for his example not the character of good people, but the nature of that barbarous and perverse nation.[92] Giraldus had never been particularly fond of the Welsh, and he never felt at home with them.[93] The fact that he was deserted by his fellow canons when pleading his case at Rome brought out again this attitude which had already been manifest in his *Descriptio Kambriae*, and which had slightly softened for only a short time when he was the champion of Welsh ecclesiastical independence. Master Giraldus had many grievances against the Welsh. When they gave an oath, one could be almost sure that they would break it, an experience also shared by Master David of Oxford.[94] They did not hesitate to tell lies if it served their interests. William de Capella in his acquisition of the church of Llanhamlach had proved the point forcefully. William was supported in his transaction by the perjury of (Welsh) priests who in this respect were no better than the lay people.[95]

---

[90] *Ep. Acts*, i, D 535.

[91] *Brecon Cartulary*, pp. 115–17; for the date *Ep. Acts*, i, D 442. He also attests a document together with Giraldus (the nephew), archdeacon of Brecon, *Brecon Cartulary*, p. 87.   [92] Below, p. 18, ll. 296–301.

[93] Cf. M. Richter, *Giraldus Cambrensis*, pp. 61–86.

[94] Below, p. 110, l. 605–p. 112, l. 611.

[95] 'per testes falsissimos ac periuros, et tamen presbiteros, quia qualis ibi populus, talis et sacerdos, falso probare non formidavit', below, p. 100, ll. 399–401.

Giraldus' nephew, by contrast, felt at home in Wales and with her people. He was particularly slow to learn a polished Latin or French,[96] the language of the more civilized members of society, and perhaps spoke Welsh better than his uncle. He was fond of Welsh music and spent his afternoons playing instruments, having already wasted the morning with hunting.[97] This could not find the approval of his learned uncle.

Master Giraldus also blamed Geoffrey de Henlaw. Although the bishop of St. David's was not a Welshman, nor familiar with the Welsh language, he lived well in that area by tolerating what Giraldus always castigated as particularly Welsh vices: incest and adultery, arson and the breaking of God's peace.[98] Such vices were not confined to the Welsh alone but apparently infected all the other people living in the country.[99] In times of stress, when law-abiding people would have needed the moral support of their bishop, he would withdraw from the country and prefer to live in a safer place.

The picture Giraldus drew of the Welsh was almost invariably a highly unfavourable one; as an individual, he had fought and suffered defeat for the Welsh cause. When his great hour was over, he was humiliated further; among the people responsible for this some had been Welsh. It is the weakness in his argument that he condemned the whole of the Welsh for these reasons, and that even in cases where he experienced injustice from somebody who was not Welsh he found some reason to drag the Welsh in. By that time he was an old man, and his inflexible attitude and undiscriminating invectives must be seen in this light.

The letters

In the letters which were later appended to the *Speculum Duorum*, the personality of Giraldus can be seen in a light different from the one usually cast by his predominantly literary works. Selected from his correspondence, they passed into the *Speculum Duorum* apparently without major revision. As such one cannot expect stylistic masterpieces among them, and sometimes they become a mere repetitive enumeration of facts.[100] The same argument is found in a number of letters, sometimes even restated word for word. Such an interrelation is particularly close in Epp. 5–7. For all such negative aspects there is a highly positive one: the impression that Giraldus was basically an

---

[96] Below, p. 32, ll. 526–8.   [97] Below, p. 132, ll. 954–65; p. 138, ll. 1084–90.
[98] Below, p. 258, ll. 300–11.   [99] Below, p. 278, ll. 281–4.
[100] e.g. Ep. 8, paragraphs starting with *Item*: pp. 264 ff., ll. 31, 44, 49, 52, 57, 61, 130, 137, 158, 250, 259, 294, 306.

honest man. Whether writing to people who were his friends or foes, like Gilbert, prior of Lanthony, or Geoffrey, bishop of St. David's, the issue is tackled in a similar way. Giraldus may have been wrong in his basic judgement, exaggerating the importance and the repercussions of the dispute with his nephew and the other people involved in it, but to him there was only one truth, regardless of his audience.

Ep. 1 *To Master Albinus, canon of Hereford*

Giraldus reminded Albinus of the old ties of friendship which had bound him to the chapter of Hereford. This friendship was seriously challenged by the hospitality granted to Giraldus' enemies, his nephew and Master William de Capella, a hospitality which was unaltered by his own repeated letters reminding the chapter not to tolerate evil and derogatory talks to be held about Giraldus.

The letter appear to have been written some time after Giraldus was betrayed by his nephew (1208).

Ep. 2 *To Hugh de Mapenor, dean, William, precentor, and Ralph Foliot, canon of Hereford*

He has heard that these three men supported his nephew in his evil deeds. Giraldus judged here more harshly than on another occasion[101] where he said that the dean of Hereford had openly disapproved of the nephew's acts. The dignitaries of Hereford should have known better, especially since the nephew stayed at Hereford for over a year. Giraldus was amazed that the letter he sent to his nephew (the *Speculum Duorum*) was regarded at Hereford as supporting his nephew's case, not his, which was a gross misjudgement of the realities. It was disapproved of like the *De Invectionibus* because of its alleged aggressive content. This also was unjust, because only the first few letters contained invectives, replying to other letters written in the same spirit, and the reply was written at the pope's invitation. Also that booklet (apparently part i of the *De Invectionibus*) was written at the beginning of the five-year dispute with the archbishop of Canterbury (*c.* 1200).

Why had he written the *Speculum Duorum* at all? It was to warn and enlighten other people about the wickedness of certain men. Other motives were to comfort himself as well as perhaps to induce his nephew to a change of attitude. In addition, his letter was written in the same spirit as the one which the pope had sent recently to the King of France, in which he rebuked him for ingratitude in the past.[102] Giraldus

---

[101] Below, p. 242, l. 33–p. 244, l. 49.

[102] Innocent's letter to Philip Augustus, sent probably in Sept. 1210, does not appear to have survived, cf. Lefèvre, loc. cit. [above, n. 1], p. 155 n. 1.

complained about the life of a man of letters in his age, which was much harder than ever before, because he lived in a time when malice grew. But he was sure that if his own age disliked his writings, future times would appreciate them.

The date of this letter can be approximately fixed as late 1210 or early 1211.

Ep. 3 *To Master William de Montibus, chancellor of Lincoln*

This letter is not immediately relevant to the content of the *Speculum Duorum*. In it Giraldus brilliantly defended his works against a harsh critic who had been his acquaintance during his years in Paris.[103] William had recently criticized Giraldus' Irish works which the author had given to Lincoln Cathedral. He had taken offence at passages which he regarded as obscene, where Giraldus described the vices of the Irish people. Yet the Bible was not free from passages which would fall into the same category. William also advised Giraldus that it was more congruent with his age and dignity to write theological works. To this the author replied in an admirable way. Firstly, his historical works had been written in his earlier years; secondly, authorities like Jerome and Augustine had praised historical writing and not merely restricted themselves to the study of the Bible. Thirdly, his Irish works, and foremost the first part of the *Description of Ireland*, were not free from theological interpretation and had for this reason earned the praise of Archbishop Baldwin. Apart from all this, his historical works were of the highest quality. Their originality made them far superior to many works: 'For, as it were, there is already a super-abundance of theological books, and even more are being added to the overflowing pile. These are concoctions of all sorts of different books and are taken from the outstanding works of great writers, then presented as though they were something new, but with some artificial rearrangement and a change of title. In fact these modern booklets are not truly genuine, for they are patched together from the earlier original works of others.'[104] The distinctive feature of his Irish and Welsh works was the new subject, which would undoubtedly secure them a place of honour in future ages. Giraldus advised the chancellor either to stop criticizing or to return the books to the author immediately.

From internal criteria it is impossible to date this letter. It may have been written at any time before the death of William de Montibus in 1213.

---

[103] *Op.* i, p. 93; an analysis of this letter in Huygens, *Latomus*, 26, 1965, pp. 90–100.
[104] Below, p. 172, ll. 61–6.

Ep. 4 *Prologue to a sermon on St. Stephen*

This is a curious piece of writing in the appendix to the *Speculum Duorum* and impossible to date. It bewails the dark hours which are over the Church and in this way mirrors the mood which pervades the *Speculum*. The text of this prologue has recently been edited.[105] With its theological subject, it does not do much credit to Giraldus' abilities in this field, nor to the clarity of his thoughts. The sermon for which the prologue was written has apparently not survived.

Ep. 5 *To John, prior of Brecon*[106]

This letter is particularly interesting in that it is addressed to a friend of Giraldus who was not involved in the dispute. It is more moderate and balanced in its arguments than most of the other letters.

Giraldus enclosed a transcript of the letter which his nephew had sent to Pembroke and in which he had defended his actions, a letter which, though written by the nephew, breathed the spirit of his tutor, William de Capella. He also enclosed a copy of his reply, so that John could judge for himself whether Giraldus really had published slander about his enemies. He pointed out that his nephew Giraldus as well as another nephew from Ireland had offended him undeservedly, but not yet to the fatal effect which they intended. Whereas the nephew from Ireland had promised to change his behaviour towards his uncle for the better, the Welsh nephew predicted further trouble. It was only a slight comfort that in this way Giraldus was forced to strengthen his own position.

The nephew and his tutor William refused to submit to arbitration, which had allegedly been proposed by the Bishop of St. David's, but of which Giraldus had not heard at all. What had been considered was an attempt at a personal reconciliation before the following Whitsun, while the question of the rightful occupation of the various incomes should rest for the time being. This was all that had been discussed with the diocesan bishop, and this the nephew refused. He had already shown faithlessness when at Lincoln he had promised (before his departure for Wales) to return about Michaelmas (29 September), but had not come before Candlemas (2 February). Among the lies spread by the nephew the gravest possibly was to say that Giraldus had resigned all his revenues

---

[105] R. B. C. Huygens, 'Deux sermonnaires médiévaux; Tétère de Nevers et Giraud de Barri. Textes inédits', *Studi medievali*, x, 3, 1969, pp. 271–96.

[106] Brecon, Benedictine priory, dedicated to St. John the Evangelist, founded *temp.* Henry I by Bernard of Newmarch, cf. David Knowles and Neville Hadcock, *Medieval Religious Houses, England and Wales*, 2nd edn. (London, 1971), pp. 52, 60.

to the archbishop of Canterbury and had received appropriate compensation. Was it not obvious that he would not have done so since he had had his nephew installed as his successor? The transaction between the archbishop and Giraldus had concerned only his promise to renounce the metropolitan claim of St. David's. At that time it had been arranged that Giraldus should retain the administration of all his income in Wales to which his nephew was later to succeed.

Complaining about Master Giraldus' letter, the nephew called the *Speculum* (= mirror) a *Spiculum* (= arrow-head). If only he would learn something from that book which Master Giraldus would prefer to call a 'book of correction and complaint'. Again[107] he referred to the letter of Innocent III to the French king which was not unlike his own letter to his nephew. An attempt by the young Giraldus to draw his brother William to his side, by appealing to their family solidarity and pointing out how unfavourably their mother had been described by Giraldus, was unsuccessful. If his family had been brought into discredit by this, how much more had the nephew done to justify the negative impression given by the *Speculum Duorum*. After all, a life of quarrels and disputes was not Giraldus' free choice. If it were left to him, he would live in retirement and try to correct his own life as well as he could. Yet the nephew boasted that he had to spend half of his income to defeat his uncle who was old and decrepit; he overlooked the fact that other people like William Fichet[108] or Philip had regarded Giraldus as no longer dangerous but later came to ask his pardon.

Giraldus by that time was so sensitive that he defended himself in advance against a charge which had not even been raised against him: that he had acted badly in finally abandoning his plea in Rome. Although he compared his attempts and achievements on this issue to the labours of Hercules, it would appear that he was not invulnerable here, and that the potential charges perhaps represent the voice of his own conscience.

Giraldus predicted no quick and sudden end to the dispute, mainly because by that time he himself had learnt the lesson of the past and had become more cautious or even pessimistic. Once peace had returned to the Church (i.e. after the lifting of the Interdict) their dispute should be settled in an orderly way. Only then could he receive satisfaction from his nephew.

This letter might have been written any time between late 1210 or early 1211 and the lifting of the Interdict in 1214.

[107] Cf. above, n. 102.
[108] Cf. also below, p. 98, ll. 356–79.

Ep. 6 *To Geoffrey, bishop of St. David's*

This letter of complaint to Geoffrey goes far beyond the role the bishop played in the dispute over the archdeaconry of Brecon. It recalls minor incidents like offensive conduct by the bishop's chaplain, Osbert, towards him. Osbert had recently gone over to the nephew. At Abergavenny, when this became apparent, Giraldus was confronted with something else unpleasant: a report by his nephew spreading slander about him throughout Wales. The effect was that the bishop favoured the nephew, especially over the administration of the archdeaconry and prebend, together with the living of Tenby. Not that he always sided with the young against the older men; when Meiler, a canon of St. David's, had suffered ingratitude from his son as Giraldus had from his nephew, the bishop had brought about a reconciliation. Master Giraldus pointed out once more the bishop's inconsistency over Tenby. In the preceding year, at Llanddew, shortly after Michaelmas, the bishop had persuaded Giraldus to allow his nephew to be the rector of the church, retaining the vicarage for himself and paying the nephew a small pension. The bishop had on that occasion promised that he would immediately induct Giraldus into corporal possession by proxy; after Christmas he found an excuse not to do so: during Lent Master Giraldus came to Llawhaden (the residence of the bishop, near Haverfordwest), but the bishop put off the matter again by pretending that Philip, prior of Pembroke, did not feel sure he would receive the money due to him from Tenby. But it turned out instead that the delay was caused by an appeal against Giraldus. Shortly before Whitsun, when Giraldus came to Llanthony Prima, the bishop had to admit that the nephew had appealed against this investiture. Now Giraldus bluntly accused the bishop of persuading the nephew to launch the appeal. The matter was worse, since the profits of the vacant church of Tenby had been uncanonically withheld from the future vicar.[109]

The bishop had exhibited a similarly false attitude over the administration of the archdeaconry. At Llanthony Prima he and Osbert had given testimony that at Newbury (in 1203) the bishop had accepted Master Giraldus in the perpetual and free administration of the archdeaconry and the prebend of Mathry (Mathry was the richest prebend at St. David's). Later the bishop gave the excuse that he had not positively agreed to the composition of 1203 in words, although it could

[109] Below, p. 214, ll. 109–15. Giraldus appears to refer to *Decret. Greg. IX*, I, 31, 4, a decretal by Pope Alexander III (*JL* 8889); for a brief discussion of the practice in England at that time cf. F. M. Powicke and C. R. Cheney. edd., *Councils and Synods*, ii, 1 (Oxford 1964), pp. 44 f.

be argued that he had tolerated the practice for at least five years. Later again he maintained that previously he had pointed out that the nephew could do the administration himself. This version was not only untrue but highly unlikely, because, since the archbishop of Canterbury had agreed to Giraldus' terms, the bishop-elect, a few days before his consecration, would not have contradicted his future superior.

Master Giraldus had proof of Geoffrey's anger towards him, for in the preceding year the nephew had boasted to his brother William that Geoffrey would never forgive Giraldus because of a letter which he himself had fabricated in Lincoln against Geoffrey from various notes of Giraldus'.[110] But how could the bishop have taken these forgeries seriously?

From the archdeaconry, the prebend (Mathry), and the church of Tenby which were withheld from him, Giraldus lost more than 50 marks annually; yet even greater was his moral loss. The unnatural situation had already lasted four years. Shame fell upon people who would do such a thing and those who would support it. Only the common hatred of Giraldus apparently kept the bishop and the nephew together. But by this the bishop became guilty since by virtue of his office he should promote harmony, not discord. He was obviously liable to hate Giraldus first because of his virtues, but more because he had had a decisive influence in Geoffrey's promotion to the bishopric. Where there should have been gratitude, there grew only hatred. Things would not be so desperate if this were the only shortcoming of the bishop, but he uncanonically[111] alienated church property, the little that had been left by his predecessors, he issued new charters less favourable than the old ones, and thus destroyed the trust which should have been the badge of the relationship between a bishop and his subordinates. Giraldus ends the letter promising to continue writing about his difficulties.

The letter was written four years after the nephew had appealed against his uncle, thus c. 1211.

Ep. 7 *To the prior of Lanthony [Secunda]*[112]

Similar to Ep. 5, this letter informs a person not involved in the dispute. Giraldus had hoped for a long time that the bishop of St.

---

[110] Cf. also below, p. 142, l. 1138–p. 144, l. 1166.

[111] Most of the quotations from canon law are also found in other works of Giraldus, cf. below, Appendix. Such complaints are commonplace at that time.

[112] Llanthony Prima, Monmouthshire, priory of Augustinian canons, dedicated to St. John the Baptist, founded c. 1103–8 by Hugh de Lacy, removed c. 1136 to Gloucester where Lanthony Secunda (now commonly referred to as Lanthony by Gloucester)

David's might have a correcting and salutary influence on the archdeacon of Brecon. But he did not doubt any longer that the bishop was
not only unsympathetic, but was in fact the initiator of the whole
rebellion. Friends of Giraldus ought not be surprised if he should lose
his temper in future. Geoffrey had initially tolerated the nephew's
wicked appeal launched at Hereford, although at that time the dean
of Hereford had pointed out that such conduct could not possibly be
tolerated. The appeal had been repeated at Brecon, involving Giraldus' own house at Llanddew, the administration of the archdeaconry,
and later, at St. David's, the prebend of Mathry. The bishop was at
Llanthony Prima and did not do anything to prevent this. Giraldus
thereupon appealed to Rome, since there was no archbishop of
Canterbury, normally the first competent person to appeal to. Even
earlier, the bishop had shown his bias against Giraldus. For while he
was away in Ireland (1204–5), Osbert, archdeacon of Carmarthen,
had seized part of Giraldus' income of the prebend of Mathry, without
any legal action being taken; the bishop, in his 'benevolent' attitude
towards Giraldus had tolerated the seizure of two or three churches in
south-west Wales then belonging to Giraldus. Similarly, the chapters of
Elfael, Maelienydd, and Buellt in the north-eastern corner of the archdeaconry had informed him at a meeting at Llowes (*Locheis*) that the
bishop had seized property of the archdeacon there amounting to
five or six marks while Giraldus was at Rome (1206). On Giraldus'
complaint the bishop asked to send the nephew over to discuss the
affair; the nephew and his tutor William de Capella were eager to go,
planning their betrayal already.

Giraldus did not like the idea of releasing his nephew from his studies
for this relatively simple and straightforward matter. But the bishop
preferred illiterate subordinates anyway, since they were easier to come
to terms with, and therefore would not take such an objection seriously.
Giraldus pointed out that his official Thomas of Hay was competent to
act as his representative, but the bishop stubbornly insisted on the
presence of the young archdeacon. After Giraldus had received a reply
from Rome and orders to summon the nephew and his tutor, he went to
Wales, where the bishop assured him of his good intentions. Giraldus
reminded the prior of Lanthony that he had already told him personally

was established as a cell of Llanthony Prima in 1137 by Miles of Gloucester, and dedicated to the Virgin Mary. Cf. Knowles and Hadcock, *Religious Houses*, 2nd edn., pp.
151, 164–5. Cartularies of Llanthony are in the Public Record Office, listed in G. R. C.
Davis, *Medieval Cartularies of Great Britain* (London, 1958), nos. 530–41. Parts of
them have been published, Eric St. John Brooks, *The Irish Cartularies of Llanthony
Prima & Secunda* (Dublin, 1953), Irish MSS. Commission.

how these good intentions of the bishop's had waned at successive meetings. He then recalled the bishop's dubious behaviour over the church of Tenby.[113] It was especially annoying that whereas the bishop had pretended not to have time to induct Giraldus to Tenby, he had had time at once to induct the nephew; all people to whom the bishop might have been indebted were quickly rewarded, but not Giraldus, to whom the bishop in the end owed his promotion.

This was not the only unlawful act. Despite the pope's command not to do anything to prejudice the metropolitan claim of St. David's, the bishop appeared to have bound himself irrevocably to Canterbury.

In the face of all that it was ridiculous of Geoffrey to complain that Giraldus wrote derogatory letters about him. The author declared his willingness to defend all his statements at a fair public trial. But he had not yet achieved the complete detachment to suffer plain injustice without taking objection. Yet the bishop went further, trying to prevent Giraldus from entering Wales altogether, whether he wanted to pursue his private interests or to preach to the people. This hurt particularly because it was done by subversive means and could not easily be detected. It was shocking to see such conduct from a bishop who should act differently for the reputation of his office. Would it not have been better had such a man remained in the monastery where he came from rather than be a bishop in a foreign barbarous country, a bishop who in no respect worked for the benefit of his diocese? As a perfect Christian, Giraldus should love his enemies, he admitted; but he could not yet show such detachment and therefore hated injustice and people who would promote it.

This letter would appear to have been written c. 1213. It shows long passages which have already appeared in the preceding Epp. 5 and 6.

Ep. 8 *To Geoffrey, bishop of St. David's*

This letter does not have anything to do with the dispute covered in the *Speculum Duorum*. It points out the defects of the bishop and may be similar to those about which Geoffrey had complained.[114] It is the third letter of its kind, but the second one to survive.

First there is the alienation of church property. A mere list may suffice: Landegof (*Landegof*),[115] taken from Nicholas Avenel; Brawdy (*Brewidi*), converted into knights' fees; Llanddewi in Gower and Llangyfelach (*Langauelach*) given to his son;[116] the vills of Llangadog

---

[113] Cf. above, p. xliv.   [114] See the preceding letter.
[115] *Op.* iii, pp. 132, 349.
[116] Ep. 8, p. 262, ll. 16–18; according to Ep. 7, p. 252, ll. 195–6, this son was Archdeacon Osbert of Carmarthen.

(*Lancadoch*) and Llandygwydd (*Landegewith*); Ystrad Dewi (*Stratdewi*); Trallong (? Trallwng Cyfyn, *Tralan*) and Llanddew. Then there was extortion of money; the neglect of his duties as pastor; the disregard of lawful appeals; the open favouring of simony, as in the case of Cwm Hir;[117] the failure to force monks to stay in their monasteries; the unlawful extortion of money from his clerics.

Certainly, the clergy of St. David's would not like to have again bishops who came from English monasteries like the last two.[118] They had had better experience with other bishops who had been secular clerics like the last but one. According to Giraldus, that one, David fitzGerald, was exemplary in his relations with his clergy, hardly visiting them at all, thus not burdening them with procuration, and only on rare occasions asking for their financial support. It is known from other sources that this bishop[119] was not the perfect shepherd Giraldus wanted to make him into, but perhaps he did not oppress his clerics unduly, simply because he did not care about them. What Giraldus had to say of the last two bishops of St. David's he had often said before: they were acceptable to Canterbury simply because they were Englishmen in Wales who, regardless of their personal qualities, would therefore follow the archbishops of Canterbury obediently. That the Welsh clerics disapproved of this situation became apparent when *c.* 1208 Bishop Geoffrey promised to take up the metropolitan claim of St. David's and was given some money readily. He took the money, but never went to Rome. There were other, similarly unjust acts of squeezing money from subordinates, as in the case of the deanery of Elfael.

What Giraldus had to say about episcopal visitations did not flatter Geoffrey either; his visitations were too frequent, as frequent in fact as those an archdeacon should perform.[120] Unfortunately the bishop visited only the houses of the priests, and left the churches to the archdeacons. He did not cover only distant parts of the diocese where a visitation with a greater number of companions might be justified, but also moved within limited areas, going from Lamphey (*Launtefei*) to Stackpole (*Stakepole*), to Carew (*Kairreu*), and to Tenby, in Pembrokeshire, or between Llanddew (*Landu*), Llanfilo (? *Lanbiliaue*), Bronllys (*Brenleis*), and Mara (probably identical with Mara Mota, manor nr. Llangors/Llanfihangel Tal-y-llyn) in Brecknockshire. The

[117] Cwm Hir, Cistercian abbey in Maelienydd, founded in 1143, refounded in 1176, cf. Knowles and Hadcock, *Religious Houses*, 2nd edn., pp. 112, 115.

[118] Peter de Leia, bishop 1176–98, had been a Cluniac.

[119] David fitzGerald, bishop 1148–76, Giraldus' uncle, about whom a highly unfavourable contemporary account has survived, 'A new edition of the so-called Vita Dauidis Secundi', ed. M. Richter, *BBCS* xxii, 3, 1967, pp. 245–9.

[120] See below, p. 270, l. 160–p. 272, l. 166.

bishop and his numerous entourage were interested only in the procurations, and did not care for ecclesiastical duties. Whereas in other
places archdeacons would take over the function of a bishop, here the
roles were reversed.

When the lay magnates oppressed the clerics and imprisoned their
relatives, as had been the case with the prior of Brecon, the bishop did
nothing to help the oppressed, except when those of them who held
several churches resigned one. Such bishops should be deposed. For
in time of stress and war when his influence would be urgently
needed, Geoffrey withdrew to England far from the battlefield and
thereby delayed the course of justice. Even with the Cistercian Order,
acclaimed throughout the world as one of the pillars of the Church, the
bishop made no exception and insisted on high payment for performing
his duties. The abbot of Cwm Hir complained about this conduct to Rome
and received satisfaction, but not everybody had such powerful friends.

Even in peacetime Geoffrey did not care about the spiritual welfare
of his flock, neither personally, for which he was not qualified in any
case, since he did not speak Welsh, nor through an interpreter. That
this was possible had been shown by Archbishop Baldwin when he
preached the crusade in Wales with the help of an interpreter. But
Geoffrey's sole interests were material, directed towards 'milk and wool'.
Giraldus hoped that he might perhaps have helped to change Geoffrey
by his admonition, as Peter had changed from a person denying the
Lord to a penitent, or as Paul from someone who first persecuted but
then preached.

There is no reliable internal criterion as to when this letter was written
but it was certainly before the lifting of the Interdict, perhaps late in
1213 or early in 1214.

Result

In his correspondence, Giraldus showed himself as a vehement critic
of the reality in ecclesiastical life which he encountered. His criticism
seems to have been justified at times, especially over the way in which
the bishop acted over the church of Tenby: according to Giraldus, the
bishop treated the archdeacon of Brecon more kindly than his uncle
over a point where personal considerations should not have played any
part at all. It is, however, always advisable to keep in mind that the
reader is presented with only one aspect of the controversy, the view of
the man who was allegedly wronged.

Quite apart from this point, the *Speculum Duorum* as a whole will
interest the Church historian for another reason. The controversy in

which Giraldus was involved gives some insight into the administration
of the Church at the diocesan level, a field where information at that
time is normally rare. If in a diocese like St. David's, which was then
little controlled by Canterbury,[121] the administration worked relatively
well, one can assume that the situation in the more closely supervised
English bishoprics was at least equally positive.

Giraldus, like some other twelfth-century archdeacons, did little
work in the archdeaconry personally, and this was at a time when the
archdeacons were still generally regarded as the principal assistants of the
bishop in the administration of the see.[122] It was not until later, during
the course of the thirteenth century, that many of their original duties
came to be delegated to other officers, principally the bishop's official.
Nevertheless, Giraldus appointed representatives to carry out his work
and he appears to have supervised and instructed them closely.[123]
The annual visitation of churches by the archdeacon or his representatives appears to have been a regular feature under Giraldus.[124]
He refers to 'his officials' in 1198, but of particular interest is the record
of the appointment of Thomas of Hay as his general official in 1204,
for this is one of the earliest instances where the identity of an archdeacon's official is known.[125] It is interesting, too, to note that it was
taken for granted that such officials could delegate their functions to
rural deans or other persons.

The reader of Giraldus' work also gets at least a glimpse of the
machinery of the rural deaneries at work. In a letter to the chapter of
St. David's dating from spring 1198 he recalls that he deposed a rural
dean, Joscelin by name, for abuse of his position.[126] Administration by

---

[121] The first metropolitan visitation to the Welsh dioceses occurred only in 1284 and
was executed by Archbishop John Pecham.

[122] Cf. the decretal of Pope Innocent III, *Decret. Greg. IX*, I, 23, 7.

[123] *Op.* i, p. 251, written in Lent, 1197.

[124] An archdeacon, under normal circumstances, should not visit more frequently,
according to a decretal of Pope Alexander III, *Decret. Greg. IX*, I, 23, 6.

[125] Below, p. 248, l. 140–p. 250, l. 142: 'scripsimus episcopo nos Thomam personam
de Haia generalem officialem nostrum per archidiaconatum de Brechene . . . constituisse.' Thomas was presumably a local man, deriving his name from Hay, deanery
Brecon. His position gave rise to a dispute because the archdeaconry was held by
Giraldus fitzPhilip but administered by Master Giraldus who commented: 'sed scire
debuit, quoniam administrator publicus et perpetuus officialem suum propria auctoritate constituere . . . potest', p. 250, ll. 148–50; on the role of the official at that
time cf. C. R. Cheney, *English Bishops' Chanceries, 1100–1250* (Manchester, 1950),
p. 145 n. 6.

[126] *Op.* i, p. 325; Giraldus in this case perhaps exceeded his powers, although according
to a decretal of Pope Innocent III, there was much uncertainty at the diocesan level
about the respective competence of the various officers regarding the rural deans:
Decret. Greg. IX, I, 23, 7: 'Subsequenter postea quaesivisti, utrum decani rurales, qui
pro tempore statuuntur, ad mandatum tuum solum, vel archidiaconi, vel etiam utriusque institui debeant vel destitui si fuerint amovendi. Ad hoc breviter respondemus,

the archdeacon with the assistance of the rural chapters is mentioned several times, in terms which imply that such practice was readily accepted and that it worked efficiently.[127] Giraldus once reported that certain local chapters—presumably the ones in the rural deaneries—had informed him of a particular action by the bishop,[128] and that he had taken the matter up.

Of equal interest are the remarks about visitation by the diocesan bishop. We can disregard at this point the critical comment that such visitations were made for the wrong reasons. It is, however, surprising to hear that the bishop allegedly visited too frequently, with the regularity of an archdeacon.[129] Although canon law by that time had established some general rules concerning the practice of visitation,[130] no specific regulation had as yet been passed establishing how often the bishop should visit the parishes in his diocese. Yet it was generally understood that he should visit less frequently than the archdeacon, and the normal complaint, which we also find occasionally in Giraldus,[131] was that the bishop failed to visit as often as was desired. Giraldus' remarks give ground for some speculation, especially since Bishop Geoffrey does not appear to have been an over-conscientious pastor. Did he visit the churches in his diocese because this was already a well-established practice, or did he have more time to undertake such visitations because he was not called to work in the royal administration as much as other bishops? A more plausible explanation may, perhaps, be found in the desirability of procurations. Abuse of procuration, with which Giraldus charged Bishop Geoffrey, was a complaint as old as visitations themselves.

Giraldus also mentioned other current abuses which the papacy tried hard to abolish in the thirteenth century. His own case is an excellent example, and he gave others in order to justify himself, illustrating that churches and major and minor ecclesiastical offices were handed down in a family from father to son, or to other close relatives, an abuse which Giraldus unashamedly called 'an old tradition of the church of St. David's'.[132] Pope Innocent III tolerated, but only just,

quod . . . quum commune eorum decanus officium exerceat, communiter est eligendus, vel etiam amovendus.'

[127] Below, p. 244, l. 54.   [128] Below, p. 246, ll. 102 ff.
[129] Below, p. 272, ll. 194–6.
[130] Notably the Third Lateran Council of 1179, *Decret. Greg. IX*, III, 39, 6 and the Fourth Lateran Council of 1215, *Decret. Greg. IX*, III, 39, 23.
[131] Below, p. 262, ll. 21–2.
[132] Below, p. 256, ll. 250–2. Elsewhere they have been called, more appropriately, 'formidable customs of [local] class-exclusiveness', see G. Barraclough, *Papal Provisions* (Oxford, 1935), pp. 52–60, at p. 58. The passing on of ecclesiastical offices to relatives and friends, by hereditary right, as it were, as well as its abuse by the young

the irregular transaction by which the archdeaconry of Brecon was passed on from uncle to nephew, but his successors were less lenient in this. The bishop's efforts to take away one of the churches of an incumbent who held several[133] were called unjust by Giraldus. The abolition of pluralism was one of the main tasks facing the Church in the following century.[134]

It should be kept in mind that Giraldus wrote the *Speculum Duorum*, which is concerned incidentally with matters of Church administration, at the time when the English Church lay under an interdict.[135] If more information were available, the diocese of St. David's would be an interesting case study, because its bishop remained in the diocese throughout the years of the Interdict. Although Church government was disturbed by this ecclesiastical censure, it still continued. Furthermore, there is not a single instance in our text which suggests any intervention by the king or his representatives in the affairs of St. David's at this difficult time. While this confirms what has been established by Professor C. R. Cheney on the subject, we can go beyond his remarks by pointing to two appeals to Rome made at that time and taken up, as far as one can tell, without delay.[136] It is perhaps due to the nature of the *Speculum Duorum*, which is not concerned, in the first place, with the administrative aspect of Church life, that no more light is shed on the impact of the Interdict. That it was felt even in Wales there can be no doubt. Giraldus' frequent allusions to it are more than mere rhetorical figures of speech, but, unfortunately, detailed information is not forthcoming.

The legal sources

The *Speculum Duorum* and the letters are full of quotations from the Bible, the Church Fathers, and from legal sources, notably the *Corpus*

beneficiaries, in twelfth-century England was severely criticized in the satirical treatise 'Tractatus Nigelli contra curiales et officiales clericos', *The Anglo-Latin Satirical Poets and Epigrammatists of the Twelfth Century*, ed. T. Wright, R.S. 59, 1872, 2 vols., i, 153–230. The stories told there, pp. 172–4, are akin to those bewailed by Giraldus, although the moral behind them is quite the opposite.

[133] Below, p. 276, ll. 250–8.

[134] Cf. A. Hamilton Thompson, 'Pluralism in the Medieval Church', *Associated Architectural Societies Reports*, no. 33, pp. 35 ff.

[135] For general remarks, Henri Maisonneuve, 'L'interdit dans le droit classique de l'église', *Mélanges Louis Halphen* (Paris, 1951), pp. 465–81; also C. R. Cheney, 'King John and the Papal Interdict', *Bull. of the John Rylands Library*, xxxi, 1947, pp. 295–317.

[136] Below, p. 246, ll. 72–7, and p. 250, ll. 156–8; also the reference to the appeal launched by the abbot of Cwm Hir against Bishop Geoffrey, below, p. 280, ll. 299–304. Of course we do not know the exact dates of these appeals, which would make the point even more interesting, since Cheney quotes a letter from Pope Innocent III dated 29 Oct. 1210, stopping a case until the Interdict should be removed, loc. cit., p. 309.

Iuris Civilis and Gratian's *Decretum*. The work stands or falls with this body of quotations, since it is one of Giraldus' main arguments that he was justified in being upset by his nephew's conduct by pointing to the authority of others who made statements to a similar effect.

The classical quotations support a point which has been made long ago and should be repeated once more: Giraldus was well versed in the writings from the classical period, and in this he proved to be a good example of what is known as the renaissance of the twelfth century.[137] Less attention has been paid in the past to the great body of quotations from canon law in his works. Not that preoccupation with canon law was unusual at that time, but it was and had long been the field of the specialist rather than the historian or even the theologian. That a man of Giraldus' background should quote from canon-law sources with apparent ease should be pointed out specifically.

Giraldus had studied law during his second stay at Paris, between 1177 and 1179.[138] He would appear to have made good progress rather quickly and soon took to teaching himself. His lectures *in causis decretalibus* were well attended, and in 1179 he was even suggested as a successor to Master Matthew of Anjou, when that teacher was called to the Third Lateran Council. How far Giraldus magnified his own achievements is impossible to say. The only example of his lecturing preserved in his autobiography does not go beyond a conventional argument. Giraldus felt strongly that he still lacked adequate training in the schools of Bologna, and it is not known whether he was ever able to study there.

In 1179, he returned to England, and in later years was attached to Lincoln. It was then that his works showed for the first time traces of his legal training. The best single example for this is perhaps the *Gemma Ecclesiastica*, completed before 1199, which in long passages is heavily indebted to the *Decretum* of Master Gratian. This work was by then easily accessible for reference at any major place of learning, so its use by Giraldus is not surprising. More significant is that Giraldus

---

[137] His style 'was influenced, not by a single prose author, ancient or medieval, or by any single poet, but rather by all the writers whose works he at any time read and enjoyed', G. J. E. Sullivan, 'Pagan Latin Poets in Giraldus Cambrensis', Ph.D. thesis, University of Cincinnati, 1950, p. 35. This statement requires some modification, since in the *Speculum Duorum*, the *Gemma Ecclesiastica*, and other works Giraldus is indebted greatly to Petrus Cantor, especially the *Verbum Abbreviatum*, a debt which he also acknowledges in the present work (cf. below, p. 148, ll. 1256–8). This influence has been pointed out by other historians; cf. E. M. Sanford, 'Giraldus Cambrensis' debt to Petrus Cantor', *Medievalia et Humanistica*, iii, 1945, pp. 16–32, and A. Boutemy, 'Giraud de Barri et Pierre le Chantre. Une source de la *Gemma Ecclesiastica*', *Revue du moyen âge latin*, ii, 1946, pp. 45–62.

[138] *Op.* i, pp. 45 ff.

kept up with the post-Gratian development in canon law as well, making reference even to the Fourth Lateran Council.[139] It is the ease with which he quoted decretal letters which shows Giraldus' interest in the most recent developments of Church jurisdiction. He claimed himself to possess copies of decretal letters,[140] and he also had the opportunity to inspect and copy from a collection of the decretals of Pope Alexander III before 1199.[141] Besides quoting the *Decretum* and decretal letters in his works, he used them for practical purposes as well. The earliest example known is in a letter to Hugh, bishop of Lincoln, written after 1194, where he made reference to a letter of Pope Alexander III to the archbishop of Canterbury from the year 1180[142] to support his claim to a benefice. This shows that Giraldus was able to keep in touch with the more recent developments of canon law while he was in England, and presumably the cathedral school of Lincoln offered the best facilities.[143]

Giraldus was not a specialist in canon law, and the implications of various divergent legal decisions, which he only knew from the decretals, may have puzzled him at times. Yet that he kept up his interest in these modern trends shows on the one hand that he was an unusually interested and versatile historian, and on the other hand that England with her cathedral schools made it possible for interested people to follow the new developments in the Church without having to leave the country.

An interesting, even though not typical, example of Giraldus' legal thinking is provided in a chapter of the *De Invectionibus*.[144] In it Giraldus discussed how far he had been justified in pursuing his metropolitan claim in Rome although his fellow canons of St. David's had withdrawn their support. He took allegations mainly from the *Code* and the *Digest*, but also from the *Decretum*, from the canons of the Third Lateran Council, and from decretals.[145] We have shown above that part v of the *De Invectionibus*, which contains this chapter, is of quite late origin. There is no indication that Giraldus put forward such legal support for

---

[139] *Op.* iv, pp. 304 ff.

[140] *Op.* i, pp. 237-8, Ep. xi, xii.

[141] 'epistolam Papae Alexandri III . . . legimus et inter alias eiusdem papae decretales scriptam, satis et vidimus et habuimus', *Op.* ii, p. 41. The decretal letter in question, *Plene nobis innotuit*, to the bishop of Arras, was not received in the decretals of Gregory IX, the *Liber Extra*; it is found in Migne, *P.L.* 200, 1324, no. xli (*JL* 13748).

[142] *Op.* i, p. 265, Ep. xxii, *Decret. Greg. IX*, 1, 3, 2.

[143] Cf. S. Kuttner and E. Rathbone, 'Anglo-Norman Canonists of the Twelfth Century', *Traditio*, vii, 1949-51, pp. 279-358.

[144] v, 20, pp. 199-201.

[145] The passage has received attention from S. Kuttner, 'Les débuts de l'école canoniste française', *Studia et documenta historiae et iuris*, iv. 1938, pp. 193-204.

his claim in Rome in this form, and indeed it would not fit into the proceedings there at all, because he never had a real chance to unfold his claim fully. The passage thus appears as an afterthought.[146] Kuttner believed that Giraldus held this *plaidoyer* in Rome in 1202, although there is no real evidence for this. It does not seem to have been part of the *De Rebus a se Gestis*, yet it is found in the *De Invectionibus* and later in the *De Iure*.[147] As such it is evidence not so much of the beginnings of a canonist school in France but rather of the continuing growth of canonist studies in England.[148]

In the *Speculum Duorum* proper the quotations from canon law are fewer in number than those from the Digest. Furthermore, they do not give any better understanding of the case itself. It was a case more suitable for moral arguments, and a basically civil case at that. The function of the few canon-law quotations is more to illustrate what had been said in other words before. But the collection of letters gives much more evidence for Giraldus as an amateur in legal studies. Here it is especially the first letter to bishop Geoffrey of St. David's which brings a number of allegations. In this letter Giraldus enumerates to Geoffrey the duties of a bishop according to the teaching of the Church. Naturally the argument is basically moral, but it has specific legal implications. So the bishop should be, first and foremost, a servant and an administrator of the goods attached to his see. He should be a good pastor to his flock and not demand more subjection than is absolutely necessary. He should not be unduly proud of his position, which is not as much exalted over that of a priest as some bishops thought. It was not the act of the consecration alone that made him a bishop worthy of the title, but he would have to show himself worthy of the office and position by his behaviour. It is significant that all these quotations come from an early period of the Church,[149] a time when a bishop

---

[146] Cf. *De Invect.*, p. 199: 'argumenta que ad hoc in curia Romana uel introducta fuerant uel introduci poterant.'

[147] *Op.* iii, pp. 278 ff.

[148] A very full and valuable introduction to legal studies in England in the twelfth century is provided by Eleanor Rathbone, 'The Influence of Bishops and Members of Cathedral Bodies in the Intellectual Life of England, 1066–1216' (Ph. D. thesis, typescript, London, 1935). On the law school at Lincoln, ibid., pp. 150–8. It was in the latter half of the century that Lincoln figured prominently in the field of theology.

[149] The most recent quotation, in fact, dates from A.D. 829 (c. 4, C. XII, q. 5); cf. below, the list of quotations. Giraldus touched here upon a problem which was passionately debated by the canonists of his time and even later: whether the episcopal office was an *ordo* different from the priesthood. Giraldus defended the traditional view which denied such difference, but with the writings of the canonist Huguccio the opposite view began to gain ground, to win the day in the thirteenth century. Cf. R. P. Stenger, 'The Episcopacy as an *Ordo* according to the Medieval Canonists', *Mediaeval Studies*, xxix, 1967, pp. 67–112, esp. 77 ff.

was meant to be little more than a *primus inter pares* among the priests. It was quite a general phenomenon, furthermore, that bishops showed more arrogance in their office than they should have done, and Giraldus' charges against Geoffrey can be traced throughout the preceding century. He did not even try to find new arguments for his special case, but copied parts of a letter which he had sent two decades earlier to Bishop Peter of St. David's.[150] The earlier letter he had taken into the *Symbolum Electorum*, which again shows that he attached a more permanent validity to his arguments.

That Giraldus made use in his letters of his earlier correspondence can also be shown by one example of verbal repetition. In the *Speculum Duorum* and in four of the appended letters he brought one and the same group of three quotations with incorrect attributions, though it should be remembered that all the letters circle around the same question: one from the Corpus Iuris Civilis: 'Ratihabitio mandato comparatur'[151] and two from Gratian: 'Error cui non resistitur approbatur, et veritas cum minime defensatur opprimitur'[152] and 'Negligere cum possis perturbare perversos nichil est aliud quam fovere, nec caret scrupulo societatis occulte, qui manifesto facinori desinit obviare.'[153] The quotations of the two canons from Gratian in Giraldus' letter to the prior of Lanthony Secunda[154] may have come in this way into the *History of Llanthony*.[155] This work shows the same wrong attribution of the canons as does Giraldus (*Ignatius* for *Innocentius*, *Innocentius* for *Eleutherius*). There are other indications that Giraldus kept in close contact with the priors of Lanthony Secunda. He was a friend of prior Roger.[156] He had been educated at St. Peter's at Gloucester before he went to study in Paris *c.* 1162, and he may well have established then first contacts with near-by Lanthony Secunda (by Gloucester). It is interesting to notice, that in his *Itinerarium Kambriae* (completed *c.* 1192) Giraldus copied an important passage directly from the *History*

---

[150] *Op.* i, pp. 218–26, for which see *infra*, Appendix, pp. 284–5; also *Op.* iv, pp. 307–11, where he attempts to arrive at a synthetical view of the problem.

[151] Dig. 50. 17. 152.

[152] D. 83, c. 3, a canon by Innocent, in Giraldus wrongly Ignatius.

[153] c. 55, C. 2, q. 7, a canon by Eleutherius, in Giraldus wrongly Innocent.

[154] The recipient was probably a man called Gilbert who flourished *c.* 1207–*c.* 1217, cf. Eric St. John Brooks, ed., *The Irish Cartularies of Llanthony Prima & Secunda*, Irish MSS. Commission (Dublin, 1953), p. ix.

[155] B.M. Cotton MS. Julius D x, ff. 31ʳ–53ᵛ, printed (ff. 32ᵛ–50ʳ only) Dugdale, *Mon. Angl.* (London, 1849) vi, pp. 128–34. A direct dependence of the *History of Llanthony* seems to be ascertained by the fact that the *History* does not only give the quotations as does Giraldus, but even takes the phrase 'presertim cum ad hoc ex officio teneatur' as part of the quotation (ff. 51ᵛ–52ʳ) which is not part of the canon proper, but a comment on it, the origins of which cannot be traced beyond Giraldus.

[156] Cf. *Op.* i, pp. 245–8.

of Llanthony,[157] and the rest of his account of Llanthony also drew heavily on the same source.

The nature of the manuscript

It has been necessary to discuss all the foregoing points before one can approach the most interesting aspect of the *Speculum Duorum*, namely how the manuscript grew under the constant revisions by the author. A special feature of the work is that it shows the reader how Giraldus actually composed one of his works.

As is the case with most of Giraldus' works, the *Speculum Duorum* has been preserved in one single manuscript, but whereas in other instances one can reasonably assume that there were once several copies, it is possible that the present manuscript of the *Speculum Duorum* (and the *De Invectionibus* for that matter) is the only one that ever existed. Thirty years ago, Yves Lefèvre, in the first full analysis of the codex, came to the conclusion: 'Nous devons donc avoir dans ce manuscrit le premier brouillon du *Speculum Duorum*.'[158] This hypothesis that the manuscript is the author's working copy makes more sense than the conclusion reached earlier by W. S. Davies (who had never seen the original manuscript in Rome) that it was made from two earlier versions, one of which consisted of the primitive text alone, the other being a full copy, containing both the primitive and the additional texts. As Lefèvre pointed out, it is hard to credit that a scribe copying from a fair text should produce a manuscript as disorganized as the present one. If our manuscript is, therefore, to be regarded as a working copy, close examination of it is of particular interest, as it may throw light on the working-methods of medieval authors in general, and of Giraldus in particular.

The present analysis is concerned exclusively with the *Speculum Duorum* proper, that is parts i and ii of our text. The letters appended in the third part present hardly any difficulties. They appear to be straightforward copies of actual letters sent by Giraldus to a number of people; in a few places a phrase or a sentence was added in the margin, or an editorial note was put in by the author, but there the corrections end. The situation regarding the first two parts is different. Here even a superficial glance shows that the text is divided into two layers, which we have called the primitive text and the additions. Palaeographical evidence

[157] *Op.* vi, pp. 37 ff., cf. *Mon. Angl.* vi, p. 129; also M. Richter, *Giraldus Cambrensis*, pp. 79 f.
[158] Loc. cit. [above, n. 1], p. 170.

establishes that the primitive text was written by a single scribe, while
the additions show a number of hands. Furthermore, the slight attempts
at rubrication of the primitive text as well as the generally careful writing
indicate that the primitive text was originally meant to be a fair copy.
Most of the additions, then, would appear to represent a second layer of
the text, written at another time, by other scribes. They can be generally
divided into two kinds: those written in the margin of the primitive
text, and those copied on separate pieces of vellum which were later
added to the manuscript. Such fragments supply roughly one-third
of the codex,[159] the other two-thirds being written on the original
gatherings.[160]

The first important problem which presents itself is that of the nature
of the primitive text. Is this, as it purports to be, an unadulterated copy
of the original letter which Master Giraldus sent to his nephew?
Superficial evidence suggests that it is, since the text shows at the
beginning and at the end the forms which are normally found in a letter:
the sender, Master Giraldus, writes to the nephew,[161] the work ends with
the valedictory formula,[162] and the nephew is addressed in the second
person plural. Other evidence, however, indicates that the original letter
had undergone revision and had been augmented. In particular there are
a number of passages which speak *of* the nephew in the third person
and not *to* him in the second person,[163] an inconsistency which makes the
Speculum Duorum rather unsatisfactory in form. Furthermore, some
passages contain more information than would seem necessary in a
letter to someone directly involved in the dispute.[164] Also on two
occasions cross-references to subsequent passages in the primitive
text are given.[165] All these factors indicate that the primitive text is
more than a strict copy of the original letter, and suggest that the
Speculum Duorum was intended to assume the character of a treatise
written for the benefit of many rather than a letter addressed to an
individual. Whether or not any parts of the original letter were omitted
in the same process is impossible to determine.

Since the primitive text thus appears to differ from the original letter,
it is necessary to distinguish as accurately as possible between the time of
the composition of the letter and the copying of the primitive text, which

---

[159] Folios 51, 53, 57, 67, 69, 70, 71, 75, 76.
[160] Folios 50, 52, 54, 55, 56, 58, 59, 60, 61, 62, 63, 64, 65, 66, 68, 72, 73, 74, 77.
[161] Below, p. 2, ll. 4–5.   [162] Below, p. 152, l. 1329.
[163] Notably p. 8, ll. 104–31; p. 14, ll. 236–7; p. 18, ll. 282–3, 301–6; p. 20, l. 347–
p. 22, l. 352; p. 84, ll. 125–9; p. 84, l. 142–p. 86, l. 153; p. 88, ll. 188–206; p. 96,
ll. 332–8; p. 142, l. 1138–p. 144, l. 1201, etc.
[164] Below, p. 18, ll. 301–6.
[165] Below, p. 20, l. 331: 'ut infra dicetur'; p. 22, l. 361: 'de quo satis dicetur inferius'.

was no longer identical with the letter, into the codex. The letter was written to the nephew after the betrayal at Hereford; it was composed at the earliest after the Interdict had been laid over England (1208), at the latest before the death of Walter Map (1 April *1210–12*). It was not copied into the codex before 1216, the year in which Pope Innocent III died, which is referred to in the *De Invectionibus.*

The additional text also shows interesting features. Most of what was written on separate pieces of parchment and later added to the manuscript refers to the nephew in the third person, further illustrating the transitional state of the *Speculum Duorum* between a letter and a treatise. The pieces vary very much in format: two[166] are of the same size as the other folios in the codex, and the text is written in double columns; these pieces seem to have been written not before the copying of the primitive text, adopting its general features, but the other leaves are much smaller and the text is in almost all cases written across the whole width. The content of the latter may give some further information about the composition of the manuscript. Most of them contain material which was certainly not in the letter to the nephew, namely stories which could illustrate his behaviour by examples relating to other people. Such stories, which could easily be taken into the text by introducing them with an 'item', etc., were perhaps collected by Giraldus quite separately from the composition of the *Speculum Duorum* and later inserted into the manuscript. Examples are folios 51ᵛ, 53ʳ (this is a more complicated case, cf. Fig. 2: there are three pieces altogether, no. 2 being separate, followed by no. 3 which contains a full story as well but which now leads on to two independent, complete stories on no. 1), 57ʳ, 67ʳ/ᵛ, 76ᵛ (the first story only). I suggest that these pieces are the *cedule* which Giraldus refers to repeatedly,[167] i.e. pieces of parchment with information on them, probably the medieval equivalent of the record cards of the modern scholar. It is known that Giraldus kept short notes, perhaps quickly jotted down on small pieces of parchment by himself, or dictated to a scribe, about anything of interest to him.[168] He informs us about a collection of notes which he kept wherever he worked, and they seem to have formed the basis of his literary work.[169]

The inserted pieces of parchment contain the great bulk of the

---

[166] Folios 70, 75.

[167] Below, p. 82, l. 90; p. 88, l. 210; p. 92, l. 256; p. 142, l. 1146; p. 144, l. 1178; once spelt, *scedula* p. 120, l. 750.   [168] Below, p. 78, l. 20.

[169] *Cedula* in this context would be slightly less technical than the same term used in different contexts, cf. above, n. 87; on the term see W. Wattenbach, *Das Schriftwesen im Mittelalter* (Leipzig, 1896, 3rd edn.), pp. 60, 198 n. 4, 232, 273, and Emin Tengström, 'Die Protokollierung der Collatio Carthaginensis', *Studia Graeca et Latina Gothoburgensia*, xiv, 1962, pp. 35–49.

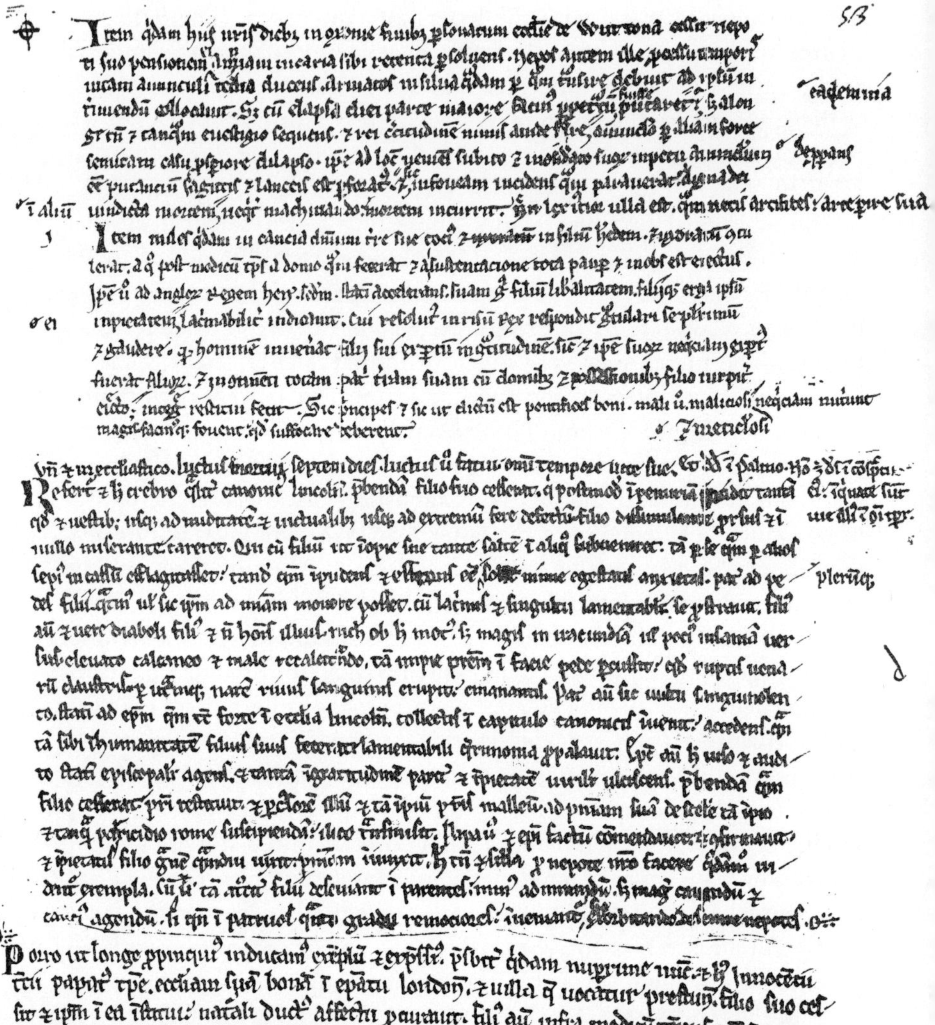

FIG. 2. Folio 53 recto

additions to the primitive text. They vary in length between a few lines[170] and several pages.[171] There are instances where the author felt it necessary to change the primitive text which followed on from these additions,[172] and in these cases the additions were certainly included in the codex after the primitive text had been copied. However, that they were not necessarily *written* after the primitive text had been copied is shown by another example: whereas it is contended that the death of Pope Innocent III is the *terminus a quo* for the copying of the primitive text, one addition on a separate piece of parchment refers to him as being still alive.[173]

The marginal additions present fewer problems. In almost every case they consist of quotations from the Bible, Church Fathers, or classical authors, and in this impersonal as well as timeless character they could have been written into the codex at any time after the primitive text was written. They vary a great deal in length, and sometimes are also to be found on the additional pieces of parchment. In some instances it is quite clear that they were written after these pieces had been inserted into the codex and thereby give testimony of the considerable time which elapsed between the commencement and completion of the manuscript in its present form. The existence of the marginal additions in this form makes it clear that the author never completed the revision of the manuscript. The result is that the present codex is a working copy which is difficult to transcribe, particularly because of the great number of cross-references.

An outline of the development of one unusually long and complex additional passage, together with reference to the accompanying figures, will serve to exemplify both the growth of the manuscript as a whole and the difficulties involved in the transcription. Folio 70, though an addition, is a full page, written in double columns. It is continued on f. 70ᵛ, which refers to another addition, i.e. f. 69ʳ (Fig. 3), which was written on a separate piece. This addition originally ended with *facultatem prestat* (third line from the end of f. 69ʳ), but it now carries on to the end of f. 69ʳ and is continued on the verso, not however at the top but on line 11. It has to be assumed therefore that the upper part of f. 69ᵛ had been filled before this extension was made. Folio 69ᵛ (Fig. 4) started originally with *Gratus ob hoc*[174] and finished with *sit scola sola.*[175] It

---

[170] Folio 57ʳ, p. 38, l. 649–p. 40, l. 664.

[171] The longest one is f. 70ʳ/ᵛ, plus f. 69ʳ/ᵛ and f. 71 (1); cf. p. 110, l. 580–p. 122, l. 804.

[172] e.g. p. 104, l. 462, with the marginal words *ut ad rem revertamur*, cf. Fig. 1, f. 66ᵛ, col. 2, line 5.

[173] Below, p. 14, l. 242: 'Nunc et huius Innocencii tercii papatus', cf. fig. 2, no. 3, lines 1–2.   [174] Below, p. 122, l. 797.   [175] Below, p. 122, l. 804.

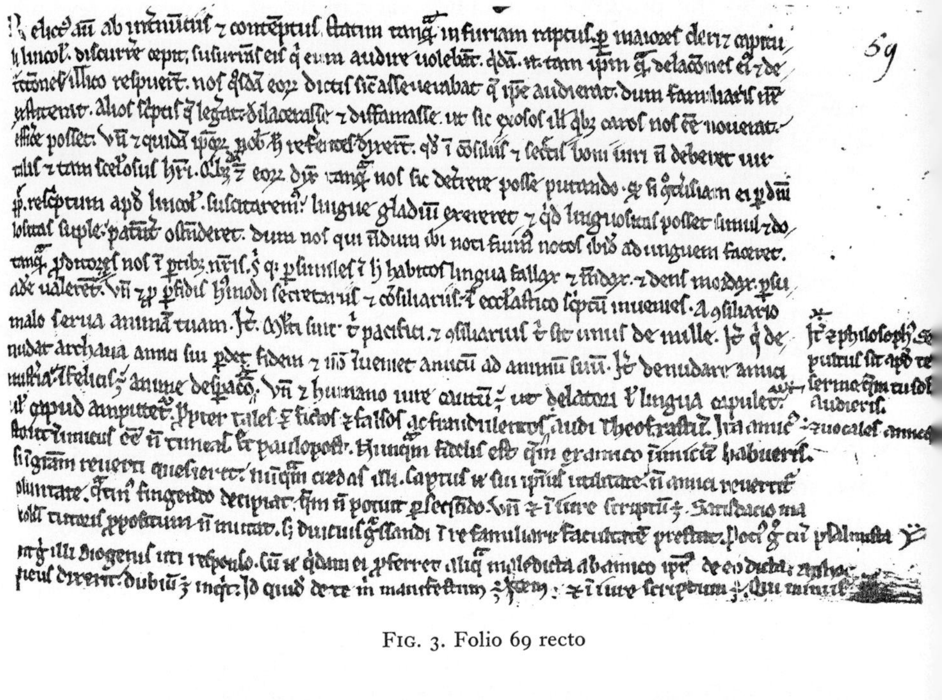

59

Fig. 3. Folio 69 recto

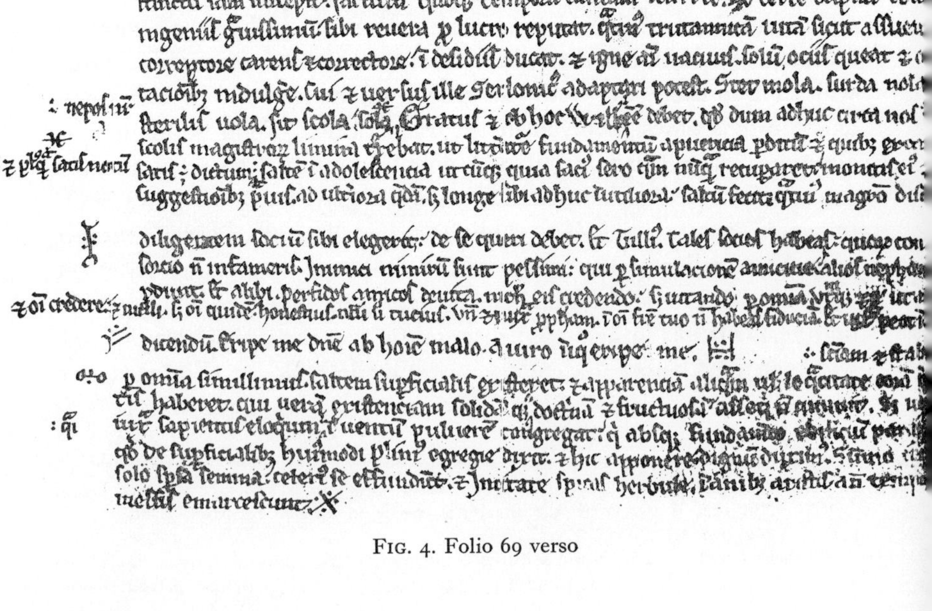

Fig. 4. Folio 69 verso

was followed by a *Gratus et ob hoc*,[176] which, however, could not be written continuously since in the meantime the extension from f. 69ʳ had been copied. Later, Giraldus decided to put the (originally second) *Gratus et ob hoc* before the *Gratus ob hoc* while leaving the text unchanged, which now sounds clumsy. In turn f. 69ᵛ branches off into f. 71ʳ (no. 2). Folio 71ʳ no. 1 (the verso is blank) is the continuation of the end of f. 70ᵛ. It is not easy to convey the complexity of these transitions, but it

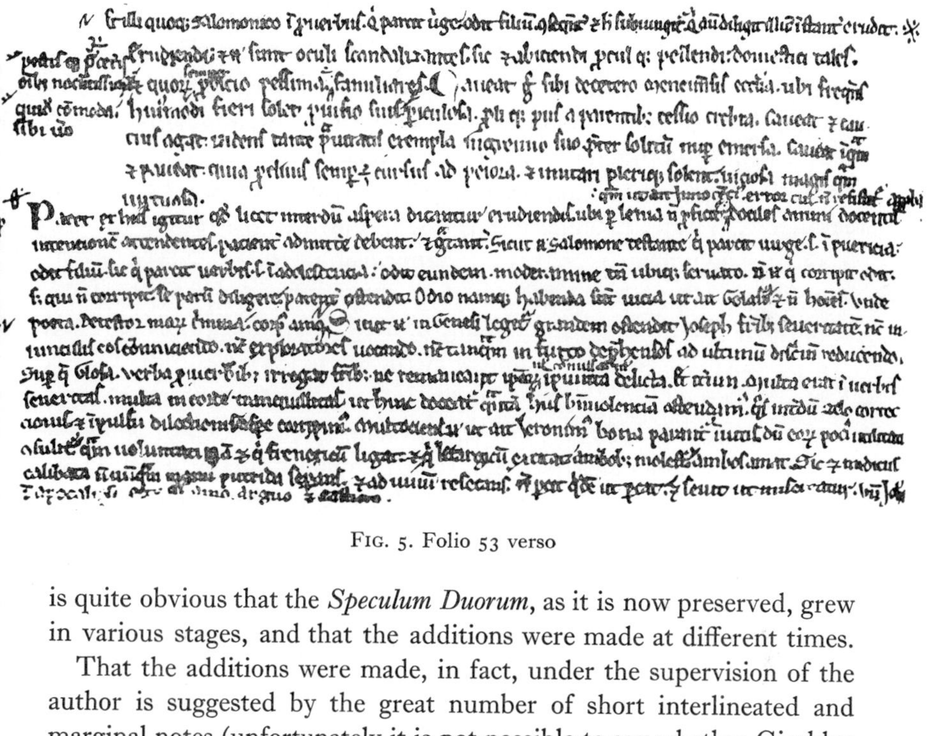

FIG. 5. Folio 53 verso

is quite obvious that the *Speculum Duorum*, as it is now preserved, grew in various stages, and that the additions were made at different times.

That the additions were made, in fact, under the supervision of the author is suggested by the great number of short interlineated and marginal notes (unfortunately it is not possible to say whether Giraldus wrote these additions himself, although it is likely that he did so in some cases). Additions of this kind may be classified as *not essential* to the grammatical sense of the text but as stylistic improvements or attempts to make the text more clear (cf. Fig. 5). The instances are too numerous to be listed here in full, but the reader can form an impression for himself by looking for short phrases or words printed in ⌐ ¬ in the Latin text. Examples are: *iam, scilicet, tamen, recte, sic, itaque, semper, quoniam*, or of a more specific nature like *sed non in audientia, Huberto, Lincolniensi canonico, de quo nobis est sermo* etc. Short emendations of this kind are so numerous that it is very unlikely that a copyist could

176 Below, p. 120, l. 775.

have left them out when he wrote the primitive text into the codex. In addition, they are so inessential that no person other than the author would think it desirable to insert them. It seems, therefore, most likely that they were included on Giraldus' initiative; that he reread the primitive text in the present manuscript and found it unsatisfactory.

A different type of very short interlineations arises from the fact that the primitive text was originally a copy of rather poor quality, written by a scribe who was not very well versed in Latin, and that it was later corrected in parts without covering all the original mistakes. Letters and syllables were added in order to correct a word, and at time the tense of a verb was changed, or it was switched from the singular into the plural. A number of examples will be given below, the correction in each case being printed in italics: ant*h*onomasice (p. 4, l. 34); ciba*vi*mus (p. 4, ll. 53–4); educa*vi*mus (p. 4, l. 54); provexi*mus* (p. 4, l. 55); creavi-*mus* (p. 4, l. 55); habund*ancia* (p. 8, l. 136); recalci*tracio*ne (p. 10, l. 156); conglu*ti*nat (p. 20, l. 344); abho*mi*nantur (p. 20, l. 345); iuven-*tu*te (p. 44, l. 729); anima*rum* (p. 46, l. 771); *p*arricida (p. 66, l. 1103); *a*pperimus (p. 78, l. 6); Lambili*au* (p. 80, l. 58); *a*libi (p. 82, l. 106); scorpi*onis* (p. 86, l. 167); monstr*a*bit (p. 88, l. 181); *deaura*tis (p. 90, l. 234); ade*oque* (p. 98, l. 357); su*r*gere (p. 102, l. 435); ab*s*tracto (p. 106, l. 525); terebat (p. 120, l. 776); equi*ta*turam (p. 126, l. 846); *in*mobilis (p. 126, l. 864); modu*l*os (p. 138, l. 1089); sint*h*omatum (p. 146, ll. 1232–3); puta*vi*mus (p. 210, l. 59); re*s*istitur (p. 222, l. 268). There are other instances where words essential to the understanding of the text had been left out and were later added: *fuisse, eadem via, deproperans* (p. 16, ll. 262 and 264); *non* (p. 18, l. 305); *murem* (p. 28, l. 452); *pater* (p. 36, l. 589); *contra* (p. 62, l. 1059); *quod* (p. 64, l. 1078); *proposuimus* (p. 110, l. 605).

Such corrections as these pose two problems: what was the nature of the text from which the scribe wrote, and did the scribe write from dictation or from a copy which he had before him? The first question may be answered by referring to other passages in the work of Giraldus where it is revealed that he kept copies of his letters which he could then produce on suitable occasions.[177] Some such copies were incorporated in his *Symbolum Electorum*, others were appended to the *Speculum Duorum*. They were either fair copies of the finished letters, or drafts; if they were drafts they were either written by Giraldus himself, perhaps heavily abbreviated, or dictated to a scribe, either spontaneously or from previously existing notes. We have already seen that the primitive text of the *Speculum Duorum* is not identical with the original letter to the

---

[177] Below, p. 82, ll. 78–9; also *Op.* i, p. 265.

nephew but an enlarged version. Whether the scribe copied from a text which was in front of him, or whether he wrote from dictation, there were enough transitional stages between the first version and the primitive text in the codex for a number of mistakes to be introduced.

Diagramatic representation of the way in which the text reached its present form:

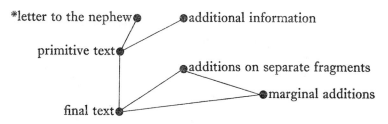

It happened frequently that a word or a syllable was written twice in error and this was corrected on revision. Examples: *eadem* (p. 66, l. 1118); *certo vos* (p. 164, l. 64); *solum* (p. 172, l. 57); *eloquiis* (p. 176, l. 6); *ut* (p. 182, l. 119); *faciens* (p. 196, l. 122); *et nos clericos alios* (p. 208, l. 21); *si* (p. 214, l. 109); *placere* (p. 218, l. 178); *et* (p. 216, l. 152); *elinguis* (p. 224, l. 299); *et excessus* (p. 236, l. 479).

In some instances words were copied which did not belong to the text, or which had no place where they were written, providing evidence of misunderstanding. Examples: *equos ipsos* (p. 2, l. 29), two words which do not occur again near that place; *et uxoratum* (p. 16, l. 270), the words occur in the text shortly afterwards and were thus originally misplaced, but the mistake was recognized by the scribe at once; *cum* preceded the *apud* (p. 94, l. 285), which may have come in as a mistake from the shortly following *nobiscum*; *duplici* (p. 106, l. 509), written by mistake, with the scribe possibly starting the same line again (cf. *duplici* in line 508); *cuivis* (p. 126, l. 868) was wrongly placed by the scribe after *merito* while it should have come a little earlier, and it was therefore added as a marginal note in the correct place; *se* (p. 148, l. 1244) was originally misplaced, but the mistake seems to have been recognized by the scribe immediately.

In other cases, also, the text was faulty but was later emended. These are mistakes which are easier to understand if one assumes that the text was written from dictation, since they involve words which sound similar, although it is not possible to establish whether such mistakes came in when the text was dictated for the first time, and therefore were in the copy from which the scribe wrote, or whether the scribe of the present manuscript wrote from dictation. Examples:

eruendi (p. 18, l. 307) read originally *erudiendi* but was later corrected;
volente instead of *valente* (p. 40, l. 663); *tam* instead of *tanquam* (p. 202,
l. 234); *sunt* instead of *sit* (p. 234, l. 431); *tormenter* instead of *tormenta*
(p. 236, l. 475).

There is, however, one example of error which can hardly be explained
as a result of writing from dictation, but which seems to point undoubtedly to the conclusion that the scribe who wrote the primitive
text copied from a text in front of him. The primitive text breaks off
in the middle of a word and a considerable portion had to be added on
the top of the page in the margin (the words in the margin are given in
italics): 'Sepe quem non correxit ob*iurgacio, emendat pudor. Et alibi in
eodem: Ingenuorum ingenia facilius educat verecundia quam metus
exsuperat et, quos tormenta non vincunt, interdum vincit pudor.* Proinde
remedium saltem . . .' (p. 42, ll. 704–7).

Thus it would seem to be more likely in the light of this example
that the scribe wrote from a copy which was in front of him, not from
dictation, and also that the text from which he copied was abbreviated,
and that he failed to expand some of the abbreviations correctly. Nevertheless there is no certainty, and the matter is complicated by the
possibility that the text may in parts have been written from dictation
at a stage which preceded the copying of the primitive text.

CHRONOLOGICAL TABLE OF
THE LIFE OF GIRALDUS

(italics indicate approximate dates)

1146	Giraldus de Barri born at Manorbier Castle, Pembrokeshire
1162–1174	student at Paris, then return to England
1175	appointment to the archdeaconry of Brecon (diocese St. David's)
1176	unsuccessful candidate for the election to the bishopric of St. David's.
1177–1179	student at Paris
1179–1182	representative of the bishop of St. David's in the diocese
1183	first visit to Ireland
1184	entry into the royal service as a clerk
1185	second visit to Ireland (with Prince John)
1188	(Lent) tour of Wales (with Archbishop Baldwin of Canterbury)
1194	retirement from court, studies at Hereford and Lincoln
1199	29 June election to the see of St. David's (short) third visit to Ireland
1199–1203	three journeys to Rome to defend his election
1203	April 15 election declared invalid by Pope Innocent III *December 6* final agreement between Giraldus and Archbishop Hubert Walter of Canterbury *December 7* consecration of Geoffrey of Henlaw as bishop of St. David's *December 11* at Newbury Giraldus resigns the archdeaconry of Brecon in favour of his nephew
1204–1205	fourth visit to Ireland
1206	pilgrimage to Rome
1207	retirement at Lincoln
1208	appeal of his nephew and Master William de Capella against Giraldus at Hereford
1223	death of Giraldus (? in the diocese of Lincoln)

TABLE OF THE WORKS OF GIRALDUS

(All dates are approximate. Where there was more than one
edition, reference is made only to the earliest one)

Works of uncertain dates

Catalogus Brevior
De Giraldo Archidiacono Menevensi
Retractationes
Symbolum Electorum
Vita Sancti Hugonis
Vita Sancti Ethelberti
Vita Sancti Remigii
Poems
Letters

Lost works of Giraldus

Mappa Kambriae
De Vita Sancti Caradoci (preface preserved)
De Fidei Fructu Fideique Defectu

Work wrongly attributed to Giraldus

Vita Davidis II Episcopi Menevensis

BIBLIOGRAPHY

The greater part of the literature on Giraldus published before 1958 has been listed in Eileen A. Williams, 'A Bibliography of Giraldus Cambrensis', *National Library of Wales Journal*, xii, 1961–2, pp. 97–140. Below are assembled all those titles which either were not mentioned in this bibliography or have appeared since.

BATE, A. K., 'Walter Map and Giraldus Cambrensis', *Latomus*, xxxi, 1972, pp. 860–75.

BERGES, Wilhelm, 'Girald von Wales', *Die Fürstenspiegel des hohen und späten Mittelalters* (Schriften der Monumenta Germaniae Historica, 2, Stuttgart, 1938, reprinted 1952), pp. 143–50.

BEST, Edward E., 'Classical Latin Prose Writers quoted by Giraldus Cambrensis', Ph.D. thesis, University of North Carolina, 1957 (unpublished).

HIBBERD, Lloyd, 'Giraldus Cambrensis and English "Organ Music"', *Journal of the American Musicological Society*, viii, 1955, pp. 208–12.

—— 'Giraldus Cambrensis on Welsh popular singing', *Essays on Music . . . in Honor of A. T. Davison* (Cambridge, Mass., 1957), pp. 17–23.

HOLMES, Urban T., 'The *Kambriae Descriptio* of Gerald the Welshman', *Medievalia et Humanistica*, New Series 1, 1970, pp. 217–32.

HUMPHREYS, Dorothy, 'Some Types of Social Life as shown in the works of Gerald of Wales', B.Litt. thesis, Oxford, 1936 (unpublished).

HUYGENS, R. B. C., 'Une lettre de Giraud le Cambrien à propos de ses ouvrages historiques', *Latomus*, xxvi, 1965, pp. 90–100.

—— 'Deux sermonnaires médiévaux: Tétère de Nevers et Giraud de Barri. Textes inédits', *Studi medievali*, x, 3, 1969, pp. 271–96.

LEFÈVRE, Yves, 'Un brouillon du XIIᵉ siècle: le manuscrit 470 du fonds de la reine Christine. Étude sur quelques inédits de Giraud de Barri', *Mélanges d'archéologie et d'histoire*, lviii, 1941–6, pp. 145–77.

MARKS, U. T., 'Gerald the Naturalist', *Speculum*, xi, 1936, pp. 110–24.

MARTIN, F. X., 'Gerald of Wales, Norman Reporter on Ireland', *Studies*, 58, 1969, pp. 279–92.

MISCH, Georg, 'Die autobiographische Schriftstellerei des Giraldus Cambrensis', *Geschichte der Autobiographie*, II, ii, 2 (Frankfurt, 1962) pp. 1297–1479.

RICHTER, Michael, 'The *Life of St. David* by Giraldus Cambrensis', *Welsh History Review*, iv, 1968–9, pp. 381–6.

—— *Giraldus Cambrensis* (Aberystwyth, 1972). This study was previously published in three articles in the *National Library of Wales Journal*, xvi–xvii, 1969–72.

Ryan, M. T. 'The Historical Value of Giraldus Cambrensis' *Expugnatio Hibernica*', M.A. thesis, University College, Dublin, 1967 (unpublished).

Schnith, Karl, 'Betrachtungen zum Spätwerk des Giraldus Cambrensis *De Principis Instructione*', *Festiva Lanx* (München, 1966), pp. 53–66.

Stewart, James, '*Topographia Hiberniae* by Giraldus Cambrensis: A Contribution to a Folkloristic Commentary', Thesis for the degree of Filosofie Licentiat, University of Uppsala, 1966 (unpublished).

Sullivan, Brother Gerald J. E., 'Pagan Latin Poets in Giraldus Cambrensis', Ph.D. thesis, University of Cincinnati, 1950 (unpublished).

SPECULUM DUORUM

Incipit speculum duorum et utile cognicionis, correctionis, conquestionis et commonicionis instrumentum

PRIMA PARS INCIPIT

MAGISTER Giraldus de Barri Giraldo archidiacono de Brechene,
5 nepoti suo, et vere a nepa dicto, salutem et salutacionem quam meretur.
Scripsistis nobis quod propter equorum carenciam ad nos termino
statuto et fide firmato venire non potuistis. Equos autem ad eundum
Meneviam et Martru et Aberteivi ad opera prodicionis perpetranda
satis habuistis. Ad redeundum vero Lincolniam ob fidei pacta servan-
10 dum, quam tempore ⌈iam⌉ ad minus certum est lapsam esse, equos
habere non potuistis. Supplicastis etiam litteris eisdem quod fraudi
vestre hoc non imputetur. Set quomodo fraudem transgressionis huius
adeo abhorrere se fingit et simulat qui tam manifestam prodicionis
plus-quam-fraudem et tam enormis scandali notam nec notare curat
15 nec vitare laborat, tanquam festucam ⌈scilicet⌉ in occulo videns et
trabem non attendens? Qua scilicet nota non solum Lincolniam et
Herefordiam atque Meneviam et Walliam totam, verum etiam Hiberniam, *pernicibus* semper *alis* fama volante, quia contagiosa quoque
turpia esse solent et enormia, iam contaminavit.
20 Rogastis etiam ut equos vobis mitteremus, set illos quos vobis in
discessu vestro accomodavimus turpiter per incuriam, ne per industriam
dicamus, exulceratos et fame affectos (nec mirum quoniam et equos
absque pabulo et pueros absque viatico eosque qui per totum autum-
pnum vobis in blado colligendo et collocando, quos ad hoc de Lincol-
25 nia in Walliam transmisimus, fideliter laboraverant absque stipendiis
debitis et etiam expensis ad redeundum!) nobis valde curialiter remisi-
f. 50va stis. | Equos etiam eosdem, cum vos et sarcinas vestras usque Brechene
detulissent, cum apud Landu quiescendum aliquandiu et a laboribus
respirandum nostri putarent, a stabulo sibi iam preparato et a pueris

1–2 Incipit . . . instrumentum *rubrica*; commonicionis *e* communicionis *corr.* V
3 Prima pars *rubrica in margine*; *post* Prima pars *verbum truncatum*: incipit?
29 *post* putarent *deletum est* equos ipsos

2. commonicionis] Cf. *Op.* i, p. 422, ll. 12 f.: *Speculum Duorum commonitorium et consolatorium*; also *Op.* i, p. 414, ll. 26–7.
15–16. Cf. Matt. vii, 3; Luke vi, 41.
18. Cf. Virgil, *Aeneis* iv, 180: (*Fama*) *pernicibus alis*, and *Aeneis* xi, 139: *Fama volans*.

Here begins the Mirror of Two Men, a useful Manual for Recognition, Correction, Complaint, and Exhortation

PART ONE

MASTER Giraldus de Barri to Giraldus, archdeacon of Brecon, his nephew—a word justly derived from the Latin for a scorpion—the greeting and salutation he deserves.

You wrote to us that it was because of lack of horses that you were unable to come to us at the appointed time as you promised. However, you were sufficiently well provided with horses to go to St. David's, Mathry, and Cardigan to perpetrate your acts of treachery. Yet you could not get horses to return to Lincoln to honour the terms of the contract—a contract which has now, without a shadow of doubt, lapsed with the passage of time. In this same letter you begged that this be not attributed to deceit on your part. But how does a man feign and pretend that he is appalled at the deceit of this offence, when he neither cares to note nor strives to avoid such an incontrovertibly deceitful—more than deceitful—act of treachery, and the disgrace of such an outrageous scandal, as if he sees the mote in his eye and ignores the beam? Indeed, since 'rumour always flies on swift wings', and scandals and outrages normally spread like the plague, by the disgrace of this scandal he has contaminated not only Lincoln, Hereford, St. David's, and the whole of Wales, but also Ireland; for scandalous and outrageous actions are normally contagious. You even asked us to send you horses, but those which we provided for you on your departure, you very politely returned, covered with sores as a result of neglect—I would almost say by intention—and suffering from starvation. (This is not surprising, since you sent the horses back without fodder, and the stable-lads without travelling money; and those men we had specially sent from Lincoln to Wales, who had worked faithfully for you through the harvest, gathering and stacking the corn, you sent back without their rightful wages or even expenses for the return!) When those very same horses had carried you and your baggage as far as Brecon, and when our servants were thinking of resting them for a short while and giving them a respite from their labours at Llanddew, Ralph, the nephew of your tutor—a man whom we have fed with our bread, just as we have a great many other ungrateful and useless characters—drove them in a despicable fashion with sticks

30 nostris ad hoc purgato necnon et a domo quam fecimus (set dicere
possumus: *sic vos non vobis* etc.) nepos magistri vestri Radulphus,
quem pane nostro sicut et alios ingratos et inutiles pavimus plurimos,
baculis et virgis turpiter eiecit, dicens et alta voce proclamans quod non
equi magistri Giraldi, set equi domini, et tanquam ant⌐h⌐onomasice
35 Domini et dominatoris magni, locum illum haberent et ibi starent,
talem quippe erga nos animum habens puer qualem et magister.

Nolumus ergo ad talem locum equos vel pueros nostros de cetero
mittere, ubi et equi fame afficiuntur et a stabulis turpiter eiciuntur, ubi
et pueri, contumeliis affecti, non cum honore debito suscipiuntur, sicut
40 Eneas, qui et avem vobis de Hibernia tulit, et Iohannes, iniuriis affecti
et a magistro vestro eiecti fuerunt, sicut et ortolanum nostrum, quem
de Anglia ad curiam emendandam venire fecimus, idem magister,
cuncta magistrans ibi et ministrans, in iniuriam nostram magnam et
vestram quoque, si cognoscere sciretis et ausi essetis, gladio, sicut
45 accepimus, super capud eius extracto, quem certe ubi maius opus
extiterat non bene traxit, set pocius perdidit ⌐quin immo et hostibus
reddidit⌐, vinculis ferreis compedivit, nec aliud in causa fuit nisi quod
de dampno nostro, quod ab ipso et suis tam in domo quam in orto nobis
49 tociens fieri vidit, loqui tantum ausus fuit. Ad talem itaque locum non
f. 50ᵛᵇ sunt equi nostri mittendi, non pueri, | donec Deus meliora providerit.

Nec adeo mirum ⌐tamen⌐ de garcione pessimo, infideli per omnia et
ingrato; set hoc magis admirandum quod nepos noster tam naturalis,
qui dulces nobiscum capiebat cibos, immo quem non solum ciba⌐vi⌐-
mus et educa⌐vi⌐mus, verum etiam in redditus amplos promovendo de
55 tam exili provexi⌐mus⌐ et quasi de nichilo creavi⌐mus⌐, tam scelerose
contra nos et cum scandalo tanto recalcitrare presumpsit, tanquam illo
ewangelico et in hoc evidenter impleto: *Qui manducat panem meum,*
levabit contra me calcaneum suum.

Et de magistro quoque vestro haut dissimiliter obstupendum, cui,
60 ut vos bonis disciplinis imbueret et non pravis, tanta contulimus et
tam utiles in omnibus extitimus, quin immo, sicut ex sequentibus
palam erit, cui omnibus que possidet adquirendis vel causa efficiens
vel efficax ad minus occasio fuimus, cui et vitam etiam ⌐non nunquam,
ut nostis,⌐ conservavimus: tam infidelem econtra se reddidit et tam
65 ingratum, quod illud in psalmo scriptum in eius sit persona satis evidenter impletum: *Homo pacis mee, in quo speravi: qui edebat panes meos,*

60 ut vos] *V* vos ut *postea transpositum*　　　62 cui] *V* qui

---

31. Epigram of Virgil: *Sic vos non vobis nidificatis aves, Vitae Vergilianae,* ed. Diehl
(Bonn, 1911), p. 35, 25–8 (Donatus).
57–8. John xiii, 18.　　　　　　　　　　　　　　　66–7. Ps. xl, 10.

and rods from the stable which had been prepared for them, and had been cleaned out for this purpose by our stable-lads—in fact, even from the home we had made (but we may quote Virgil: 'Thus ye birds build your nests, but not for yourselves'); and he bellowed and shouted at the top of his voice that the horses of Master Giraldus were not to occupy that space, nor to be stabled there; only the horses *of his* lord, as if antonomastically he were the Lord God Almighty himself. Indeed, the son entertains the same feelings towards us as the tutor.

It is not, therefore, our desire in future to send either our horses or our stable-lads to a place where our horses are both starved and turned out of their stables in a disgraceful fashion, and where, too, our stable-boys are subjected to insults, and are not received with the respect due to them, like Aeneas, who even brought you a bird from Ireland, and John: they were both unjustly treated and thrown out by your tutor. So, too, in the case of our gardener, whom we sent from England to set your court-yard to rights: this same tutor who directs and manages everything there to our detriment as well as yours, if you had the sense and courage to admit it, drew his sword at his head (so we have heard). Naturally, he did not draw his sword with any skill when there was a more pressing need, but rather 'mislaid' it—in fact he actually gave it to the enemy. He then chained him up in iron fetters, for no other reason than that the gardener had only dared to remark on the losses which he saw so frequently being sustained by us at the hands of him and his cronies both in the house and in the garden. Therefore, our horses and our stable-lads are not to be sent to a place like this, until the Lord improves things.

I am not, however, so surprised at that wicked groom, an ungrateful and unfaithful wretch in every respect; but it is the more astonishing that our nephew, as one close to us, who used to eat sweet bread with us, indeed, whom we have not only fed and educated, but have also raised from abject poverty by providing for his preferment to rich revenues, and have, as it were, created from nothing, should have dared to kick us in the teeth so wickedly and so maliciously, as if the verse of the Gospel had also clearly been fulfilled in this case: 'He that eateth bread with me, shall lift up his heel against me.'

In a similar way, too, the conduct of your tutor beggars description: we have conferred so much upon him and have been so helpful to him that he might imbue you with good and not bad manners: for him, as will be clear from what follows, we were the efficient cause, or at least the effective reason for his acquiring all he possesses; and we have even saved his life on more than one occasion, as you know. Yet he, in return for this, has shown himself to be so unfaithful and so ungrateful that

magnificavit super ⌐*me*⌐ *supplantacionem.* ⌐Et illud quoque Salomonis
in Proverbiis per contrarium: *Ne moliaris amico tuo malum, cum in te
habeat fiduciam.* ⌐Et illud eiusdem et ibidem, non per antifrasim, set
70 expresse: *Qui delicate nutrit servum suum, postea illum senciet contu-
macem.* Et illud Ysaie: '*Filios enutrivi et exaltavi, ipsi vero spreverunt
me.* Unde et cum poeta dicere potui:

Non exspectato vulnus ab hoste tuli.

Et iterum:

75 *Que venit indigne pena, dolenda venit.*
⌐*Iam pacior telis vulnera facta meis.*⌐

Et ⌐*cum*⌐ Psalmista sepius ad Dominum hunc versum orando proponere: *Custodi me a laqueo quem absconderunt mihi et ab scandalis
operancium iniquitatem.* ⌐Et tanquam Ieremie verbum ad Sedechiam
80 regem in hunc modum assumere: *Viri pacifici tui seduxerunt te et
recesserunt a te.*

Unde super illud in Ewangelio: *Trademini autem a parentibus et
fratribus et cognatis et amicis,* etc., Expositor: *Minorem dolorem mala
ingerunt que ab extraneis inferuntur; plus enim in nobis ea tormenta
85 seviunt que ab illis patimur de quorum mentibus presumebamus, quia cum
dampno corporis mala nos cruciant amisse caritatis.* Hinc est enim quod
de Iuda, traditore suo, per Psalmistam Dominus dicit: *Et quid si
inimicus meus maledixisset mihi, supportassem utique. Et si is qui oderat
me super me magna locutus fuisset, absconderem me utique ab eo. Tu vero
90 unanimis homo, dux meus et notus meus.*⌐ Nos igitur hupupe quodammodo que nidificat in stercoribus ⌐*suis*⌐ similes extitimus; nepos autem
noster cuculum, qui nutritores suos, cum adultus fuerit, devorare solet,
expresse representat.⌐

Super hac autem supplantacione per magistrum excogitata et per
95 discipulum docilem in talibus effectui mancipata per visionem quandam
premuniti satis fuimus, sicut de inopinatis rerum eventibus plerumque
consuevimus. Videbatur enim nobis quod nepos ille noster tanquam in
lecto nostro, cuius porcionem non modicam ei concessimus, nobiscum
preter solitum constitutus, partem lecti maiorem occupans ⌐*ex toto*⌐

69–72 *haec additio legitur tota in f.* 52ʳ   82–90 Unde super illud . . . notus meus
legitur in f. 52ʳ

68–9. Prov. iii, 29.   70–1. Prov. xxix, 21.   71–2. Isa. i, 2.
73. Ovid, *Her.* vi, 82; cf. *infra,* Ep. 6, p. 238, 521.
75. Ovid, *Her.* v, 8; cf. *infra,* Ep. 4, p. 182, 95.
76. Ovid, *Her.* ii, 48: Heu ! patior . . .
78–9. Cf. Ps. cxl, 9: *Custodi me a laqueo, quem statuerunt mihi: et a scandalis operan-
tium iniquitatem,* and Ps. xxx, 5: *Educes me de laqueo hoc, quem absconderunt mihi.*
80–1. Cf. Jer. xxxviii, 22: *Seduxerunt te et praevaluerunt adversum te viri pacifici tui
. . . et recesserunt a te.*

it is clear enough that that passage of the Psalm: 'For even the man of my peace, in whom I trusted, who ate my bread, hath greatly supplanted me', has been fulfilled in his character. An inverted form of this is found in the Proverbs of Solomon: 'Practise not evil against thy friend, when he hath confidence in thee.' Again in the same book of the same author, put clearly and not in an inverted form: 'He that nourisheth his servant delicately from his childhood afterwards shall find him stubborn.' Again in Isaiah: 'I have brought up children and exalted them, but they have despised me.' So then I could agree with the poet who says: 'The wound I have borne is from an unexpected enemy.' And again: 'The pain that comes undeserved / Is a matter of sorrow.' 'Now I bear wounds / By my own hands inflicted.' When praying to the Lord, we could speak this verse with the Psalmist: 'Keep me from the snares, which they have laid for me: and the gins of the workers of iniquity. I could, too, take up the words of Jeremiah to King Zedekiah in the following way: 'The men of peace have deceived thee, and have departed from thee.'

So, on this verse in the Gospel, 'And ye shall be betrayed by your parents, and brethren, and kinsmen, and friends, etc.', the Commentator remarks: 'Troubles that are inflicted by strangers cause us less pain; for the torments we suffer from those whose thoughts we took for granted rage more bitterly within us, because, as well as the physical injury, the pains of the love that is lost causes us agony.' Hence what our Lord spoke of his betrayer, Judas, by the Psalmist: 'For it was not an enemy that reproached me; then I could have borne it: neither was it he that hated me that did magnify himself against me; then I would have hid myself from him. But it was thou, a man my equal, my guide and mine acquaintance.' In some ways we are like the hoopoe who builds her nest in her droppings, while our nephew clearly resembles the cuckoo who, when he is fully grown, usually devours his foster-parents.

However, we had sufficient presentiment of this deceit—a deceit thought up by the tutor and put into effect by the pupil, an apt pupil in such matters—since we dreamt of it, as we usually have done where unexpected events are concerned. For we dreamt that that nephew of ours was in bed with us (contrary to our usual custom) and, though we gave him plenty of room in it, he was taking up more than his fair

---

82–3. Luke xxi, 16. Cf. *infra*, Ep. 4, p. 182, 107–8.
83–4. Bede, *In Lucae evangelium expositio* xxi, 16 (Migne, *P.L.* 92, cols. 586–7). Quoted also *infra*, Ep. 4, p. 182, 108–10.   87–90. Ps. liv, 13–14.
91. Cf. *infra*, Ep. 6, p. 234, 462.

f. 52ra nos totis viribus expellere nitebatur.| Et dum in hac quasi lucta ali-
101 quandiu versaremur, cum ille nos expellere pararet et nos in thoro
nostro nos retinere vellemus, tandem ab occulis nostris con⌐ten⌐cio
talis sompnum excussit.

⌐Vidimus et aliam de eodem ⌐postea⌐ visionem. Cum enim nun-
105 ciasset nobis pluries post discessum suum primum se ad nos in brevi
reversurum et fidei prestite federa servaturum, videbatur nobis in
sompno quod, cum essemus in Wallia et quidam clerici nostri de mandato nostro ad nos venirent ad visitandum quandam ecclesiam nostram,
vidimus inter alios quendam equitantem capite more Walensico tenui
110 pallio et virgeis ac variis lineis discolorato desuper cohoperto et panno
dextro trans humerum sinistrum proiecto, et, querentibus nobis quis-
nam esset Walensis ille, responsum est quoniam nepos noster archidiaconus erat. Ipse vero, quam cito ad nos clamare potuit, quesivit
ad quid vocaremus eum et vexaremus, quia sine ipso satis visitacionem
115 illam fieri posse dicebat. Cui cum responderemus a nobis ipsum non
fuisse vocatum: 'Possum', inquit, 'ergo reverti'; cui diximus: 'Potes,
et presertim etiam in habitu tali' (non enim discorditer ipsum a nobis
discessisse visio recolebat). Et statim, lora regirans, via qua venerat
reversus est. In crastino vero sociis et amicis nostris ad nos venientibus
120 visionem retulimus, dicentes eis nepotem nostrum in brevi quidem
venturum, set non minus discorditer quam ante recessurum. Vestis
igitur illa discolor et varia, levis et inordinata, levem eius animum,
varium et incompositum designavit. Quod autem se vexari conquestus
est, signare potuit quod corpori magis et desidie datus, tam corporis
125 laborem excercitando quam animi quoque studiis honestis indulgendo,
cum nec hunc nec illum fugere laborem nos unquam consueverimus,
semper abhorrere soleat et recusare. Quod vero tam promptulus statim
ad revertendum fuit et nos relinquendum, et reversionem eius talem
secuturam in brevi designavit et mores eius ex parte, quoniam a puerili-
130 bus annis usque in hodiernum nunquam ubi quacumque occaisiuncula
procul a nobis esse poterat propinquus esse volebat, indicavit⌐.

Quam detestabilis etiam bonis viris contra parentes et sanguine
propinquos, qui suorum securitatem ⌐et utilitatem⌐ per cessiones huiusmodi tam naturaliter tamque sollicite procurarunt, talis videatur recal-
135 citracio, ex responso decani Lincolniensis Rogeri, viri fidelis et boni,
discreti quoque et eruditi, verbo vestro quod *ex habun⌐dan⌐cia cordis*

104–31 *haec additio* (Vidimus et aliam . . . indicavit) *legitur in f. 51^v*   133 *post*
qui *deletum est* ad   134 procurarunt] *V* procuraverunt *expunxit* -ve-

136–7. Matt. xii, 34; Luke vi, 45; also quoted *infra*, pp. 26, 40, 118, 156.

share and was trying to oust us with all his might. While we were engaged for some time in this wrestling-match, so to speak—he ready to push us out and we resolved to keep our head on the bolster—this fight eventually roused us from our sleep.

We also had another dream about him afterwards. When he had announced to us time and again after his original departure that he would return to us in a short time and honour the terms of the contract that had been given, we dreamt that, when we were in Wales and some of our clerks were coming to us at our request to visit one of our churches, we saw someone riding among the others. His head was covered after the Welsh manner with a thin cloak, brightly coloured with striped and variegated cloths, on top, and the right-hand side of this cloak was thrown over his left shoulder. When we asked the identity of this Welshman, the reply was given that it was our nephew, the archdeacon. As soon as he was within hailing distance, he asked the purpose of our summons and the reason for our troubling him, as he claimed it was possible for this visitation to take place without him. When we replied that he had not been summoned by us, he said, 'I can go home, then', and we replied, 'You can; especially in an attire like that.' (For the dream did not recall that we had parted at odds.) Immediately turning his horse around, he went back the way he had come. On the following day we related the dream to visiting friends and companions, telling them that our nephew would come in a short while, but that his departure would be no less discordant than before. That multicoloured, variegated, frivolous, and disordered dress signified the fickleness, the changeability, and the disorder of his mind. The fact that he complained that he was troubled could have signified that he was given over to sluggishness and slothfulness and was in the habit of avoiding and even refusing to indulge in physical activity, as well as in decent intellectual study, though we have never been in the habit of shirking the hard work of the one or the other. The fact that he was so ready to leave us and return immediately signified that he would go away in a short time and showed up those ways of his, since from his childhood days up to the present he never wished to stay close to us, when, given the slightest pretext, he could be as far away from us as possible.

How detestable respectable men consider recalcitrance of such a kind towards parents and kindred, who have so naturally and so carefully acquired security and advantage for their own kindred by resignations of this nature, you could have judged from the reply which Roger, dean of Lincoln, made to that remark of yours, for 'out of the abundance of the heart the mouth spake', in the hearing of many (and he

os emisit, in audiencia facto non modica, perpendere potuistis. Cum
enim ⌜in eiusdem hospicio⌝ redditus vestros vocaretis illos qui vobis
per operas nostras sic fuerant assignati, statim cum indignacione magna
140 subiecit: 'Redditus vestros dicitis quasi per probitatem vestram ad-
quisitos; si talis essetis qualis esse deberetis et bene vobis in verbo
prospiceretis, nunquam eos quamdiu vixerit vel voluerit hic patruus
vester, qui tam sibi quam vobis totum perquisivit, redditus vestros vel
vocitare vel etiam reputare deberetis.'

145   Unde et vir ille, et vir revera virilis animi, virque virorum per-
paucorum, cum fratrem suum uterinum in amplos reditus iam promo-
visset longeque maiores ei conferre proposuisset, et ille processu
temporis recalcitrare cepit, adeo ipsum incontinenti non solum ab
hospicio, verum et ab animo pariter et amore prorsus abiecit, quod, cum
150 episcopi Lincolnienses ob eius honorem atque favorem illum in ecclesia
Lincolniensi canonicare vellent, non permisit dicens et asserens se in
ecclesia qua ille canonicus esset nunquam decanum fore; unde et tam
f. 52rb inexorabiliter | ad correctionem plurium et castigacionem abhominatus
est ipsum, quod nunquam in conspectum ipsius nedum in consorcium
155 illum postea venire sustinuit. Set ad maiorem etiam talium detesta-
cionem, quotiens de fratre suo vel similibus ingratis et recalci⌜traci⌝one
notatis coram se mencionem fieri contingere solet, non aliter ipsos
quam proditorum nomine vel nota vocitandos censuit vel denotandos.

    Ad hec etiam archidiaconus Oxoniensis, magister Walterus Mapus,
160 vir eruditus, eloquens et facetus, audiens cessionem hanc a nobis sic
factam, statim in audiencia plurium dixit nos minus circumspecte
minusque discrete in hoc egisse neque tot cessionum huiusmodi exempla
prava quot viderat ipse nos vidisse, ⌜sufficere tamen nobis ad cautelam
de rege Henrico secundo et filiis suis perniciose nimis erga patrem
165 agentibus nostri temporis exempla debuisse⌝. Illud etiam in Ecclesiastico pluries proponere consuevit: *Melius est ut filii tui te rogent quam
te respicere in manus filiorum.* Veridicum autem tam ipsum fuisse quam
etiam filium Syrac Iesum in facto suo tam facinoroso nepos noster
⌜aperte⌝ comprobavit.

170   Relatum est etiam post facinus istud, et apud Lincolniam sepe
refertur, de presbitero quodam in Anglia qui diebus nostris ecclesiam
suam bonam cesserat filio suo, putans ut iustum foret ad consilium suum
tam ecclesiam quam filium se quamdiu viveret et vellet habiturum.

166-7. Ecclus. xxxiii, 22.

is a faithful and true man, as well as prudent and learned). When in his lodging you were calling your own those revenues which had been assigned to you by our own efforts in such a fashion, he immediately replied with great indignation: 'You speak of those revenues as if you had acquired them as a result of your own virtue; if you were as you ought to be and thought properly about what you were saying, you should never call or even consider them your own as long as your uncle lives or wishes, since he has acquired everything as much for himself as for you.'

So when that man—a truly noble man, a man as few men are—had promoted his own uterine brother to considerable revenues and had promised to confer many more on him, and the brother began to kick against him as time went by, immediately he not only sent him packing, but excluded him from his love and his thoughts to such an extent that he prevented the bishops of Lincoln from making his brother a prebendary in Lincoln cathedral as a mark of honour and respect for himself when they wanted to, and asserted that he himself would never be dean in the church where the other was canon. So, in order to correct and convert others, he hated his brother so completely—a fact which many people thoroughly disapproved of and tried to correct—that he never afterwards allowed him to come into his sight nor even into his company, but, as a mark of even greater detestation of such men, whenever mention happened to be made of his brother or similar ungrateful, notorious recalcitrants, it was his considered opinion that they should be called or addressed by nothing else than the name or title of 'betrayer'.

When that well-educated, eloquently elegant man, Master Walter Map, archdeacon of Oxford, heard of the resignation that we had carried out after this fashion, he immediately said in the hearing of many that we had acted with little circumspection and prudence in this matter, and we had not seen as many terrible examples of this kind of resignation as he had. The examples of King Henry II and his sons, who treated their father absolutely disgracefully, ought to have sufficed as a contemporary lesson. He frequently quoted this text from Ecclesiasticus: 'For better it is that thy children should seek thee, than that thou shouldst stand to their courtesy.' However, with his own criminal enterprise our nephew clearly proved that the archdeacon had spoken the truth as much as Jesus, son of Sirach.

Later a crime was told—and indeed is still often told—at Lincoln of a certain priest in England, who, in our lifetime, gave up his well-endowed church in favour of his son, thinking, as would be right, that he would have both his church and his son as he wanted them there

Filius autem concubinam in brevi postea superinduxit, cuius instinctu
175 paulo post a domo sua quam ipse fecerat patrem eiecit. Set quoniam ei
ab episcopo diocesiano, miserante penuriam patris et filii facinus de-
testante, eiusdem ecclesie data fuit administracio plena, filius, ut
f. 52ᵛᵃ episcopi factum eluderet et patrem modis | omnibus mendicare com-
pelleret, Cisterciensis ordinis habitum assumens, ex nequicia magis et
180 indignacione quam devocione sicut ex postfacto claruit, monastice
regule se subiecit. Episcopus autem, hoc audito, misertus adhuc patris
inopie; erga quem pia gerens viscera ab ecclesie patrono ut bonis eius
more solito ⌜quamdiu viveret⌝ cuncta ministrando senex ille susten-
taretur laudabiliter impetravit. Quod cum ad filium, non presbiteri,
185 set verius diaboli, fama nunciante pervenit, habitum incontinenti
reiecit domumque suam et ordinem relinquens et ad remota trans-
migrans in patria nunquam postea comparuit.

O quociens nepos noster, et vere a nepa dictus, et huic in nequicia
valde propinquus, dicere quasi comminando consuevit quod antea
190 monacus fieret quam correctionis nostre doctrineque iugum et discipline
frenum diucius sustineret, quatinus inopiam ei sic generaret qui copiam
ipsi et opulenciam tanto studio procurarat. Adeo namque correpcionis
semper impaciens fuerat et correctionis quod etiam, cum ⌜aliquociens⌝
de verborum suorum inepcia corriperetur, silencium sibi mensium
195 duorum vel trium indicebat, tanquam pitagoricos discipulos, qui per
quinquennium in scolis silebant, sequi volens. Set illi per pacienciam
et prudenciam, ut taciti melius audirent et plus discerent, hoc faciebant;
iste vero per maliciam atque nequiciam, ut nec etiam in verbis et sermone communi, qui nulla ⌜recte⌝ loqui lingua noverat, emendacionem
200 suscipere posset. Igitur apud ipsum inter stultiloquium et nulliloquium
nichil erat medium.

f. 52ᵛᵇ Quidquid autem de redditibus acci|deret per operam nostram
obtentis, utinam hodie monacus esset, set monacus bonus, et non
qualis ille predictus, habitum, non animum mutans, et monasterium
205 deserens, non autem maliciam derelinquens! Sacius enim foret, et
longe sacius, hominem mundo mortuum ⌜esse⌝, ubi nec boni nec mali
memoriam de se relinqueret ullam, quam sic superstes existens, nec
disciplinatus nec morigeratus, set sceleri pocius et prodicioni per omnia

195–6. Cf. Seneca, *Ep. moral.* v, 12 (Ep. lii): *apud Pythagoram discipulis quinque annis
tacendum erat.* See also *infra*, Ep. 4, p. 176, 4.

as long as he lived or wished. However, not long afterwards, his son took a mistress, and at her instigation shortly afterwards evicted the father from the home which he himself had made. The whole administration of the church was made over to him by the diocesan bishop, who pitied the penury of the father, and hated the crime of the son. To get round the action of the bishop, and to make his father a complete pauper, the son took the habit of the Cistercian order, and submitted himself to the monastic discipline, out of malice and anger rather than piety, as it later transpired. However, when the bishop heard this, he had even more pity on the poverty of the father—to whom he showed great compassion—so that he arranged with the patron of the church in a laudable manner that the ageing father should enjoy the benefits he was used to by administering everything until his dying day. When the rumour of this reached the ears of the priest's son—it would be more true to describe him as the Devil's own son—he immediately laid aside the habit, and, relinquishing his home and order, he went away to distant parts, and never again appeared in his homeland.

How often has that nephew of ours—the word is truly derived from the Latin for a scorpion, for he resembles this man very much in his wickedness—how often has he kept threatening as it were that he would become a monk sooner than put up any longer with the yoke of our correction and teaching, and the art of discipline, so that he might impoverish the man who had taken such pains to procure his wealth and riches! He was, indeed, always so intolerant of our rebuke and reproof, that when he was occasionally reproved for his inability to express himself, he used to relapse into silence for two or three months, as if he wanted to emulate the Pythagorean students who did not speak for five years in their schools. But they did it out of patience and for a purpose, so that by their silence they might hear better and learn more: he, however, did it out of spite and peevishness, so that he might not have his speech and conversation corrected, as being one who could not speak any language properly. Thus for him there was no half-way point between talking rubbish and saying nothing.

Whatever might become of the revenues, which we obtained by our diligence, would that he were a monk today—a good monk and not like the aforementioned, who changed his habit but not his heart, and left the monastery behind him, not the malice! It would be better, far, far better for a man to be dead to the world, in a place where he would leave behind no trace of himself, either for good or ill, than to survive in such a way, undisciplined and disobedient, but rather with a devotion to crime and treachery in every respect, marked by the stains of

datus perpetueque infamie nevo notatus, suis omnibus generique toti
210 summo dedecori foret et dolori.

⌜⌜Unde et in Ecclesiastico: *Luctus mortui septem dies, luctus vero fatui omni tempore vite sue.* Et David in psalmo: *Non est Deus in conspectu eius, inquinate sunt vie illius in omni tempore.*⌝

Refertur et hoc crebro, qualiter canonicus Lincolniensis prebendam
215 filio suo cesserat, qui postmodum in penuriam incidit tantam quod et vestibus usque ad nuditatem et victualibus usque ad extremum fere defectum, filio dissimulante prorsus et in nullo miserante, careret. Qui cum filium, ut inopie sue tante saltem in aliquo subveniret, tam per se quam per alios sepius incassum efflagitasset, tandem, quoniam impudens
220 et effrons esse ⌜plerumque⌝ solet nimie egestatis anxietas, pater ad pedes filii, quatinus vel sic ipsum ad misericordiam movere posset, cum lacrimis et singultu lamentabili se prostravit; filius autem, et vere diaboli filius, et non hominis illius, nichil ob hoc motus, set magis in iracundiam vel pocius insaniam versus, elevato calcaneo et male recalci-
225 trando, tam impie patrem in facie pede percussit quod, ruptis venarum claustris, per utramque narem rivus sanguinis erupit emanantis. Pater autem, sic vultu sanguinolento, statim ad episcopum, quem tunc forte in ecclesia Lincolniensi, collectis in capitulo canonicis, invenit accedens, quantam sibi inhumanitatem filius suus fecerat lamentabili queri-
230 monia propalavit. Episcopus autem, hoc viso et audito, statim episco-paliter agens et tantam ingratitudinem pariter et impietatem viriliter ulciscens, prebendam quam filio cesserat patri restituit et percussorem illum et tam impium patris malleum ad penitenciam suam de scelere tam impio et tanquam parricidio Rome suscipiendam ilico transmisit.
235 Papa vero et episcopi factum commendavit et confirmavit et impietatis filio gravem, quandiu vixit, penitenciam iniunxit. Hec tamen et similia pro nepote nostro facere quodammodo videntur exempla. Cum ⌜et⌝enim tam atrociter filii deseviant in parentes, minus admirandum, set magis cavendum et caucius agendum, si quando in patruos, quanto gradu
240 remociores, inveniantur ⌜sic⌝ exorbitando desevire nepotes.⌝

⌜Porro, ut longe propinquius inducamus exemplum et expressius, presbiter quidam nuperrime nunc, et huius Innocencii tercii papatus tempore, ecclesiam suam bonam in episcopatu Londoniensi et villa que vocatur Prestun' filio suo cessit et ipsum in ea institui naturali
245 ductus affectu procuravit. Filius autem, infra modicum tempus patris

211–81 *hae tres longae additiones* (Unde ... nepotes; Porro ... fecit; Item quidam ... deberent) *leguntur in tres schedulis quibus factum est folium 53ʳ*

211–12. Ecclus. xxii, 13.   212–13. Ps. x, 5.

everlasting wickedness, and becoming an utter disgrace and cause of shame to his friends and all his family alike.

Thus it is written in Ecclesiasticus: 'The mourning for the dead is seven days: but for a fool all the days of his life.' And David says in the Psalm: 'God is not before his eyes: his ways are filthy at all times.'

The following tale is frequently repeated of how a canon of Lincoln had given up his prebend in favour of his son, and afterwards fell into such a state of poverty that he was without clothes to the point of nakedness, and without food almost to the point of starvation, while his son pretended not to notice and was without pity. After he had begged his son, in vain, both directly and through others, to relieve his poverty, to some degree at least, in the end he prostrated himself at the feet of his son in a pitiful fashion (for fear of extreme poverty is normally beyond shame and decency), weeping and sobbing, trying to move his son to pity perhaps in this way. However, the son—a true son of the Devil and certainly not of this man—was by no means moved by this; instead he turned to anger—or rather to madness—and raising his heel he kicked his father full in the face, so wickedly that it ruptured the blood-vessels, and streams of blood gushed forth from both nostrils. His face covered with blood, the father immediately revealed the extent of his son's inhumanity towards him in a pitiful complaint to the bishop, whom he chanced to discover in Lincoln cathedral since there was a meeting of canons in the chapter-house. When the bishop heard of it and saw the evidence, he acted as a bishop should, and sternly punished the son's enormous ingratitude and impiety: to the father he restored the prebend, which he had ceded to the son; the youth who had given his father such a hammering he sent to Rome to do penance for this impious crime, near to parricide. The pope praised and confirmed the action of the bishop, and imposed a severe penance on the son for his impiety for the rest of his life. These and similar cases seem to set an example to our nephew. For if even sons maltreat their fathers in such a dreadful fashion, there should be less need for astonishment, but greater care and caution should be taken whenever nephews are seen to be cruel to their uncles by going astray in such a manner, since the relationship is less close.

Furthermore, to give an example that is far closer and more to the point, very recently—in fact during the pontificate of the present pope, Innocent III—a certain priest ceded to his son his well-endowed church in a place called Preston in the diocese of London and, prompted by fatherly affection, ensured that he should be installed there. However, after a short while the son, finding his father's life a burden, allowed

vitam fastidio ducens, inopem eum et egenum vilemque demum et abiectum secum aliquandiu fore sustinuit. Set paulo post a se prorsus
eiectum a domo quam ipse fecerat pium patrem filius ipsius irrevocabiliter proturbavit. Pater autem, tanquam ad ultimum confugiens
250 remedium, apostolorum limina petens et ad pedes pape se prosternens,
rem gestam et suam erga filium humanitatem et eius erga ipsum crudeli-
tatem ei cum lacrimis et singultibus indicavit. Papa vero, paterna pietate
commotus et efficaciter afflicti statim misertus, per iudices et executores
optimos ab eodem in partibus suis electos, et filium incontinenti ob
255 ingratitudinem amoveri et patri ecclesiam denuo conferri eumque restitui
in integrum ilico fecit.⌉

⌐Item quidam hiis nostris diebus in Oxonie finibus personatum
ecclesie de Wuttona cessit nepoti suo, pensionem ⌐ei⌝ an⌐n⌝uam, vicaria
sibi retenta, persolvens. Nepos autem ille, processu temporis vitam
260 avunculi tedia ducens, armatos in silva quadam, per quam transire
debuit, ad ipsum interimendum collocavit. Set, cum elapsa diei parte
maiore facinus perpetratum ⌐fuisse⌝ putaret, ⌐eadem uia⌝, set a longe
tamen et tanquam e vestigio sequens, et rei certitudinem nimis avide
scire ⌐deproperans⌝, avunculo per aliam forte semitam casu prospe-
265 riore dilapso, ipse ad locum veniens subito et inconsiderato suorum
impetu avunculum esse putancium sagittis et lanceis est perforatus et,
⌐sic⌝ *in foveam incidens quam paraverat*, digna Dei vindicta mortem
⌐in alium⌝ nequiter machinando mortem incurrit. ⌐*Nec enim lex* iustior
ulla est quam necis artifices arte perire sua.⌝

270 ⌐Item miles quidam in Cancia dominium terre sue tocius in filium
heredem et uxoratum contulerat, a quo post modicum tempus a domo
quam fecerat et a sustentacione tota pauper et inobs est eiectus. Ipse
vero, ad Anglorum regem Henricum secundum statim accelerans, suam
erga filium liberalitatem filiique erga ipsum inpietatem ⌐ei⌝ lacrima-
275 biliter indicavit. Cui resolutus in risum rex respondit gratulari se
plurimum et gaudere quod hominem invenerat filii sui expertum
ingratitudinem sicut et ipse suorum nequiciam expertus fuerat filiorum
et incontinenti totam patri terram suam cum domibus et possessionibus,
filio turpiter eiecto, integre restitui fecit. Sic principes et sic, ut dictum
280 est, pontifices boni; mali vero maliciosi ⌐et meticulosi⌝ nequiciam
nutriunt magis facinusque fovent quod suffocare deberent.⌉

270 *post* tocius *deletum est* et uxoratum   270–87 Item quidam . . . deberent
scriptum est alia manu

---

267. Cf. Ps. vii, 16: *et incidit in foveam quam fecit*; also Prov. xxvi, 27: *Qui fodit
foveam, incidit in eam.*   268–9. Cf. Ovid, *Ars Am.* i, 655–6.
279–81. et sic . . . deberent] This late addition to the text refers back to *supra*, lines
230–6 and 252–6, which also were not in the primitive text.

him to stay with him for some time in a state of poverty and impoverishment, and, ultimately, contempt and humiliation. But shortly afterwards this impious son threw his pious father from the home he had made and drove him out once and for all. The father, however, sought the ultimate remedy: hurrying to Rome, he threw himself at the feet of the pope, and, weeping and sobbing, told him of the affair, and of his goodness towards his son, and his son's cruelty towards him. The pope, with paternal concern, immediately had compassion on the poor man, and through the agency of honest local people, chosen by the man as papal judges and sequestrators, caused the son to be dismissed immediately for his ingratitude, and the church to be made over to the father again, and the father to be reinstated there once more fully.

Similarly, in our own lifetime, in the vicinity of Oxford a man ceded the rectorship of the church of Wootton to his nephew, paying him an annual stipend and retaining the vicarage for himself. The nephew, as time went by, finding the life of his uncle an inconvenience, posted armed men to kill him in a wood which the uncle had to pass through. But when, after the greater part of the day had passed, he thought that the crime had been committed, he went to the place along the same path, intending to follow at a distance and in his footsteps, as it were, hurrying in his eagerness to learn whether the crime had been committed. The uncle, with better fortune, had escaped by going along another path, and when the nephew reached the spot, his men, taking him for his uncle, suddenly and unexpectedly attacked him and riddled him with arrows and spears. Thus he fell into the trap he himself had prepared, and, as a just punishment from heaven, met his death wickedly contriving death for somebody else. There is no law more just than that those who trade in murder should be hoist by their own petard.

Similarly, a knight in Kent had transferred the ownership of all his land to his married son and heir: shortly afterwards he was thrown out of the home he had made, and his livelihood, as a beggar and pauper. He immediately hastened to Henry II, King of England, and in tears told him of his liberality to his son and his son's impiety towards himself. The king burst into laughter, and replied to him that he was pleased and delighted that he had discovered a man who had experienced ingratitude from his son, just as he, too, had suffered wickedness from his own sons. He immediately had the son thrown out in disgrace, and all the land, as well as the cottages and possessions, restored *in toto* to the father. In this way act princes, and, as has been said, good bishops: the wicked, the malicious, and the dreadful, on the other hand, foster wickedness, and nurture the crimes that they ought to suppress.

Huius ⌜itaque⌝ nepotis nostri effectum est opera quod iam in exemplum apud Lincolniam positi sumus et proverbium, adeo quidem ut,
cum ibi persone ecclesiastice plures propinquos suos in reditibus suis
285 naturali motu vel per cessiones tales vel modis aliis promovendi fixum
animo propositum habuissent, a suis postea super hoc sepe conventi
contra excipiant et constanter abnuendo contradicant, dicentes quod
factum nepotis magistri Giraldi de Barri, quia malicia cotidie magis ac
magis exuberat et habundat, caucius amodo circa talia negociandum
290 ceteros evidenter instruxit, illud quoque poete proponentes ⌜vel proponere valentes⌝ :

> *Felix quem faciunt aliena pericula cautum.*

Et illud:

> *Erudiunt plerumque bonos exempla malorum.*

295 Et illud philosophi: *Ruina precedencium posteros docet et caucio est
semper in reliquum lapsus anterior.* Et tamen, quamvis contra excepci-
ones huiusmodi replicent illi a bonis exempla fore sumenda, et non a
f. 54ʳᵃ malis et male morigeratis, nec a barbaris | presertim et perverse nature
nacionibus, propter pravi tamen exempli tam vehemenciam quam
300 recenciam proficere non possunt, set maledictiones crebras in capud
auctoris tam mali exempli tamque nocivi ex corde refundunt. Nec
solum Lincolniam facinoris huius exemplum contaminavit, verum
etiam Herefordiam, ubi in audiencia magna nepotis contra patruum tam
naturalis fabricata et facta appellacio fuit, necnon et Walliam totam et
305 Hiberniam aliaque loca plurima, per que facti, quod supprimi ⌜non⌝
potuit, fama volavit et volabit, ad scelera similia provocavit. Ve igitur
homini per quem scandala tot venerunt! ⌜Eruendi etenim sunt oculi
scandalizantes; sic et abiciendi proculque pellendi domestici tales et,
quorum ⌜semper⌝ prodicio pessima ⌜pestisque pre ceteris omnibus
310 nocentissima⌝, familiares.

Caveat ergo sibi de cetero Menevensis ecclesia, ubi frequens huiusmodi fieri solet provisio, suis ⌜quidem commoda, sibi vero⌝ periculosa,
prolique piis a parentibus cessio crebra. Caveat et caucius agat, videns
tante pravitatis exempla in gremio suo preter solitum nuper emersa.

---

307 Eruendi] *V* Erudiendi *expunxit* -di-   307–16 *haec additio legitur in f. 53ᵛ*

292. Quoted by H. Walther, *Lateinische Sprichwörter*, no. 8952.
294. Not identified.
295–6. Ennodius, *Vita B. Epiphanii episcopi Ticinensis* (Migne, *P.L.* 63, col. 227);

The result of the action of this nephew of ours is that we have already become a proverbial example at Lincoln; so much so that when many a cleric set their minds on promoting their relatives to their incomes out of natural affection, either by similar resignation or in other ways, and when these relatives then come again and again to see them about this, they take exception and constantly reject and deny it, arguing that, since the nephew of Master Giraldus de Barri revels in and overflows more and more each day with wickedness, his action has clearly taught them to be more wary in negotiating such matters. They quote, or could quote, the poet: 'Happy is the man whom others' perils teach to be cautious'; and this one, too: 'The examples of the wicked are generally a lesson to the good'; and this statement of the philosopher: 'The downfall of past generations teaches the future generations: the former sinner is more cautious in future.' And though the common rejoinder to these exceptions is that examples should be taken from the good, and not from the wicked and immoral, and especially from barbarians and people whose nature is degenerate, they can make no headway, as much as a result of the strength as the freshness of the bad precedent; but they pour out a stream of curses from their hearts on the head of the man who set such a wicked and harmful precedent. The example of this crime has infected not only Lincoln, but also Hereford, where at a great assembly the natural appeal of the nephew against his uncle was fabricated and made. Similar crimes have also been provoked by it in all Wales and Ireland, and a great many other places across which the tale of the crime has flown (and will fly)—for it cannot be suppressed. Woe to the man by whose agency so many sins have come to pass. For, just as when your eyes offend you, you should pluck them out, so, too, you should cast out and drive away such servants and relations; their treachery is always the most base, and their destructiveness is the most harmful in comparison with all others.

Let the church of St. David's beware for her own sake in future; there provisions of this kind take place so frequently—provisions which are advantageous to her flock, but harmful to herself; and resignations are frequently made by pious parents in favour of their offspring. Let her beware, I repeat, and proceed with greater caution in the light of the unusual precedents that have arisen lately in her own bosom. Let her

---

this quotation also occurs in *De Vita Galfridi Archiepiscopi Eboracensis* (*Op.* iv, p. 420, 14–16), in *Expugnatio Hibernica* (*Op.* v, p. 399, 11–12), in *Descripti Kambriae* (*Op.* vi, p. 224), and *infra*, part ii, 1208–9.

306–7. Cf. Matt. xviii, 7: *vae homini illi, per quem scandalum venit.*

307–8. Cf. Matt. xviii, 9: *Et si oculus tuus scandalizat te, erue eum, et projice abs te*; cf. also Matt. v, 29.

315 Caveat, inquam, et paveat, quia proclivis semper est cursus ad peiora
et imitari plerique solent viciosa magis quam virtuosa.⌐

Et tamen tam naturalis hic nepos noster et tam moralis, quatinus
aliquo fuco facinus suum colorare posset erroremque suum utcumque
quo tueretur haberet, *ad excusandas excusaciones* extraneis et ignaris
320 dicere consuevit quod ob iracundiam nostram et acerbitatem nimiam
nemo nobis assistere, nemo nos potuit sustinere, ac si aperte dixerit:
'Si procul abcessero, si hominem quem nullus tolerare poterit ego
reliquero, nemo miretur!' Cui responderi potuit, ⌐et vere responderi,⌐
quod a nullis sapientibus nullisque discretis ac bene morigeratis, set a
325 fatuis tantum et indoctis, quorum hic ductor et magister suus doctor
est, discordare solent mores nostri. Cum enim illum et alios indociles
et incorrigibiles docere vellemus et verbis corrigere, non verberibus,
⌐quoniam⌐ ingenua nimirum ingenia magis verba timent quam verbera,
329 qui nec verberum et virgarum in puericia correctionem habuit, nec
f. 54ʳᵇ verborum in ad|olescencia castigacionem admittere voluit, qui nec tunc,
ut infra dicetur, per timorem, nec postea per pudorem aut amorem,
disciplinam amplexus fuit, restat ut, indisciplinatus permanens et indomitus pariter et indoctus, correptorem omnem et correctorem, qui
se reddidit incorrigibilem, gravem reputet et acerbum, iuxta illud in
335 Sapiencia: *Gravis est nobis ad videndum; dissimilis enim nobis est vita
ipsius,* ubi et suppleri potest: ideoque displicet nobis doctrina ipsius.
Et nos e diverso supplere possumus quia disciplina talium non nobis
solum, set et bonis omnibus est disciplina. ⌐Unde et Propheta de talibus:
*Odio habuerunt corripientem in porta, et loquentem perfecte abhominati
340 sunt.* Et ⟨in⟩ Ecclesiastico: *Quam aspera est nimium sapiencia indoctis
hominibus et non permanebit in illa excors.* Et in Ecclesiaste: *Verba
sapientum sicut stimulus, et quasi clavi in altum defixi.* Et in eodem:
Perversi difficile corriguntur, et stultorum infinitus est numerus. Item
et in Ecclesiastico: *Qui docet fatuum quasi qui conglu*⌐ti⌐*nat testam.*⌐
345 ⌐Item et in Proverbiis: *Abho*⌐mi⌐*nantur iusti virum impium, et ab-
hominantur impii eos qui in recta sunt via.*⌐

Solet etiam hic nepos noster ea solum verba nostra, que rodere
utcumque et asperitatis arguere poterat, cuiusmodi monitoria reputabat
omnia et correctoria, quamquam summa cum lenitate prolata, firme

340 in] *V omisit*

---

319. Ps. cxl, 4.   335–6. Wisd. ii, 15.   339–40. Amos v, 10.
340–1. Ecclus. vi, 21.   341–2. Eccles. xii, 11.   343. Eccles. i, 15.
344. Ecclus. xxii, 7.   345–6. Prov. xxix, 27.

beware, and let her tremble, since the path to greater crime is always a
headlong one, and most men are more inclined to imitate acts of wickedness than acts of virtue.

In order to be able to add colour to his crime by deceit and to have
some means or other of defending his error, this nephew of ours,—such
a natural man and so upright—'to excuse his excuses', was in the
habit of telling strangers and those ignorant of the facts that no one
could help us and no one could stand us, because of our bad temper and
sarcasm: as if he had openly said: 'No one will be surprised if I go
away, if I leave a man whom no one can bear.' The rejoinder could
have been made—and it would have been true—that our habits do not
usually clash with the wise, the prudent, and the well-mannered, but
only with the foolish and the stupid, whom he leads in body, and his
tutor leads in spirit. When we wanted to teach him (and other unteachable and incorrigible characters), we punished them with a tongue-
lashing, rather than a lashing with canes, since gentlemen—certainly
the intelligent—fear a tongue-lashing more than a thrashing. He
neither had a thrashing with the cane and birch as a boy, nor was he
willing to receive a tongue-lashing in adolescence, and, since he did not
take to teaching then through fear, as we will relate below, or afterwards through shame or love, the inevitable result is that he is permanently undisciplined, unbroken, and untaught. Since he has shown himself to be incorrigible, he thinks that anyone who reproves and
rebukes him is dour and bitter. It is rather like the verse in the Wisdom
of Solomon: 'He is grievous unto us even to behold; for his life is not
like other men's', which we can supplement with: 'for this reason his
principles displease us.' We can supplement this by saying the opposite,
for the education of such men is a lesson not only for us, but also all
upright men. The prophet says of them: 'They have hated him that
rebuketh in the gate: and have abhorred him that speaketh perfectly';
and in Ecclesiasticus: 'Instruction is very unpleasant to the unlearned:
he that is without understanding will not remain with it'; and in
Ecclesiastes: 'The words of the wise are as goads, and as nails deeply
fastened in'; and in the same book: 'The perverse are hard to be corrected and the number of fools is infinite.' The same thought is expressed
in Ecclesiasticus: 'He that teacheth a fool is like one that glueth a
potsherd'; and in Proverbs: 'The just abhor the wicked man, and the
wicked loathe them that are in the right way.'

This nephew of ours is in the habit of committing to memory only those
words of ours which he could disparage in some way or other and accuse of
tartness of which kind he considered all admonitory and reproving words

350 memorie commendare ea⌐que⌐, tanquam ad rumen sepe revocando et
depravando, cum nichil tam benedictum quod non possit malignitas
⌐pervertere et⌐ depravare, in nostram suggillacionem perverse recitare.
Cui poterat quidem ex adverso responderi: *Set male* quod *recitas,*
incipit esse tuum. ⌐Unde de talibus rex et propheta David: *Qui*
355 *retribuunt mala pro bonis, detrahebunt mihi, quoniam sequebar bonitatem.*
Et alibi: *Locuti sunt adversum me lingua dolosa et sermonibus odii*
circumdederunt ⌐me⌐ et expugnaverunt me gratis.—Et posuerunt ad-
versum me mala pro bonis, et odium pro dilectione mea.⌐ Nec mirum
tamen si diaboli naturam, qui malis hominum tam dictis quam factis
360 retinendis atque notandis semper intendit et nunquam bonis, diabolici
generis illius, de quo satis dicetur inferius, germen non imitari non
possit. Scriptum est enim et ore divino pronunciatum: *Vos ex patre*
diabolo estis et opera patris vestri facitis. Super quod Expositor: *Non*
est maledictio vel obiurgacio, quia correctio.

365 ⌐Patet ex hiis igitur quod, licet interdum aspera dicantur erudiendis
ubi per lenia non proficitur, ⌐quoniam, ut ait Innocencius, *error cui*
non resistitur approbatur⌐, dociles animi docentis intencionem attendentes pacienter admittere debent et gratanter. Sicut enim, Salomone
testante, *qui parcit virge*, scilicet in puericia, *odit filium*, sic qui
370 parcit verbis, scilicet in adolescencia, odit eundem; moderamine tamen
ubique servato, non enim qui corripit odit, set qui non corripit se
parum diligere patenter ostendit. *Odio namque habenda sunt vicia*, ut
ait Gelasius, *et non homines.* Unde Poeta:

Detestor morum crimina, corpus amo.

375 ⌐Et illi quoque Salomonico in Proverbiis: *Qui parcit virge, odit filium,*
consequenter et hoc subiungitur: *Qui autem diligit illum, instanter*
erudit.

Proinde et quoniam Heli filios suos Ofni et Phinees tepide nimis
tam arguebat quam erudiebat, et quoniam illi doctrinam patris non
380 attendebant, divinitus ulcione secuta et filii gladiis in bello capta
ab Azotis archa domini corruerunt; et pater, suscepto rumore, sella
protinus aversa, retro cadens, confracto cerebro miserabiliter expiravit!⌐

365–82 *hae additiones* (Patet . . . erudit) *leguntur in f. 53ᵛ; additio sequens* (Proinde . . .
expiravit) *legitur in margine f. 52ᵛ*

<hr />

353–4. Cf. Martial 1, 38, 2: *Sed male cum recitas, incipit esse tuum.*
354–5. Ps. xxxvii, 21.   356–7. Ps. cviii, 3.   357–8. Ps. cviii, 5.
362–3. Cf. John viii, 44: *Vos ex patre diabolo estis, et desideria patris vestri vultis*
facere.
363–4. Not identified.

to be, even though they had been delivered with the utmost gentleness, ruminating upon them often and distorting them, he used to repeat them sneeringly to mock us; for there is nothing so blessed that malice cannot corrupt and distort. We could answer him by retorting: 'The evil which you recite starts to be your own.' As King David, the prophet, said of this: 'They that render evil for good have detracted me because I followed goodness'; and elsewhere: 'They spoke against me with deceitful tongues and compassed me about with words of hatred and have fought against me without cause; and they repaid me evil for good and hatred for my love.' It is not, however, surprising that this spawn of that family of the Devil (of which much will be spoken later) must inevitably imitate the nature of the Devil, who is always intent on retaining and marking wicked words and deeds, and never the good. For the words of the Lord in Holy Writ are: 'You are of your father the Devil and you do the works of your father.' Over this the Commentator has written: 'This is not a curse or abjuration, since it is a reproof.'

It is, then, clear from this that, although harsh words are said to those that are to be taught when there is no profit in using gentle words (for, as Innocent says, 'The sin that is not resisted is approved of'), docile minds, understanding the purpose of the teacher, ought to accept them with patience and thanks. As Solomon says: 'Assuredly he that spareth the rod' (that is, in childhood) 'hateth his son': so, too, he who spares his words (that is, in adolescence) hates him. But moderation should be observed in all things, for he that rebukes does not hate, but he that does not rebuke clearly shows that he has too little affection. As Gelasius says: 'We should hate the sin, not the sinner', and the poet: 'I hate corrupt morals, I love the person', and also in the Proverbs of Solomon: 'He that spareth the rod hateth his son', and, following this, he adds: 'But he that loveth him correcteth him betimes.'

So, too, because Eli rebuked and taught his sons, Hophni and Phinehas, in an all too slapdash fashion, and since they did not follow the instruction of their father, divine retribution followed: the sons fell to the sword in battle, when the Ark of the Lord had been captured by the men of Ashdod. When the father heard the report, he immediately upset his seat, and, falling backwards, he broke his skull and expired miserably.

366–7. Gratian, D. LXXXIII, c. 3; cf. also *infra*, Ep. 5, p. 192, 45, and further references given there.
369. Prov. xiii, 24.
372–3. Cf. Gratian, D. LXXXVI, c. 2 (Leo): *Odio habeantur peccata, non homines.*
374. Not identified.   375–7. Prov. xiii, 24.   378–82. Cf. 1 Sam. iv, 5–6.

Sicut enim in Genesi legitur, grandem ostendit Ioseph fratribus severitatem, nunc in vinculis eos convinciendo, nunc exploratores
385 vocando, nunc tanquam in furto deprehensos, ad ultimum discrimen reducendo, super que Glosa: *Verba pro verberibus irrogat fratribus, ne remaneant ipsorum ⌐vel commissa vel⌐ inpunita delicta.* Et iterum: *Multa erat in verbis severitas, multa in corde tranquillitas, ut hinc doceatur quantam hiis benevolenciam ostendamus quos interdum zelo*
390 *correctionis et impulsu dilectionis aspere corripimus.*—*Multociens enim, ut ait Ieronimus, bona parantur invitis, dum eorum pocius utilitati consulitur quam voluntati.* Nam et qui freneticum ligat, et qui letargicum excitat, ambobus molestus, ambos amat. Sic et medicus, calibata non-
395 nunquam manu putrida separans et ad vivum resecans, non parcit quidem ut parcat et sevit ut misereatur. Unde Iohannes in Apocalipsi: *Ego quos amo arguo et castigo.*⌐

Ut autem ad vos alloquendum iam revertamur, nosse nunc ergo pro
f. 54va certo potestis et manifeste perpendere vera fu|isse proverbia de vobis ab ineunte etate dicta et quasi vaticinia nostra, sicut iam opere sub-
400 sequente probastis, ⌐⌐nimia⌐ ueritate subnixa⌐. Considerantes enim olim indolem puericie vestre ⌐tam illaudabilem⌐ cervicemque tam flexibilem et agilem et capud oblongum et tam tornatile occulosque leves et instabiles et os larvosum moresque perversos et a natura paterna prorsus alienos, dicere dolendo consuevimus, quasi cum Apostolo:
405 *Sine causa laboravimus et laboramus in isto.* Nichil enim nostre nature, nichil paterne vel etiam fraterne maturitatis aut gravitatis scurilitas ista pretendit. Unde et una cum Marciali Coco dicere potuimus:

Lubricus aspectus faciesque incerta, Macrine,
Ostendunt nobis te nimis esse levem.

383–97 *reliquum additionis* (Sicut . . . castigo) *legitur in f. 53^v*

383–6. Cf. Gen. xlii–xliv.
388–90. Not identified.
386–7. Not identified.
390–2. Not identified.
397. Rev. iii, 19.
405. Cf. Gal. iv, 11: *Timeo vos, ne forte sine causa laboraverim in vobis.*
408–9. Marcialis Cocus] This epigram is not Martial's, but by Godfrey of Winchester (*c.* 1050–1107), also known as Martialis Cocus: *The Anglo-Latin Satirical Poets and Epigrammatists of the Twelfth Century,* ed. Thomas Wright (R.S. 59, 1872), 2 vols., ii, p. 122: *Lubricus aspectus, facies incerta, Macrine | Significant nobis te nimis esse levem. | Est speculum mentis facies, oculique revelant | Qualia sunt intus mens animusque hominis.*

For as we read in Genesis, Joseph displayed great severity towards his brothers: at one time he bound them in chains, at another he called them spies, at another time he brought them into the utmost disrepute as if they had been caught in the act of theft, on which the Commentator says: 'He inflicted a tongue-lashing on his brothers in return for their thrashings, so that their crimes should neither be secret nor remain unpunished.' Furthermore, 'great was the sternness in the words, great was the peace in the heart, so that from this the extent of the goodwill we show to those we occasionally rebuke sharply out of zeal for correction, as from the promptings of affection, might be taught.' 'For often', as Jerome says, 'good is done to those who do not appreciate it, since one has regard for their benefit more than their wishes.' For the man who ties up the madman, and the man who stimulates the lethargic man, provokes both of them, but loves both of them. So, too, the doctor, with a hand of steel, while cutting out the infected part, sometimes cuts down to the living flesh; he does not spare, in order to spare: he causes pain, in order to be merciful. This is why John says in the Apocalypse: 'As many as I love, I rebuke and chasten.'

To return to addressing you personally: you may now, therefore, be perfectly sure and may clearly infer that the predictions made about you from an early age were true, and our prophecies, as it were, were founded too much on truth, as you proved from your subsequent action. When we considered your childhood traits which were so unpraiseworthy, your neck which was so flexible and agile, your head which was so long and rounded, your shifty and flickering eyes, your cynical mouth, your corrupt morals, which were opposed to your father's nature, we used to say in sorrow, to quote the Apostle: 'I have bestowed labour upon him in vain.' For that coarseness of yours shows nothing of our nature, your father's or even your brother's maturity or seriousness. So we could have agreed with Martial Cocus: 'Your slippery look, your ambivalent expression, Macrinus, show us that you

---

Giraldus quotes the genuine Martial occasionally, though infrequently, calling him either simply Martialis or Martialis Cocus, so, e.g., *Op.* vi, p. 162; *Op.* viii, pp. 82–3, cf. Sullivan, op. cit., pp. 174–5. For further information on Godfrey of Winchester cf. Max Manitius, *Geschichte der lateinischen Literatur des Mittelalters*, Handbuch der klassischen Altertumswissenschaft 9. 2. 3, Band 3 (München, 1931), pp. 769–71, and Paul Lehmann, *Pseudo-antike Literatur des Mittelalters*, Studien der Bibliothek Warburg, Heft 13 (Leipzig–Berlin, 1927), p. 16. Attention should be drawn to a manuscript of Martial's poems from the time of Giraldus which he may have known: Corpus Christi College, Cambridge MS. 236.

410 ⌐Et cum Cassiodoro senatore, loquente de adolescente Iuliano apostata:
Non est sperandum, inquit, *de eo cui in iuventute sunt hec, cervix in-*
flexibilis, oculi vagi et discurrentes, nares minas et iniurias spirantes et
humeri iactantes.⌐ Solebamus ob hoc multociens, si recolitis, cum ad
paternam maturitatem et moralitatem vos provocaremus, et vos econtra
415 semper ad scurilitatem natura fermentata, forcior omni doctrina, com-
pellebat, exemplum ponere de gallina que pullum anatis per suum
laborem et longam ovis incubacionem tandem cum aliis exclusum, et
suum reputans, ab aquis et paludibus, quas iugiter innatat et frequentat,
ad campestria voce monitoria et passibus sollicitis frustra revocat et
420 invitat; facile ⌐nimirum⌐ est istud nostre sollicitudini frustratorie similiter adaptari. ⌐Si modici quippe fermenti ad massam corrumpendum
magnus est effectus, quid ubi multum exuberat et nimis habundat?⌐

Item infra dies octo postquam archidiaconatum et prebendam vobis
conferri procuravimus, natura perversa que redundat in vobis compel-
425 lente, dixistis, quoniam *ex habundancia cordis loquitur os*, quod, sicut
David de Barri, nepos noster, operatus est in Hibernia contra nos,

f. 54ᵛᵇ reditus magnos quos ei contulimus sibi occupando et | nichil inde nobis
respondendo, sic facere sciretis quandoque velletis. Set utinam moralitatem ac maturitatem et fidem nepotis illius imitaremini! Ecce verbum
430 illud huius tam cito dictum, et natura impellente, nec ludicro tamen,
set serio prolatum, iam nunc ad velle pervenit et actum. Unde non
iuvente verbum illud, set nature pocius violente fuisse maturior etas,
in nullo mutata vel meliorata, manifeste declarat, propter quod ⌐etiam⌐
verbum, cor manifestans et naturam, viginti marcarum ecclesiam tunc
435 vobis quoque nostro beneficio conferendam et iamiam in ianuis ad
hoc paratam amisistis.

⌐Sic itaque lingua blesa et quanquam ex toto fere defectiva, garrula
tamen et prepropera, nobis quidem bene, set vobis male, tunc garriendo
balbuciebat. Quod enim de maioribus que vobis minus discrete con-
440 tulimus, quoniam innaturali pariter et ingrato, iam fecistis, doctrina

---

430 hujus] *V* hui   437–48 *haec additio legitur in margine f. 55ʳ*

410–13. In his *Historia Tripartita*, bk. vii (Migne, *PL*, 69, col. 1065), Cassiodorus
quotes Gregory of Nazianc and writes: *Tunc igitur non frustra consideravi virum* [i.e.
Iulianum]. *Non enim fortuiter ista conspexi; sed faciebat me cautum inconstantia morum*
eius et excessus uberior . . . Nullum enim signum in eo mihi utile videbatur. Cervix inflexi-
bilis, humeri jactabiles, oculi currentes, huc illucque directi et furiose respicientes; pedes
impatientes, nares spirantes injurias atque contemptum, schemata risibilia, et hoc ipsum
semper habentia; risus incontinens et quasi subbulliens; consensus et negatio simul, ratio
nulla ratione consistens . . .
421–2. Cf. 1 Cor. v, 6: 'Modicum fermentum totam massam corrumpit', and
Tractatus Nigelli contra curiales et officiales clericos, ed. T. Wright, *The Anglo-Latin*
Satirical Poets etc. (R.S. 59, 1872), i, p. 188: 'Sicut enim contingit ex modico fermento
totam massam corrumpi . . .'. Cf. also *Itinerarium Kambriae* (*Op.* vi, p. 22).

are too fickle.' We can also use the words of the senator Cassiodorus, speaking of the young Julian the Apostate: 'We must not rely on somebody', he said, 'who in his youth has this: an unbending neck, wandering and hasty eyes, nostrils breathing threats and insults, and swaggering shoulders.' For this reason, if you recall, when we urged you to emulate your father's maturity and decency, and on the other hand your spoilt nature which was stronger than all the teaching in the world constantly urged you on to coarseness, we used to give the example of the hen that, thinking that a duckling, which has been hatched with the rest by her efforts after a long incubation, is her own, tries to call it back and entice it off the pools and marshes it constantly frequents back on to the dry land with words of warning and running around anxiously, but all to no avail. It is not difficult to interpret this in the light of our own vain anxiety. If the effect of just a little yeast to leaven the dough is great, what happens when it is present in vast quantities?

So within a week of our arranging for the archdeaconry and prebend to be transferred to you, at the instigation of that corrupt nature with which you are overflowing, you said (for the mouth speaks from the fullness of the heart) that you knew that whenever you wanted you could act against us in exactly the same way as our nephew, David de Barri, acted against us in Ireland; he did it by claiming for himself the rich revenues which we granted him, and by giving us no account of them. But I wish you would imitate the decency, morality, and trustworthiness of that nephew! (That statement of his, uttered Oh! so hastily and impelled by his nature, and put forward not in jest, but in all seriousness, has now reached the point of being carried out at will!) Your more mature years, which have by no means changed or got better, clearly prove that that statement was not one of youth, but rather of an impetuous nature: and because of this statement, which revealed your heart and your nature, you have lost a church worth twenty marks, which was to be transferred to you out of kindness on our part, and was on the point of being prepared for this purpose.

So, too, your lisping tongue, which, though it is nearly completely defective, is none the less garrulous and glib, stuttered garrulously, nicely for us and not so nicely for you. What you have already done about those benefits we bestowed on you all too rashly—as you are unnatural and ungrateful—you would certainly have done and perpetrated

425. Matt. xii, 34; Luke vi, 45.
437–8. lingua blesa] Cf. Disticha Catonis 3, 4: 'Sermones blandos blaesosque cavere memento'; for a similar use of the term cf. *Symbolum Electorum* (*Op.* i, p. 297, 34), *De Invectionibus*, ed. W. S. Davies, p. 106.

prava monente et natura perversa sequente, de illa procul dubio ecclesia, si res ex proposito processisset, haut dissimiliter actum nunc et
perpetratum esset. Bene igitur lingua blesa tunc garriebat, bene naturam
promens tunc balbuciebat. *Mos etenim est,* sicut ait Simacus, *ut*
445 *balbucientes plus loquantur; affectant enim copiam pudore defectus.* Unde
et Ieronimus noster in talium sugillacionem ait: *Discat quandoque
tacere qui nunquam didicit loqui.* Et alibi: *Multi cum loqui nesciant
tacere non possunt.*⌉ Porro si verbum illud aut simile, ⌈pravi⌉ cordis
archana revelans, paucis ante diebus emissum fuisset, in statu quo
450 vos invenimus, exili satis et humili absque dubio adhuc essetis.

Item cum apud abaciam de Thornolmia nobiscum vos anno preterito
duximus, tanquam ⌈murem⌉ in pera aut serpentem in sinu, ibi canonicis
domus, quia nos laudabant in eo quod benefeceramus vobis, dixistis
econtra, ⌈set non in audiencia nostra⌉, quod nunquam vobis bene-
455 feceramus, set magis redditus vestros vobis auferre volebamus, si
possemus, tanquam dedecus esset vobis si per operas nostras redditus
habere videremini, qui nunquam tamen per vos aliquos adquisistis;
set ecce quemadmodum priori tanquam puericie verbo consonat et
hoc in iam adulto; nec mirum quia nec in minimo etatis beneficio a
460 natura mutato.

Item dixistis pluries scriptoribus et ribaldis apud Lincolniam ⌈qui
post discessum vestrum id per villam pupplicaverunt⌉ quod reditus
f. 55ʳᵃ vestros cito in manu vestra habere | volebatis et sub custodia senis
illius non amplius esse sustinendo et tanquam illud poete dicendo:

465   *Ille semel raptos nunquam dimittet honores?*

Iactitastis etiam coram eisdem et aliis, similibus vobis in moribus
et studiis, nos nisi per assensum vestrum et ad nutum magne maiestatis et generositatis vestre Walliam intrare vel etiam appropiare non
ausos ·fore. Ideoque voluntati vestre resistere nobis tutum non esse
470 dicens etiam et asserens quod, si contrarii vobis essemus, curtas et
artas vias nostras in Wallia curtus avunculus vester ille pararet. Sicut
autem hic nepos noster, sic quondam et consobrinus, abbas scilicet
Sancti Dogmaelis, utroque nimirum nos supplantare nitente, archiepiscopo et archiadversario nostro ⌈Huberto⌉, iactitando proposuit

466-7 moribus et studiis] *V* studiis et moribus *postea transpositum*

444-5. Symmachus, lib. i, epist. 76, MGH AA 6, 1, 1883, p. 33: *Natura rerum est
ut qui balbutiunt plus loquantur; adfectant enim copiam pudore defectus.*
446-7. Not identified; see, however, Jerome, *In Ezechielem* i, 4 (Migne, *P.L.* 25, col.
42): 'Eiusdem sit sapientiae et tacere et loqui pro tempore': closer, however, is Isidore,
Sententiarum Libri tres, ii, 29 (Migne, *P.L.* 83, col. 629): 'Imperiti, sicut loqui nesciunt,
ita tacere non possunt.'   447-8. Not identified; but cf. note on 446-7.

where that church was concerned, had the matter gone beyond the planning stage; for your principles urged wickedness, and your nature pursued corruption. Your lisping tongue chattered on well then: your tongue stuttered well, revealing your true nature. For, as Symmachus says, 'It is usual for stammerers to say more, for their garrulity is a result of the shame they feel for their defect.' So, too, Jerome jokes at the expense of such men: 'May every man who has never learned to speak learn when to be silent', and elsewhere: 'Though many do not know how to speak, they cannot be silent.' Furthermore, if that statement or any similar one that revealed the secrets of your wicked heart had been uttered a few days sooner, without any doubt you would still be in the same position we found you in—impoverished and humble.

Again last year, when we took you with us to the abbey of Thornholme, like a mouse in the sack, or a serpent in the bosom, since the canons of the house were praising us for the benefits we had conferred upon you, you rebutted them—though not in our hearing—saying that we had never conferred any benefits on you, but that it was our desire, if possible, to rob you of your revenues, as if it were a matter of shame that you, who have never acquired any revenues by yourself, should appear to hold your revenues as a result of our efforts. Look how this remark of your mature years accords with the previous remark as it were of your youth. It is not surprising, since you have not changed from your old nature in the least by the benefit of age.

Again, you often said to scribblers and satirists at Lincoln (and after your departure they publicized it throughout the city) that you wanted to have your revenues in your hand quickly, not letting them stay any longer in the custody of that old man, as if, to quote the poet, 'He will never give up honours once he has taken them'.

You even boasted in their presence, and in that of others like you in morals and ideas, that we would never dare to enter, or even approach Wales except with your consent and at the pleasure of your great majesty and lordship. You said that it was not safe for us to oppose your will, and asserted that if we were to oppose you, that uncle of yours would make our journey in Wales a short and brief one. In just the same way as this nephew of ours tries to destroy us, so once upon a time our cousin, the abbot of St. Dogmaels, boastingly promised and vowed to Hubert, our archbishop and archadversary, that the archbishop should keep us out of England through his power, if he could, and he himself

---

451. Thornholme Priory, Lincs., priory of Augustinian canons, founded perhaps by King Stephen, cf. Knowles and Hadcock, *Religious Houses* (1971 edition), pp. 144, 176.
465. Lucan, *Pharsalia* i, 317.

475 et promisit quod ab Anglia nos per potenciam suam archipresul, ⌜si posset⌝, arceret et ipse nos a Wallie finibus absque dubio procul expellendo fugaret. Pro talibus enim, ⌜carne propinquis et corde longinquis⌝, ait Propheta: *Unusquisque se a proximo suo custodiat, et in omni fratre suo non habeat fiduciam, quia omnis frater supplantans supplantabit,*
480 *et omnis amicus fraudulenter incedet,* etc. Pro utroque tamen cum poeta dicere poterimus et exclamare:

Quid feret hic tanto dignum promissor hiatu?

Quemadmodum enim iste, qui maioris erat auctoritatis, generositatis et potestatis, itinera nostra per Walliam impedire plus quam aries unus
485 nec potuit, nec id unquam ⌜etiam⌝ attemptare presumpsit, sic haut dissimiliter et modulo suo minor hec vesica tumescens per acum
f. 55ʳᵇ modicam satis et exilem explosa crepabit et, vento inflacionis | emisso, tumor ille subito detumescet et evanescet.

Item dixistis et Lincolnie coram pluribus in solario nostro, qui non
490 magis ob hoc vos appreciabantur, set longe minus, quod, ubi archidiaconum vos fieri fecimus, dixeramus vobis quatinus ad habendam administracionem nos presentaretis, set obaudiendo et surdam ad hoc aurem faciendo aliasque divertendo recessistis. O quam curiale dictum et quam naturale, fictum tamen et falsitate compactum! Simile quoque
495 quandoque dixistis in Wallia priori de Brechene, variando tamen in hoc et varium, ob hoc sicut in aliis, et versipellem vos ostendendo, quod nos quidem ad administracionem presentastis, set non perpetuam. Nec bonus vir ille dictum hoc aut dicentem approbavit. Ceterum quid moror exemplis inepciarum vestrarum quorum me turba fatigat? Talia
500 fuerunt tunc dicta et tam naturalia futuros eventus presagiencia eorumque habundanti ex corde prenuncia. Et talia nunc sunt opera talium sermonum subsecutiva. Qualis enim puer, talis et puber: unde et a simili qualis adolescens et iuvenescens, talis credendus fore senescens et a natura non recedens.
505 Quid etiam de larvis dicemus et irrisionibus vestris, a quibus corrigi vel castigari vos prava natura non permisit? Nunquam pater vester larvosus fuit; nunquam enim vel illum vel fratrem vestrum optimum Willelmum de Barri vel semel, si bene recolimus, larvam facere vidimus; ⌜consobrinus autem ille vester nature perverse⌝ larvosus et derisor est.
510 Quare? Quia Bascrevillanus est. Scriptum est autem: *Qui corripit*

507 vestrum optimum] *V* optimum vestrum *postea transpositum* 509 *haec additio scripta est in rasura* 510 *post* autem *deletum est* Qui corripit derisorem injuriam sibi facit, et alibi

478–80. Jer. ix, 4.

would certainly worst us by driving us away from Wales. Indeed the aim of both was to oust us. The prophet speaks of such, who are close in blood but distant in love: 'Take ye heed every one of his neighbour, and trust ye not in any brother: for every brother will utterly supplant, and every neighbour will walk with slanders', etc. We could have quoted the poet in either case, and exclaimed: 'What could this promiser gain that was worth wasting so much breath?' For, just as this man, who was of greater authority, nobility, and power, was not able to prevent our journey through Wales any more than one tup could, and he did not even dare try it, so, too, in the same way this bloated bag of wind, this inferior imitation of his model, the abbot, will be burst by a short thin needle, and will go bang, and, when all the hot air has gone, that over-inflated pride of his will suddenly go down and disappear.

Again, at Lincoln in the presence of quite a few in our sollar you said (to their greater disapproval, not their approval) that when we had had you made archdeacon, we had told you to present us to the administration, but you stopped listening and, turning a deaf ear to it, and directing your attention elsewhere, you withdrew. What a pretty speech, and how in character! But invented and chock-full of lies! It was the same, too, in Wales when you said to the prior of Brecon, that you had presented us to the administration, but not for all time, varying the story, and showing yourself to be changeable and cunning in this as in other matters. But that excellent man approved neither of the speech nor of the speaker. But why do I waste my time on the examples of your follies, when their numbers weary me? Such were your utterances, and so much in character were they, foretelling future events, and prophetic from the fullness of your heart. So, too, are your actions now, following in the wake of such statements: for as the child is, so is the boy. Hence by analogy, as is the youth and the man, so (we must believe) will be the man as he grows old, never departing from his nature.

What are we to say of your sarcasm and mockery of which your bad character has not allowed you to be cured or chastened? Your father was never sarcastic; for, if our memory serves us correctly, we never saw either him or that excellent brother of yours, William de Barri, act sarcastically. But that cousin of yours with his corrupt nature is sarcastic and scornful. Why? Because he is a Baskerville. However, it is written: 'Whoever rebukes the ungodly, brings down hatred upon

482. Horace, *Ars Poetica* 138.
510–11. For the quotation which has been cancelled as well as for the one which has been preserved cf. Prov. ix, 7: *Qui erudit derisorem ipse iniuriam sibi facit; et qui arguit impium, sibi maculam generat.*

impium, sibi parit odium. Et illud eiusdem, Salomonis scilicet: *Non*

f. 55ᵛᵃ *amat pestilens* | *eum qui se corripit*, set increpaciones omnes exosas habet.
⌐Item et in Proverbiis: *Qui erudit derisorem ipse sibi iniuriam facit,*
et qui arguit impium generat maculam sibi. Item et ibidem: *Qui odit*
515 *increpaciones, insipiens est.* Et illud eiusdem: *Sapientiam atque doctri-*
nam stulti despiciunt.⌐ Proinde et larvas vestras derisorias, quas in
nostra natura non novimus ⌐et quas dediscere non potuistis⌐, sepe
notando, dicere vobis consuevimus quod neminem verius quam vos
ipsum deridere et delarvare et in propriam quoque faciem vestram,
520 si fieri posset, expuere deberetis, qui totum tempus vestrum preteritum
dedistis perdicioni, totum ⌐vero⌐ tempus instans et imminens nunc
dare studetis prodicioni. *Iustum est nimirum*, sicut ait Democritus,
ut ridentes rideantur. Cum enim erudicioni ⌐vestre⌐ totis nisibus intendere deberetis, turpi totum studium impendistis hactenus et im-
525 penditis prodicioni, quia vere puer indisciplinatus et pullus indomitus,
qui nec litteris indulsistis, nec linguam latinam, aut etiam gallicam,
addidicistis, nec linguam puerilem ac blesam exuistis, nec maturitatem
ullam aut moralitatem induistis. Sola igitur prodicione, magistro
vestro dictante, et natura perversa se promte ad hoc applicante, pre-
530 cellere studuistis. Unde non solum extraneos, verum et nos ipsos,
quociens dicta, vel theologica vel philosophica, vel etiam curialia
verba et faceta, que viri eruditi venerari, admirari, et magnopere amplecti solent, in puppli⌐c⌐a audiencia proponeremus, vos delarvantem
et vos deridentem C⌐h⌐amitam vocabamus, versus hos pronunciando:

535   *Cham ridet*
                            Dum nuda videt
                         Pudibunda parentis.
                               Iudei
                            Risere Dei
540   *Penam pacientis.*

Unde, sicut Caimite dicuntur fratrum interfectores, sic C⌐h⌐amite dici
solent patrum et parentum derisores. Porro, si patruum vestrum, et tam
utilem vobis patruum, iam infatuatum et delirum, alii deriderent, si de
544 paterna natura quicquam in vobis esset, defectus ipsius seniles pocius |

f. 55ᵛᵇ deflere deberetis quam deridere. Nec mirum tamen si Bascrevillani
parentum sint derisores, qui eorumdem scilicet ⌐frequenter⌐ esse solent
persecutores.

521 *post* tempus *deletum est* et

511-12. Prov. xv, 12.   512. Cf. *infra*, note on 514-15

himself.' And again from the same author, Solomon: 'A scorner loveth not one that reproveth him', but hates all reproof. Again we find in Proverbs: 'He that reproveth a scorner getteth to himself shame, and he that rebuketh a wicked man getteth himself a blot'; again in the same book: 'He that hateth reproof is brutish', and this quotation of the same author: 'Fools despise wisdom and instruction.' So when on many an occasion we observed your mocking sarcasm, which we do not find in our own nature, and which you could not unlearn, we used to say to you that you should mock and be sarcastic about no one more than yourself, and, were it possible, should spit in your own face. You devoted all your time in the past to mischief, and now you aim to devote all your time in the present and in the future to treachery. 'It is indeed right', as Democritus says, 'that the mocker be mocked.' For when you should have been devoting all your efforts to your education, you spent and spend all your energy on base treachery; for, indeed, you were an undisciplined brat and an unbroken colt, who neither devoted yourself to literature, nor learned either Latin or even French, nor rid yourself of your childish lisping, nor assumed any mature or decent outlook. At treachery alone were you eager to excel, under the tuition of your tutor, and with the keen urgings of your own wicked nature. So, when you mocked and derided not only strangers but also ourselves, whenever in public we uttered theological or philosophical points, or even polite witticisms which educated men usually respect, admire, and love greatly, we called you a Chamite, and quoted the following lines: 'Ham laughs when he sees his father naked. The Jews laughed when they saw God suffering pain.' So, just as those who kill their brothers are called Chaimites, so those who deride their parents and fathers are usually called Chamites. Furthermore, were others to mock your uncle—an uncle so useful to you—as a buffoon and idiot, if there were any of your father's nature in you, you should lament the failings of your uncle's old age, rather than deride them. But it is not surprising that the Baskervilles, who are very frequently the persecutors of their parents, should be their mockers.

513–14. Prov. ix, 7. This addition corrects the quotation given earlier (*supra*, 510–11), which is not a genuine quotation.

514–15. Prov. xii, 1.

515–16. Prov. i, 7.

522–3. Not identified.

535–40. Quoted by H. Walther, *Lateinische Sprichwörter*, no. 2710.

541–2. Giraldus and his scribe had to give the name of Cain as Chaim (cf. *infra*, part ii, lines 1099 and 1132), which makes the descendants of Cain into *Chaimite* and thus makes the pun *Chaimite–Chamite* (i.e. descendants of Cham) possible.

Cum itaque merito ridendi sint derisores, hoc precipue ridendum et
hostili quoque irrisione dignissimum quod ille qui deflendus est amicis
550 omnibus et deridendus inimicis quique in sibilum ac stuporem et
maledictionem datus est universis, passim cunctos et absque delectu,
tanquam splenetico morbo laborans, quod revera tamen magis ex
innata malicia ⌜et nequicia necnon et impericia⌝ quam morbi materia
prodit, tam amicos ridet quam inimicos, cum multociens tamen illud
555 ei Senece frustra dicere consueverimus: *Odibilem facit hominem risus
aut superbus et clarus aut furtivus et malignus aut alienis malis evocatus.*
Unde Salomon: *Risum reputavi errorem,* ubi et hoc supplendum,
indiscretum scilicet vel iniquum. Primus itaque derisor ⌜patriarche⌝
Nohe maledictionem patris in se provocavit et in filios suos servitutem
560 induxit. Helisei quoque longo post tempore derisores ultrices ursi de-
vorarunt. ⌜Item audi Salomonem in Parabolis. *Preparata sunt derisoribus iudicia dampnacionis et mallei percucientes stultorum corporibus.*
⌜Et in eodem: *Oculum qui subsannat patrem . . . effodiant eum corvi de
torrentibus et comedant illum filii aquile.*⌝ Item ⟨in⟩ Ecclesiastico: *Ne
565 derideas hominem in amaritudine.* Et in libro Iudicum irrisores tribulis
et spinis comminuit Gedeon. Et in Ebraica veritate: *Beatus vir qui
non abiit in consilio impiorum et in via peccatorum non stetit et in cathedra
derisorum non sedit.*⌝ Ex quibus exemplis ⌜perspicue⌝ perpendi potest
quam accepti sint Deo parentum suorum et maiorum derisores.
570 Preterea querere sepius consuevimus **quare pater** vester et fratres
ambo, quociens simul essemus, nunquam a latere nostro discedere
volebant, semper nobis adherebant, semper narrantis aliquid vel loquen-
tis ab ore pendebant. Vos autem a puerilibus annis et usque modernum
tempus semper pro posse procul a nobis et nunquam prope, semper
575 remotus nec solum a nobis et nostra, verum etiam ab omni doctrina
f. 56ʳᵃ laudabili et non propinqus, sicut | nunc est videre, esse voluistis,
tanquam illo prophete versu et verbo in vobis manifeste completo:
Tu vero odisti disciplinam ⌜et⌝ *proiecisti sermones meos retrorsum.*
Que ergo racio tante diversitatis? Certe morum hinc concordia magna,
580 et inde discordia. *Omnis enim amicicia vera provenit,* ut ait Seneca,
ex morum concordia. Sicut enim veri galline pulli eam e vestigio

564 in] *V omisit*

555–6. Not identified.   557. Eccles. ii, 2.   558–9. Cf. Gen. ix.
560–1. Cf. 2 Kings ii, 23–4.
561–2. Prov. xix, 29: *Parata sunt derisoribus iudicia et mallei percutientes stultorum
corporibus.*
563–4. Prov. xxx, 17.   564–5. Ecclus. vii, 12.
565–6. Cf. Judg. viii, 7.

Since, then, the derider deserves to be derided, it must be especially laughable, and deserve the most savage derision, that that man, who is to be lamented by his friends, and to be derided by his enemies, and who is an object of contempt, stupefaction, and curses to all, laughs at absolutely everyone without distinction, both friend and foe alike, as if labouring under some sickness of the spleen. In fact, this sickness arises from innate malice, wickedness, and ignorance rather than physical sickness. Yet, time after time, we used to quote Seneca at him, though to no avail: 'Proud and ringing laughter, or secret and malicious laughter, or laughter caused by someone else's troubles makes a man odious.' So Solomon says: 'I said of laughter, it is mad', to which one must add, that is, indiscriminate or unfair laughter. Thus the first man to deride the patriarch Noah brought his father's curse on his head, and brought slavery on his sons: and much later too, those who mocked Elisha were devoured by bears in revenge. Again, listen to the words of Solomon in the Proverbs: 'Judgements are prepared for scorners, and stripes for the back of fools', and again in the same author: 'The eye that mocketh at his father, let the ravens of the brooks pick it out and the young eagles eat it.' Again we find in Ecclesiasticus: 'Laugh no man to scorn in bitterness', and in Judges Gideon cut in pieces the mockers with the thorns of the wilderness and with briars; and the Psalm: 'Blessed is the man that walketh not in the counsel of the ungodly, nor standeth in the way of sinners, nor sitteth in the seat of the scornful.' From this it can clearly be noted how acceptable to God are those who mock their parents and elders.

Moreover, we frequently asked why, whenever we were with your father and both your brothers, they never wanted to leave our side, but always stayed close, always hung on to our words when we were telling a tale, or were saying something. You, however, from your childhood years right up to the present day, always wanted to be as far away from us as possible, never close to us. As can now be seen, you always wanted to keep aloof not only from us and our teaching, but also every teaching worth its salt, never involved in it, as if to fulfil the words of the verse of the prophet: 'Thou hatest instruction, and castest my words behind thee.' What is the reason for this great difference between us? Surely, the harmony of moral outlook on the one hand, and the discord on the other. For, as Seneca says: 'True friendship is the result of a harmony of moral behaviour.' For just as the true chicks of the hen

---

566–8. Ps. i, 1, in the translation of Jerome, *Divina Bibliotheca, Liber Psalmorum* i, 1 (Migne, *P.L.* 29, col. 119).

578 Ps. xlix, 17.   580–1. Not identified.

subsequntur et propius accedunt, sic falsi et adulterini, aliene nature morem gerentes, procul ad paludes semper abcedunt.

585 Ad cumulum autem malicie vestre tocius et nature perverse probacionem et illud accedit quod, a paterna natura ex toto degenerans et peiorem materne nature partem assumens et sequens, furti quoque scelere detestando et, quoniam erga nos, conduplicato vos iam irremediabili culpa contaminastis, dum patruo vestro, et qui vobis plus quam ⌜pater⌝ exstitit, quem etiam dominum vestrum verbo vocatis et ore,
590 set non opere, probatis, Propheta dicente: *Si pater ego sum, ubi honor meus? Si dominus ego sum, ubi est timor meus?* Tali namque patruo et domino cartas suas super terris prebende de Martru et ecclesie de Landu olim nostra diligencia perquisitas, necnon et litteras domini pape super irritandis resignacionibus persecucionis tempore factis, non solum in
595 iniuriam nostram, set etiam suam, *in celum os* ponendo, furtive subtraxistis. ⌜De talibus enim dicit Psalmista: *Et dilexerunt eum in ore suo et lingua sua mentiti sunt ei. Cor autem eorum non erat rectum cum eo; nec fideles habiti sunt,* etc. Et alibi: *Ore suo benedicebant et corde suo maledicebant.* Et hoc quoque: *Vana locuti sunt ad proximum suum;*
600 *labia dolosa in corde et corde locuti sunt.* Item et in Evangelio: *Populus hic labiis me honorat. Cor autem eorum longe est a me.* Unde et Balaamite dici possunt qui ⌜verbum⌝ bonum habent in ore, et non in corde vel ⌜in⌝ opere.

De hiis autem qui parentibus committere furta presumunt, audi
605 Salomonem in Parabolis: *Qui subtrahit aliquid a patre vel a matre, particeps homicide est.* Quanto magis et qui a patruo longe utroque parente commodiore? In Decalogo quoque furtum omnino non fieri, nedum parenti, septimum constat esse mandatum: *Non furtum facies.*⌝

Ad mentem etiam revocare vos volumus, quod tociens vobis in-
610 culcare solemus, quod et in vestra natura vidimus olim ⌜et notavimus⌝,
f. 56ʳᵇ set et nunc plenius impletum esse videmus, illud verbum | quod miles quidam modestus et prudens ⌜de partibus illis⌝, cui nomen Ernaldus, cognomine Rheting, patri vestro Flandrensica lingua de ⌜viro quodam tam sanguine vobis quam moralitate convinctissimo⌝ quondam apud
615 Haverfordiam dixit. Cum enim simul intuerentur in eum et tam gestus eius quam actus indiscretos et incompositos considerantes admirarentur, querenti patri vestro a milite ⌜predicto⌝ quid ei super hoc videretur,

---

613–14 *haec additio scripta est in rasura*   617 *haec additio scripta est in rasura*

590–1. Mal. i, 6.   595. Cf. Ps. lxxii, 9.   596–8. Ps. lxxvii, 36–7.
598–9. Ps. lxi, 5.   599–600. Ps. xi, 3.
600–1. Matt. xv, 8, and Mark vii, 6, quoting Isa. xxix, 13.
601–3. Cf. Num. xxiii.   605–6. Prov. xxviii, 24.   608. Exod. xx, 15.

follow in her tracks and keep close, so the chicks from another brood assume the habits of a different nature, and always stray far away into the marshes.

The fact that, in completely abandoning all trace of the character of your father, and assuming and pursuing the worse half of your mother's character, you have defiled yourself with unpardonable guilt by the detestable crime of theft—doubly detestable since it was against us—adds to the list of all your wickedness, and adds to the proof of the degenerate state of your character. For, with an eye to glory, you stole the deeds of the lands of the prebend of Mathry and the church of Llanddew, which we had obtained long ago by our diligence, and letters of the Lord Pope about the invalidation of the resignations made at the time of the trial (a crime not only against us but also against him) from your uncle, who has been more than a father to you: whom with your own lips you call your master, but do not prove it by acting accordingly. As the Prophet says: 'If then I be a father, where is mine honour? And if I be a master, where is my fear?' This is the uncle and master you robbed! The Psalmist says of such men: 'Nevertheless they did flatter him with their mouth, and they lied unto him with their tongues. For their heart was not right with him, neither were they steadfast', etc. Elsewhere: 'They bless with their mouth, but they curse inwardly', and this, too: 'They speak vanity every one with his neighbour, with flattering lips and with a double heart do they speak.' Again we read in the Gospel: 'This people honoureth me with their lips; but their heart is far from me.' Thus they might be called Balaamites, since they have fair words on their lips, but not in their hearts and in their doings.

Listen to what Solomon says in Proverbs about those who dare to commit theft against their parents: 'Who robbeth his father or his mother, the same is the companion of a destroyer.' How much more true is this of one who robs his uncle who has been more liberal than either parent. In the Decalogue theft is completely forbidden, to say nothing of theft from parents; the Seventh Commandment reads: Thou shalt not steal.'

We want to recall to your mind that we are so often in the habit of driving the point home that long ago we saw and noted in your character (and indeed we now see that it has been fulfilled only too completely) what a knight from those parts, a moderate and sensible man, called Ernaldus Rheting, once said in Flemish at Haverfordwest to your father of a man who was very close to you in both blood and moral outlook. For when they were both looking at him and considering in amazement his flamboyant and disordered conduct and activities, your father asked

respondit mixturam re vera in eo male factam maleque dispensatam
fuisse, nimium enim de grisia lana appositum fuisse dicens et de nigra
620 nativa parum asserens, etiam se nunquam capam pluvialem habere
velle de panno ex tali mixtura confecto, curialiter alludens mixture lana-
rum colorum diversorum ex quibus Haverfordie panni fieri solent et
innuens aperte per similitudinem istam maternam naturam pessimam
in predicto ⌈non nominato, set notato⌉ nimis habundare et de paterna
625 parum; subiecit etiam, quasi dolendo plurimum et plangendo, se
quoque pariter signo crucis quasi pre admiracione signando: 'In hunc
modum, Deus omnipotens, quantum infortunium accidit domino meo
et nobis omnibus (de Ricardo scilicet, filio Tancardi, viro magno suis
diebus et suis in finibus atque magnifico, loquens), quod ipse nunquam
630 uxorem nisi de diabolico genere illo ducere potuit.' Hic nempe ⌈pre-
notatus⌉, a Bascrevillana natura non degenerans, unde semper filii
patres et e diverso strangulare pro posse solebant, et patrem invitum
monacari et matrem, quantum poterat renitentem, cum utriusque male-
dictione monialem fieri fecit.

635   Multociens quoque vir ille predictus, scilicet Ernaldus, et alii de
Fiandrensico genere viri, robusti et de feodo Haverfordie ⌈quondam⌉
f. 56ᵛᵃ feodati, dicere solent et plan|gendo dolere, quod filios domini sui in
tenera et puerili etate tam agiles statim et tam leves conspexere, dicentes
et asserentes pueros tam promtulos inprimis et tam exiles ad robustam
640 paterne nature gravitatem ac maturitatem statureque grandis et pulcre
proceritatem, vero vaticinio quidem, sicut hodie est videre, ⌈vix⌉ pro-
venturos.

    Proinde qualiter primevus ille filiorum, quem nominare non curamus,
patriam prodens et hostili incendio pariter et rapine tradens, comperta
645 nequicia statim tam propter verecundie tante confusionem quam etiam
ulcionis regie formidinem et timorem, tanquam sibi ipsi manum ini-
ciens, quia *viri sanguinum et dolosi non dimidiabunt dies suos* et quoniam
virum iniustum mala capient in interitu, mortem suam accellerare non
abhorruit, tota satis provincia novit. ⌈Ad hec etiam Ricardo, Tancardi
650 filio, Ierosolimam iam secundo profecto, dictus ille filius eius, si tamen
filius, quoniam vel ab alio genitus, vel in cunis forte mutatus, vel
potius expresse diabolicam materne nature melancoliam imitatus, sepe
in audiencia dicere consuevit: 'Utquid de peregrinatione longinqua'
(de patre loquens rusticus ille) 'rediret? Utquid anni seniles eius terram
655 amplius occuparent?' Item, reverso viro predicto et vere suis diebus

624 *haec additio scripta est in rasura*
649–64 *haec additio legitur in f. 57ʳ*

630–1 *haec additio scripta est in rasura*
  655 viro] *V* viiro

647. Ps. liv, 24.

648. Ps. cxxxix, 12.

the aforementioned knight what he thought of him. The knight replied
that in his case the mixture was badly made and badly put together;
for, he said, there was too much grey wool, and too little native black
wool: he would never, he asserted, wish to have even a rain-hood of
a cloth composed of such a mixture. This was a witty reference to the
mixture of wool of different colours, from which the cloth at Haverfordwest is usually made. In this comparison he was clearly referring to the
excess of his mother's atrocious traits, and the lack of his father's in the
aforementioned—who is not named, but is well known. He also added,
as if in grief and sorrow, and also crossed himself, as if to show his
amazement, and spoke as follows: 'God almighty, what a disaster for
my lord' (he was speaking of Richard fitzTancred, a great and mighty
man in his own day and in his own land) 'and all of us, that he could
never take a wife apart from one of that Devil's own breed.' That
aforementioned man in no way gave up the Baskerville tradition of
sons trying to stifle their fathers, and vice versa, as much as possible;
he forced his father to become a monk against his wishes, and his
mother to become a nun, though she resisted with all her might, with
the curses of both of them.

On more than one occasion, too, the aforementioned Ernaldus, and
other stout Flemings, who had been in the fief of Haverfordwest, used
to say in sad lamentation that they noticed that the children of their
master were so hasty and fickle in their youth, and said and asserted
that the children, starting off so nimble and so thin, would hardly
grow up to reach the solid gravity and maturity of their father's
character, and the grandeur of his impressive and handsome figure—
a true prediction as is to be seen today.

For example, the eldest of the sons, whose name we do not care to
mention, betrayed his country, and handed it over to enemy fire and
plunder. When his treachery was discovered, immediately, as much from
the shame of such a great disgrace as from the fear and terror of the
king's revenge, turning his hand against himself as it were, he did not
hesitate to hasten his own end; for 'bloody and deceitful men shall
not live out half their days', and 'evil shall hunt the violent man to
overthrow him', as the whole area knows well enough. In addition to
this, after Richard fitzTancred had already set out a second time for
Jerusalem, this alleged son of his—if indeed he is his son: for he was
either sired by someone else, or perhaps changed in his cradle, or more
probably he was imitating the devilish spite of his mother's side—often
used to say in public: 'Why should he return from his long pilgrimage?'
(The buffoon was speaking of his father.) 'Why should the old man rule

virilis animi viro, cum dictus ille diaboli magis quam hominis illius
filius cum hominibus et amicis, ut mos est, obviam ei veniret, statim
ut in personam patris, qui vir procerus quidem et personalis erat,
oculos coniecit, coram secretariis suis quibusdam coequitantibus, qui
660 postmodum ⌐hec¬ retulerunt et multo minus ipsum ob hoc appreciati
fuerunt, in huiuscemodi verba prorupit: 'Utquid senex iste reverti
curavit? Diabolus ipsum ad nos reduxit.' Et sic *ex habundancia cordis
ore loquente* nec se ullatenus occultare v⌐a¬lente, Bascrevillana, qua
repletus erat, in ipso natura comparuit¬.

665 Sequens autem et etate secundus, set pravitate primus, priori
quoque tam stature modicitate quam nature perversitate cum augmento quoque simillimus, quam naturalis fuerit quam liberalis et
quam fidelis suo in loco pagina forsan subsecutiva declarabit. Unde et
a sapiente quodam, metrico versu, satis eleganter dictum est:

670 *Plus gravitatis habent res que cum tempore crescunt.*
Rara solet subitis rebus inesse fides.

Plangentibus autem tociens nobis atque dolentibus, et quasi cum
Apostolo conquerentibus quod *sine causa laboraverimus in vobis,*
verba nobis consolatoria dicere, ut mos est, plerique solebant, asserentes
675 mores illos tam perversos et gestus incompositos etatis beneficio maturi-
oris futuris temporibus penitus exuendos et mutandos; quibus respondere consuevimus: 'Cur non ergo frater eius primevus, scilicet
f. 56ᵛᵇ Willelmus, cuius in|dolem bonam et maturitatem naturaliter insitam
a puerilibus annis cum gaudio notavimus et approbavimus, mores et
680 modos optimos etatis maleficio non mutavit? Sicut enim ille maturitatem
innatam et moralitatem quam puer adhuc tener ilico pretendit usque
in hodiernum cum augmento servavit, sic iste scurilitatem, instabilita-
tem, perversitatem et indocilitatem, quas a materna, omine sinistro,
natura contraxit, a puericia statim in ipso notatas, et, non absque
685 mentis angustia, frustra virga sepe cohibitas et repressas, quia *naturam*
expellas furca, etc., crescentibus semper et invalescentibus perversis
moribus, et hoc nature viribus, que vix et difficile vinci solet, inseparabili quidem et immutabili, proh dolor! pertinacia servat.
Item quociens quasi plangendo preteritorum iacturam temporum

663 valente *e* volente *corr. V*

662-3. Matt. xii, 34; Luke vi, 45   668. suo in loco pagina] Cf. *infra,* 1127-8.
670-1. These two lines are also quoted in other works by Giraldus, e g. *Gemma*
Ecclesiastica (*Op.* ii, p. 302), *Topographia Hibernica* (*Op.* v, p. 143), and *De Vita*
Galfridi Archiepiscopi Eboracensis (*Op.* iv, p. 419), and they are invariably attributed
to a *sapiens,* cf. H. Walther, *Lateinische Sprichwörter,* no. 21709b. The *sapiens* in

the land any further?' Again, when the father, indeed a man of virile temper in his time, returned, that so-called son (the son of the Devil, rather than this man's) went to meet him, as is the custom, with his friends and cronies. As soon as he set eyes on the figure of his father, who was a tall and stately man, in the presence of some of his confidants who were riding with him (and later reported what went on and appreciated him the less for it), he burst out with something like this: 'Why has this old man bothered to come back? The Devil has brought him back to us.' Since 'out of the abundance of the heart the mouth spake' and was no longer able to conceal itself any further, the Baskerville spirit, with which he was filled, was revealed in him.

The following pages will reveal how in character, how generous and trustworthy, was the next brother, his junior in age, but his senior in wickedness, and, when he grew up, very similar to the elder in the smallness of his stature and the depravity of his character as well. A poet expressed this rather elegantly in verse: 'Things which grow with the passing of time have greater importance. Reliability is usually rare in things which suddenly spring up.'

However, when we were painfully lamenting, as we often did, and, as it were, sharing our grief with the Apostle, that 'we have laboured in vain in you', a great many people, as is usual, spoke words of comfort to us: they said that your depraved moral outlook and disorderly behaviour would completely disappear and change in the future with the benefit of greater maturity. We usually gave the following answer to them: 'Why, then, has not his elder brother, William, whose good character and maturity, which came naturally to him, we have noted with pleasure and approval from his childhood years, altered his excellent manners and conduct with the ravages of time? For, just as he, when growing up, has maintained and increased the innate maturity and decency which he showed as a young boy, to the present day, so, too, the other one, to our sorrow, with an unshakeable and unchangeable tenacity retains the coarseness, the fickleness, the immorality, and the pigheadedness which he has inauspiciously inherited from his mother's side: these we had already noticed in his childhood, and, stricken at heart, we subdued and repressed with the rod—in vain, for 'though you drive out nature with a pitchfork', etc., yet his wicked ways, his natural inclinations grew greater and gained in strength; for these are usually conquered only after much difficulty and ado.

question is, no doubt, Giraldus himself; cf. also *infra*, Ep. 4, note on p. 180, l. 79 s.v. *sapientis*.
673. Gal. v, 11.
685–6. Horace, *Epist.* i, 10, 24; also quoted in *Speculum Ecclesie* (*Op.* iv, p. 141, 22).

690 vestrorum dicere consuevimus quod infortunio vestro et incommodo
maximo nos contigit a Lincolnia primum per turbacionem illam et
inquietudinem magnam inter archiepiscopum Cantuariensem Hubertum
et nos peccatis urgentibus exortam discessisse. Tunc etenim ibi nobiscum ⌈per curam et sollicitudinem nostram⌉ puer existens et litteris ac
695 moribus per timorem et virgam, sicut illa quidem etas exegit, si non ea
interrupcio facta fuisset, affatim inbueremini. Quorum quidem amborum postea factus quippe tanquam pullus indomitus et vere puer
indisciplinatus, literature scilicet et moralitatis, parum nempe tunc
per timorem ob brevitatem temporis et iniuriam turbacionis nec per
700 amorem postea vel pudorem quicquam addiscens, cum dampno vobis
gravissimo et dedecore vestris immenso, iacturam incurristis, cum tamen
f. 58ʳᵃ non nunquam, quem | non emendat in puericia timor, emendare soleat
in adolescencia pudor et, quem non corrigit virga, corrigat interdum
erubescencia. Unde Ieronimus in libro epistolari: *Sepe quem non*
705 *correxit ob⌈iurgacio, emendat pudor.* Et alibi in eodem: *Ingenuorum*
ingenia facilius educat verecundia quam metus exsuperat et, quos tormenta
non vincunt, interdum vincit pudor.⌉ Proinde remedium saltem a
Domino, ceteris omnibus deficientibus, postulanti crebro vobis cum
Psalmista dicendum foret: *Bonitatem et disciplinam et scientiam doce*
710 *me,* etc. ⌈Sicut enim bona est *castigacio Domini in matutinis,* sic
et doctoris. Et sicut *bonum est iugum Domini ferre ab adolescencia,*
sic et doctoris.⌉ Scriptum est ⌈enim⌉ in Ecclesiastico: *Filii tibi sunt?*
Erudi illos et curva illos a puericia illorum. Et in eodem: *Curva cervicem*
filii tui in iuventute, tunde latera eius, dum puer est, ne forte induret et
715 *non credat tibi, et erit dolor anime tue.* Alioquin iuxta Salomonem:
Adolescens iuxta viam suam incedens, et cum senuerit, non discedet ab
ea. Et in Genesi: *Sensus et cogitacio hominis ab adolescencia sua in*
malum prona est. Unde et Augustinus: *Maius est impium iustificare*
quam celum et terram creare. Maius est enim recreare quam creare.
720 Unde et abbas Bernardus: *Facilius est informare rudem quam reformare*

705–7 *haec additio scripta est in margine*; ob *scriptum est in brevi rasura*

704–5. Cf. Jerome, *Epist.* 108 (Migne, *P.L.* 22, col. 897): *ut quem obiurgatio non*
correxerat emendaret pudor; quoted also in *De Principis Instructione* (*Op.* viii, p. 12).
705–7. Jerome, *Epist.* 66 (Migne, *P.L.* 22, col. 642).
709–10. Ps. cxviii, 66.
710. Cf. Ps. lxxii, 14: *Et fui flagellatus tota die et castigatio mea in matutinis.*
711. Cf. Lam. iii, 27: *Bonum est viro, cum portaverit iugum ab adolescentia sua.*
712–13. Ecclus. vii, 25.
713–15. Cf. Ecclus. xxx, 12: *Curva cervicem eius in iuventute et tunde latera eius dum*
infans est . . .
716–17. Prov. xxii, 6.
717–18. Cf. Gen. viii, 22: *Sensus enim et cogitatio humani cordis in malum prona sunt*
ab adolescentia sua.

Again, how often, bemoaning the waste of your early years, have we been in the habit of saying that it was unfortunate and very disadvantageous for you that it happened that we had to leave Lincoln for the first time as a result of that dispute and great disagreement between Hubert, archbishop of Canterbury, and ourselves, which arose from the promptings of sin! For, even at that time when you were a child there with us under our care and guidance, you would have been thoroughly taught your letters and good manners through fear of the rod, as that age demands, had not that interruption occurred. Indeed, afterwards in both these respects you became an unbroken colt, so to speak, and indeed an untutored brat. Then, the lack of fear failed to teach you literature and manners, because of the lack of time and the harmful effect of the disturbance, and love and respect certainly taught you nothing afterwards; all this waste was to the greatest detriment of yourself and the immense shame of your family, although respect in adolescence usually corrects the man whom fear does not chasten in childhood, and shamefacedness will usually rectify the man whom the rod does not improve. Thus Jerome writes in his book of letters: 'Often the man who has not been corrected by chiding is improved by shame.' Elsewhere in the same book he writes: 'Shame teaches the minds of the noble more easily than fear overcomes them, and sensitivity to their shortcomings often subdues those whom torture does not subdue.' Thus, when all else fails him who often asks the Lord at least for a remedy, it should be said to you with the words of the Psalmist: 'Teach me goodness, discipline, and wisdom', etc. For just as the reproof of the Lord is good in the morning, so, too, is that of the teacher, and just as it is right to bear the yoke of the Lord in adolescence, so, too, is it right to bear that of the teacher. For it is written in Ecclesiasticus: 'Has thou children? Instruct them and bow down their neck from childhood'; and in the same book: 'Bow down his neck while he is young, and beat his sides while he is a child: lest he grow stubborn, and regard thee not, and so be a sorrow to thee.' Elsewhere in Solomon we find: 'Train up a child in the way he should go, and when he is old, he will not depart from it.' And in Genesis: 'For the imagination of man's heart is evil from his youth.' So, too, Augustine says: 'It is harder to make righteous the wicked than to create heaven and earth, for it is harder to re-create than to create'; so, too, the Abbot Bernard: 'It is easier to teach the untaught, than to

---

718-19. Cf. Augustine, *Tractatus in Iohannem*, lxxii, 3 (*Corpus Christianorum* 36, 1954, p. 509, ll. 14-15): *intellegat qui potest, iudicet qui potest, utrum maius sit iustos creare quam impios iustificare*.

720-1. This is also quoted by Giraldus in *Gemma Ecclesiastica* (*Op.* ii, p. 194).

perversum. Item Salomon: *Literarum erudicione senectuti viaticum preparatur et disciplinata iuventus etatem confert fructuosam.* Unde Ieronimus: *Radix litterarum amara est, fructus vero dulcis.* ⌐Item Salomon in Parabolis: *Accipe, fili, disciplinam . . . ut addatur tibi*
725 *sciencia et torques collo tuo.* Set ecce qualiter vir docilis et industrius non animi tantum, verum etiam corporis ornamenta meretur.⌐ Item ⟨in⟩ Ecclesiastico: *Que in iuventute tua non congregasti quomodo invenies in senectute tua?* Unde papa Eugenius cuidam electo illiterato: *Fili, vacasti iuven⌐tu⌐te; sterilem habebis senectutem; nunquam in vita mea*
730 *promoveberis.* ⌐Hoc itaque verbum pape verbo Prophete consonare videtur, qui ait: *Quia scienciam reppulisti, repellam te, ne sacerdocio fungaris mihi.* Set o quam expressa nimiaque veritate subnixa! Hec in vobis et similia sepe notavimus et anxie recoluimus.⌐

Ad reparandum tamen utcumque tempus perditum et ⌐hominem⌐
735 perversum quoquo modo reformandum plurimum elaborantes, quam-
f. 58ʳᵇ quam incassum, statim post promocionem | vestram quam procura-vimus, ut denuo sermonem ad vos dirigamus, studio et doctori congruo vos assignantes, formam vobis discendi et libros audiendi, litteratu-ram quoque pre cunctis amplectendi et moralitatem ac maturitatem
740 assequendi scriptam reliquimus, precipientes quatinus frequenter in-spiciendo formam illam et discendi et continendi ac vos gerendi modis omnibus sequeremini. De Hibernia quoque, ubi moram postea per biennium fecimus, quociens litteras vobis et nuncios misimus, semper eandem formam ingeminantes et inculcantes, cum verbis monitoriis
745 et exortatoriis, ne sine causa laboraverimus in vobis, scriptam ad vos destinavimus. Reversi vero formam illam tociens et tam solicite datam nec in litteris et doctrinis nec in moribus aut gestibus vel in minimo repperimus assecutum, set, biennali spacio post tot monita tam verbis quam litteris inaniter facta, sicut et reliquo tempore, toto prodicioni
750 dato et preceptore vestro ac doctore relicto, novissimum in vobis erro-rem sicut usque in hodiernum diem, quamquam ex contingentibus adhibendisque remediis nichil omiserimus, semper invenimus longe

---

723–6 *haec additio* (Item Salomon . . . meretur) *legitur in margine f. 56ᵛ*   727 in] *V omisit*

721–2. This is also quoted by Giraldus in *Topographia Hibernica* (*Op.* v, p. 191).

723. Quoted by Giraldus in *Topographia Hibernica* (*Op.* v, p. 191) and in *Itinerarium Kambriae* (*Op.* vi, p. 75). In his introduction to *Op.* vi, pp. lxv f., Dimock mentions incorrect attributions by Giraldus. The present quotation, attributed to Solomon, does not occur in the Vulgate, neither does the other quotation noted above (cf. *supra*, note on 721–2). The present quotation is given by Dimock as Jerome, *Epist.* 125, *Ad Rusticum: De amaro semine literarum dulces fructus carpo.* But we find in Jerome, *Epist.* 107 (Migne, *P.L.* 22, col. 867) a quotation which is also of interest: *ut radicis amaritudinem dulcedo fructuum compensaret.*

reform the wicked.' Again Solomon: 'The study of letters makes provision for later years, and a youth of dedication brings forth fruit in old age.' Thus Jerome says: 'The roots of learning are bitter, but the fruit is sweet'; again Solomon in the Proverbs: 'My son, hear the instruction . . . so that knowledge be bestowed upon you, and chains about thy neck.' But see how the man who is docile and hard-working, deserves honour not only with his mind, but also his body; again in Ecclesiasticus: 'If thou hast gathered nothing in thy youth, how canst thou find any thing in thine age?' So, too, Pope Eugenius said to a certain illiterate elect: 'My son, you were idle in your youth, you will have a barren old age, you will never be promoted in my lifetime.' This statement of the pope seems to accord with the word of the Prophet, who says: 'Because thou hast rejected knowledge, I will also reject thee, that thou shalt be no priest to me.' How clear and well founded on the truth are these statements! These and similar ones we have often noted and anxiously reflected on in your case.

We took great pains, however, to make up lost time by some means and reform a wicked man in some way or other, though to no avail. To come back to you: immediately after your promotion, which we procured for you, we assigned you to study under a suitable teacher, and left a written plan for your teaching: listening to books, studying literature above all, and aiming for morality and maturity. We took care that under frequent inspection you followed that plan for your education, behaviour, and conduct in every way. Whenever, too, we sent you letters and messages from Ireland, where we stayed for a couple of years afterwards, we always reiterated and stressed the same plan and we set it down in writing for you with words of advice and encouragement, lest we should labour without reason on you. When we returned, we found that you had not followed that plan, which we had given you so frequently and so carefully, either in your letters and studies, not even in your manners and conduct, or in the smallest point, but two years after our advice had been offered in vain time and again both by word of mouth and by letter—two years devoted, like all the time afterwards, to treachery after you had deserted your guide and mentor—we always found the last error in you (just as is the case nowadays) that was far worse than the first one, though we omitted no possibility, and left no remedy untried. This is not surprising: for except the Lord build the house,

724–5. Cf. Prov. i, 8–9: *Audi, fili mi, disciplinam patris tui . . . ut addatur gratia capiti tuo et torques collo tuo.*
727–8. Ecclus. xxv, 5.
728–30. Presumably an oral tradition attributed to Pope Eugenius III (1145–53).
731–2. Hos. iv, 6.

priore deteriorem. ⌐Nec mirum tamen quia *nisi Dominus edificaverit domum in vanum laboraverunt qui edificant eam.* ⌐Unde Ieronimus super

755 Matheum: *Frustra laborat doctor nisi Deus faciat ut proficiat.* Cui consonat et illud Prophete: *Frustra percussi filios vestros, disciplinam enim non receperunt.*⌐ Qui vero sepe corripitur et non corrigitur, diligenti quoque grave nimis est honus et insuave. Unde et in Moralibus vox Ecclesie: *Quos corrigere nequeo, quasi supra dorsum porto.* ⌐Item

760 et in Ecclesiastico: *Harenam et salem et massam ferri facilius est portare quam hominem imprudentem et fatuum et iniquum.*⌐

Set forte nepos noster in illud quandoque Salomonis inciderat: *Qui apponit scienciam, apponit laborem; et cor intellegens tinea est ossibus.* Unde, quoniam tam animi quam corporis laborem semper abhorruit, et

765 qui nec res suas exteriores nedum ossa vel medullas unquam tinea demoliri pro posse sustinuit, et sciolus ob hoc et studiosus esse recusavit. Ideoque noluit intelligere, ut bene ageret. Sciat autem scriptum esse quoniam ignorans ignorabitur et quoniam affectata ignorancia non excusat, set condempnat.⌐

770 Possumus itaque cum Propheta dicere in persona medicorum et custodum angelorum, qui medici sunt anim⌐arum⌐: *Curavimus Babilonem et non est curata, non sanata; derelinquamus eam.* Super quod Glosa interlinearis: *In infirmitate desperatam.* Unde et: *Opera periit et inpensa.* In texto quoque subditur: *Et eamus unusquisque in terram*

775 *suam.* Hoc enim medicorum est proprium quod, ut egrum considerant desperatum, statim eum abeundo relinquunt. Argumentum hinc etiam

f. 58ᵛᵃ sumi potest | quod angeli custodes homines sibi deputatos derelinquunt obstinatos. ⌐Cui et illud in Parabolis consonare videtur: *Vocavi et renuistis; extendi manum meam* (⌐scilicet⌐ ad opera consilii boni) *et*

780 *non fuit qui aspiceret. Despexistis omne consilium meum et increpaciones meas neglexistis.*⌐ Sic ergo sibi ex toto sunt relinquendi qui non possunt emendari.

Unde et philosophi quoque responsum cuidam gibboso roganti ut corrigeret in eo quod corrigendum videret et hic non incongrue a nobis

785 assumi potest: *Corripere,* inquit, *te possum; corrigere non possum.*

753–69 *hae additiones* (Nec mirum tamen . . .) *leguntur in margine f. 58ʳ usque ad* quandoque Salomonis; *quod sequitur* (inciderat . . . condempnat) *legitur in margine f. 56ᵛ* 771 animarum *e* anime *corr.* V

753–4. Ps. cxxvi, 1.   755. Not identified.   756–7. Jer. ii, 30.
759. Cf. Gregory the Great, *Moralia in Iob,* xiii, 1 (Migne, *P.L.* 75, col. 1017): *Quos corrigere non valet tolerat, facta peccantium supra dorsum portat.*
760–1. Ecclus. xxii, 18.
762–3. This quotation attributed by Giraldus to Solomon does not occur in the Vulgate; cf. *supra,* note on 723.
768. ignorans ignorabitur] Cf. 1 Cor. xiv, 38: 'Si quis autem ignorat, ignorabitur.'

they labour in vain that build it. Thus Jerome says in his Commentary on Matthew: 'The teacher labours in vain, unless God ensures that progress is made.' This statement of his agrees with that of the Prophet: 'In vain have I smitten your children; for they received no correction.' The man who is often reproved, but not corrected, is also a very severe and unpleasant burden on the man who loves him; so, too, the voice of the Church in his homilies: 'Those I cannot correct, I carry as a burden on my back'; again, too, in Ecclesiasticus: 'Sand and salt, and a mass of iron is easier to bear than a man without sense, that is both foolish and wicked.'

But at length our nephew chanced to come across that passage of Solomon: 'Whoever takes up knowledge, takes to toil; and the understanding heart is a gnawing worm in the bones.' Thus, since he disliked mental strain as much as physical strain, and was one who could under no circumstance bear his skin, let alone his bones and marrow, to be destroyed by a worm, for this reason he refused to be enlightened and studious. So he refused to learn to act decently. He should know, however, that it is written that the ignorant will not be known, and that deliberate ignorance is not an excuse but a condemnation.

So, then, we can agree with the prophet on the role of doctors and guardian angels, who are the doctors of souls; 'We would have cared for Babylon, but she is not healed: let us forsake her'; on this the interlinear gloss runs: 'past hope in sickness', so the trouble and expense was useless. The text goes on: '. . . and let us go every one into his own country.' For this is the practice of doctors: when they consider a sick man past hope, they immediately retire and leave him. The argument can even be carried on from this: guardian angels abandon the men entrusted to them if they turn out obstinate. The passage of Proverbs seems to agree with this: 'I have called and ye refused; I have stretched out my hand (that is to works of good counsel) and no man regarded; but ye have set at nought all my counsel, and would none of my reproof.' Thus, then, those who cannot be corrected are to be totally abandoned.

So, too, we could take up without any incongruity the reply of the philosopher to a hunchback who asked him to straighten him out on the points he saw in need of straightening out: 'I can reprove you', he said,

771–2. Jer. li, 9.

773. Glosa interlinearis] Cf. Rabanus Maurus, *Exp. super Ieremiam* lib. xvii (Migne, *P.L.* iii, col. 1164): *a medicis desperantur.*

773–4. Cf. Macrobius, *Saturnalia* 2, 4, 30: *Opera et impensa periit.* This line is also quoted in the *Tractatus Nigelli contra curiales et officiales clericos*, ed. T. Wright, *The Anglo-Latin Satirical Poets* etc. (R.S. 59, 1872), i, p. 167, l. 14; cf. *infra*, part ii, ll. 1044, 1311.   774–5. Jer. li, 9.   778–80. Prov. i, 24–5.

785. Not identified; cf., however, Walter Map, *De Nugis Curialium*, ed. T. Wright (London, 1850), p. 71: 'quia corripi potest, corrigi autem non nunc.'

Haut aliter enim qui gibbum indocilitatis et prave moralitatis ab ineunte etate strumosum habet corripi quidem potest, corrigi vero non potest. Unde et Salomon in Ecclesiaste: *Considera opera Dei, quia nemo corrigere possit quem ille despexerit.* ⌐⌐Proinde et proverbialiter dici

790 solet quia felix puer et fortunatus facile docetur et doctrinatur; quid autem ex contrario contingat, Salomon aperte declarat.⌐ ⌐Ideoque simul cum Ieronimo de cetero senciamus, qui in Prologo super Esdram ait: *Frustra ad aliquid eniti neque aliud fatigando nisi odium querere, extreme demencie est.* Qui similiter et super Osee prophetam ait:

795 *Grandis miseria ubi, quia desperatur emendacio, non adhibetur correctio.*⌐

Verum tamen ⌐utinam⌐ in persona pocius Effraim cum Propheta nepos noster dicere posset: *Castigasti me et eruditus sum, quasi iuvenculus indomitus,* quod et Glosa sic explanat: *Multis laboribus scilicet et verberibus ad emendacionem denique perductus.* Ubi et paulo post in

800 texto quo subiungitur: *Confusus sum et erubui quoniam sustinui obprobium adolescencie mee.* Plerosque nimirum, quos nec virga correxit nec iurgia, propria processu temporis emendavit erubescencia.

⌐De talibus itaque gaudendum, qui, quasi desperati diu, tandem tamen ad emendacionem accedunt, quoniam, ut ait Ieronimus, *plus*

805 *terram diligimus que post spinas exaratas fructus uberes producit quam que nullas spinas habuit, set tamen exculta fertilem segetem gignit.* Et Dominus in Evangelio: *Dico vobis quod gaudium erit in celo coram angelis Dei super uno peccatore penitenciam agente quam super nonaginta novem iustis qui non indigent penitencia.*⌐⌐

810 Ceterum in adultis etiam, dum tamen humilibus perditi fuerint ingeniis et docilibus, sermo doctrine capit et fructum facit, sicut in illa peccatrice felici apparuit, que *sedens secus pedes Domini audiebat verbum illius,* et in Apostolo, qui ad pedes Gamalielis se dicit et gloriatur legem audisse. In elatis autem et inflatis, quia vas tumidum infusa

815 repellit et quoniam in malivolam animam sapiencia non introibit, firmas et fructuosas figere radices sciencia nequit. Superbis quippe resistit Deus, humilibus autem dat graciam et parvulis prestat sapienciam. Et de tumore collium descendit humor ad ima convallium. Set unde superbit et unde tumescit, unde doctrinam respuit, per quod

788–9. Eccles. vii, 14.

793–4. Jerome, *Praefatio in Ezram* (Migne, *P.L.* 28, col. 1403). Jerome writes: '*Frustra autem, ut ait quidam, neque aliud . . .*' The *quidam* in this context is used in the same way by Sallust (*Jugurtha,* 3): *Frustra autem niti neque aliud f. n. o. q. e. d. e.*

795. Not identified.

797–8. Cf. Jer. xxxi, 18: *Audiens audivi Ephraim transmigrantem: castigasti me . . .*

798–9. Glosa] Cf. Jerome, *Commentarium in Ieremiam Prophetam,* vi, ch. xxxi (Migne, *P.L.* 24, col. 878c): '*Quasi iuvencus indomitus, sive sicut vitulus, et non didici, hoc significat quod multo labore atque verberibus eruditus sit, ut ad poenitentiam converteretur, et non profecerit.*'

'but I cannot straighten you out'; similarly he who from his youth has had a scrofulous hump of indocility and perverse ways can be reproved, but he cannot be straightened out. Thus, Solomon says in Ecclesiastes: 'Consider the work of God: for who can make that straight which he has made crooked?' This, too, is usually expressed proverbially: 'A lucky and fortunate child is easily taught and instructed.' However, Solomon clearly spells out what happens in the opposite case. So, then, in future we shall hold the same views as Jerome, who says in the preface to Ezra: 'It is utter madness to labour at a subject in vain and to seek nothing but hatred for your efforts.' He also speaks similarly on the prophet Hosea: 'It is a matter of great sadness that when correction is not used improvement is given up as useless.'

But, oh that our nephew could say like Ephraim in the words of the prophet: 'Thou hast chastised me, and I was chastised, as a bullock unaccustomed to the yoke.' The gloss explains this as follows: 'He was corrected with great difficulty and with thrashings.' A little later in the text this, too, is added: 'I was ashamed, yea, even confounded, because I did bear the reproach of my youth.' Indeed, most of those whom neither the rod nor reproaches correct are improved by shamefacedness as time goes by.

It is, then, a matter of joy that those who have been given up as hopeless for so long reach the point of mending their ways. For, as Jerome says: 'We prefer that land which produces a rich crop after the removal of thistles to that which has no thistles but none the less when cultivated produces a rich crop.' And our Lord says in the Gospel: 'I tell you that there will be more joy in heaven among the angels of God for the one sinner that repenteth than for the ninety and nine just men which do not need repentance.'

Yet even in adulthood, as long as the minds are humble and docile, a sermon on discipline has its effect and bears its fruit: just as happened in the case of that blessed sinner who sat at the feet of the Lord and listened to his words, and in the case of the Apostle who said and boasted that he had heard the Law at the feet of Gamaliel. Since a full pot will not take any more, and since wisdom will not enter a malicious soul, knowledge cannot plant firm and fertile roots in the haughty and pompous. For God takes a stand against the proud. For the Lord gives grace to the humble, and offers wisdom to the mean. Water flows from the uplands into the lowest of the valleys. But what is the source of his haughtiness? What is the source of his pomposity? Why does he turn

---

800-1. Jer. xxxi, 19.   804-6. Not identified.   807-9. Luke xv, 7 and 10.
812-13. Luke x, 39.   813-14. Cf. Acts xxii, 2.

820 bonis omnibus se confusibilem reddit? In quibus, inquam, suffragiis confidere presumit, qui nichil unquam per se, ut de fortune donis primo loquamur, adquisivit, nichil omnino, ut de nature bonis subnectamus, in se virtuosum, vel laudabile nichil prorsus, nisi scelerosum et vile, pretendere potuit?

825 Illud ergo Trogi Pompei hic inserere dignum duximus: *Veteres*
f. 58ᵛᵇ *imaginem sapiencie | pre foribus omnium templorum pingi et hec verba consuevere inscribi:*

> *Usus me genuit, peperit memoria;*
> *Sophiam me vocant Grai, vos Sapienciam.*

830 Semper stultos homines odi; cultores scienciarum opido fovi. Item querunt me mali et non inveniunt. Oderunt Sapienciam. Set si oderunt, quomodo querunt? Querunt ipsam non propter ipsam. Querunt enim in doctrina, non in vita. Verbis eius inflati, et sic ab ea magis alieni. De illis ergo quid dicetur, qui sapienciam et scienciam adeo oderunt?
835 Quod nec etiam illam vel istam querunt nec verbis inflati nec sentenciis saginati?

Ad hec etiam, ut ad vos iterum sermo dirigatur, qui tam amplam sermoni nostro ⌜stiloque et calamo⌝ materiam prebuistis, ⌜set utinam bonam!⌝ quociens ad moralitatem, ⌜laude dignam,⌝ et maturitatem
840 vos inducere frustra nitentes, et ad mores ex convictu formandum et quedam *cum prima resec*andum *crimina barba* vos invitare volentes, cum bonis ambulandum, bonis et discretis adherendum diximus et exempla huiuscemodi proponendo monita dedimus. In libro Sapiencie: *Qui cum sapientibus graditur sapiens erit, amicus vero stulti similis erit*
845 *ei.* ⟨Et in⟩ Ecclesiastico: *Cum viro sancto assiduus esto.* Et in psalmo: *Cum sancto sanctus eris et cum viro innocente innocens eris.* Et Poeta: *Semper te melioribus offer.* Et Cato: *Cum bonis ambula.* Vos autem non solum in puericia, verum etiam in etate adulta, innate scurilitati morem gerentem et bonam doctrinam omnem aspernantem, cum
850 eruditis fere nunquam, cum garcionibus autem et histrionibus, quia *similia similibus gaudent,* semper invenimus. Cui hec et similia dolentes

---

839 laude *scriptum est in rasura*   845 Et in] *V omisit*

---

825. Trogi Pompei] The attribution of the following ten lines to Trogus Pompeius is perhaps based on a mistake by Giraldus, since it could not be traced in his works; cf., however, the notes on *infra*, 825–7; 828–9.

825–7. Veteres . . . inscribi] John of Salisbury, *Policraticus*, ed. C. C. I. Webb, 2 vols. (Oxford, 1909), i, p. 257.

828–9. Aulus Gellius, 13, 8, 3: *Usus me genuit, mater peperit Memoria; Sophiam vocant me Grai, vos Sapientiam.* In the form quoted by Giraldus (omitting *mater*), the lines also occur in John of Salisbury, *Policraticus*, cf. *supra*, note on 825–7.

840. ad mores ex convictu formandum] Cf. *infra*, note on 847–8.

841. Cf. Juvenal, *Sat.* 8, 166: *Quaedam cum prima resecentur crimina barba.*

his nose up at teaching? Why does he show himself to be in a state of confusion where everything good is concerned? On what foundation, I ask, does he presume to rely? For he has never acquired anything by himself, if we are referring to his chance gifts, and he has been able to show absolutely no trace of anything virtuous or praiseworthy, or anything, moreover, except that which was wicked or vile, if we are discussing his natural gifts.

We think it right at this point to insert this quotation from Trogus Pompeius: The ancients used to put a statue of Wisdom at the entrance of all their temples, and to inscribe these words: 'Experience was my father, Memory was my mother. The Greeks call me Σοφία, you call me Wisdom.' I have always hated stupid men. I have fostered those greatly who cherish wisdom. Moreover wicked men search for me, but do not find me. They hate wisdom, but if they hate it, why do they seek it? They do not seek it for its own sake. For they seek it in word, not in life. They are filled with the words, and so they are further estranged from it. What then is to be said of those who hate wisdom and knowledge? They seek neither one nor the other, since they are crammed with neither the words nor the opinions.

In addition to this (to address our sermon to you again—for you have provided considerable material for our words, as well as our pen and pencil, though I wish it had been good material) whenever we made vain attempts to educate you up to praiseworthy behaviour and maturity, and wanted to encourage you to form your character from social intercourse, and to get rid of some of your wickedness with your first beard, we told you to seek the company of upright men, and associate with upright and wise men; we offered you precepts of the following kind in advice: in Proverbs: 'He that walketh with wise men shall be wise; but a companion of fools shall be destroyed.' And in Ecclesiasticus: 'Be continually with a godly man.' And in the Psalms: 'With the perfect man thou wilt shew thyself perfect, with the pure thou wilt shew thyself pure.' And the poet: 'Give yourself up to better men', and Cato: 'Walk with the upright.' However, we always found you not only in childhood, but also as an adult yielding to your innate coarseness, and despising every kind of good teaching, and hardly ever associating with the upright, but rather with louts and actors: for birds of a feather flock together. This and similar advice we often used to give him:

844–5. Cf. Prov. xiii, 20: *Qui cum sapientibus graditur, sapiens erit; amicus stultorum similis efficietur.* 845. Ecclus. xxxvii, 15. 846. Ps. xvii, 26. 847. Horace, *Epist.* i, 2, 68.

847–8 Cato] This is quoted also in Petrus Cantor, *Verbum Abbreviatum*, chapter 70 (Migne, *P.L.* 205, col. 206): *Unde Cato: Ambula cum bonis, quia a convictu mores formantur*; also quoted in *Symbolum Electorum*, ep. 28 (*Op.* i, p. 302); *Topographia Hibernica* (*Op.* v, 153, 168). Cf. *infra*, part ii, 243–4 and 339–40.

851. Macrobius, *Saturnalia* 7, 7, 12; cf. *infra*, 993.

f. 59ra proponere | sepe solemus: *A convictu mores formantur.—Corrumpunt bonos mores colloquia prava*, vel metrice sic:

> *Colloquium pravum mores corrumpit honestos.—*

855 *Qui picem tangit coinquinabitur ab ea.—Cum electo electus eris et cum perverso perverteris.* Et in Ecclesiastico: *Cum fatuis ne consilium habeas; non enim poterunt diligere nisi qui ipsis placent.* Et illud Ieronimi: *Qualis quisque est talium consorcio delectatur.* Et illud eiusdem: *Illum habeas comitem cuius sermo, habitus et incessus sint doctrina virtutum.* ⌐Item et 860 Paulus: *Separate vos ab omni fratre inordinate ambulante.*⌐

O quam dissimilem optimus ille Willelmus de Barri, tociens dictus tociensque dicendus et semper nobis ad meliorum exempla reservandus, in puerili etate nil puerile gerens, se semper exhibuit! Cum enim bonus vir ille et sanctus Baldewinus, Cantuariensis archiepiscopus, Walliam 865 olim ob crucis obsequium, nos quoque cum ipso tunc ducendo, peragrasset et apud Haverfordiam provincie tocius populus ad audiendum sermonem eius accurreret, puer predictus, vix duodennis adhuc existens, non cum paribus colludere gestiens, set in tanta turba et tam conserta ad sedendum propius et audiendum, tanquam cum Domino 870 in medio doctorum sedente et interrogante, laudabili in puero prudencia se ingessit. Et, quod laude dignum etiam et admiracione, visa ibidem et audita que magis occurrebant memorabilia et discretis quoque viris notabilia, plurimis postmodum annis evolutis, iam miles effectus et adultus, recitare memoriter et referre solebat. Cum etiam tunc continue 875 ad equitandum et a patria doctrine causa, ut fieri solet, primo exeundum f. 59rb nobis a patre traditus | esset et Walliam postea totam et Anglie quoque partem non modicam in comitatu archiepiscopi, qui indolem eius bonam, maturitatem innatam et moralitatem postea secutam certis indiciis presagientem statim et redolentem, valde commendabat, nobiscum 880 transpenetraret, quecumque vel a nobis vel ab aliis dicta faceta vel narraciones curialitati accommodas audire poterat, non deridendo quidem, non delarvando, set diligenter ascultando, tam memoriter

---

852. *A convictu m. f.*] cf. *supra*, 840 and 847–8.

852–4. *Corrumpunt b. m. c. p.*] 1 Cor. xv, 33. Cf. H. Walther, where one finds under no. 3597: *Corrumpunt mores bonos colloquia prava*, there a dactylic hexameter. Giraldus transforms the quotation of 1 Cor. into a different dactylic hexameter which occurs also in Petrus Cantor, *Verbum Abbreviatum*, chapter 70 (Migne, *P.L.* 205, col. 206).

855. Cf. Ecclus. xiii, 1: *Qui tetigerit picem inquinabitur ab ea.* The quotation occurs also, in the same form as here, in John of Salisbury, *Policraticus*, ed. C. C. I. Webb, i, p. 323.

856–7. Ecclus. viii, 20; also quoted by Petrus Cantor, *Verbum Abbreviatum*, chapter 70 (Migne, *P.L.* 205, col. 206).   857–8. Not identified.
858–9. Not identified.

860. Cf. 2 Thess. iii, 6: *Ut subtrahatis vos ab omni fratre ambulante inordinate.*

863–7. An allusion to Archbishop Baldwin of Canterbury preaching the crusade in

'Habits are formed by social intercourse'; 'Evil communication corrupts good habits'; or, in verse, 'Evil communication corrupts an honest character'; 'He that toucheth pitch shall be defiled therewith'; 'With the pure thou wilt shew thyself pure, and with the perverse thou wilt shew thyself froward', and in Ecclesiasticus: 'Advise not with fools; for they cannot love but such things as please them'; and in Jerome: 'Everybody enjoys the company of men similar to himself'; and again: 'Choose as your companion the man whose habit, speech, and gait teach virtue'; again, also Paul: 'Withdraw yourselves from every brother that walketh disorderly.'

How different did that excellent man, William de Barri, who has been mentioned often, and will be mentioned again, and will be used by us as an example of what is better, show himself to be! As a child he never acted childishly. For when that upright and holy man, Baldwin, archbishop of Canterbury, came to Wales to preach the Crusade (we accompanied him as well) and the people of the whole area came to Haverfordwest to hear his sermon, the aforementioned lad, though he was hardly twelve years old, had no desire to play with his contemporaries, but was eager to sit in that huge and packed throng and listen, as if with our Lord, when he sat in the midst of the teachers, and questioned them, and he conducted himself with a wisdom that was praiseworthy for his age. And what really deserves praise and admiration, after years had elapsed and he had grown up and become a knight, he could recount and retell from memory what he had seen and heard there—everything that was memorable and worthwhile to wise men. He had been committed by his father to our care then for riding continuously and to leave his homeland for the first time for his education, as is usually the case, and he travelled through all Wales and a not inconsiderable part of England with us in the company of the archbishop, who strongly commended him for his good character, which gave a clear indication and immediate foretaste of his innate maturity and subsequent behaviour. Whatever courteous words were uttered by us or by others, or whatever polite anecdotes he could hear, he committed to memory, not despising or sneering at them, but listening to them carefully, so that, many years later, when we had forgotten all about them, he repeated and retold them with an eloquent ease, and he jogged our

Wales in Lent 1188, which Giraldus described in great detail in his book *Itinerarium Kambriae* (*Op.* vi).

868. Cf. Horace, *Ars Poetica* 159: . . . *gestit paribus colludere.*

869–70. Cf. Luke ii, 46.

861–85. A story of a similar 'good boy' is told by Walter Map, *De Nugis Curialium*, ed. T. Wright (London, 1850), p. 138.

retinebat quod ea multis postmodum annis, a nostra memoria prorsus
elapsa, suavi eloquencia narrans et repetens nobis ad memoriam pariter
885 et gloriam de tali nepote non modicam revocaret.

Constanter itaque dicere possumus et indubitanter asserere quod,
si paternam olim aut fraternam hanc indolem imitari vel in minimo
prava vos materna natura permitteret, non solum patruum vestrum tam
proximum vobis et tam proficuum, qui tot terras et tot regiones tam
890 animose et tam virtuose peragravit, tot hominum mores vidit, tantum
audivit tantumque retinuit, verum etiam extraneum quemlibet seni
illi persimilem, quatinus multis adquisita laboribus tanquam absque
labore perquirere possetis, totis sequi nisibus totisque amplecti viribus
cum summo desiderio curaretis. Non enim ociose, non sine causa sic
895 poeta librum suum inchoavit:

> *Dic mihi, musa, virum capte post menia Troie,*
> *Qui mores hominum multorum vidit et urbes.*

Unde et in Ecclesiastico: *Si videris sensatum evigila ad illum et gradus
hostiorum ⌜eius⌝ exterat pes tuus.* Et in eodem: *Ne despicias narracionem*
900 *sapientum, et in proverbiis illorum conversare. Ab ipsis enim disces doctrinam
intellectus.* Et paulo post: *Non te pretereat narracio seniorum; etenim
ipsi didicerunt a patribus suis: quoniam ab ipsis disces intellectum et in
tempore necessitatis dabis responsum.* Item et in eodem: *Fili, si at-*
f. 59ᵛᵃ *tenderis | mihi, disces; et si accommodaveris animam tuam, sapiens eris;*
905 *et si inclinaveris aurem tuam, excipies doctrinam; et si dilexeris audire,
sapiens eris. In multitudine seniorum sta et sapiencie eorum coniungere.*
⌜Item et in libro Iob: *In senibus est sapiencia et in multo tempore pru-
dencia.*⌝ Item et⌜David⌝ in psalmo: *Quanta audivimus et cognovimus
ea: patres nostri narraverunt nobis.* Et in Deuteronomio, ⌜Moysi
910 scilicet cantico⌝: *Interroga patrem tuum et annunciabit tibi; seniores
tuos, et dicent tibi.* ⌜Et alibi de Ioseph: *Constituit eum dominum domus
sue et principem omnis possessionis sue. Ut erudiret principes eius sicut
semetipsum et senes eius prudenciam doceret.*⌝ ⌜Unde et versus illos
Virgilianos verbumque Enee ad filium Aschanium vobis, adhuc puero
915 nec dum penitus desperato, quoniam et meritis nostris ⌜laboribusque
laudabilibus⌝ sors, ut videbatur, non ⌜eque⌝ responderat, dicere consuevimus:

> *Disce puer virtutem ex me verumque laborem,*
> *Fortunam ex aliis,* etc.

896–7. Horace, *Ars Poetica* 141–2. The lines are the first two verses of the translation
of the *Odyssey.*   898–9. Ecclus. vi, 36.   899–901. Ecclus. viii, 9–10.
901–3. Ecclus. viii, 11–12.   903–5. Ecclus. vi, 33–5.
907–8. Cf. Job xii, 12: *In antiquis est sapientia et in multo tempore prudentia.*

memory and at the same time brought us not inconsiderable pride for having such a nephew.

So we can assert firmly and without any shadow of doubt that, were the wickedness of your mother's side to allow you to imitate this quality of your father and brother even to the slightest extent, it would be your greatest desire to strive to emulate and with all your might to cherish not only your uncle, who is so close to you and so good to you but any stranger who resembles your old uncle—who has wandered so eagerly and virtuously through so many countries and regions, and has seen so many of mankind's customs, and has heard and re-membered so much. In this way you could acquire without exerting yourself what he has acquired under great hardship. It was not with-out purpose or reason that the poet started his book as follows: 'Tell me, Muse, of the man who after the capture of the walls of Troy saw the ways and cities of many men.' So, too, we find in Ecclesiasticus: 'If thou seest a man of understanding, get thee betimes unto him, and let thy foot wear out the steps of his doors.' Again in the same work: 'Neglect not the discourse of the wise, and be conversant with their proverbs, for of them thou shalt learn instruction', and shortly after this: 'Miss not the discourse of the aged, for they also learned of their fathers: because from them thou shalt learn understanding, and thou shalt answer in time of need.' Again we find in the same book: 'My son, if thou wilt attend to me, thou shalt learn, and if thou wilt apply thy mind, thou shalt be wise. If thou wilt incline thine ear, thou shalt receive instruc-tion, and if thou love to hear, thou shalt be wise. Stand in the multitude of the ancients that are wise, and join thyself to their wisdom'; again in the book of Job: 'With the ancient is wisdom, and in length of days understanding.' And again David in the Psalms: 'Which we have heard and known, our fathers have told us', and again in Deuteronomy, the song of Moses: 'Ask thy father, and he will shew thee; thy elders, and they will tell thee.' And elsewhere of Joseph: 'He made him lord of his house, and ruler of all his substance: to bind his princes at his pleasure, and teach his senators wisdom.' So, too, when you were a child, not as yet given up for lost, since our fate seemed not to respond justly to our deserts and praiseworthy efforts, we used to repeat those lines of Virgil—the speech of Aeneas to his son Ascanius: 'My child, learn virtue from me and honest toil, and your fortune from others', etc. So, too, we find in Cassiodorus: 'It is very hard for an industrious man

908–9. Ps. lxxvii, 3.   910–11. Cf. Deut. xxxii, 7; which has *maiores* for *seniores*.
911–13. Ps. cxlvii, 21–2.
918–19. Virgil, *Aeneis* xii, 435–6; also quoted in *De Invectionibus*, vi, 15 (*Op.* i, p. 170; ed. Davies, p. 217), on the same nephew.

920 Unde et Cassiodorus: *Grave nimis est ut fructu laboris sui vir fraudetur*
industrius et cui debetur pro sedulitate pariter et strenuitate premium,
cece illius domine vel errore devio vel adversante ⌜*malicia*⌝ *dampnum et*
dispendium paciatur iniquum. ⌝

Non hic autem magister Iohannes Blundus, iuvenis eloquens et
925 eruditus, ignoravit maiorum suorum et seniorum scienciam atque doctrinam, non aspernans, set viribus totis amplectens. A quo cum aliquociens quereremus quantam in ·Francia moram fecisset, qui Francorum
lingua tam recte, tam delicate et delectabiliter, tanquam materna sibique
nativa loquebatur, respondit se nunquam mare Gallicum transfretasse,
930 set ab avunculis suis, duobus viris litteratis et eloquentibus, magistro
Roberto Blundo et magistro Waltero, ⌜Lincolniensi canonico,⌝ qui
diu in Francia studiis indulserant, se tam literaturam in Anglia quam
etiam ydioma Gallicum addidicisse nec se minorem operam ad hoc
quam ad illam adhibuisse. Quinimmo, quociens ab illis verbum aliquod
935 Gallicum, elegans et defecatum rudique Anglorum a Gallico et fecu-
lento longe alienum, prolatum audivit, statim illud vel stilo vel calamo
memorie tenaci commendavit nec animo placatus esse potuit donec idem
verbum loco postmodum et tempore coram avunculis suis et in audiencia
suavi et vernanti eloquio suo in casu pronunciasset. Unde, quod illi,
940 remotis in partibus, laboribus et lucubracionibus multis adquisierant, hic
nepos eorum in patria sua, ad pedes eorum sedens et audiens eisque
f. 59ᵛᵇ iugiter assistens, id sibi quidem ingenio docili studioque laudabili | et
diligencia perutili bonus emulator et imitator comparavit.

Item Ieronimus: *Antistenes cum gloriose docuisset rethoricam, So-*
945 *crates dixit discipulis suis: 'Abite et magistrum querite. Ego iam solum*
eloquentem repperi, qui plures sapientes audivi.' Statimque Socrates,
venditis que habebat, nichil sibi plus quam palliolum reservavit et, pedes
Antistenem insecutus, studium consummavit. Huius Antistenis Diogenes
ille famosissimus sector fuit, Alexandro rege potencior et humane nature
950 *victor. Cum autem Antistenes discipulorum nullum reciperet et perseveran-*
tem Diogenem dimovere non posset, novissime clava minatus est ei nisi
abiret. Cui ille caput subiecit dicens: 'Nichil est tam durum quod a mellito
fonte dividat cinicum.'

Hii igitur et horum similes, senioribus et sapientibus assistentes,
955 quia doctrinam et sapienciam summopere dilexerunt, se quoque

920–3. Cassiodorus, *Variarum Liber*, ii, *Epist.* 21 (Migne, *P.L.* 69, col. 557) writes:
Grave nimis est ut fructu laboris sui fraudetur industrius, et cui debet pro sedulitate con-
ferri praemium, dispendium patiatur iniustum.

924. Iohannes Blundus] It is possible that this is the famous Aristotelian scholar
John Blund who died in 1248. For the few known data of his life, not including this
present reference, see D. A. Callus, 'The Treatise of John Blund *On the Soul*', *Autour*
d'Aristote, Recueil d'études de philosophie ancienne et médiévale offert à Monseigneur

to be robbed of the fruits of his labour, and for a man who deserves a reward for his application and hard work to suffer harm and loss unjustly from the devious wanderings or vicious malice of that blind mistress, Fate.'

However, this young man, Master John Blund, an eloquent and learned man, did not ignore the wisdom of his elders and betters, and did not look down upon learning, but embraced it wholeheartedly. When, on occasions, we asked him how long his sojourn in France had been—for he spoke French so correctly, so pleasantly, and so delightfully, as if it were his mother tongue—he replied that he had never crossed the Channel, but had learnt both the literature and the language in England from his uncles, Master Robert Blund, and Master Walter, canon of Lincoln—both educated and eloquent men, who had long studied in France—and he had devoted as much time to the literature as to the language. Moreover, whenever he heard them utter some elegant and pure French phrase, which was very different from the rough, corrupt French of the English people, he immediately, in order to remember it more easily, made a note with a pen or a pencil, and was not satisfied in his own mind, until he had uttered the word later correctly in context, in the presence and hearing of his uncles, in his pleasant, lively, and eloquent manner; so, what they had acquired in foreign parts with great effort and considerable lucubration, this nephew of theirs—a fine and zealous imitator—acquired for himself at home, sitting at their feet, listening to them and keeping constant company with them, because of his docile nature and laudable zeal, and his eminently proper diligence.

So, too, Jerome says, 'When Antisthenes taught rhetoric in his splendid fashion, Socrates said to his pupils, "Go and search for the master. I, who have studied under many wise men, have found him to be the only eloquent man." Socrates himself also promptly sold all his possessions, and, keeping nothing more than a meagre cloak, sat at the feet of Antisthenes and completed his studies. That very famous man Diogenes was a follower of this Antisthenes, who was more powerful than King Alexander, and overcame human nature. When, however, Antisthenes would not receive any of his pupils, and could not get rid of the persistent Diogenes, he finally threatened him with a club if he did not go away. Diogenes bowed his head to him with the words: "There is nothing so harsh that it can cut off the cynic from the source of honey." '

A. Mansion (Louvain, 1955), pp. 471–95. See also Iohannes Blund, *Tractatus de Anima*, ed. by D. A. Callus and R. W. Hunt, Auctores Britannici Medii Aevi, ii (London, 1970).

944–53. Cf. Jerome, *Adv. Iovinianum* ii (Migne, *P.L.* 23, col. 318), not verbatim: more correctly, Antisthenes was the pupil, Socrates the teacher.

doctos et sapientes multis vigiliis multisque laboribus, set fructuosis
et utilibus, reddiderunt. Unde Tullius ad filium, enumeratis multis
et maximis doctrine atque sciencie commodis, ait et quasi ex predictis
inferendo subiunxit: *Quare effice et elabora ut excelleas.* Laborem
960 enim et lucubram more nepotis nostri in studio fugere evidens inercie
signum est et ignavie magne. Proinde et Seneca, ne iners aut ignavus
repperiretur, se testatur longe plus olei ad lucubrandum quam vini
ad potandum expendisse.

964   Item, ut ad vos iterum apostrophemus, ⟨ad⟩ patrem vestrum et fra-
f. 60ʳᵃ trem optimum, a quorum memoria difficile disce|dimus, revertamur.
Verba que pater filio pluries dicere solebat hic repetemus. Dicebat
enim plurimum ei cavendum ne de Bascrevillana natura perversa
quicquam insitum in ipso comperiret, quia, si hoc (quod absit!) acci-
deret, terram suam ipsum iure hereditario contingentem, quamquam
970 ei auferre non posset, adeo destruendam ab ipso priusquam decederet
et deformandam assertive promisit, quod longo post tempore in statum
reduci et reformari non valeret. Facilis autem ad castigandum fuit cui
nichil omnino perverse nature illius et tam exose, totum per Dei gratiam
occupans hominem, melior natura reliquit.

975   De hoc etenim hominum genere dicere consueverat rex Henricus
secundus quia, si tantum vir unus de Bascrevillanis, sicut *avis unica
fenix*, in mundo foret et non plures, totam mundi massam et machinam
tantillo fermento contaminandam fore et corumpendam.

Ad memoriam quoque revocare potestis qualiter monacus Sagiensis,
980 de Normannia oriundus, cum abbate suo nobiscum apud Lincolniam
existens, in audiencia pupplica dixit summopere vobis cavendum fore
ne materni generis in vobis natura prevaleret. Noverat enim ille genus
vestrum utrumque, puta qui in partibus nostris, cellula scilicet de
Pembroc, diutinam paulo ante moram fecerat. Notaverat enim in
985 hospicio nostro, ubi simul cum abbate fuit, gestus vestros leves et
illaudabiles et a paterne nature gravitate laudabili et maturitate longe
alienos, in quo duo perpendere poteritis: quam commendabilis, etiam |
f. 60ʳᵇ apud extraneos, natura sit illa, sibi non incognita, a quo mores vestri
ex toto discordant, et quam sit ea detestabilis quam expresse repre-
990 sentant.

Quicquid autem alii vel dicant vel senciant, mores sue nature con-
sonos et conformes, quamquam pravos penitus et perversos, cuilibet

964 ad] *V omisit*   966 solebat] *V* solet

959. Cicero, *Fragmenta* E, ix, 1, ed. C. F. W. Müller.
961–3. Not identified.
976–7. Cf. Ovid, *Amores* 2. 6. 54: 'Et vivax *phoenix, unica* semper *avis*.'
977–8. Cf. *supra*, 421–2.

These, therefore, and others like them, associated with their elders and the wise, since they admired their teaching very greatly, and with great vigilance and great effort, but fruitful and useful, became educated and wise. Thus, when Cicero was listing the many very great advantages of education and wisdom, he said to his son, as if basing his premiss on our previous argument: 'Therefore, work and toil so that you may excel'. For to avoid hard work and long hours in study after the manner of our nephew is a clear indication of laziness and gross idleness. Likewise Seneca, to avoid the charge of sloth or idleness, states that he consumed far more oil when working at night than wine when drinking.

To address ourselves once more to you directly: let us return to your father and your admirable brother (we are loath to refrain from mentioning them). We will repeat here the words which the father was often wont to say to his son. He used to say that his son had to take very great care that he should find no trace whatsoever of that Baskerville wickedness in him, because if this were to happen—perish the thought—although he could not take the land away from him, since it was his by hereditary right, he promised to destroy and ruin it to such an extent that it could not be restored to its former state for a long time afterwards. However, he was amenable to reproof: for his better nature, which, by God's grace, filled the whole man, left no trace of that wicked and detestable side in him.

King Henry the Second used to say of that family that if only one of the Baskervilles and no more were left in the world, like the single bird, the phoenix, the whole mass and complex of the world would be befouled and polluted by that speck of corruption, small though it was.

You can also call to mind how a monk, a Norman from Séez, who was staying with us at Lincoln with his abbot, said in public that you should take very great care lest the nature of your mother's side get the upper hand in you. For he knew both sides of that family of yours: not long ago he had stayed in our area (in fact, at the cell at Pembroke). For, when he was our guest along with the abbot, he had observed your foolish, unpraiseworthy habits—habits which are totally alien to the laudable seriousness and maturity of your father's character. From these you will be able to conclude two things: how commendable on the one hand to strangers is your father's character, of which he was not unaware, and with which your habits are in total disagreement, and how detestable is that which they clearly portray.

983–4. cellula scilicet de Pembroc] The Benedictine priory in Monkton, known as Pembroke priory, a cell of Séez, was founded c. 1100 by Arnulph de Montgomery, cf. Knowles and Hadcock, *Religious Houses* (1971 edition), pp. 56, 73.

I

absque dubio, quia *similibus semper similia gaudent* longe pre ceteris, censura commendat. Unde et vos infamis illius et scelerosi avunculi
995 vestri, cuius infra natura describitur, nec non et consobrini vestri notabilis illius gestus leves et agiles moresque conformes, bonis omnibus et bene morigeratis detestabiles, plurimum approbare et pluries commendare consuevistis. Patris autem vestri et fratris optimi moralitatem, maturitatem et gravitatem, vestris nempe moribus omnino contrarias,
1000 nunquam nobis audientibus vel semel etiam vel exiliter commendastis.

Dicebat etiam de filio bono pater optimus quod, postquam miles fuit et uxoratus, nunquam ipsum verbo vel facto vel etiam gestu, patris quippe naturam et imaginem expresse gerens, vel semel in iram provocavit nec umquam aliter aut imperiose magis se in domo patris
1005 habebat, cum dominus tamen et heres existeret, nisi quod pater, ut decuit, administrabat, quam si extraneus esset in domo paterna et stipendiis eius, ut alii, sustentatus, propter quod et patris benedictionem tociens affectuosam quidem et effectuosam, ⌐ut ita dicamus¬, atque efficacem, sicut et hodie patet, cum *diligentibus Deum omnia cooperen-*
1010 *tur in bonum*, et precipue finalem optinere promeruit. Cum autem ille, qui heres erat et dominus in domo paterna, tam mitis extitit tamque modestus, vos, qui nichil nisi per graciam nostram, nichil per probitatem
f. 60ᵛᵃ aut virtutem propriam | obtinuistis, nec tam firmus est status vester in collatis, maxime cum nec discrecio vigeat in vobis nec erudicio nec
1015 quicquam, nisi prodicio, ut tociens diximus, et temporis perdicio, quin vacillare de facili possit et titubare, quomodo vos, nisi prava impellente natura, tam cervicosum, tam indiscretum et tam indomitum ostendere presumitis et ostentare?

Scire vos etiam ad hec volumus venerandis legibus et imperialibus
1020 cautum esse sanctionibus quod ob ingratitudinis odibile vicium et detestabile malum filii et heredes exheredantur et liberti quoque in servitutem revocantur.

Nobis autem non sic de nutritura, set longe secus longeque peius accidit, quoniam non semel in die, set tociens cotidie continueque fere
1025 per mores et modos adversos, gestus et actus atque sermones paterne nature ex toto contrarios, per discursus leves et scurilitates, per larvas crebras et larvosas derisiones, quas in nostra nunquam natura cognovimus, per indolem quoque perversam penitus et indocilem, tanquam

993. Macrobius, *Saturnalia* 7, 7, 12, cf. *supra*, 851.
995. cuius infra natura describitur] Cf. *infra*, 1126 ff.   1009–10. Rom. viii, 28.

But whatever others may say or think, it is certain that every man's judgement approves morals consonant and conformable with his own, be they ever so corrupt and evil, since like rejoices in like above all other things. Thus you used to approve completely and commend frequently the silly, fickle habits and morals of that infamous and criminal uncle of yours, whose character will be described below, and also that notorious cousin of yours, since they conformed to your own, though they were abhorrent to all decent, civilized men. However, the morality, the maturity, and the seriousness of your father and your excellent brother you never once commended in the slightest degree in our hearing, since they were at complete odds with your own morality.

Your excellent father used to say of his good son, that after he was knighted and married, because he clearly took after his father's character and appearance, he never on any occasion provoked him to anger by word, deed, or conduct, nor did he ever conduct himself in any different fashion or in an excessively lordly manner in his father's home, though he was the lord and heir, save that, as was right, his father had the administration, as if he were a stranger in his father's home, and like others dependent on wages from his father. As a result of this on many occasions he deserved to earn his father's affectionate, and, so to speak, effective, efficacious blessing, as is evident today, since 'to them that love God all things work together unto good', especially his final blessing. While, however, he who was the heir and lord in his father's house, was so mild and moderate, you, who have obtained nothing, except thanks to us, and nothing by your own goodness or virtue, and whose position in what you have received is not so secure, especially since there is in you no trace either of erudition or learning, or for that matter of anything except, as we have often repeated, treachery and time-wasting to prevent your standing from vacillating over a trifling matter!—the way in which you have ostentatiously presumed to show yourself as thick-skinned, thick-headed, and uncouth can be nothing but the impulse of your depravity.

In addition to this, it is our desire that you know a warning is given in venerable laws, as well as in imperial sanctions, that sons and heirs are disinherited, and freedmen re-enslaved, for the hateful crime, the detestable sin of ingratitude.

You have shown your ingratitude to us, not so much in respect of your upbringing, but in a different and much worse respect, since you ceaselessly irritated and annoyed us by your morals and bad manners, attitudes and actions, and conversations, which are completely contrary to your father's character: by your flippant discourse and jokes,

studio nitens ad hoc toto, nos irritare et exacerbare non cessastis. Unde
1030 et maledictionem quam pater aut patruus vel nepoti, cui plus quam pater
extitit, ingratissimo per omnia et scelerosissimo, dare poterit, per
nequicias omnes et pravitates enormes ac prodiciones turpes, tanquam
perdicionis filius et prodicionis, in capud vestrum exaggerastis.

Propter quod ea que de filio perdicionis in psalmo scripta sunt et
1035 filio ⌐quoque⌐ prodicionis hic adaptari possunt: *Dilexit maledictionem*
et veniet ei; et noluit benedictionem et elongabitur ab eo. Et induit male-
dictionem sicut vestimentum, et intravit sicut aqua in interiora eius, et
sicut oleum in ossibus eius.

1039   Novit itaque Deus quod, qui ante discessum vestrum assidua fuimus
f. 60ᵛᵇ in rixa | et anxie mentis angustia, corrigere quippe volentes incorri-
gibilem, iuxta illud Sapientis: *Eice derisorem et exibit iurgium cum*
ipso, summa procul dubio postea sumus tranquillitate gavisi, ⌐et
satis, Deo dante, dapis habentes rixeque multo minus malicieque et
iracundie,⌐ tanquam procelloso erepti e pelago, iam secure navigantes,
1045 in portu salutis et pacis constituti.

Refert autem Tullius in libro de senectute quod *quatuor robustos filios,*
quinque filias, tantam domum, tantas clientelas Appius regebat et cecus et
senex; intentum enim animum tanquam arcum habebat nec languescens
succumbebat senectuti; tenebat non modo auctoritatem, set etiam imperium
1050 *in suos; metuebant eum servi, verebantur liberi, carum omnes habebant;*
vigebat in illo mos patrius et disciplina. Ita senectus honesta est si se ipsam
defendit, si ius suum retinet, si menti mancipata est, si usque ad ultimum
spiritum dominatur in suos.

Nos autem ob unius venenosi capitis et cervicosi nequiciam domun-
1055 culam nostram exilemque familiam et exiguam regere non potuimus
et more solito ac debito proinde et pacifice gubernare, presertim adhuc
nec ceci, nec decrepiti vel deliri.

Qualiter autem hec senum quorumdam vicia vitari debeant, Tullius ibidem docet dicens: *Pugnandum tanquam* ⌐*contra*⌐ *morbum et sic*
1060 *contra senectutem. Habenda racio valitudinis: utendum excercitacionibus*
modicis; tantum cibi et pocionis adhibendum ut reficiantur vires, non
opprimantur. Nec vero corpori solum subveniendum est, set menti atque
animo multo magis. Nam hec quoque, nisi tanquam lumini oleum infundas,

1036 induit] *V* induet

1033. John xvii, 12. This expression is applied to Judas.
1035–8. Ps. cviii, 18.
1041–2. Cf. Prov. xxii, 10: . . . *exibit cum eo iurgium.*
1046–53. Cicero, *De Senectute* xi (37).
1059–70. Cicero, *De Senectute*, xi (35–6).

by your constant sarcasm and your cynical mockery, which we have never observed in our character: by your completely perverse intractable disposition, as if applying all your zeal to this end—this you did not once a day, but many times each day, in fact, almost constantly. Thus you have also heaped the curse which a father or uncle (who has been more than a father) could invoke upon the head of a nephew who has been ungrateful and wicked in every respect, as a result of all the instances of his wickedness, his terrible depravity, his wicked deceit, as if he were the very son of perdition and deceit.

For this reason the words written in the Psalm of the son of perdition and deceit can be adapted here: 'He loved cursing, so let it come unto him; he delighted not in blessing, so let it be far from him. As he clothed himself with cursing like as with his garment, so let it come into his bowels like water, and like oil into his bones.'

God knows then that before your departure we were in a continual state of strife and mental anguish, since we wished to correct the incorrigible. It is virtually the words of the Sage: 'Cast out the scorner, and contention shall go out with him'; and without doubt afterwards we revelled in our peaceful existence. And, by God's grace, having enough of the wherewithal, and much less strife, spite, and anger, we were like those saved from a stormy sea who, having come through safely, are set in the harbour of safety and tranquillity.

Cicero, in his book *On Old Age* relates that Appius, though old and blind, governed four sturdy sons, and five daughters, a great house and a great patronage. He kept his mind as taut as a bowstring and did not grow weary and slip into dotage. He retained not only his authority, but also his command over his household. His slaves feared him, his children respected him, and everyone held him dear. His country's customs and discipline were strong in him. Thus old age is honourable, if it takes care of itself, if it maintains its rights, if it is in possession of its wits, if it keeps its rule over its household to its last breath.

We, however, were not able to govern our tiny house and our small and confined family circle because of the wickedness of one poisonous and thick-skinned member: we were not able to guide it providently and peaceably in its usual and proper manner, although we were not blind, decrepit, or a dotard.

In the same book, Cicero teaches us how these failings in certain old men are to be avoided; he advises: 'Old age is to be fought against like a disease, and a strict regimen of health is to be kept to. Moderate exercise is to be taken, and as much food and drink to be taken as may invigorate the strength, not suppress it. One must not only aid

1064 *extinguntur senectute. Et corpora quidem excercitacionum defatigacione* |
f. 61ʳᵃ *ingravescunt; animi vero excercitando levantur. Nam quos ait Cecilius*
comicus stultos senes, hos significat credulos, obliviosos, dissolutos. Que vicia
sunt non senectutis, set inertis ignavie et sompniculose senectutis. Ut enim
petulancia, ut libido magis est adolescencium quam senum, nec tamen
omnium adolescencium, set non proborum, et sic ista senilis stulticia que
1070 *deliracio appellari solet senum levium est, non omnium.*

Tales itaque senes, qui iugi studio talique continuo excercitacionis
animorum utuntur remedio, deliracionis vicia non incurrunt. De
cuiusmodi Varro hec exempla ponit. Masinissa, rex Numidie, ante omnes
homines senectute admirabilis, nullo unquam imbre, nullo frigore
1075 capud contexit; idem aliquot horis in eodem vestigio perstare solitus,
donec iuvenes simili labore fatigaret. Item Gorgias interrogatus cur
centesimum et septimum ageret annum et cur tam diu viveret: *Quia*
nichil habeo, inquit, *propter* ⌐*quod*⌐ *senectutem meam accusem.*

De talibus itaque senibus, qui animi excercicio et sobrietatis quoque
1080 commodo, remediorum omnium maximo, senectutis vicia prescripta
vel omnino vitant, vel, ut minime officere possint, levant ac mitigant,
sciens nos esse, nepos noster moram rumpere maluit et, longe tempus
anticipando, cum crimine et infamia nostros ante diem in annos incurrere, quam vel deliracionem nostram cum laude et modestia vel
1085 etiam defunctionem exspectare.

Ut autem apercius occulata fide videre possitis ex quam diversis
naturis compacti fueritis et confecti, duos vobis homines proponimus,
Willelmum de Barri fratrem vestrum, cuius memoria nobis suavissima,
⌐et alterum, consobrinum scilicet seu consororinum vestrum, quem ex-
1090 pressius notificare, nisi per circumstancias agnosci possit, non curavi-
f. 61ʳᵇ mus⌐, quorum ille, paternam | sequens naturam, et a Deo dilectus est,

---

1075 contexit] *V* contegit; perstare] *V* prestare　　　1089–91 *haec additio scripta est*
in rasura usque ad seu con-; *reliquum* (sororinum . . . curavimus) *legitur in margine*

1065–6. The phrase is borrowed from *Hereditas* by Meandrus, imitated by Cecilius.
　　1072–6. Cicero] *De Senectute*, x, 34: . . . *nullo imbri, nullo frigore adduci ut capite*
operto sit. Varro is one of the participants of the dialogue which takes place in *De*
Senectute. More correctly, Giraldus quotes from Valerius Maximus, *Factorum et*
dictorum memorabilium libri novem, bk. viii, chap. xiii, 1: *Massinissa Numidiae rex,*
hunc modum excessit, regni spatium sexaginta annis emensus, vel ante omnes homines
robore senectae admirabilis. Constat eum, quemadmodum Cicero refert libro qui de se-
nectute scripsit, nullo unquam imbre, nullo frigore, ut caput suum veste tegeret, adduci
potuisse. Eumdem ferunt aliquot horis in eodem vestigio perstare solitum, non ante moto pede
quam consimili labore iuvenes fatigasset. This last sentence gives interesting additional
information about the endurance of Masinissa, his being capable of standing on one
foot for hours, which is not mentioned in Cicero. Valerius Maximus would appear to
draw from another source, since he says explicitly: *ferunt* ('it is said'). Giraldus thus
should not have attributed this sentence to Varro, and thereby not to Cicero. He
knows Valerius Maximus very well (cf. *infra*, part ii, notes on 826–8; 936–7; 938–9).

the body, but, even more so, the wit and the intelligence. For unless, as it were, you pour oil into the lamp, they fade in old age. And indeed, the body wearies as a result of the fatigue of exercise, but the mind is stimulated by exercise. For by those whom the comic poet Caecilius calls stupid old men he means the credulous, the forgetful, and the remiss. These failings are not of old age, but of idleness and sloth and sluggish old age. For just as insolence and lust are greater in the young than in the old, yet not in all the young, but only in the dissolute, so too, this senile stupidity, which is normally called dotage, is found in worthless old men, not in all.'

Such old men, then, as avail themselves of sedulous study and the lasting remedy of mental exercise, do not incur the failings of dotage. Varro gives us the following example of such a man. Masinissa, King of Numidia, admirable in his old age above all men, never covered his head during any rain or frost. He was in the habit of standing on the same spot for several hours, until he wearied young men with the same task. Again, when Gorgias was asked the reason why he was in his hundred and seventh year, and why he was living on so long, he said, 'Because I have nothing to blame on my old age.'

Thus, with the knowledge that we resemble such men, who by mental exercise, and the advantage of sobriety—the best remedy of all —either completely avoid the aforementioned failings of old age, or, in order that they may have the minimum harmful effect, alleviate and temper them, our nephew preferred to brook no delay, and considerably anticipating the course of time, to launch an attack upon our old age accompanied with defamatory allegations, rather than await, praised for his modesty, either our senility or our decease.

However, in order that you may be able to see more clearly the diversity of the characters from which you are made up and composed, we set two men before you, your brother William de Barri (the recollection of whom is very pleasant to us) and your cousin (whom we have not cared to identify more clearly, if he cannot be identified otherwise). Of these, the former took after his father and was beloved of God, as can

---

What may have happened is this: When Giraldus took down these moral examples to add them to his stock of quotations, he attributed these remarks on Masinissa to the source mentioned by Valerius Maximus, i.e. Cicero; but this was correct only for part of the quotation. At a later date, when using the quotation, he had forgotten that he had taken it from Valerius Maximus, and he attributed it *in toto* to Cicero.

1076–8. Cicero, *De Senectute*, v, 13. Only Gorgias' reply is quoted literally. In fact, Giraldus again follows Valerius Maximus, who, unlike Cicero, reports this anecdote concerning Gorgias immediately after the one mentioned in the preceding note. Cf. Valerius Maximus, *Factorum et dictorum memorabilium libri novem*, bk. viii, chap. xiii, 2: *Nam cum centesimum et septimum ageret annum interrogatus quapropter tandiu vellet in vita remanere: 'Quia nihil, inquit, habeo quod senectutem meam accusem.'*

sicut humano iudicio presumi potest, et ab hominibus dilectus pariter
et approbatus, quia, sicut de sancto quodam legitur, necesse enim erat
ut quem Deus gracia perfuderat ab hominibus diligeretur; iste vero
1095 materna et matertere vestre natura plene refertus, sicut et vos vestre,
quam sit graciosus et vel a Deo dilectus (secundum presentem iusticiam
dicimus) vel ab hominibus satis apparet, et plusquam satis, qui transacto vicennio cruce signatus, et abiecta quondam tam cruce quam etiam
uxore legitima, quam et turpi crimine falso forsan diffamavit, iam quidem
1100 factus adulter pupplicus et de magnis et amplis terris tam in Hibernia
quam etiam in Anglia et Wallia turpiter et viliter ⌐est⌐ exheredatus.
Et, ut illud maternum genus amplius extolleret et magnificaret, se
quoque degenerem in nullo probaret, tam p⌐ar⌐ricida quam etiam
matricida demum effectus, dum utrumque mundo mori, ut diximus,
1105 renitentem prava intencione coegit.

Tantum ergo scelus hominis istius a proximis suis et necessariis
taceri non potuit, nec alterius bonitas digna preconio supprimi potuit
aut subticeri. Duo namque fratres eius, milites, ⌐natu minores,⌐ de
prescriptis duobus in audiencia magna ⌐quandoque⌐ loquentes fra-
1110 trisque sui mores perversos plurimum detestantes et plangentes, alte-
riusque liberalitatem et fidelitatem multum commendantes, in multa
audiencia verbum istud emiserunt: 'Mirum quod homini, quem patria
tota diligit, laudat et veneratur, aeris inclemencia gravis oves omnes
et animalia cuncta sic ademit. Illi vero, quem totus nec immerito
1115 mundus exosum habet, nec pecudum aut pecorum nec etiam armentorum
ex communi fere temporis intemperie ulla penitus dampna persensit.'|

f. 61ᵛᵃ Vos igitur in hoc consobrino vestro, moribus et modis, natura
nimirum eadem operante, vobis simillimo, tanquam in speculo con-
siderare potestis, quem etiam et in hoc vicistis quod longe cicius in
1120 patruum quam ille in patrem, sciens quippe moram plerumque periculosam, magna providencia, set maiori tamen inpaciencia tam im-
piger ad turpia insurexistis. Verum Salomone testante: *Hereditas ad
quam ⌐in principio⌐ festinatur, in novissimo benedictione carebit.* Quod
ad utrumque vestrum referri potest, ad illum expresse, ad vos ⌐autem⌐
1125 per simile.

1092 hominibus *e* omnibus *corr. V*   1094 ab] *V* ad   1108 *additio scripta in*
rasura   1118 *post* eadem *deletum est* eadem

be assumed by men's opinion of him, and equally beloved and approved of by all his fellow men, since, as is said of a holy man, it was inevitable for the man on whom God had liberally bestowed his grace to be loved by his fellow men. This cousin of yours, however, takes after his mother (your aunt), just as you take after yours. Just how full of grace or beloved of God he is we can indicate from his present fate, or is sufficiently—indeed more than sufficiently—proved by his fellow men: twenty years after taking the Cross, he renounced both the Cross and his legitimate wife, whose reputation he destroyed with a foul and perhaps fictitious charge, and being by then a public adulterer he was disinherited in shame and disgrace of large and extensive estates in Ireland, England, and Wales. And to exalt and magnify his mother's family more fully, and to prove that he had in no way degenerated from it, he was finally stained with the sins of matricide and parricide, since, with evil persistence, he compelled both his mother and his father to die to the world, in spite of their resistance, as we have said before.

As the gravity of the crime of the latter could not be hushed up by his relatives and dependants, so the goodness of the former—goodness worthy to be noised abroad—could not be suppressed and covered up. For his two younger brothers, who were knights, spoke of the aforementioned two in the hearing of many, cursing and bewailing at great length the corrupt morals of their brother, and praising the other's liberality and fidelity highly. They uttered the following statement in the hearing of many: 'It is amazing that the inclemency of the weather robs one man, whom the whole country loves, praises, and reveres, of all his pregnant ewes, and all his animals, while the other, whom the whole world hates—not without cause—has suffered hardly any loss in ewes, flocks, or cattle, from the inclemency of the weather that has afflicted just about everyone.'

You can see yourself in this cousin of yours, who resembles you in morals and manners (since nature clearly does the same thing twice) as if in a mirror; yet you excel him in the following respect: for you were by far the quicker off the mark in your wickedness against your uncle than he against his father, since with great foresight you were aware that delay is generally dangerous: yet you turned with great foresight, but with even greater impatience, so zealously to wickedness.

as Solomon testifies: 'An inheritance may be gotten hastily at the beginning, but the end thereof shall not be blessed.' This can be applied to both of you—to him expressly: to you by analogy.

1093–4. Not identified.   1104. ut diximus] Cf. *supra*, 609–34.
1122–3. Prov. xx, 21.

In alio quoque generis eiusdem viro scelerosissimo et sanguine vobis proximo, cuius nomen, ne paginam nostram contaminet totam, apponere non curavimus, vos et naturam vestram tanquam in altero similiter speculo contemplari poteritis, qui nec patri, dum vixit, nec
1130 fratri primevo fidelis aut tractabilis fuit, qui et fratrem iuniorem uterinum pariter et germanum turpi prodicione decepit et, tam statum eius quam ordinem pervertendo, fortunam ipsius pinguem prius in macilentam et tranquillam in turbulentam, inaudita finibus in nostris malicia, mutare coegit. Qui nec dominis suis unquam nec vicinis aut proximis
1135 fidem portavit, ⌐monacorum malleus et predo perniciosus tociusque religionis et honestatis persecutor festinus et hostis scelerosissimus.⌐ Qui et sororum pudiciciam infestavit et nature ipsius iura simul ac federa, quod horribile magis est et abhominabile Deoque odibile et detestabile, violare non abhorruit, turpe nimirum a puericia reputans si quam turpitudinem
1140 unquam relinqueret intemptatam, primus et solus hiis nostris diebus ⌐qui⌐ puplica nota Walliam nostram illo nephando crimine maculavit.

⌐Longanimis autem expectator Dominus, et in obstinatos tamen interdum etiam in tempore gravissimus ultor, ipsum, ubi firmius stare putabat, titubare permisit et exheredatum penitus a nido perturbari,
1145 ubi et unde tot enormia commisit et a patria tota, quam turbaverat tociens et intoxicaverat, turpiter expelli digna quidem ultione sustinuit.⌐ ⌐Quique, dolore repletus et angustia, miseram animam paulo post in terra aliena pauper et inops exhalavit.⌐

f. 61ᵛᵇ   Ad fratrem autem vestrum optimum ut revertamur, dum in cu|nis
1150 adhuc infans iaceret, veniens Meilerius Henrici filius, qui et postea iusticiarius Hibernie fuit, vir probus et magnus nosterque consobrinus, ut puerum recenter natum videret, sicuti mos est, et visitaret, considerato diucius et diligencius vultu ipsius patri simillimo, sicut in puero perpendi potuit et notari, facetum satis et iuxta dicentis inten-
1155 cionem iam veritate completum, cum astancium risu pariter et applausu verbum hoc emisit: 'Nichil in hoc puero materne nature revera videmus. Totus enim noster est proprius, in quo nichil sibi vendicet alienus. Unde nec etiam matri sue porciunculam aliquam in ipso, nisi ferri igniti probetur examine, concedemus.' Qui vos autem et vestram
1160 naturam diligenter attendunt, dicunt e contrario vel dicere possunt patrem vestrum, tam discretum tamque modestum, nullam in vobis tam dissimili porcionem omnino, nisi ferri calentis vel aque frigentis iudicio probatum fuisset, vendicare potuisse.

1126–48. This man is Robert fitzRichard fitzTancred, who died in 1211; cf. W. S. Davies, 'Giraldus Cambrensis, *Speculum Duorum*', *Arch. Camb.* 83, 1928, p. 126 n. 2. 1127–8. cuius nomen . . . curavimus] Cf. *supra*, 668.

You will be able to contemplate both yourself and your nature in a second mirror, so to speak, in another criminal of this family (I do not care to add his name for fear of soiling the page completely). While he was alive, neither to his father nor to his elder brother was he faithful or tractable: he, too, deceived his younger brother, born of the same mother and father, with vile treachery, and, subverting both his status and rank, he forced his brother's fortunes from former riches to disgrace, and from peace to strife, with a viciousness unheard of in our area. He kept his word neither to his lords, his neighbours, nor his relatives. He was a hammer and pernicious robber of monks, he was the worst persecutor and the most ready enemy of every aspect of religion and piety. He also debauched his sisters' chastity, and, this is the more detestable and abominable, and is hateful and detestable to God, he did not hesitate to violate the laws and contracts of nature herself. Clearly from childhood, thinking it a disgrace to leave any vileness untried, he was the first and only one during our times to dishonour our Wales with the public scandal of that unspeakable crime.

However, the Lord is patient and longsuffering, and yet even in time he takes terrible revenge occasionally upon the obstinate; he let him stumble when he thought he was in a stable position, and had him disinherited and thrown out of the nest from which he had perpetrated his enormous crimes, and had him totally exiled from his homeland which he had so often violated and debauched—a just punishment. And he full of sorrow and in dire straits, breathed his last in a foreign land, an impoverished pauper.

Let us return to your admirable brother: while he was a child still in his cradle, our cousin Meiler fitzHenry, an honest, great man (he afterwards became Justiciar of Ireland), came to see and visit the newly born child, as is the custom; he considered long and hard the similarity of his features to his father's (as can be seen and observed in a child) and to the amusement and applause of the bystanders, he uttered the following witty remark, which has now proved to be true, exactly as the speaker meant it: 'In this child we can indeed find no trace of his mother's side, for he takes completely after our side. No stranger can lay claim to anything in him for himself. So, we will not even concede that there is the slightest little bit of his mother in him, unless it be proved by the ordeal of the red-hot iron.' However, as far as you are concerned, those who pay close attention to your character can or do say the opposite: your father's discretion and moderation could have laid claim to absolutely no part of you, since you are so unlike him, unless it were proved by the ordeal of hot iron or cold water.

Item et hoc etiam ad laudem quam meruistis accedit, quod sicut
1165 doctores ab ineunte etate singulos respuens demum et relinquens et
tanquam pullus indomitus frenum detrectans fugere consuevistis quibus
omnibus vestra disciplina semper inventa est displicina, magistrum
quoque David Walensem, cognatum vestrum, cuius vos doctrine
pariter et custodie ad reparandum utcumque tempora perdita fide bona
1170 commisimus, per iniurias et contumelias sicut ceteros apud Beverlegam
f. 62ra reliquistis. Quem etiam, quia nobis sub archi|diaconi nomine quando
scripsit, conviciis et probris affectum pugno flandrensico grandi et
grosso, tanquam neronianus revera discipulus, impie percutere voluistis. Qui mores etiam vestros et modos doctrineque defectus et defectuum
1175 causas nobis describendo litteris suis luce clarius enucleavit sibique
defectus illos non imputandos, set magis indoli vestre prave et nature
indocili atque rebelli, sicut et nunc patet, palam et aperte propalavit.
Quam etiam vestri descripcionem veritate fuisse subnixam facinora
vestra subsecutiva nunc manifeste declarant.

1180 Ad consummandam quoque nature prave nequiciam et explicandam
doctrine rebellionem indomitam et indomabilem, quatinus ad plenum
erumperet innata perversitas, que claudi non potuit amplius et occul-
tari, nunc denique magistrum vestrum et dominum cum scandalo
maximo et exemplo pernicioso infamieque nevo perpetuo per Angliam,
1185 Walliam nec non et Hiberniam diffuso non minus scelerose et contagiose
quam iniuriose deseruistis. Propter quod non solum terras illas, verum
etiam et universas ad quas facti illius facinorisque vestri tam egregii
fama pervenerit, quia semper contagiosa sunt turpia et viciorum imita-
trix natura, duplici exemplo pravo contaminastis, dum et prolem, ut in
1190 parentes insurgant, animare quidem et armare curastis et parentes
quoque, ut filiorum ac prolis profectui minus intendant, premunistis.
f. 62rb Cum enim utraque sint pessima, peiora certe studia pravi|tatis sunt
quam opera. Hec etenim casualia plerumque sunt et correctioni ac-
comoda; illa vero, que ex premeditacione proveniunt et industria,
1195 inseparabilia videntur et ⌐quasi⌐ naturaliter inserta. Verum igitur
apparet, quod dici solet, quia non tantus est amor prolis in parentes
quantus et parentum in prolem. Sicut enim humor a stipite in ramos
ascendit, set non a ramis ad truncum revertitur, sic amor a parentibus
in prolem ascendit, set non sic in parentes iterum a prole descendit.

1200 In hoc itaque nostro facto vestroque facinore subsecuto palam et

Again, it reflects on the praise you deserve that you used to reject and desert individual teachers at an early age, and avoid them like an unbroken colt pulling at the bridle: they all found your disciplining displeasing to themselves. At Beverley you left Master David the Welshman, your kinsman, to whose teaching and custody we committed you in all good faith, to make up for whatever time you had lost; you insulted and abused him, just as you did the rest. You heaped insults and reproaches on him because on occasions he wrote to us as archdeacon, and you wanted to strike him in an impious fashion with a big, fat Flanders fist, like a true pupil of Nero. When he described in his letters your morals and manners, your educational deficiencies and the reasons for them, he put it trenchantly, as clear as daylight, and revealed openly and plainly that those deficiencies were not to be imputed to himself, but to your depraved character and unteachable and rebellious nature, as is now obvious. That this description of you is founded on truth, your subsequent crimes now clearly show.

To consummate the wickedness of your depraved character, and to perfect your unconquered and unconquerable rebelliousness against teaching, so that your innate frowardness, which could not be checked or contained any further, might burst out fully, you have now at last wickedly and virulently no less than insultingly deserted your teacher and master with the greatest scandal, giving a pernicious precedent; and the eternal blemish of your infamy has spread abroad throughout England, Wales, and Ireland. By these two depraved precedents you have contaminated not only those lands, but also every land on earth where the news of that action and that unprecedented crime of yours has reached, since villainy always spreads like the plague and it is natural to imitate vice. You have taken care to encourage and arm children to rise against their parents, and you have forewarned parents to take less thought for the advancement of their sons and offspring. For, although both of these are very dreadful crimes, wickedness as a policy is indeed worse than wickedness of action, since the latter is, for the most part, a matter of chance and is open to correction. But the former, which is the result of premeditation and deliberate choice, seems to be irremovably and, so to speak, naturally implanted. What is usually said appears to be true: the love of offspring for parents is not as great as that of parents for their offspring. For, just as moisture rises from the roots to the branches, and never returns from the branches to the trunk, so, too, love descends from parents to offspring, but does not rise to the parents from the children.

The truth of this is clearly proved in this action of ours and that

aperte veritas ista declaratur. Nos etenim vestram, ut satis est notum,
promocionem et securitatem in posterum, ne post dies nostros egestatem
ullatenus incurreretis, set pocius ut mundanis opibus et copiis atque
opulenciis afflueretis, efficaci studio procuravimus. Vos autem e con-
1205 trario, ut in rebus ac reditibus quos tanta cura in vos congessimus
nullam auctoritatem, nullam omnino potestatem haberemus, quin
immo quatinus patruum vestrum, et plus quam patrem qui vos erumpnis
genuit et in paupertate reliquit (hic autem ab inopia vos eripuit et, quod
longe plus est, ut litteris ac moribus excelleretis, tantis, quanquam ina-
1210 niter, studiis invigilavit), hunc, inquam, patruum talem vobis ac tantum, ˹ut˺ in senio mendicum vel enormiter egenum redderet prava
natura vestra, quam exuere, quam mutare, quam expellere nulla unquam furca, quamquam ferrea et fortiter calibata, prevalebit, perversa
simul cum doctrina totis nisibus elaboravit.
1215   O quamdiu Willelmus de Barri frater vester et nepos noster, non
quidem a nepa dictus, set nature bone per omnia datus, in domo
paterna vivere posset, donec patrem suum, quamquam heres et dominus,
f. 62ᵛᵃ uxorem | habens et filios ac filias familiamque propriam, set ex toto
patri, sicut et ipsemet erat, deditam et devotam, a domo sua turpiter
1220 eiceret et terras suas contra patrem occuparet! Magis etiam patruo
gratus et obnoxius in omnibus esse deberetis, nisi nature perversitas
repugnaret, qui vobis ex sola quicquid habetis et unde tumescitis
contulit gracia, quam ille patri, in cuius bona ex iure hereditario successit et primogenitura.
1225   Quanta nimirum sit cura parentibus exibenda, docuit Dominus non
verbo solum dicens: *Honora patrem tuum et matrem tuam ut sis longevus*
super terram, set etiam exemplo, dum a cruce matrem discipulo commendavit. Super quem locum Expositor ˹ait˺: *Docet ut a piis filiis*
impenditur cura parentibus. Unde et Apostolus: *Si quis suorum curam*
1230 *non habet parentum, infidelis est et infideli deterior.* Id ipsum quoque de
senioribus quibuslibet sanguine propinquis et tanquam in loca parentum succedentibus affectusque paternos suis minoribus vel maiores
etiam et efficaciores ostendentibus non immerito quidem intelligi dedit.
Quin immo quanto necessitudo sanguinis minor ˹et genialis iunctura
1235 remo˺cior, tanto et gracia maior ˹ac cumulacior˺ et gratitudo debetur
obligacior. ˹De ciconiis et hic notandum duximus quod adeo nutriture

---

1234–5 et genialis *scriptum est in rasura,* junctura remo- *in margine*

1226–7. Exod. xx, 12.   1227–8. Cf. John xix, 27.
    1228–9. expositor] Glossa Ordinaria (Migne, *P.L.* 114, col. 422A): Et *docet ut a piis*
filiis impendatur cura parentibus.

subsequent crime of yours. For, as is very well known, by our effective assiduity we obtained your promotion and security for the future, so that you should not meet with any need after our time, but rather have abundant worldly wealth, resources, and riches. However, your wicked nature as well as your corrupt teaching, which no fork, though it were of well-forged steel, will have the strength to root out, exerted all its efforts in order that we should have no authority or power over the affairs and revenues which we had heaped on you with such lavish care: moreover, it strove to make your uncle, who has been such a great help to you, a beggar or exceedingly impoverished in his old age—an uncle at that who has been more than a father, since your father sired you in wretchedness and left you in poverty, while your uncle rescued you from poverty, and, far more important, took pains, though to no avail, that you should excel in letters and morality!

Oh, how long would your brother and our nephew, William de Barri (who is not a viper in the bosom, but endowed with an excellent nature in every respect), how long would he be able to live in his father's house before he would cruelly reject his father from his own home and take over his estates, flying in the face of his father, although he was lord and heir with a wife, sons and daughters, and a household of his own, completely devoted to his father as he was! You should be even more grateful and obedient in every respect to your uncle than he was to his father, if the wickedness of your character did not prevent it, since your uncle gave you whatever you have, and the reason for your pride, out of the goodness of his heart only, while he succeeded to his father's wealth by the law of hereditary succession and primogeniture.

The Lord taught the extent of the love to be shown towards parents not only by word, saying: 'Honour thy father and mother that thou mayst be long-lived upon the land', but also by example by commending on the cross his mother to the disciple. On this the Interpreter says: 'He teaches that love should be shown to parents by good children.' So, too, the Apostle says: 'But if any provide not for his own, he hath denied the faith and is worse than an infidel.' Not undeservedly did he mean this to be understood to refer to older men who are related and are *in loco parentis*, and show fatherly feelings, or even greater and more effective feelings, to their young. Moreover, the less the tie of blood, and the more remote the tie of birth, the greater is the grace, and the more obliged should be the gratitude. We think the following feature of storks to be worth consideration: they show such concern in the feeding of their

1229–30. Cf. 1 Tim. v, 8: *Si quis autem tuorum et maxime domesticorum curam non habet, fidem negavit et est infideli deterior.*

pullorum invigilant, ut in ipsa nutritura penne eis decidant adeo ut
volare non possint. Unde et pulli iam maturi, donec parentibus denuo
penne succreverint, eos vice versa nutriunt et sustentant. Argumentum
1240 quod affectum grandem filii erga parentes habere debent⌐.

Ad hoc autem exemplum de iure imperiali sumptum, plenum equitate
et pietate, hic apponere et huic adaptare casui preter rem non putavimus,
ubi et cautum reperitur in hunc modum. Piorum imperatorum emanavit
auctoritas, ut etiam earum rerum que in tempestate maris levande
1245 navis causa eiciuntur dominium non amittatur; non enim eas quis eo
animo abiecit quod habere nolit, set quod periculum effugere possit;
f. 62ᵛᵇ unde et qui res ipsas lucrandi | animo abstulerit furtum committit.
Sic et qui naturali quodam impulsi motu propinquis suis res ac reditus
suos cedunt ⌐et tanquam abiciunt⌐, non ea intencione id faciunt quod
1250 quamdiu vixerint aut voluerint habere nolint, vel quod spontaneam
inopiam incurrere velint, set ut sui, pocius in posterum per operam
ipsorum securiores effecti, paupertatis incommodum ⌐atque periculum⌐
effugere possint.

Ad degenerem quoque naturam vestram astruendam et hoc accedit,
1255 quod illum magistrum vestrum, scilicet Capre Willelmum sive Capelle,
cuius instinctu, natura cooperante, tot simul notas et culpas furti,
fraudis, fidei transgressionis, ingratitudinis et prodicionis cum perpetua
infamia in tenera etate iam incurristis, dans fidem, ex quo tam docilis
in hiis tam cito fuistis, vos multum in talibus annis ulterioribus, vita
1260 comite, profecturum, quod illum, inquam, magistrum post discessum
a nobis, ob doctrinam et instructionem talem, ecclesiam, vestes quas
vobis dedimus ⌐bonas⌐ et ecclesie porcionem largiendo, ⌐tanquam rebus
omnibus per eius operam laudabiliter et optime gestis⌐, preter solitum
remunerastis.

1265 Novimus autem ex quo fonte insolens et insolita largitas et liberalitas
ista provenit, quatinus illum, scilicet quem prescriptorum doctorem
habuistis et instigatorem, eundem in posterum ad parta tuendum, si
opus acciderit, tanquam pugilem habere possitis validum et defensorem.
Valorem autem illum apud viros eruditos valde revera invalidum
1270 (set magnus et beatus monoculus etc., quam parum vobis valebit!)
tempora forte futura videbunt. ⌐Nec mirum ⌐id forsan alicui videri
poterit⌐, si vir elinguis, nulla quippe recte loqui lingua prevalens,
virum linguosum, cuiusmodi tamen in terra nec dirigi quidem nec

1271–2 *haec additio* (Nec mirum . . .) *scripta est in margine*; id *scriptum est in rasura,*
forsan . . . poterit *ss.*

1243–7. Cf. *Dig. Iust. Augusti*, ed. Th. Mommsen (Berlin, 1870), 14, 2, 8: *De Lege
Rodia de Iactu.* The same passage is quoted in *De Principis Instructione* (*Op.* viii,
p. 120, lines 21–7). Similarly also Ivo of Chartres, *Prologus in Decretum* (Migne, *P.L.*

chicks that in feeding them their feathers moult, so much so that they are unable to fly. So when the chicks are mature they nourish and feed their parents in return until their feathers grow again. This is proof that children ought to have a strong regard for their parents.

In addition to this, we can cite an example taken from Imperial Law, full of justice and piety, which we consider apposite and adaptable to this case; there a provision is found in the following words: 'The authority of the just emperors has decreed that the ownership of those things which are thrown overboard to lighten the ship in a storm is not lost. For one does not throw them overboard with this intention because one does not want to keep them, but in order to be able to escape the peril. Thus, whoever takes them with a view to profiting from them commits theft.' So, too, those who cede (and, as it were, throw overboard) their goods and revenues to their relatives under the impulse of natural affection, do so not because they do not want to have them as long as they live or wish, or because they wish to incur self-wrought ruin, but in order that their relatives may be more secure for the future by their efforts, and may be able to escape the inconvenience and perils of poverty.

The fact that it was at the instigation of that tutor of yours, William (the son of the Goat or Kid) and with the co-operation of your nature that you rushed wholeheartedly into the disgraceful sins of theft, fraud, breach of trust, ingratitude, and betrayal with continual infamy at a tender age helped in the forming of your degenerate nature and gave the promise that, since you were so docile in these arts, you would progress well in such things in your later years, as time went by. This tutor of yours you rewarded unusually after leaving us by giving him a church, clothes (which we had given you—good ones at that) and part of the benefice of a church, for his teaching and instruction, as if all had turned out admirably and excellently as a result of his efforts.

However, we are well aware of the reason for your insolent and unusual generosity and liberality: it is so that you might be able to keep him as a sturdy fighter in your defence, and to watch over your gains for the future, if there is a need; for you have him as the teacher and instigator of what we have been writing about. However, the future will see his prowess not particularly strong in the eyes of educated men. (But in the kingdom of the blind . . . How little will that help you!) It is not remarkable, indeed—it could be seen by anyone—that a man without the ability to express himself correctly in any language should

---

161, col. 54): 'Sicut enim ii qui mare navigant tempestate urgente, navique periclitante, anxiati quaedam exonerant, ut caetera salva permaneant, ita . . .'

diligi solent, ut pro se loquatur, secum tanquam os suum circumducat. 1275 Scriptum est ⌐tamen⌐ in Parabolis: *Remove a te os pravum et detra-hencia labia sint procul a te. Oculi tui recta videant et palpebre tue pre-cedant gressus tuos.* Non enim a Domino datum est os istud, ⌐cui pravitas omnis atque dolositas longe aliena et semper exosa⌐, sicut Moysi, causanti quod impedicioris lingue fuerit, datus est Aaron, qui 1280 pro eo loqueretur, sicut in Exodo legitur, dicente ei Domino: *Loquetur Aaron pro te ad populum et erit os tuum.*⌐ Set ecce qualiter cum natura f. 63ʳᵃ prava concordat in omnibus | doctrina perversa et ex tali concordia, quia qualis doctor talis discipulus, conglutinatur hec amicicia.

1280–1 loquetur Aaron] *V* Aaron loquetur *postea transpositum*

1275–7. Prov. iv, 24–5. 1280–1. Exod. iv, 16.

take around with him as his 'mouth' a talkative man of the type who can neither be guided nor loved on earth to speak for him. It is written in Proverbs: 'Put away from thee a froward mouth, and perverse lips put far from thee. Let thine eyes look right on, and let thine eyelids look straight before thee.' That 'mouth' of yours was not given to you by the Lord, to whom all wickedness and guile is totally alien and always detestable, in the same way that Aaron was given to Moses to speak for him, for he complained that he suffered from a speech impediment. As we read in Exodus, the Lord told him: 'Aaron shall be thy spokesman unto the people, and he shall be to thee a mouth.' But see how his corrupt teaching is in every respect in harmony with your depraved nature, and from this harmony this friendship has been cemented: 'Like master, like pupil.'

SECUNDA PARS

De Capre Willelmo sive Capelle

PORRO, quoniam *inimici hominis domestici eius* et quia nulla res tam
nociva sicut familiaris inimicicia, quemadmodum in hoc nostro nunc
5 patet negocio ut ad unguem intus, scilicet et in cute, vir virulentus
dinosci possit, qualem se nobis exibuit post tot beneficia, palam a ⌐p⌐peri-
emus, quatinus, si ⌐vobis⌐ cavere nolueritis, quia talis et tam inutilis
nobis extitit, plenius ei retribuatis. Preter prodicionem itaque nobis
factam in hoc quod vos abduxit, immo seduxit, dum vos perpetuo in-
10 famem reddidit, quod nobis aperte constat, set apercius vobis, et preter
decem marcas quas a nobis habuit in hoc biennio ut vestre erudicioni
intenderet et preteritorum temporum vestrorum iacturam quoquo modo
redimeret et repararet, quoniam alias opera ipsius non indiguimus, tres
marcas de nostris et plures falso nimis et fraudulenter optinuit, marcam
15 scilicet unam, quam transacto biennio ad equum suum falvum emendum
ei tradidimus, quam apud Lincolniam nunc ultimo nobis abiurare
paratus fuit, sacramentum etiam vestrum simul cum suo nobis ad hoc
optulit, de vobis nempe tanquam de se ipso ad fas omne nephasque
confidens, cum tamen super marca, ei tunc tradita, certi essemus et
20 postea per notulas nostras inventas et scripta nec non et servientum
assercionem magis super hoc certificati.

    Item, cum Lincolniam ultimo venit, duodecim solidos, quos nobis
f. 63ʳᵇ tunc reddere debuit, de blado nostro | quod ad cervisiam suam auxili-
atricem faciendam acceperat estate proxima et dimidiam marcam in
25 denariis cum dictis et scriptis ad computacionem super hiis et aliis nobis
faciendam, cuncta dolose suppressit nec mencionem aliquam inde fecit.

    Unde, cum apud Landu per totam estatem illam moram faceret
seque sororesque suas et concubinam, simul cum ecclesia comparatam,
⌐quamquam inpudicam et inpurissimam⌐ familiam⌐que⌐ totam illuc
30 translatam de grangia nostra, nobis ignorantibus, sustentaret, quia dici
proverbialiter solet quod panis fatui citius comeditur et comestione
consumitur, quociens nobis apud Lincolniam litteras mittebat, semper
mandabat et, tanquam fidelis, nobis valde quasi premuniendo consule-
bat quod parcius expenderemus et in grangia nostra de Landu parum

---

2 De Capre . . . Capelle *rubrica*   25 dictis] *V* dicis

3. Mic. vii, 6, taken up by Matt. x, 36.

PART TWO

William (the Whoreson) de Capella

SINCE 'a man's enemies are they of his own household', and since nothing is as harmful as the enmity of friends, as is clear from this affair of ours, in order that a malicious man can be recognized perfectly in the flesh, we shall reveal clearly his attitude to us after we had helped him so much, so that, if you have no desire to take heed for yourself, you may repay him more fully for the harm he has done us. Apart from betraying us in the manner in which he alienated, indeed seduced, your affection, while at the same time making you eternally notorious, a fact that is clear enough to us, and even clearer to you, and apart from the ten marks which we had given him during the past two years to spend on your education and somehow to recover and redeem the time you have lost, since we did not require his work for anything else, he has obtained by exceedingly false and fraudulent means three marks and more from our household. One of these marks which we gave him at the end of the two years to buy his dun horse, he was prepared to deny to us at Lincoln this last year, and even offered us your as well as his own oath on it, relying on you, as if you were he, in everything legal and illegal, though we had no doubts over the mark given to him, and afterwards received confirmation of it from the entries in our memoranda, and in addition from the statements of our servants.

Again, the last time he came to Lincoln, he deceitfully concealed the twelve shillings from our corn, which he ought to have repaid then (he had taken this last summer to give an ale-feast for his helpers) and the half-mark in pence with verbal and written promises—this was to make an audit for us over these and other matters. No other mention of these was made from that date on.

He stayed at Llanddew all that summer and sustained himself, his sisters and his concubine, whom he had taken when he received the church, though she was a shameless hussy, and his whole household, which he had transferred there without our knowledge, from our farm (there is a proverbial saying that the bread of the fool is all too soon wasted and consumed by squander). Whenever he sent letters to us at Lincoln, he always advised and, as if he were a faithful steward, strongly counselled us to spend less, and not to expect too much from our farm

35 confideremus. Sciebat enim ipse quid de grangia nostra fecerat et quid
cotidie faciebat et, quia parum nobis ⌈inde⌉ relicturus erat, pro custode
quippe consumptor effectus in fraudes et furta, fide per totum commu-
tata. Unde et effectum est ut, que communibus annis decem marcas
ad minus vel etiam quindecim, aliis autem viginti aut plures reddere
40 nobis grangia consuevit, vix hoc anno et sub hoc custode quinque
vel sex, computatis omnibus, reddere potuit, cum tamen autumpno,
blado bene collecto et collocato, plene referta fuisset. ⌈Unde et cum
Propheta dicere possumus: *Maledictus qui opus domini facit fraudulenter*⌉.

45 Quamvis etenim proverbialiter dici soleat non minus cautos homines
esse quam latrones, custodes tamen ipsos quibus et indubitata fides est
habita et summa rerum tota commissa, dum tamen perfidi fuerint et
fraudulenti, custodire posse et a domesticis hostibus rem servare late-
49 brisque ab omnibus et lateribus pravis rem salvare, sine fundo quidem
f. 63ᵛᵃ prudencia foret et tanquam inexhaustus sapien|cie puteus.

Cum enim ille qui omnia novit, scrutator quippe cordium et cognitor
quoque cogitacionum, rei sue familiaris furem custodem haberet et
ultro talem admitteret et sustineret, dampna domestica et furta fami-
liaria quis vitare valebit? Set, quoniam in misteriis et ministeriis pactum
55 racio diversa reformat rei sue servande, quam poterit quivis curam
inpendat, quatinus, si totum salvare nequeat, minorem tamen quam
possit iacturam incurreret.

Item cum B., presbiter de Lambili ⌈a⌉u marcam unam nobis debitam
nuper ad reddendum paratam haberet et Willelmus hoc sciret, statim
60 illuc properans, dixit marcam illam sibi a nobis debitam et ad ei solven-
dum assignatam, et comminatus est ei et appellavit, ne alii traderetur,
et sic a presbitero meticuloso marcam nostram extorsit. Set ecce fides
tociens nobis prestita bene servata, et per 'salvis salvandis', quam semper
adiectionem sacramentis suis et fidelitatibus prestandis fraudulenter
65 adicere solet, bene salvata!

Item, cum de tribus marcis, quas ei nunc ultimo apud Lincolniam in
solutum marce promisse concessimus, quas scilicet pro equo nostro
vendito apud Brechene susceperat, cum quarta quoque quam ei tunc
condonavimus ad se scilicet adquietandum erga militem de mercimonio
70 ecclesie quam emerat cum capella, pulcra ei visa nimis et candida, quod
totum tamen, priusquam prodiciones eius erga nos tot compertas

63 nobis prestita] *V* prestita nobis *postea transpositum*

---

43. Jer. xlviii, 10.   51–3. Cf. John xii, 6.   63. Cf. *infra*, 480.

at Llanddew, as if forewarning us. For he knew what he had made, and what he was making every day of our farm, and that he was going to leave us all too little: for, indeed, he had become a destroyer instead of a keeper, and his honesty became deceit and theft. The result was that while our farm used to give us a return of at least ten or even fifteen marks in normal years, and in others twenty or more, this year with this keeper it could hardly give a return of five or six all told, although, when the grain had been collected and garnered, there should have been a complete glut at harvest. So we can also say with the Prophet: 'Cursed be he that doeth the work of the Lord deceitfully.'

Though it is often said proverbially that men are no less wary than thieves, it would be a mark of fundamental prudence, drawn, as it were, from the ever full well of wisdom, that one should guard the guardians themselves, in whom one has absolute trust, and to whom all one's possessions are entrusted, though they are deceitful and untrustworthy, and preserve one's property from domestic enemies, and keep it safe from all kinds of subterfuges and unscrupulous associates.

When God who is aware of everything, who examines everyone's heart, who judges everyone's thought, had a thief as the warden of his household, and moreover accepted and sustained such a man, what man will be able to avoid loss to his property and theft from his goods? But, since a different way of thinking reshapes the manner of his service and administration, let him take whatever pains he can to preserve his property, so that, if he should be unable to save everything, he would, however, incur the least possible loss.

Again, when B., priest of Llanfilo, had got the one mark which he owed us to repay us, and William got to hear of this, he immediately hurried off in that direction and said that we owed that mark to him and that it had been set aside to pay him. He threatened and cajoled him not to give it to anyone else, and in this way he extorted our mark from the frightened priest. But consider how well he kept his trust, which he so frequently protested to us, and, on the principle that what is saved is to be preserved, how well did he preserve his trust, which full of deceit he constantly appealed to when swearing his oaths or swearing his loyalty.

Again, there is the matter of the three marks which we gave him last year at Lincoln, in payment for the promised mark, and which he had in fact taken for the sale of our horse at Brecon, as well as the quarter which we remitted to him to discharge himself from a knight for the sale of a church which he had bought, with a chapel, which he thought very beautiful and fair. The letters patent which testify that all this took

habuimus, factum fuit, litteras patentes hoc testificantes, quibus nostrum
sigillum et suum appensum fuerat, in custodiam domini prioris de
74 Brechene tradere debuisset, non illi quidem eas, set sacriste domus
f. 63ᵛᵇ tradidit, sicut prior | postea nobis rescripsit, et easdem infra quindecim
dies, cum audisset nos scelera ipsius apud Lincolniam comperisse,
resumpsit, cum apud priorem tamen tanquam in sequestro ex communi consensu nostro et condicto reservari debuissent, quarum etiam
transcriptum penes nos reservatum, ut melius hominem noscatis, vobis
80 destinare curavimus.

Item cum apud Lincolniam nunc ultimo, priusquam fraus eius detecta
fuisset, sigillum nostrum ei traderemus ad litteras nostras signandum,
variis personis variaque ad loca transmissas, tanquam domestico et
familiari nostro, persuasit nobis quia negocia nostra plurima tam in
85 Anglia quam in Wallia facere tunc debuit et etiam usque Meneviam et
Pembrochiam transire ad quod et expensas a nobis accepit ad obviandum
vobis si, illuc eundo, malignari velletis sicut ⌈et⌉ fecistis. Quo tamen non
ivit, set vos instructum ab eo, immo destructum verius, ut libere et sine
impedimento debaccari possetis et excogitata communiter scelera per-
90 petrare, transmisit. Persuasit, inquam, ut cedulas duas vel tres, vacuas,
set signatas, secum ad cautelam portaret. Credidimus ei, sicut iurato
nostro, et cui fidem tanquam nobis ipsis tunc habuimus. Ipse vero, sicut
pueri nostri, qui cum ipso ad sigillandum tunc erant, nobis postea
testati sunt, quinque vel sex cedulas vacuas sigillavit. Comperta vero
95 nequicia postmodum ipsius, scripsimus priori de Brechene, super hiis
et aliis nequiter et fraudulenter ab ipso erga nos gestis, et ut ipsum inde
conveniret, et precipue quod cedulas illas, sive vacuas sive inscriptas, |
f. 64ʳᵃ sigillo nostro signatas, ei traderet, quod ipse facere renuens, nichil
super hoc certum, nichil nisi in dolo, respondit. Ecce et hic fides bene
100 servata! Ecce et cui fides habenda est magna!

Item fide firmavit coram sociis nostris et viris bonis, scilicet Petro de
Hungeria et magistro Thoma, quod vos contra festum Sancti Michaelis
ad nos reduceret, consilioque nostro stare faceret, aut a vobis ex toto
discederet. Affidavit etiam quod, si vos fraudulenter erga nos agere et
105 a consilio nostro exire videret et recedere, statim id nobis nunciaret, set
nichil horum fecit; quin immo vos apud Herefordiam et ⌈al⌉ibi appellare
et vos⌈met⌉ appellando diffamare, longe plus vobis in hoc nocens quam
nobis, valde fideliter instruxit.

106–7 *additio scripta in* rasura

---

101. Petro de Hungeria] A man of this name occurs also in *Rotuli Hugonis de Welles,
Episcopi Lincolniensis, 1209–1235*, ii (Canterbury and York Society, 1907), *passim*.

place before we discovered his numerous treacheries against us, and to which both our and his seals had been appended, he ought to have handed over to the keeping of the prior of Brecon; he did not give them to him, but handed them over to the sacristan of the house, as the prior later informed us, and within a fortnight, when he heard that we had found out in Lincoln about his crimes, he took them back, though by common agreement and decision between us they should have been kept in the safe-keeping of the prior. We have had a copy of them, which we kept for ourselves, sent on to you, so that you may recognize the man's character better.

Moreover, last year at Lincoln, before his deceit had been detected, when we gave him our seal to seal our letters, which were sent to different persons in different places, as though he were a dependant of our own household and our trusted friend, he persuaded us that he ought to handle most of our affairs both in England and Wales, and that he ought to go even to St. David's and Pembroke. For this reason he received expenses from us to meet you, in case, by his going there, you wished to stir up trouble, as in fact you did. However, he did not go there, but sent you, instructed, or rather subverted, by him, so that you could run riot freely and without restraint, and perpetrate the crimes you had worked out between you. He persuaded us, I repeat, to let him carry two or three empty but sealed schedules, in case he needed them. We trusted him like a liege man of ours, and one in whom we placed our trust at that time as if he had been ourselves. In fact, he put the seal on five or six empty schedules, as our servants, who were with him to seal them, later testified to us. When we afterwards discovered his knavery, we wrote to the prior of Brecon about this and that man's other acts of wickedness and perfidy towards us and told the prior to come to terms with him, and particularly that he should hand over to the prior those schedules, whether empty or completed, that bore our seal. This William refused to do, and gave no definite answer, apart from a deceitful one. How well he kept his faith in this matter! What a man to place so much trust in!

Moreover, he gave his oath in the presence of Peter of Hungary and Master Thomas, both friends of ours and upright men, that he would bring you back to us by Michaelmas, and make you abide by our counsel; otherwise he would leave you completely. He even swore that if he saw you playing the traitor to us, and withdrawing from and forswearing our counsel, he would immediately inform us; but he did none of this. This faithful steward told you to make appeals at Hereford and elsewhere, and by appealing to spread your fame; by so doing he did more harm to you than to us.

Qualis autem magistri fides, talis et discipuli, qui in manu domini
110 decani Lincolniensis coram multis et magnis personis, priusquam discederet, fidem dedit, quod ante festum Sancti Michaelis Lincolniam ad nos
rediret.

Preterea quam sepe magister discipulum, quasi ludicro, sub ioco tamen
et risu verum dicendo, nequam et versutum et de toto genere suo scele-
115 rosissimum vocitare solebat, tanquam approbans et ad hoc quodammodo provocans versipellem eius naturam et perversam recalcitrandi
voluntatem. Pullum quoque vos anatis crebro ludendo et cachi⌐n⌐nando
vocitare solebat, tanquam tamen in derisionem nostram quoniam hanc
120 vestre nature similitudinem adaptare consuevimus. Innuens etiam in
f. 64ʳᵇ hoc et memorie vestre, quam doctrine talis capacem novit | et tenacem,
forcius imprimens et infigens quod, sicut pullus adulterinus fugax est
semper et aberrans, sic et vobis, aliene nature, qua replemini, morem
gerenti, fugere quam cicius a nobis, sicut et ⌐nunc⌐ videri potest, et
aberrare, ne et exorbitare dicamus, expedire.

125 Item, cum egregius ille magister et doctor fraudium et commentor
prodicionum, consumptis frustra cautelis omnibus et ingeniis ad equos
habendum, quibus nepotem nostrum cum sarcinis suis abduceret sicut
paraverat, demum, in excogitata nequicia ne deficeret, ad miram ver-
suciam se convertit. Persuasit enim nobis, post longas meditaciones et
130 exquisitas argucias (nec mirum, cui fidem in omnibus tunc habuimus),
quatinus equos nostros ad vendendum in Walliam, ubi longe melius eos
quam in Anglia vendi posse dicebat, per ipsum, qui eos bene servari et
inpinguari et postea vendi bene procuraret, transmitteremus. Quo facto,
cum apud Brechene perventum esset, depositis sarcinis suis, statim
135 equos nostros a domo nostra, quam construximus, turpiter eiecit et
graviter exulceratos per incuriam, aut pocius industriam, ut de cetero
nobis inutiles forent, et fame affectos, sine pabulo quippe et expensis
laborem eorum bene remunerando, quod Iudei vel gentilis fieri iumen-
tis ad usum cuiuspiam fidei concessis non deberet, domino et magistro
140 nepos et magister remiserunt. Set ecce fides ab utroque bene servata et
promissio facta, sicut et alie, bene completa!

Poterant ergo, sicut et absque dubio fecerant, risus multos et cachinnos
f. 64ᵛᵃ magnos simul emittere, quod senem illum, | iam quasi delirum et fraudi-
bus undique circumventum, adeo nunc infatuarunt et, veluti prestigiis
145 utendo mirandis aut verius commoditate viri simplicis et creduli nimis

However, as far as trust was concerned, it was a case of like master, like pupil. For before he went he gave his oath in the hand of the dean of Lincoln, in the presence of many important men, that he would return to us at Lincoln before Michaelmas.

Furthermore there are the many occasions when the master jokingly— though in the guise of a laugh and a joke he was speaking the truth— used to call his pupil a crafty good-for-nothing and the worst of all his family, as if approving of and encouraging his cunning nature and his perverse proclivity for recalcitrant behaviour. Again, sniggering and joking, he frequently used to call you a duckling, as if making a joke at our expense, since we often applied this image to you. Even in this matter he was hinting at your memory which he knew to be capable of retaining such teaching, and was pressing and driving home more forcibly the point that, just as the bastard chick is always flighty and straying, since you have a totally different nature from ours, you found it convenient to escape from us as quickly as possible, as can now be seen, and to stray, not to say turn aside, from the path of virtue.

Moreover, when that outstanding master, that teacher of perfidy, that inventor of treacheries, had vainly used all his trickery and all his wit to get horses to take away our nephew with his baggage, as he had planned, finally, with deliberate perfidy, he resorted to a magnificent device, so that he should not run short. After considerable planning and subtle arguments (not surprisingly, since we trusted him) he persuaded us to send our horses to be sold in Wales, where, he argued, they could be sold for a far better price than in England, with him in charge, to keep them well groomed and fattened up and so to get a good price. When this had been done, and they had arrived at Brecon, and their baggage had been unloaded, he immediately in a disgraceful fashion turned our horses out of the stable which we had built for them. Then the nephew and his tutor sent them back to their lord and master, with shocking sores, as a result of neglect, or rather by intention, so that they would be useless to us in future, and starved, without fodder and expenses to re- quite their labour—a thing which ought not to be done to animals be- longing either to Jew or Gentile which have been entrusted to anyone's care and protection for work. How well both of them kept their trust! How well they performed this promise they had given, just like others!

They could have given vent to many a coarse laugh, as no doubt they did, that they had now made such a fool of that old man, who was already a buffoon, and surrounded by deceit on all sides, and impudently and perfidiously bewitched him using some sort of miraculous magic, though it is nearer the truth to say that they over-abused the goodwill

abutendo, non minus impudenter quam infideliter sic incantarunt (viri, inquam, qui nec alios decipere, presertim in hac etate, volebat nec ab aliis, precipue tot sibi beneficiis et tantis et tam multipliciter obligatis, se decipiendum ullatenus fore credebat), quod predo perfidus et raptor
150 inprobus predam hominis, set predonem sponte sequentem, rapinam quoque, set rapi quidem ultro volentem, et ut nichil intactum relinquatur, coram oculis eius in vehiculis ipsius et vecturis honeratis quidem, et non honoratis, furta simul et furem asportavit. Verum, si verus est vates,

155 *non habet eventus sordida preda bonos.*

Set o quam veridicum de Brechene tunc decanum Ricardum invenimus, qui de moribus et modis magistri illius, set non nisi scelerum tamen et prodicionum, nos tociens premonuit et, ut nobis caveremus ab ipso, sepius premunivit, set quod ille nobis fide bona predixit, nos, magis ex
160 invidia dictum quam veritate credentes, fidem verbis non adhibuimus, verum palponi magis quam veritatis ⌐in hoc⌐ preconi tunc aures et animum applicuimus. Habet enim, ut ait Tullius, assentacio iocunda principia, eadem vero exitus amarissimos affert.

⌐Adeo namque proditor ille se verbis ubique blandum exibuit, adeo
165 promtulum ad obsequia cuncta et officiosum, ut sibi animum nostrum sic firmius allicere posset et, opportunitatis demum occasione captata, scorpi⌐onis⌐ cauda gravius pungeret improvisum, quod, biennii spacio quo nobis adhesit, vix etiam semel ore vel opere nos offenderet aut in aliquo molestaret. Habent enim assentatores huiusmodi velut apes
170 mel in ore et aculeum in dorso. Habent, tanquam scorpiones, caput blandiens et caude puncturam venenosam. Unde Psalmista: *Molliti sunt sermones eius super oleum, et ipsi sunt iacula.* ⌐Et in Parabolis: *Simulator ore decipit amicum suum.* Item et ibidem: *Homo qui blandis sermonibus et fictis loquitur amico suo rete expandit pedibus eius.* Cui con-
175 sonat et illud Zenonis: *Malum hominem blande loquentem agnosce tuum*

152 oculis] *V* occulis, *c expuncto*   156 Ricardum *scriptum est in rasura*
159 premunivit] *V* premonuit *postea correctum*   160 verbis *scriptum est in rasura*
164–87 *haec additio* (Adeo . . . caveas) *legitur in margine inferiore f. 64ᵛ*   172 *haec additio legitur in margine f. 65ʳ.*

155. Ovid, *Amores* i, 10, 48.
162–3. Cf. Cicero, *De Amicitia* xxvi, 97; not verbatim, but in this sense.
171–2. Ps. liv, 22.   173. Prov. xi, 9.
173–4. Cf. Prov. xxix, 5; *Homo qui blandis fictisque sermonibus loquitur amico suo rete expandit gressibus eius.*
175–6. Zeno] Giraldus quotes most likely from a florilegium, possibly the one wrongly attributed to Caecilius Balbus, *De Nugis Philosophorum*, ed. E. Woelfflin (Basiliae, 1855), which will be referred to in the following notes (for the wrong attribution cf. Schanz–Hosius, *Geschichte der römischen Literatur*, Handbuch der Altertumswissenschaft, 8, 1, fourth edition (München, 1927), pp. 262–3). In this case, however,

of a simple, credulous man—and that a man who neither wished to deceive others, especially at his age, nor believed that he would ever be deceived in any way by others, especially those indebted to him by many, great, generous benefactions, for this treacherous plunderer and wicked looter carried off his prey in the form of a man, though the prey followed the plunderer of his own accord, and his loot, though the loot wanted to be taken of his own accord, and in order to leave nothing untouched, he carried off in one fell swoop both the stolen goods and the stealer before his eyes in his own carts and wagons, loaded down, but not honest. But, if the poet is correct, 'Ill gotten gain does not prosper'.

But we have discovered how truthful Richard, the dean of Brecon at that time, was: he often warned us of the morals and ways of that tutor, which were concerned with nothing but crime and treachery, and often forewarned us to take heed for ourselves where he was concerned; but we believed that what he told us in all good faith was based on jealousy rather than the truth, and did not give his words any credence, but lent our ears and our attention to the wheedler rather than the guardian of the truth in this matter. For, as Cicero says, flattery has a sweet beginning, but leads to a bitter end.

That treacherous creature was such a smooth talker, and so ready and willing to carry out his duties, that he was able to win our heart over to him in this way, and finally, taking advantage of an opportunity, he struck unexpectedly and more viciously than a scorpion's tail, since, during the two years he was close to us, he hardly offended us by word or deed, or annoyed us in any respect even once. For flatterers of this kind are like bees: they have honey on their tongues, but a sting at the rear. Like scorpions they have a beguiling head, but a venomous bite in their tail. As the Psalmist says: 'His words are smoother than oil, and the same are darts'; and in Proverbs: 'The dissembler with his mouth deceiveth his friend'; and again in the same book: 'A man that speaketh to his friend with flattery and dissembling words spreadeth a net for his feet.' The following quotation of Zeno also is in keeping with this: 'Recognize that an evil man with a smooth tongue is a snare for you.'

the quotation does not agree verbatim with the printed version which has: *Malum hominem blande loquentem innocentum laqueum esse.* The exact quotation occurs, however, in Walter Burley, *De Vita et Moribus Philosophorum,* ed. H. Knust, Bibliothek des litterarischen Vereins in Stuttgart 177 (Tübingen, 1886), p. 96, lines 13–14. Although this work was composed more than a century after the *Speculum Duorum,* it appears to derive from a manuscript transmission close to the one from which Giraldus quotes; cf. also R. B. C. Huygens, 'Zu Idung von Prüfening und seinen Schriften "Argumentum super quatuor questionibus" und "Dialogus duorum monachorum" ', *Deutsches Archiv,* 27, 1971, 544–55, at 554.

laqueum esse. Et illud Teofrasti: *Amicum blandum cave, cuius amarum est semper, quod fuerit dulce.*⊓ ⌜Item Beda: *Qui veneni poculum porrigit, labium calicis melle tangit, ut quod dulce est presenciatur, ne quod mortiferum est timeatur.* Item Anselmus: *Ille difficile vitatur, qui in labiis*
180 *bona portat et in corde mala occultat.* Item et Cato: *Parce laudato, nam, quem tu sepe probaris, una dies qualis fuerit monstr⌜a⊓bit amicus.*⊓ Et in Ecclesiastico: *Est qui nequiter se humiliat et interiora eius plena sunt dolo.* Item et Marcialis:

> *Virus adulator dulci sermone refundit,*
185 > *Irretire volens quem facit absque metu;*
> *Set, dum blanditur vox blesa et dulcia verba*
> *Supra oleum mollit, tunc tibi tu caveas!*⌝

Item in discessu a nobis hoc ultimo, cum in equis, ut diximus, et expensis nostris magister et discipulus versus Walliam properarent,
190 ut appellationem quam contra nos conflaverant ad supplantacionem
f. 64ᵛᵇ nostram valde naturalem liberius apud Herefordiam | formare valerent et firmare, duos pueros nostros, quos ad equos nostros servandum cum ipsis misimus, per aliam premittere viam, causas nectendo falsas et conflictas, ne concepte scilicet fraudis explicacioni et quasi vesice inflate
195 explosioni aliqui ex nostris interessent, modis omnibus sunt conati. Set, cum pueri nostri ab equis nostris, quorum deputati custodie fuerant, discedere nollent, magnus ille fraudium doctor et commentor ad aliam decipulam se convertit; vocans enim pueros nostros seorsum tanquam ad consilium et secretum, dixit eis quod eo die apud Herefordiam coram
200 domino Menevensi episcopo et Herefordensi capitulo discipulus suus, scilicet archidiaconus, ipsum, quia cum domino ipsorum, scilicet magistro Giraldo, fideliter stabat nec ab eius obsequiis aliquatenus averti poterat, Romam appellare volebat, quatinus scilicet sub hoc decepcionis nubilo pueri circumventi contra ipsum et non contra nos appellatum
205 esse putarent, et ita factum illud et facinus nobis nequaquam nunciarent. Set ecce fraus et fictio ⌜valde⌝ pulcra, et fides ab utroque bene servata!

Item, ut perfectius hominem noscatis, presbiter, pater Willelmi, in lecto egritudinis qua decessit, nobis revelavit quod nunquam resignaverat ecclesiam suam de Lanhamelac neque cesserat illam Willelmo,
210 sicut ipse iactabat, set tantum cedulam vacuam ab eo traditam puella

177–81 *haec additio sic legitur:* Item *post additionem praecedentem in margine f. 65ʳ; quod sequitur* (Beda: 'Qui . . . amicus') *in margine superiore f. 64ᵛ*   206 pulcra *scriptum est in rasura*

176–7. Teofrastus] This quotation occurs in the so-called Caecilius Balbus (cf. note on 175–6) xv, 12, p. 25.

And Theophrastus: 'Beware of a flattering friend: his gall is what should have been sweet.' Again we find in Bede: 'The man that offers a draught of poison touches the lip of the cup with honey in order that the sweetness may be tasted first, lest what is lethal be feared.' Again Anselm says: 'The man whom it is difficult to avoid is he that bears a fair report on his lips, but conceals the malice in his heart'; and Cato: 'Be sparing in your praise, for time will show what has been the man you often esteem.' In Ecclesiasticus we find: 'There is one who humbleth himself wickedly, and his interior is full of deceit.' Martial expresses the same thought: 'The flatterer spews out his poison with honeyed tones, since he wants to ensnare the man he has made confident; but when his lisping tongue flatters, and makes his words smoother than oil, then be on your guard!'

When they left us last time, and both master and pupil were hastening towards Wales on horseback, as we have said, and at our expense, so that they could make and strengthen the appeal they had concocted against us at Hereford, to deceive us very simply and freely, they tried all means to send our two grooms, whom we had sent with them to look after the horses, ahead along another route, by concocting false and conflicting reasons, lest any of our servants should take an interest in the unfolding of the deceit they had devised, and, as it were, the bursting of the swollen bladder. But when our grooms refused to abandon our horses, which they had been put in charge of, the great master and author of falsehoods resorted to another trick; he called our grooms to him as if to take them into his confidence, and told them that his pupil, the archdeacon, wanted to appeal to Rome against him that day at Hereford in the presence of the lord bishop of St. David's and the chapter of Hereford, since he was faithful in the service of their lord, Master Giraldus, and could not relinquish his service in any respect, with the result that our grooms were tricked by the fog of deceit into believing that the appeal was being made against him, not us, and they therefore failed to report that fact and flagrant misconduct to us. What a pretty piece of lying and deceit! How well both kept their trust!

Moreover, to give you a clearer picture of the man, William's father, the priest, told us on his sick-bed (where he died) that he had never resigned or ceded his church at Llanhamlach to William, as he claimed, but that a chambermaid, with whom William had dealings, sealed only

177–9. Not identified.   179–80. Not identified.
180–1. Cato] Disticha Catonis 4, 28, *Poetae Latini Minores*, ed. Aemilius Baehrens, Teubner (Lipsiae, 1881), vol. 3, p. 233.
182–3. Ecclus. xix, 23.
184–7. These lines do not occur in the works of Martial.

quedam de camera, cum qua rem habebat, sigillo veteris Willelmi de
f. 65ʳᵃ Oildebof signavit et hoc fuit illa quam sibi postea simul cum | ecclesia
marcis plurimis comparavit.

Item cedulam illam, vel aliam, quia forte plures per eandem tales
215 habuit, apud Lincolniam super presentatione sua ad ecclesiam illam
et institutione a clerico nostro, qui gravem penitentiam pro fraude tali
a confessore suo postea suscepit, inscribi fecit, quod et vos forsitan non
ignorastis. ⌐Quin immo ut invitus scriberet persuasistis, non principalis
quidem fraudis huius et falsitatis auctor, set consentaneus ⌐tamen⌐
220 docilisque discipulus, tam fautor in omnibus quam adiutor.⌐

Super tale itaque fundamentum fidele edificium construi posse
putatis? Proinde, cum ius in re prorsus nullum haberet, quod pro
ecclesia illa dedit et capella sequaci, a capra diminutive dicta, unde
agnomen adventicium nunc primum est, ex re sortitur, empcio fuit
225 aperta, et non redempcio. *Ex fructibus igitur* hiis et huiusmodi *cogno-*
scetis eum.

Mirum autem quod sub pondere tanto ecclesie illius sic adquisite et
iuxta capellam sive capram tam criminosam ⌐per quam et miles adulter
neci expositus et maritus zelator ⌐ac zelotipus sive zelotes nimis⌐
230 prodicioni datus⌐ securos potest carpere sompnos.

Ad hec etiam apud ecclesiam ita comparatam et capellam ⌐consecuti-
vam, principalem tamen, non accessoriam⌐, convivio vobis ab ipso
parato, Willelmus coram pueris nostris, ostentans ocreas suas, more
procaci tensas in altum cum calcaribus ⌐de⌐aura⌐t⌐is, tanquam hironice
235 et derisorie in pupplica audiencia dixit: 'Has ocreas dedit mihi magister
Giraldus, et hanc ecclesiam, ut dicit, mihi dedit.' Ad quod respondemus
quia nec a nobis nec ab alio ei data fuit ecclesia illa, quoniam non data
quidem erat, set manifeste comparata. Ad quam etiam comparacionem
magister Giraldus bene scotum suum apposuit, in quo et se quoque
240 sotum ostendit et decepcioni accommodum, qui tredecim marcas aut
quattuordecim in hoc biennio (decem enim sponte, tres autem residuas,
aut quatuor fraudulenter et furtive subtractas) adiecit, immo verius
abiecit. | Talia igitur a tali doctore discere poteritis et *a convictu* pariter
et prava doctrina *mores* formare iuxta illud: *Si videbas furem, currebas*
245 *cum eo; et cum adulteris porcionem tuam ponebas.* ⌐*Os tuum habundavit*
malicia, et lingua tua concinnabat dolos⌐.

---

234 deauratis] *V* aureis *postea transformatum in* deauratis   239 scotum] *V*
scoctum, *c expuncto.*

211–12. Willelmi de Oildebof] For this incident see *supra*, pp. xxxvi–xxxvii.
225–6. Cf. Matt. vii, 20: *Igitur ex fructibus eorum cognoscetis eos*; also Matt. vii, 16.

an empty schedule, which he had given to her, with the seal of the elder William de Oildebof, and it was this that he later acquired for himself with the church for a considerable amount of money.

Again that schedule, or another, since he happened to hold more of the same kind, he had filled in at Lincoln with his presentation to the benefice of the church and his installation by our clerk, who received a heavy penance afterwards from his confessor for this forgery. Perhaps you were not unaware of this. Indeed, you persuaded him to write it, though he did not want to; he was not the initial instigator of this deceitful forgery, but an accomplice and willing pupil; indeed he aided and abetted it. Do you think, then, that a reliable structure can be built on such foundations? Moreover, since he had absolutely no right in this affair, what he gave for the church and the accompanying chapel (derived from the Latin diminutive for a whore, from which he happens to get his extraordinary nickname), was a clear purchase, not repurchasing. Thus by his fruits, fruits of this kind, ye shall know him.

It is amazing that he can rest quiet in his bed at night with the weight of that church on his conscience, particularly as it was acquired in such a way, and a chapel like the wicked whore through whom an adulterous knight was exposed to death, and a zealous, jealous zealot of a husband was betrayed.

In addition when he was holding a banquet for you at the church he had thus acquired, and the accompanying chapel, which is, however, independent, not subordinate, in the presence of our grooms, William was showing off his thigh boots, saucily waved his gilded spurs in the air, and said in public hearing in derisive and sarcastic fashion: 'Master Giraldus gave me these boots, and, as he says, he gave me this church.' Our rejoinder to this is that that church was given to him neither by us nor anyone else, since it was not in fact given, but clearly 'acquired'. Indeed Master Giraldus added his payment to this 'acquisition'—indeed he proved half-witted and open to deception in this matter, since he added, or rather threw away, thirteen or fourteen marks during these two years (ten of his own accord, and the remaining three or four fraudulently and furtively stolen). Such, therefore, is what you could learn from such a teacher, and you could mould your character from intercourse with him, and from his depraved teaching, according to the principles of 'If thou didst see a thief thou didst run with him, and with adulterers hast thou been a partaker. Thy mouth has abounded with evil, and thy tongue framed deceits.'

243–4. Cf. *supra*, part i, 840, and *infra*, 339–40.
244–6. Ps. xlix, 18–19.

Preter has autem quatuordecim marcas, ad dictam empcionem adiectas, in quibus totum, sicut accepimus, ecclesie cum capella precium extitit ⌐adimpletum⌐, bullas domini pape semel et iterum ad hoc ei
250 perquisivimus, que quidem ad terrorem ad minus simul cum familiaritate nobiscum contracta, nequicia nempe illius nondum plene comperta, parti adverse fuerunt. Et preter hec etiam domino Menevensi episcopo litteras deprecatorias pluries pro ipso destinavimus, set testimoniales nequaquam, quas tamen ipse sepius a nobis instanter et impudenter
255 efflagitabat. De postulacione vero tociens a nobis pro ipso facta, cum fraus et falsitas tota nobis, tam ex patris confessione quam etiam cedule vacue, set signate apud Lincolniam inscripcione, indubitata veritate constaret, et litteris etiam domini pape perquisitis, cum omne quod contra conscienciam agitur edificet ad gehennam, graviter inde deliqui-
260 mus et, penitencia nobis ob hoc iniuncta, sub ieiuniis adhuc et disciplinis laboramus.

Non solum autem ei ad ecclesiam illam qualiquali mercimonio et quoquo modo sic obtentam tantum iuvamen adiecimus. Verum etiam vitam quandoque, cum iuvenes scilicet de Kenardesle ipsum coram
265 nobis gladiis extractis invaserunt, conservavimus; fauvellum quoque suum trium marcarum aut quatuor equum, cum gladio suo, quem sicut pugil egregius et gladiator eximius ⌐statim⌐ hostibus reddiderat, et capello et harnesio toto, ei tunc reddi fecimus. Quod si forte non con-
f. 65ᵛᵃ cesserit nec ob insolenciam ita fuisse professus fuerit, in similem | forte
270 casum in absencia nostra per rei ipsius experienciam adhuc incidere poterit.

Primum enim erga nepotem ipsorum, puerum tunc, personam scilicet ecclesie de Kenardesle, deceptum ab ipso fraudulenter et circumventum, scelus eius apparuit. Haut dissimiliter quoque vestram nunc
275 ⌐non puericiam quidem, set⌐ impericiam, redditus vestros vobis mutilando, sibique firmius alliciendo, qui nunquam opera vel sua vel vestra aliquos hactenus vobis adquisitis, decepcione dolosa pariter et scelerosa circumvenit. Sic etiam quicquid habet, quoniam et ecclesiam de Lanhamelac sibi per cedulas, ut dictum est, adulterinas, per testes falsissimos
280 et aperta periuria, quorum testium primus et previus falsitatis, viam aliis et iter prebens, fuit presbiter ille Fichetus, demum etiam ad turpitudinis cumulum, sciens quippe quoniam *unde habeas querit nemo, set oportet habere*, non absque scandalo gravi per simoniacam empcionem, nec tamen occultam, set manifestam, adquisivit.

270 absencia] *V* abscencia   275 non] *legitur tantum* i *in extrema margine, sed debemus legere* n *mutilatum caesura, quia aliter non comprehenditur* set

282–3. Juvenal xiv, 207; quoted also *infra*, 1186, with further cross-references.

However, in addition to the fourteen marks given for the aforementioned purchase, which, as we have heard, was the total purchase price for the church and the chapel, we acquired bulls from the Lord Pope for him for this purpose on one and more occasions; these, indeed, were less frightening to the opposing party in view of his familiarity with us, since his wickedness had not yet fully come to light. In addition to this we frequently sent intercessory letters on his behalf to the lord bishop of St. David's, though no letters of attestation, which he continually and impudently demanded from us. As far as the demand we frequently made on his behalf is concerned, when it was clear to us, both from his father's confession and the entry in the empty schedule that had been sealed at Lincoln, that the fraud and forgery had a basis in indisputable truth, and even from the letters of the Lord Pope we acquired, since everything that is done against the dictates of conscience leads to hell, we have sinned greatly in this, and up to this day, since a penance has been put upon us for this offence, we are labouring under fasting and discipline.

However, we did not only give him considerable aid for that church, whatever the terms and means of its acquisition. We also saved his life when those youths from Kinnersley drew their swords and attacked him in our presence. We also had his horse worth three or four marks, as well as his sword, which this great fighter, this extraordinary swordsman, had immediately handed over to his enemies, and his cap and equipment returned to him intact. If he perhaps will not admit, or will not confess, that it occurred thus on account of his insolence, with his experience of this affair he will still perhaps be able to meet with similar danger in our absence.

His criminality first came to light in the case of their nephew, then a youth, the parson of the church of Kinnersley whom he dishonestly deceived and cozened, and in the same way he took advantage of your inexperience, although you are no child any longer, with his treacherous and criminal deceit, by clipping your revenues, and insinuating himself more firmly into your confidence, though you have never acquired any revenues for yourself either by his or your own efforts. This is the way he acquired everything he has, since he acquired the church at Llanhamlach, as has been said, by bastardized schedules, by false witnesses, and clear perjury; the first of these witnesses, the forerunner of the deceit, who showed the way for the others, was that priest Fichet. Finally, as the consummation of his wickedness, in the knowledge that 'nobody will ask where you got it from, but you ought to have it', with considerable scandal he acquired it by simony—not underhand, but blatantly.

285 Item apud Lincolniam nobiscum tanquam mus in pera vel serpens
in sinu constitutus, ubi concamerarii fuistis et concubicularii, dicere
plerumque palam et publice consuevit, set tamen in absencia nostra,
quia non opporteret vos nisi ungere tantum ocreas vestras et possetis
a patruo vestro quicquid velletis optinere. Sciebat enim quod inepciis
290 vestris et maliciis, per prudenciam atque modestiam scandalum, si fieri
posset, extinguendo, totis vellet nisibus obviare; verum quam pronus
et patiens extitit ac pacificus (quia *beati pacifici*!) ad scandalum, priusquam exortum fuerat, evacuandum et supprimendum, quamquam, ut
prodiret in brevi, iam conceptum! ⌐Propter quod, indiciis variis hoc com-
295 perto, quod Iude proditori dictum est a Domino, vobis aliquociens dicere
consuevimus: *Quod facis, fac cicius!*⌐ Tam pertinax forsan animique tam
f. 65ᵛᵇ |vindicis ad ulciscendum cum scandalo tanto scelus emersum ceterosque
ab exempli pernicie tam pravi deterrendum poterit quandoque videri!

Set ecce qualiter verbis hiis et similibus ad recalcitrandum, ut officia-
300 lis vester et plus-quam-magister fieret, modis omnibus vos instigare
parabat, quatinus etiam in aqua turbida melius piscari posset, qui, etiam
in aqua clara et limpida, nimis bonam hactenus, per fraudes tamen et
falsitates multas et crebras, apud nos invenit piscacionem. Verum de
duabus ripis amodo circa nos sicut consuevit non piscabitur. Apud vos
305 autem et de ripa vestra quam melius poterit de cetero piscetur et venetur!
Primo namque decipi, ut ait Seneca, *incommodum est, secundo stultum, tercio*
turpe. Semel enim exustus, nedum sepius, ignem veretur. Unde poeta:

> *Qui semel est captus fallaci piscis ab hamo,*
> *Omnibus unca cibis era subesse timet.*

310 Sacius est itaque sero quam nunquam penitere et ˈproverbialiter dici
solet quod empta per iacturam sapiencia vix ab animo elabi, set tanquam
in habitum verti et perpetue memorie infigi solet.

Item proditor hic noster et seductor vester, sciens quia qui minima
contempnit paulatim deficit, sciens etiam quoniam ex multis modicis
315 magnus acervus erit, sciens quod exigua lucra, dum tamen plurima, si
non perficiunt, prosunt tamen et proficiunt, iuxta illud:

> *Et que non prosunt singula, multa iuvant,*

sciens et illud: *Et si non recte possis, quocumque modo rem,* apud

---

285 *post* Item *deletum est* cum   296 forsan] *V* sorsan

292. Matt. v, 9.   296. John xiii, 27.
301. Cf. Walter Map, *De Nugis Curialium*, ed. T. Wright (London, 1850), p. 242:
in aqua turbida piscantur uberius.
306–7. Not identified; but quoted also (*orator*) by John of Salisbury, *Epp.* 177,
254 (Migne, *P.L.* 199, cols. 172, 297).   308–9. Ovid, *Pont.* 2, 7, 9–10.
314–15. Cf. Ovid, *Rem.* 424: *de multis grandis acervus erit.*   317. Ovid, *Rem.* 420.

Again, when he was at Lincoln with us like a mouse in a sack, or a serpent in the bosom, when you were sharing rooms and chambers together, he used to say openly and publicly with many witnesses, though never in our presence, that you only had to polish your boots, and you could get whatever you wanted from your uncle. For, indeed, he knew that he wished with all his heart to rid you of your stupidity and wickedness, by crushing, if possible, the scandal with wisdom and moderation; but how ready, how patient, what a peacemaker ('Blessed are the peacemakers') he was to get rid of and crush scandal before it sprang up, though it had already been conceived and was soon to break out! For this reason, when this had come to light by a variety of means we occasionally used to tell you what our Lord told Judas his betrayer: 'That which thou dost, do quickly.' It will be seen how single-minded and how quick was his intention to avenge a crime that oozed scandal, and deter the rest from this depraved and pernicious example.

But see how, with these and similar words he set about inciting you by all means to kick over the traces, so that he might become your official, and more than your tutor, so that he could get even better fishing in troubled waters, when he found, even in the clear, untroubled waters of your household, the fishing to be very good, with many frequent frauds and forgeries. But he will not fish from the two banks on either side of us as he used to do. But in future let him fish and hunt from your bank, which he can do much better! As Seneca says: 'To be deceived once is inconvenient, to be deceived a second time is stupid; a third time it is downright criminal.' Once burnt (to say nothing of more than once) twice shy. As the poet says: 'The fish that has once been caught by a hidden hook fears a bronze hook in all food.' It is better then to repent late than never, and there is a proverbial saying that the mind rarely forgets wisdom dearly bought: it becomes part of one's habit; it is buried deep in one's memory for ever.

Again this man, who betrayed us and suborned you, knowing that the man who takes no heed of trifles gradually goes short, knowing that a huge heap will result from the accumulation of many little things, knowing that low interest rates, as long as they are numerous and if they are not paid off, make a considerable profit (as the poet says, 'Things that in isolation do not help much, taken together can be profitable') and knowing that 'you should carry on however you can, even if you cannot do it legally', when he was dressed for travelling at our hospice

318. Cf. Horace, *Epist.* i, 1, 66: *Si possis, recte, si non, quocumque modo rem.* Also quoted by Giraldus in *De Iure et Statu Menevensis Ecclesie* (*Op.* iii, 131), *Itinerarium Kambriae* (*Op.* vi, 81), and *Speculum Ecclesie* (*Op.* iv, 156 and 227).

f. 66ra Lincolniam in hospicio nostro, ubi se cotidie pane | nostro reficiebat,
320 iam ad iter accinctus, ut gladio bono predam suam, si opus in via foret,
defendere posset, qui male tamen capud proprium, quandoque urgente
necessitate, defendit, ubi etiam nec gladium suum, quoniam hostibus
reddidit, ausus unquam extraere fuit, gladium nostrum lumbardicum,
quoniam exploraverat bonum et bene calibatum, plicabilem quoque et
325 convertibilem pro suo, vili ac pessimo et rubigine consumpto, per se
mutare presumpsit nostrumque gladium talem in sua vagina suumque
talem in nostra clam et occulte, quin immo furtive ⌜quidem et scelerose⌝
transposuit. Hoc autem per pueros nostros ad partes illas transmissos,
qui gladium nostrum apud Brechene cum ipso postea viderunt et etiam
330 in domo nostra apud Landu recognoverunt, suumque rubiginosum apud
nos postmodum in non suo loco repertum, nobis indubitanter innotuit.

Absit autem quod nepos noster furti talis crimine turpi contaminetur;
scimus tamen quod tam furti illius, quoniam in camera sua et ipso
vidente perpetrati, quam ceterorum, sicut de cartis nostris, litteris et
335 bullis nobis ibidem furtiva scelerositate subtractis, principalis auctor,
machinator et protractor, excogitator et doctor ille magister erat;
discipulus autem, ad has disciplinas et similes ingeniosus et docilis
valde, conscius ⌜quidem⌝ omnium et fautor ac particeps fuit; nec
mirum, ⌜quoniam⌝ *a convictu* pariter et doctrina, nec repugnante natura,
340 *mores* trahens. Unde illud in psalmo: *Si videbas furem, currebas cum
illo*, etc. ⌜Et super illud Ieremie: *Nolite tacere super iniquitatem eius*,
etc., dicit Expositor: *Qui enim tacendo consentit, particeps est culpe*
f. 66rb *simul et pene.*⌝ Set ecce ⌜quemadmodum⌝, qui in mino|ribus talis
extitit, qualis in maioribus sit habendus, fidem dedit et, qui super
345 pauca se tam fidelem exibuit, qualiter super multa sit constituendus
evidenter ostendit.

Item, quoniam originalis ei natura donat et dictat ut lingue plurimum
habeat et fidei parum, nuper in partibus illis et in domo nostra et in
presencia vestra et iuxta vos sedens, cui dicta ipsius omnia et facta,
350 etiam in contumeliam nostram emissa, displicere non poterant, pueris
nostris illuc transmissis loquens minaciter, et cum fastu grandi capud
et collum torquens atque retorquens, in huiuscemodi verba prorupit:
'Quid putat magister Giraldus reditus nostros nobis auferre et nos ita
suppeditare? Longe secus erit. Faciemus enim et ⌜(pupplice potest)⌝

339–40. a convictu ... mores trahens] Cf. *supra*, part i, 840.
340–1. Ps. xlix, 18.   341–2. Jer. li, 6.

in Lincoln, where he was daily filling his belly with our food, in order to provide himself with a sword with which he could defend his booty, if need be on his travels, though, when the necessity arose, he defended himself like a coward, and never even dared draw his own sword (he gave it to the enemy), had the audacity to expropriate our Lombard sword, since he had found it to be a good, well-tempered sword and a very suitable substitute for his own, which was cheap, worthless, and completely rusty. This sword of ours he transferred to his sheath, and his own to ours, in a sneaking, underhand, not to say thievish and rap-scallion, fashion. We had positive proof of this from our grooms who had been sent to that region and saw him wearing our sword at Brecon, and even recognized it at our home at Llanddew, and when his rusty sword was later found at Lincoln, not in its right place.

Now, we hope that there is no implication that our nephew is sullied with the foul crime of this theft. We do know, however, that that tutor of his was the principal instigator, architect, and planner, contriver and instructor of that theft, since it was planned in his room and in his presence, just as he was of the others, like the criminal theft of our charters, letters, and bulls; however, his pupil, who is talented and teachable where teaching like this is concerned, aided, abetted, and encouraged everything; this is not surprising since his character was formed from association with him and his teaching and without any resistance from his nature. As the Psalmist says, 'if thou didst see a thief thou didst run with him', etc.; and in Jeremiah, 'be not silent upon her iniquity', etc., over which the commentator says: 'He that gives his tacit consent, shares the guilt and the punishment.' But consider how it has shown truly that a man who has such qualities in minor matters is to be regarded in major matters, and clearly shows how a man who has been trustworthy in a few matters is to be put in charge of many.

Moreover, since his basic nature endows him with and forces him to have too much garrulity and too little trustworthiness, while he was recently in that area sitting by you in our house and in your presence, since neither his words nor his deeds, even though they slighted us, could upset you, he spoke menacingly to our servants who had been sent there and turning his head and neck this way and that with great presumption he burst out: 'Why does Master Giraldus think of robbing us of our revenues and preventing us from having them? It will go very ill for him. We will bring it about, and perhaps publicly urge that

341–3. Cf. *infra,* Ep. 8, p. 278, 272–4.
342–3. Expositor] Rabanus Maurus, *Expositio super Ieremiam,* lib. xvii (Migne, *P.L.* iii, col. 160B): '*Qui enim tacendo consentit* perversa voluntate . . . *particeps est* delicti eius et consors vindictae.' 344–5. Cf. Matt. xxv, 21.

355 suggeremus, quod domino regi quingentas marcas absque mora pacabit
et sic aliquandiu forsan ab ipso pacem habere poterimus. Nunquid enim
adeo bene ad⌐eoque⌐ fortiter ab ipso ut Willelmus Fichet aut Thomas
de Haia nos defendere non poterimus?' In quo dicto nobis occurrunt
notabilia duo: et quod per propriam minime, set per regiam solum se
360 nobis obsistere posse reputat virtutem, et quod duobus clericis illis,
quibus benefeceramus, ut patria novit, ingratis tamen et infidelibus se
tercium ipsis in hoc ⌐con⌐similem, quoniam ingratum pariter et infidelem, connumerare non erubuit. Videat autem ille, si sapiat, quem
finem illi duo de scelere suo sint in posterum assecuturi; et tunc vel
365 imitabiles in hoc reputet ipsos vel aspernabiles. Multa namque danda
sunt tempori, nedum etiam tempestati. Non enim quod differtur ideo
semper et aufertur. Dum etenim luget, ⌐ut⌐ nunc, et laborat ⌐anglicana⌐
ecclesia, matri nostre condolentes, tanquam inscii in multis esse debemus
f. 66va et ignari, et omnes fere | iniurias dissimulare, donec rex ille regum, in
370 cuius manu corda sunt regum, dies indulserit sereniores. De Willelmo
vero Ficheto, iniurioso nobis olim et infideli, et hoc tanquam impune,
quem ⌐in exemplum⌐ ceteri sumunt et secuntur, quia semper imitabilis error, preter iam dicta et alia quoque, racio pactum reformat. Ina-
nis enim est actio quam inopia debitoris excludit. Multi namque sunt
375 in Wallia tales et illi Ficheto non dissimiles, qui magnis et probis viris
et dictis contumeliosis iniurias graves et factis ⌐fatuis ac⌐ facinorosis
iacturas grandes faciunt pluries et facere possunt, condigne vero vel
de conviciis satisfacere vel etiam dampna illata resarcire nullatenus
possunt. Verumtamen, quoniam interdum respondendum est stultis et
380 castigandi sunt fatui, ne sibi sapientes esse videantur, forte Fichetus,
aliquo adhuc tempore, fatuitatem suam, ulcione secuta etsi non condigna, recognoscet.

Porro periculosum est quantolibet iure (et quam manifesto!) ⌐contra⌐
tales, et vel in Wallia natos, vel diucius conversatos, causam habere, non
385 propter hec solum, set ob hoc etiam quia non ea que causa desiderat
tantum, set magis quod opinionem ledat, conviciis coram iudicibus
scaturientes, tanquam histriones impudici et impudentes, proponere
curant. ⌐Quibus tamen iuxta inpericiam suam et inprudenciam respondere viros industrios non decet. Unde Ieronimus in libro episto-
390 lari: *Non prodest cause, set nec honestati competens est neque modestie,*

390-1. Not identified.

he will immediately placate his majesty the king with 500 marks, and then perhaps we will be able to get some peace from him. For cannot we defend ourselves against him as well and as boldly as William Fichet or Thomas of Hay?' Two important points spring to our mind in this statement: that he thinks that he will be able to resist us not with his own, but with the king's strength, and that he does not hesitate to number himself as a third counterpart in this matter to those two ungrateful and unfaithful clerks, whom, as everybody knows, we benefited, since he is equally ungrateful and unfaithful. Had he any sense he could see the outcome of their criminal activities: then he would make up his mind whether these two are to be imitated or despised. One should leave a great many things to the test of time, to say nothing of the proper season. What is put off is not always lost. While the Church in England grieves, as now, and is in turmoil, we grieve with our mother, and we must be, as it were, ignorant and unaware of many things, and hide almost all our injuries until that King of Kings, in whose hand are the hearts of all kings, grant happier times. Reasoning reforms the opinion of William Fichet, who was at one time slanderous and unfaithful to us, and that without being punished, and whom the others take as an example and imitate, since sin is always imitated, apart from the other reasons given. The deal which the poverty of the man who owes the money precludes is invalid. There are a great many in Wales like that Fichet who are frequently making and are able to make grave assaults on honest and upright men with their slanderous statements and causing great loss by their foolhardy and criminal deeds, but can in no way gain suitable pleasure from their slanders, or redress the damages inflicted. However, since from time to time some rejoinder has to be made to fools, and the foolhardy have to be put in their place, in case they think themselves wise, perhaps at some future date Fichet will recognize his folly, when justice, though not the justice he deserves, catches up with him.

Moreover, it is dangerous to bring a case against such people, whether born in Wales, or having come to Wales, whatever the justice (and how manifest it is!), not only for these reasons, but also because like shameless and impudent actors they take pains to put to the court not that which is strictly relevant to the case, but rather that which is biased opinion, pouring forth slanders before the judges. Careful men ought not to reply to them in the light of their inexperience and lack of wisdom. As Jerome says in the Book of Letters: 'It does not help the case, nor is it in keeping with honour and moderation, to slander slanderers,

maledicentibus maledicere et adversarium talione mordere.⌐ Cum autem
demum ad contestandum processum fuerit et perventum, quicquid
expedire cause crediderint, promte probare vel agendo vel excipiendo vel
etiam replicando sunt parati, non maiorem quippe in sacramento cor-
395 poraliter prestito quam in verbo simpliciter emisso vim ponentes.
Unde et in foro pupplico contradictoria duo, dum tamen utcumque
proficere posse putaverint, proponere simul et semel atque probare nec
f. 66ᵛᵇ verecundantur nec verentur. Sicut et iste Capre Willelmus, sive | Capelle,
institutionem suam in ecclesia de Lanhamelac factam, per testes falsis-
400 simos ac periuros, et tamen presbiteros, quia qualis ibi populus, talis et
sacerdos, falso probare non formidavit.

⌐Unde cum nos presbiteros ⌐duos⌐ de partibus illis, quos nominare
non curavimus, super debitis quibusdam et rebus nostris alienatis
rescripto domini pape per iudices in Anglia quandoque conveniremus,
405 accepto per aliquem, quem bene novimus et qui magis tamen ex officio
lites et discordias sopire deberet quam fovere, quod nos per idem rescriptum non minus efficaciter reconvenire possent, statim inito consilio
animoque resumpto, scientes quippe se ad quidlibet probandum testibus
habundare posse, parati fuerant incontinenti coram iudicibus eisdem
410 super decem marcarum redditu quondam uni ipsorum debito et alteri
centum solidorum, fide mediante, promisso nos, si lis procederet,
reconvenire. Cum tamen, Deo teste, qui omnia novit, super hoc vel
illo, non solum mencio nunquam, set nec etiam cogitacio facta fuisset,
sic itaque iuris remedium, ubi nequicie virus habundat, ad iniquum
415 trahi compendium, vel magis dispendium potest. Et tam ex fidei defectu
quo nil turpe, dum tamen utile, reputatur, quam prava plerumque
⌐terre ipsius⌐ consuetudine fieri solet.

Utinam autem, ut comoda parumper disgressio fiat, viri in clero
constituti, et maxime ⌐parcium illarum⌐ presbiteri, qui vite viam
420 ceteris et iter exempli prebere tenentur, decretum illud Euticiani pape
cum effectu advertere velint! *Audivimus quosdam periurii scelus parvi-
pendere et levem periuris penitencie modum imponere.* Qui pocius nosse
deberent talem de periurio penitenciam imponendam, et non minorem,
qualem et quantam, de adulterio vel homicidio sponte commisso aut

391 Cum autem *scriptum est in rasura*   402–61 *haec additio legitur in schedula qua*
factum est folium 67ʳ   419 *propter caesuram paginis legitur* parcium ill *quod sequitur*
prima pars litterae a

400–1. qualis ibi populus, talis et sacerdos] Cf. Hos. iv, 9; 'Et erit sicut populus, sic
sacerdos.' This is a saying popular among Christian authors, and it would be rash to
point to any single one as inspiring Giraldus; it occurs, however, also in John of
Salisbury, *Policraticus*, bk. v, ch. xvi (ed. C. C. I. Webb, 2 vols. (Oxford, 1909), vol. i,
p. 579, l. 23): 'sicut populus, sic et sacerdos.' For John's influence on Giraldus more

and retaliate by using your opponent's tactics.' When it finally comes to the point at issue they are ready to prove whatever they believe helpful to their case, either by acting upon it, by objecting, or even by replying to it, giving no more importance to the oath they have given corporally than to a word just spoken. Thus in a public court they do not hesitate or fear to put forward and prove two contradictory views at one and the same time, as long as they think they are able to gain from them in some way or other. Thus William de Capella, that whoreson, had no hesitation in falsely proving the fact of his institution in the church of Llanhamlach by false and perjured witnesses, though they were priests —for in Wales, it is true to say, the priests are as bad as the people.

So, when on one occasion we summoned by judges in England two priests from that area, whom we do not care to name, with a rescript from the Lord Pope over the matter of certain debts and the sale of our possessions, we learnt from somebody, whom we know well, and who ought by virtue of his office to suppress litigation and discord rather than foster them, that they could no less effectively resummon us using the same rescript. This plan was immediately entered upon and taken up with a will, and knowing that they could get plenty of witnesses to prove absolutely anything, they were prepared to resummon us immediately before the same judges, if the case proceeded, in the matter of a revenue of ten marks which was once owed to one of them, and a hundred shillings promised on oath to the other. Though, as God is our witness—and he knows everything—there could not only never have been made any mention but not even any thought of one or the other. Thus the remedy of the court, when the poison of wickedness abounds, can be made a short-cut—or rather a roundabout way—to injustice. And thus as much from the lack of faith as the wicked habits of most men on earth it usually comes about that nothing is considered wicked as long as it is profitable.

However, to make our digression useful, we pray that men in the tonsure, especially priests of that area, who are bound to show the way of life and provide a leading example to the rest, would be willing to pay effective attention to that decree of Pope Eutychianus: 'We have heard that certain people pay scant heed to the crime of perjury, and impose a light form of penance on perjurors.' Who ought to know better than they, that they ought to impose the same penance for perjury as for adultery, or intentional homicide or other criminal offences, and not a smaller

generally see Wilhelm Berges, *Die Fürstenspiegel des hohen und späten Mittelalters* (Schriften der MGH 2, Stuttgart, 1938, reprinted 1952), pp. 143–50, 294, and *passim*.
   421–2. Gratian, C. XXII, q. 1, c. 17.

425 ceteris viciis criminalibus? Item et illud Fabiani pape: *Quicumque se
periuraverit vel alios sciens in periurium duxerit, quadraginta dies in pane
et aqua et septem sequentes annos peniteat, et nunquam sit sine penitencia et
nunquam in testimonium recipiatur.* Non solum hec autem, set et alia
capitula multa, causa xxi et xxii, contra periuros invenies horribilia.
430 Quis enim magis videtur Deum contempnere quam qui, in ipso peccato
quod contra Deum pe⌐r⌐petrat, in animam suam Deum ultorem et
iudicem invocat, dicens: 'Sic me Deus adiuvet, et hec sancta'?

Porro, qui ad sacramentorum omnium maximum et dignissimum
conficiendum et sumendum a lecto meretricio dampnabilique cubiculo
435 et tam plectibili contubernio mane cotidie su⌐r⌐gere ⌐sacerdos⌐ non
abhorret et tantum facinus tam indigne perpetrare, quomodo vel periurium vel aliud quodcumque dampnabile crimen abhorrebit? Verum,
cum peccatum quodlibet, grave presertim et diutinum, pondere suo
ad aliud trahat et plus quam idre capita pariat, quid miseri expectant?
440 Quid vindice ⌐districti⌐ iudicis *iram in diem ire sibi thesaurizant*? Cur
non magis, capud criminum in ipsis omnium, fomitem et fomentum
ac fundamentum, libidinem non extingunt? Nunquid enim, sicut *rusticus expectat dum defluat ampnis,* ⌐*at ille labitur et labetur in omne
volubilis evum*⌐, sic presbiter ⌐,*vel reprobus*⌐, expectat dum defluat
445 humor, at ille labitur et solito cursu labetur in evum? Qui ergo cursum
hunc tam consuetum et fluxum tam diutinum ac luxum tam noxium
reprimere voluerit ac cohibere, ⌐testante Augustino, qui ait: *Ex quo
semel aperti sunt rivuli seminis, intolerabilis est molestia carnis.*⌐ Iuxta
doctrinam sapientis: *Minus comedat, minus bibat; plus oret, plus*
450 *laboret.* ⌐Et iuxta sentenciam versuum horum:

Funde preces, plora, legito, meditare, labora.
Quod prosit fac tu pede vel sermone vel actu.

Item:

Plango quod amisi, quod commisi, quod omisi,
455   *Quod reus incurri, quodve malum merui.*

Vitam emendare et vas mundare laboret.⌐ Et sic passibus hiis incedens,

---

428–61 lia *et quod sequitur* (. . . reddat) *legimus in f. 67ᵛ*   444 presbiter *scriptum
est in rasura*

425–8. Gratian, C. XXII, q. 5, c. 4, attributed to Gelasius and others.
433–61. This passage is found almost verbatim in the *Gemma Ecclesiastica* (*Op.* ii,
pp. 190–1). In the present text, the passage occurs in an addition and has been heavily
corrected and expanded. This poses a serious chronological problem because it has
always been assumed that the *Gemma* had been completed by Giraldus before 1198.
It would be difficult to explain why the scribe of the *Speculum Duorum* did not copy

one? Again there are the words of Pope Fabian: 'Whoever perjures himself, or knowingly incites others to perjury, should spend the next seven years and forty days on bread and water, and he should never be without a penance, and never be taken on oath.' You could find many other terrifying paragraphs (*Causae*, xxi and xxii) against perjurors as well as these. For who seems to despise God more than the man who calls God into his soul as an avenger and judge of that very sin which he has committed against God, with the words: 'Thus may God aid me and these sacred words'?

Furthermore, how will any priest who every morning does not hesitate to rise from the bed of a whore, a punishable association in a damnable bedroom, to take and make the greatest and most noble of all sacraments and does not hesitate to commit such a disgraceful crime draw back from perjury or any other damnable crime? But, when any sin, especially a serious long-lasting crime, gravitates towards another one under its own weight, and sprouts more heads than the Hydra, what can the wretched people do? Why do they 'store up for themselves for the day of wrath' the punishing wrath of the absolute judge? Why do they not rather wipe out in themselves lust, the chief, the kindling, the tinder, the basis of all crimes? Why does the priest or reprobate wait for the *humour* to stop following while it sweeps on and will sweep on in its usual bed for all time, just as the peasant waits for the river to stop flowing, while it rolls on and will roll on its swirling way for all eternity? So, he ought to be willing to suppress and check a course so habitual, a flood so constant, a debauchery so harmful; as Augustine testifies, 'Once the courses of seed are opened, the discontent of carnal lust is intolerable'; similarly the philosopher teaches: 'Let him eat less, let him drink less; let him pray more, let him toil more.' Similarly there is the thought of these verses: 'Pour forth prayers, weep, read, meditate, toil. Do what is profitable when you walk, speak, or work'. Again: 'I lament what I have missed, committed, and omitted, what I am guilty of, or what evil I have deserved.' Let him strive to change his life and scour the pot.

---

the text straight from the *Gemma* if it existed there already in its final form at the time when he was writing. Could it be the case that a final version of the *Gemma* was made late in Giraldus' life and that the passage under discussion passed, not from the *Gemma* into the *Speculum*, but from the *Speculum* into the *Gemma*?

440. Rom. ii, 5, and cf. Ps. cix, 5; also Wisd. i, 15: *Dies irae, dies illa*.

442–4. Horace, *Epist.* 1, 2, 42–3.

447–8. Not identified.

449. The *sapiens* is presumably again Giraldus, cf. *supra*, note on part i, 670–1.

451–2. Noted by H. Walther, *Lateinische Sprichwörter*, no. 10077a, quoted also in the *Gemma Ecclesiastica* (*Op.* ii, p. 191, 24–5.)

454–5. Quoted by H. Walther, *Lateinische Sprichwörter*, no. 21550a, quoted also in the *Gemma Ecclesiastica* (*Op.* ii, p. 191, 27–8).

calore spiritus, non ariditate corporis vel defectu etatis, desicet in se
fontes libidinis, ut denique virum, viam felicitatis aggressum, virtus
insignem et excelsum Deoque carum et acceptum, non voluptas vilem
460 et humilem et abiectum perpetuaque pena dignum et dampnabilem,
reddat.⌐

Proinde, ⌐ut ad rem revertamur,⌐ plerique viri, prudentes et discreti,
non vinci a malo volentes, set pocius in bono malum vincere preeligentes,
vilium hominum excessus et minutorum huiusmodi, ⌐sepius⌐ etiam in
465 se factos tanquam culicum morsus, qui pungere quidem possunt, emendare vero non possunt, contempnere magis et tanquam oculis clausis
talia preterire quam aut iniuriosos tales in ius vocare aut vindictam
accelerare dignum duxere, iuxta illud poete:

Dignum te Cesaris ira nullus honor faciet,
470 et illud:

Quo stetit equatur campo collataque nescit
Maiestatem acies; minuit presencia famam.

Item, cum Henricus clericus, cognatus eius, ⌐de quo nobis est sermo⌐,
et a cognacione non degenerans, in hospicio nostro Lincolniensi in
475 furto deprehensus fuisset manifesto, illi per quem id compertum et
detectum putabat mortem ob hoc ⌐Capre Willelmus⌐ multociens est
comminatus. Set ecce qualiter ei furti turpitudo displicuit! Et ecce
qualiter qui panem nostrum cotidie comedebat de dampno nostro et
rei familiaris detrimento valde dolebat! Et ecce fides in omnibus hiis
480 bene servata et per 'salvis salvandis' bene salvata! Quin immo, quoniam
ipse dampna nobis facere, quamquam inmeritis, modis omnibus paratus
fuerat, similia nobis ab aliis fieri, et ab hiis precipue quorum forsan
consors et particeps erat, non abhorrebat, illud nempe poete non
484 ignorans:

f. 68ra *Exilis domus est, si non | et multa supersunt.*
Et fallunt dominum et prosunt furibus.

Novimus autem cur tantis nisibus lucrum suum cum dampno nostro
facere sic modis omnibus, quia, et si non recte, quocumque modo moliri
quidem et machinari non cessabat. Noverat enim se, post empcionem
490 capre sue sive capelle, societatem nostram seu familiaritatem, cum ad
nos id pervenisset, sicut consueverat, non habiturum. Ideoque, quoniam
parcere non norunt fugitivi, presertim fide carentes et scelerosi, quicquid rapere potuit, vel manifeste vel occulte, rapuit et asportavit. Et ob
hoc quoque cum ceteris furtis et fraudibus predo in hoc manifestus et

463. Cf. Rom. xii, 21: *Noli vinci a malo, sed vince in bono malum.*
469. Lucan, *Phars.* iii, 136-7.   471-2. Not identified.   480. Cf. *supra*, 63.

If he enters on this path, he will dry up the springs of lust by the warmth of his spirit, not by the drying up of his body or the decrepitude of old age, with the result that, if he starts on the way of happiness, virtue will make him an outstanding and exalted man, beloved and accepted by God, while lust would make him worthless, low, and abject, damned and deserving everlasting punishment.

Accordingly, to return to the subject, a great many wise and prudent men, who have no desire to be overcome by evil, but rather choose to overcome evil by good, consider it best to ignore the excesses of worthless men, and insects of this kind, which they frequently inflict upon them, like gnat bites, which can annoy, but not change, and pass them by with eyes closed rather than either bring such mischievous characters to justice or hasten their punishment. As the poet says: 'No honour will make you worthy of Caesar's wrath'; again: 'The drawn-up battle-line is levelled to the plain it stood on, and knows no greatness; presence reduces glory.'

Again when Henry, the clerk, a relative of the one we are talking about, who has in no way lost those family traits, was caught red-handed while stealing in our hospice at Lincoln, William, the whoreson, frequently threatened with death the man through whom he thought it had been discovered and detected. How the disgrace of theft displeased him! How badly this man, who used to eat our bread daily, used to deplore our loss and the impairment of our household! How well he kept his trust and how well he preserved it, on the principle that what is safe is to be saved! Nay rather, since he himself was prepared to cause damage to us, though we did not deserve it, by every means, he did not have any qualms about similar damages' being caused to us by others, especially those he was possibly hand in glove with. Indeed, he cannot be unaware of what the poet says: 'A house is poor, if there is not a great superfluity which deceives its lord and profits thieves.'

However, we know why he exerted all his efforts to fill his own pockets at our expense, since he did not cease his efforts and machinations on the grounds of if you cannot do it properly, do it by whatever means you can. For he knew that, after the purchase of that his chapel, he would not enjoy our society or company, as he had been used to, when this reached our ears. Thus, since runaways, especially criminals and those lacking faith, do not know how to be merciful, he stole and carried off whatever he could steal either openly or secretly. For this reason, too, as well as the rest of his thefts and deceits, this red-handed plunderer and

---

485–6. Horace, *Epist.* i, 6, 45–6. The second line is quoted in a corrupt way. In Horace it runs: *Et dominum fallunt et prosunt furibus. Ergo . . .*

495 fur improbus nepotem nostrum abduxit, quatinus de cetero ei adherere
cum nobis non posset, et ⌜quasi⌝ cum catulo ad libitum ludere et,
plus-quam-magister et officialis, suis in clero et capitulo lucris intendere
et bursam implere et preterea, quod non pro modico reputavit, a mercimonio suo non longe distare valeret, set, adepto in hunc modum quasi
500 commodo multiplici et emol⌜u⌝mento non simplici, ventrem suum
honerare de die cum archidiacono posset, et eundem exhonerare de
nocte cum cadavere suo ei delectabile foret. Unde videns clericus
quidam Walensis ipsum circa nepotem nostrum sic plus-quam-magi-
strum in omnibus ⌜existere⌝ et lucris capitulorum ad opus suum in-
505 sacianter inhiare, coram pluribus dixit: 'Magister Giraldus de Barri
non nepoti suo, sicut speravit, set magis magistro Willelmo de Capella
archidiaconatum de Brechene dedit.'

Item, facto quoque mercimonio sic duplici, tam ecclesie scilicet quam
f. 68ʳᵇ capelle, statim ad nos decipiendum, quin immo multiplici arte | usus
510 est ⌜et⌝ cautela; cum summa namque festinacione, ne rumor ad nos
per alium ante veniret, Lincolniam protinus accelleravit. Et de capella,
unde agnomen iam ex re sortitur, mercimonium subticendo penitus,
contractum super ecclesia factum, palliato vocabulo tamen pacis et
quietis redempcionem vocans, quamquam cum gravamine magno, ad
515 quod amicorum ⌜suorum⌝ et dominorum auxilio opus ei fore propone-
bat, supplicans humiliter et largicionis nostre, de qua precipue confide-
bat, devote graciam efflagitans, ⌜quoniam effrons est egestas, et quem
nichil pudet dum modo iuvet⌝, nobis revelare non erubuit. Qui, suscepto
statim a nobis auxilio, largo quidem et amplo ac minus discrete collato,
520 fideli tamen nostro et speciali clerico utilique per omnia valde nobis
instrumento futuro, sicut ⌜tunc⌝ credidimus, dato per quod utriusque
mercimonii, tam principalis quam accessorii, cum paulo ante perceptis,
a toto gravamine potuit facillime respirare, tot ⌜, inquam,⌝ beneficiis
honoratus et a debitorum sarcinis exhoneratus, scelerosus tamen in
525 omnibus et ingratus, ab⌜s⌝tracto nepote nostro, cum furtis rerum
aliarum et rapinis, tanquam ⌜ultimum⌝ nobis 'vale' dicturus, et tamen
se reversurum predamque reducturum fide mediante pollicitus, a nobis
vir vulpinus, et longe plus quam vulpina dolositate repletus, corpore
simul et corde recessit. Simul ergo cum Propheta dicere possumus:
530 *Seminavimus triticum et spinas messuimus*, et cum Ihesu filio Syrac:
Non agnoscetur in bonis amicus, nec abscondetur in malis inimicus.

509 *post* capelle *V scribit* duplici *iterum, sed falso*　　515 dominorum] *V* domi-
niorum, i *expuncto*

496. So also 652–3, 1125, Ep. 7, p. 248, 128–9.
530. Cf. Jer. xii. 13: *Seminaverunt triticum et spinas messuerunt.*
531. Ecclus. xii, 8.

lawless thief carried off our nephew, so that he would no longer be able
to side with us in future, and would be able to play with the pup at will;
as his official and more than tutor, he would be able to give his attention
to the profits from the clergy and chapter, and line his pockets; moreover—and this he thought no small matter—he would not be a long way
from his business, but once he had acquired his manifold comforts in
this way as well as an elaborate emolument, he would be able to fill his
belly by day with the archdeacon, and it would be delightful for him to
unburden it by night with only his own corpse as witness. Thus when
a Welsh priest saw this tutor, who was more than a tutor, hovering about
our nephew in every action, and listening insatiably for the profits of
the chapters for his own work, he said in the presence of many: 'Master
Giraldus de Barri has given the archdeaconry of Brecon not to his
nephew, as he hoped, but rather to his tutor Master William de Capella.'

Moreover, after he had completed the shady deal over the church as
well as the chapel in this way, he immediately used his dexterous skill
and trickery in order to deceive us; for he hastened to Lincoln straight
away at top speed, lest gossip about it reach us from any source but
himself. He said absolutely nothing about the deal over the chapel from
which he in fact gets his surname, but had no qualms about revealing to
us the contract that was made over the church; using honeyed phrases
he called it the purchase of peace and quiet, though at great expense, for
which he suggested he would need the help of his friends and masters,
and he humbly requested and devoutly begged the favour of a loan from
us, on which he particularly relied—poverty bears a bold face, and has
absolutely no shame about anything, as long as it helps. He immediately
accepted our aid, which was large and sufficient, and conferred, albeit
with too little forethought, upon our faithful and special clerk, who
would be a very useful tool for us in any contingency—or so we thought
at the time. Through this, as well as the payments made shortly before,
he could very easily have gained a breathing-space from the whole
burden of both the principal and the subsidiary deal. Loaded with so
many bounties, and relieved of the burden of his debts, though an ungrateful rapscallion in every respect, as if to say 'Goodbye' to us for the
last time, he carried off our nephew, as well as robbing and stealing
other property, and promising on his oath that he would return and
bring back his booty, this foxy man, in fact a man with more craftiness
than a fox, departed from us both in body and heart. So we can agree
with the Prophet when he says: 'We have sown wheat and reaped
thorns'; and with Jesus son of Sirach: 'A friend shall not be known in
prosperity, and an enemy shall not be hidden in adversity.' Aristotle has

⌐Item et Aristotiles: *Difficile est in re prospera amicos probare, in adversa vero semper facile.*⌐

Multociens tamen hic proditor noster et rerum omnium, tanquam
535 Iugurta secundus, simulator varius et dissimulator, verbis coram nobis
asperis et acerbis inepcias vestras acriter arguens et obiurgans ac
reprehendens, ab errore vos revocare et retinere velle videbatur. Set
f. 68ᵛᵃ quicquid super hoc ab illo simu|latorie vel ab aliis vere et suasorie
⌐, non autem persuasorie,⌐ cantatum de die fuerat, totum ipse de nocte
540 auribus vestris, in camera quippe vobiscum et cubiculo collocatus eodem,
discantabat, formans ac firmans concepto in scelere docilem nimis in
talibus animum vestrum. ⌐Sicut et in psalmo scriptum est: *Iniquitatem
meditatus est in cubili suo; astitit omni vie non bone, maliciam autem non
odivit.* Item et in Proverbiis: *Qui corripit hominem, graciam postea
545 inveniet apud eum, magis quam ille qui blandimentis decepit.*⌐

Nec mirum tamen, quamquam multis admirandum, quod ille per-
suasor vobis magis efficax fuit solus et turpium et de nocte, quam veri
amici vestri plurimi de die clara et laudabilium, cum nova novissimis
hiis diebus inter vos duos videatur tanquam amoris copula iam reperta,
550 tam forti bitumine conglutinata, quod nulla materia nulloque ⌐sit⌐
unquam menstruo sanguine dissolvenda, verum, quoniam uno assidue
et ubique fere thoro tanquam inseparabili collocata, non absque nota
apud nonnullos, ⌐et⌐ quoniam qui famam negligit crudelis est et quicquid inhonestum probabiliter fingi potest caveri magnopere debet et
555 evitari, ⌐docente Apostolo *ab omni specie mala abstin*endum fore,⌐
a probis ⌐quidem⌐ et honestis viris non approbanda.

Ad hec etiam Lincolnia, parum ante discessum vestrum, fide tociens
ab ipso tam promte quoque et tam devote prestita, de vos reducendo et
consilio nostro pro posse stare faciendo vel a vobis, ut diximus, dis-
560 cedendo, ecclesiam⌐que de Langan⌐, ut in nullo vobis obnoxius foret
vel astrictus, resignando, putantes promissa ipsius hec omnia vera, presertim fidei religione firmata, diximus ei quod, si sic et cum affectu tali
ad nos rediret, quamdiu in hospicio nostro nobiscum esset et comes
individuus nobis existeret, dimidiam marcam marce prius ei promisse
565 annuatim ad ipsum, dum circa nos esset vestreque doctrine intenderet,
vestiendum adiceremus. Ipse vero, sicut accepimus, iam nunc in Wallia

---

544–5 postea inveniet] *V* inveniet postea *postea transpositum*　　　553 quoniam
scriptum est in rasura　　555 *per caesuram marginis ablatae sunt hae litterae:* d (docente),
o (omni), l (mala)　　　560 obnoxius foret] *V* foret obnoxius *postea transpositum*

---

532. Aristotiles] Cf. the so-called Caecilius Balbus, *De Nugis Philosophorum* (1855),
xv, 6 (p. 25): *Aristoteles dixit: Difficile est in re prospera amicos probare, in adversa semper
facile.*
542–4. Ps. xxxv, 5.

the same idea: 'It is hard to prove one's friends at times of success, but it is easy in times of trouble.'

Very often this betrayer of ours, this hypocrite and dissembler in every respect, like a second Jugurtha, bitterly attacked, reproached, and censured your stupid behaviour with sharp and bitter words in our presence, and apparently wanted to check and bring you back from the error of your ways. But whatever he had been harping upon during the day in this deceitful manner, or whatever others had been harping on in a truthful and suasory though not persuasive manner, he refuted completely at night in your ears, since he shared the same chamber and bedroom as you, forming and strengthening your resolve over this crime—a resolve which was completely inclined to this sort of affair. It is just as the Psalm says: 'He hath devised iniquity on his bed: he hath set himself on every way that is not good; but evil he hath not hated'; and in Proverbs: 'He that rebuketh a man shall afterwards find favour with him, more than he that by a flattering tongue deceiveth him.'

It is not, however, surprising, though many find it so, that the incitement to crime of that one man at night was more effective than exhortations to an admirable way of life of your very many true friends in broad daylight. For a strange sort of bond of love between the two of you has come to light lately, which is bonded as if with a strong glue, since it can be broken by no material object and no menstrual blood, but, since it is continually, as it were, consummated in an inseparable marriage almost everywhere, it is notorious among a great many people, and since a man who pays no heed to reputation is a barbarian, and since he is probably able to think up anything dishonest, it ought to be watched and avoided: as the Apostle teaches, we should avoid all forms of evil, it is to be disapproved of by all upright and honourable men.

In addition to this, shortly before your departure from Lincoln, he frequently gave his oath so readily and so devoutly, that he would bring you back and make you abide by our counsel, as much as possible, or, as we have said, he would leave you and resign his church at Llangan, so that he would be in no way obliged or bound to you. We thought all his promises were true, especially since they were made under oath, and we told him that if he came back to us thus and with such affection, as long as he was with us in our hospice and was our inseparable companion, we would give him half a mark annually in addition to the one promised earlier, to robe him, for as long as he was with us and concerned with your education. However, as we have heard, he is now

544–5. Cf. Prov. xxviii, 23: . . . *qui per linguae blandimenta decipit.*
555. Cf. 1 Thess. v, 22: *Ab omni specie mala abstinete vos.*

f. 68ᵛᵇ pupplice iactitat | quod annuum viginti solidorum redditum ei con-
tulimus, inter logicas proposiciones ⌜(nec mirum, quoniam a primo
statim limine logicam salutavit)⌝ male distinguens et simplicem cate-
570 goricam pro condicionali et ypotetica sumens.

Contra personam etenim de Kinardesle, cognatum nostrum, non
maiorem inprimis excercende fraudis adinvenit occasionem; set vali-
diorem et robustiorem ad dedecus suum et dampnum, si magister ille
cedularum adulterinarum per aliquam de nostris, quas dolose optinuit
575 et detinet, cedulam falsam et falso inscriptam hoc ausus fuerit attemptare, quia dolus dolum attrahit et audaciam prestat, remedio contra
fraudes huius modi iam reperto, Deo dante, inveniet defensionem. Set
ecce qualiter hic vinea plantanda et qualiter in homine, fide carente,
spes est et fiducia ponenda!

580 ⌜Pluries tamen hic proditor noster, quamquam tot turpibus irreti-
tus, more scelerosorum omnium, qui tanto nequiores sunt et nequiciis
notabiliores, tanto presumptuosiores et ad dissimulandum ac modis
omnibus excusandum longe ⌜pro⌝mciores, in audiencia plurima coram
pueris nostris post discessum vestrum primum in Wallia iactitando,
585 dicebat quod, quam cito Lincolniam ad nos rediret, statim ipsum in
pristinam familiaritatem et societatem et ad mensam nostram et etiam
discum proprium valde gratanter admitteremus et quoniam omnes
presumpciones nostras, quas contra ipsum habuimus, uno sacramento
Walensico facile satis evacuaret. Verum in utroque promisso, sicut et
590 in aliis omnibus, Lincolniam veniens mendax apparuit. Quoniam por-
tam nostram, ad quam, tanquam rebus omnibus erga nos optime gestis,
simulator quippe varius et dissimulator audacter et impudenter accessit,
intrare non potuit, nec etiam discipulus suus intravit, quia sine magistro,
quamquam revera tali magistro qualem depinximus, ei tamen insepara-
595 biliter adherens, intrare recusavit. Sacramentum quoque suum excu-
satorium, quod in capitulo Lincolniensi optulit instanter et ingessit,
quatinus periurio plectibilique magis quam piaculari flagicio,⌜se⌝ sic
purgare posset inpurissimum, non admisimus, monentes ipsum quatinus sacramenta prius prestita de nepote nostro ad consilium nostrum
600 reducendo vel ab ipso recedendo, et cetera prescripta plurima primum
adimplere curaret, prius scilicet quam aliud offerre de novo presume-
ret, quia | sacramenta terre illius ignorare non debuimus, que, cuius-
modi sint et quanti ponderis, tam remotis in partibus quam propinquis,
per experienciam plurimam et periculosam nos satis agnoscere posse
605 ⌜proposuimus⌝. Qualiter etiam magister David Oxoniensis, pauperista

580–738 *haec longa additio* (Pluries . . . perniciem nati) *scripta est in f. 70ʳ et 70ᵛ*
602 *f. 70ʳᵇ*

boasting in public in Wales that we gave him an annual revenue of twenty shillings. He cannot tell the difference between the propositions of logic: he takes a simple categorical for a conditional and hypothetical. This is no surprise, since he said farewell to logic before entering its portals.

He discovered an opportunity of practising his deceit, that was initially no greater, against the parson of Kinnersley, an acquaintance of ours; but if that tutor has the gall to try this with another false schedule with a false entry from those counterfeit schedules of ours which he stole fraudulently and now holds (trickery attracts trickery and wears a bold face), he will discover the cure for deceits of this kind and, God willing, he will find the defence stronger and more powerful to his disgrace and loss. But consider how one should plant one's vines here, and how one ought to place one's hopes and trust in a man bereft of faith.

Though embroiled in so many criminal activities, after the manner of all criminals, who are the more wicked and notorious for their wickedness, the more presumptuous and ready to dissemble and make any sort of excuse, this betrayer of ours frequently said boastingly in the hearing of many in the presence of our servants after your first departure to Wales, that as soon as he returned to us at Lincoln, we would at once gladly receive him into our company and society at our table, even our high table. He also said that he would easily obviate all the misconceptions we had of him by one Welsh oath. However, on his return to Lincoln he proved himself a liar in both these promises, as in all others. For this treacherous deceiver and dissembler was unable to enter the door which he boldly and impudently approached, as though all our business had been carried out excellently, and his pupil did not enter, since he refused to enter without his tutor; though it was the sort of tutor we have depicted, he was none the less inseparable from him. We refused to hear his excusatory oath which he immediately offered and presented at the chapter of Lincoln, to be able to clear himself of perjury and his penal rather than sinful crime. We told him to see that he performed his former oaths about bringing back our nephew into our counsel or himself leaving him, and his other promises, before he should have the audacity to offer us another one, since we ought not to be ignorant of that country's oaths, the nature and weight of which we suggested we were sufficiently well able to recognize by our own frequent and perilous experience both far and near. We publicly revealed that tale of Master David of Oxford which is nowadays sufficiently well known:

605. pauperista] The term is taken to indicate the followers of Vacarius, cf. F. de Zulueta, ed., *The Liber Pauperum of Vacarius*, Selden Society 44, 1927, p. xviii.

probus et acutus, semel in Wallie finibus advocacionis officio fungens,
propter clientum suorum et testium eorum tot periuria tam passim et
tam irreverenter exibita, quorum et ipse non inscius erat, reversus in
Angliam et a Deo visitatus simulque compunctus et penitencia ductus,
610 incontinenti monasterium intravit et habitum religionis assumpsit, satis
hodie divulgatum esse puplice propalavimus. Qualiter etiam et per
qualia vel qualium sacramenta simul cum cedulis adulterinis institucionem suam in ecclesia de Lanhamelac factam, Willelmus iste falso
probavit, satis notum existere proposuimus. Cuius etiam falsitatis hec
615 certa probacio, quod presbiter pater eius, in egritudine constitutus extrema, cum nos super ingressu suo in ecclesiam de Lanhamelac minus
canonico certificaret, consilio nostro ecclesiam eandem in manu decani
de Brechene Ricardi imminente puncto letali resignavit, quod quidem,
si prius ipsam Willelmo cessisset, sicut ipse mentitur, et resignasset,
620 non iterum hoc fecisset nec opus fuisset. Ex hoc etiam constare potest
presbiteros omnes et clericos, per quos et patris cessionem et suam
institucionem in dicta ecclesia factam probare presumpsit manifeste
periuros et ob hoc simul cum ipso perpetuo notabiles et infames
habendos.

625   Cum igitur a nobis sacramenta sua sic parvipendi conspiceret, | per
que tam a furtis et fraudibus cunctis quam sceleribus universis se purgare facillime posse putabat et tam a pecunia subtracta quam etiam
infamia contracta, que vix aboleri solet, iuxta poeticum illud:

Pena potest demi; culpa perhempnis erit,

630 se prorsus immunem efficere, qui blande primum incesserat, ut, more
solito, nos deciperet, ⌐Salomone testante, qui ait: *Cum submiserit*
vocem, ne credas ei; septem enim nequicie in corde ipsius, et propheta
David: *Molliti sunt sermones eius super oleum, et ipsi sunt iacula,*⌐
statim ut scorpius cauda pungere cepit, dicens ad internuncios, viros
635 eruditos et discretos, quos ad nos miserat, consolares et amicos nostros,
et in pedes a sessione prosiliens, nepotem nostrum archidiaconum, ibi
tunc presentem et totum audientem, nunquam, nisi ipso prius recon-
ciliato, nobis reconciliandum fore, et hoc, tanquam discipulum suum
ad fas omne nephasque pro nutu flectere potens, constanter et confiden-
640 ter asseruit. Prohibuit etiam et, alta voce proclamans, appellavit quod
nepotis nostri curam, ut consuevimus, et reddituum quos ei contulimus
administracionem de cetero nullatenus haberemus, quod audientes, viri

625 *f.* 70va

---

629. Ovid, *Pont.* i, 1, 64; cf. *infra,* Ep. 5, 157 and Ep. 6, p. 222, 253–4; also quoted
by Giraldus elsewhere (*Op.* i, p. 215; *Op.* iv, pp. 173, 352; *Op.* viii, p. 181).

he was an honest and acute man and a legal expert who once performed the duty of advocacy in Wales. Because of the numerous, widespread, irreverent perjuries of his clients and witnesses, of which he was not unaware, he returned to England; he had a vision from God, felt remorse, and inspired by penitence immediately entered a monastery and took the cloth of religion. We suggested that it was sufficiently well known by what oaths and by whose oaths as well as counterfeit schedules that William of yours proved his institution in the church of Llanhamlach. The positive proof of this deception is the fact that when his father, the priest, who lay dying on his sick-bed, assured us that his entry into the possession of the church of Llanhamlach was far from canonical, on our advice at the very point of death he resigned the church to the keeping of Richard, dean of Brecon; had he formerly ceded and resigned it to William—as William mendaciously claims—he would not have done it a second time: there would have been no need. From this evidence it can be stated as a fact that all the priests and clerics through whom he had the temerity to prove his father's resignation and the fact of his institution to the church were clearly perjurors and for this are to be regarded as infamous and deserving censure once and for all.

When he realized that we thought nothing of those oaths of his, by which he thought he could very easily exonerate himself of all his thefts and frauds as well as all his crimes, and clear himself of the money he had stolen and the infamy he had earned (and that can scarcely be disposed of: as the poet says, 'The punishment can be removed, but the guilt is for ever'), though he had started in his pleasant manner, to deceive us, as he usually did (as Solomon testifies: 'When he shall speak low, trust him not; because there are seven mischiefs in his heart'; and the Prophet David: 'His words are smoother than oil, and the same are darts'), immediately he began to stab with his sting like a scorpion. He addressed himself to the intermediaries, educated, wise men, fellow scholars and friends of ours, whom he had sent to us, and leaped to his feet, and said that our nephew, the archdeacon, who was there present and listening to everything, would never be reconciled to us, unless he himself was reconciled beforehand. He firmly and confidently asserted this as if he had the power to turn his pupil to every kind of right or wrong at will. He even forbade, and, shouting at the top of his voice, prayed that in future we should not have the guardianship of our nephew, as we used to, and the administration of the returns which we had

---

631–2. Cf. Prov. xxvi, 25: *Quando submiserit vocem suam, ne credideris ei: quoniam septem nequiciae sunt in corde illius.*
633. Ps. liv, 22.

qui missi fuerant et ab ipso missi incontinenti responderunt, ei dicentes nunc perspicuum esse presumpciones magistri Giraldi contra ipsum
645 veras existere et appellaciones alias, tam apud Herefordiam quam alibi in hunc modum a discipulo suo vel aliis factas, per ipsum fuisse fabricatas. Novit enim quia, si nepos noster ad nostrum rediret consilium, nec ipse per archidiaconatum, ut nunc est, plus-quam-magister existeret, quin immo potestatem ibi nullam haberet, nec frater eius presbiter,
650 comperta iam amborum nequicia, pinguem ecclesie de Landu vicariam amplius optineret. Ideoque totam hanc maliciam et tanti scandali notam, quatinus in aqua turbida bene piscari et ut ludere cum catulo commode possit, indubitanter est machinatus.

ᴦRelictus autem ab internunciis et contemptus, statim tanquam in
655 furiam raptus, per maiores cleri et capituli Lincolniensis discurrere cepit, susurrans eis qui eum audire volebant (quidam enim tam ipsum quam delaciones eius et detracciones illico respuerunt) nos quosdam eorum dictis, sicut asseverabat, que ipse audierat dum familiaris noster extiterat, alios scriptis que legerat, dilacerasse et diffamasse, ut sic
660 exosos illis quibus caros nos esse noverat, efficere posset. Unde et quidam ipsorum, nobis hec referentes, dixerunt quod in consiliis et secretis viri boni non deberet vir talis et tam scelerosus haberi. Quibus ᴦ-damᴵ etiam eorum dixit, tanquam nos sic deterrere posse putando, quod, si controversiam ei per domini pape rescriptum apud Lincolniam
665 suscitaremus, lingue gladium exereret, et quid linguositas posset ('simul et dolositas', suple) patenter ostenderet, dum nos, qui nondum ibi noti fuimus, notos ibidem ad unguem faceret, tanquam proditores nos in partibus nostris, sibique persimiles in hoc habitos, lingua fallax et mendax et dens mordax persuadere valerent. ᴦPoterant igitur illi
670 Diogenis uti responso. Cum enim quidam ei proferret aliqua maledicta ab amico ipsius de eo dicta: *An hoc amicus meus dixerit, dubium est,* *inquit. Id quidem de te mihi manifestum est.* Item et in iure scriptum est: *Qui minus diligentem socium sibi elegerit, de se queri debet.* Et Tullius: *Tales socios habeas, quorum consorcio non infameris. Inimici nimirum*
675 *sunt pessimi, qui per simulacionem amicicie alios nepharie produnt.* Et alibi: *Perfidos amicos devita, nichil eis credendo, set vitando per omnia.*

654 *haec additio legitur in schedula qua factum est folium* 69ʳ   662 viri boni] *V* boni viri *postea transpositum*   669 *haec additio scripta est in margine f.* 69ʳ *usque ad* Qui minus; *quod sequitur* (diligentem socium . . .) *scriptum est in f.* 69ᵛ   672 Item *scriptum est in rasura*

670. Diogenes] Apparently taken from the so-called Caecilius Balbus, *De Nugis Philosophorum*, xxiv, 3, p. 28: *Diogenes, cum quidam ei perferret aliqua maledicta ab amico eius de eodem dicta: An haec amicus dixerit, dubium est, inquit, id quidem de te manifestum est.*
672. in iure] Inst. iii. 25. 9: *Nam qui parum diligentem socium sibi adsumit, de se queri debet.* Giraldus quotes this also *Op.* i, p. 206, 2–3.

granted to him. When the men who had been sent—sent by him—
heard this, they immediately replied that it was clear that Master
Giraldus' assumptions about him were true, and that the appeals that
were made at Hereford and elsewhere by his pupil and other people had
been concocted by him. For he knew that if our nephew came back into
our fold, he would not have his super-tutelary powers in the archdeaconry, as is now the case, but would rather have no power, nor would
his brother, the priest, obtain the rich vicarage of the church of Llanddew
any further, when the wickedness of both of them was discovered. So he
clearly stirred up all his wickedness, and the notoriety of this great
scandal, to be able to fish well in troubled waters, and to play with the
pup at his ease.

When left in contempt by the intermediaries, he immediately, as
if seized by rage, began to run among the elders of the clergy and
chapter of Lincoln, whispering to those who wished to listen to him (in
fact, some were heartily sick of him, his vices, and his slanders there).
He claimed that we had defamed and slandered some of them by word
of mouth, which he had heard when he had been our companion, and
others in writing which he had read so that he could make us hateful to
those to whom he knew we were dear. So, some of them reported this to
us and said that such a wicked criminal should not share the counsels and
secrets of a good man. As if he thought he could frighten us, he told
some of them that if we brought him to trial at Lincoln with the rescript
of the Lord Pope, he would bare the blade of his tongue and show the
power of a quick tongue (to say nothing of sharp practice), and he would
make us (since we were not yet known there properly) known to a hair,
as if his fallacious and lying tongue and biting tooth could persuade them
that we were traitors in our own country, and to be regarded as the same
as himself in that respect. They could have used to him a reply of
Diogenes: for when someone told that man of some malicious remark
a friend had made of him he said: 'I am not sure whether my friend said
this. It is obvious to me that it concerns you.' It is also written in the
law: 'A man who chooses himself a friend who does not love him ought
to complain about himself.' Cicero says: 'You should choose friends by
whose company you will not be disgraced. Those who wickedly betray
others under the guise of friendship are by far the worst enemies'; and
elsewhere: 'Shun treacherous friends by putting no trust in them but by

673–5. Cf. Cicero, *Post reditum ad Quirites* 21: . . . *quoniam me quattuor omnino
hominum genera violarunt, unum eorum, qui odio rei publicae, quod eam ipsis invitis con-
servaram, inimicissimi mihi fuerunt: unum, qui per simulationem amicitiae me nefarie
prodiderunt . . .*
676. Cf. Cicero, *Post reditum ad Quirites* 21: . . . *sic ulciscar facinora singula, quem*

⌐*Utrumque etenim*, ut ait Seneca, *malum et omni credere et nulli; set omni quidem honestius, nulli vero tucius.* Unde et iuxta Prophetam: *In omni fratre tuo non habeas fiduciam.* Et iuxta poetam:

680   *Cognatum fratremque cave carumque sodalem.*⌐

Unde et pro perfidis huiusmodi secretariis et consiliariis in Ecclesiastico scriptum invenies: *A consiliario malo serva animam tuam.* Item: *Multi sint tibi pacifici; et consiliarius tibi sit unus de mille.* Item: *Qui denudat archana amici sui, perdet fidem et non inveniet amicum ad animum* 685 *suum.* Item: *Denudare amici misteria infelicis est anime desperacio.* ⌐Item et philosophus: *Sepultus sit apud te sermo quem tu solus audieris.*⌐ Unde et humano iure cautum est ut delatori vel lingua capuletur vel capud amputetur. Propter tales, etiam fictos et falsos ac fraudulentos ⌐et vocales, amicos⌐ audi Theofrastum: *Ita amicus esto, ut inimicus esse* 690 *non timeas.* Et paulo post: *Nunquam fidelis est quem ex amico inimicum habueris et, si in graciam reverti quesierit, nunquam credas illi. Captus enim sui ipsius utilitate, non amici revertitur voluntate, quatinus fingendo decipiat, quem non potuit persequendo.* Unde et in iure scriptum est: *Satisdacio malivolum tutoris propositum non mutat, set diucius grassandi* 695 *in re familiari facultatem prestat.* Pocius ergo cum Psalmista dicendum: *Eripe me, Domine, ab homine malo; a viro iniquo eripe me.*⌐ ⌐Et cum eodem sic orandum: *Domine, libera animam meam a labiis iniquis et a lingua dolosa.*⌐

Ceperunt etiam ambo, doctor et discipulus, acriter in hoc discessu suo 700 comminaciones contra nos emittere multas. Primo, quia thesauris nos | habundare noverant magnis, et valde nummosos et pecuniosos nos esse sciebant: potestati pupplice, que talia non recusat, suggererent quatinus pecuniam grandem olim fisco debitam, ut aiunt et asserunt, a nobis extorquerent. Secundo, quod ecclesiis quibusdam in Wallia, quarum

677 *haec additio quoque scripta est in f.* 69ᵛ   681 *hic redimus ad f.* 69ʳ
695–6 *dicendum* et quod sequitur *legimus in f.* 69ᵛ *nec non et additionem sequentem* (Et cum eodem . . . dolosa)   699 *hic redimus ad f.* 70ᵛᵃ   700 *f.* 70ᵛᵇ
701 nummosos] *V* mummosos   704 extorquerent] *V* extorquerent, *sed falso* nt *expuncto*

ad modum a quibusque sum provocatus: malos cives rem publicam bene gerendo, perfidos amicos nihil credendo atque omnia cavendo. These quotations from Cicero (673–5 and 676) occur also in *Symbolum Electorum* (*Op.* i, 206 and 295) and in *Speculum Ecclesie* (*Op.* iv, 159), there with the quotation of 678–9.
    677–8. Cf. Seneca, *Ep. mor.* i. 3: *Utrumque enim vitium est et omnibus credere et nulli, sed alterum honestius dixerim vitium, alterum tutius.*
    678–9. Cf. Jer. ix, 4: *et in omni fratre suo non habeat fiduciam.*
    680. Ovid, *Ars Amatoria* i, 753.
    682. Cf. Ecclus. xxxvii, 9: the Vulgate does not contain the word *malo*.
    683. Ecclus. vi, 6.   683–5. Cf. Ecclus. xxvii, 17.   685. Ecclus. xxvii, 24.

completely avoiding them.' As Seneca says: 'It is equally wrong to trust everyone and to trust no one; it is more honourable to trust everyone, though it is safer to trust no one.' This is similar to what the prophet says: 'Trust not any brother of yours', and close to what the poet says: 'Beware of your associate, your brother and your dear companion.'

So, you will find in Ecclesiasticus a text about treacherous secretaries and counsellors of this kind: 'Beware of an evil counsellor'; again: 'Be in peace with many; but let one of a thousand be thy counsellor'; again: 'He that discloseth the secret of a friend loseth his credit and shall never find a friend to his mind'; again: 'To disclose the secrets of a friend leaveth no hope to an unhappy soul.' Again, the philosopher says: 'Let the conversation which you alone have heard be buried deep in your heart.' Thus secular law warns that a denouncer should lose his tongue or his head. Concerning such feigned, false, fraudulent, and loquacious friends consider Theophrastus' statement: 'Be such a friend that you are not afraid to be an enemy'; and a little later: 'The former friend whom you have as an enemy is never trustworthy, and if he wants to get back into your favour, you should never trust him. For a man deceived by his own usefulness will not return at the will of a friend, so that he will cheat by deceit the man he cannot cheat by pursuing him.' So, too, it is written in the law: 'Making amends does not alter the evil intention of the warrantor, but gives greater chances for thievish designs in the estate.' Therefore one should rather quote the words of the Psalmist: 'Deliver me, O Lord, from the evil man: rescue me from the unjust man.' And one should pray with him: 'O Lord, deliver my soul from wicked lips and a deceitful tongue.'

Both teacher and pupil began to utter a great many bitter curses against us on their departure. First, because they knew we had great treasures, and they knew that we were very wealthy and rich: they would suggest to the public authorities, who never turn down such things, to extort a large sum, which they claim we once owed to the exchequer. Secondly, they threatened that we would be completely deprived of some

686. philosophus] This word is attributed to Socrates in the so-called Caecilius Balbus, *De Nugis Philosophorum*, xxiii, 3, p. 27: Socrates: *Sepultus apud te sit semper sermo quem solus audieris.*

687. humano iure] Giraldus appears to allude to Anglo-Saxon law. The passage nearest in content is in II Cnut 16 ('Si quis alium iniuste accusaverit, ita ut accusatus perditurus sit propter *delatio*nem accusantis pecuniam aut vitam, et accusatus se inde purgaverit, delator sit reus *lingue* sue . . .', F. Liebermann, ed., *Die Gesetze der Angelsachsen*, 3 vols. (Halle, 1903–16), i. p. 321; cf. also pp. 67, 203, 566).

689. Theofrastus] This also occurs in the so-called Caecilius Balbus, op. cit. xv, 11, p. 25: *Ita amicus esto, ut inimicus esse non timeas.*

693–5. in iure] Dig. 26. 10. 6.   696. Ps. cxxxix, 2.   697–8. Ps. cxix, 2.

705 nepoti nostro quondam personatum cessimus et ob securitatem utrimque
maiorem, presertim etiam ipsius utilitatem quam modis omnibus
procuravimus, nos pensionarios ei constituimus, privandos nos ex
toto minabantur. Tercio, quod tam archidiaconatus quam prebende,
a tempore quo redditus istos ei contulimus, quantum annuatim inde
710 suscepimus districte a nobis audire volebat; verum non minus alienum
vel admirandum hoc esse videtur, nisi quoniam lingua, licet balbuci-
ens et blesa, cor manifestat, quam si lagena vel olla, contra figulum
insurgens et intumescens, super racione reddenda cur vel amplam
⌐ipsam¬ in imo ⌐fecerit¬ vel artam in summo vel etiam quantas in luti
715 composicione fecerit expensas, convenire contendat.

Porro nepos talis, et vere a nepa dictus, qui nutritori suo talia iam
fecit et se facturum quoque deteriora promittit, dum *ex habundancia
cordis os* verba pronunciat et proponit, tam cuculum, ut diximus, qui
nutritorem suum devorat, aperte representat, quam de illorum quoque
720 natura, quam sequitur expresse, quorum semper min⌐o¬res, ut tociens
diximus, cum adulti fuerint, maiores strangulare nituntur, esse se
probat et manifeste declarat.

Ad maiorem etiam huius nostri nepotis confusionem, si quo modo vel
quocumque remedio corrigi posset, quod non credimus, vel ad aliorum
725 saltem in posterum qualemcumque cautelam, de Ioas, rege Iuda, pone-
mus exemplum, qui Zacariam, filium Ioiade, qui eum, ne cum regio
semine toto necaretur, absconsum nutrierat et postea regem fecerat,
quoniam de idolatria postmodum ipsum increpabat, occidi fecit. Sic
etiam, ut propius exempla petamus, Nero Cesar Senecam, preceptorem
730 suum, quoniam ab atrocitate nimia ipsum revocare et ad clementiam
eum monitis salubribus et scriptis inclinare volebat, neci exponere
non abhorruit.

Set ecce quam odiosa est obstinatis etiam salubris increpacio, que
sola, quamquam plus lenis quam aspera, inter nos et nepotem nostrum
735 tante discordie causam dedit! Pereant ergo viri virulenti et devoratores
ac parricide cuculi! Pereant pessimi et ingrati imitatores Ioab sangui-
narii! Pereant etiam neroniani discipuli in necem erudiencium et perniciem nati!

⌐Ad hec autem et hoc adicimus, quod, sicut ad ianuas hospicii
740 nostri Lincolniensis, non minus inpudenter quam inprudenter, tanquam
re bene gesta per omnia, se doctor et discipulus ingerere presumpse-
runt, sic, et eadem inpudencia, non minus quam ante, contumaciter et

---

725 Iuda *scriptum est in rasura*   739–56 *haec additio scripta est in prima duarum
schedularum quibus factum est folium 71ʳ ab alia manu*

churches in Wales the parsonage of which we had once given to our nephew, and had made ourselves the payers of his pension for the greater convenience of both parties and especially for his benefit, which we looked after in every way. Thirdly, he wanted to have an accurate account from us of how much we received annually from the arch-deaconry and prebend from the time we had given the revenues to him. But this appears to be no less strange or remarkable, except that his tongue, though stammering and inarticulate, reveals his heart, than if the flagon or jug rises in anger against the potter and tries to come to an agreement about giving an account of why he either made it large at the bottom or narrow at the top or even how great an expenditure he made in mixing the clay.

Furthermore, this nephew, a word truly derived from the Latin for a scorpion, who has done such things to his foster-parent and promises to do even worse, since 'out of the abundance of the heart the mouth speaks', clearly resembles the cuckoo, as we have said, which devours its foster-parent. Clearly he has proved and shown that he has derived his character from theirs, which he obviously follows, since, as we have often said, when the chicks grow up, they strive to choke the older birds.

To increase the shame of this nephew of ours, if he could be corrected in any way or by any means (we have no hope of that) or at least to give a warning to others in future, we offer the example of Joash, king of Judah, who had Zechariah, son of Jehoiada, killed: he had reared Joash in secret, to prevent the royal line dying out, and had afterwards made him king, and later attacked him for his idolatry. In the same way, to give a more pertinent example, Nero Caesar had no qualms about killing Seneca, his mentor, because he wanted to divert him from his excessive savagery and lead him on to the path of mercy with his salutary admonitions and writings.

But consider how hateful even a salutary rebuke is to the pig-headed! This alone, though more soft than bitter, has caused this great controversy between us and our nephew. Damn vicious, destructive men, and cuckoos who kill their fathers! Damn these base, ungrateful imitators of bloody Joab! Damn these pupils of Nero, born to bring death and destruction to their teachers!

We would add the following fact to the above: just as the tutor and pupil had the gall to approach the gates of our hospice at Lincoln in a no less impudent than imprudent fashion, as if the whole affair had ended well, so, too, with no less impudence than before did they withdraw

717–18. Cf. Matt. xii, 34; Luke vi, 45.
725–8. Cf. 2 Chron. xxii–xxiv.

discorditer recedentes, ad quandam ecclesiam nostram in Anglia per
aliam viam quam venerant hospitandi causa diverterunt. Nec mirum,
745 quoniam attrite frontis est avaricia et, quantumcumque in loculis
habeat, semper egena propriis⌐que⌐ parcens iugiter aspirat ad aliena.
Ubi et ⌐tunc⌐ a clericis nostris laute satis et splendide ⌐sunt⌐ exhibiti
et cum honore suscepti, simulantes quippe ⌐et mencientes⌐ se ad
graciam nostram et concordiam ex toto iam reversos, et literas etiam
750 nostras eis pretendentes ex aliqua forte scedularum predictarum, quarum
copiam habent, solita falsitate fabricatas. Norunt etenim quod inimicos
suos, iuxta Petri Alphurni sentenciam, modis omnibus et comedendo
et consumendo et devorando, ac fabricando quoque, quod tamen
ultimum hoc non ad Petri quidem, set ad ipsorum sentenciam spectat
755 (quia *dolus an virtus, quis in hoste requirat?*), totis gravare nisibus quisque tenetur.⌐⌐

Propter hec igitur et alia turpia nimis et enormia hominis istius opera,
si de patris optimi natura, qui tam fidelis et tam naturalis extiterat
adeoque infidelitatem in aliis et dolositatem omnem semper abhorre-
760 bat, quicquam in vobis existeret, tam ipsum quam alios sibi similes
et scelerosos omnes ipsumque pre ceteris cunctis, qui vestram adole-
scenciam tot turpibus notis commaculavit, exosos plurimum et non diu
domesticos aut familiares haberetis, quod, si tales aut talia diu vobis
adheserint et placuerint, materne nature peiorisque partis eiusdem
765 melancolia pessima vos plenum esse pro certo proha⌐be⌐tis. Tunc enim,
quanto scelerosiores fuerint homines, tanto vobis absque dubio fient
familiariores. Tunc etenim turpia vobis cuncta placebunt et nepharia:
f. 72ra naturalia cuncta et laudabilia displicebunt. | Et sic moralitatem quam
vel ex natura prava vel doctrina ⌐vel⌐ pocius utraque hactenus preten-
770 distis usque in senium et extremum quoque spiritus alitum, nisi
Dominus vos in fine respexerit, innata perversitate prosequemini.

Gratus itaque vobis Willelmus esse debet, quod mores eius et modos,
qui vobis placent plurimum et placebunt, per quod et carior nobis
existet, iam ex parte depinximus et propalavimus.
775 ⌐Gratus et ob hoc Willelmo ⌐nepos noster⌐ esse debet, quod, dum
adhuc circa nos in scolis magistrorum limina t⌐e⌐rebat, ut litterature
fundamentum, a puericia perditum (et quibus ex causis satis est dictum

---

745 quoniam] *V* qoniam *scriptum in rasura*   754 ultimum hoc] *V* hoc ultimum
postea transpositum   757 *hic redimus ad f. 68ᵛ*   765 prohabetis] *V* probatis
postea correctum   775–86 *haec additio scripta est in f. 69ᵛ*   775 et] *V* etiam
postea correctum   Willelmo *scriptum in rasura*

in a disgraceful and discordant fashion, and turned aside to one of our churches in England for hospitality by a different route from that by which they had come. This comes as no surprise, since greed wears a bold front, and, whatever it has in its pockets, it is always in need, and is mean with its own property and perpetually lusts after others'. There and then they were accorded a splendid and praiseworthy welcome and were received with honour by our clerks, since they pretended and lied that they were back in our favour and peace was restored, and even gave them letters from us, forged with their usual deceit, possibly from one of the aforementioned schedules, of which they have a considerable supply. They know that, according to the precept of Peter Alphonsus, everyone is bound to use all his efforts to harm his enemies in every way, by consuming, laying waste, and destroying, and also forging, though this last is not Peter's, but it fits in with their precept (for who looks whether it is craft or courage the enemy is using?).

Because of these and other excessively base and outrageous doings of this man, if there was any trace in you of your admirable father's nature—and he was faithful and natural and always hated absolutely all unfaithfulness and cunning in others—you would regard him and all other scoundrels like him, but him above all, as hateful, since he ruined your adolescence with such disgusting scandals, and would not keep them for long as servants or familiars. If such characters and such activities are associated and please you for long, you can be quite sure that you are full of the dreadful madness of the worse side of your mother's nature. Then, the more criminal men are, the more familiar they will certainly be to you. Then every vice and wickedness will delight you: and everything natural and praiseworthy will displease you. Thus with your innnate wickedness, you will follow your ethical code which you have either from your wicked nature or education, or more likely from both, to your old age, and dying day, unless God looks upon you in the end.

Thus William ought to be grateful to you, since we have to some extent depicted and revealed his morals and habits, which are so very pleasing and will be so very pleasing to you, and for this reason he will be dearer to you than to us.

Our nephew likewise ought to be grateful to William, because, while he was still wearing down his tutors' doorsteps in the schools near us, to regain at least in adolescence basic literature, which he had lost since his young days (enough has been said about the reasons for this and more

752. Petri Alphurni] This seems to be Petrus Alphonsus, but the quotation cannot be traced in his works.   755. Cf. Virgil, *Aen.* ii. 390.

⌐et plus quam satis notum¬), saltem in adolescencia utcumque, quia
sacius sero quam nunquam, recuperaret, monitis eius et suggestionibus
780 pravis ad ulteriora quedam, set longe sibi adhuc inutiliora, saltum
fecit, quatinus magistro discipulus per omnia simillimus saltem super-
ficialis existeret et apparenciam aliquam vel loquacitate coram imperitis
haberet, qui veram existenciam solidamque ⌐scientiam et stabilem¬
doctrinam et fructuosam assequi non curavit. Set vere, iuxta sapientis
785 eloquium, ⌐quasi¬ *in ventum pulverem congregat, qui absdue funda-*
mento edificium parat. ⌐Et hoc similiter: *In loco solido fabrica robusta*
construitur. Quibus et illud evangelicum et veritatis ipsius verbum consonare videtur: *Omnis qui audit verba mea et non facit ea, similis est viro*
stulto, qui edificavit domum suam super arenam; et descendit pluvia, et
790 *venerunt flumina, et flaverunt venti, et irruerunt in domum illam, et cecidit*
et fuit ruina eius magna. Propter quod et illud antiquum Sibille vaticinium nostris videtur evidentissime diebus adimpletum: *Venient,* inquit,
dies, et ve illis quibus leges oblitterabunt scienciam litterarum.¬ Unde
quod de superficialibus huiusmodi Plinius egregie dixit, et hic apponere
795 dignum duximus: *Summo,* inquit, *solo sparsa semina celerius se effundunt*
et imitate spicas herbule: inanibus aristis ante tempus messis emarcescunt.

Gratus ob hoc etiam eidem et longe gracior esse debet, quod, preter
mendas tot et maculas indelebiles quas eius instinctu iam suscepit,
iacturam quoque temporis tantam incurrit, quod certe dampnum,
800 docilibus ingeniis gravissimum, sibi revera pro lucro reputat, quatinus
trutannicam vitam, sicut assuevit, correptore carens et correctore, in
desidiis ducat et, igne animi vacuus, solum ociis queat et ocitacionibus
indulgere. Cui et versus ille Serlonicus adaptari potest:

Stet mola, surda nola, sterilis vola, sit scola sola.¬

805　　Ex illa quoque natura vobis et hoc accedet, ut illos qui magis utiles
vobis fuerint et proficui magis exosos et infestos habeatis. Unde quanto
Willelmus fraudulencior nobis et infidelior fuit vel etiam in posterum
fuerit, tanto cariorem ipsum nature illius inpulsu habere debetis. Set
forte futuris adhuc quandoque diebus convertetur dolus eius in caput
810 eius et in verticem ipsius iniquitas eius descendet.

786 *haec additio scripta est in secunda schedula qua factum est folium 7 1ʳ*　　793 *hic
redimus ad additionem scriptam in f. 69ᵛ*　　797–804 *hic redimus ad initium additionis
scriptae in f. 69ᵛ; quod hic sequitur* (Gratus ob hoc . . . scola sola) *scriptum est ante id
quod superius hic editur* (Gratus et ob hoc Willelmo) *sed postea transpositum est ab
auctore ipso per litteras a et b scriptas in margine*　　797 *eidem et longe gratior
scriptum est in rasura*　　805 *hic reditur ad f. 7 2ʳ*

785–6. This does not occur in Walther, *Lateinische Sprichwörter.* Is the *sapiens*
again Giraldus? Cf. *supra*, 449 and part i, 670–1.

than enough attention has been paid to them), on the ground that it was better late than never, on his corrupt advice and promptings he leapt at other interests, though far less useful to him, with the result that the pupil was completely similar to his tutor, at least superficially, and because of his talkativeness he gave an appearance of it to the unexperienced, though he did not bother to pursue the true reality, actual knowledge, and real, fruitful education. But in reality, as a philosopher eloquently puts it, 'the man who builds a house without foundations is virtually heaping dust for the wind'. And similarly, 'a sturdy building is constructed on a firm spot'. The following passage from the Gospel, the word of absolute truth, has the same underlying thought as these two: 'And everyone that heareth these my words, and doeth them not, shall be like a foolish man that built his house upon the sand. And the rain fell and the floods came and the winds blew: and they beat upon that house. And it fell: and great was the fall thereof.' For this reason that ancient prophecy of the Sibyl can clearly be seen to have been fulfilled in our time; she said: 'The time will come, and woe to them for whom the laws wipe out the knowledge of letters.' Thus we also think it worth while to add what Pliny said beautifully of such superficial characters: 'Seeds scattered on the top of the soil and small shoots resembling ears of corn develop too rapidly: and they wither away with barren ears before the harvest time.'

He ought to be grateful, even more grateful, to him, because apart from the many faults and indelible blemishes which he gained at his prompting, he also wasted so much time: this loss, which is very serious to docile minds, he considers in fact a gain for himself, with the result that he leads the life of a hobbledehoy in idleness, as he is used to, without anyone to reprove or rebuke him, and lacking a fire in his belly, he is only able to indulge in a life of ease and inactivity. The following verse of Serlon can be applied to him: 'Let the millstone stop, let the bell be deaf, let the hand be empty, let there be leisure alone.'

It was an additional aspect of that nature of yours that those who were most useful and valuable to you, you baited and harassed. Thus, the more treacherous and unfaithful William was to us, or will be in future, the dearer you should regard him with your natural instincts. But perhaps at some future date his guile will rebound against his own head, and his wickedness will come down on top of him.

786–7. See note on 785–6.   788–91. Matt. vii, 26–7.   792–3. Not identified.
795–6. Not Pliny, but Quintilian, *Inst.* 1. 3. 5: *sparsa sunt semina . . . ante messem flavescunt.*   804. Serlon de Wilton, ed. Jan Öberg, 76, 2.

Quod enim nos plus quam hominem exosos habeatis, qui vobis plus homine proficui fuimus, non solum in hoc egregio nostre supplantacionis exemplo, illud poete vaticinium verum esse testante:

Filius ante diem patrios inquirit in annos,

815 sicut in Absalone patuit et, ut propius exempla petamus, in filiis regis Anglorum Henrici secundi, quorum tamen nec ille nec isti diu detestando facinore tali sunt gavisi, Salomone quoque testante in Parabolis, quoniam: *Hereditas ad quam in principio festinatur, in novissimo benedictione carebit,* verum ex hoc quoque, quod a puerilibus annis usque in 820 hodiernum diem nunquam nobis adherere, nunquam nobis assistere, sicut pater vester, ut dictum est, et fratres optimi, patri consimiles,

f. 72rb facere consueverunt, animo vestro, moralitatem, maturitatem, et doc|trinam omnem omni tempore respuenti, sedere potuit aut placere, natura quippe tociens dicta semper ad contraria, semper ad adversa vos pro-
825 pellente.

Unde et illud Valerii Maximi de Pompilio, qui capud Ciceronis amputavit, quod pro capite ipsius in Capitolio peroraverat, et hic videtur inserendum: *Pompilius neminem odit nisi cui plurimum debet. Periculosum est ergo multa beneficia in aliquem conferre, quia, cum* 830 *turpe est non reddere, volt non esse cui reddat.* Unde Seneca: *Es leve facit amicum, grave vero et grande facit inimicum.*

Mirum autem et mira nature corrupcio, quod, qui heredes sibi procreant aut successores ⌐etiam¬ per cessiones vel alio modo sibi fieri sollicite curant, illos eosdem eo ipso hostes sibi peiores et capitales per 835 beneficia parant ac pariunt inimicos. Illi enimvero, quatinus in bona universa parentum atque maiorum ilico irrumpere possint, vite ipsorum invidentes et more tocius inpacientes, mortem ipsorum iam desiderant eamque nonnulli machinari quidem ac moliri non formidant. Set nonne suspensis hii persimiles, qui odio inexorabili illos semper exosos habent 840 et capitaliter persequuntur, quorum opera tam suspendio liberati quam patibulo, et vite denuo redduntur et humano consorcio restituuntur?

⌐Accidit autem aliquando suspensum quendam, militis, ut fertur,

815 Absalone] *V* Absolone   842–52 *haec additio scripta est alia manu in schedula qua factum est f. 71ᵛ*

---

814. Ovid, *Metam.* i, 148.   818–19. Prov. xx, 21.

826. Valerius Maximus] Giraldus refers to Valerius Maximus v, 3, 4, ed. Kempf (1888), p. 237, l. 27–p. 238, l. 15. The person in question is C. Popilius (not Pompilius, as Giraldus writes his name) Laenas, whom Cicero had freed, by his eloquence, from a very dangerous situation, and who in turn took delight in killing Cicero with his own hand. Giraldus does not quote from Valerius Maximus directly, but instead uses Petrus Cantor, *Verbum Abbreviatum*, ch. 139 (Migne, *P.L.* 205, col. 337). Cf. also the note on Ep. 6, p. 224, 282–5 *infra*.

The fact that you should hate us more than any man, since we were more valuable to you than any man, is proved in the first place by the matter of that supreme precedent of your deceiving us, which proves that the prophecy of the poet is true: 'The son inquires how old his father is before his time', as was clear in the case of Absalom, or, to give a closer parallel, in the case of the sons of Henry II, King of England: however, neither he nor they rejoiced for long in their detestable crime; as Solomon bears witness in Proverbs: 'The inheritance gotten hastily in the beginning, in the end shall be without a blessing.' In the second place, it is proved by the fact that from your earliest years up to the present day you could never bear being near us, or stand our company, as your father, as we said, and your admirable brothers who are like your father, were in the habit of doing. You must have determined and made up your mind—a mind that at all times rejects morality, maturity, and all education—because your nature which has been mentioned so often always urged you to do the contrary and to do the opposite of what we wished.

It seems appropriate to insert the words of Valerius Maximus about Pompilius, who executed Cicero, which were uttered on the Capitol in the funeral oration over his head: 'Pompilius hated no one except the man he owed the greatest debt to.' It is, then, dangerous to do anyone many good turns, because when it is disgraceful not to repay, he does not wish that there be a man to whom repayment has to be made. As Seneca says: 'A small loan makes a friend, but an important and large one makes an enemy.'

It is amazing—an amazing aberration of nature—that those who beget heirs for themselves, or take pains to get successors to themselves by means of resignations or any other means are making them into worse enemies for themselves, and creating mortal enemies by their acts of munificence. And so that they can make greater inroads into all the wealth of their parents and elders, since they hate them living and brook no delay, they long for their death and not a few have no qualms about contriving and engineering it. But do they not resemble those sentenced to hanging, who always hate—hate inflexibly—and persecute with a deadly hatred those by whose efforts they have been saved from death both on the gallows and the gibbet, given back life, and restored to society?

It happened once, as the story goes, that a man sentenced to hanging

829–30. Periculosum est . . . reddat] Petrus Cantor, *Verbum Abbreviatum*, ch. 139 (Migne, *P.L.* 205, col. 337B).

830–1. Seneca], Seneca, *Epist.* 19. 11: *Leve aes alienum debitorem facit, grave inimicum.* This quotation likewise occurs in Petrus Cantor, *Verbum Abbreviatum*, ch. 139, and again *infra*, Ep. 6, p. 224, 287–8.

beneficio transeuntis a patibulo deiectum et a mortis urgentis incomodo
liberatum, eundem postea militem foro puplico propter equum sibi ab
845 eo sublatum, ut asserebat, capitaliter inpetiisse. Quem miles demum, ob
id duello victum, denuo ad suspendium duxit et equi⌈ta⌉turam suam,
quam mira malicia petere presumpsit, digno Dei iudicio ei restituit.
Haut aliter Capre Willelmo, cui capud reddidimus, similique nos ob
hoc odio persequenti, forsan adhuc accidere poterit, quatinus mortis
850 maturacionem, quam per nos amisit, per aliquos forte nostro dolori
atque dedecori condolentes, etsi non opera nostra, non voluntate, quandoque recipere queat et iuxta merita reperire.⌉

⌈Est itaque perspicuum, sicut nequicie, sic et ignavie signum maxime,
quod filii tales et nepotes, de propria virtute non confitentes, nil prorsus
855 sua vel opera vel opere perquirere, nil maiorum suorum cura quesitis
unquam adicere curant, set tantum partis insistere, et, tanquam immunes
aliena ad pabula fuci, paratis inhiare contendunt; et sic parentes aut
patruos etate provectos, bona ipsorum nunc ex parte mutilando, nunc
totaliter occupando, vel enormiter ipsos apporiare, vel etiam domibus
860 eiectos propriis ex toto, more cuculorum, qui suos demum nutritores
devorant, vitalibus ante diem horis et auris toto desider⌈i⌉o privare
nituntur.⌉

Facere quoque videtur ad hec, quod in hospicio nostro Lincolniensi,
ceteris nobis assurgentibus cunctis, sepe solus in banco ⌈in⌉mobilis,
865 tanquam magnus dominus, set non in hoc laudabilis nimis, sedere
presumpsistis, acsi tante maiestati vestre tali assurgere seni non con-
veniret, cum tamen extraneo ⌈cuivis⌉, quamquam nec boni quippiam
nec mali merito, capiti cano, quod magna fuit quondam capitis re-|
f. 72ᵛᵃ verencia cani, naturali iure quodam et consuetudine simul approbato,
870 iuvenes assurgere teneantur. ⌈. . . . . et hoc repperitur: *Coram cano
capite consurge et honora personam senis.*⌉ Cum igitur etati cuilibet
longeve sua reverencia sit exibenda, cur solum nostra senectus inter
ceteras omnes vobis, nisi et quoniam vos creavit, tam aspernabilis?
⌈Verum quod responsum est cuidam dicenti: 'Qua fronte tam cervicose
875 te erga me geris, qui te ex nichilo creavi?' nobis respondere potestis.
Dictum est enim econtra: 'Si ⌈tu⌉ de nichilo me creasti ⌈et ego⌉ de
nichilo tibi serviam.' De duobus autem malis sacius esset de nichilo
servire quam in malo servire vel etiam in non male meritos totis
maliciose nisibus desevire.⌉
880 Facit ad hoc etiam, quod apud Lincolniam in camera nostra coram

844 puplico] *V* pubplico, b *expuncto*   845 inpetiisse] *V* inpeciisse   853–62 *haec*
additio prima manu scripta est in margine f. 72ʳ   868 *post* merito, cuivis *expuncto*
869 approbato] *V* approbata *postea correctum*   870 *huius additionis primam lineam*
abstulit caesura marginis folii   872 sit *scriptum est in rasura*   cur *scriptum est in rasura*

was cut down from the gallows and released from imminent death by the goodwill of a passing knight: afterwards he prosecuted capitally the knight in a public court for stealing a horse from him, as he claimed. The knight won the case, and took him out to be hanged again, and by a judgement worthy of God restored to him his harness which he had the remarkable gall to sue for. Perhaps it could turn out just the same with William, the whoreson, whose life we saved and who on account of this persecutes us with a similar hatred; perhaps it could happen that he may be able to meet an early death, which we saved him from, as he justly deserves, at the hands of others who are sympathetic to our pain and shame, though it would not be our doing, or wish.

The obvious sign of the wickedness and very great cowardice of such sons and nephews is that they do not rely on their own courage and take no trouble to get anything further by their own efforts or doings, and to add to what they have gained by the diligence of their elders, but only try to stick to what they have, and, like useless drones, feeding on others' food, they long for a ready-made profit. When their parents and uncles are at an advanced age they sometimes partly ruin their property, and sometimes totally take it, and either exert all their efforts to impoverish them entirely, or even throw them out of their own homes, and like cuckoos who in the end devour their foster-parents, deprive them of their lives before their time.

In addition to this, when you were at our hospice in Lincoln, when all rose in our presence, you often had the temerity to remain seated on your bench, like some great lord, though not one to be praised, as if it inconvenienced your majesty to rise to this old man, though young men are bound by a natural law and accepted custom to rise for any grey-haired stranger, regardless of whether he deserves good or ill, since at one time there was great respect for grey hair. As one finds written: 'Rise in the presence of a grey-haired man, and honour the person of an old man.' Since, then, they ought to show respect to old age of any description, why are only we in our old age among the rest so despicable to you, unless it is because we have created you? What is the reply to anyone who asks 'Why are you so impudent towards me? I have made you from nothing'? You can give the reply. It is: 'If nothing is what you made me from, nothing is the service you will get from me.' Of the two evils the better is to give no service than to give wicked service, or even to rant and rage maliciously with all one's strength against those who do not deserve ill.

In addition to this in our chamber at Lincoln in the presence of a

plurimis, manum vestram ad bibliotecam nostram extendens super quodam inter cetera plurima nobis imposito, vos, tanquam excusando et rem negando, iurastis, non requisitus tamen, set repentinus, in quo etiam, ut notum pluribus et certum erat, ultro tunc periurastis. Statim-
885 que tumide nimis et superbe alta voce proclamastis quod non propter nos vel honorem nostrum, set propter priorem de Thornolmia, qui presens tunc aderat, ne tale quid sinistrum de vobis existimaret, hoc fecistis, tanquam priorem quempiam vel etiam abbatem plus quam nos revereri seu venerari plusve diligere vel honorare deberetis. Ibidem
890 etiam, interrupto colloquio nostro necdum finito, cum fastu grandi sur-gens, solus precipitanter et indignanter exihistis et tanquam minaciter et contumaciter abcessistis. Set quanti vel quantus esse potest olle tumor contra figulum, quesumus, et fictorem aut factorem suum?

Talis namque tumor talisque fuit superbia prima, set potenti dextera,
895 cui resisti non potest, repente gravissima, ut satis est notum, ulcio data et terribilis in imum a tam alto est ruina secuta. In hiis igitur omnibus notis olithos (hoc est: nosce te ipsum), per hec aliis, et hiis similia, intus ad unguem et in cute notum, et notis huius modi sepe notatum et a pro-bis viris pro fatuo pariter ac pravo reputatum. ⌜Cui et versus ille in
900 psalmo non incompetenter adaptari potest: *Homo, cum in honore esset, non intellexit; comparatus est iuventis insipientibus et similis factus est illis.* ⌜Et in Para⌜bolis⌝: *Da stulto honorem et non intelliget.* Unde et ibidem: *Sicut qui mittit lapidem in acervum Mercurii, ita qui tribuit insipienti honorem,* super quod Glosa: *Per acervum Mercurii intellige
905 idolatriam, et honorem suple scilicet ecclesiasticum. Suggillantur enim qui dignitates ecclesiasticas carnaliter distribuunt.*⌝ Honorem tamen illum qui tibi tumorem hunc parit nulla penitus tumentis probitas, set dili-gentis et promoventis indignum et impium facilitas, ne et fatuitas
f. 72ᵛᵇ dicamus, sibi inepte comparavit.⌝ | Ut autem in fine verum materni
910 generis peiorisque partis eiusdem quasi primipilum et signiferum vos probare possetis, in discessu vestro tanquam ultimum, nobis 'vale' dicturi, osculum a nobis vos et magister vester non minus impudenter quam fraudulenter et infideliter extorsistis, dum osculum Iude domino ac magistro porrexistis. *Pravum* quippe *cor hominis et inscrutabile,*
915 *quis cognoscet illud?* Quibus statim hec verba subiunximus: si fides utrimque vera, tunc benevolencie est osculum et dilectionis; sin autem

884 periurastis] *V* peierastis   910 signiferum] *V* signififerum

897. ipsum] *NOTIS OLITHOS* is glossed *nosce te ipsum*: evidently an allusion to *gnothi seauton* of Delphos. Are we not faced with a corrupt form of writing: *NOTI SOUTHOS*? This ingenious suggestion was put to me by my colleague Paul Burguière. [Y. L.]; see also B. Bischoff, 'The Study of Foreign Languages in the Middle Ages', *Speculum* 36, 1961, p. 216.

great many people you placed your hand on our Bible and gave your
oath over one of many accusations made against us, as if to explain
yourself and to deny the whole affair: you were not asked to do so,
but did it suddenly, and thus, as many knew for sure, you perjured
yourself even more gravely. Immediately, puffed up with pride, you
shouted at the top of your voice that you did not do it for us or out of
respect for us, but for the prior of Thornholme, who was there at the
time, lest he should think ill of you, as if you should revere and respect,
love or honour any prior or even any abbot more than us. There, too,
you interrupted our conversation, though it had not ended, and rising
with great arrogance, you stormed out alone in indignation and left
threatening and blustering. But, we might ask, what power has the anger
of the flagon against the potter, its creator and maker?

Such was your anger, such was your initial pride; but sudden and
towering vengeance, as everyone knows, has a powerful right hand which
cannot be resisted, and great is the plunge into the depths that follows
from such a height. Among all these censures γνῶθι σεαυτόν (that is:
know thyself); by these and others like them, you are known and recognized in perfect detail; you have often been attacked with rebukes of this
nature: honourable men regard you as a wicked fool. That verse of the
Psalm can be applied perfectly in your case: 'Man when he was in
honour did not understand: he is compared to senseless beasts and is
become like them.' In Proverbs: 'Give honour to a fool and he will not
comprehend it'; in the same: 'As he that casteth a stone into the heap of
Mercury, so is he that giveth honour to a fool.' The gloss over this
is: 'For the "heap of Mercury" understand "idolatry", and add "ecclesiastical" to "honour". It is an attack on those who divide church honours
in a worldly manner.' It was not the goodness within this boaster, but
his ability of picking and promoting what was unworthy and impious,
let us not say folly, which in its inept way gained that honour which begets
this haughtiness in you. In order that you could prove that you were
a true front-ranker and standard-bearer of your mother's family and the
baser element of that family, on your departure you and your tutor,
impudently, deceitfully, and faithlessly took a last kiss from us, as if to
say 'farewell' to us, while you gave a Judas kiss to your lord and master.
For man's heart is deceitful and wicked: who can know it? We immediately added these words: if the trust on either side is true, then it
is a kiss of goodwill and love: but if on the other hand crime and deceit

900–2. Ps. xlviii, 13 or 21.
902. This does not occur in the Vulgate.
903–4. Prov. xxvi. 8.   904–6. Not identified.   914–15. Jer. xvii, 9.

scelus et fraus, sub osculo tecta, in actum post eruperint, nequicie est
osculum ⌜istud⌝ et prodicionis. Nec mirum si purum hominem, inscium
futurorum eventuum et cordium ac cogitacionum prorsus ignarum
920 nimisque familiaribus credulum, sui prodiderint et deceperint, cum
scriptum sit: *Inimici hominis domestici eius.* Et alibi Propheta: *Unus-*
quisque se a proximo suo custodiat, et in omni fratre suo non habeat fidu-
ciam, quia omnis frater supplantans supplantabit, et omnis amicus frau-
dulenter incedet, et vir fratrem suum deridebit et veritatem non loquetur.
925 Et in eodem: *Nam et fratres tui et domus patris tui etiam ipsi pugna-*
verunt adversum te et clamaverunt post te plena voce ne credas eis cum
locuti fuerint tibi bona. Item et hiis consonat illud poete:

> *Cognatum fratremque cave carumque sodalem.*

Non hoc, inquam, mirum, ex quo Deus et homo, cunctipotens et
930 cuncti⌜s⌝ciens ac cunctividens, a discipulo suo se tradi permisit.

Hoc ergo mirandum, hoc vehementer obstupendum, quod de tali
f. 73ʳᵃ patre tam naturali tamque | fideli, tam maturo in omnibus et tam morali,
filius talis, tam innaturalis et tam infidelis omnique moralitate bona
carens et maturitate, nasci potuit aut geniali linea propagari. Unde et
935 illud Valerii Maximi de filio Scipionis degenere dictum et hic apponere
preter rem non putavimus: *Scipionis Affricani Paulini nobilissimi filius*
ita virtute et moribus a patre degeneraverat, ut preturam ab eo tollerent.
Sic quoque filius Quinti Fabii, unde philosophus quidam: *Dii boni,*
quas tenebras de fulmine nasci passi estis?
940 ⌜Item Iozie, regi Iuda, qui regum illorum omnium optimus fuit,
successit filius eius Ioas, rex pessimus, ideoque a Pharaone Nechao
deiectus et in Egipptum ductus et frater eius Ioachim ei substitutus.
Item Samuel propheta fidelis Domini fuit, et iudex iustus a Domino
constitutus; filii autem eius Iohel et Abia iudices erant iniquissimi,

---

932 tamque] *V* tamque que; que *repetitur in initio f. 73ʳᵃ*   936 Scipionis] *V*
Scipii   942 substitutus] *V* substitututus

---

921. Mic. vii, 6, and Matt. x, 36.   921–4. Jer. ix, 4–5.
925–7. Jer. xii, 6.
928. Ovid, *Ars Am.* i, 753, quoted also *supra*, 680.
936–7. Cf. Valerius Maximus, *Factorum et Dictorum memorabilium libri novem*, III
v, 1, dealing with Cn. Scipio, the son of the elder Africanus, who was shamefully
imprisoned and whom later on his relatives prevented from taking his seat in the
tribunal although he had succeeded in being elected praetor.
938–9. Cf. Valerius Maximus, as quoted in the preceding note, III, v, 2. The son of
Quintus Fabius Maximus was deprived of his heritage because he was not worthy of it.
The sentence which Giraldus attributes to 'a certain philosopher' is by Valerius
Maximus, who ends in this way paragraph 1 (cf. the preceding note): *Di boni, quas*
tenebras e quo fulmine nasci passi estis! Here, as earlier on (cf. *supra*, note on part i,

veiled beneath a kiss later burst into action, that is a kiss of wickedness and betrayal. It is not surprising that a man's own friends and servants betray and deceive a pure man, unaware of the future, completely ignorant of their hearts and thoughts and excessively trusting in his servants, since it is written: 'A man's enemies are his servants.' As the Prophet says: 'Let every man take heed of his neighbour, and let him not trust in any brother of his: for every brother will utterly supplant, and every friend will walk deceitfully. And a man shall mock his brother, and he will not speak the truth.' And in the same work: 'For even thy brethren, and the house of thy father, even they have fought against thee and have cried against thee with full voice. Believe them not when they speak good things to thee.' That passage of the poet has the same underlying thought as these: 'Beware of your associate, your brother, and your dear companion.' This, I repeat, is not surprising since God and man, all-powerful, all-knowing, and all-seeing, allowed himself to be betrayed by his disciple.

It is then amazing, is absolutely bewildering that from such a father, so natural, so trustworthy, so mature in every way and so moral could be born such a son, so unnatural, so untrustworthy, so lacking in every kind of good morals and maturity, or could come from such a noble line. So we consider it not inappropriate to append that remark of Valerius Maximus of the degenerate son of Scipio: 'The son of the most noble Scipio Africanus Paulinus had degenerated so much from the courage and morals of his father, that they took his praetorship from him.' The son of Quintus Fabius was similar. A philosopher said of him: 'Good gods, what shadows did you allow to be born from the lightning?'

In the same way Josiah, King of Judah, the best of all those kings, was succeeded by his son Jehoahaz, the worst king, and for this reason he was deposed by Pharaoh-nechoh, taken to Egypt, and his brother Jehoiakim was substituted for him. Again, Samuel was a faithful prophet of the Lord and a just judge appointed by the Lord; however, his sons Joel and Abiah were the most unjust judges; and their wickedness

1072–6) one can follow Giraldus' way of working. He found, and perhaps wrote down in a summary way, the anecdotes dealing with the son of Scipio Africanus and the son of Fabius, for his collection of excerpts on moral questions: there he indicated that they had been taken from Valerius Maximus. Then, on the same note, he transcribed the exclamation with which Valerius Maximus had concluded the paragraph dedicated to Scipio. This sentence, copied again out of context, appeared to him suitable for a quotation, but he has forgotten that it is by Valerius Maximus just like the rest of the anecdotes. Then Giraldus attributes the saying to 'a certain philosopher', which is a safe way of avoiding a wrong attribution.

940–2. Cf. 2 Kings xxiii, but the king is called Joachaz, not Joas.
943–6. Cf. 1 Sam. viii.

945 quorum etiam iniquitas occasionem dedit filiis Israel petendi regem
a domino.�

Multis igitur signis et indiciis indolem pravam redolentibus, quod
dolentes in vobis plangere consuevimus, vos detestabili natura reple-
tum a puerilibus annis usque in adultos comprobare soletis. Quorum
950 hic quedam, quasi sub epilogo recapitulata tanquam in calce libelli,
videre poteritis et dolere. Primo, quod semper indocilem, semper
omnis doctrine bone contemptorem, sicut est hodie videre, vos exibu-
istis. Deinde, quod fatuorum semper et garcionum, seniorum nunquam
et sapientum, consorcia dilexistis. Set, quociens inter discretos nobiscum
955 ad hoc ductus et constitutus ut verbis doctrinalibus et narracionibus
curialibus atque facetis intenderetis, tociens vel picturas vel aves aliave
frivola domus inspicere, quoniam *oculi sapientis*, ut ait Salomon, *in
capite eius*, ⌐hoc est stabiles et non incerti, *oculi vero stultorum in
finibus terre*, hoc est vagi per devia et errabundi,⌐ vel cithare cordis ad
960 modulos rudes eliciendum digitos apponere, vel cum canibus aut catis
vel etiam pueris ludere vosque, non puerum nunc et pusillum, set
f. 73ʳᵇ grandem iam et adultum, viris bonis et | discretis fatuum ostendere
consuevistis, cum certissimum indolis bone sit indicium sapientibus et
sensatis velle libenter assistere eorumque verbis aures attentas et animum
965 applicare. Preter leves etiam et inutiles vestros ad frivola queque discursus bone moralitati ac maturitati valde contrarios, preter larvas
occultas risusque malignos et furtivos, alienis malis evocatos, preter in-
crepacionis impacienciam et incorrigibilem in omnibus obstinaciam,
preter illiteraturam nimiam et fere laicam ac popularem, preter lin-
970 guarum omnium precipueque duarum, latine scilicet et gallice, que
pre ceteris apud nos prestant, impericiam, preter puerile blese lingue
vicium, per incuriam grandem, immo et ignaviam vilem ac plectibilem,
nondum exutum, set tanquam affectatum et gratum, de die in diem magis
habundans augmentatum, preter hoc etiam, quod semper a nobis, sicut
975 et a doctis omnibus, et plus quam ceteris a nobis, procul abesse et nunquam propius assistere vobis desiderio fuit, preter hoc quoque, quod
nunquam bona commemorans, semper autem, more maligni illius et
hostis antiqui, male retractans ⌐et commemorans⌐, proclivis ad peiora
fuistis, preter hec, inquam, omnia, de quibus singulis satis dictum est
980 supra, de genere illorum, qui se invicem infestare iugiter, exheredare
quoque et supplantare, necnon et strangulare non cessant, quos tociens

957 sapientis *scriptum est in rasura*

957–8. Eccles. ii, 14.   958–9. Prov. xvii, 24.

gave a reason for the children of Israel to ask for a king from the Lord.

You used to give many indications and signs stinking of your depraved character—a fact that we used to lament in you—that you were absolutely full of a detestable nature from your childhood years until your adulthood. You will be able to see and lament some of these repeated like an epilogue here at the end of the book. In the first place there is the fact that you have always shown yourself to be unteachable and contemptuous of all good education. Secondly, there is the fact that you have always enjoyed the company of fools and scoundrels, not old and wise men. But whenever you went and stayed with us in the company of intelligent men so that you might turn your attention to words of instruction and polite and witty stories, you always used to inspect pictures, or birds, or other trivia of the household—as Solomon says: 'The eyes of a wise man are in his head' (that is stable and not fickle) 'but the eyes of fools are in the ends of the earth' (that is wandering, devious, and rambling)—or to try your hand at the lute, to pick out coarse tunes, or to play with dogs, cats, or even boys, though you were not a little boy, but a grown-up adult, and you used to act the fool to upright intelligent men, although the desire to associate with, listen to, and give one's attention to the conversation of wise and sensitive men is regarded by them as the surest indication of good character. Apart from your fickle, useless susceptibilities for any trivia, which are strongly opposed to good morals and maturity, apart from your secret derision, your spiteful furtive laughter, caused by others' troubles, apart from your intolerance of rebuke, and your totally incorrigible obstinacy, apart from your gross lack of literacy, which was almost secular and vulgar, apart from your ignorance of all languages, especially the two most current with us, Latin and French, apart from the childish fault of lisping, which you have not got rid of because of your gross negligence and vile, execrable idleness, but which rather has got more and more abundant from day to day, as if it were something dear and pleasant, apart from the fact that you always desired to keep your distance from us, just as you did with all educated men, and in fact further from us than the rest, and had no desire to stay in our company, apart from the fact that you never recalled good things, but, like that ancient, malignant enemy, you distorted them and recalled them in an evil light and always had an inclination towards more wicked activities; apart from all these, I say, of which we have said enough individually above, it is clear that you belong to the members of that brand which is continually and ceaselessly persecuting, disinheriting and supplanting and killing each other in

nominare tedio duximus, vos esse manifestat, et vere de maximis unum,
quod omnes quos in illa turbacione nostra gravi et grandi contra archiepiscopum Hubertum tantaque potentum ac magnatum persecutione
985 magis adversantes habuimus et contrarios, illos statim, et postquam
f. 73ᵛᵃ vos | promovimus, et antequam ipsos in pacem nostram et graciam
suscepimus, familiares et domesticos habuistis, tanquam ⌜ad⌝ nostram
supplantacionem et exclusionem, iam nunc factam, et ex tunc revera
faciendam animo conceptam, promtos habere possetis, tam adiutores
990 quam fautores.

Facit ad hoc etiam, quod eosdem et alios, qui in assumpta rebellione
vos fovent tanteque nequicie favent, consiliarios habetis precipuos et
secretarios, qui etiam, ut quasi vobis fidelius obsequi viderentur et vos
quoque firmius involvere niterentur, et quoniam, ut mos, populis sempeʳ
995 venturus amatur, et quoniam gaudent novitate moderni, et quia mutare
dominos plebs indocta cotidie vellent, quamquam deteriore fere semper
condicione, eoque precipue quia tucius cum catulo luditur quam cum
cane vetusto, contra nos, ut dicitur, appellarunt et vos etiam, quatinus
facinus quos inquinat equet, quin immo ut magis ingratum maior
1000 infamia fedet et, que nullo nit⌜ro⌝, nulla fullonis herba, dilui poterit,
macula notet, contra tantum amicum et tam proximum tamque proficuum appellare fecerunt.

Unde et tociens vobis dictus tociensque dicendus et semper ad
peiora vocandus Capre Willelmus sive Capelle, scelerum illorum sicut
1005 et aliorum omnium doctor eximius et protractor, quatinus et fraudem
conceptam effectui mancipare, et tamen erga nos se fidem utcumque
f. 73ᵛᵇ servare apud imperitos et minus acutos videri posset, hac ar|te
processit. Cum clerici in capitulo contra nos alii per eius doctrinam,
sedente nepote nostro pro tribunali et tanquam iudice magno et gravi,
1010 iam appellassent et sedenti, tanquam in trono ⌜principi⌝, fidelitatem
precise iurassent, in quo et contra sacramentum coram nobis antea
prestitum, tam sic iurando quam appellando, manifeste venerunt, et
periurium incurrerunt, unde rumores forsan adhuc audire poterunt.
Hiis, inquam, sic patratis, set verius perpetratis, surgens ille magister
1015 talium, et manu silencium indicens, in huiusmodi verba prorupit:
'Audio, inquit, quod contra magistrum Giraldum, cuius et clericus sum
et iuratus, hic agitur. Proinde et pro ipso et pro iure suo in omnibus ad
domini pape presenciam appello et terminum talem appellacioni con-
stituo.' Eoque dicto rem fictam magis quam serio factam, nec veram
1020 agi, set simulatoriam et fraudulentam, sub ficti risus et fraudulenti subsequenter significancia, tanquam re bene gesta propalavit, acsi aperte

994 involvere] *V* invuolvere, u *expuncto*.   1011 precise] *V* prescise

turn—we consider it too much of a bother to name them so often. In fact you are clearly one of the greatest, since all of those whom we had as our opponents and adversaries during that dreadful great trial of ours against Archbishop Hubert, and the persecution of the potentates and magnates, after we promoted you, and before we accepted them into our company and favour, you immediately took as your friends and servants, as if you would be able to have them at hand as helpers and promoters for the supplanting and exclusion of us which you had already planned to put into effect, as you now have done.

In addition to this you have them and others who encourage you now that you have taken up the rebellion and favour your great wickedness as your special companions and aides. In order that they might appear to be more faithful servants and strive to involve you more deeply, as is said, they appealed against us, since it is usual for an up-and-coming man to be loved by the mob; and since they delight in the novelty of the modern, and since the untaught masses daily want to change masters, though it is nearly always for the worse, and especially because it is always safer to play with the pup than the old dog, they have made you appeal against a great, close, and useful friend, so that the crime may put those it stains into the same position, and so that the greater infamy may pollute one who is more disliked, and mark with a blemish which can be removed neither by washing nor by dyeing.

Thus William de Capella whom we have often called, and will often call, a whoreson, and whom we call by even worse names, that consummate teacher and discoverer of those crimes and all others, has used such skill that he has been able to put the deceit he conceived into effect, while at the same time appearing to keep his trust with us, at least in the eyes of the inexperienced and less perspicacious. When the clerks on his instructions appealed against us in the chapter, when our nephew was sitting before the tribunal like some great and mighty judge, and had sworn fidelity to him sitting like a prince on a throne, they clearly went against the oath they had previously given to us, both by swearing and appealing in this way, and committed perjury, and the gossip about this will still be heard. When all this had been achieved, or rather stage-managed, that tutor of theirs rose and called for silence with his hand, and spoke as follows: 'I hear that action is being taken against Master Giraldus, whose clerk and liege-man I am. On his behalf and on behalf of his privileges I appeal to the presence of the Lord Pope.' When he had said this he revealed that the whole affair was trumped up rather than made in earnest and was not a true action, but false and counterfeit, with a show of a false and feigned smile, as if it had turned out well,

diceret: 'Totum faciamus, set nichil tamen facere videamur.' Set ecce qualiter fatuis sub nubilo tali fraus velata, discretis autem multis indiciis et circumstantiis non celata. Verumtamen verus est vates, de talibus

1025 loquens et dicens:

> *Si latet ars prodest: affert deprensa pudorem.*

Pluries tamen vobis dicere consuevimus quod, si quandoque natura-

f. 74ra liter obediendi et obsequendi patruo, qui vobis plus-quam-|pater extitit, vos titillacionem sentire contingeret, hoc proprie paterne nature

1030 ascriberetis; quociens autem recalcitrandi et iugum ac frenum modi modestieque detrectandi vos libido perculerit, ex materna id provenire natura procul dubio perpenderetis. Item qui ad recalcitrandum nobis, qui tales et tanti vobis extitimus, vos instigaverint, quatinus et in aqua turbida melius piscari possint et cum scandalo maximo perpetue⌐que⌐

1035 infamie nevo vos maculaverint, illos inimicos vobis et infideles indubitata veritate noveritis; qui vero ad obediendum eique modis omnibus obsequendum, qui vobis tam utilis extitit, consilium dederit, illum vos et honorem vestrum deligere pro certo scire possetis.

Quociens autem hec et alia vobis doctrinalia et premonitoria dicere

1040 consuevimus et in natura indoci⌐li⌐ atque rebelli sermones nostros capere non posse consideravimus, hec et similia subnectere plangendo solemus, et primo illud a Macrobio de Saturnalibus introductum, de corvo ⌐diu⌐ scilicet indocili, tandem tamen facto casualiter utili: *Opera perit et inpensa.*

1045 Et illud poete:

> *Non profecturis littora bobus aro.*

Et hoc vulgare:

> *Laterem lavo, et litus aro.*

Et hoc Serlonicum:

1050 > *Unda lavat lateres, bos litus arat, sine re res.*

Et illud quoque populare:

> *Ablue, pecte canem: canis est et permanet idem.*

f. 74rb Et illud Prophete expresse | vobis aptandum: *Si mutare potest Ethiops pellem suam, aut pardus varietates suas, et vos poteritis benefacere, cum*

1055 *didiceritis malum.* Ubi et hoc suppleri poterit: 'prava operante pariter tam natura quam doctrina.'

1026. Ovid, *Ars Amatoria* ii, 313.   1033–4. Cf. *supra*, 301.

1042–4. Cf. Macrobius, *Saturnalia* II, iv, 29–30. The text by Macrobius makes clear the allusion which is obscure in Giraldus: *Sublimis [Augustus] Actiaca victoria revertebatur. Occurrit ei inter gratulantes corvum tenens quem instituerat haec dicere: 'Ave, Caesar, victor, imperator.' Miratus Caesar officiosam avem viginti milibus nummum*

as if to say, 'Let us do everything, but let us appear to do nothing.'
Consider how this deceit was shrouded in mist for the stupid, but not
concealed from the wise because of the many indications and the circumstances. The poet speaks the truth who says of such: 'If the art is concealed, it betrays: when discovered, it causes shame.'

We often used to tell you that, if you ever happened to get any pleasure from obeying and serving your uncle, who has been more than
a father to you, in the natural way, you would put it down to your own
father's nature; whenever the desire to kick against the pricks and drag
the yoke and reins of moderation and modesty struck you, you would
certainly consider that it came from your mother's nature. So those who
have urged you to kick against us, though we have been so important to
you, so that they may get better fishing in troubled waters, and mark
you with the greatest scandal and blemish of eternal infamy, you should
undoubtedly recognize as your enemies and unfaithful to you; however,
the man who counselled you to obey and serve in every way, the man
who has been so useful to you, you ought to be able to know for sure
that he loves you, and cares for your honour.

Although we used to give these and other words of instruction and
advice and realized that it was not in your unteachable and rebellious
nature to be able to understand our conversation, we now console our grief
with thoughts of this kind: first Macrobius in *De Saturnalibus*: 'Work
and expense is wasted', where he mentions the crow which is stupid for
a long time but is finally made useful occasionally; the verse of the poet:
'I plough the shore with oxen, but to no effect'; the popular verse: 'I am
washing the stones, and ploughing the shore'; the verse of Serlon: 'The
wave washes the brick, the ox ploughs the shore, but the business is to
no purpose', and another popular verse: 'Wash, comb the dog: but he's
a dog and will stay the same'. That passage of the prophet is clearly
adaptable to you: 'If the Ethiopian can change his skin or the leopard
his spots, you also may do well though you have learned evil.' To which
might be added, 'Since both nature and education worked for evil in you'.

*emit . . . Salutatus similiter a psittaco, emi eum iussit. Idem miratus in pica hanc quoque
redemit. Exemplum sutorem pauperem sollicitavit ut corvum institueret ad parem salutationem. Qui, impendio exhaustus, saepe ad avem non respondentem dicere solebat: 'Opera
et impensa periit* [I have wasted my time and my expenses].' *Aliquando tamen corvus
coepit dicere dictatam salutationem. Hac audita dum transit, Augustus respondit: 'Satis
domi salutatorum talium habeo.' Superfuit corvo memoria, ut et illa quibus dominum
querentem solebat audire subtexeret: 'Opera et impensa periit.' Ad quod Caesar risit emique
avem iussit quanti nullam adhuc emerat.*   1046. Ovid, *Tristia* v, iv, 48.
    1048. Cf. Terence, *Phorm.* 186: *laterem lavo.*
    1050. Serlon de Wilton, ed. Jan Öberg, 76, 1 (cf. *supra*, note on 804).
    1052. Quoted by H. Walther, *Lateinische Sprichwörter*, no. 141.
    1053-5. Jer. xiii, 23.

Ad hec etiam, quod ex nature vicio, non iuvente lubrico, vel etiam ludicro prescripta provener⌐i⌐nt enormia cuncta, ex hoc clarescere potest, quod a puericie vestre moribus olim ac gestibus etas adhuc in
1060 nullo discordat adulta, et quod gena barbata tociensque resecta nondum ulla resecavit crimina prima, cum scriptum sit tamen et poetica moralitate pronunciatum:

> Quedam cum prima resecentur crimina barba.

⌐Unde Ieronimus: *Errores adolescentie etas matura condempnat.* Item
1065 et Boecius: *Res quidem puerilibus auribus accommodatas senior philosophie tractatus eliminat.* Maledicta igitur est arbor que nullum omnino fructum facit. Et maledictus est fructus quem nunquam emendat maturitatis effectus.⌐ ⌐Ipsa quoque veritate id testante et dicente: *Omnis arbor que non fecerit fructum bonum excidetur et in ignem mittetur.* Unde
1070 ad emendacionem, vel serotinam, invitans, auctor ait:

> Non lusisse pudet, set non incidere ludum.

Iuvenilis etenim excusabilis est levitas, cum laudabilis fuerit ipsa maturitas:

> Tunc prima est inculpabilis etas,
1075 > Cum ludis ponunt tempora metas.⌐

Verumtamen de vobis et emendacione vestra, quamquam sera, valde curiosi et, tanquam de non suo fetu, ut dictum est, res decepta, solliciti, pluries post discessum vestrum a nobis hunc ultimum pueros nostros ad partes illas, tanquam exploratores et non transfugas, mittere consue-
1080 vimus, qui, ad nos reversi, querentibus nobis de statu vestro et quibus ibi studiis moram faciendo indulgeretis, retulerunt nobis quod, surgens a lecto cotidie valde mane circiter primam, arcum ilico cum sagittis et missilibus arripiens, arti sagitifere semper fere venandisque leporibus valde frequenter, usque ad tempus prandii et ultra, indulsistis. Et cum
1085 quereremus utrum aliqua diei vel noctis hora libris inspiciendis et
f. 74ᵛᵃ clericalibus studiis vos indulgere viderent, responderunt | quod, preter predicta, sagittandi scilicet et venandi, studia, non aliis vos intendere viderunt, nisi post cenam et usque ad vesperam, nec non et cubandi horam, citharis Walensicis ad barbaros utcumque mod⌐ul⌐os elicien-
1090 dum manus et digitos adaptare. ⌐Sicut ergo Ciceronis est verbum: *Plurimus mihi sermo est cum libris meis,* sic et nepotis nostri: 'Plurimus mihi cum sagittis et citharis ceterisque inepciis meis sermo est.'⌐ Set ecce qualiter a puericie vestre studiis et moribus supra descriptis

---

1068–75 *haec additio scripta est alia manu*   1083 sagitifere] *V* sagitiffere, f *expuncto*
1086 preter] *V* pter

1063. Juvenal, *Sat.* viii, 166; cf. *supra*, part i, 841.

In addition to this the fact that all the outrageous scandals which we have been writing about are the result of that useless, lubricious, not to say ludicrous fault in your nature, can be shown from the following fact that your adult years in no way clash with the morals and habits of your childhood, and the fact that though you cut back your beard so often, in your adulthood you never cut back your original crimes, though there is the poetic precept: 'Some crimes should be cut back with the first beard.' As Jerome says: 'Maturity despises the errors of adolescence'; and Boethius: 'The more mature reflections of philosophy get rid of the things that delight a child's ears.' The tree that bears absolutely no fruit is cursed. And the fruit which is not improved by the effects of ripening is cursed. As the truth of God testifies: 'Every tree that bringeth not forth good fruit shall be cut down and shall be cast into the fire.' So, the author urges repentance, though late, with the words: 'It is not the fact that you have played about that is a matter of shame, but the fact that you do not put an end to your games.' The levity of youth is excusable, when the mature years are praiseworthy. 'The early years are without blame, when time puts an end to the games.'

But we were often curious and worried about you and your repentance, though late, like the proverbial instance of the tree deceived by unnatural fruit, and after this last departure of yours we frequently used to send our servants to that area as scouts, not deserters. They came back to us, and, when we asked them about how you were and what studies you were spending your time upon, they told us that you used to get up very early—about dawn—every day, take your bow, arrows, and darts and almost always spend your time on the art of archery, and very frequently on hunting the hare until breakfast and later. When we asked them whether they saw you spending any time of the day or night reading books and on your clerical studies, they replied that they never saw you spending time on any other studies apart from archery and hunting, which we have mentioned, except that after dinner you turned your hand to the Welsh lute and tried to get some barbarous tunes from it, until evening and even bedtime. While Cicero says, 'Most of my conversation is with my books', our nephew says, 'Most of my conversation is with bows and arrows, lutes, and the rest of my foolish

---

1064. Cf. Jerome, *Comm. in Ecclesiasten*, xii (Migne, *P.L.* 23, col. 1005): *adolescentiam senectute commutet* [*Israel*].

1065–6. Not identified.   1068–9. Matt. iii, 10 and vii, 19.

1071. Non lusisse . . . ludum] Horace, *Ep.* i, xiv, 36. *Non lusisse . . . metas* also quoted by Giraldus in *Topographia Hibernica* (*Op.* v, p. 200), *Symbol. Elect.*, Ep. xxvi (*Op.* i, 288, 22).

1074–5. Not identified; also quoted in *Topographia Hibernica* (*Op.* v, 200).

1091. Not identified.

etas adulta et gena barbata, frivolis solum et inutilibus, iugiter intendens,
1095 prava et perversa nimis operante natura, discordare non potest.

Scriptum est autem in Genesi de Ismaele, filio Abrahe, quod adultus
factus est iuvenis sagittarius, et de Esau, filio Ysaac, quod factus est
vir venator; set raro vel sagittarios vel venatores in bono Scriptura sacra
commemorat. Item de Chaim et Lamech primis homicidis, et cum
1100 fratricidio bigamie vicio et adulterio simul adiecto, lineari propagine
Iubal descendens, pater canencium in cithara et organo musiceque con-
sonancie describitur inventor fuisse, quatinus labor pastoralis, a Iabel,
fratre suo natu priore, ordinatus et ornatus, quasi in delicias verteretur.
Unde poeta:

1105   *Titire, tu patule recubans sub tegmine fagi*
        Silvestrem gracili ⌜(vel *tenui*)⌝ *musam modularis* ⌜(vel *meditaris*)⌝ *avena.*

In hac igitur opera et opere tali, quid aliud nisi, et in iuvenibus quoque,
deliracio quedam in lira declaratur, et vite levis ac lubrice oblectacio
pariter et ostentacio, unde Propheta: *Usquequo deliciis dissolveris filia*
1110 *vaga?* Sic, et a simili, 'usque quo deliciis dissolvetur filius vagus?'
⌜Propter quod et Alexander Macedo, dulcisonam forte citharam audiens,
cordas eius statim incidit; requisitus autem cur hoc fecisset, respondit
sacius esse cordas incidi quam corda.⌝ |

f. 74vb   Preteriri quoque et hoc non debet, qualiter, viso recalcitrandi, quod
1115 olim conceperat, tempore iam idoneo et consilio quoque a magistro dato,
nacta scilicet hoc audendi occasione ob altercaciones quasdam inter
officiales nostros et episcopales in absencia nostra factas super obven-
cionibus et proventibus inter episcopum et archidiaconum nec recte,
ut visum est nostris et ⌜forsitan⌝ vere, nec legitime divisis, nepos noster
1120 ad asperius inde scribendum nos excitare non cessavit, dicens et sepius
inculcans dedecus esse magnum si tales iniurias et tantas nobis et ipsi,
qui in ⌜nostra⌝ custodia fuit, irrogatas, ne in consequenciam traherentur,
clausis oculis per ignaviam transiremus, quatinus scilicet exacerbato sic
episcopo, quoniam obsequium amicos, veritas odium parit, et quoniam
1125 cum catulo ludere solet iocundius esse, et quoniam in aqua turbida
piscacio bona, conceptum facinus, ipso favente, promcius et liberius
effectui mancipare valeret.

⌜Verumtamen oculum hunc non simplicem in viro ⌜⌜(utinam bene!)⌝⌝
perfecto, probo ⌜quoque⌝ ac discreto, simplicitatis et veritatis amico,

---

1111 dulcisonam] *V* dulcissonam, s *expuncto*

1096–9. Cf. Jerome, *Commentarium in Michaeam*, ii, v (Migne, *P.L.* 25, col. 1201):
'Quantum ergo possum mea recolere memoria, numquam venatorem in bonam partem
legi. Ismael et Esau venatores fuerunt.'

pastimes.' Consider how your adult years, since you got your beard, in concord with your depraved and corrupt nature, are unable to go against the studies and habits of your youth which we have described above, and are continually concerned only with the frivolous and useless.

It is written in Genesis that Ishmael, son of Abraham, grew up to be a young archer, and Esau, son of Isaac, grew up to be a huntsman; but rarely does Holy Writ mention archers or huntsmen in a good light. Again Jubal, a direct descendant of Cain and Lamech, the first murderers, as well as bigamists and adulterers, is described as the father of those who sing at the harp and organ, and the inventor of harmonious music, with the result that shepherding—a job regulated and made distinguished by his elder brother Jabel—was turned into a lascivious activity. As the poet says: 'Tityrus, lying in the shade of a spreading beech-tree, you play woodland music on your slender oaten pipe.' In this action and activity what else is shown other than, as in your youth, a craze for music and the delight and vanity of the soft and easy life? As the prophet says: 'Unto what delight wilt thou become dissolute, fickle daughter?' So, in a similar way, we can say, 'Unto what delight wilt thou become dissolute, fickle son?' For this reason, when Alexander of Macedonia happened to hear a sweet-sounding harp, he immediately cut its strings. When asked why he did this, he replied that it was better for its strings to be cut than the heart-strings.

We must not ignore how he saw a suitable occasion for kicking against the pricks, as he had once decided, and counselled by his tutor, he took the opportunity to risk it because of disputes between our officials and the bishop's that had arisen in our absence over incomes and proceeds that had been incorrectly, and, as seemed to be the case to our officials, illegally divided between the bishop and the archdeacon. Our nephew continually urged us to write with a certain amount of asperity; he frequently drove home the point that it was a great disgrace that because of idleness we should pass over with eyes closed such great damage to ourselves and to him, who was under our protection, to prevent them becoming a precedent, so that by angering the bishop he could more easily and rapidly put into effect the crime he had dreamt up with his prompting, since flattery makes friends, and the truth causes hatred, because it is generally more pleasant to play with the pup, and because fishing is good in troubled waters.

1096–8. Cf. Gen. xvi and xxv.   1099–1103. Cf. Gen. iv.
1105–6. Virgil, *Bucolica* i, 1–2.   1109–10. Jer. xxxi, 22.
1111–13. Not identified; also referred to in the *Topographia Hibernica* (*Op.* v, 156).
1125. in aqua turbida] Cf. *supra*, 301, 1033–4.

1130 sciente nimirum ⌐quoniam⌐ *qui ambulat simpliciter ambulat confiden-*
ter, cuius nempe mores omnino cum bonis, quamquam eiusdem iam
pridem vita cum malis ⌐quoniam Abel esse renuit quem Chaim malicia
non exercet⌐, vir animo duplex et dolosus frustra quesivit.⌐ Set ecce
quam indolis egregie factum in facinus conversum; ecce ad quale
1135 studium eius ingenium et quam laudabile datum! Unde cum Propheta
non semel, set sepius dicere possumus: *Seminavimus triticum et spinas*
messuimus.

⌐Ad hec etiam, quod nimie nequicie et nequitatis innate nimis evidens indicium fuit, literas omnes ad eius instanciam, ut diximus, et ob
1140 archilevitice dignitatis honorem, quem ei minus caute contulimus in
solita et debita integritate, pariter ac libertate, servandum, a nobis
emissas, quibus tam episcopi quam archidiaconi iura, nobis olim arte
simul et usu non incognita, certo cercius ab invicem distinximus atque
utriusque ⌐propria⌐ ab alio non usurpanda evidenter explanavimus,
1145 cotidie mane, dum nos vel in ecclesia vel in scolis extitimus, nepos iste
noster, clam intrando cameram nostram, revolutis libris ac cedulis
nostris, puta cui nimirum aditus ad secretiora nostra cuncta patebant,
manu propria, sicut ipse pluries postea minus discrete iactitavit, tanquam re bene et laudabiliter in hoc gesta, maliciose transcripsit easque,
1150 postmodum simul tanquam in libellum consertas et toxico magistri sui
conglutinatas, ubi et de veneno suo non modicam, ut credimus, partem
adiecit, dicto dioces⌐i⌐ano episcopo, ad animum eius contra nos ex-
asperandum et conceptum facinus, episcopo sibi sic placato et in nos
exacerbato, tucius aggrediendum, tanquam ipsi fidelis, set nobis, cui
1155 plus debebat, ⌐quia quicquid alicui preter merita bona et beneficia,
etiam inmoderate, collata deberi potuit⌐, penitus ⌐ingratus et⌐ infidelis, acerba quidem et aspera libamenta premisit. ⌐Que utinam,
sicut prava fuerant et perversa, sic tanquam frivola et vana apud
modestie virum et paciencie, et cuiusmodi de fonte illa manarunt,
1160 quoniam *arbore de tali talia poma cadunt,* ⌐non⌐ ignorantem, et quam
fidem in homine fidei tenerime ipse invenire posset certissimis abhinc
indiciis coniectare valentem, suscepta fuissent, nec pontificis animum,
quem nichil amplecti decet preter honestum quique illud Apostoli
ignorare non debuit: *Noli vinci a malo, set vince in bono malum,* ad

---

1138–1218 *haec additio scripta est alia manu in magna schedula qua factum est folium*
75ʳ et 75ᵛ   1143 distinximus] *V* distincximus   1157–66 *haec additio scripta*
est in margine f. 75ʳ alia manu   1160 ignorantem] ignor *scriptum est in rasura*

1130–1. Prov. x, 9.
1136–7. Cf. Jer. xii, 13, and *supra,* note on 530.

But this deceitful rogue vainly put the evil eye on a righteous (would he were absolutely!) man, who was honest and wise, a lover of simplicity and truth, who knew that the man who walks in simplicity walks in confidence, and whose morals were among the good, though his life to that time was among the wicked, since he refused to be an Abel whom Cain does not vex with wickedness. Consider how the action of that noble character was turned to crime. Consider what study he turned his mind to and how laudable was his gift. So we can say with the Prophet, not once but many times: 'We have sown wheat and reaped thorns.'

In addition to this there was another clear indication of his excessive wickedness and innate dishonesty. While we were either in church or at school, every morning that nephew of ours secretly entered our chamber, unrolled all our books and schedules (because to him the entrances to all our secrets lay open) and with his own hand, as he often later boasted with all too little discretion, as if it had been a job well done and deserving praise, he transcribed all the letters which we had sent at his insistence and to keep the honour of his archidiaconal dignity, which we had granted him with too little caution, in its usual, proper state of immunity as well as freedom; in these we distinguished positively and individually the rights of a bishop and an archdeacon, which we once knew quite well by skill and practice, and we clearly explained that the individual rights of each were not to be usurped by the other. They were afterwards put together into a pamphlet and collected with the poisonous malice of his tutor (and, we believe, he added a considerable part of his own venom), and he sent this bitter and biting sample to the diocesan bishop, to stir up his wrath against us; once he had pleased the bishop in this way, and angered him against us, to start on the course of the crime he had thought up in greater safety, as if he was faithful to the bishop and totally ungrateful and unfaithful to us, to whom he owed more (for what could he have owed to anyone except the goods he deserved and the benefices, conferred even excessively?). Just as these writings had been wicked and depraved, we wish that they had been accepted as frivolous and vain by a man of moderation and toleration, who was aware of the sort of source they came from, because fruit of a kind comes from a tree of its kind, and who could conjecture from these very clear signs what faith he could find in a man of very little faith, and we wish that he had not stirred up the bishop's mind to foster such wicked, outrageous, and pernicious crimes by his example, since the bishop ought

1160. arbore de tali talia poma cadunt] A frequent proverb with many variations, cf. H. Walther, *Lateinische Sprichwörter*, nos. 1257a, 1260, 5132, etc.
1164. Rom. xii, 21.

1165 turpia fovendum et enormia exemplo⌐que⌐ tam perniciosa commovissent.⌐

Preterea, quod indubitanter post Iude prodicionem scelera cuncta, sua immanitate pariter et inhumanitate, longe transcellit, nepos hic noster scripta historica de diversis materiis olim a nobis edita parum
1170 ante discessum suum plus solito, set maliciose magis quam studiose, revolvens, quia parum lectioni aut libris intendere consuevit, quecumque vel ipse vel magister suus | de hospicio nostro et mensa nostra capitales, nobis quidem de ipsis nil tale ⌐tunc⌐ verentibus aut suspicantibus, insidias uterque pretendens, tanquam in maiorum suggilla-
1175 cionem, sicut interdum fieri solet, emissa, veluti pape et curie romane, regum quoque et principum nostrorum, quorum, etsi boni sint mores, quia nichil humanum omnino perfectum, fieri tamen possent meliores, valde diligenter ambo in cedulis suis exceperunt, quatinus, si tam ⌐s⌐celerose paulo post occupata pacifice tenere non possent, statim de
1180 libris nostris nos accusare et, tamquam telis propriis nos impetere et vulnerare nitentes, apud utramque potestatem nos, tanquam maiestatis reos pubplice deferrent, sicut iam minati sunt pluries et minantur, quatinus vel sic nobis abster⌐r⌐itis silencium inponere possent, et tunc occupata, etsi non recte, quocumque modo, quippe quos nichil pudet
1185 dummodo iuvet, iuxta poeticum illud:

Unde habeas querit nemo, set oportet habere,

saltem turpiter cumque capello qui deleri non potest et capella quoque, set delebili, retinere valerent.

Set nonne nepos hic talis, etsi aliud quicquam in causa non esset,
1190 set cetera sepulta vicia forent, hoc unico scelere se vere a nepa tam natum esse probaret quam nominatum? Nonne ⌐et⌐ hos ambos, magistrum et discipulum talem, in tanta familiaritate circa nos habitos, quia revera familiares inimici et domestici semper pestilentissimi, tanquam mures in pera vel pocius serpentes in sinu, nimis inprudenter enutrivi-
1195 mus? Discant ergo ceteri hoc nostro exemplo caucius de cetero negociari. Quamquam igitur istorum utrique proprie nimis, precipue tamen et magis proprie, nepoti tali, propter iura nature pariter et nutriture ab ipso violata, illud Marcialis Coci poterit adaptari, qui | ad quendam apostrophando ⌐viciosissimum⌐ satis lepide satisque facete sic ait:

1200 *Mentitur qui te viciosum, Zoile, dicit:*
Non viciosus homo es, Zoile, set vicium.

1172 *hic legitur in f.* 75rb   1181 *maiestatis*] *V* magestatis *postea correctum*
1196 *post* nimis *legitur in margine haec additio:* possit utrumque *quae comprehensibilis*
non videtur   1198 *hic legitur in f.* 75va

to pursue nothing but the honourable, and should not have forgotten the Apostle's precept: 'Be not overcome by evil: but overcome evil by good.'

Moreover, since he certainly far surpassed all the crimes since the betrayal of Judas in his barbarism and inhumanity, that nephew of ours studied more than usually, a little before his departure, the historical writings on various topics which we once published, out of malice rather than keenness, since he usually gave but little attention to reading and books, and whatever we said in our hospice or at table either he or his tutor claimed to be a plot punishable by death, though we then feared or suspected nothing of this about them, as if we had said these things to affront our betters, as occasionally happens—such as the pope, the Roman curia, and our kings and princes: for though their morals are good, since nothing mortal is absolutely perfect, they could be made better. They made very careful excerpts in their schedules, so that, if they could not keep peacefully what they stole shortly afterwards, they would immediately try to accuse us from our own books, and, as it were, to attack and wound us with our own weapons, and they would denounce us for treason to the powers temporal and ecclesiastical, as they have often threatened and still do. Since they are ashamed of nothing as long as it helps them (as the poet says: 'No one will ask where you got it from, but you should have it'), their intention was to be able to impose silence on us by scaring us away in this manner, so that they could then hold on to what they had taken, although not of right, by whatever means, along with the small goat which cannot be destroyed and also with the destructible chapel.

Surely, even if there was nothing else in his case, but all the rest of his faults lay buried, by this one single crime our nephew would prove that he is both born from and named after the scorpion. Surely we have raised these two all too foolishly, the master and the pupil, whom we had as friends, like mice in a bag, and snakes in the bosom, since in fact friends and servants are the most vicious enemies? Let others learn from this example of ours to conduct their business more carefully in future. We could apply that quip of Martialis Cocus properly to both of them, but in fact it could be applied more properly to our nephew because of his violations of the law of nature and guardianship: he addressed a particularly wicked character in the following sharp and witty way: 'Zoilus, the man who calls you wicked is a liar. You are not a wicked man, Zoilus, you are wickedness personified.' The witticism,

1186. Juvenal, xiv, 207, cf. *supra*, 282–3; quoted also in *Speculum Ecclesie* (*Op*. iv, p. 156) and in *De Iure et Statu Menevensis Ecclesiae* (*Op*. iii, 131).
1193. Cf. Mic. vii, 6, and Matt. x, 36: *inimici hominis domestici eius*.
1200–1. Martial, *Epig*. xi, 92.

Illud autem comicum de servo quodam nequissimo et sub eodem tropo similiter emphatice dictum illi magistro tali poterit non incompetenter adaptari: *Davus est ipsum scelus.*⌐

1205 ⌐Caveant itaque prudentes et caucius agant, et quos tanquam in sinu secum enutrire voluerint intus et in cute primum agnoscant et hec sapientum eloquia mente reponant: *Felix quem faciunt aliena pericula cautum.—Erudiunt plerumque bonos exempla malorum.—Ruina precedencium posteros docet et caucio est semper in reliquum lapsus anterior.*

1210 Verum, quia *pravum* est *cor hominis et inscrutabile, quis cognoscet illud?* Domestici proditoris insidias, cui fides in omnibus habita et cui de secretis nichil absconditum, quis evitare vel precavere valebit?⌐

⌐Verum, etsi ab homine scelus hoc impunitum forte transiret, credere non possumus quod a vindice summo et iudice sup⌐p⌐remo tam

1215 turpium et tam detestabilium ulcio non sumeretur, quoniam, ut ait Jeremias, ⌐qui⌐ *pacem cum amico suo loquitur et occulte ponit ei insidias. Numquid super hiis non visitabo, dicit Dominus? Aut in gente huiuscemodi non ulciscetur anima mea?*⌐

Sane movere quempiam poterit cur talem qualem ⌐nepotem⌐ hunc

1220 ⌐nostrum⌐ depinximus, non solum adultum, set et puerum, tantopere postmodum promovere curavimus. Ad quod respondemus quia patris eius optimi et fratris nostri primevi gracia, qui nos, inter ultima verba

f. 77ʳᵃ nobis cum lacrimis | dicta, pro ipso tam affectuose rogavit, quoniam ei nomen nostrum in baptismo dederat ipsumque propter nos et ob

1225 fiduciam nostri litteris addixerat, eius promocioni, quem nostre totaliter cure commendabat, pro loco et tempore intenderemus. Propter hoc, inquam, et non propter indolem ullam vel naturam quam in eo videremus bonam, quia non nisi detestabilem semper et perversam eius profectibus invigilavimus.

1230 ⌐Unde venerabilis Menevensis antistes Gaufredus, vir litterati ingenii et discreti, ⌐in partem neutram adhuc declinans⌐, nepotem hunc nostrum ⌐in primis⌐ intuens, et per gestuum suorum ac sint⌐h⌐omatum motus ac modos naturam hominis plene perpendens, puta qui preter ceteras scienciarum dotes plurimas in naturalibus et phisicis facultatibus

1235 erat excellentissimus, nobis secreto loquens: 'Adolescens, inquit, iste, nisi freno vestro cohiberetur, nimis effrenis et indomabilis procul dubio foret.' Ille autem non longo post tempore, frenum nostrum prorsus

---

1205–12 *haec additio scripta est eadem manu atque praecedens* 1213–18 *hanc additionem scripsit alia manus* 1217 in gente] *V* ingentem 1219 *hic redimus ad* f. 74ᵛ, *scriptum prima manu* 1230–40 *haec additio legitur in schedula qua factum est folium 76ᵛ*

1204. scelus] Allusion to Terence, *Andria*, but not verbatim, cf. l. 607: *ubi illic est scelus . . .* 1207–8. Cf. *supra*, notes on part i, 292–4.

which was made in the same emphatic fashion about a particularly wicked slave, could quite competently be applied to that tutor of yours: 'Davus is crime itself.'

Let wise men take care and let them act with greater caution, and let them recognize those whom they wish to adopt into the bosom of their family both inwardly and externally. Let them take to heart the precepts of the philosophers. 'The man whom others' perils make cautious is fortunate.' 'The lessons of the wicked very often teach the good.' 'The disaster of former generations teaches future generations, and the former sinner is always more cautious in future.' But, since the heart of man is deceitful and wicked, who can know it? Who can avoid or forecast the plot of a domestic betrayer who has been completely trusted and from whom no secret had been hidden?

But, even if this crime were to go unpunished by man, we cannot believe that revenge for such wicked and detestable crimes would not be taken by the highest punisher and the supreme judge, since as Jeremiah says, 'with his mouth one speaketh in peace with his friend, and secretly he lieth in wait for him. Shall I not visit them for these things, saith the Lord? Or shall not my soul be revenged on such a nation?'

Indeed, it could be asked why we took such pains at all to promote such a nephew as that of ours we have depicted both as an adult and as a child. We reply that it was for the sake of his excellent father, our eldest brother, who among his last tearful words to us pleaded affectingly on his behalf, since he had given him our name at his baptism, and because of us and his faith in us he had destined him for the arts, that we should give our attention at the right time and place to his promotion, since he commended him completely to our care. For this reason we supervised his progress, not because we saw any good character or nature in him, since we saw nothing but a detestable and wicked character.

So, Geoffrey, the venerable bishop of St. David's, an educated and wise man, who, when still impartial, looked at that nephew of ours, and gave full consideration to the nature of the man by the actions and manners of his habits and symptoms (remember, apart from the rest of his very many knowledgeable gifts he was unsurpassed for his natural and medical abilities) told us in private: 'That lad will certainly be unrestrained and uncontrollable, unless he is curbed by you.' However, not long afterwards by casting off completely our curbs,

---

1208–9. Ennodius *Vita S. Epiphanii* (Migne, *P.L.* 63, col. 227); cf. also *supra*, part i, 295–6.

1210–11. Jer. xvii, 9; cf. *supra*, 914–15.   1216–18. Jer. ix, 8–9.

abiciens, et tanquam iuvencus indomitus discipline pariter et doctrine iugum omne detrectans, verbum viri boni atque periti nimia veritate
1240 complevit.⌐

Pro talibus itaque nepotibus, quibus promovendis, quamquam indignis, in clero constituti viri magni et dignitate conspicui nimis indulgere solebant, papa Alexander tercius dicere consuevit, aliis ut liberius reprehenderet, se connumerando: *Filios nobis Deus abstulit,*
1245 *nepotes autem diabolus dedit.*

⌐Audiamus etiam quid in talium et tam carnalium suggilacionem Ieronimus dicat: *Multa nos,* inquit, *facere cogit affectus et, dum corporum propinquitates respicimus, corporis et anime creatorem offendimus. Multi nempe, dum parentum miserentur, animas perdiderunt.* Proinde,
1250 sicut iusto Dei iudicio, per filios illegitime vel etiam illicite genitos vexari plerumque videmus, in terris et ob terras, progenitores; sic et qui suorum promociones per cessiones aut procuratas utcumque, carne, non spiritu revelante, successiones, que sine peccato vix provenire solent, tantopere curant, per eosdem sic promotos vexari pereque con-
1255 tingit et turbari.⌐

⌐Item, quoniam precentoris Parisiensis magistri Petri tam vita quam doctrina imitabilis nobis esse videtur, verbis suis propriis, que in Summa sua que Verbum Adbreviatum dicitur ad hec inducit, et hic utemur. Ait enim: *Consanguineis dabis de proprio, de patrimonio scilicet tuo, non*
1260 *Christi sanguine ipsius adquisito, cuius dispensacio credita est ecclesiasticis viris, ut illud pauperibus distribuant. Ob hoc enim precepit Dominus in lege, ut talis eligatur sacerdos qui dicat patri et matri: Nescio vos. Set numquid consanguineo meo, et bono et probo, non dabo de patrimonio crucifixi? Non, ut eum erigas columpnam ecclesie sive in ecclesia propter*
1265 *perniciem exempli. Non enim consideratur quod bono dederis, set quod consanguineo, ut illud trahant in exemplum* gracie, ita ut, quod tu das gracie, alii exemplo tui dabunt nature. De patrimonio vero Christi consanguineo probo dare poteris ad sustentacionem. *Gratis enim confertur. Unde et pocius gracie, immo soli gracie, debet conferri, non nature,*

1244 *post* liberius, se *expunctum est*   1246 *haec additio scripta est in f. 76^v*
1256–81 *haec additio, quae sequitur praecedentem in f. 76^v, scripta est alia manu*
1256 *In voce* Item *littera* i *praevisa est ut rubricata, sed non effecta est*   1260 cuius *et quod sequitur legimus in f. 75^v*

1244–5. Petrus Cantor, *Verbum Abbreviatum,* chapter 71 (Migne, *P.L.* 205, col. 211). The same quotation occurs in the *Gemma Ecclesiastica* (*Op.* ii, p. 304) and in the *Vita S. Remigii* (*Op.* vii, 66).

1247–9. Ieronimus] Jerome, *Ep.* lxiv, 4, *Ad Fabiolam de veste sacerdotis* (Migne, *P.L.* 22, col. 610): *Multa nos facere cogit affectus carnalis; et dum corporum propinquitates respicimus, corporis et anime creatorem offendimus.* This quotation would appear to have been taken not directly from Jerome's correspondence, but from Petrus Cantor,

and like an unbroken beast shrugging off the yoke of discipline and education completely, our nephew proved as only too true the statement of an honourable and experienced man.

Pope Alexander III, counting himself among the rest, so that he might find fault more easily, used to say of such nephews whose promotion great men of the clergy and men of outstanding dignity used to take pains over, though they were unworthy: 'God has robbed us of our sons, but the Devil has provided us with nephews.'

Consider what Jerome says to rebuke such men given to worldly pleasures: 'Affection makes us do many things, and, when we consider relationships of the flesh, we offend the creator of the body and the soul. There are many who, while feeling pity for their parents, have lost their souls.' Thus, by God's strict judgement, we find that a great many sires on earth have been troubled on account of their estates by sons whom they have illegitimately or even illicitly begotten. In the same way, too, those who take pains over the promotion of their relatives by resignations or successions caused by the promptings of the flesh, not the spirit, which can rarely be done without sinning, are troubled and disturbed by those they promote.

Since we hold in esteem the life and teaching of Master Petrus Cantor of Paris, we will use here his words which he introduced on this subject into the 'Summa' which is called the *Verbum Abbreviatum*. He says: 'Give to your relatives from what is your own, i.e. from your own patrimony, not from what you have acquired by the blood of Christ. The dispensation of this is entrusted to men of the Church to be distributed to the poor. For this reason the Lord commands in the law to choose the priest who tells his father and mother: "I know you not." But why shall I not give to a relative of mine who is upright and honest, from the patrimony of the Crucified? Not if it means your setting him up as a pillar of the Church and in the Church; because of the infectious result of the precedent. The point is not that you give it to a good man, but that you give it to a relative, so that they make it an example of grace, with the result that, what you give for merit, others, following your precedent, will give for natural affection. You will be able to give to an honest relative from Christ's patrimony for his sustenance. This is given free. Thus you ought to give it rather for grace, and grace alone, not natural

---

Verbum Abbreviatum, chapter 71, *De suggestione carnalis affectus* (Migne, *P.L.* 205, col. 210D).

1259–66. Petrus Cantor, *Verbum Abbreviatum*, chapter 47 (Migne, *P.L.* 205, col. 149), with minor variations.   1264. Deut. xxxiii, 9.

1268–77. Petrus Cantor, *Verbum Abbreviatum*, chapter 47 (Migne, *P.L.* 205, col. 149), with minor variations.

1270 *carnalitati. Unde in Vitis patrum: Mi abba, dabone elemosinam parenti,*
filio vel consanguineo?—Respondit Abas: Non.—Quare, mi aba?—Quia
modicum sanguinis te trahit. Vicio nunquam dederis, quia paria sunt
indignis dare et demonibus immolare. Sic enim diligendi sunt peccatores,
ut non diligantur eorum errores. Item, si dispensatores rerum multitudinis,
1275 scilicet septem diaconi ab apostolis constituti, *laucius quibusdam, quia*
consanguineis, distribuissent, credo quod eodem fulmine percussi essent
a Petro, quo Ananias et Saphira. Nos igitur quia, carne revelante, non
spiritu, garcioni indolis a puerilibus annis abiectissime et per omnia
desperatissime, columpnam erigi in ecclesia procuravimus, digno Dei
1280 iudicio, temporali flagello gravique cum scandalo et rerum detrimento
puniti sumus.⌐

Quociens igitur, ut ad vos verba vertamus, animum vestrum natura
perversa pungit et ad scelerosa propellit, literas istas pre manibus et
oculis in secreto tanquam speculum habeatis, in quo mores et modos ac
1285 gestus vestros inspicere possitis, et sic eos vel mutare prorsus, si fieri posset, quoniam omni doctrina longe forcior est natura, vel saltem minuere
et mitigare curetis. Quod, nisi feceritis, set pocius passibus assumptis
et assuetis hactenus incedere perstiteritis, dampno vobis et dedecori
vestris existens, totus in trenos ire poteritis. Et illud quoque prophete
1290 vere quidem in vestra persona pronunciare: *Ve mihi, mater mea.*
Quare genuisti me similem tibi, virum rixe, virum discordie, virum ne-
quicie, et ignominie in universa terra? Et illud eiusdem: Maledicta dies
f. 77ʳᵇ *in qua natus sum, dies | in qua peperit me mater mea. Maledictus vir qui*
annunciavit patri meo, dicens: Natus est tibi puer masculus, et quasi gaudio
1295 *letificavit eum.* Et post pauca: *Quare enim de vulva egressus sum, ut*
viderem laborem et dolorem et consumerentur in confusione dies mei?
⌐Item, et iuxta doctrinam Salomonis in Parabolis, ⌐hiis ad hanc verbis
utentis⌐: *Cave ne gemas in novissimis et dicas: Cur detestatus sum*
disciplinam et increpacionibus non adquievit cor meum, nec audivi vocem
1300 *docencium me et magistris non inclinavi aurem meam? Set pene fui semper*
in omni malo.⌐

Parvas litteras nostras primo vobis post discessum vestrum missas
nimie brevitatis arguistis ⌐: parvum amicum parvas vobis litteras misisse,
solita parvi capitis discrecione rescribendo. Verius autem, ut credimus,

---

1270 Vitis] *V* Vitas   1282 *hic redimus ad f. 77ʳ*   1297–8 *haec additio* (hiis
. . . utentis) *scripta est alia manu*

1290–2. Cf. Jer. xv, 10: *Vae mihi, mater mea: quare genuisti me virum rixae, virum*
discordiae in universa terra!
1292–5. Jer. xx, 14–15.

affection and fleshly relationship. As it says in the *Lives of the Fathers*:
"My Lord Abbot, shall I give alms to a parent, son, or relative of mine?"
"No", said the abbot. "Why not, my Lord Abbot?" "Because a mere
blood relationship urges you. You should never yield to this vice, since to
give to the undeserving and to sacrifice to the devil are equal sins."
Sinners are to be loved in such a way that it is not their sins which are
loved. Again if those dispensers of the people's possessions, the seven
deacons appointed by the apostles, were to have given more lavishly to
some because they were relatives, I believe Peter would have struck them
with the same bolt with which he struck Ananias and Sapphira.' Because
of the promptings of the flesh, rather than the spirit, we tried to set up
a scoundrel, who from his childhood years has had a most despicable
character, as a pillar in the Church, and because of this, by God's judgement, which we deserved, we were punished with a temporary scourging
and with a terrible scandal and loss of property.

To return to you: whenever your wicked nature makes its presence
felt in your mind, and pushes you on to the path of crime, keep this
letter at hand for your private examination like a mirror, in which you
can see your morals, manners, and habits, and thus be able to change
them, if it can be done (for nature is far stronger than any teaching),
or at least moderate and temper them. But if you do not do this, but
rather persist in going along the path you started on and have grown used
to, to your own loss and the disgrace of your family, you can go to hell.
You will be able to pronounce the Prophet's curse over yourself: 'Woe
is me, my mother! Why hast thou borne me like unto you, a man of
strife, a man of contention, a man of wickedness and disgrace to all the
earth?' And again: 'Cursed be the day wherein I was born: let not the
day in which my mother bore me be blessed. Cursed be the man that
brought the tidings to my father, saying: A man child is born to thee:
and made him greatly rejoice'; and a little later: 'Why came I out of the
womb to see labour and sorrow, and that my days should be spent in
confusion?' Again, as Solomon teaches in Proverbs in the following
words: 'And beware thou mourn not at the last and say: Why have I
hated instruction, and why has my heart consented not to reproof; and
why have I not heard the voice of them that taught me, and not inclined
my ear to the master? I have almost always been in all evil.'

You complained that the short letter we sent you a little after your
departure was too brief. You wrote back with the usual wisdom of that
tiny head of yours that a mean friend had sent a mean letter. You should,

1295–6. Jer. xx, 18.
1298–1301. Prov. v, 11–14.

1305 doctorem prodicionis amicum vobis modicum et discipulum perdicionis pariter et prodicionis, tam docilem in hiis et tam ingeniosum et
industrium, amicum sibi ipsi minimum, quin immo et maximum absque
dubio reputare potestis inimicum⌐. Ideoque ⌐litteras⌐ nunc longiores
habeatis. Materiam namque scribendi diffusam nobis, cum inopinatis
1310 simul rerum eventibus, doctor talis et discipulus iam dederunt. Quoniam
enimvero *opere* simul *et inpense per*dite dampnum hominisque tocius,
quod plus est, perditi dolor inportune verba ministrat et quoniam,
ga⌐r⌐rula semper et in hoc solo fortis, scaturire solet sermone senectus,
⌐quamquam tamen, Ieronimo testante, *librum epistola redolere non*
1315 *debeat*⌐, litteras in epistolam et epistolam accipiatis in libellum conversam. Speculum ergo latum et grande ⌐missum est vobis, in⌐ quo vultus
suos ambos, nature tamen magis quam nativitatis, simul poterunt
doctor et discipulus contemplari.

Scimus autem quod litteras istas magistrum et discipulum, etsi non
1320 plene, tamen ex parte, depingentes, ultrix statim flamma consumet.
Verum per tot manus et ora iam volitarunt et volitabunt, quod comburi
quidem poterunt, ⌐consumi vero et prorsus⌐ aboleri nullatenus poterunt.
⌐Diligencius enim pluribus ex causis preter prescriptas scripsimus
⌐hic⌐ et diffusius, quatinus ad unguem hii duo per hec dinosci possint
1325 ⌐eorumque mala sibique similium melius de cetero vitari ipsique per
hec utrumque corrigi et nos quasi querulo carmine consolari⌐ et, quamquam nobis ista valere nequeant ad medelam, multis tamen in posterum
ea ⌐forte⌐ legentibus proficere possint ad cautelam.⌐

Utinam bene, et longe melius quam speremus, valere possitis!

1330 EXPLICIT SPECULUM DUORUM

1316 *haec additio scripta est postquam* in *rasum est*   1330 Explicit Speculum
duorum *rubrica*

1311. Cf. Macrobius, *Saturnalia* II, iv, 30; cf. *supra*, note on part i, 773–4, and on
part ii, 1042–4.   1314–15. Not identified.

however, we believe, think it more true that the teacher of treachery is a slight friend, and the pupil of ruination and treachery, who is so docile, clever, and industrious in matters like this, is the worst friend to himself and, in fact, is certainly his worst enemy. For this reason, you may now have a longer letter. For this tutor and pupil as well as the unexpected turn of events have already given a considerable amount of material for our writings. Since the loss of work and wasted expense and, what is more important, the grief for the loss of the whole man has persistently helped the flow of words, and since garrulous, and in this case, sturdy old age, usually pours forth a torrent of words (though, as Jerome testifies, 'A letter should not smell like a book'), accept the letter that has become an epistle, and the epistle that has become a book. Therefore we offer you a wide and large mirror in which both tutor and pupil can contemplate the features of their nature rather than their natural faces.

However, we know that the flame of revenge will immediately consume this letter which depicts master and pupil, though not completely, yet to some extent. It has passed and will pass through so many hands and by word of mouth, that it can indeed be burnt, but in no wise can it be truly consumed or altogether destroyed. For various reasons, apart from those mentioned, we have written more carefully and at greater length, so that these two can thereby be recognized, so that the crimes of them and those like them can be seen more easily in future, that they may be rebuked, and finally that we may be consoled by our song of lamentation and, though they can have no remedial effect for us, that they may serve as a warning to all those who may perhaps read it in future.

It is our prayer that you may prosper and prosper far better than we hope.

HERE ENDS THE SPECULUM DUORUM

En tibi quam bellum dat dicta capella capellum
Mensque secuta dolum, tendens ad turpia solum.
Si tibi mens, inquam, fuerit maturior unquam,
Nosces quod nequam tibi rem non fecerit equam,
1335 Cuius germana, multis meretricula plana,
Filia presbiteri, tua propria gaudet haberi.
O quam iactura gravis et commercia dura
Pro re tam vana, tam vili, perdita fama!
Sic decet ingratum non unum ferre reatum:
1340 Te, miser, emenda, mundans te duplice menda.
Sic mage sordescunt, sic semper crimina crescunt,
Ni cito deleta maiori sorte repleta.

1331 *hoc poema scriptum est alia manu*

Oh, what a pretty chaplet that chapel gives you,
   And a mind that pursues guile and is intent on wickedness only.
Were you to have a more mature attitude
   You would realize that it could not make an unfair affair fair.
Your sister, a priest's daughter, whom many use as a downright whore,
   Is glad to be thought of as your own.
What a heavy waste! What hard bargaining,
   For such a trivial, cheap matter, lost reputation.
Thus, an ungrateful wretch should not bear one charge.
   You wretch, mend your ways, clear yourself with a second sin.
Thus they grow filthier: thus crime increases,
   Unless it is quickly destroyed and filled out again with greater things.

EPISTOLARUM PARS

1

f. 78ra *Magistro Albino Herefordensi canonico*

DILECTO suo et utinam digne diligendo magistro Albino Herefordensi canonico magister Giraldus de Barri salutem.

Non absque stupore mentis ad aures nostras pervenisse noveritis,
5 adversarios nostros, immo proditores nequissimos, quorum erga nos tam ingratitudinem apertam quam et nequiciam, ex toto detectam per litteras nostras Herefordensi capitulo semel et iterum super hoc missas, ignorare non potuistis, vestros ⌈non solum⌉ contubernales, verum et conmensales nuper effectos. Nec mirum tamen quod auditorium vestrum
10 et scole doctrinam, que communis omnibus, tam discolis scilicet quam domesticis, esse solet, eis ut ceteris indulsistis; sed hoc revera non mediocriter admirandum nulloque prorsus fuco coloris excusandum, quod eos in hospitio vestro, sicut accepimus, tanquam individuos nocte dieque socios quasi in iniuriam nostram gravem et pristine contemptum
15 amicicie, cum in eodem pectore plene et perfecte simul ac semel contraria consistere nequeant, admisistis. Nec enim ullatenus accidere potest quin eorum, quorum a nobis licet inmeritis tam corda quam corpora simul aversa sunt et adversantia, ora quoque maledica et labia |

f. 78rb dolosa, quoniam *ex habundantia cordis* in verba simul et convitia lingua
20 plerumque resolvi solet, nostri crebrius in audientia vestra, precipue post pocula et hora minus sobria, delationem personent et detractionem. Sicut ergo *duobus dominis* Veritate testante *nemo* perfecte *potest servire*, sic et contrariis omnino moribus, cum omnis vera et constans amicicia proveniat ex morum concordia, unus atque idem animus fideliter ap-
25 plicari non solet.

Ceterum et si veterem amicum fastidio ducens, mutare iam amiciciam moderne novitatis vicio dignum duxeritis, in alios tamen quam adversarios eius, qui paulo ante vobis non displicuit, tam manifestos et tam

---

3 de de Barri *V*   22 potest perfecte *transposuit V*

---

2. Dilecto . . . diligendo] Cf. Ep. 8, 2.
10–11. Cf. Thomas à Kempis, *Serm. ad novicios*, 3, ed. Pohl, *Op.* vi, 1905, p. 23,
9–11: *Qui non vult audire magistrum ut bonus discipulus, hic cum dyscolis verberabitur*

THE LETTERS

[1.] *To Master Albinus, canon of Hereford*

MASTER Giraldus de Barri sends greetings to his beloved (if only he were worthy of that love!) Master Albinus, canon of Hereford.

We should like you to know that it is to our utter amazement that we have heard that our enemies, those most criminal traitors, have recently become not only your comrades but even guests at your table. You could not have been unaware of their open ingratitude towards us, as well as their evil-mindedness, which we revealed completely in more than one letter sent by us to the chapter of Hereford. Although it is not surprising that you have been as kind to them as to anyone else, with your attention and with the teaching of the school, which is open to all, annoying and good pupils alike, yet it is all the more surprising and is excusable by no possible argument, that you have admitted them under your roof, so we understand, as personal friends, day and night. This is a serious personal affront and an insult to our former friendship, since such contradictory attitudes cannot exist harmoniously in one man. Nor can it happen otherwise that, now that they have turned and are turning away from us spiritually and physically (though we deserve better), their spiteful tongues and deceitful lips resound repeatedly in your hearing with scandalous denunciations against us, especially when they are barely sober after a drinking bout; for out of the fullness of the heart the tongue generally breaks into abusive speech. For, just as the truth testifies, no man can perfectly serve two masters, so one and the same attitude of mind cannot be applied consistently to completely opposite ethics, because all true and lasting friendship is produced by a shared moral code.

But even if you should grow tired of an old friend and consider it worth while to change our friendship in this fashionable way, it would have been more fair and decent for the change to have been made in the first friendship towards others than such clearly treacherous enemies of

ut asinus rudis (cf. ibid. 14, p. 104, 13–15: *quod sepe . . . contingere solet tepidis et dyscolis discipulis*). For the original meaning of *dyscolus* see note on Ep. 4, 5.
12. fuco] Cf. Ep. 2, 17; Ep. 7, 277; Ep. 8, 43, 53, 266; *supra*, part i, 318.
13–14. Cf. Ep. 2, 15.
18–19. labia dolosa] Ps. xi, 3 and xxx, 19.   19 habundantia cordis] Matt. xii, 34; Luke vi, 45.
22. Matt. vi, 24 = Luke xvi, 13.

perfidos, prime amicicie fieri mutationem decentius quidem et honestius
30 foret. Porro in Ecclesiastico legitur: *Ne derelinquas amicum anticum,*
novus enim non erit similis illi, et in Sidonio: *Vetustos sodales pro recentium*
novitate non fastidias. Alioquin sic videbere amicis uti ut floribus, tam diu
gratis quam recentibus. Vos itaque videritis. Novit enim deus, qui omnia
34 novit, quia si vobis aut cuidam dilecto nostro similis, quod absit, casus
f. 78ᵛᵃ acciderit, | nullum apud nos omnino proditores huiusmodi refugium
invenirent, nullum a nobis nisi revertendi quamcicius et resipiscendi
consilium prorsus haberent, sed tanquam ethnicos interim et publicanos
tam a nostris quam proborum virorum consortiis omnibus longe alienos
habendos eos absque dubio censeremus.
40   Utinam diu et bene valere possitis et amicicie federa, presertim antique
et non antiquate, firma constantia conservare velitis.

---

29 prime *scripsi coll.* 14–15 et 40] primam *V*

30–1. Ecclus. ix, 14.
31–3. in Sidonio] Ep. iv, 14, 4; *MGH*, AA, viii, 1887, p. 66, 21–3.
33–4. Cf. Ep. 5 265–6; Ep. 8, 113.
40. = Ep. 2, 113–14 = Ep. 5, 279 = Ep. 6, 531; cf. Ep. 8, 354 ff.; *supra*, part ii,
1329.

the man who was recently not displeasing to you. Besides, as it says in Ecclesiasticus: 'Forsake not an old friend: for the new will not be like to him'; and in Sidonius: 'Do not reject old friends for the novelty of the new, but cherish friends as flowers, the old as well as the new.' See yourselves in this light. For God, to whom everything is known, knows that if anything like this should happen to you or anyone dear to us—which God forbid—traitors of this kind would find no shelter under our roof and would certainly receive no further advice, except to return as quickly as possible to their senses. But until then we would certainly regard them as publicans and Gentiles, to be kept far away from us and from all contact with upright men.

It is our prayer that you enjoy good health in future and be willing to uphold and strengthen the bonds of a friendship, especially one which is old, not outdated.

2

*Hugoni decano et Willelmo precentori et Radulfo Folet Here-
fordensi canonico*

SCIRE vos volumus ad aures nostras commeantium relatione pervenisse,
quod nepotis nostri archidiaconi de Brechene, qui aliquantulam apud
5 Herefordiam nuper inter vos moram fecit, mores, modos ac gestus et
conversationem plurimum approbastis, multum quoque mirantes tam
vos quam alii, nos iuvenem tam modestum et tam bene morigeratum
verbis et scriptis tam acerbis corripuisse. Sed utinam nos pocius
9 acerbitatis nimie et delacionis iniurie argui possemus et vere, quam ille
f. 78ᵛᵇ indolis prave et moralitatis perver|se! Verum spacio brevi et tanquam
in transitu per exterioris hominis composi⟨ti⟩onem nequit vel in modico,
nedum ad unguem, interior homo cognosci. Scriptum est enim: *Pravum
cor hominis et inscrutabile, quis cognoscet illud?* Per longam autem insimul
cohabitationem, annuam scilicet vel maiorem, moramque diutinam et
15 individuam nocte dieque conversationem mores hominis et vere nature
qualitas perfectius, ut nostis, et verius perpenduntur. Apparentiam
namque sophisticam plerique pretendere solent, fuco liberalitatis in
verbis et vultu innatam animi nequiciam arte quadam, sed tamen ad
horam, dissimulantes: *nichil* enim *simulatum,* ut ait Symachus, *valet
20 esse diuturnum,* quia revera *quicquid assumitur, proprium non putatur.*
De Iugurta legitur quod simulator fuerit omnium rerum et dissimulator.
Ubi autem vera liberalitas et constans veritas, ibi locum non habet
huiusmodi varietas, sed quibus hec desunt, illis quidem simulatione
opus est et palliatione, per quas tamen coram prudentibus et discretis
25 diu latere non possunt: scriptum est enim quia *frustra rete iacitur ante
f. 79ʳᵃ oculos penna|torum.*

Preterea quidam apud vos, sicut accepimus, epistolam nostram nepoti nostro transmissam et exuberante materia in librum conversam
famosum, ut fertur, libellum vocant, tanquam in nepotis nostri favorem

---

1. Hugh de Mapenor and William Foliot were suggested as candidates for the
bishopric of St. David's in 1203, *Op.* iii, p. 321.
5. nuper] Cf. Ep. 1, 4–9.
7. morigeratum] Cf. *supra,* part i, 324, 997.
12–13. Jer. xvii, 9.   15. Cf. Ep. 1, 13–14.
17. See note on Ep. 1, 12.
19–20. Symachus] *Ep.* i, 1, 6, *MGH,* AA, vi, 1883, p. 2, 21–2: *Omnis quippe osten-
tatio non caret suspicione mendacii, quia quidquid adsumitur, proprium non putatur.*
nichil . . . diuturnum] Cf. Ep. 7, 146–7.

[2.] *To Hugh, the dean, William, the precentor, and Ralph Folet, canon of Hereford*

IT is our desire that you know that we have learnt by report from travellers that you have displayed complete approval of the conduct, manners, and conversation of our nephew, archdeacon of Brecon, who recently sojourned briefly with you at Hereford. You and others are surprised that we have misrepresented this quiet, well-behaved young man with such bitter works and words. But we would rather that we might be found guilty of using too much bitterness and unjust denunciation—and rightly—rather than that he be found guilty of having a corrupt nature and a perverted character. Yet the true self cannot be known even in part, let alone completely, by outward appearances and in a short time during a fleeting visit. For it is written: 'The heart is deceitful above all things and wicked: who can know it?' A man's habits and the quality of his true nature are more perfectly and precisely assessed, as you know, after a long association with him, for a year or more, and by long and close contact with him and conversation at all times of the day. Most people can with a certain, albeit temporary, skill give the impression of wisdom, by disguising their innate wickedness under a mask of affability in the way they talk and look, but they cannot keep it up. For, as Symmachus says: 'Nothing that is a pretence can be kept up for long; since in fact whatever is put on cannot be accepted as sincere.' It is written of Jugurtha that he was a hypocrite and dissembler about everything. Furthermore wherever there is a true noble spirit, and complete integrity, there is no place for inconsistency of this kind, but those who lack it surely need a veneer of falseness and secrecy. However, by these means they cannot stay concealed for long from wise, distinguished men. For it is written: 'The net is spread in vain before the eyes of them that have wings.'

Besides, certain of your circle, so we understand, say that the letter we sent to our nephew (a letter now grown into a book, such was the abundance of material) is a libel; they take it in our nephew's

21. Sallust, *Cat.* v, 4: *Quoius rei lubet simulator ac dissimulator* (= Catilina!); cf. *supra*, part ii, 535, 592.

24–5 (cf. 95). Cf. Ep. 7, 59–60, 137, 172–3.

25–6. Prov. i, 17.

27 ff. Cf. *Symbolum Electorum*, i, 8 (*Op.* i, p. 228, 19 ff.).—epistolam . . . conversam] the *Speculum Duorum*, cf. *supra*, part ii, 1315–16.

29. Cf. Justinian, *Cod.* 9. 36.: 'De famosis libellis'.

30 (qui utinam vere favorabilis in omnibus et apud omnes et valde com-
mendabilis esset, quia revera nemini in mundo, ne sine causa laboraverimus, in ipso tam gratum hoc foret sicut et nobis) et nostram quoque non
obliquam, non indirectam, sed pocius apertam sugillationem, sicut et
alii ibidem librum nostrum *De Invectionibus* intitulatum ratione tituli
35 solum dampnabilem censere volebant. Quibus confutandis satis alias
et alibi responsum fuit, quia tam delicati lectores et tam scrupulosi
libellum *De Invectionibus* Tullii in Salustium et Salustii in Tullium
simili censura dampnabilem reddant, sic et satiricos omnes, morum
assertores laudabilium et contrariorum reprehensores, sic et Ieronimi
40 libros universos, in quibus tam cardinalium quam prelatorum ecclesie
quantumlibet magnorum vicia palpanda non duxit, sic et historias tam
ecclesiasticas quam Romanas necnon et alias cunctas, in quibus historica
veritate pariter et severitate de bonis bona, de malis vero bonis contraria
f. 79rb refe|runtur.

45 Sciant etiam illi, qui in librum *De Invectionibus* tituli intuitu solum
tam acriter invehuntur, quod licet due vel tres epistole prime invective
videantur, sequens tamen opus alia prosequitur et utiliora. Sed mos est
in scripturis a principiis libros denominari, sicut liber Moysi *Genesis*
vocatur, quoniam a mundi generatione inchoatur: modicum tamen
50 auctor in hoc moratur.

Nec mirari quoque vel indignari quispiam debet, si nos provocati
scriptis iniuriosis, ut ex prima patet epistola, et etiam a papa ad rescri-
bendum invitati, verbis verba rependimus et talionis lege respondimus,
cum iuxta comicum illud *qui pergit dicere quod vult, audiet quod non vult*:
55 nondum enim tante perfectionis iter arripuimus, ut pro malis ubique
bona reddendo et illud apostoli per omnia adimplendo: *Noli vinci a
malo, sed vince in bono malum*, et illud apostolorum principis: *Non
reddentes malum pro malo vel maledictum pro maledicto, sed econtrario
benedicentes*, possimus omnino tam indecentium in nos confictione
60 tamque turpium obiectione et in tanta audientia non moveri. Unde ⌈ut⌉

33–44. The same argument, 88 ff. and Ep. 3, 6–21 (Ep. 2, 42–3 = Ep. 3, 8–9).
34–5. Cf. 45 and 97.
35–6. alias et alibi] See *Epistola ad Stephanum Langton* (*Op.* i, pp. 406–7); cf. Ep. 3,
11–22.
36. Cf. Ep. 5, 157; Ep. 7, 214.
42–3. Cf. Ep. 3, 8–9, and *De Iure et Statu Menevensis Ecclesie* (*Op.* iii, p. 373, 12–13).
43. de bonis bona, de malis vero bonis contraria] see the Archpoet, i, 14, 3–4:
redditurus ad pondus proprium | bona bonis, malis contrarium. In his *Speculum Ecclesie*
(*Op.* iv, p. 293) Giraldus quotes verses 11 and 12 of the famous 'Confession': *Tertio
capitulo memoro tabernam . . . deus sit propitius huic potatori.* See also R. B. C. Huygens,
'Die Gedichte von Gillebert', *Sacris Erudiri*, xiii, 1962, pp. 519–86 (Introduction).
45–6. Cf. 34–5 and 96–7.
54. Terence, *Andria*, 920. The same quotation in Ep. 7, 218, *Symbolum Electorum*,
i, 8 (*Op.* i, p. 228, 25–6), and *De Invectionibus*, ed. W. S. Davies, p. 89, 30–1.

favour, and as an insult, moreover, neither indirect nor sly, but open and direct, to us. (If only he could please everyone in every respect and were worthy of praise; this would please no one as much as us, showing that we have not worked in vain!) Likewise, other friends of yours wanted to condemn our book *De Invectionibus* solely because of the title. Enough has already been said elsewhere to disprove their case, as such sensitive and exacting readers should express similar condemnation of the *De Invectionibus* of Cicero against Sallust and of Sallust against Cicero. They should also condemn those who wrote satires, the defenders of worthy behaviour and censors of the opposite, who are in the same position; and the works of Jerome, in which he did not believe in playing down the vices of quite a number of cardinals and leading prelates of the Church; and the historians of Rome and of the Church and of everything else in which, with strict regard for historical accuracy, the good are called good and the evil the opposite.

For those who inveigh against our *De Invectionibus* solely because of its title ought to know that only the first two or three letters seem full of invective, but the rest of the work follows different, more positive lines. But it is the custom in literature to name a book after its first section, just as the book of Moses is called Genesis, since it begins with the creation of the world; but the writer deals only briefly with that subject.

Nor ought anyone to be surprised or indignant that we returned word for word, under provocation from unfair attacks in writing, as is clear from the first letter—and what is more, we were asked to reply by the pope—and our reply was in accordance with the principle of *lex talionis*; as the comic playwright says: 'He who continues to say what he wishes, will hear what he does not wish.' For we have not taken the path of a perfection so great that, by returning good for evil everywhere, and by fulfilling in everything that saying of the Apostle: 'Be not overcome by evil, but overcome evil by good', and that of the leader of the apostles: 'Not rendering evil for evil, not railing for railing, but contrariwise blessing', we can remain altogether unmoved by such a fabricated charge against us of base behaviour, particularly in such company. So

---

55 ff. Cf. Ep. 7, 230–2 and 325 ff. (55, *pro malis*: Rom. xii, 17: *nulli malum pro malo reddentes, providentes bona*). See Ep. 7, 327–8, and *supra*, part ii, 463, 1164.

56–7. Rom. xii, 21; = Ep. 5, 273–4 = Ep. 6, 533–5 = Ep. 7, 327–9.

57–9. 1 Pet. iii, 9.

60–2. *Invectiva*, 1, 1, ed. Kurfess, *Appendix Sallustiana*, 1950, p. 8, 7 and 8, 13–p. 9, 1. The same quotation in the preface to the *De Invectionibus* (i, p. 11, 19–23, ed. Davies, p. 82, 19–22): *Unde et verbis Ciceronis in Invectionibus contra Salustium hic uti liceat: Si forte . . . introduxit.*

et verbis Ciceronis utamur in Salustium: *Si forte offendimini, patres*
f. 79va *conscripti, iustius illi quam michi succen|sere debetis, qui inicium introduxit.*
Ceterum si et hoc obiciat aliquis, quod *post inimicicias ire meminisse*
malorum est, scire pro certo vos volumus et per vos ceteros, quod, extante
65 adhuc et annis postea pluribus archiadversario nostro (quoniam anno
laboris nostri primo, qui per quinquennium post et amplius duravit),
editus in curia libellus hic erat et in publico coram domno papa eiusque
mandato et cardinalibus ⟨in⟩ consistorio primum lecta fuit epistola prima
tam acriter in nos et tam mendaciter emissa, et consequenter responsalis
70 illa secunda cunctorumque communiter applausu commendata plurimum
et approbata.

Nunc autem ad illos, qui libello nostro famosum nomen imponunt,
respondere curavimus: sicut enim a delationis inmunes sunt culpa, qui
falsis omissis tantum veris insistunt, sic et qui super ingratitudinis
75 vicio querimoniam deponendo et ne in simile incidant incomodum tam
presentes quam posteros premuniendo et variis ac veris exemplis et
auctoritatibus, fictis ac falsis omni ex parte remotis, fideliter erudiendo
f. 79vb ad hec solum intendit, ab infamantis est | crimine prorsus inmunis,
presertim vero cum conquerendi intuitu, quatinus nos utcumque quasi
80 querulo carmine consolemur, et corrigendi, quatinus nepos noster
crebra verorum inspectione et ad animum revocatione saltem ob vere-
cundiam emendetur, et premuniendi ceteros, ut in casibus similibus
discant decetero caucius negociari, cum hoc, inquam, affectu solum
et proposito singula proponantur, non infamandi, quia *quicquid agant*
85 *homines, intentio iudicat omnes,* quamquam tamen aliqua revera, immo
pleraque videantur inserta, que male meriti maleque morigerati et
prorsus ingrati famam et opinionem non inmerito ledere possint.

Verum eodem intuitu censuraque consimili epistolam domni pape
nuper Francorum regi directam, que sic incipit: *Non absque dolore*
90 *recolimus,* illi quoque famosum libellum vocare poterunt, quoniam

---

64 certo vos *bis, alt. del.* V   69–70 illa responsalis *transposuit* V

63–4. *Disticha Catonis,* 2, 15, 2; the same quotation in the *Descriptio Kambriae,* 2, 9
(*Op.* vi, p. 223, 11).   64. Cf. Ep. 5, 18–19, and 7, 7; *supra,* part i, 1019.
65 (–71). archiadversario nostro] Hubert Walter, archbishop of Canterbury, author
of the first letter in the *De Invectionibus* (1. 1) (see line 68), the second letter (*re-*
sponsalis illa secunda: 69–70) being Giraldus' answer. Cf. Ep. 7, 205–6 and *De Iure et*
Statu, etc., 6 (*Op.* iii, p. 307, 20): *archiadversario instigante;* cf. *supra,* part i, 474.
79–80. Cf. Ep. 4, 13; Ep. 6, 3 and 520; *supra,* part ii, 1326.
84–5. Cf. the *Iocalis,* ed. Lehmann, *Sitzungsberichte,* München, Phil.-hist. Abt.,
1938, Heft IV, 5, p. 60, 44: *Quidquid agant homines, intencio iudicat omnes;* J. Werner,
Lateinische Sprichwörter und Sinnsprüche des Mittelalters, 2nd edn., 1966, p. 102, no.
172: *Quidquid agunt . . .; Bibliotheca Casinensis,* iv, 1880 (Florilegium), p. 194, col. 2:
Sola voluntatis forma monetat opus | Quicquid agant homines, intentio iudicat omnes; the
pentameter also in Simon Mulart (s. xv): *De ortu, victoria et triumpho domini Karoli*

we may borrow the very words of Cicero against Sallust: 'If you are greatly displeased, senators, your anger would be more justly directed against the man who is the source of it rather than against me.'

But if anyone objects that it is wrong to cast up old grievances after a broken friendship, it is our desire that you, and others through you, realize clearly that this pamphlet was compiled in the Roman curia while our archenemy was alive and for a number of years after that (during the first year of our labours which lasted for five years and more). Furthermore the first letter, composed with such bitterness and full of distortions against us, and next the second in reply, strongly commended and approved by the general applause of all, were read out initially at the command of the Lord Pope, before himself and the consistory of cardinals.

Now, however, it is our concern to reply to those men who call our pamphlet libellous; for, just as men are free from the sin of false testimony if they stress the truth and ignore falsehood, similarly, too the man who complains of ingratitude as a vice and warns his contemporaries and posterity so that they may not meet with similar distressing circumstances and who painstakingly educates them by citing true-life examples and by quoting various authors, cases which are far removed from all invention and falsehood, and devotes himself solely to these things is altogether free of the charge of slander. For the purpose of this book is to complain—so that we are comforted somehow with this plaintive song; and to reform—so that our nephew, by seeing the truth frequently and keeping it in mind, should be set on the right course by truthfulness; and to warn others—so that they should learn to act with greater circumspection in future when similar circumstances arise: since, I say, the individual charges are put forward with this idea and intention alone, not of slandering, because 'whatever a man does he is judged by his intentions', although truly, however, some of the charges, indeed most of these included, appear to be of the kind which could not undeservedly damage the reputation and standing of an unworthy, badly behaved, and ungrateful person.

Libellous is what those people can call the letter which the Lord Pope recently sent to the King of France, written with the same view and containing similar criticism. It begins: 'It is not without grief that we

ducis Borgundie moderni, ed. P. C. Boeren, *Twee Maaslandse dichters in dienst van Karel de Stoute* (The Hague, 1968), p. 201 n. 5.

86. Cf. Plautus, *Epidicus* 607: *male morigerus*; cf. note on 7, and *supra*, part i, 298.

88 ff. See note on 33–44.

88–96. The same letter (which is now lost) is alluded to in Ep. 5, 132–6; cf. Introduction, pp. xl, xliii.

super imperatoris ingratitudine, ab ipso tanto creati studio, conqueritur, plurima proponens ibidem ab eo contra spem acta et preter merita ipsius tanta, quibus ad eius sublimationem, ut notum est satis, per decennium 94 iam et amplius tanto studio laboraverat, tanquam a penitus ingrato f. 80ra perpetrata, quibus fa|ma ipsius apud probos omnes et discretos, ad quos ea pervenerint, graviter ledi poterit et obfuscari. Sic ergo delibe- rant, qui ad oculum iudicant et qui iuxta Ieronimum nichil ipsi cudere norunt, sed ab aliis edita dente mordaci dilacerare contendunt. Quin etiam in prologo super Esdram ait: *Librum nostrum non efferatis in* 100 *publicum nec fastidiosis cibos ingeratis superciliumque vitetis eorum, qui iudicare tantum de aliis et ipsi facere nichil noverunt.* Unde et illud Senece non incompetenter hiis adaptari potest: *Lividi lectoris malicia dictionem sanam et insanam pari revolvit appetitu, non minus appetendo despecta que rideat quam electa que laudet.*

105 Proinde et scriptorum moderni temporis sicut et antiqui gravis est conditio, sed tanto modernorum gravior, quanto de die in diem malicia maior, quod laboribus suis et scriptis, quamquam egregiis, se coevis et coetaneis suis tantum exosos reddunt. Unde Ieronimus in prologo priori: *Frustra quidem ad aliquid eniti nec aliud fatigando nisi odium* 110 *querere, extreme dementie est.* Unicum itaque nobis et similibus remedium restat, ut qui lucubris et laboribus nostris presentibus placere non possumus, saltem posteris et *post fata, cum suus ex merito quemque* f. 80rb *tuebi*tur *honor,* displicere non debeamus. Uti|nam diu et bene valere possitis.

100 superciliciumque, *del. alt.* ci, *V*

---

91. Cf. Ep. 5, 21–2; Ep. 6, 180; Ep. 7, 47–9, 233–4, 284.

95. See note on 24–5.

97. iuxta Ieronimum] Cf. *Prologus in librum Isaiae* (Migne, *P.L.* 28, col. 826B): . . . *nos quoque patere morsibus plurimorum, qui stimulante invidia quod consequi non valent despiciunt.* Cf. 34–5 and 45–6.

98. Cf. Ep. 3, 81–2.

99–101. *Praef. in libro Ezrae,* ed. *Biblia sacra iuxta latinam vulgatam versionem* viii (Rome, 1950), pp. 4, 5–6. Cf. *infra,* 109–10.

101–4. This sentence is always attributed to Seneca: *Op.* i, p. 417, 34–418, 2 (*De Libris a se Scriptis*), *Speculum Ecclesie* 4, Preface (*Op.* iv, p. 262, 25–7), *Expugnatio Hibernica,* Preface (*Op.* v, p. 213, 15–18), *Descriptio Kambriae,* 1, Second Preface (*Op.* vi, p. 164, 7–10) and always the last part of the quotation is as follows: *non amplius concupiscens electa que laudet quam despecta que rideat.* The words have been taken not from Seneca, but from Sidonius, Ep. iii, 14, 2, *MGH, AA,* viii, p. 51, 18–20: *Nam qui maxume doctus sibi videtur, dictionem sanam et insanam ferme appetitu pari revolvit, non amplius concupiscens* erecta *que laudet quam despecta quae rideat.*

105–8. Cf. R. B. C. Huygens, *Accessus ad Auctores, Bernard d'Utrecht, Conrad d'Hirsau: Dialogus super Auctores* (Leiden, Brill, 1970), p. 66, 201–6 (note).

109–10. in prologo priori] p. 4, 2–3 (see note on 99–101). Cf. *supra,* part i, 792–4, and *Symbolum Electorum* i, xxiv (*Op.* i, p. 287, 2): *Magna enim dementia est . . .*

110–13. See note on Ep. 3, 78–83.

111. lucubris] Cf. Isidorus, *Etym.* 20, 10, 8.   113–14. See note on Ep. 1, 40.

recall . . .'. For he complains of the ingratitude of the Emperor, whose
election he had secured with such pains; and in the same work he
quotes the numerous unexpected things the Emperor did—things which
he himself did not deserve: for, as is well known, he had laboured for
ten years or more to raise him to his exalted position—just as if they
were acts of great ingratitude which could seriously damage his reputation in the eyes of all decent and honest men who heard them. For those
who judge by appearances think in this way and, according to Jerome,
can thrash out nothing original themselves, but instead try to tear
others' products to pieces with biting comment. In his commentary
on Ezra he even says: 'Do not drag my book before the public gaze
and do not force food on the fussy. Avoid the arrogance of those who
can only pass judgement on others and have no talent themselves.' It
would not be unfitting to add the following words of Seneca: 'The
malicious and spiteful reader devours good and bad style with equal
eagerness, as much to laugh at the mistakes as to praise the finer points.'

Accordingly, the position of writers of the present, just as of the past,
is serious, but it grows even more serious for the modern writers as
spite increases daily, since their works and writings, however excellent,
make them odious to their contemporaries. As Jerome says in an earlier
prologue: 'It is indeed a waste of time for anyone to strive at anything
and to seek nothing but hatred by hard work. That is the height of
madness.' And so there is only one remedy for us and those like us:
as we cannot please men today with our laborious studies, at least we
should not displease posterity after our death, when each man's worth
will defend him according to his merits.

It is our prayer that you enjoy long and good health.

3

Magistro Willelmo Lincolniensis ecclesie cancellario

SATIS admirari non potuimus quod vir, quem bonum et benignum
fama predicat, libros nostros Hybernicos, *Topographiam* scilicet et
Vaticinalem Expugnationis Historiam, olim ecclesie Lincolniensi in uno
volumine datos a nobis, quos antea plurimum commendare consuevit,
5 nunc, ⌐sicut⌐ accepimus, ratione materie dampnare presumit, quoniam
alicubi inter cetera de vitio gentis illius agitur cum bestiis coeundi, de
bestiis quoque ad mulieres accedentibus, historica veritate simul et
severitate, que veris quidem iuxta res gestas parcere non novit, cum
tamen ibi circumcisis labiis verbisque decentibus et honestis tam
10 inhonesta materia satis honeste sit tractata. Bibliotecam igitur censura
simili propter plurima materie turpis inserta iudex talis dampnabilem
dicat et folia illa, sicut de nostris libellis censuit, in quibus turpia continentur, ut de Sodoma et Gomorra subversis et subversionum causis
et paulo ante de Sodome civibus angelos sibi exhiberi ad cognoscen
15 dum efflagitantibus et in domum Loth certatim ob hoc irruentibus,
et in Levitico de muliere que accesserit ad omne pecus ascendi ab eo,
f. 80ᵛᵃ simul cum pecore interficienda, et in Epistola Pauli de | masculorum
concubitoribus et mulieribus cum mulieribus turpitudinem operantibus
et aliis in hunc modum in sacra scriptura multis, in quibus sicut nec
20 veritati, sic neque verborum parcitur inhonestati. Resecentur itaque
folia et abiciantur et que talia continent dampnentur universa!
Preterea dixistis theologica nos scribere debere et hoc pocius maturitatem nostram decere. Cui respondemus quod viridis etatis et iuventutis
nostre fuerunt hec opera, nec historice materie hactenus intacte noticia
25

---

17 ea *V*   24 viridilis *V*

2. Cf. Ep. 6, 419–20.
3–4. Cf. *Epistola ad capitulum Herefordense* (*Op.* i, p. 409, 8–10): *Topographiam
Hibernicam et Vaticinalem Hybernice Expugnationis Historiam, opera duo scilicet et
diversa, sed uno volumine conserta.*
6–7. Especially chapters 2, 23, and 24 of the *Topographia* (*Op.* v, pp. 110–111).
On other such scandalous subjects, see the first preface to the *Vaticinalis Expugnationis
Historia* (*Op.* v, pp. 209–10).
6–21. See note on Ep. 2, 33–44 (8–9 = Ep. 2, 42–3).
9. Cf. Ep. 6, 147.
10. circumcisis labiis] perhaps from Jerome, *Ep.* xviiiA, 15–16, *CSEL,* 54, 1910,
p. 95, 16–p. 96, 3.
11–22. See note on Ep. 2, 35–6.
13. folia illa] *sc.* dampnabilia (esse).

[3.] *To Master William, chancellor of the church of Lincoln*

O U R amazement could not have been greater that a man, whom public opinion proclaims to be good and kind, should now, so we hear, dare to condemn our books on Ireland (namely *The Topography* and *The Prophetic History of the Conquest*) on account of the subject matter—books which we gave in one volume to the church of Lincoln, and which he used to praise highly—just because somewhere in them the vice of these people (the vice of coupling with beasts and of beasts' coming to women) is dealt with with strict historical accuracy, which cannot spare the truth as far as the facts are concerned; though, none the less, such an indecent subject matter was dealt with decently enough there by the use of restrained speech, and seemly, proper vocabulary. A critic like this, therefore, should by the same criterion claim that the Bible is to be condemned on account of the inclusion of a considerable amount of obscene material. For there are pages which contain disgusting things similar to those he thought objectionable in our books: for example, the overthrow of Sodom and Gomorrha, and the reasons for it; and, a little earlier, the demands of the citizens of Sodom that the angels be shown to them to be known, and their attack on the house of Lot for this purpose. And the instruction in Leviticus that any woman who allowed herself to be mounted by a beast should die along with the animal; and in Paul's epistle, the disgusting acts of men lying with men and women with women. There are many other examples of this kind in Holy Writ in which neither the truth nor the indecent language is spared. So, cut out these pages and throw them away and destroy everything which contains such material.

Besides, you have said that we ought to write theological works and that this would be more becoming to our maturity. Our reply to this would be that these works were written when we were young and inexperienced and they were not without praise in the eyes of sound

14. Gen. xix, 24–5, cf. xiii, 13, and *passim*.
15–16. Gen. xix, 1–11.
17–18. Lev. xviii, 23: *Mulier non succumbet iumento nec miscebitur ei, quia scelus est,* and xx, 16: *Mulier quae succubuerit cuilibet iumento, simul interficietur cum eo.* In the *Topographia Hibernica,* 2, 24 (*Op.* v, p. 111, 15–18, *De leone mulierem adamante*), Giraldus writes also: *Unde et in Levitico scriptum est: 'Mulier que accesserit ad omne pecus ascendenda ab eo, mulierem interficietis et pecus morte moriatur': rei enim sunt.*
18–19. Cf. Rom. 1, 27, and 1 Tim. i, 10.

nec scolastici stili elegantia recte iudicantibus illaudabilia. Nec inter
auctores et scriptores minimum locum historici tenent. Unde et
Ieronimus et Augustinus et agiographi nostri inter opera sua cetera
hystorias quoque sui temporis suorumque finium accurate scripserunt:
30 non enim solam semper Bibliotecam ruminare volebant. Quedam etenim
precipue facienda et alia quoque ducebant non omittenda; unde nec
Origenes ille famosissimus inter primos et tempore primus et eruditione maximus, nec Ieronimus noster nec Augustinus aut Hylarius, nisi
litterature solide podio firmoque arcium fundamento suffulti, tam valide
35 in sacris scripturis ecclesie columpne vel hereticorum ⌐mallei⌐ fuissent
tam victoriosi.

Ad hystoriarum autem et historicorum commendationem audiatur |
f. 80ᵛᵇ illa Senece tanquam huius opere descriptio: 'Hystoria', inquit, 'est antiquitatis autoritas, testis temporum, via vite, vita memorie, nuntia
40 vetustatis, lux veritatis'.

Ad hec etiam in libro nostro Hybernico, quem ratione preassignata
tam subtili dampnabilem iudicastis, quamquam iuvenilibus annis
editum, presertim in distinctione prima, ubi de avibus agitur earumque
naturis, theologicas diligens lector invenire poterit tam moralitates quam
45 allegorias non ineleganter adaptatas; quas cum bonus vir ille sancteque
memorie, litterature quoque tam eximie Cantuariensis archiepiscopus
Baldewinus coram se lectas audisset, quesivit a nobis an aliquam ab

26 Hec V

26. Cf. *Speculum Ecclesie*, 3, 1 (*Op.* iv, p. 143, 2): *scholastico stilo*; *Vaticinalis Ex-*
pugnationis Historia, First Preface (*Op.* v, p. 209, 4–5: *Scholastici stili elegantie omnium*
unica laus est et uniformis; *Itinerarium Kambriae*, First Preface (*Op.* vi, p. 7, 25):
scholastico stilo . . . digerere.   26–7. See note on 37–40.
27–30. Cf. *De Rebus a se Gestis*, 2, 14 (*Op.* i, p. 71, 16): *ab agiographis nostris* (see
note on 45–52); *Epistola ad capitulum Herefordense* (*Op.* i, p. 418, 19–20): *Origenes et*
Ieronimus ceterique agiographi nostri; ibid. p. 416, 23–9: *Adiciendum hoc etiam et nota*
non indignum arbitror, quod tam Origenes quam Ieronimus et Augustinus, quamquam in
sacris scripturis transferendis pariter et exponendis tam utili labore desudaverint, historias
tamen temporis sui plurimas, tam ecclesiasticas scilicet quam et alias quoque memoratu
dignas, tractare non omiserunt.
30–1. Cf. *Epistola ad capitulum Herefordense* (*Op.* i, p. 417, 2–8): *Quedam igitur*
oportet facere, veluti sacris utriusque Instrumenti paginis, presertim autem medullis evan-
gelicis . . . attentius invigilare, et alia tamen . . . nullatenus omittere.
33–6. Cf. Petrus Cantor, *Verbum Abbreviatum*, Migne, *P.L.*, 205, col. 26A: *Hiero-*
nymus et Gregorius . . . validi mallei hereticorum Augustinus et Hilarius . . .
37–40. Cf. *Epistola ad capitulum Herefordense* (*Op.* i, p. 417, 12–17): *Ad historicorum*
namque commendationem moralis ille philosophus, Seneca scilicet (see note on Ep. 4, 162),
historie descriptionem talem non inelegantem emisit: 'Historia est antiquitatis auctoritas,
testis temporum, lux veritatis, vita memorie, magistra vite, nuntia vetustatis; also in
De Iure et Statu, etc. 7 (*Op.* iii, p. 333, 17–22): *Nec enim inter auctores et scriptores*
egregios ultimum historici locum tenent (see 26–7). *Ad historiarum nempe commendatio-*
nem audiatur illa Senece tanquam huius opere descriptio: 'Historia', inquit, 'est antiqui-
tatis auctoritas, testis temporum, via vite, vita memorie, nuncia vetustatis, lux veritatis';
also the First Preface of the *Vaticinalis Expugnationis Historia* (*Op.* v, p. 213, 19–

judges, either for dealing with historical subject-matter, as yet untouched, or the elegance of a scholarly style.

Historians do not hold the lowest rank among authors and writers. For Jerome and Augustine and our hagiographers have written among other things accurate histories of their age and area. For they did not want to concentrate always exclusively on the Bible; they thought that certain subjects should receive special attention and others, too, should not be overlooked. Neither Origen, that most famous of the chief writers, the earliest in time and foremost in learning, nor our Jerome, nor Augustine, nor Hilary would have been such strong pillars of the Church, with their theological books, and such successful hammers of heretics, if they had not had such a sound basis and firm grounding in literature and the arts.

Listen to what Seneca has to say in praise of historians and history; it is almost a description of my book: 'History', he says, 'is the judgement of the past, a witness of the times, a pathway for life, life to tradition, a messenger from antiquity, the light of truth.'

Furthermore, in our volume on Ireland, which you criticize so subtly for the reason given above, the diligent reader will be able to find both theological morals and allegories, drawn with no inconsiderable skill, especially in the first part which deals with birds and their habits, despite the fact that it was a work of our youth. For when this book was read out to Baldwin, archbishop of Canterbury, that good man of sacred

---

22): *Historia namque est antiquitatis auctoritas, testis temporum, lux veritatis, vita memorie, magistra vite, nuntia vetustatis*; Second Preface of the *Descriptio Kambriae* (*Op.* vi, p. 164, 15–17): '*Historia namque*', ut ait Seneca, '*est antiquitatis auctoritas, testis temporum, lux veritatis, vita memorie, magistra vite, nuntia vetustatis*. The saying is not by Seneca (like many other quotations ascribed to him by Giraldus), but by Cicero, *De oratore*, ii, 9, 36: *Historia vero, testis temporum, lux veritatis, vita memoriae, magistra vitae, nuntia vetustatis, qua voce alia nisi oratoris immortalitati commendatur?*

41–5. Chapters 12–20 of book i of the *Topographia Hibernica* (*Op.* v, pp. 34–53) are dealing with birds, their nature and allegorical significance; cf. in the *Ep. ad cap. Herefordense* (*Op.* i, p. 409, 14–16): *in Topographia nunc missa, in Distinctione prima ... tractatum de avibus earumque naturis et allegoriis etiam adaptatis.*

45–52. The same story is told in the *De Iure et Statu Menevensis Ecclesie*, 7 (*Op.* iii, pp. 334–5), and in the *Ep. ad cap. Herefordense* (*Op.* i, p. 410, 1–14): *... circiter editionem dicte Topographie primam et libri recitationem in publica cleri audientia per triduum solemniter Oxonie factam, cum archiepiscopus Cantuariensis Baldewinus, vir quidem valde litteratus et in sacris scripturis affatim eruditus, dictum de avibus earumque naturis et allegoriis assignatis tractatum coram se lectum quandoque relectumque diligenter audisset, quesivit utrum evidentiam aliquam ad allegorias illas sic assignandum ab agiographis et expositoribus nostris* (see note on 27–30) *habuissem, cumque responsum accepisset quod revera penitus nullam, nisi quod solum gratia divina concessit, subiecit vir ille bonus atque benignus: 'Nec mirum, quia certe eodem spiritu quo et ipsi!'* Baldwin is also presented as a great admirer of Giraldus' works in the *De Rebus a se Gestis*, 2, 20 (*Op.* i, pp. 79–80): *Tam Giraldi ab archiepiscopo quam styli ipsius commendatione*; there the archbishop is stated to have tried to persuade Giraldus to become the official historian of the Third Crusade.   45. Cf. 72.

expositoribus nostris evidentiam ad hec habuissemus, et cum responsum acciperet quod omnino nullam, nisi sicut deus nobis indulsit, statim
50 adiunxit: 'Certe eodem spiritu quo et ipsi!' Iudicavit autem non ut lividus aut delator, sed ut benignus et iustus litterati laboris commendator.

Item si theologica tantum opera queritis et alia contemptibilia iudicatis, quatinus in aliquo vobis et examini vestro placere possimus,
55 *Gemmam* nostram *Ecclesiasticam* maturioribus annis elaboratam et
f. 81ʳᵃ ecclesie Lincolniensi cum *Vita* quoque | *sancti Remigii*, similiter a nobis tractata, transcursis iam annis plurimis datam, in qua theologice solum et canonice scripture resultant, oculo benigniore respiciatis.

Scire vos etiam volumus quod predicta scripta nostra hystorica, que
60 adeo nunc parvipenditis, longeviora et longe cariora multis, ut credimus, immo sicut pro certo scimus, in posterum erunt quam scripta plurima, que theologica et theologice facultati tanquam ex superhabundanti et superflue superaddita, ex aliorum scriptis undique corrogata et transpositionibus quibusdam artificiosis et titulorum mutationibus ex
65 magnorum virorum laboribus egregiis excerpta et quasi de novo nunc fabricata, sed verius quidem artificialiter innovata, quatinus ex aliorum operibus antiquis et autenticis consuta sic nuper opuscula et dignis laudem adimere et indignis adquirere queant.

Nos autem ex materia hactenus illibata Hybernicas et Walensicas
70 finium nostrorum historias iuvenilibus annis tractare curavimus et tanquam ex cortice durissimo et testa nondum effracta vel cuiquam pervia abditos extrahere nucleos et in lucem edere non ineleganter elaboravimus.

74 Porro quoniam scripta quantumlibet egregia lividis ingeniis auctore
f. 81ʳᵇ superstite pla|cere non possunt, nos opera nostra dum vivimus contra emulorum morsus litteris et scriptis, sicut ex prohemio patet *Vaticinalis Historie* primo, defendere pro posse curavimus et curamus, absque ⟨dubio⟩ credentes, quin immo et certi existentes, quod apud posteros et *post fata, cum* livore cessante *suus ex merito quemque tuebitur*
80 *honor*, ipsa se sua dignitate defendent, et que nunc placere nequeunt,

---

57 solum *bis* V, *pr. del.*   64 artificiocis V   65 excerpta *ex* excepta *corr.* V
67 consulta V

---

72. Cf. 45.
78–83. (Cf. Ep. 2, 110–13.) This conviction has been formulated after Ovid, *Amores*, i, 15, 39–40, cf. the First Preface to the *Itinerarium Kambriae* (*Op.* vi, p. 5, 17 f.): *iuxta illud poete: 'Pascitur in vivis livor, post fata quiescit | cum suus ex merito quemque tuetur honor'*; (*Pascitur . . . quiescit* also in the *Verbum Abbreviatum* (see note on lines 33–6), 52A); last Preface to the *Expugnatio Hibernica* (*Op.* v, p. 411, 19–23): *ut . . . humanam per opuscula nostra gratiam, si literarum decus quandoque resurgat et in statum*

memory and so well versed in literature, asked us whether we had borrowed from our commentators. When we replied that we had received no help, except from God, he remarked: 'You must have had the same source of inspiration as they!' As you see, he did not take the stand of a hostile critic but of a kind, just patron of literary labour.

However, if it is only theological works you want and any other kind you consider should be disregarded, so that we may satisfy you and your examination in some respect, look more kindly upon our *Gemma Ecclesiastica* which we worked upon in our more mature years and which we gave some years ago to Lincoln cathedral, together with the *Life of St. Remigius*, another work of ours, which resounds with exclusively theological and canonical references.

It is also our desire that you should know that the above historical works of ours, which you now consider so trivial, in time to come will, as we believe and, indeed, know for certain, survive for a very long time, and be more valued than very many works. For there is already a superabundance, as it were, of theological books, and even more are being added to the overflowing pile. These are concoctions of all sorts of different books and are taken from the outstanding works of great writers, then presented as though they were something new, but with some artificial rearrangement and a change of title. In fact these modern booklets are not truly genuine, for they are patched together from the earlier original works of others; they are attempts to snatch the reputation from the deserving and attach it to the undeserving.

We on the other hand took pains in our youth to distil the histories of Ireland and Wales, our home grounds, from hitherto untouched material and managed to extract the hidden pearls, as it were, from the hardest shells, as yet unbroken and still unravished, and bring them out, not unskilfully, to the light.

Furthermore, since books, however outstanding, cannot please spiteful minds while the author is still alive, we are taking care—and always have—to defend our books by pen and paper from the biting attacks of rivals while we are still living, as is clear from the first preface to the *Prophetic History*. We firmly believe and indeed know for certain that with posterity there will be no spite after our death, and a man's honour will serve as his defence according to his merits. Their writings will protect themselves by their own worth, and the works which cannot please now will truly be unable later to displease really. Just as now they

redeat, saltem in posterum, cum suus ex merito quemque tuebitur honor, assequamur; also in the *De Invectionibus*, v, 11 (i, p. 137, 6–8, ed. Davies, p. 192, 5–6) and in the *Speculum Ecclesie*, 2, 33 (*Op.* iv, p. 107, 22).

tunc revera displicere non poterunt, et sicut nunc undique mordaci dente roduntur et laniantur, sic dignis tunc demum laudibus et preconiis extollentur.

Aut itaque libellos prescriptos rodere de cetero et verbis minus dis-
85 cretis dilacerare cessetis, aut ipsos auctori suo quam cicius resignare curetis. Valete.

84 Haut *V*

81–2. Cf. Ep. 2, 98.

are bitten and torn to pieces with sharp teeth, so later they will be praised to the skies as they deserve.

So stop snapping at these books and tearing them apart so rudely, or else kindly return them to the author as quickly as possible.

Farewell.

4

Ante sermonem de sancto Stephano quasi preparatio quedam seu prefatio

Semper ego auditor tantum, nunquamne reponam? Vexatus tociens et
tanto tempore, tanquam ergo Pittagoricus discipulus iam per quinquen-
5 nium inter vos et amplius silens nec *inter olores canoros anserem strepere*
sinens, sed pocius maiori modestia maiorum eloquiis locum prebens, ad

f. 81ᵛᵃ quorundam instantiam quos pati repulsam indecens foret, | nunc saltem,
quia sacius sero quam numquam, quamquam vix et invitus os et
linguam in verba resolvo. Sit itaque nobis, qui de Christi athleta forti et
10 prothomartire preclui deo dante dicturi sumus, hodierne diei publica
materies, sed privati iuris. Verumtamen quoniam id, quod habundat in
corde, etiam importune plerumque redundat atque resultat in ore,
quatinus in primis quasi querulum carmen venia petita premittatur:
turbat hodie mentis sabbatum et vehementer inquietat nimie tribulati-
15 onis, que nunc ecclesiam remotis in partibus et propinquis, capiti
nempe simul et membris insultans, tam graviter et tamen inaniter
urget et artat, incomodum. Ut enim ex malis huiusmodi bonum aliquod
eliciat, deus ad hoc quos amat arguit et castigat, filios, quos recipit,
flagellat acrius et fatigat, quatinus, ad intellectum vexatione data et ⟨ad⟩
20 adulationis gloriam vel etiam conversionis gratiam persecutorum rabie
diucius dissimulata, passi iniurias et afflicti de fornace tribulationis
auro demum et obrizo purissimo puriores exeant et in conspectu
domini electis preciosiores existant. *Durum est* igitur *contra stimulum*
24 *calcitrare*, durius et presumptuosius invincibilem vinci posse putare. |

f. 81ᵛᵇ Dicente namque et vere dominatore domino, qui vincit, qui regnat, qui
imperat, qui *rex* est *regum et dominus dominantium*, quin immo *cuius*

---

3 nunquam ve *V*   6 eloquiis *bis, alt. del. V*   13 quarulum *V*   24 invincibi *V*

---

3. Juvenal, *Sat.* i, 1–2.
4. Cf. Ennodius, ed. Vogel, *MGH*, AA, vii, 1885, p. 245 (no. 334), 4–5: *Solve ergo Pythagoricam taciturnitatem* . . . See also next note, and *supra*, part i, 195–6.
5. Virgil, *Buc.* 9, 36 (*argutos*) quoted in Symmachus, *Ep.* 1, 1, 4, ed. Seeck, *MGH*, AA, vi, 1883, p. 2, 2–3: *Liceat inter olores canoros anserem strepere*, cf. *De Rebus a Se Gestis*, 2, 2 (*Op.* i, p. 47, 6–11): . . . *ne solus inter vos anomalus videar neve solus loquentibus aliis taciturnitate pre ceteris Pythagoricus discipulus inveniar* (= 4), *elegi potius loquendo ridiculus quam tacendo discolus* (see note on Ep. 1, 10–11) *inveniri. Quam igitur vocem inter olores canoros clamosus anser* (= 5) *emittet?*
8. Cf. *supra*, part ii, 779: *sacius . . . numquam*; cf. 6, 318, and *De Invectionibus*, Preface, ed. Davies, p. 82, 17: *vix et invitus*.

[4.] *A Preface or Preparation to a Sermon on St. Stephen*

AM I always to be a listener, and make no reply? I have been pestered so often and for such a time, and like some Pythagorean pupil keeping a five-year or more silent vigil among you, I have not allowed 'the goose to honk among the singing swans', but rather, with greater modesty, I have yielded to the eloquence of my betters. Now, at least, at the insistence of some people—for it would be wrong for them to suffer the indignity of a refusal—better late than never, I shape my mouth and tongue to speech, though rather reluctantly. Since we are, God willing, to preach on Christ's great champion and proto-martyr, may our subject for today be public, though a matter of private law. However, as that which fills our heart even resounds and re-echoes in my mouth, so that, by your leave, our sermon is prefaced by this sort of plaintive song: Today the sabbath is disturbed and haunted by a disquietude and a great tribulation—a tribulation which is now heavily, though vainly, oppressing and crushing the Church in lands far and near, attacking both head and limbs at the same time. For the Lord, in order to bring some good from troubles of this kind, reproves and chastens those he loves, and he bitterly scourges and tires the sons whom he receives so that, when torture is applied to the perception, and the long-feigned frenzy of the persecutors for the glory of worship and the grace of conversion, after suffering injuries and being afflicted by the furnace of tribulation they finally come forth purer than gold, even than the purest refined gold, and stand more precious than the chosen in the eyes of the Lord. 'It is hard', then, 'to kick against the pricks', but it is harder and more presumptuous to think that the unconquerable can be conquered. This, too is what the Lord, truly the Almighty, said, he who conquers, rules, and commands, he who is King of kings and Lord

13. See note on Ep. 2, 79–80.   14. mentis sabbatum] Cf. 168.
15–17. Probably an allusion to the Interdict, cf. Ep. 5, 256.   17–18. Cf. 103.
18–19. Cf. Heb. xii, 6: *Quem enim diligit dominus castigat, flagellat autem omnem filium quem recipit*, and Rev. iii, 19: *Ego quos amo arguo et castigo*.
19. Cf. Isa. xxviii, 19: *sola vexatio intellectum dabit auditui*.
20–1. Cf. 70–1.   23–4. Acts ix, 5 (= xxvi, 14).
25–6. Cf. *Introitus Epiphan.*: *Ecce advenit dominator dominus* (Isa. iii, 1, and x, 16). Cf. the tricolon of the 'Laudes': *Christus vincit, Christus regnat, Christus imperat*: E. H. Kantorowicz, *Laudes Regiae* (Berkeley and Los Angeles, 1946) pp. 1–12, 14 ff., and *passim*; B. Opfermann, *Die liturgischen Herrscherakklamationen im Sacrum Imperium des Mittelalters* (Weimar, 1953), pp. 35 ff., and *passim*.
26. 1 Tim. vi, 15 = Rev. xix, 16.
26–7. Luke i, 33 (*Ordo Missae*: Credo).

regni non erit finis quique *regnabit in eternum et ultra* et *potestas cuius*
potestas eterna, que non auferetur, et regnum quod non corumpetur: Ecce ego
vobiscum sum usque ad consumationem seculi, adversus ecclesiam ecclesie-
30 que fidem, hiis ultimis mundi diebus tam gloriose manifestatam et per
exquisitam ac benignissimam Christi misericordiam, qua salvos nos
fecit, hoc tempore gratie tam gratiose et tam habunde revelatam, quis
prevalebit? *Porte inferi non prevalebunt adversus eam.* Et ut prophetarum
ex parte verbis utamur: *Quis est iste qui dixit ut fieret, domino non iubente?*
35 *Dominus enim exercituum ipse decrevit et quis preiudicare presumet, et*
si manus eius extenta, quis avertet eam? Dominus novit conatus hominum, quoniam vani sunt. Ecclesie namque plantam Christi sanguine
⟨irrigatam⟩ olim ac rubricatam adeoque firmissime fundatam et in-
convulse radicatam, quis vel exstirpare vel etiam ad modicum infirmare
40 valebit? Vexari poterit ad horam in terris plantatio celestis, evacuari
f. 82ʳᵃ vero nullatenus aut enervari, concuti poterit adversis fluctibus | in-
gruente procella Petri navicula verique Noe salvatrix archa, quati vero
non poterit aut dissolvi. Cum enim excitatus a sompno summus ille
gubernator fuerit, imperabit *ventis et mari* et fiet statim *tranquillitas*
45 *magna.* Sicut ergo palma, sic et ecclesia, palmam utique vere repre-
sentans, quia palmam ubique finalem auctore domino victoriose
reportans, quanto plus premitur in radicibus, tanto copiosius in ramis
exsurgit et excrescit in frondibus; etsi plerisque tamen ipsa videatur
mora molesta—quia longanimus expectator dominus idemque malorum
50 denique gravissimus ultor sicut et bonorum omnium benignissimus
retributor, suis absque dubio temporibus longe uberior fiet in fructibus.
Eius itaque disposicioni cum spe certissima et infallibili fidutia totum
committatur, *cuius providentia in sui dispositione non fallitur* quique
per prophetam suum ait: *Michi vindictam et ego retribuam, quoniam*
55 *ipsi* revera *cura est de* nobis, *qui non derelinquit sperantes in se* nulloque
nos tempore deserit, nisi prius fuerit a nobis ipse desertus, *nec unquam*
sua gubernatione destituit quos in soliditate sue dilectionis instituit. Unde
et in Ecclesiastico: *Scitote quia nullus speravit in domino et confusus est,*

---

40 evacuare *V*　　　　41 concut *V*

27. Exod. xv, 18.　　　　27–8. Dan. vii, 14.　　　　28–9. Matt. xxviii, 20.
31–2. Cf. Tit. iii, 5: *Secundum suam misericordiam salvos nos fecit.*
33. Matt. xvi, 18.　　　　　　　　　　33–4. See notes on 79 and 122–3.
34. Lam. iii, 37.
35–6 (cf. 39–40). Isa. xiv, 27 (*et quis poterit infirmare?*).
36–7. Ps. xciii, 11: *Dominus scit cogitationes hominum, quoniam vanae sunt.*
39–40. See note on 35–6.
44–5. Mark iv, 37–9; Matt. viii, 26: *Imperavit ventis et mari et facta est tranquillitas*
magna.
49. Cf. *supra*, part i, 1142.

of lords', 'whose kingdom shall have no end' and 'who reigneth for ever
and evermore', 'whose power is an everlasting power that shall not be
taken away: and his kingdom that shall not be destroyed': 'And behold,
I am with you, even to the consummation of the world.' When the Lord
says this, who shall prevail against the Church, against the faith of the
Church, shown so gloriously even in these last days of the world, and
graciously and openly revealed at this time of grace, by the excellent
and most blessed mercy of Christ by which we are saved? 'And the
gates of hell shall not prevail against her', and, to employ the words of
the prophets in part, 'Who is he that hath commanded a thing, when the
Lord commanded it not?' 'For the Lord of hosts hath decreed and who
dares to prejudge it? And his hand is stretched out, and who shall turn
it away?' The Lord himself knows that the attempts of men are vain.
For the plant of the Church was once watered and reddened with the
blood of Christ, and was very firmly planted and deeply rooted. Who,
then, can either uproot it or harm it to the slightest extent? The heavenly
colony on earth could be troubled briefly but it cannot be got rid of, or
weakened; the ship of Peter, and true Noah's saving ark could be
buffeted by the onrushing waves when the storm broke, but they
could not be capsized or sunk. When that heavenly steersman is roused
from his sleep, he will command 'the wind and the sea', and at once
there will be 'a great calm'. The Church is like the palm, and indeed
truly reflects it, for everywhere it carries the ultimate palm of victory at
the instigation of the Lord. The more the roots are trampled, the greater
will be the branches and leaves. Though the delay seems long to most
people—for the Lord is patient and long-suffering and metes out the
sternest justice to the wicked just as he metes out the richest rewards to
the good—without doubt in its own good time it will be far more fruitful. Let all be committed to his disposing with the surest hope and unshakeable faith: 'His providence faileth not in his orderings'; he spake
by the prophet, 'Revenge is mine, I will repay', indeed his care is for us;
'he hath not forsaken them that hope in him', and he never deserts us,
unless we desert him first; nor has he ever deprived of his guidance
those he has founded on the said foundations of his love. So, too, in
Ecclesiasticus: 'Know ye that no one hath hoped on the Lord and hath

53. *Dom. VII post Pent.* Oratio.
54. per prophetam *should be* per apostolum (cf. 107): Rom. xii, 19; Heb. x, 30.
54-5. I Pet. v, 7: *Quoniam ipsi cura est de vobis.* Judith xiii, 17: *Laudate dominum deum nostrum, qui non deseruit sperantes in se.*
56-7. *Dom. II post Pent.,* Oratio: *Numquam* [*Nec unquam* Giraldus, cf. 61 *nec ulla* / *nulla*] *tua gubernatione destituis, quos in soliditate tuae dilectionis instituis.*
58-9. Ecclus. ii, 11-12 (. . . *quis enim permansit in mandatis eius et derelictus est?*).

f. 82rb *permansit in | mandatis eius et derelictus.* Ut enim summam totam sub
60 brevitate concludam: non claudetur nobis misericordie ianua, nisi
prius ex nostra fuerit clausa malitia, *quia nec ulla nobis nocebit adversitas,
si nulla dominetur iniquitas.* Labor igitur, ut ait Gregorius, protrahitur
pugne, ut sic amplius crescat corona victorie. Proinde et cum propheta
Nahum dicere quandoque deo dante poterimus: *Celebra, Iuda, festivitates*
65 *tuas et redde Altissimo vota tua, quia non adiciet ultra ut pertranseat in te
Belial: universus interibit.* Super hunc enim locum expositor: *Si quando
fuerit gravis persecutio et dei ultio demum in eius adversarios apparuerit,
dicamus ad ecclesiam: 'Celebra, Iuda, festivitates tuas', et cetera.* Sed
quoniam *misericordia domini plena est terra,* cuius etiam *misericordia*
70 *superexaltat iuditio,* cum peccatores omnes et presertim ecclesie persecutores, districto dei iudicio, quod evitari non poterit aut mutari, vel
converti necesse sit vel everti, domino tamen, *cui proprium est misereri
semper et parcere,* paterna clementia propiciante gratiamque suam
misericorditer, ubi vult et quando vult, inspirante, qui ait: *Nolo*
75 *mortem peccatoris, sed magis ut convertatur et vivat,* favorabili presump-
tione atque probabili, que benignius in dubiis †interpretali, conversio
f. 82va denique seque|tur et non eversio.

Preterea, quia nunquam sola veniunt scandala, sed iuxta metricum
illud sapientis eloquium:

80 *Semper adest homini quo pectoris ima gemiscant,*
ne possit plena prosperitate frui.
Gaudia nunc luctu, nunc mutat amara secundis
versans humanas sors inopina vices.
Sola venire solent et vix et sero secunda
85 *et simul et subito semper amara fluunt,*

preter tantas et tam varias temporis huius, immo verius tempestatis

76 interpretali] *latet corruptela*

61–2. *Feria VI post Cineres,* Oratio super populum: *Quia nulla [nec ulla* Giraldus, see
note on 56–7] *ei nocebit adversitas, si nulla ei dominetur iniquitas.*
62–3. If Giraldus quotes correctly, I cannot find the passage. But cf. Gregory
the Great, *Dial.* 3, 19, Migne, *P.L.* 77, col. 269B: *Sine labore certaminis non est palma
victoriae;* also *Moralia in Iob,* 8, 7, Migne, *P.L.* 75, 808CD: *Unde et electus . . . tanto
fidentius spe tendit ad praemium, quanto nunc robustius perdurat ad laboris incrementum
. . . Subsequentis vitae praemiis tanto se remunerari largius conspicit, quanto pro amore
illius quotidianis se mortibus verius impendit;* ibid. 10, 19, col. 941C: *Quia igitur nunc
per tribulationem seritur, ut post gaudii fructus metatur, tanto maior fiducia mentem
roborat, quanto hanc fortior pro veritate afflictio angustat.* 64–6. Nahum i, 15.
66. expositor] Jerome, *In Nahum,* Migne, *P.L.* 25, col. 1243A, quoted from the
Glossa Ordinaria. Cf. *infra,* 108 and Ep. 8, 273, 327. 69. Ps. xxxii, 5.
69–70. Jas. ii, 13: the Vulgate has *iudicium,* so Giraldus perhaps has in mind Augustine, *De perfectione iustitiae hominis* 34, *CSEL,* 42, 1902, p. 35, 12 (*iudicio*).

been confounded, and hath continued in his commandment and hath been forsaken.' To put it in short: the doors of his compassion are not closed against us, unless they are first closed by our own wickedness —for no harm will come to us if no wickedness dominates us. As Gregory says, the toil of battle is protracted, so that in this way the crown of victory may be greater. Eventually, God willing, we will be able to say, in the words of Nahum the Prophet: 'O Judah, keep thy festivals and pay thy vows to the Lord, for Belial shall not pass through thee again; he is utterly cut off.' Over this passage the interpreter has added: 'If there is ever a heavy persecution, and the wrath of the Lord avenges itself upon his enemies, let us say to the Church: "O Judah, keep thy festivals", etc.' But since 'the earth is full of the mercy of the Lord, whose mercy exalteth itself above judgement', though it is necessary to convert, or overthrow, sinners, especially persecutors of the Church, with the rigorous judgement of God, which cannot be escaped or altered, since the Lord, 'whose property it is always to have mercy', forgiving with his fatherly clemency and compassionately inspiring his grace when and where he wishes, says, 'I desire not the death of the wicked, but that the wicked turn from his way and live' with favourable and conclusive early action, which can be explained as being the better course in doubtful cases, in the end conversion, not overthrow, will result.

Moreover, scandals never come in ones, but in the eloquent words of that wise poet: 'There is always something that causes a man to groan in the depths of his heart, which prevents him from enjoying complete prosperity. Blind chance, changing man's lot, at one time brings joy from grief, at another bitterness from prosperity. Times of prosperity come rarely, singly, and late; times of bitterness come together suddenly and always.' Thus, in addition to the great variety of ills of these times

70–1. Cf. 20–1. 72–3. *Missa defunctorum*: Oratio.
74. Cf. John iii, 8: *Spiritus ubi vult spirat*.
74–5. Ezek. xxxiii, 11.
78. nunquam sola veniunt scandala] (Matt. xviii, 7 and Luke xvii, 1) Cf. Ep. 5, 162–3, cf. Ep. 6, 55.
79. sapientis] Giraldus himself (!) is meant, and he quotes his own verses, with or without a fourth distich, in other works of his: *Speculum Ecclesie*, 4, 19 (*Op*. iv, p. 304): *Unde et metricos sapientis cuiusdam versus hos . . . hic apponere preter rem non putavimus: Semper . . . fluunt. Ergo ubi nil varium, nil vanum nilve nocivum | sint ibi fixa tibi spes, amor atque fides*; Prologue of book ii of the *De Vita Galfridi* (*Op*. iv, p. 386): *Sed quidem ut metricis cuiusdam versibus sapientis ad hec utamur* (see notes on 33–4 and 122–3): *Semper . . . fluunt* (from this passage quoted by Walther, *Lateinische Sprichwörter und Sentenzen des Mittelalters*, iv, 1966, no. 27890a); *Itinerarium Kambriae*, 1, 4 (*Op*. vi, p. 51 n. 3): *Unde et a quodam sapiente dictum est: Sola venire . . . fluunt*; also in the *Topographia Hibernica*, 3, 49 (*Op*. v, p. 193): *Semper . . . fluunt*; in the *Symbolum Electorum*, 2, 5 (*Op*. i, pp. 354–5): *Semper . . . fides*; and in the letter to Stephen Langton (see note on 141–2), ibid. p. 403 (and n. 1): *Semper . . . fides*. See also *supra*, part i, 669; ii, 449, 784.

iniurias fere iam communiter inflictas, ad malorum cumulum et tam
inique perversitatis pariter et adversitatis augmentum, que spetialius nos
tangit et angit nosque directe, etsi minus recte, respicit et despicit, in-
90 testina discordia premit et penetrat ad precordia nec animum extra se
factum et tanquam in extasim raptum aliud quicquam utiliter agere sinit,
dum propriis nimirum et inopinatis adeo pressa molestiis et oppressa et
presertim ingratitudinis impie vulnerata telis, ultra quam credi possit,
mens indignata et consternata stupescit. Tam recens etenim plaga, tam
95 repentina et tam inopina, quia *que venit indigne pena, dolenda venit,*
nullum omnino remedium consolationis admittit. Et si vultus exterior,
ne vel austeritatem nimiam pretendere videatur vel accidiam, spem
f. 82ᵛᵇ simulet | interdum et hilaritatem, quod intus agitur deforis quasi
velamine quodam ex industria tegens, propter exempli tamen perniciem
100 tam detestabilis et tam pravi et indelebilem tanti scandali notam ac
mendam, que tam atra nevi fuligine, quam nullo nitro nullaque fullonis
herba diluere quantalibet purgatoris cura valebit, adeo ignominiose
et nostros maculat et nos molestat, *aliquisque malo* sit ut *usus in illo*
que multos quidem ut cautius negotientur premuniendo castigat,
105 propter hec, inquam, interna voluntas asperis et amaris tristicie motibus,
quamquam occultis, trans modestiam angustatur. Unde et super illud in
ewangelio Mathei: *Trademini autem a parentibus et fratribus et cognatis*
et amicis expositor: *Minorem mala dolorem ingerunt que ab extraneis*
inferuntur: plus enim in nobis ea tormenta seviunt, que ab illis patimur,
110 *de quorum mentibus presumebamus,* ubi et nos supplere poterimus, nec
inmerito: quorum promotionem totam tanto studio procuravimus,
quia, preter dampna corporis, seu possessionis, cum iactura omnium
gravissima *mala quoque nos cruciant amisse caritatis.* Ideoque 'cum
f. 83ʳᵃ iactura gravissima', quia | fraterna dilectio saluti tam necessaria per
115 iniuriam gravem semel amissa, et maxime que aut scandalum pariat aut
alias nimis enormiter offendat, vix ullo reparari ad plenum tempore
queat. Propter hec igitur supra modum *anxiatus est super me spiritus*
meus et *in me turbatum cor meum.*

Porro, ut Egyptios interdum spoliare liceat et in sacre scripture saculis

---

108 mala minorem *transposuit V*   119 ut *bis V, pr. del.*

95. Ovid, *Heroides* v, 8 (*indigno*), cf. Ep. 6, 522 and *supra*, part i, 75.
96–8. Cf. 129–30.
101–2. Jer. ii, 22: *Si laveris te nitro...*; Mal. iii, 2: *herba fullonum* = Ep. 6, 249–50;
supra, part ii, 1000.
103. Ovid, *Met.* 2, 332: *aliquisque malo fuit usus in illo.*
106–13. in ewangelio Mathei] Luke xxi, 16, see note on 54!—expositor (see note on
66): *Glossa Ordinaria,* Migne, *P.L.* 114, col. 334D–335A: *Maius tormentum, cum aliquis*
ab illis patitur, de quibus presumebat, quia cum damno corporis mala cruciant amissae
caritatis. Cf. *supra*, part i, 83–6.   117–18. Ps. cxlii, 4.

or rather tempests, which have come upon us all, to add to the heap of sins, and to increase the dreadful perversity and adversity, which affect and distress us more especially and concern and trouble us directly, though unjustly, internal discord weighs heavily on us, and pierces to the vitals, and does not allow our mind to do anything useful when it is carried out of itself in a sort of ecstasy. At the same time, our mind relapses into an angry and perplexed silence, burdened and oppressed by its own unsought troubles, and especially wounded by the weapons of impious ingratitude for more than could be believed. This recent blow, so sudden, so unexpected, admits absolutely no cure and consolation, since the undeserved pain is to be grieved over. If my outward appearance at present feigns hope and cheerfulness, carefully clothing my inner feelings on the outside, as it were, lest it appear to be excessively austere or acid, my inner desire is constrained, more than is proper, by hard and bitter feelings of sorrow, though they are hidden. My inner joy, I say, is constrained, because of the curse of this detestable and depraved example, and because of the indelible stain and blot of this terrible scandal—a blot which disgracefully mars our friends and grieves us, as if with a black dye-stain which cannot be removed with soap or any dye-stuff, whatever pains the washer take, and, so that there may be some use in that trouble, it teaches and forewarns many to proceed with greater caution. Thus in the Gospel according to St. Matthew we find: 'And you shall be betrayed by your parents and brethren and kinsmen and friends.' Over this the interpreter has written: 'The troubles caused by strangers give less pain: more intensely do those pains rack us which we suffer at the hands of those whose attitude we had presupposed.' To this I would add, not without reason, 'of those whose whole promotion we have effected with such zeal', since, apart from missing the physical presence, or the possession along with the most painful loss of all this we also suffer the pains of the love that has been lost. I say 'the most painful loss of all', because once brotherly love, so necessary for salvation, is lost through some insult, especially when it stirs up a scandal, or harms other relationships gravely, it can scarcely be restored to its original state in any length of time. So, then, 'my spirit is in anguish with me' and 'my heart within me is troubled' beyond measure.

Moreover, let us, as it were, rob the Egyptians, and put their sacred

---

119. On the subject of the *spoliatio Egyptiorum* see H. de Lubac, *Exégèse médiévale: Les quatre sens de l'Écriture*, i, 1 (1959), pp. 290–304 (more literature is quoted in R. B. C. Huygens, *Accessus ad Auctores, Bernard d'Utrecht, Conrad d'Hirsau: Dialogus super Auctores* (Leiden, Brill, 1970), note on p. 130, 1820 ff.) See also *infra*, note on 123–4.
119–20. Compare the story of the cup of Benjamin: Gen. xliv, 1–13.

120 vasa eorundem preciosa reponere et ⟨cum⟩ Origene atque Ieronimo
elegantia ethnicorum et ethicorum locis competentibus dicta recolere
sacreque doctrine studiis inserere, precipue vero cum fas sit et expediat
undecumque proficere, ⌜quicquid enim ubicumque bene dictum est, meum
est, inquit Theologus⌝, audiamus, si placet, post classis amisse dis-
125 persionem et tam piam hospitis naufragi, sicut in libro Eneidos legitur,
suorum consolationem, hanc scilicet: *Durate et vosmet rebus servate*
secundis: o passi graviora, dabit deus hiis quoque finem, et paulo post:
Forsan et hec olim meminisse iuvabit, quid auctor in continenti subiungat
in hunc modum: *Talia voce refert curisque ingentibus eger spem simulat*
130 *vultu, premit alto corde dolorem*. Haut aliter et nos aliud quidem in facie
gerimus palamque pretendimus et aliud interius anxia mente sustinemus,
nec mirum: dum ad vulnera nostra tam cruda tamque crudelia, de-
decoris quidem atque pudoris amaritudine confusibili multo forcius
f. 83rb absque dubio quam | rerum dampnis inflicta, doctas etiam adhiberi
135 medentium manus vehementia doloris pariter et indignationis non
permittit, ut ita brevi eloquio paucisque verbis pateat aperte quod
patimur, dedecore medullitus longeque molestius quam dampno
movemur. Illud autem solacium aliquod cum amaritudine tamen ad-
mixta adhiberi potest, quod ingratitudo talis nunquam letos sortitur
140 effectus.

Sane fors fiet ut dies longa quandoque plenius hebetet laxatum dolorem, siquidem malis fere cunctis finis de tempore venit: semper enim
remedium oblivio doloris est, quia quod ratione non possumus, temporum prolixitate sepelimus omnisque diuturnitate simul et longevitate

---

121 ennicorum *V*, cf. *Ep. 1, 37*   133 amaritudinem *V*   139 adhibere *V*

121. Cf. *Symbolum Electorum*, 1, 28 (*Op.* i, p. 297, 25–6) and *Speculum Ecclesie*,
3, 6 (*Op.* iv, p. 159, 12–13): *hec . . . et his similia . . . ethnicorum et ethicorum*.

122–3. Cf. *Gemma Ecclesiastica*, 1, 34 (*Op.* ii, p. 108, 24–6): *Quoniam, ut poete verbis*
ad hec utamur (*supra*, 33–4, and note on 79), *cum fas sit, ut ait philosophus, undecumque*
proficere . . . See also next note.

123–4. The *theologus* mentioned in this addition is Seneca, *Ep.* 16 (= ii, 4), 7, ed.
Reynolds, i (Oxford, 1965), p. 43, 11–12: *Quidquid bene dictum est ab ullo, meum est.*
The whole sentence has been taken from Petrus Cantor, *Verbum Abbreviatum*, Migne,
PL, 205, col. 25A: *Quidquid enim ubicumque bene dictum est, meum est, inquit Theologus*
(*Quicquid . . . meum est*, also col. 73B) (cf. K. Nothdurft, *Studien zum Einfluss Senecas*
auf die Philosophie und Theologie des zwölften Jahrhunderts (Leiden, 1963), pp. 44, 148).
The same words are also found in the *Symbolum Electorum*, 1, 24 (*Op.* i, p. 287, 11–20
(18–19)): *Eoque remedio preterita utcumque delicta sanemus et derelicta compensemus, ut*
dicta poetarum moralia et philosophorum, quibus tantopere olim indulsimus, elegantiora
queque ad memoriam revocata quasi gemmas auro laudibus divinis inseramus, et sic spoliando
Egyptios (= 119) *et ditando Hebreos vasa aurea et argentea mutuo accepta in tabernaculi*
structuram congeramus: quicquid enim ubicunque bene dictum est, meum est, inquit Theo-
logus (= 123–4), *licitum enim et liberum est undecumque proficere* (= 122–3). On
Giraldus' use of Petrus Cantor see *supra*, part ii, 1256–8, and E. M. Sanford, 'Giraldus
Cambrensis' Debt to Petrus Cantor', *Medievalia et Humanistica*, iii, 1945, pp. 16–32,

vessels in the sacks of Holy Scripture, and recollect together with Origen and Jerome the elegant sayings of pagan moralists from suitable passages, and add them to the studies of holy teaching, indeed, especially since it is right and useful to profit from any source whatsoever (the theologian says, 'Whatever has been well said, whatever it be, it is mine'). Let us hear the pious words of comfort the shipwrecked stranger spoke to his men after the scattering and loss of the fleet, as recorded in the book of the *Aeneid*, which runs as follows: 'Hold out and reserve yourselves for good fortune: you who have undergone more serious hardships, God will put an end to these, too', and shortly afterwards: 'It may be that some day you will recall these with pleasure.' And immediately the author adds the following: 'So he spoke and though bowed down by the weight of his cares, he feigned a look of hope on his face, and kept his sorrow deep in his mind.' In the same way we show and offer to the public gaze one emotion on our face, while deep in our suffering heart we hold another one. This is not surprising: the vehemence of our sorrow and anger does not allow us to apply the hands of healing to our raw, sore wounds—wounds made cruel much more, certainly, by the distressing bitterness of shame and dishonour than by the loss of property. So, to reveal our sufferings to the public gaze briefly and in a few words, we are distressed deep at heart much more by the dishonour than by the loss. The following comfort can be offered, though it is laced with bitterness: such ingratitude has the lot of never having a joyful outcome.

Doubtless there will be the chance that a length of time will eventually deaden the pain more when it is easier, if indeed there is an end in time to almost all troubles. Forgetfulness of pain is always the cure, since that which we cannot bury by reasoning, we bury with the passing of time, and all affliction grows old and fades after a long duration and

---

and A. Boutemy, 'Giraud de Barri et Pierre le Chantre. Une source de la *Gemma Ecclesiastica*', *Revue du moyen âge latin*, ii, 1946, pp. 45–62.

125–30. Virgil, *Aen*. i, 207, 199, 203, and 208–9, see *supra*, 96–8. Also *De Invectionibus*, 6, 24 (*Op*. i, p. 184, 3–5, ed. Davies, p. 228, 3–5) and *Expugnatio Hibernica*, 1, 23 (*Op*. v, p. 267, 27–8).

132–4. See note on Ep. 6, 209–10.

141–2. Cf. the letter to Stephen Langton (see note on 79), p. 402, 14–29: *Illud quoque poeticum ad mentem vestram revocandum:* '*Quod male fers, assuesce: feres. Mala cuncta vetustas | lenit*' (= 146), *et illud quoque moralis philosophi* (see note on 162): '*Fors fiet ut dies longa quandoque hebetet laxatum dolorem* (cf. Seneca, *ad Marciam*, 8, 1: *Dolorem longa dies consumit*), *siquidem malis fere cunctis finis de tempore venit* (= 141–2). *Interim autem, dum recens est anxietas, frigent forte verba solantium nec aures applicat consiliis etiam bonis surdus ex multis iniuriis animus* (= 155–6). *Unde poeta:* '*Dum furor . . . furori.*' '*Quis matrem . . . aptus eris*' (=150–4).

144. Cf. *Corpus Iuris Civilis*, ed. Krüger, 1928, p. 567 (a), *Dig*. 36. 1. 22 *in fine:* . . . *prolixitate temporis.*

145 senescit et evanescit afflictio. Quibus et consonat aperte poeticum illud:
Quod male fers, assuesce: feres. Mala cuncta vetustas | lenit, quoniam
effice ut assuescas: nichil assuetudine maius, | difficilem facilem facit as-
suetudo laborem. Item et illud quoque poete eiusdem, qui testante
Seneca ludendo seria scribens nunquam in bene dicendo destitit, hiis
150 concordare videtur: *Dum furor in cursu est, currenti cede furori,* et illud:

> *Quis matrem nisi mentis inops in funere nati*
f. 83ᵛᵃ   *flere vetet? Non hoc illa | monenda loco est.*
> *Accedes melius tunc, cum sua vulnera tangi*
> *iam sinet et veris vocibus aptus eris.*

155 Interim ergo frigent verba solantium nec aures applicat consiliis etiam
bonis surdus ex tot iniuriis animus. Accedit ad hec etiam quod, preter
iam dicta, studii fructum animique grandia conantis et ardua profectum
turbat nimium et pre cunctis adversis sensibiliter magis infestat,
memorie scilicet detrimentum, maximum quidem inter cetera multa
160 senilis etatis incomodum, cuius eximius ille poeta in pastorali poemate
suo breviloquio gaudens sic meminit: *Omnia fert etas, animum quoque*;
et moralis ille philosophus egregius, de quo mentionem iam fecimus,
in libro suo *Declamationum* et libri fere principio de memoria loquens
et huic concordans ait: *Cum multa iam mihi senectus ex me desideranda*
165 *confecerit, oculorum aciem retruderit, aurium sensum ebetaverit, nervorum*
firmitatem fatigaverit, inter ea que retuli memoria res est ex omnibus animi
partibus delicata magis et fragilis, in quam senectus primum incurrit.

Cum itaque mentis tranquille serenitatem tot adversa prepediant et
f. 83ᵛᵇ perturbent cumque preter hec, quod nobilis ocii | lumen tantis tenebris
170 obnubilat et obfuscat, amplius de die in diem debilitata fatiscat et

---

146 vetustas *e* vetustustas *corr.* V

---

146. Ovid, *Ars Am.* ii, 647–8 (*feres bene; multa vetustas | lenit*). The same quotation
in the *De Principis Instructione*, 1, 5 (*Op.* viii, p. 17, 16–17). See also note on 141–2.

147. Ovid, *Ars Am.* ii, 345: *Fac tibi consuescat: nil adsuetudine maius.*

147–8. *Catonis Monosticha*, ed. Baehrens, *PLM*, 3, 1881, p. 240, 70 (*Durum etiam
facilem . . .*).

148–9. Cf. Seneca (the philosopher), *Nat. Quaest.* 3, 27, ed. Gercke (1907), p. 129,
15: . . . *ille poetarum ingeniosissimus* . . . ; Seneca (the father), *Decl.* 2, 2, 8, ed. Müller
(1887–8), p. 133, 11–12: *habebat ille comptum et decens et amabile ingenium* . . . In
his *Speculum Ecclesie* (3, 8: *Op.* iv, p. 173, 1–3) Giraldus refers to Ovid in the same
way: *ut ait gentilis ille poeta nobilis, qui Seneca testante nunquam in bene dicendo destitit:*
'*Pena potest demi, culpa perennis erit*' (*Ex Ponto*, i, 1, 64, see notes on Ep. 5, 156, and
Ep. 6, 252–4).

150–4. Ovid, *Rem. Am.* 119 (*Vita Sancti Hugonis*, 1, 8 (*Op.* vii, p. 104, 30), and
Rem. Am. 127–8 and 125–6, cf. *Topographia Hibernica*, 3, 12 (*Op.* v, p. 157, 10–14):
'*Quis matrem . . . loco est*' Igitur: '*Dum dolor . . . currenti cede dolori* [!], | *tempore cum
residet, iam medicina valet.* See also note on 141–2.

length of time. The following passage from the poet clearly concurs with this view: 'Grow used to that which is hard to bear: you will bear it. The passing of time assuages all ills.' So 'ensure that you get used to them: nothing is more effective than habit, habit makes the difficult task simple'. The following passage of the same poet, who, according to Seneca, wrote serious poetry in fun, and never ceased speaking wisely, seems to agree with these views. 'When madness runs wild, give way to the running madness.' And the following: 'Who but the witless would forbid a mother to weep at her son's burial? She is not to be advised there. You will get on better when she lets her wounds be touched and your voice has a truthful ring.' In the meantime, therefore, words of consolation are like ice, and our heart turns deaf ears to counsel, good though it be. In addition, apart from what has just been mentioned, the process is aggravated by loss of memory, the greatest curse among many others of old age: this disturbs to a great extent and more than all misfortunes perceptibly impairs fruits of study, and the progress of intelligence which is attempting the sublime and difficult. The outstanding poet has put this briefly, delighting in his own epigrammatic style, in his pastoral poem. Age carries all away, as well as the intelligence. And that outstanding moral philosopher, whom we have already mentioned, speaking of memory almost at the beginning of his book of Declamations, says in agreement with this view: 'Though my old age has put an end to many desirable things, though it has blunted the sharpness of my eyes, and dulled the sense of my hearing, and weakened the strength of my sinews, among those which I have mentioned, memory of all the parts of the mind is the most delicate and fragile: this is what old age attacks first.'

Since, then, so many curses trouble and disturb the tranquil peace of my mind, and since in addition to these (for the noble light of leisure is darkening and fading into shadow) our power of memory

155–6. See note on 141–3.

161. Virgil, *Buc.* 9, 51 (*Symbolum Electorum*, 1, 31, *Op.* i, p. 323, 10); *Gemma Ecclesiastica*, 2, 8 (*Op.* ii, p. 205, 30); *De Principis Instructione*, 1, 21 (*Op.* viii, p. 146, 3).

162. moralis ille philosophus egregius] Cf. *De Rebus a se Gestis*, 2 (*Op.* i, p. 47, 2: *moralis Seneca noster;* also *Symbolum Electorum*, 1, 24 (*Op.* i, p. 284, 1): *philosophum gentilem Senecam*; ibid. p. 417, 13–14 (*De libris a se scriptis*): *moralis ille philosophus, Seneca scilicet* (see notes on 141–2 and Ep. 3, 37–40); same page, 34–5: *moralis ille philosophus egregius Seneca*.

162. iam] 148–9.

164–7. Seneca, *Controversiae*, ed. Müller (1887), i, pref. 2, p. 2, 1–5.

168. Cf. 14.

169. Cf. *De Iure et Statu Menevensis Ecclesie*, 7 (*Op.* iii, p. 333, 9–11): *lectioni deditus* [Giraldus himself] *et otio nobili, ad posteritatis gratiam sibi comparandam legendo, scribendo totum mentis acumen applicuit.*

defectum acceleret, annis quoque senilibus et laboriosis pregravata
plurimum iam fere succumbat in nobis consuete nimirum efficatie
viribus evacuata nimis cellula memorialis, postulat id pagina presens et
desiderat quatinus, his prelibatis ut res ipsa suo decetero cursu securius
175 explicetur, *oculis* nunc *subiecta fidelibus* in hoc auditorio vestro, gratie
vestre beneficio et lectoris officio, propaletur.

Qui michi ministrat, me sequatur et cetera, ut alibi.

175. Horace, *Ars* 181.   177. John **xii**, 26.

weakens daily and grows weary, and hastens the loss, and greatly burdened by wearisome years of senility, is now almost gone, robbed of the strength of its useful prowess, the present age desires and demands that this be revealed now before the scrutiny of the eyes of the faithful, in your hearing here, with the aforementioned to expedite this affair for its future course, with the benefit of your grace, and the service of the reader.

'If any man minister to me, let him follow me', etc., as elsewhere.

5

Iohanni priori de Brechene

VENERABILI viro et in Christo dilecto Iohanni priori de Brechene
magister Giraldus de Barri salutem in domino.

Litteras, quas nepos noster egregius, liberalis et naturalis ad partes
5 de Pembroch quasi contra nos et *ad excusandas excusationes* erroneas
⟨direxit⟩, manu quidem sua scriptas et studio magistri sui, qui os suum
est et lingua, dictatas, vestre discretioni pariter et dilectioni transmittere
curavimus simul cum litteris nostris responsalibus, per quas perpendere
9 poteritis aperte, preter cetera quidem indicia multa, que satis et plusquam
f. 84ra satis audistis hactenus et vidistis, mo|res hominum et naturas, qui in
dominum suum et magistrum et utrique proficuum, cum domino non
honor unus, sed omnis inpendi debeat, tam mendaciter scribunt, cum
etiam, si lesi fuissent a nobis et graviter lesi vel dicto, ut aiunt, vel
scripto, multum tolerare deberent et ire mitigationem pacienter expectare
15 et non statim dominum seu iuste sive iniuste motum ac mordentem
canina rabie remordere et ad talionem ilico reddendum tanquam a pari
contendendo festinare.

Scire vos etenim et in primis volumus et per vos tam ipsos quam
alios, quibus litteras istas ostendetis, quod infortunio quodam et For-
20 tune cece malicia, duorum nepotum nostrorum innaturalium nimis
et ingratorum, quos nutrivimus et ample beneficiavimus et quasi de
nichilo creavimus, unum in Hybernia et alterum in Wallia, toxicum
venenatum iam gustavimus, non letale tamen ut cupiunt cuculi nostri,
in perniciem nutritoris, quantum in ipsis est, educati, quibus tedio
25 est vita nostra, quia nos tyriacam salutiferam ad hec venena per dei
gratiam apposuimus et efficacius apponemus, quamvis tamen sacius
fuisset et longe sacius providentia previa ante lesionem occurrere et
sibi precavere quam post causam vulneratam remedium querere. Unus
f. 84rb tamen nepotum illorum, Hybernicus | scilicet, quociens ad nos venit
30 vel nuntios mittit ad nos vel nos ad ipsum, cum omni humilitate se

---

5 excusandas] ex *ss. V*   7 transmittere] ns *ss. V*

---

4. Cf. 20, and Ep. 6, 102; *supra*, part i, 304, 317, etc.
5. Ps. cxl, 4; *supra*, part i, 319.
6–7. Cf. Ps. xlix, 19: *Os tuum abundavit malitia et lingua tua concinnabat dolos*; see
note on Ep. 6, 299–300.   10–11. Cf. 108–9, 238.
16. ad talionem . . . reddendum] Cf. 133, 276–7; Ep. 6, 26, 176–7; Ep. 7, 205 (but
also Ep. 7, 319); Ep. 8, 73, 87.

[5.] *To John, prior of Brecon*

MASTER Giraldus de Barri sends greetings in the name of the Lord to the venerable John, prior of Brecon, beloved in Christ.

Our own excellent and gracious nephew characteristically sent a letter to Pembroke accusing us and 'to make excuses for sinful excuses', written in his own hand and dictated by his tutor, who is his mouth and tongue. We have taken the trouble to send it along with our own reply for your consideration and delectation. Apart from the many other indications of which you have seen and heard more than enough already, these will help you to get a clear grasp of the behaviour and character of the men who write such lies against their own lord and master, to whom both are indebted, as a master should be given his due not in one matter only but in every respect. Also if they have been hurt by us—even hurt seriously—either by something we have said, as they claim, or by something we have written, they ought to be very tolerant and wait patiently for our anger to evaporate. They ought not immediately to rush to snap back at their master like wild dogs, whether he has lost his temper justly or unjustly and snapped at them and hurt their feelings. Nor ought they to repay like with like, as if it were a struggle of equals.

For it is our desire that you in particular learn, and that those men as well as others to whom you show these letters learn from you, that by some bad luck and the malice of blind Fortune we have tasted the cup of poison, served up by our two very unnatural and ungrateful nephews, whom we brought up and amply provided for, and whom we have created from nothing, as it were, one in Ireland and the other in Wales. This drink was not fatal as our young cuckoos who were drawn to harm their foster parent, as is the nature of these birds, would wish. These young men find our life a hindrance, because by God's grace we have applied and shall apply in future a more effective healing antidote to this poison, although it would have been wiser by far to have foreseen the danger and to have taken timely precautions than to seek a remedy for injuries received. For whenever one of these nephews (we mean the Irish one) comes to us or sends us messages or when we send to him,

---

18–19. Cf. Ep. 2, 64.
19–20. Fortune cece] very frequent, cf. Otto, *Sprichwörter*, 694.
20. innaturalium] cf. 4.   21–2. See note on Ep. 2, 91.
24. Cf. 237–8.
25. tyriacam (= theriacam), cf. Pliny, *Nat. Hist.* xx, 24, 100 (264).

culpabilem in excessibus suis recognoscit et causas quasi urgentes
adnectens et veniam petens se nobis satisfacturum in omnibus et
obsecuturum tanquam domino et patruo firmiter compromittit; alter
autem, Walensicus scilicet, immo verius Flandrensicus, si mala fecit,
35 se longe deteriora facturum tanquam potentie vir magne, sed verius
dementie maioris et nequitie, cum comminatione promittit—nec
mirum tamen, ubi animo nequam ex natura et ⟨in⟩ malum prorsus
admisso monitores addant etiam calcaria cotidie nequiores, sed nequicia
prodeat in publicum inmoderata, maxime vero cum ille, qui ab initio
40 tante malicie tantique scandali seminario obviasse pontificaliter et
emergentia tanquam Ydre capita obruisse viriliter et contrivisse debuisset
ac potuisset, quasi clausis oculis, ne dicamus conniventibus, et sub
quadam dissimulatione cuncta pertransit. Verum in iure cautum esse
dinoscitur quia *ratiabitio mandato comparatur*, cui et consonat aperte
45 canon ille Ignacii pape: *Error, cui non resistitur, approbatur et veritas*
cum minime defensatur, opprimitur, et ille Innocencii quoque: *Negligere*
f. 84ᵛᵃ *cum possis perturbare per|versos, nichil est aliud quam fovere nec caret*
scrupulo societatis oculte, qui manifesto facinori desinit obviare, precipue
quidem cum ad hoc ex officio teneatur. Quid etiam in fautores dis-
50 cordiarum et fotores statuant canones, satis est notum. Porro nisi tam
magnos Ylion hostes habuisset et impugnatores, non tanta repugnantium,
Hectoris scilicet et Troili, laus fuisset. Unde poeta: *Hectora quis nosset,*
felix si Troia fuisset? Ardua per preceps gloria stravit iter.

Nunc autem ad litteras eodem zelo et studio, quo contra nos actum
55 est, conceptas et fabricatas respondebimus. Quod enim in primis
scribunt, se arbitrio bonorum virorum nullatenus supponere velle,
nec eorum etiam, quos loco suo domnus episcopus ad hoc assignavit,
dicimus quod ad arbitrium quodlibet vel quorumlibet nos episcopus
non astrinxit, sed ut infra terminum illum et pascha proximo subsecuti-
60 vum coram ipso, si ad hoc intendere posset, vel his, quibus vices suas
in hoc committeret, compareremus simul cum nepote nostro peroptimo

34 Flandensicus *V*   41 ydrie *V*   52 noscet *V*

40. pontificaliter] Cf. Ep. 7, 28, 132, and *supra*, part i, 230–1: episcopaliter agens.
41. Cf. *supra*, part ii, 439.   42–3. Cf. Ep. 7, 49–50.
44–9. The same quotations occur in Ep. 6, 139, 268–73, Ep. 7, 66–71, Ep. 8, 266–72;
also in *De Rebus a se Gestis*, 2, 14 (*Op.* i, p. 71, 3–10), *De Iure et Statu Menevensis*
Ecclesie, 4 and 7 (*Op.* iii, p. 219, 23–9 and p. 363, 11–18) and *Topographia Hibern In*
3, 30 (*Op.* v, p. 177, 8–14). They have been taken from the *Dig.* 50, 17, 152:*ica*,
maleficio ratihabitio mandato comparatur, and from Gratian, c. 3 D. LXXXIII (*Item*
Innocentius: Error . . . obviare) and c. 55 C. II q. 7 (*Item illud Eleuterii papae: Negligere*
. . . obviare) (the words *precipue . . . teneatur* in all the above-mentioned quotations
are not part of the canon, cf. Introduction, p. lvi). In the Letters the attributions
are always to Ignatius papa (!) and to Pope Innocent; in *De Rebus a se Gestis* and in
De Iure et Statu etc., ch. 4, it is to Innocent only, as in Distinctio 83; in *De Iure* etc.,

with all humility he admits his transgressions and seeing good reason asks for forgiveness and promises to give us satisfaction in all things and to obey us strictly, as his uncle and benefactor. But when the other (the Welsh, or rather Flemish one) behaves badly, he boasts that he will do far worse, threatening like a man of great influence, but in truth he is more like a fool and a felon. And no wonder, since his advisers, who grow more evil daily, add fuel to a mind already aflame with wickedness; but immoderate wickedness will come to light, especially since the man who (as bishop) should have and could have taken measures from the beginning against such malice and scandal, and like a man should have cut off these Hydra's heads as they grew, in fact shut his eyes to, or even connived at it and tolerated it all, pretending not to see. For as the law warns: 'Approbation comes close to authorization'; which is clearly in keeping with the canon of Pope Ignatius: 'To fail to correct an error is to approve it, and to fail to defend truth is to repress it'; and the canon of Innocent: 'Not to correct when possible those who have gone astray is tantamount to encouraging them. Nor is the man who fails to take action against a patent crime free of the suspicion of being secretly in league with it.' This is even more true when he is bound to do so by virtue of his office. Furthermore what the canons decide against patrons of discord is well enough known. Indeed, if Troy had not had such mighty foes to attack them, the praise for its defenders, Hector and Troilus, would not have been so great. As the poet says: 'Who would have heard of Hector if Troy had not been in trouble? The road to fame is steep and is strewn with difficulties.'

Now, then, we shall reply to the letter which was thought out and fabricated with the same eagerness and enthusiasm with which they acted against us. For, as they write in the first place, they will not subject themselves to the arbitration of upright men—not even of those whom the Lord Bishop had appointed to act on his behalf in this matter; our reply is that the bishop has not constrained us in any arbitration of anybody at all, but that we should appear before him after that date and following next Easter, if that were convenient for him, or else before others whom he would appoint to act in his stead. With us should

ch. 7, they are to Innocent (*Error*, etc.) and Ignatius (*Negligere*, etc.), in the *Topographia Hibernica* to Innocent (*Error*, etc.) and to Eleutherius (*Negligere*, etc.). See also (for 44) in Peter of Blois, *Canon episcopalis*, Migne, *P.L.* 207, col. 1101A, and (for 45 [Innocentius] and 45–8) in the *Causa inter Cantuariensem archiepiscopum et episcopum Londoniensem*, Materials for the History of Thomas Becket, ed. Robertson, R.S. 67 (1875–85), iv. p. 215, 7–9 and 14–17. Also *supra*, part i, 366–7.

49–50. Cf. Ep. 6, 266–7.

52. poeta] Ovid, *Tristia* iv, 3, 75 and 74. The same quotation in *De Invectionibus*, 5, 4 (see note on 230–1), *De Iure et Statu Menevensis Ecclesie*, 3 (*Op.* iii, p. 205, 6–8), and *Expugnatio Hibernica*, 2, 28 (*Op.* v, p. 365, 9–10).

Willelmo de Barri, cui scamonie revera nichil adheret, ceterisque probis
viris cognatis communibus et amicis, temptaturi scilicet si per eorum
64 operas et diligentias discordia tanta posset ullatenus in concordiam
f. 84vb revocari, et ut interim quod tenebat quo|vismodo quisque teneret nec
aliquo rescripto vel instrumento a curia Romana seu aliunde perquisito
contra alium quis uteretur, et hoc tantum in manu domni episcopi
diocesiani fuit fide mediante firmatum. Unde cum et hoc facturum se
nepos ille noster nunc abneget, de primo quidem est falsitatis et menda-
70 cii manifestus assertor, de secundo vero fidei inverecundus et impudens
est transgressor, sicut et apud Lincolniam fuit, cum in manu domni
decani maioris ecclesie coram multis et magnis tanti capituli viris
fidem dedit se contra festum sancti Michaelis proximo futuri Lincolniam
ad nos rediturum: qui demum circa Purificationem beate Virginis illuc
75 venit et tunc quidem sicut recedendo, sic et revertendo perversus.
Proinde et tunc quidem ad minus tempore fuit lapsa fides. Scribit
tamen sicut criminosi, qui quod obiciendum sibi verentur, primum
aliis imponunt, nos in manu domni episcopi fidem dedisse, quod nec
dicto nec scripto ipsum decetero lederemus. In quo mendax est aperte
80 sicut et in ceteris, quia nec linguam episcopus nec stilum, in quo est
solacium nostrum, cohibere potuit nec ullam etiam super hoc mentionem
fecit, sed de facto solum et ut nepos quod occupaverat tam naturaliter
et tam liberaliter, interim in pace teneret nos constrinxit. Unde et in
f. 85ra hoc | sicut et in aliis fere cunctis se per omnia mendacem ostendit.
85 Dicit etiam et mendaciter dicit ac scribit, quod redditus illos, quos
nunc repetimus, coram archiepiscopo Cantuariensi resignatos abiura-
vimus et compensationem aliam in redditibus aliis ab ipso recepimus.
Sed que nos, quesumus, ad hoc necessitas compelleret aut constringeret,
cum post concordiam inter archiepiscopum et nos factam diebus aliquot,
90 ipso quidem archiepiscopo, deo teste, plurimum in primis admirante
et propositum nostrum dissuadente, nepotis nostri promotionem minus
discrete procuravimus? Sed ad hoc revera faciendum lacrime patris
optimi, in verbis ultimis nobis factis pro ipso cum precibus effuse, magis
quam indoles ulla filii pessimi compulerunt.
95   Quod et de compensatione scribunt, per hoc similiter falsum esse
constat, quia notum est illis, qui concordie inter nos et archiepiscopum
facte intererant, quod ipse, licet nos soli in causa dignitatis ecclesie

70 asse//tor (*ras.*) V

---

66. Cf. 107–8.   73 (cf. Ep. 6, 60). festum sancti Michaelis] 29 September.
74. Purificationem beate Virginis] 2 February.

come our very fine nephew, William de Barri, who is not involved in the unpleasant side of this, and the other upright men—relatives, neighbours, and friends—who should make every effort, somehow to restore this dissension to harmony, using all their wit. Meanwhile each side should hold on to what he has, and should not make use of a mandate or other document procured from the Roman curia, or any other source, against the other. This was all that was agreed upon, in good faith, with the blessing of the diocesan bishop. And so, since that nephew of ours now refuses to do even this, in the first place he is clearly an advocate of lies and falsehood, and in the second place he is shamelessly and callously breaking his trust, just as he did at Lincoln when he gave his word to the dean of the cathedral, before a number of important men of that great chapter, that he would return to us at Lincoln by next Michaelmas. In the end he arrived there about the Purification of the Blessed Virgin, and then, indeed, he was just as wicked on his return as he was on his departure. On this occasion he caused us to lose faith in him by this delay alone. Moreover he writes like the guilty man who is the first to impute to others the blame which he fears will be laid against him, saying that we had given a promise to the Lord Bishop not to attack him in future either in words or in writings. In this, as in other things, he is obviously a liar, because the bishop could not prevent us from speaking or writing (this is our consolation). Nor did he ever mention any such thing, but in fact only bound us to accept that our nephew should hold on provisionally in peace to what he had taken over so freely and unscrupulously. In this as in almost everything else he shows himself to be a consistent liar. Furthermore, he claims— and what he says and writes is untrue—that under oath before the arch- bishop of Canterbury we resigned those incomes which we are now reclaiming, and that we received compensation from him in other incomes. But what necessity, we ask, would force or compel us to this, when we procured the promotion of our nephew with too little discretion a few days after the agreement between the archbishop and ourselves, while that very same archbishop, as God is our witness, was at first very surprised and tried to dissuade us from our proposal? We were moved to do this for our wretched nephew, not because he in fact deserved it, but because his dear father, when he last spoke to us, with tears in his eyes pleaded with us on his behalf.

What they write about the compensation is untrue for the same reason, for those who were present at the agreement between the archbishop and ourselves know that, since we were left standing alone on the issue of the dignity of our church, after all the others had been corrupted and

nostre tunc essemus, ceteris cunctis per corruptionem abstractis, sexaginta marcatas reddituum se nobis in Anglia daturum, ut ab eius vexa-
100 tione cessaremus, firmiter pepigit. De quibus et XX marcatas ante
obitum suum suscepimus et adhuc tenemus. Litis igitur hec redemptio
f. 85ʳᵇ fuit et | non reddituum vel commutatio vel compensatio. Per hoc etiam
id patere potest, quod reddituum nostrorum in Wallia, ad quos ibi
nepotem nostrum promoveri curavimus, coram archiepiscopo et episcopo
105 nostro aliisque viris magnis et multis, administrationem nobis quamdiu
vellemus et gubernationem communi consensu et auctoritate reservavimus.

Item dicit et scribit quod litteris a curia Romana vel aliunde perquisitis ipsum vexare contendimus, tanquam falsarii crimen in dominum ac patruum suum sibi tam proficuum valde naturaliter oblique
110 contorquens. Sed utrum vere sint littere an falso perquisite, forsan
adhuc in rei experientia quandoque comperiet. Credimus tamen quod
nepos noster, ut ipsum in aliquo saltem excusemus, verbi illius virus,
per notarium suum omni nequitia notabilem appositi, pocius non
averterit quam sciens et prudens, in hoc tamen inprudens, id per
115 industriam annotaverit.

Notarius etiam ille, notis non innoxiis tam notabilis aliosque notabiles reddens, ut litteraturam ostentet in aliquo, qua funditus caret,
de tragedia mentionem in litteris facit, sed hoc quasi pro nosti quo
quodam, quoniam hec leta sui discipulique | principia more tragedico
120 mestum et amarum, ut tales agressus decet, finem et exitum deo dante
consequentur. Item de quodam libello nostro mentionem faciens,
Speculum, ut verbis alludat tanquam retor bonus, in *Spiculum* trans-
vertit, sed que sit exornatio, qua sic abutitur qui rethoricam nunquam
audivit, credimus quod non novit, et si nomen coloris illius ipsum ex
125 usu forte magis quam arte nosse contigerit, sub qua specie tamen
exornationis illius, cum littera scilicet in litteram convertitur, scimus
pro certo quod prorsus ignorat. Utinam autem turpia, quibus liber
ille redundat et ex veris certe, non ex fictis, quem ipsi *Speculum* aut
Spiculum vocant, nos autem *Correctionis librum et Conquestionis*, tan-
130 tum ea et similia perpetrasse aut perpetrare formidarent, quantum in
scriptis abhorrent adnotata!

Domnus papa in epistola, quam nuper scripsit, super imperatoris
ingratitudine conqueritur, ad cuius procurandum promocionem per
decennium et amplius hanelavit. Siqua ibi reperiuntur, quibus fama

119 princia *V*   121 faciens *bis, alt. del. V*   127–8 ille liber *transposuit V*

107–8. Cf. 66.   108–9. See note on 10–11.
118–19. nosti quo quodam] Cf. 146, 163–4 (note); *supra*, part ii, 402–3.
121–7. Cf. Giraldus' use of this *color* in Ep. 6, 193–8, and 239–40.
128. Cf. 2 Cor. vi, 6, or 1 Tim. i, 5, or 2 Tim. i, 5: *non ficta*.

withdrew their support, the archbishop solemnly gave his word to assign incomes to us in England to the value of sixty marks, if we would stop troubling him. Before he died we received twenty marks of this income, and we still have this sum. This payment covered that issue, and was not a cash compensation for other incomes. Thus, it is also quite clear that we have reserved for ourselves for as long as we wish, by common agreement and with general acceptance, the administration of our incomes in Wales to which we had our nephew assigned on that occasion, in the presence of the archbishop, our bishop, and many other worthy men.

He also says and writes that we have tried to annoy him through letters, obtained from the Roman curia and other sources, and he twists the truth, accusing us, who as his master and uncle are so spontaneously beneficent to him, of forgery. But whether the letters were procured by fair means or foul he will see in time when the matter is put to the test. However, we believe, to give our nephew credit at least to some degree, that he failed to avoid the poison of that statement issued by his notary—a man noted for his wickedness—rather than that he deliberately wrote it with malice aforethought, though he was not farsighted in this matter.

That notary—so notorious for his criminal reputation and who makes others notorious—in order to show a smattering of literature, of which he lacked the fundamentals, refers to 'tragedy' in his letter, but only on behalf of someone you know: for these first moves which went so well for him and his pupil, with God's help will end, as tragedies do, in sorrow and bitterness, as befits such a fine start. Moreover, he referred to a certain pamphlet of ours: to make a play on words, as if he were a good rhetorician, he twisted *Speculum* into *Spiculum*, but we believe that this man, who has never had a rhetorical lesson, does not know what *exornatio* is, though he misuses it in this way, and if he happens to know the name of this trope, by accident rather than skill, we are absolutely convinced that he does not know under what category of *exornatio* the substitution of one letter for another comes. However, would that they had feared to have perpetrated, or to perpetrate, these and similar wickednesses with which that book, which they call a *Speculum* or *Spiculum*, and we *A Book of Correction and Complaint*, is stuffed (from fact, not fiction) as much as they shun them when they are written down.

In a letter, which he has recently written, our Lord Pope complains of the ingratitude of the Emperor, whose promotion he has exerted every effort to achieve for ten years or more. Anything found there, by which the reputation of the Emperor should be justifiably denigrated,

129. Cf. *supra*, part i, 1–2.   132–6. See note on Ep. 2, 88–96.   133. See note on 16.

f. 85vb   inperatoris merito denigrari debeat, sibi quidem et non scripto | imputet
136   aut scriptori. Parabola hec est libelli nostri.

Item mentionem facit litteris suis nepos noster de beneficiis suis
ecclesiasticis canonice, ut dicit, adeptis—sed utrum supplesset, ut
mendax in hoc sicut in aliis dictis suis appareret: per probitatem suam
140   et non per alterius gratiam perquisitis!

Item scribit nepos ille nepoti nostro Willelmo de Barri et, quamquam
fratri, sibi per omnia tamen in cute simul et extra longe dissimili, de
genere suo materno per scripta nostra, ut asserit, ignominiose diffamato,
matrem quoque communem sepe commemorans et inculcans, quatinus
145   illum erga nos per litteras et suggestiones ac dilationes iniquas exaspe-
rare queat, sicut et alium quempiam quandoque fecit, quemadmodum
ex post facto patuit et adhuc patet. Sed frustra quidem ad hoc nititur,
quoniam inter nos et hunc nepotem amiciciam nature conformitas et
morum concordia sic firmavit, sicut ex altera parte nature diversitas
150   et morum discordia fedus amicicie dissociavit.

Item dicit et scribit quod per scripta nostra genus suum est diffa-
matum. Dicimus autem econtra et verius dicimus, quia longe magis
f. 86ra   per facta propria, quamvis nichil inde scriptum foret, et facinora | sua.
Infamia namque iuris aboleri utcumque per principem potest, facti
155   vero infamia nunquam: quis enim cohibere potest ora populi mur-
murantis? Unde poeta: *Pena potest demi, culpa perhennis erit.*

Delicati sunt igitur et indiscreti, qui delinquere graviter et enormiter
volunt et tamen ora loquentium manusque scribentium compescere
querunt. Illud autem Ieronimi pocius et propensius hii tales advertant:
160   *Si fama anno preterito de te mentita fuit vel certe si verum dixit: cesset
vicium, cessabit et rumor.*

Ad hec etiam, quia nunquam sola veniunt scandala (sed *ve homini,
per quem scandalum venit*), in curia notati cuiusdam quia notabilis,
notati quidem non nominati, minores omnes sicut et maiores de novo
165   nos lacerant et inter nos et nostros moventes discordiam et foventes,
aquam antea limpidam et claram, ut melior fieri piscatio possit turbare
non cessant. Sic corbini communiter crocitant et clamitant sicut et
veteres corvos crocitare prius audierant. Sed cur adeo lesa caritate,
que lesio gravis est nimis et periculosa penitusque saluti contraria,
170   exosos nunc habent et invisos nil tale meritos vel merentes, quia deo

---

142. Cf. Persius, *Sat.* iii, 30: *intus et in cute.*   146. See note on 118–19.
    156. Ovid, *Ex Ponto*, i, 1, 64, see notes on (Ep. 4, 148–9 and) Ep. 6, 252–4; *supra*,
part ii, 629.   157. See note on Ep. 2, 36.
    159. Ieronimi] *Ep.* 54, 13, 4, *CSEL*, 54, p. 480, 11–12. The same quotation occurs
in the *Symbolum Electorum*, 1, 28 (*Op.* i, p. 303, 6–10): *Ieronymus tamen in libro epistolari solatium his prestare videtur, dicens: Si fama . . . rumor.*

he should attribute to himself, not to the writing, or the writer. This is a parable relating to our pamphlet.

Again, in his letter, our nephew refers to his ecclesiastical benefices acquired, as he claims, canonically—but I wonder whether he should have added (to prove himself a liar in this matter as in the rest of his utterances): acquired by his own sanctity, and not thanks to anyone else.

Again that nephew writes to our nephew, William de Barri, who, though his brother, is none the less far different superficially and inwardly, of his mother's family, which, as he says, has been shamefully maligned by our writings: he also frequently mentions and insists that they share the same mother, to be able to embitter him towards us by letters, insinuations, and unfair exaggerations, just as he does with anyone else whenever he wishes, as became clear subsequently, and is clear today. But he labours his point in vain, since the natural affinity and similarity of moral outlook has strengthened the friendship between us and this nephew, just as in the case of the other the natural diversity and dissimilarity of moral outlook has destroyed the bonds of friendship.

Furthermore, he says in his letter that his own family is being maligned in our books, to which we reply—and with greater justification —that it was defamed much more by his own behaviour and actions, even if nothing were written about it. For while a legal disgrace can be removed at any time by the prince, once something has been done it cannot be undone. For who can stop the people from talking? As the poet says: 'Remove the punishment, but the guilt remains.'

Therefore, those who wish to commit an outrageous crime and still try to bind and gag those who would talk or write about it, are overbearing and unreasonable. It would be more fitting for such men as these to turn to Jerome: 'If last year's slander about you was untrue, or if indeed it spoke the truth: let the vice cease, and the gossip will cease.'

Scandals never come singly—but woe to the man who causes a scandal. At the court of somebody well known as a public figure (who shall remain anonymous), young and old alike bedevil us anew, causing trouble between us and our followers. They never cease to stir up water that had been previously clear and limpid so that they can fish more successfully. Young ravens scream and caw in chorus as they have heard the old ravens do. God is my witness that 'I know nothing against myself. Yet am I not hereby justified' in their eyes. Why do they hate us now and envy us, although we have never deserved this and do

162–3. Matt. xviii, 7; Luke xvii, 1 (cf. Ep. 6, 55): see note on Ep. 4, 78; *supra*, part i, 306–7.   163–4. See note on 118–19, and *supra*, part i, 624.
  166–7. Cf. Ep. 6, 44–6, 295–6; *supra*, part ii, 301–2, 652, 1125–6; Walter Map, *De Nugis Curialium*, 5, 7, ed. James, 1914, p. 254, 14.

f. 86rb teste *nichil michi conscius sum* (*nec* tamen apud illos | *in hoc iustificatus sum*)? Aliam igitur huius malicie tante causam erga nos videre non possumus, nisi quia forte gravis sum eis ad videndum, gravior etiam ad vivendum. Dissimilis est enim eis vita nostra. Vivere tamen adhuc

175 aliquamdiu et in pace vivere et retro acta deflere vitamque corrigere vellemus, quod et summopere desideramus, si permitterent. Sed inimicus homo, bonis semper invidens propositis, tritico nostro puro, domesticorum maxime nostrorum utens malicia tanquam instrumento, zizania superseminavit.

180   Preterea, ut ad nepotem nostrum revertamur, qui tam amplam nobis scribendi materiam prebet et utinam in bonis, dicit et publice iactitat, quia medietatem reddituum suorum, sed per nos, ut credimus, adeptorum, quatinus operas nostras bene remuneret, ad nos vincendum expenderet: dedecus enim ei maximum, ut asserit, foret, suggerente

185 quoque magistro suo, si ab illo vinceretur in hac causa, vetusto scilicet et vexato quasi deliro et infatuato et ab omnibus victo, Willelmum quoque Fichet inter alios nominans et Philippum falsum diaconum ac tyneosum tanquam victores, sed se non minus in hoc mendacem quoque quam maliciosum ostendit. Victi namque fuerunt hii ambo et

f. 86va non | victores, si victi censendi fuerint qui magnorum virorum inter-
191 ventu flexisque genibus et cum lacrimis veniam petunt, et si merito victor habendus fuerit qui pocius in tali casu, ubi superbia convertitur in humilitatem, misericordiam exercet quam vindictam. Summum namque victorie genus est, ut ait Seneca, vindicare potuisse, sed in

195 victos tamen misericordiam exercuisse. Hec est enim leonina nobilitas. Unde poeta:

> *Quo quisque est maior, magis est placabilis ira*
> *et faciles motus mens generosa capit.*
> *Corpora magnanimo satis est prostrasse leoni:*
200 > *pugna suum finem cum iacet hostis habet.*
> *At lupus et turpes instant morientibus ursi*
> *et quecumque minor nobilitate fera est.*

Item et Stacius:

> *Ut leo, Massili cum lux stetit obvia ferri,*
205 > *tunc ungues, tunc arma citat; cum decidit hostis*
> *ire satis super est vitamque relinquere victo.*

190 fuerint] fcīerint *V*

171–2. 1 Cor. iv, 4.

172–6. Cf. Ep. 7, 200–4, 248–50 (173, cf. *supra*, note on part i, 335–6).

177–9. Matt. xiii, 25: . . . *venit inimicus . . . et superseminavit zizania in medio tritici* . . . ; cf. Ep. 6, 276; Ep. 7, 287, and *infra*, 275–6.

not now, and why do they thrust kindness aside, an act which is all too serious and dangerous and altogether unsalutary? We can see no other cause for such malice against us except perhaps that 'it is hard enough for them to see me; it is harder for them to live with me'. For our life is unlike theirs. Yet we would like to live for a while in peace, regret the past, and improve our life. This would be our greatest wish, if only they would let us. But the enemy, always envious of good intentions, sowed tares among our good seed, taking advantage of the malice of our family.

Furthermore, to return to our nephew, who provides us with plenty of material to write about (if only it were in his favour!): he boasts publicly that to crush us he would spend half of his income, which, however, he gained with our assistance, in order to repay our kindness, so we believe. For it would be extremely disgraceful, as he puts it (his tutor also suggested the idea), if he were to be defeated in this issue by that frustrated old man, who is almost foolish, insane, and has been defeated by everyone else. He names amongst others William Fichet and Philip, that lying, loud-mouthed deacon, as triumphing over us, but in this matter, too, he proves himself no less mendacious than malicious. For these two were the victims rather than the victors, if people have to be regarded as victims when they ask for pardon at the request of important men, crying on bended knee, and if some one should rightly be regarded as victor, who, when pride turns to humility, practises mercy rather than revenge. 'For it is the highest form of victory', says Seneca, 'to have been in a position to take revenge, but to have shown mercy to the vanquished. For in this lies the lion's nobility.' As the poet says: 'The greater a man is, the more easily his anger is stilled, and the noble mind understands the slightest hints. It is enough for the noble lion to have felled his victim; the fight comes to an end when the enemy is laid low. But the wolf and the cowardly bear menace the dying, and every beast that is less noble.' And as Statius says: 'As when the lion is faced by a flashing Massylian blade, then he uses his claws, then he uses his defences: when the foe is fallen his anger is satisfied and he spares the life of the victim.'

186–7. Cf. *supra*, part ii, 281 and 357–82.

193–5. Cf. (Ps.-Seneca, =) Martin of Braga, *Formula vitae honestae* (= *De quattuor virtutibus cardinalibus*), ed. C. W. Barlow (New Haven, 1950) (*Martini episcopi Bracarensis Opera omnia*), p. 241, 7–8: *vindictam putabis vindicare potuisse: scito enim honestum et magnum vindictae esse genus ignoscere.* Cf. *supra*, part i, 1163, and *infra*, note on Ep. 7, 269–71.

197–202 and 204–6. Ovid, *Tristia* iii, 5, 31–6 and Statius, *Thebais*, viii, 124–6 (*ire supra satis est*); both quotations also occur in *De Principis Instructione*, i, 7 (*Op.* viii, p. 23, 11–12: the editor does not give the quotations in full there).

Sin autem dixerit livor et obiecerit quod in causa, propter quam tantum laboravimus tociensque Romam transmigravimus, non optinuimus, sed pocius a spe cecidimus, respondemus, quod nemo tam fortis,
210 quem non possit potentia maior opprimere nec elephas tam robustus aut camelus tam gibbosus, quem non valeat sarcina nimium gravis et inmoderata moles obruere, quoniam, ut ait Agellius, sine culpa mole sarcine vincitur, qui ad portandum onus, etsi impar, tamen devotus,
f. 86ᵛᵇ occur|rit. Item et Seneca: *Magnarum rerum etsi successus non fuerit,*
215 *honestus tamen est ipse conatus.*

Veruntamen tantus agressus et tam pertinaciter perseverans tantusque dignitatis ecclesie sue zelus, etsi finem debitum ac desideratum non plene fuerit consecutus, transire non debet illaudatus. Unde et in libro *Methamorfosios*, ubi Archieloi cum Hercule pugna describitur, ait
220 poeta, animosum quamvis et presumptuosum viri commendans agressum: *Vinci non tam turpe fuit, quam contendisse decorum,* et in eodem, Phetontis tanquam epitaphium scribens: *Hic situs est Pheton, currus hauriga paterni | quem si non tenuit, magnis tamen excidit ausis;* idem et alibi:

225   *Ut desint vires, tamen est laudanda voluntas:*
        hac ego contentos auguror esse deos.
        Hec facit ut veniat pauper quoque gratus ad aram
        et valeat ceso non minus agna bove,

et idem alibi: *Careat successibus, opto, | quisquis ab eventu facta notanda*
230 *putat,* et illud eiusdem: *Non est in medico semper relevetur ut eger: | interdum docta plus valet arte malum.* Item et Aristotiles: *Nec medicus semper sanabit nec orator semper persuadebit; sed si ex contingentibus nichil omiserit, satis utrumque propositam dicemus habere disciplinam.*
f. 87ʳᵃ Intestinum igitur est bellum et detestabile nimis, viscera | tanquam
235 in ventrem coniurata, dum nepos patruum iuvenisque senem ad pugnam provocat et senilibus annis nostris sibique tam inutilibus tam iuveniliter insultat et tanquam cuculus alter mordaciter et voraciter insurgit in nutritorem suumque sibique tam proficuum totis querit prosternere nisibus promotorem. Audiat tamen illud Ieronimi ad Augustinum et

234 *ante* tanquam *del. est* tam *V*

---

212. Agellius (= A. Gellius)] Quotation not identified.
214-15. Ps.-Seneca, *De moribus*, 85, ed. Haase, *Supplementum* (1902), p. 63; cf. *De Iure et Statu Menevensis Ecclesie*, 3 (*Op.* iii, pp. 204-5): *Item et illud Senece: In arduis aggressibus etsi non sequatur effectus, laudabilis tamen est ipse conatus.*
221. Ovid, *Met.* ix, 5-6 (*nec tam | turpe fuit vinci*).
222-3. Ovid, *Met.* ii, 327-8.
225-8. Ovid, *Ex Ponto*, iii, 4, 79-82 (*et placeat*).
229-30. Ovid, *Heroides*, ii, 85-6. The same verse is quoted in the *De Iure et Statu*

But should malice raise the objection that we have not succeeded in the cause on which we have spent such labour and travelled so often to Rome, but that we have despaired, we reply that nobody is so strong that superior power cannot defeat him, nor is the elephant so mighty or the camel so hump-backed that a heavy or excessive load cannot knock him down. For as Agellius says, 'the man is guiltless who is beaten by the weight of the burden, when he is willing to carry it, though not equal to it.' Similarly Seneca says: 'It is honourable to have attempted such things, even without success.'

So great an enterprise, carried out with such determination and such enthusiasm for the dignity of his church, should not be passed over without praise, although the desired result, which should have been achieved, was not fully realized. As the poet says in the *Metamorphoses* when the fight between Hercules and Achelous is described, in praise of the bold and arrogant attack of the man: 'It was not so shameful to have been beaten as honourable to have fought.' And in the same book he writes the epitaph for Phaethon: 'Here lies Phaethon, the driver of his father's chariot. Although he did not succeed in holding it, he died with great braveness.' And again elsewhere: 'Although strength is lacking, a willing spirit is to be praised. I prophesy that the gods will be content with it. This makes the poor man come well received at the altar. And he may have influence by the slaughter of a lamb no less than an ox.' And again elsewhere: 'In my opinion, may whoever thinks deeds are to be judged by their outcome be unsuccessful.' And from the same poet: 'A doctor is not always able to heal a patient; the illness is sometimes stronger than the skilful learning.' And again in Aristotle: 'The doctor will not always be successful nor the orator always convincing; but if they leave out nothing proper, we shall say that both have the necessary skill.' Therefore, it is a most detestable family feud, as if the intestines had conspired against the stomach, when a nephew challenges his uncle, the young challenging the old, and does harm to us so childishly in our old age, we who are now so useless to him; and when, like the cuckoo, he boldly and greedily stands up against the one who reared him and with strong blows tries to knock down his own generous benefactor. Then he should keep and bear in mind the words of Jerome to Augustine:

Menevensis Ecclesie, 3 (*Op.* iii, p. 204, 26–7) and (with the lines quoted above (52–3) and in 230–3) in the *De Invectionibus*, 5, 4 (*Op.* i, p. 129; ed. Davies, p. 186, 4–15).

230–1. Ovid, *Ex Ponto*, i, 3, 17–18, cf. Werner–Flury, *Lateinische Sprichwörter und Sinnsprüche des Mittelalters* (1966), no. 158. See also note on 229–30.

230–3. See note on 229–30 (231–3 not identified, but cf. *supra*, part i, 751–2).

234. Cf. Sallust, *Cat.* 5, 2. Cf. Ep. 7, 281–4.   237–8. Cf. 24.   238. See note on 10–11.

239–40. Jerome, *Ep.* 102, 2, *CSEL*, 55, 1912, p. 236, 10: *Memento . . . quod bos lassus fortius figat pedem* (= Augustine, *Ep.* 68, 2, *CSEL*, 34, 1895, p. 242, 11).

240 animo reponat: *Memento quod bos vetulus forcius pedem figit!* Confidimus
autem in domino, qui iudex est iustus et vindex virtuosus, quod tantam
maliciam non relinquet in terris inpunitam et quod eius virtute, *a quo*
bona cuncta procedunt et talionem pravi suscipiunt, minitantem capiti
nostro clavam clava maiori retundemus et ⟨quod⟩ tam enorme facinus in
245 posterum et tam exemplo perniciosum ac contagiosum in consequentia
non trahetur per dei gratiam efficiemus.

Gradatim tamen ad hoc et non saltim accedemus, sed fidei per
omnia pactum adimplentes modestieque pariter et fame nostre con-
sulentes, quid amici communes super pace reformanda et scandali
250 tanti macula delenda ac diluenda proficere possint attemptabimus, et
modum ac modestiam nostram ac liberalitatem, quam post dedecus
tantum et dampna suscepta tam male merito et tam ingrato, si resipisceret, exhiberemus, generi nostro primum in Wallia, deinde in
f. 87ʳᵇ Hybernia propalabi|mus. Postmodum etiam ordine suo totum in
255 capitulo Herefordensi necnon et Lincolniensi sicut et episcopis Anglie
maioribus, quam cito dominus ecclesie Anglicane pacem dederit,
proponetur eorumque consilio, quibus non ignoti sumus nec causa
nostra incognita, quoniam *arma tenenti | omnia dat, qui iusta negat,*
perperam actum deo dante corigetur, quatinus et sic, ubi culpam
260 invenerint incorrigibilem et obstinatam, illum merito culpabilem
reputent omnes et illaudabilem, et cum lis *suo Marte* decurrerit, si a
causa forte ceciderit et sinistrum calculum reportaverit, cum etiam
interdum honeste cause, nedum turpissime varia sint fata et valde
ambigua, minus ab omnibus plangi debeat, quin immo verius tanquam
265 iniqus et obstinatus dignus habeatur hostiliter irrideri. Novit tamen ille,
qui omnia novit, quem testem ad hoc inducimus, quod si contra mentem
loquimur, gravem, quod absit, in nos ultorem provocamus, quia voluntatem et animum habuimus certoque cum hoc proposito iuxta fidei
prestite pactum ad amicorum examen accessimus, quatinus ab utroque,
270 tam magistro scilicet quam discipulo, si resipisceret, post illata dampna
f. 87ᵛᵃ et dedecora tanta, probra, minas et convitia satisfactionem | etsi non
condignam, modestam tamen et honestam susciperemus et nolentes,
si locus adesset et occasio iusta, vinci a malo, sed vincere pocius in bono

243 pravam *V*　　　　245 pernicium *V*　　　　272 codignam *V*

242-3. *Dominica V post Pascha*: Oratio.
256. See note on Ep. 4, 15-17.　　　　258. Lucan, *Phars.* i, 348-9.

'Remember an old ox treads more firmly.' But we trust that God who is the just and the rightful avenger will not let such evil go unpunished on earth, and that, in his mercy, 'from whom all blessings flow', the wicked too shall be punished. When a man brandishes a club at our head, we shall return the blow with a bigger club, and, with God's help, we shall make sure that such a wicked deed, so evil in its example and so infectious in its results, will not be prolonged.

We shall approach this step by step, and not precipitately, fulfilling our promises in every way, thinking of our dignity as well as our reputation; and we shall try out whatever our friends can do to make peace, and to destroy and wipe out the traces of such a crime. We shall make known to our family both in Wales and Ireland our approach, the modesty and kindness which (even after suffering such shame and such great loss) we would show such an undeserving and ungrateful man, if he became reasonable. Once the Lord has restored peace in the English Church, everything will be discussed as it should be in the chapter of Hereford as well as of Lincoln, and also before the more important bishops of England. With the advice of those people to whom we and our cause are well known, what has been done wrong will be put right, with God's help, since just as 'the man who refuses justice gives everything to the one who is armed', in the same way, when all discover that the fault is incorrigible and irremovable, they will rightly regard him as blameworthy and wicked, when the dispute has taken its course without help from others; and if by chance he loses the case, and and judgement is given against him, since sometimes the fate of honourable, let alone base, causes is variable and highly uncertain, he should be pitied the less by everybody. Indeed he would rightly be, he would deserve to be, laughed to scorn as an unyielding reprobate. For he who knows everything, and whom we invoke as our witness, knows that if we speak against our better conscience we call down an avenger —Heaven forbid!—upon us. For we had the desire and intention, and we have submitted this fixed plan to the judgement of our friends according to the terms of the agreement: namely that we should receive satisfaction, even if not complete, at least measured and honourable, from both of them, the tutor as much as the pupil (should he return to his senses after inflicting such shame and losses, reproaches, threats, and insults). For if the opportunity and a suitable occasion presented themselves, since we do not want to be defeated by evil, but rather to

261. Cf. Ovid, *Met.* iii, 122–3: ... *furit omnis turba suoque | Marte cadunt subiti ...*
262. Cf. *Dig.* vii, 62, 10: *Si actor ... deteriorem calculum reportaverit.*
265–6. See note on Ep. 1, 33–4.   273–4. See note on Ep. 2, 56–7

malum, ad pacis et concordie comodum cum utriusque partis honore
275 tenderemus. Sed inimicus ille, de quo diximus, et hostis antiqus
tritico nostro purissimo lolium suum adiungere et ad corumpendum
olei nostri dulcedinem totam toxicum suum venenatum admiscere
non cessat.

  Utinam diu et bene valere possitis.

   275. de quo diximus] 177–9.   276–7. See note on 16.
   279. See note on Ep. 1, 40.

overcome evil with good, we would aim for the benefits of peace and
harmony, with the rights of both parties. But the adversary whom
we mentioned before, that enemy of old ever adds his tares to our wheat
and his deadly poison to contaminate the flavour of our oil.

We wish you good health for a long time to come.

6

Galfrido Menevensi episcopo

INTER varias querimoniarum causas tanquam ultimis olor in angustiis
ad queruli carminis solacia multifarie conpulsi, conquerimur in primis
de amico nostro Osberto canonico et capellano vestro, erga quem, novit
deus, animum non habuimus nisi bonum et benignum nec habere
5 volumus, quod cum ultimo vobiscum fuimus, apud Abergeven' scilicet,
videns quendam clericum nostrum nobiscum equitantem mane, dum nos
vobiscum in itinere fuimus, quesivit ab eo si nullo alio modo victum
perquirere sciret, quam sic nobiscum per patrias equitando et terras
9 circumeundo, tanquam non | aliud faceremus quam trutannico more
f. 87ᵛᵇ circumcirca deambulare.

Cui respondemus, quod aliquem vidimus, quem claustro ⌈quiescere⌉
decentius foret, non minus quam nos, sed etiam longe plus per Angliam
et Walliam discurrentem, et quia nos in optimo statu quietis fuimus
et adhuc forsan essemus, nisi nostrorum proditio, quibus benefecimus,
15 statum nostrum mutasset et quietem nostram in laborem et studium
nostrum ⌈tanquam⌉ in stadium convertisset. Putabant enim, ut credimus, nos senio confectos nullique rei nisi banco solum vel lecto amplius
aptos. Sed si ipse clericum illum tali dissuasione a nobis abstraeret
aut nos ipsum a vestris, quod absit, obsequiis abduceremus, credimus,
20 immo et scimus, quod duos vel tres canonicos et capellanos, si velletis,
loco illius habere possetis et nos clericos alios loco illius, sicut hactenus
habuimus, habere possemus.

Preterea et de hoc quoque conquerimur, quod cedulam illam famo-
sam, coram nobis apud Abergeven' lectam, ex frivolis et falsis omnino
25 confictam, sed ad nos diffamandum quasi talione reddita pro modulis
suis pariter et deterrendum confectam, per monasteria | et varia, per
f. 88ʳᵃ que transit, loca in publica audientia legi facit ad infamiam nostram et
ignominiam sic dilatandam et amplificandam, causas etiam adversario-
rum nostrorum per omnia iustificando et nostram in omnibus intentionem
30 depravando. Sed pereat palefridus ille, quamquam emptus ex nostro,
tam suaviter ambulans ⌈eique a nepote nostro ad alliciendum datus⌉,
propter quem preter merita nostra tam iniquum et amarum erga nos

21 *post* velletis *deletum est* et nos clericos alios (= 22) *V*

---

2. Cf. Ep. 7, 173–5.
2–3. On the 'swan-song' see Cicero, *Tusc.* i, 30, 73; Ovid, *Met.* xiv, 430; (Martial,
Ep. xiii, 77).

[6.] *To Geoffrey, bishop of St. David's*

LIKE a swan in his dying moments we are driven in various ways to seek the solace of a song of grief. The first and foremost of our various reasons for complaint concerns our friend Osbert, canon and a chaplain of yours, towards whom we have not had and do not want to have anything but good and kindly intentions. Our complaint is that when we were last with you at Abergavenny, noticing one of our clerics who was riding with us early in the morning, while we were travelling with you, he asked if he knew no other way of earning a living than riding round the country in our company, and touring, as if we did nothing else but wander round and about like a beggar.

We reply to him that we saw someone for whom it would be better to stay quiet in the cloister, since he travelled through England and Wales, not less, but much more than we did: we were at complete peace, and would perhaps still be, had not the treachery of our 'friends', whom we aided, upset our condition and changed our peace into toil, and our study into a stadium. For, we believe, they thought that we were bowed down with old age, and suitable for nothing but a bench or a bed. But, if he would rid us of that cleric with arguments like that, or, heaven forfend! we should remove him from your services, we believe, and indeed we know that, if you wished, you could have two or three canons and chaplains in his place, and we could have other priests in his place, as we have had so far.

We also have further grounds for complaint: that famous document, which was read in our presence at Abergavenny—a document completely fabricated from lies and trivia, but concocted to defame and frighten us, as if he were paying his debt according to his capacities—he has read in public in the monasteries and the various places through which he passed, to enlarge and extend our infamy and disgrace; he even completely justified the cause of our adversaries and utterly distorted our point of view. But damn that pretty prancing horse, though it was bought from our money, and given to him by our nephew to appease him. Because of it his attitude towards us is so unfair, bitter,

---

3 (and 520). See note on Ep. 2, 79–80.　　　　　　　　　5–6. Cf. 35–6.
10. trutannico more (beggarly, rascally). Cf. *Descriptio Kambriae*, 1, 3 (*Op.* vi, p. 168, 7): *enarratio . . . trutannica potius quam historica*, and *Vita S. Hugonis*, 2, 4 (*Op.* vii, p. 123, 5): *trutannicum et fictitium* (false, lying), and *De Iure et Statu*, etc. 1 (*Op.* iii, p. 145, 28–9): *trutannice vivere et more trutannico . . . vitam producere*; cf. *supra*, part ii, 801.　　　26. See note on Ep. 5, 16.　　　31 (42, 55, 152). Cf. *supra*, part ii, 735–8.

animum gerit et caritate tam vacuum. Novit enim deus quod erga
35 ipsum vel alium de vestris animum non nisi serenum habemus vel
habere volumus et sincerum.

Non mirum igitur, si proditores nostri pessimi et inimici, domestici
scilicet et intestini, in nequicia sua contra nos concepta dudum et
incepta tam temerarii existant et pertinaciter obstinati, cum illum
40 assidue (quia nocte dieque) contra nos et pro se, comitem vobis in-
dividuum, cubicularium et consiliarium, suasorem habeant et susur-
ronem. Pereat ergo palefridus ille.

Nec mirum etiam, si de ecclesia de Tynebeh, sicut et archidiaconatus
44 et prebende administratione necnon et aliis quibusdam, aquam |
f. 88ʳᵇ turbidam bibimus, que quidem nisi turbata fuisset, limpidissima foret.
Sed in aqua turbida solet esse piscatio bona, sicut et apud Tinebeh nunc
apparet.

Turbatio namque similis et discordia, que inter Meilerium canonicum
et filium suum, cui similiter prebendam suam cesserat, apud Meneviam
50 nuper emersit nostri nepotis exemplo, per operam vestram et ponti-
ficalem diligentiam, quia nullus turbator rem impedivit (modicum enim
ex turbatione tali lucrum surgere potuit, quia non piscatio ibi tam bona
sicut apud Tinebeh ⌜fuit⌝, ubi pisces habundant, et palefridus etiam
ibi locum non habuit), cito in serenitatem et concordiam reversa fuit.
55 Pereat ergo palefridus ille, per quem scandala tot venerunt.

Eidem quoque et ⌜eius⌝ ascensori imputandum et hoc esse videtur,
quod super dicta ecclesia de Tynebeh tam varie est erga nos actum et
tam contrarie post acta responsum, que responsa quidem quasi sub
epilogo repetere preter rem non puta⌜vi⌝mus: qualiter in primis apud
60 Landu parum post festum sancti Michaelis anno preterito cum in-
f. 88ᵛᵃ ductione | vestra, ne dici, quod absit, debeat seductione, personam
fieri ecclesie predicte concessimus, vicaria nobis per pensiunculam
annuam eidem reddendam manu vestra data et canonica quoque ob-
edientia a nobis inde suscepta. Dixistis nobis, quod nos in corporalem
65 ecclesie possessionem per aliquem clericorum nostrorum de partibus
illis, quia tunc versus Meneviam ire parati fuistis et nos versus Lincolniam, statim induceretis; qualiter post natale per quendam puerum
nostrum et per litteras vestras nobis apud Lincolniam mandastis, non
tutum fuisse investituram illam tunc fecisse propter Falconem, qui

34 gerit animum *transposuit* V   59 putavimus] vi *ss.* V   63 eidem *in ras.* V

35–6. Cf. 5–6.
37–8. Cf. Mic. vii, 6 (= Matt. x, 36): *inimici hominis domestici eius.* Cf. 126.
44–6 (= 295–6). Cf. Ep. 5, 166–7.   48–9. Cf. Ep. 7, 241.
55. See note on Ep. 4, 78.

and devoid of love, though we do not deserve it. God knows that our attitude to him, and any other servant of yours, is peaceable and sincere; we would wish it to be no other.

It is, then, no surprise that our wicked and inimical betrayers (intimate members of our household) are so bold and persistently obdurate in the criminal enterprise they conceived and began against us long ago, since they have him, your inseparable companion, chamberlain, and adviser, whispering and insinuating constantly (day and night) against us, and on their behalf. So damn that horse.

It is even no surprise that we drink the troubled waters of the church at Tenby, just as we do of our administration of the prebend and the archdeaconry, to say nothing of certain other affairs. These waters could be of the clearest, had they not been stirred up. But fishing is usually good in troubled waters, as indeed now seems to be the case at Tenby.

A similar trouble and discord, which recently came to light at St. David's, following the example of our nephew, between Canon Meiler and his son, to whom he had ceded his prebend in a similar way, was swiftly resolved into peace and concord by your efforts and episcopal diligence, since there was no one to stir up the trouble. For only a moderate gain could be made from such trouble, since the fishing was not as good there as it was at Tenby, where there were plenty of fish, and the horse was not involved. So, damn that horse, the cause of so many scandals.

The following, it would seem, should also be laid at the doors of him and his mount: the action over the said church at Tenby is so different where we are concerned, and the response so different after the actions: indeed, we consider it not to be beside the point to repeat these responses as a sort of epilogue. First for example at Llanddew shortly after Michaelmas last year at your suggestion, let us not say seduction (perish the thought!), we agreed to become parson of the aforementioned church, and the vicarage was given to us with your hand (with a small annual pension to be given to him) and taken up with canonical obedience by us. You said you would immediately induct us to the corporeal possession of the church through one of our clerics from that area, since you were then about to go to St. David's and we to Lincoln. Then, after Christmas, you informed us at Lincoln by means of one of our servants and your letters that it was unsafe for the installation to have taken place then because of Falco, who had again taken up the

59–62 ff. qualiter . . . concessimus, *etc.*] Cf. Ep. 7, 169–71, 256–68.
60. festum sancti Michaelis] 29 September; cf. Ep. 5, 73.
59–64. Cf. Ep. 7, 166, 175–7.
69. Falco] Also named in *De Iure et Statu Menevensis Ecclesie*, 7 (*Op.* iii, p. 349, 19).

70 bailliam terre illius de novo susceperat, cum tamen ediverso nobis et
aliis visum esset, propter id pocius et precipue, ne ille vel alius rem
impedire posset, totum esse perficiendum; qualiter etiam in Quadragesima sequente cum apud Lanwadein ad vos venimus, illi rationi
dilationis facte, quoniam exilis valde fuerat, non innitentes, respondistis:
75 propter appellationem prioris de Pembroch et prohibitionem, ne quicquam scilicet amplius de ecclesia illa fieret, donec de pensione annua
sibi inde reddenda securitas ei facta fuerit, et cum diceremus econtra
mirum nobis videri, si prior hoc fecisset et quia cito securitas ei super

f. 88vb hoc fieri posset, precepistis ibidem officiali | vestro de partibus illis,
80 scilicet magistro M., coram archidiacono vestro Sancti David Iohanne
ibi tunc presente, quatinus quam cito securitatem illam priori feceri-
mus, investituram ecclesie illius habere nos faceret cum fructibus inde
perceptis; qualiter, cum ad priorem apud Pembroch venimus, negavit
hoc coram multis, cum iuramento quoque protestans se nunquam
85 super hoc appellasse vel prohibitionem aliquam fecisse; qualiter, cum
priori debita securitas a nobis facta fuisset, quam tamen non expeciit,
quia satis, ut dixit, de nobis securus extitit, officialem vestrum semel,
secundo et tercio per litteras et nuncios ad nos vocavimus, qui tergi-
versando ⌜diucius⌝ et subterfugiendo se quam diu potuit absentavit.
90 Tandem cum fugere non amplius posset, dixit et quasi vultu verecundo
respondit, quod appellatum inde contra nos fuerat et ne fieret hoc
prohibitum ideoque multum ei displicere constanter asseruit, seu
ficte quidem seu vere, quod negocium illud consummare non potuit.
Et cum quereremus quis esset ille appellans et prohibens, dicere
95 noluit. Cui tunc respondimus, evidenter ex hiis apparere pisces de
Tynebeh nimis sapidos esse et copiosam loci eiusdem piscationem
presertim in Quadragesima valde placitam et concupiscibilem esse;

f. 89ra qualiter demum, cum ad vos apud Lanton' in Ewias | in crastino
Pentecostes veniremus cum omni humilitate et forte nimia, que pro-
100 tervitatem ⌜adversam⌝ augere solet et insolentiam, dixistis nobis
aperte, quoniam alie rationes ad differendum excogitate dictis modis
fuerant evacuate, quod nepos ille noster tam naturalis et tam liberalis,
ne investituram illam assequeremur, apellaverat. Cui respondimus,
quoniam id, quod consilio vestro et persuasione vestra factum fuerat,
105 nocivum nobis esse non deberet et quoniam propter frivolas tales et

81 fecerimus] ce *ss.* *V*   98 apud Lanton(ei) ad vos *transposuit V*

---

98. Cf. Ep. 8, 351.   102. Cf. Ep. 5, 4.

bailiwick of that area, though, on the other hand, we and others took the opposite view: it was especially for this reason that the business should rather be completed, lest he or any other get in the way. Then, when we came to see you at Llawhaden the following Lent, without relying upon that reason for causing the delay, since it was quite trivial, you replied: it was because of the appeal of the prior of Pembroke, and the injunction preventing anything else being done concerning that church until assurance had been given to him concerning the annual pension assigned to him; and when we said in reply that we thought it remarkable that the prior should have done this, and that an assurance on this matter could be given to him quickly, there and then you ordered your official in those parts (Master M.) in the presence of John, your archdeacon of St. David's, that as soon as we would give that assurance to the prior, you would order that he should have us installed in that church with the returns. Then, when we went to the prior at Pembroke, he denied this before many, and bore witness under oath that he had never appealed over this matter, nor had he made any injunctions. Then, when we had given the required assurance to the prior—an assurance, however, which he did not require, since, as he said, he was sufficiently assured where we were concerned—we called for your official to come to us by letter and messenger once, twice, and three times; he hung back for a long time, he was evasive and absented himself for as long as he could. At length, when he could avoid us no longer, he said in reply with an apparent air of truth, that an appeal had been made against us there, and the injunction on the installation had been made. He constantly asserted, whether falsely or truthfully, that the fact that the business could not be concluded was greatly displeasing to him. When we questioned him on the identity of the appellant and prohibitor, he refused to tell us. Then we told him that it was patently obvious from this that the fish at Tenby were too tasty and the rich fishing there was very pleasant and desirable especially during Lent.

Finally then: when we came to visit you at Llanthony in Ewias the day after Whitsun in all humility—perhaps with too much humility, which normally exacerbates hostile impudence and insolence—you told us clearly (for the other reasons thought up to delay the installation had been exposed in the ways mentioned above) that that nephew of ours with his characteristic generosity had appealed against our being installed. We retorted that this act, which had been carried out at your instigation and with your connivance, should not be done to spite us, and the matter should not have been put off because of such frivolous

malivolas appellationes res differri non debuisset: semper enim suggeri poterit aliquibus ut appellent et impediant, quatinus negotia sic protrahantur et ecclesie fructus interim indebite consumantur.

Sed si iuxta decretales pape Alexandri III et aliorum plurium in hoc
110 ei concordantium, fructus ecclesiarum vacantium personis futuris reservari aut in ecclesiarum reparatione, ubi opus fuerit, expendi iubentur, quod et ubique optinere dinoscitur, ubi equitatem non suffocat iniquitas et avaricia, quanto magis rectores assignati et insti-
114 tuti, sed voluntate sola, ne dicamus cupiditate, a possessione perturbati
f. 89ʳᵇ et prolongati, ecclesiarum suarum fructibus | privari non debent!

Novimus enim, quod et satis in his et in aliis experti sumus, amplum et latum esse iudicis officium, tam ordinarii scilicet quam delegati, et quia multa expedire negotia possunt, dum ea, que iuris exilis sunt, promovere et ediverso que iuris evidentis fuerint, perturbare prevalent
120 et impedire.

Preterea libet nobis et liceat id recolere, quam varie nobis tribus vicibus, quibus ad vos venimus, responsum fuit. In primo namque adventu nostro de Lincolnia ad vos apud Ewias post destitutionem nobis factam, dixistis nobis et firmiter promisistis, tanquam pium et paternum
125 filio solacium prestans, quod coram iudicibus nostris delegatis, quia iam domestici adversarii nostri citationem unam susceperant, vos et Osbertus capellanus et canonicus vester absque dubio testificaremini, quod nos apud Neubiriam coram archiepiscopo et episcopis plurimis ad perpetuam et liberam archidiaconatus de Brechene et prebende de
130 Martru administrationem nepotis nostri presentatione suscepistis, dum tamen ad hoc per iudices compulsi essetis, quod ipsi de officio suo ex litterarum tenore facere poterant. Secundo vero cum ad vos venimus, mutatus est stilus et forsan animus, quod tamen non meruimus. Dixistis
f. 89ᵛᵃ enim tunc nobis, quod presentati quidem | vobis fuimus ad dictam
135 administrationem, sed nichil respondistis: dici tamen, ut nostis, solet quod *taciturnitas confessionem imitatur* et concessionem, presertim etiam cum ratam habueritis et sicut videbatur valde gratam, quamplurimis postmodum annis, quam exercuimus administrationem. Iuris quoque regulam esse novistis, quia *ratiabitio mandato comparatur.*
140 Tercio vero cum aliquanto elapso tempore ad vos veniremus et super hiis mentio facta fuisset, iterum mutato, sicut videbatur, tam animo

109 si *bis, pr. del. V*   113 *post* magis *delevi* ubi *utpote e 111 et 112 repetitum*
126 adversari *V*   127 testificaremini] ific *ss. V*

109. decretales pape Alexandri III] cf. *Decret. Greg. IX,* i, 31, 4 (ed. Aemilius Friedberg) (*JL* 13822). This decretal occurs in contemporary English decretal collections, cf. Charles Duggan, *Twelfth-century Decretal Collections and their Importance in English History* (London, 1963), p. 210.   126. Cf. 37–8.

and malicious appeals: for it will always be possible for it to occur to some people to make appeals and cause obstructions, so that the business is protracted, and in the meantime the benefice of the church is consumed in an unwarranted fashion.

But if, according to the decretals of Pope Alexander III and others of like mind in this matter, it is decreed that the fruits of vacant churches are to be kept for the future parsons, or to be spent on church repairs where necessary (a rule which is known to obtain everywhere where injustice and greed do not choke justice), how much more should designated and appointed rectors, who have been ousted from possession and put off by a whim, not to say concupiscence, not be robbed of the benefices of their churches!

For we know (we are sufficiently expert in these and similar matters) that the power of the judge (both judge ordinary and judge delegate) is sufficiently wide, and that they are able to expedite many matters, while they have the power to settle those where the case is slim, and, on the other hand, reverse and impede those where the case is clear cut.

Furthermore it is amusing for us to recollect (and, by your leave, to recollect it now) how varied was the reply on the three occasions we came to see you. On the first occasion on our arrival from Lincoln to see you at Ewias after our deprivation, you said and gave us the firm promise, as if giving good, fatherly comfort to a son, that you and Osbert, your chaplain and canon, would certainly testify before our judges delegate (our intimate enemies had taken out a summons): that at Newbury before the archbishop and a great many bishops you received us into the perpetual and free administration of the archdeaconry of Brecon, and the prebend of Mathry, at the presentation to the benefice by our nephew, as long as you were compelled to do this by the judges, since they could do this according to their powers and terms of reference. On the second occasion when we came to see you the style and perhaps outlook had changed, though we did not deserve it. Then you said that we were presented to you to the aforementioned administration, but that you gave no response; however, as you well know, it is often said that silence is tantamount to a confession and agreement, especially since you considered the administration which we held signed, and, as it appeared, sealed during the very many years afterwards. You also know it is a rule of law that 'ratification is proved by mandate'. On the third occasion when we came to see you after some time, and mention had been made of these matters, both the attitude, as it appeared, and

---

136. Cicero, *De invent.* i, 32, 54: *taciturnitas imitatur confessionem.*
139. See note on Ep. 5, 44–9.

in peius quam responso, dixistis nobis quod facta vobis presentatione
tali coram archiepiscopo de nobis ad illam administrationem respondistis, quod talis administratio satis a nepote nostro fieri posset in
145 capitulis suis, quod tamen responsum, si etiam tale fuisset, nostre
intentioni contrarium minime fuit, quamvis tamen, ut salva venia
vestra veritati non parcamus, verisimile videri non possit quod in tanta
consecrationis vestre recentia (quoniam quarto die post vel quinto ab
149 archiepiscopo facta, qui ibidem presens extitit et factum illud nostre
f. 89ᵛᵇ administrationis approbavit et autenticavit | et ut sic etiam fieret totum
procuravit), aliquod ibi verbum a vobis sue voluntati dissonum emit-
teretur. Pereat ergo palefridus ille, et non pereat sed resipiscat ascensor
eius, propter quem aut per quem in tanto viro et tam multis prelato
tanta potuit verborum lubricitas et dupplicitas vel etiam multiplicitas
155 inveniri. ⌈Nec mirum tamen, si is, qui multiplex et varius fuit in
religione, nunc mente mutabilis existat et intencione, ab ordine nimirum
arciore turpiter et cum scandalo descendens ad suaviorem et sic in illo
proficiens, ut, dum iterum per seculares astucias videretur ascendens,
apud districtum fuerit iudicem periculose pariter et ignominiose de-
160 ficiens, quia iuxta propheticum illud *deiecisti eos dum allevarentur* et
poeticum illud *tolluntur in altum | ut lapsu graviore ruant.*⌉

Veruntamen, quamquam palefrido, tociens a nobis et tot inprecationi-
bus devotato, totum imposuerimus, potuit et illud pocius tanto maleficio
tanteque malicie, propter quam tantis preter solitum iniuriis afficimur
165 et affligimur, causam dedisse simul cum invidia, qua sola caret miseria,
que semper pociores infestat, quod nepos ille noster anno preterito
apud Urbem Legionum coram fratre suo milite pervalido et fidelissimo
sibique per omnia dissimillimo, dicere palam non erubuit, quod nunquam Menevensis episcopus, quamdiu vitales carperet auras, nos
170 diligeret, et cum causam ab ipso quereremus: 'Propter litteras', inquit,
'vestras contra ipsum Lincolnie fabricatas, quas ei deportare curavimus.'
Cui et incontinenti respondimus, iactandum hoc ei, si discretus esset,
minime fore, quod de hospitio nostro et mensa et pane nostro, quo
f. 90ʳᵃ cotidie | vescebatur, ⌈ut cetera nunc taceantur beneficia,⌉ litteras
175 ⌈nostras⌉ ⌈presertim ad comodum suum factas et propter honoris,
quem ei contulimus, ac dignitatis, quamquam indigno, integra et illibata iura servandum,⌉ furtive subtrahendo et secreta nostra maliciose

---

145 responsum tamen *transposuit* V   152 et *bis* V

147. Cf. Ep. 3, 9.   160. Ps. lxxii, 18.
    161. Claudian, *In Rufinum* i, 22–3; the same quotation in the *Vita Galfridi*, 2, 18
(*Op.* iv, p. 419, 2–3), *De Instr. Pr.* (*Op.* viii, 153, 3–4).
    169. Cf. Virgil, *Aen.* i, 387–8: . . . *auras | vitales carpis.*
    176–7. See note on Ep. 5, 16.

the reply took a turn for the worse: you told us that we had been presented to you to the administration in the presence of the archbishop and that you replied that such an administration could be carried out well enough by our nephew in his chapters: this reply, if such it had been, was least opposed to our idea, although, saving your grace, in order that we spare not the truth, it cannot seem to fit the facts, that that same utterance at variance with its purpose should be made by you considering how recent your consecration was (for the event took place only four or five days earlier: the archbishop had done it and he was present also on that same occasion; he approved and confirmed the arrangement concerning our administration, and even had everything done in this way). So, damn that horse, and may his rider not be damned, but repent: only because of him, or through him, could such verbal slipperiness, duplicity, or even multiplicity of duplicities be found in such an important man who is set over so many. Nor, for that matter, is it surprising that he, who was so ambivalent and equivocal in his religion, is now so fickle in his design and intention: in shame and disgrace he left his excessively strict order for a more lax one, and he so proceeded in that matter that, when he was clearly getting on in the world by means of secular chicanery, he appeared before a stern judge for hazardous and ignominious default; it is similar to that prophetic verse: 'When they were lifted up you have cast them down'; and the poet's phrase: 'They were raised to heaven, that their fall might be greater.'

Yet, though we put all the blame on the horse, which we have cursed and held up to execration so often, it is more likely that the following could have given grounds for such great villainy and malice, because of which we suffer and sustain such unparalleled outrages, as well as the envy, which distress, which always troubles the stronger, only lacks: last year at Caerleon that nephew of ours said openly and without a blush in the presence of his brother—a most valiant and faithful knight and totally dissimilar to him—that the bishop of St. David's would never love us, as long as he had breath in him. When we asked him the reason, he said: 'Because of the letters you made up against him at Lincoln, which we had sent to him.' We immediately retorted that had he any sense, he ought hardly to boast of this, since by secretly stealing our letters from our hospice, board, and bread, on which he daily dined—we will not go into all the benefits on this occasion—to be able to please the prelate and spite us, and by maliciously revealing our secrets he clearly proved in this criminal escapade that he was our betrayer—and especially when the letters were to his advantage, and composed to keep unbroken and unsullied

detegendo, ut per hoc prelato placere posset et nos displicere, se
proditorem nostrum in hoc facinore manifestum esse probavit sicut
180 et in altero, quod nos scilicet, qui eum creavimus et a mendicitatis
incomodo ⌈eripere⌉ curavimus, hiis que iusto tytulo et auctoritate
magna possedimus, pravis pariter suggestionibus et corde perverso
f. 90rb temerarie quidem | et nefarie spoliare presumpsit.

Ubi et illud Laban in Genesi, qui furti Iacob arguit, ad mentem nobis
185 occurrere potuit: *Cur*, inquit, *fugisti et cur furatus es deos meos?* 'Consobrinus et gener meus et coepulator hec facere non debueras!' Sed
ecce qualiter inter alias circumstantias graves coepulationem non
omisit. Haut aliter et nos ad hunc nepotem nostrum apostrophare
poterimus: 'Cur fugisti et cur furatus es secreta mea? Nepos et nutritus,
190 coepulator ⌈et commensalis⌉ meus hec facere non debueras.' Sed
utinam ita se furti excusare posset, sicut et Iacob excusavit! Cui et
illud in psalmo aperte consonat: *Homo pacis mee, in quo speravi, qui*
edebat panes meos, magnificavit super ⌈*me*⌉ *supplantationem.* ⌈Non enim
baculum senectuti nostre iuxta spem paravimus, sed iaculum et capiti
195 nostro malleum nequicie pariter et malicie comparavimus, non podium
⌈revera⌉ sed odium, non postem sed hostem, non gaudium sed gladium,
non vinum ad letificandum, sed letale venenum magis ad suffocandum
ori nostro propinavimus.⌉

Si igitur istud in causa est, quod ille domesticus hostis noster et
200 intestinus nobis apparuit, sicut vereri quidem possumus per ea que
nimis evidenter experti sumus, tunc nichil aliud nobis remedii restat
nisi ut dies expectemus sereniores, quoniam *hora tenebrarum et potestas*
nunc est. Suis enim revera temporibus sole clarius elucente *fient ista*
palam, cupient et in acta referri, cum ea, que nunc tenebris obvolvuntur
205 et occultantur, nubibus et nebulis procul expulsis, lucis beneficio
serenioris cunctis aperta clarescent.

Novit autem deus, quod licet de archidiaconatu et prebenda et
ecclesia de Tinebeh quinquaginta marcarum aut plurium annuatim
dampna senserimus et senciamus, longe plus tamen dedecore rei ipsius
210 quam dampno movemur, qui tot iniuriis afficimur et preter merita
tanquam homo nauci aut nichili, quin immo et ab illis, erga quos

---

178 placere *bis V, alt. del.*   181 curavimus (= a)] *sequuntur* (c) Ubi ... supplantationem (*184–93*), (b) hiisque ... presumpsit (*181–3*), (d) Si igitur (*etc.*, *199*) *et in*
margine (*f. 90*): Cave quia transpositio *V*   184 Ubi] //bi *V*   200 apperuit *V*
202–3 nunc est et potestas *transposuit V*   203 fient *e* fiant *corr. V*

---

180. See note on Ep. 2, 91.
184. Gen. xxxi, 19; cf. Ep. 8, 200–1.
185. Cur ... meos] Gen. xxxi, 27 and 30. The words (185) *Consobrinus* ... (186)
debueras seem to be an addition by Giraldus.

the rights of the honour we bestowed on him and the dignity, though he was not worthy of it. It is just like the other case, when he presumed to rob us of the possessions we held by legal deed and great authority in that incontinently wicked fashion from the wicked promptings of his corrupt heart, though we made him, and had him taken from poverty.

At this point what Laban said in Genesis when he accused Jacob of theft could have occurred to us; he said: "'Why hast thou fled, and why hast thou stolen away my gods? As my relative, my son-in-law, and feasting partner, you should not have done it.' But take note, how he did not miss out, among the other serious charges, the fact that he was his table companion. We, too, will be able to address ourselves to this nephew of ours in the same way: 'Why hast thou fled, and why hast thou stolen away my secrets? As my nephew and foster-child, my table companion and my commensal, you should not have done it.' But, oh that he could give an excuse for his theft in the same way as Jacob! The following passage from the Psalm is clearly applicable to him. 'The man of my peace, in whom I trusted, who ate my bread, hath greatly supplanted me.' We have not made a support for our old age as we hoped, but a cudgel full of wickedness and spite for our head; we have not found succour, but rancour; we have not made a helper, but an enemy; we have not found pleasure, but a sword; we have drunk not wine to delight our palate, but rather a lethal poison to choke us.

If it is the case that he is our enemy in our own home and family, as indeed we can fear from the excessive treatment we have obviously experienced, then we have no other remedy than to await more peaceful times, since it is now the 'hour and the power of darkness'. For, indeed, when in its own time the sun shines more brightly, 'those deeds of yours will be revealed, and they will cry out to be referred to the court registers', since, when the clouds and mists have been blown away from those things which are now hidden and shrouded in shadow, they will be bright and shining by benefiting from the more serene light.

However, God knows, that, though we have been and still are aware of the loss of forty marks or more annually from the archdeaconry, the prebend, and the church of Tenby, we are much more upset at the shame in this matter than at the loss: we are subjected, undeservedly, to so many outrages, as if we were a trivial good-for-nothing fellow, at the

---

192–3. Ps. xl, 10.
194. Tob. v, 23 and x, 4: *baculum senectutis nostrae.* See note on Ep. 5, 121–7.
202. seneriores] Cf. 315 and Ep. 7, 75, 278. Luke xxii, 53.
203–4. Juvenal, *Sat.* ii, 135–6 (also in Petrus Cantor, *Verbum Abbreviatum,* Migne, *P.L.* 205, col. 158A).
209–10. Cf. Ep. 4, 132–4, and *passim.*

magni proculdubio meriti in aliquo quandoque fuimus articulo. Deliros
nos namque senes et fatuos esse plerique nunc reputare possunt,
quos tantis molestiis et maliciis affligi impune videntes mirantur et
215 obstupescunt, quos vivaces et validos antea viderunt et noverunt. Sed
f. 90ᵛᵃ ig|norant hii forsan aut non attendunt, quod paciencie tempus est hodie
in clero, miserie quoque et iniurie, non autem iusticie vel misericordie.

Porro quid faciant clerici miseri et minuti sub potestate constituti
et in qua tutela confidere poterunt, ubi sic affliguntur pro magnis habiti?
220 Quid enim faciet virgula deserti, ubi sic concutitur cedrus Lybani?

Sane licet annua dictorum reddituum aut plurium iactura, triennio
iam elapso vel etiam quadriennio, dampnificati simus et dampna adhuc
eadem perpeciamur, longe tamen illi nepoti nostro plus intulit dampni,
qui tam turpi prodicioni ipsius, seu dissimulando et occulte consentiendo
225 seu etiam per se vel suos aperte suggerendo, favorem adhibuit et quod
extinguere debuit, excitavit, quanto videlicet minor est rerum iactura
quam dierum: res etenim redeunt, sed irrevocabiliter tempora pretereunt. Qui ergo res ei sic contulit et tam turpi questui favorem dedit,
et tempus eidem et famam abstulit: per quinquennium enim ob hoc
230 trutannice vixit et doctrine tempus amisit, qui litteris et disciplina
tantum indiguit. Quarum etiam loco (quia peccatum, nisi mature
deletum fuerit, pondere suo ad aliud trahit: qui enim in sordibus est et
f. 90ᵛᵇ in his moratur, | amplius sordescere solet) luxus et lascivia successerunt.

Unde et comicus ille: *En quid facit ocium et cibus alienus*, item et poeta:
235 *Queritur Egistus quare sit factus adulter.* | *In promptu causa est: desidiosus
erat.* Sed de tali equitio nunquam nobis pullum donet deus. Quid enim
de tam scelerosis utrimque nisi scelus ipsum, quid de tam nequiter
iniquis nisi nequitia proveniret inmensa et inmoderata?

Preter hec etiam qui tempus abstulit, et nevo quoque deterrimo
240 ⌐pariter et teterrimo⌐ famam eiusdem occasionaliter obtenebravit,
quoniam qui ocio consensit, et vicio quodammodo causam dedit, iuxta
poeticum illud: *Ocia si tollas, periere Cupidinis arcus*, et illud eiusdem:

---

218 faciant *ex correctura ut videtur* V   233 lacivia V   237 nisi] ubi V
240 teterrimo *e* deterrimo *corr.* V

---

212. articulo] Cf. 280.
220. Cf. Ps. xci, 13; *De Iure et Statu*, etc. 1 (*Op.* iii, p. 134, 17–18).
232–3. Cf. Rev. xxii, 11.
234. Terence, *Eunuchus*, 265 (ii, 2, 34); the same quotation in the *Symbolum Electorum*,
1, 31 (*Op.* i, p. 319, 26).
235–6. Ovid, *Rem. Amoris*, 161–2, quoted (*Queritur*, Ovid: *Quaeritis*) from Petrus
Cantor, *Verbum Abbreviatum*, Migne, *P.L.* 205, 246D (cf. 297D), here and in the
Gemma Ecclesiastica, 2, 20 (*Op.* ii, p. 263, 14–15); see A. Boutemy, 'Giraud de Barri

hands, moreover, of those to whom we were undoubtedly of great worth once upon a time. A great many people can now think of us as an addled, half-witted old man, whom they are amazed and astonished to see subjected to such great vexations and acts of spite, and whom they once saw and knew as sprightly and vigorous. But perhaps they do not know, or give no heed to the fact that today it is the time of patience among the clergy, as well as of suffering and outrage, but not of justice or pity.

Moreover, what are wretched clerics with petty power to do, and what protection can they rely upon when those who are considered great are so afflicted? What is the reed of the desert to do when the cedar of Lebanon is shaken in that way?

Indeed, though we have suffered the annual loss of the revenues or more things, since three or four years have elapsed, and have so far borne this loss with patience, to our nephew, however (who, whether by dissembling or secretly condoning, or even by prompting openly himself or through his minions, has shown his approval of his vile betrayal, and, when he should have extinguished them, fanned the flames), the loss is far greater, in that the loss of possessions is less important than the loss of days: for possessions return, but time is gone for ever. For through this, the man who bestowed these possessions on him, and gave his approval to such a vile request, robbed him both of time and repute; so, then, for this reason, a man, greatly in need of literacy and discipline has lived in this beggarly fashion for five years and has lost time for his education. So one sin drags man down to another by its own weight, unless it is stopped in time (the man who is in rags and stays in them, usually gets dirtier) extravagance and lasciviousness have taken the place of literacy and discipline. So that comic poet says: 'Ah, what leisure and someone else's food can do!' The poet expresses the same idea: 'Aegisthus was asked why he became an adulterer. The answer is easy: he was bone idle.' But may the Lord never give us a colt from a stud like that. For what could come from such a pair of criminals except crime itself? What could come from the wickedly unjust except boundless, limitless wickedness?

Moreover, as he has lost time and gratuitously stained his reputation with a most foul and hideous blot, since he consented to leisure and somehow or other justified crime, his ease is reminiscent of that phrase of the poet: 'If you remove leisure, the bows of Cupid are powerless';

et Pierre le Chantre, une source de la *Gemma Ecclesiastica'*, *Revue du moyen âge latin*, 2, 1946, p. 53 (see also *infra*, notes on 242 and 243).

239-40. See note on Ep. 5, 121-7.

242. Ovid, *Rem. Amoris*, 139 (= *Verbum Abbreviatum* (see note on 235-6), 246D).

Res age, tutus eris. Pocius autem ad studii labores tam rudis et recens
esset compellendus, quam ad turpes questus et quietis ignaviam
245 alliciendus. Sed ecce quemadmodum dilexit eum.

Qui igitur nevo predicto, quamquam nature consono, simul et
dampno temporis occasionem dedit, eidem quoque iactura longe maiore
capellum contulit indelebilem, tam atra videlicet macula contra nature
pariter et nutriture necnon et promotionis iura fuliginosum, que nullo
250 nitro, nulla fullonis herba ullo unquam dilui aut deleri tempore queat.
f. 91ʳᵃ Graviter igitur uterque | lesit, sed recuperabiliter unum, irrecuperabiliter
alterum: temporis enim sicut et fame iactura perennis, iuxta illud: *Lesa
pudicicia est, deperit illa semel,* et illud ⌜*eiusdem*⌝: *Pena potest demi,
culpa perennis erit.*

255 Set ecce qualiter et quantum utrumque dilexit, tam patruum scilicet
quam nepotem. Nepos autem quare ab eo speciali dilectione diligi
deberet, aut propter corporis aut etiam animi dotes, novit deus, quia
causam videre non possumus aut rationem, nisi forsan ob hoc eum
dilexerit, quia nos ad nutum eius persequi tam promptulus fuit.
260 Propter hoc tamen et propter scripta nostra, cartas et alia plurima
nobis furtive subtracta, propter hoc etiam, quod preter fraudes tot et
prodiciones tam ingratum se nobis exhibuit et infidelem, pro certo
scimus, quod probis et fidelibus viris omnibus vilis et contemptibilis
est habendus.

265 Sed queret quis, cur filiorum discordiam pater non extinxerit aut
pontificali potestate non represserit, cum non ignoret quantam animad-
versionem in fautores dissensionum et fotores canones statuant, cum
et illud legerit, scilicet Ignacii pape: *Error, cui non re⌜si⌝stitur, approba-*
f. 91ᵛᵇ *tur et veritas cum minime defensatur, op|primitur,* et illud Innocencii:
270 *Negligere cum possis perturbare perversos, nichil est aliud quam fovere
nec caret scrupulo societatis occulte, qui manifesto facinori desinit obviare,*
presertim quidem cum ad hoc ex officio teneatur, item cum etiam
scriptum in iure noverit quod *ratiabitio mandato comparatur,* ex quibus et hoc patet, quam graviter suppremum illum pacis amatorem
275 et auctorem offendant hii precipue, qui ad hoc presunt ut prosint,
cum inter illos zizania seminant, quos ad pacis unitatem totis nisibus

---

273 in iure *ex* iniurie *corr. V*

243. Ovid, *Rem. Amoris,* 144; the same quotation in the *Gemma Ecclesiastica,* 2, 20
(*Op.* ii, p. 264, 1–2, from the *Verbum Abbreviatum* (247A), see A. Boutemy, quoted in
note on 235–6, loc. cit.) and in Ep. 8, 324 (note).
248. capellum] Note the pun on Capella (see note on Ep. 7, 314)!
249–50. Cf. Ep. 4, 101–2.
252–4. Ovid, *Heroides,* v, 104, and *Ex Ponto,* i, 1, 64. Both quotations also in the

and again, 'Get on with your business, you will be safe.' One so un-tutored and young ought to have been made to work hard at his studies rather than seduced into such wickedly profitable business and idle sloth. But look how he preferred the tutor.

He, therefore, was the reason for the blemish mentioned above (though it was in keeping with nature) as well as the wasted time; he also fitted him to his greater loss with a cap—a cap fouled in the face of all the laws of nature, fostering, and advancement with a stain so black that it cannot ever be washed away or got rid of by any soap or dye-stuff. Both, then, have done great harm: the one has done remediable harm, the other irremediable harm: for the loss of time just as the loss of reputation is for all time—it is similar to the following: 'Once honour is damaged, it dies forthwith', and 'punishment can be with-drawn, but guilt is for all time.'

But see the nature and extent of his affection for the two, the uncle and the nephew. Why the nephew comes in for such special attention from him either for his physical or mental attributes, God knows, since we are unable to see the cause or reason, except because he was so ready to persecute us at his request. Yet, because of this, and because of our writings, documents, and a great many other things that were furtively stolen from us, and because apart from his many lies and be-trayals, he has been so ungrateful and unfaithful to us, we are absolutely sure that he should be held cheap and contemptible by all honest and true men.

But the question could be asked why the father did not damp down the discord of the sons, or suppress it by his episcopal power, since he should not be unaware of the extent of the censure laid down in the canons against the supporters and fosterers of dissensions, if he had read what Pope Ignatius says: 'To fail to correct an error is to approve it, and to fail to defend truth is to repress it'; and Pope Innocent says: 'Not to correct when possible those who have gone astray is tantamount to encouraging them; nor is the man who fails to take action against a patent crime free of the suspicion of being secretly in league with it', especially when he is held to this by his office; and since he knows that it is written in law that 'approbation comes close to authorization'. From these quotations it is clear how much those in office to do good, when they sow tares among those whom they are bound to spare no effort to restore to the unity of peace, offend that supreme lover and author of peace since

Symbolum Electorum, 1, 3 (*Op.* i, p. 215, 13–17), the second also in Ep. 5, 156 (see also note on Ep. 4, 148–9) and in *De Iure et Statu,* etc., 7 (*Op.* iii, p. 352, 18).

266–7. Cf. Ep. 5, 49–50.   268–73. See note on Ep. 5, 44–9.
275. See note on 403.   276. zizania] See note on Ep. 5, 177–9.

revocare tenentur, dicente domino: *beati pacifici*, beati pedes pacem portantes.

Item queret forsan et aliquis, virum veneratione dignum et dilectione
280 et erga eundem in multis bene et maxime in promotionis articulo peroptime meritum cur pater diligere nequeat. Cui comicum illud respondere sufficiat: *Mala mens, malus animus*. Proinde et illud Valerii Maximi de Pompilio, qui caput Ciceronis amputavit, quod pro capite
284 ipsius in Capitolio peroraverat, et hic videtur inserendum: *Pompilius* |
f. 91ᵛᵃ *neminem odit, nisi cui plurimum debet*. Periculosum est ergo multa beneficia in aliquem conferre, quia, cum turpe est non reddere, vult non esse cui reddat. Unde Seneca: *Es leve facit amicum, grave vero et grande facit inimicum*. Sic igitur, et eadem ex causa eodemque ingratitudinis vicio detestabili, tam promoti quam a suspendio liberati, quia tanta
290 beneficia reddere vel nolunt vel nequeunt, quos pre ceteris diligere deberent odio letali persecuntur. Nonnullum tamen novimus, qui fautores promotionis sue quosdam iuxta facultatis modulum ample beneficiavit et remuneravit, sed utinam conventione prehabita nec artatus ad hoc nec obligatus!
295 Poterit et alia nostre persecutionis et turbationis ratio reddi, quoniam in aqua turbida solet esse piscatio bona: nec enim caritas simul et prava cupiditas regnare in eodem pectore possunt. Novimus enim et pro
f. 91ᵛᵇ certo novimus, quod nunquam nepos ille noster, quamquam iniquus | et nativa peiori ex parte nequicia plenus, iners tamen et ignavus, elinguis
300 pariter et illitteratus tantam erga nos scelerositatem esset agressus, nisi pravis suggestionibus multis et maiorum viribus innixus eiusque precipue favore suffultus, qui talium et tam turpium in loco, cui preerat, extirpator pocius et ultor quam aut fautor aut fultor esse deberet.

Miser igitur est animus meticulosus et malitiosus, emulus et igno-
305 miniosus, qui vel unicum abhorret in patria virum, litteris et eruditione non ultimum, moribus et maturitate non infimum, tanquam conversationis et vite conscium habere metuens illum, cui displicere plurimum

---

277 pacem *e* partem *corr. V*   289 detestabili *e* detestabili *corr. V*   299 elinguis *bis, pr. del. V*

277-8. Matt. v, 9; cf. Is. lii, 7; Rom. x, 15; Nahum i, 15; *supra*, part ii, 292.
280. articulo] Cf. 212.
282. Terence, *Andria*, 164 (i, 1, 137) (= Servius, *Aen*. 6, 11); the same quotation in the *Symbolum Electorum*, 1, 1 (*Op*. i, p. 205, 22-3), and 1, 28 (p. 299, 26-7).
282-5. The story of 'Pompilius' (C. Popil(l)ius Laenas) is told in Valerius Maximus, v, 3, 4, ed. Kempf, 1888, p. 237, 27-238, 15, and the words *quod . . . peroraverat* (283-4) are a reminiscence of those of Valerius Maximus: *illud se caput ferre, quod pro capite eius quondam peroraverat* (p. 238, 14-15). But the quotation in 284-5 comes (via the *Controversiae* of Seneca, 7, 2, 2, ed. Müller, 1887, p. 290, 9-10: *nullos magis odit Popillius quam quibus plurimum debet*) from the *Verbum Abbreviatum*, 337A-B (cf.

our Lord said: 'Blessed are the peacemakers': 'blessed are the feet of those that bring peace.'

Again the question might be asked why the father is unable to like the man who is worthy of respect and favour, and deserves well in many things and especially in the matter of the promotion. It is sufficient to give the following verse from the comic poet: 'An evil mind: an evil soul.' And again the remark of Valerius Maximus of Pompilius, who cut off the head of Cicero, which he made over his head on the Capitoline, seems appropriate here: 'Pompilius hates no one, except the man to whom he owes most.' It is hazardous, therefore, to confer many benefits on someone, since, because it is criminal not to repay, he wishes away the man to whom the repayment is to be made. Thus Seneca says: 'A trivial loan makes a friend, but a large and important loan makes an enemy.' So, then, for the same reason and the same detestable crime of ingratitude, both those who have been promoted and those who have been freed from the gallows pursue those whom they ought to love above all others with a deadly hatred since they are either unwilling or unable to repay such large benefits. However, we know a certain person who has amply rewarded and repaid some of those who favoured his promotion according to his means; but would that he were not bound or obliged to do this by the ordained convention.

There may be yet another reason for our persecution and harassment, since fishing is usually good in troubled waters: for love and wicked covetousness cannot hold sway at the same time in the same breast. For we know, and know for sure, that, though that nephew of ours is unjust and for the most part full of natural wickedness, he is idle and slothful, inarticulate and illiterate, and he would never have embarked on such a criminal enterprise against us if he had not been backed by many wicked suggestions and the strength of his betters, and especially urged on by the favour of that man who, in his pre-eminent position, ought to have extirpated and punished such wicked criminals, rather than encourage and support them.

That wretched soul is terrible and spiteful, envious and disreputable which hates the quite unique man in the country, who is not the last in letters and education, and not the worst in morals and maturity, as if it feared to have him who it knows does not like crime as a party to its

155B); from the same source comes 286–7, *cum turpe est . . . reddat*, and also the Seneca quotation (287–8); see also *supra*, part ii, 826–31.

287–8. Seneca, *Ep.* 19, 11: *leve aes alienum debitorem facit, grave inimicum*; see also note on 282–5.

291–3. Cf. Ep. 7, 192–3.   295–6 (=44–6). See note on Ep. 5, 166–7.
297–8. Cf. 320.   298–300. Cf. Ep. 7, 233 (and 44).
299–300. elinguis] Cf. Ep. 5, 6–7; Ep. 7, 43–4; *supra*, part i, 1272.

turpia novit, quem revera, si sincerus esset et serenus, speciali caritatis
vinculo quodam amplecti deberet et venerari.

310　Viam autem humilitatis satis ⌐hactenus⌐ ex industria pretemptavimus
et plusquam satis, plus quoque quam deceret aut expediens foret, sicut
f. 92ʳᵃ ex post factis pa|tuit et adhuc patet, propter quod pusillanimes magis
reputati sumus et contemptibiles, quoniam, ut ait Gregorius, *admonendi
sunt subditi ne plusquam expedit sint subiecti*, et cetera. Sed cum locus
315　affuerit et lux serenior illuxerit, longe diversa deo duce nobis inceden-
dum est via, magis ardua scilicet per dei gratiam et magis honesta.

　　Testem tamen illum invocamus, cui *nuda et aperta sunt omnia*, quod
vix et inviti valde vobiscum coram iudice contendemus, salvo solum
honore nostro et dedecore propulsato rerumque dampnis etsi non plene,
320　saltem honeste restauratis. Scimus etenim et pro certo scimus, si litibus
tantum et causarum controversiis inter nos disceptatio fiat, quoniam
coram iudicibus et maioribus regni tocius ordinis ecclesiastici viris illud
fiet, quod in tanti discriminis amaritudinem lis excrescet, nisi maturius
in pacis et concordie comodum negotia vergant, quod ille, cuius demum
325　promocioni favorem adhibendo finalem cum effectu calculum apposui-
f. 92ʳᵇ mus et cui nostra longe | plus valuit tam longa rebellio quam ceterorum
omnium facilis et ficta, ne et coacta dicamus, confederatio, ob diabolicum
ingratitudinis vicium totis non inmerito deici et destrui nisibus attem-
ptabitur.

330　Malorum quippe materia de die in diem amplius aumentata, dum
varie delinqui dinoscitur et multifarie: vel bona ecclesiastica dilapidando
terrasque et predia, per advenarum inepcias misere Menevensi ecclesie,
principum violentia, corpore quidem et non corde presidentium
perpauca relicta, vili commercio distraendo vel symoniacis passim
335　actibus pravis ⌐insistendo vel⌐ institutionibus institutiones contrarias
et adversas superaddendo cartasque novas in veterum preiuditia seu
prece seu precio seu favore vel metu conficiendo (cum tamen scriptura
testante *episcopus si timet, actum est de eo*) vel miserum etiam multipliciter clerum exaccionibus variis et iniuriis affligendo eumque

317 ominia *V*　　　320 *post* scimus *delevi* quia

313–14. See note on 374–6.　　　　　　　　315. serenior] See note on 202.
317. Hebr. iv, 13: *omnia autem nuda et aperta sunt oculis eius;* cf. 2 Cor. i, 23: *Ego
autem testem deum invoco . . .*
318. See note on Ep. 4, 8.　　　　　　　　　320. Cf. 297–8.
335–7. Cf. *De Iure et Statu*, etc., 7 (*Op.* iii, p. 349, 14–17): *Item super institutionibus
novis in personarum damna priorum male perpetratis et cartis novis in veterum preiudicia tam
suarum quam decessorum quoque suorum iuste et legitime premissarum emissis . . .* ; cf.
Ep. 7, 309–10, Ep. 8, 44–5.
337. prece seu precio] Proverbial (Ovid, *Fasti*, ii, 806), cf. *De Iure et Statu*, etc., 7
(*Op.* iii, p. 349, 18): *seu prece seu precio seu favore sive timore*, and Ep. 8, 304–5.

conversation and way of life; indeed, were it sincere and untroubled, it ought to embrace and respect him with a special bond of love.

However, in this respect we have sufficient and more than sufficient previous experience of the path of humility deliberately, indeed, more than would be proper and expedient, as was obvious from subsequent events and is even now obvious, for which reason we were thought to be cowardly and contemptible, since, as Gregory says, 'the underdog should be warned not to be more subject than is necessary', etc. But when the time is ripe, and the sun shines more brightly, we must, under God's leadership, enter on a far different road, a road, by the grace of God, steeper and more honourable.

Yet we call to witness him to whom 'all things are naked and open', that it is with very great reluctance that we will fight you before a judge, only to keep our honour intact, to get rid of the dishonour, and have the loss of our property restored, if not in full, then honourably. If there were a disagreement between us in the processes and the arguments of the cases (since it will happen that the trial will break out into bitter recrimination before the judges and the seniors of the ecclesiastical order of the whole country, unless the business inclines beforehand towards a convenient and harmonious peace) we know and are quite certain that because of his devilish vice of ingratitude he will not undeservedly try to overthrow and destroy us with all his might, since we have made the final and effective decision by giving approval to his promotion, and our long strife has been much more in his interest than the facile, false, not to say forced, alliance of the rest.

Indeed, the crimes grow greater from day to day, while they are known to be committed in many various ways: there are very few church goods, estates, and farms left to the wretched cathedral of St. David's because of the ineptitude of foreigners and the violence of the princes who govern with their bodily desires rather than their hearts. They are disposed of in criminal trafficking; occasional wicked acts of simony are pressed on with; opposing or adverse institutions are added on to institutions, and new deeds, precluding old ones, are drawn up whether by request, or at a price, or for fear of favour (though Scripture tells us: 'If a bishop is afraid, he is done with'). The poor clergy is subjected in many ways to the charges and insults, and left exposed defenceless and opposed

---

338. Attributed to Cyprian in the *Verbum Abbreviatum* of Petrus Cantor (317c) and in Giraldus' *Symbolum Electorum*, 1, 22 (*Op.* i, p. 260, 24–6): *Clericus vel laicus si timet, vicinus est veniae, episcopus autem si timet, actum est de eo*; in the *Gemma Ecclesiastica*, 2, 38 (*Op.* ii, p. 361, 29–30) (= *De Invectionibus*, 6, 27 [omitted in *Op.* i, p. 193], ed. Davies, p. 235, 30–1), and in the *Speculum Ecclesie*, 4, 39 (*Op.* iv, p. 352, 12). The same words are quoted in Ep. 8, 277.

340 nichilominus gravibus et assiduis laicorum direptionibus undique
f. 92ᵛᵃ oppressum et penitus indefen|sum exponendo—in tantum, inquam, sic
malicia crescet, quod, caritate utrimque perdita, fraterna dilectio saluti
tam necessaria et tam paterna quam filialis affectio, sincera in primis
et serena, vix ullo reparari ad plenum tempore queat.

345   Mirum autem, cum rebus ecclesiasticis ⌐episcopi⌐ tanquam commendatis, non tanquam propriis uti deberent, adeo ut iuxta canones
apostolorum nec etiam testamentum de rebus ecclesie condere possint,
qua fronte, qua temeritate res alienas, quia dominicas deoque dicatas,
alienare sunt ausi et dilapidare. Unde Leo papa, causa XII, q. II:

350 *Episcopus rebus ecclesie tanquam commendatis, non tanquam propriis*
utatur. ⌐Unde religiosum valde prioris cuiusdam vel abbatis ad epi-
scopium hanelantis verbum fuit: 'Plus valet', inquit, 'meum quam
nostrum', secularem ⌐nimirum animum⌐ et singularem aperte
declarans.⌐ Item et in canonibus apostolorum, causa XII, q. I: *Sint*

355 *manifeste res proprie episcopi, si tamen habeat proprias, et manifeste*
dominice, id est ecclesiastice, *ut potestatem habeat de propriis moriens*
episcopus sicut voluerit et quibus voluerit derelinquere, et cetera. Similiter
et ex concilio Yspalensi, eadem causa, q. V: *Fixum abhinc et perpetuo*
mansurum esse decrevimus, ut episcopus res sui iuris, quas aut ante

360 *episcopatum aut certe in episcopatu sed hereditaria successione adquisivit,*
f. 92ᵛᵇ *secundum au|toritatem canonicam cui vult conferat et quicquid de eis vult*
faciat; postquam autem episcopus factus est, quascumque res de facultatibus
ecclesie aut suo aut alterius nomine comparaverit, decernimus, ut non in
propinquorum suorum, sed ecclesie, cui preest, iura deveniant.

365   Mirum etiam, cum nec domini existant nec dominantes esse debeant,
quod tantam in clero tyrannidem exercere presumunt. Unde Ieronimus
ad Nepotianum, XCV. distinctione: *Esto subiectus pontifici tuo et quasi*
anime parentem ama. Sed et episcopi sacerdotes se sciant esse, non dominos,
honorent clericos quasi clericos, ut ipsis episcopis a clericis quasi episcopis

370 *honor deferatur. Scitum est illud oratoris Domicii: Cur ego, inquid, te*
habeam ut principem, cum tu me non habeas ut senatorem? Item apostolus,
XIIII. distinctione, capitulo ultimo: *Episcopi non debent esse dominantes*

---

345 episcopi *in margine scriptum hoc loco inserui*   346 deberent *in ras.* V
350 *ante* Episcopus *deletum est* Sint . . . proprias (= *354–5*) V   363 decernimus *e*
decrevimus *corr.* V   364 iura *ex* iure *corr.* V   365 *et* 402 debeant *e* debuerant
corr. V

345–417. See Appendix (I), p. 284.   348–9. Cf. 441–2.
350–1. Gratian, c. 52, C. XII, q. 2; the same phrase also occurs in 'Statuta Ecclesiae
Antiqua', xv, Migne, *P.L.* 56, col. 882A.
354–7. Gratian, c. 21, C. XII, q. 1.
358–64. Gratian, c. 4, C. XII, q. 5.

by the heavy and continual depredations of the laity on all sides. Wickedness, I say, will grow to such a point that, with the loss of charity on
both sides, brotherly love, so necessary for salvation, and fatherly, as
well as filial, affection, originally pure and untroubled, could scarcely
be restored to the full whatever the time given.

It is amazing, when bishops ought to treat church property as a trust,
not as their own, so much so that they cannot even bequeath goods of
their church in their will according to the canons of the Apostles, to
see the effrontery and temerity with which they dare to sell and dilapi-
date others' property (since they are the Lord's and are dedicated to
God). So, Pope Leo says in *Causa XII, questio ii*: 'The bishop is to
treat church property as a trust, not as his own.' Thus the pious statement of a certain prior or abbot, yearning for a bishopric: '"Mine"',
he said, 'has more force than "ours"', clearly revealing his over-secular
and selfish intention. Again in the canons of the Apostles (*Causa XII,
questio i*) we find: 'Let the personal possessions of the bishop, if he
has any personal possessions, be clearly marked, and the possessions
of the Lord (i.e. the ecclesiastical ones) be clearly marked likewise, so
that a dying bishop has the power over his possessions to dispose of
them as and to whom he wishes', etc. Again from the Council of Seville
(in the same *Causa, questio v*): 'We have set down that it is a decree to
be enforced for all time that according to canonical authority a bishop
may confer on whom he wishes, and do whatever he wishes with those
things which are his of right, which he acquired before his episcopate,
or succeeded to by hereditary right during his episcopate; however,
after he is made bishop, we decree that whatever things he has acquired
by the authority of the Church, or in the name of someone else, come
under the jurisdiction, not of his relatives, but of the church over which
he presides.'

It is remarkable that, although they are not lords and ought not to be
dominating, they presume to exercise such a tyranny over the clergy.
Thus Jerome says to Nepotianus (*Distinctio XCV*): 'Be subject to your
bishop, and love him like a spiritual father. But let the bishops be aware
that they are priests and not lords, and let them honour their clergy as
clergy, so that the clergy may honour their bishops as bishops.' The
following of the orator Domitius is well known: 'Why', he said, 'am I to
regard you as Emperor, when you never regard me as senator?' Again
the Apostle (*Distinctio XIV*, last chapter): 'Bishops should not be
masters among the clergy, but formed according to the spirit of the

367–71. Gratian, c. 7, D. XCV (= Ep. 52, 7).
372–3. Gratian, c. 3, D. XCIV (not XIIII as Giraldus has) (*gregis*).

in clero, sed forma facti gregi ex animo. Quibus et illud Gregorii consonare videtur, causa II, q. VII: *Admonendi sunt subditi ne plusquam*
375 *expedit sint subiecti, ne cum student plus quam necesse est hominibus subici,*
compellantur eorum vicia venerari, et non tantum vicia non venerari,
quin immo viciosos prelatos puplice reos deferre sub interminatione
ibidem multis capitulis invitantur, sicut ibidem caput illud: *Quapropter,*|
f. 93ʳᵃ manifeste declarat. ⌜Unde et episcopus pape: *Ubi non delinquimus,*
380 *pares sumus.* Lex enim apostolo testante *propter transgressores posita est,*
proinde et qui spiritu dei ducitur, non est sub lege.⌝

Preterea, sicut pro rebus ecclesie, puta non propriis, episcopi merito
extolli non possunt, sic et nomine episcopali immo longe minus gloriari
deberent, quo etiam presbiteros communiter noverint insigniri, ut
385 XCIII. distinctione *Legimus in Ysaia,* ubi multis exemplis docet
Ieronimus presbiteros comuniter ab apostolo 'episcopos' vocari et
quoniam omnia sacramenta omnibus presbiteris communia fuerant;
quod pauca quedam presbiteris subtracta episcopis sunt attributa, ad
hoc tantum ut aliqua essent episcopi specialia factum est. Quid tamen
390 in hoc, nisi numerositas exhonerata, paucitas vero honerata videtur?
Nichil habet episcopus in se presbiterio maius, nichil ⟨non⟩ equale:
in maximo sacramentorum et precipuo pares sunt. Sed numquid
episcopos paucitas honorabiles, presbiteros turba contemptibiles facit,
quia omne quod rarum est plus appetitur (unde pulegium apud Indos
395 pipere preciosius est)?

Cum ergo iuxta Ieronimum episcopi sacerdotes sint, non domini,
cum iuxta apostolum non debeant esse dominantes in clero, cum iuxta
Leonem rebus ecclesie tanquam commendatis, non tanquam propriis
uti debeant, ex quibus iuxta canones apostolorum nec etiam in ultima
400 voluntate liberam habent arbitrii dispositionem, cum etiam iuxta
Ieronimum olim idem presbiter qui et episcopus et in commune
f. 93ʳᵇ ec|clesiam regere debeant, unde supercilium episcopis tantum? Unde

---

384 noverint *e* noverent *corr. V*   388 attributa] attribuita (i *ss.*) *V*   394 pulegium *e* pullegium *corr. V*   402 = 365

374–6. Gratian, c. 57, C. II, q. 7 (374–5: cf. 313–14).
378. Quapropter] c. 47, C. II, q. 7.
379–80. Not identified.
380. Cf. Gal. iii, 19: *Quid igitur lex? Propter transgressiones posita est.*
385. Legimus in Ysaia] c. 24, D. XCIII, see note on 392–5.
391. The same words occur in a letter to Peter de Leia, bishop of St. David's and
predecessor of Geoffrey de Henlaw, to whom Ep. 6 is addressed (cf. Appendix, p. 284);

flock.' This passage from Gregory appears to conform to this view (*Causa II, questio vii*): 'The underdogs should be warned not to be more subject than is expedient, lest, when they desire to be subjected more than necessary, they be compelled to worship their masters' vices', and not only not worship their vices, but, moreover, they are urged, according to many chapters, to prosecute vicious prelates in public under threat of penalty, as in the same place the chapter *Quapropter* clearly shows. Again in the words of a bishop to the pope: 'When we do not transgress, we are equals.' In the words of the apostle, the law 'was made because of transgressors', in the same way that he who is led by the spirit of God is not subject to the law.

Moreover, just as bishops cannot justifiably be extolled for the possessions of the church—remember, they are not personal!—thus they ought even less to be glorified for the title 'bishop', a title which they know is used commonly for priests, as in *Distinctio XCIII, Legimus in Ysaia*, where Jerome gives us many examples of priests commonly being called 'bishops' by the apostle, and teaches that all sacraments had been common to all priests: the action of taking a few certain rites from priests and reserving them to bishops was only done to give the bishops something apart. Yet why are few in fact seen to be honoured in this respect unless it is because the many are stripped of honour? There is nothing inherent in a bishop that makes him greater than a priest, and there is nothing that makes them unequal: they are equals in the greatest and most important of the sacraments. But does scarcity make bishops venerable and abundance make priests contemptible because what is rare is more sought after? (Thus pennyroyal is more valuable than pepper among the Indians.)

Since, then, according to Jerome bishops are priests, and not lords, since according to the apostle there should not be masters among the clergy, since according to Leo they should treat church property as a trust, not as personal property, from which according to the canons of the Apostles not even in their will do they have a free disposal of their decision, since according to Jerome at one time a priest was the same as a bishop, and they ruled the church in common, what is the source of this great arrogance of the bishop? What is the source of such a lust

as in both instances the indispensable word *non* is missing, it would appear that the corruption was already in the copy from which this passage was taken. See also note on Ep. 8, 78–9.

392–5. These lines are taken from the Distinctio *Legimus in Ysaia* (see note on 385): *Quid paucitatem, de qua ortum est supercilium, in leges ecclesie vendicas? Omne quod rarum est plus appetitur. Pulegium apud Indos pipere preciosius est. Diaconos paucitas honorabiles, presbiteros turba contemptibiles facit.* The phrase *Pulegium apud Indos pipere pretiosius est* occurs also in Jerome, *Ep.* 146. 2, *CSEL* 56, 311.

dominandi tanta libido? Cur tantum preesse cupiunt et non prodesse?
Cur potius tirannidem exercent in clero quam assumpti regiminis
405 rationem, ita, ut illud Ieronimi, XCIII. distinctione, cap. *Diaconi,*
quasi studio quodam adimplere curaverint: *Nunc autem, ex quo in*
ecclesiis sicut in Romano inperio crevit avaricia, periit lex a sacerdote et
visio de propheta. Singuli quoque per potenciam episcopalis nominis (. . .)
totum, quod levitarum est, in suos usus redigunt, nec hoc solum, quod sibi
410 *ascriptum est vendicant, sed cunctis auferunt universa. Mendicat infelix*
in plateis clerus et servili opere mancipatus puplicam de quolibet poscit
elemosinam (. . .) Solus episcopus incubat donis, solus utitur ministeriis,
solus sibi vendicat universa, solus partes invadit alienas, solus occidit
universos: hinc propter avariciam episcoporum sepe odia consurgunt, hinc
415 *episcopi acusantur a clericis, hinc principium litis, hinc detractationis causa,*
hinc origo fit criminis. Omnia sunt hec verba Ieronimi et sentencie
capituli.

f. 93va　　Qualiter autem episcopi tales hec et alia sanctorum scripta,| pravos
actus eorum detestancia, absque rubore pretereunt et horrore, satis
420 admirari non possumus. Unde Ambrosius: *Sciant episcopi quia tot*
mortibus digni sunt, quot perdicionis ad subditos exempla ⌐*prava*⌐ *trans-*
mittunt. Item Ieronimus: *Non omnes episcopi sunt episcopi: Petrum*
attende, Iudam considera, ⌐*et paulo post: Qui enim in officio male vivis,*
utquid terram et locum alterius occupas? Cave ne predicacio et debita populo
425 *oracio ei pro peccato tuo subtrahatur et tu cum plebe moriaris eternaliter.*
Qui enim suis premitur, aliena non diluit. Talis enim commune opus impedit
et ideo mortaliter peccat.⌐ Idem etiam canes inpudicos dicit episcopos
tales, Iude similes et non episcopos. Item et alibi: *Vilissimus reputandus*
est episcopus, si non precellat sciencia et sanctitate qui est honore prestantior.
430 Sed quomodo ibi sanctitas, ubi sola cupiditas regnat et nulla caritas?

---

404 assumpti] p *ss. V*

---

403. preesse . . . prodesse] Augustine, *De civitate Dei,* xix, 19: *non se esse episcopum*
qui praeesse dilexerit, non prodesse: CC, 48, p. 687, 29–30. Cf. also Yves Congar, 'Quelques expressions traditionnelles du service chrétien', *L'épiscopat et l'église universelle,*
ed. Y. Congar and B. D. Dupuy, Unam Sanctam 39 (Paris, 1962), pp. 101–2. The
phrase is quoted frequently by Giraldus. On *praeesse–prodesse* cf. also St. Isidore, *De*
ecclesiasticis officiis, ii, v, 8, Migne, *P.L.* 83, col. 782c; see also *supra,* 275, and Bernard
of Clairvaux, *De consideratione,* iii, 1, 2; Peter of Blois, *Canon episcopalis,* Migne, *P.L.*
207, col. 1102D.
406–16. Gratian, c. 23, D. XCIII (411 *operi* Gratian, but *opere = operae: servili opere*
mancipatus), also in the *Symbolum Electorum,* 1, 7 (*Op.* i, p. 222, 22).
418–60. See Appendix (II), pp. 284–5.　　　　　　　　　419–20. Cf. Ep. 3, 2.
420–2. Not identified.
422–3. considera] Gratian, c. 29, C. II, q. 7 (*Ep. ad Heliodorum,* xiv, 9); see also the
next note.

for power? Why do they only desire to be at the head and not help? Why do they exercise tyrannical powers over the clergy rather than the consideration of the rule they have received? It is as if they were zealously making sure that they fulfilled the following passage from Jerome (*Distinctio XCIII*, chapter *Diaconi*): 'Now, however, since avarice has arisen in the church, just as it did in the Roman empire, the law has passed away from the priest, and the vision from the prophet. Certain people have also converted what belongs to the deacons for their own use, simply by the power of the title 'bishop', and they sell not only what is ascribed to them, but pillage everything from everyone. The priest, unlucky in his collection, and appointed to servile tasks begs public charity from anyone and everyone. The bishop alone retains sole power over gifts; the bishop alone avails himself of the administration; the bishop alone sells all and sundry for himself; the bishop alone invades others' areas; the bishop alone kills all and sundry; hence hatred often arises because of the greed of the bishops; hence bishops are accused by their priests; hence the start of litigation; hence the reason for slander; hence the start of accusation.' All these are the words of Jerome and sentences of that chapter.

How such bishops could pass over without a blush or horror these and other writings of the saints, execrating their depraved activities, we cannot be sufficiently astonished. Thus, in the words of Ambrose, 'the bishops ought to know that they deserve as many deaths as the wicked examples of treachery they have passed on to their underlings'; similarly in Jerome, 'not all bishops are bishops: think of Peter: remember Judas'; and shortly afterwards, 'you who live wickedly in office, why do you occupy the land and place of another? Take care lest the preaching and prayer owed to the people are withheld from them because of your sin, and you die for ever with the people. A man who is weighed down by his own guilt does not wash away another's. Such a man blocks the common need and, therefore, sins mortally.' The same author also calls such bishops shameless dogs and like Judas not bishops. Again he says: 'The bishop, who is of very high standing, is to be regarded as most despicable, if he is not of outstanding wisdom and holiness.' But how can there be holiness where there is only greed, and

---

423–7. paulo post] Not from Gratian nor from Jerome, but from the *Verbum Abbreviatum*, 39D, where the words *Qui enim . . . 427, peccat* follow immediately the quotation: *Quod probat Hieronymus his verbis talem alloquens sic: Non omnes episcopi sunt episcopi* (without *Petrum . . . considera*: see note on 422–3).

427–8. Cf. Gratian, c. 32, C. II, q. 7: *Unde Augustinus: Qui nec regiminis in se rationem habuit nec sua delicta detersit nec filiorum crimen correxit, canis inpudicus dicendus est magis quam episcopus*; see the Appendix (II) on l. 427–8.

428–9. Gratian, c. 45, C. I, q. 1.

In quo etsi forte scientia, cum caritate sit vacua et pocius inflat quam
edificat, non ad salutem est previa, sed magis in contrarium dans
compendia. Unde Ieronimus: *Non sciencia scripturarum notum deo*
facit, quem operum iniquitas indignum ostendit, quin immo quanto sciencius
435 *peccat, tanto gravius et damnabilius in Gehenne suplicia se precipitat.*
Ad hec etiam super illud in psalmo: *Posuisti homines super capita nostra,*
dicit Ambrosius: *Patimur interdum superiores, quos scimus tamen*
deteriores, quamquam zelo rectitudinis et non amaritudinis corripi
f. 93vb secreto | debeant, ut diximus, a subditis prelati tales, et si incorrigibiles
440 inventi fuerint, in facie ecclesie rei sunt puplice deferendi.

Qui ergo res dominicas deoque dicatas, sibi tantum commendatas,
dilapidare non formidant et possessiones ecclesiasticas turpi distraere
venalitate non cessant, unde et ecclesias ipsas, terris amplis et prediis
devota fidelium largitione ditatas olim in inmensum et dotatas, spoliant
445 incessanter et ad mendicitatem apporiant, quique in Christi sortem
electos tam tyrannice desevire presumunt gregemque sibi commissum
non solum lupis exponunt, verum etiam ipsi, qui pastores et rectores
esse deberent, lupi peiores existunt, qui, symoniacis aut paccionibus
aut actionibus ingressum habentes et ⌈a⌉ pravis iniciis declinare nulla-
450 tenus aut deviare volentes, plus tamen Giezi quam Symonem, quia
plus vendentes quam ementes, plus adimentes quam adquirentes,
expresse representare nec verecundantur nec verentur—hii omnes
absque dubio eorumque similes ex solo fidei defectu adeo enormiter
exorbitant adeoque damnabiliter a via veritatis aberrant. Nam si premia
455 iustorum post hanc vitam et penas reproborum, sicut scripture sacre
testantur, aut sperarent aut timerent, si illis, inquam, gaudia perpetua
et istis suplicia fine carentia firmissime crederent nec vacillarent,|
f. 94ra prescriptos excessus saluti tam contrarios indubitanter aut virtutis amore
declinarent aut pene perhennis ob terrorem vehementer abhorrerent
460 et evitarent.

Porro cum hec ita ⌈se⌉ habeant, quidam faventes ineptiis suis, ut
sordescant amplius et putrescant in stercore suo, sompniant sibi solacia

---

431 *ante* sit *deletum* est sunt *V*   446 *ante* gregemque *deletum* est ut *V*   451 *alt.*
plus *bis V, pr. del.*   452 verecuncundantur *V*

---

431. Cf. 1 Cor. viii, 1.   433–5. Not identified.   436. Ps. lxv, 12.
437. Ambrosius] Not Ambrose (see the note on 487–8) but Augustine (quoted in the
Glossa Ordinaria), *Enarr. in Psalmos* (65, 12), CC, 39, p. 850, 21–2.
438–40. Cf. 377–8.   441–2. Cf. 348–9.
450 (cf. Ep. 7, 307, Ep. 8, 32, 39–40). Cf. *De Invectionibus*, 6, 27 (*Op*. i, p. 194, 6;
ed. Davies, p. 235, 42): *Simoniacam labem et Gieziticam*; also *De Iure et Statu Menevensis*
Ecclesie, 7 (*Op*. iii, p. 367, 10–11): *tam Simoniacam quam Gieziticam pravitatem*; ibid.
14: *Gieziticam pravitatem vilissimam*; ibid. 21–2: *Gieziticam detestabilem ac turpissimam*
cartarum et literarum . . . venalitatem. See 2 Kings v, 20 ff.
453. See note on 512–13.

no charity? And even if there chances to be wisdom in him, since it lacks love, and blows up rather than builds, it does not lead to salvation, but rather gives the short cut in the opposite direction. Thus, according to Jerome, 'knowledge of the scriptures does not make known to God a man whose iniquitous doings have shown him unworthy, but rather, the more knowingly he sins, the more seriously and damnably does he cast himself into the punishment of Gehenna'. In addition, about the words in the Psalm: 'Thou hast set men over our heads', Ambrose says: 'We suffer meanwhile from superiors whom we know to be inferiors.' Although such prelates ought to be privately rebuked by their underlings with a zealousness for righteousness, not for bitterness, as we have said, if they are found to be incorrigible, they should be publicly prosecuted in the face of the church.

Thus, then, those who do not shrink from squandering the Lord's possessions, which have been dedicated to God, and only entrusted to them, and do not cease disposing of ecclesiastical properties in a disgraceful and venal fashion, as a result of which they unceasingly plunder the churches themselves, which once were immensely enriched and endowed with ample lands and estates by the generosity of the faithful, and despoil them to the point of penury, those who presume to tyrannize the elect of Christ, and not only expose the flock entrusted to their care to the wolves, but even they themselves, who should be shepherds and leaders, are greater wolves, who, having embarked upon their simoniacal contracts or transactions, and being unwilling in any way to turn aside or draw back from their wicked beginnings, are neither ashamed nor afraid of being more of a Gehazi than a Simon, in that they sell more than buy, spend more than acquire—all these, and those of their kind, certainly go so far astray and wander so damnably from the way of righteousness solely because they lack faith. For, if they either believed in the rewards of the just, or feared the punishment of the unjust in the afterlife, as Holy Writ testifies, and, I say, if they believed very firmly in the perpetual joys for the one and the endless tortures of the other and did not vacillate, they would certainly either turn away from the aforementioned excesses, which stand in the way of salvation, by the love of virtue, or shun and avoid them because of the fear of eternal punishment.

Moreover, since such is the state of affairs, certain people, looking with favour on their ineptitude, so that they become more foul and

462. Cf. Joel i. 17; Peter of Blois, *Canon episcopalis, id est tractatus de institutione episcopi*: *Per hanc in suis stercoribus miseri computrescunt atque peccatorum suorum bibentes urinam, gloriantur cum male fecerint et exsultant in rebus pessimis*, Migne, *P.L.* 207, cols. 1097–1112, at 1109A; cf. also note on Ep. 5, 44–9 and *supra*, part i, 91.

vana, cum tamen, omissis gravibus sicut et admissis, delictis scilicet
et derelictis, iram sibi vindicem accumulare non cessant. Incestus enim
465 puplicos et adulteria, cedes in locis sacris et incendia dissimulando
pretereunt nec populo dei scelera ipsorum anunciant nec tanquam
tubam vocem exaltant neque pro domo domini se murum opponunt,
sed persecutionis tempore fugiunt pocius et delitescunt, lucro pecuniarum totis inhiando nisibus, non animarum, dum percipere lac et lanam
470 cum cathedrali honore pariter et pontificali nimis avide concupiscunt,
curam autem debitam gregi commisso et diligenciam inpendere fere
ex toto pretermittunt. O quam inpar et quam inequale commercium,
pro modica in tempore et quasi momentanea corporis pompa mytraque
cornuta et virga baiula tam desiderata perpetuam misero spiritui simul
475 et carni, quatinus potentes in oculis suis potenter tormenta patiantur,
f. 94ʳᵇ penam comparare et tam exili | lucro et tam exiguo tam interminabile et
incomparabile damnum compensare.

Post tales igitur ingressus, quales iam depinximus, et progressus
pravosque per omnia iugiter actus et excessus et iuxta moralitatem suam
480 sibi figmenta componunt, quia, si iam lassi seculo ad monasterium,
unde sumpti forte et revera sorte magis quam arte fuerant, vel etiam
aliud denique se conferant et a malis ibidem cessent atque quiescant,
quecumque ante acta fuerit vita et quantumlibet enormis et ignominiosa,
iam in portu se navigare et tanquam rebus ⌜optime⌝ per omnia gestis
485 tutos existere confidenter asseverant. Sed questione dignum videtur,
quando rapinas omnes singulis iniuriam passis et violenter ablata re-
fundent, testante Ambrosio quia *non dimittitur peccatum nisi restituatur
ablatum.*

Verum ut pecuniarum dampna taceantur, que quidem in respectu
490 sunt modica et tamen districte pro his ratio reddenda, tot animarum
dispendia per pastoralem incuriam deperditarum, pro quibus sibi
lucrandis Christus animam suam posuit et preciosissimum quoque sanguinem suum fudit, miseri prelati tales, immo miserrimi, quomodo vel
494 quando restituent, qui suas ⌜simul et⌝ subditorum animas perpetue
f. 94ᵛᵃ damnationi et perdicioni donant? | Quam ergo rationem villicationis
sue in die tremendi iudicii sunt reddituri, ubi tremebunt angeli, ubi

---

474 baiula virga *transposuit V*   475 *ante* tormenta *deletum est* tormenter *V*
479 iugigiter *V*   et excessus *bis, alt. del. V*   483 fuerit *e* fuerint *corr. V*

464–6. Cf. Ep. 7, 304–5.   466–7. See notes on Ep. 8, 336–8.
467. Cf. Ezek. xiii, 5: . . . *neque opposuistis murum pro domo Israel.*
468–70. See note on Ep. 8, 197–249.
469. lac et lanam] Ezek. xxxiv, 3 (cf. Ep. 8, 197–205, 309).
475. Wisd. vi, 7.
487–8. The same quotation in *De Iure et Statu*, etc., 1 (*Op.* iii, p. 104, 8–9) and in

corrupt at heart, dream up vain comforts for themselves, though by disregarding and approving, abandoning, and neglecting these important issues, they are ceaselessly heaping up vengeful anger for themselves. For they conceal and neglect public incest, adulteries, and murders and arson in holy places. They neither proclaim their crimes to God's people, nor raise their voice like a trumpet, and they do not become a bulwark for God's house, but rather flee and skulk at the time of persecution, expending all their efforts on gaining money rather than souls, and all too greedily they long to get milk and wool, as well as cathedral and episcopal honour, yet almost completely neglect to give due care and attention to the flock entrusted to them. What an unjust and unfair business, when for brief, almost momentary, physical pomp, a bishop's mitre, and the longed-for crosier they heap up eternal punishment both for their wretched spirits and for their bodies, as much as these great in their own eyes suffer great torture, and when for such a meagre and trivial profit they get endless damnation beyond compare.

After the sort of beginnings that we have just described, they build up their careers, their completely depraved activities, their excesses and excuses for themselves according to their own canons of morality, because if, weary of the world, they were at last to retire to the monastery from which they had been taken, by luck and indeed chance rather than design, or some other one, and there give up their evil ways and spend a quiet life, whatever their previous life has been, however abnormal and disgraceful it has been, they would swear with confidence that they were now in harbour and safe, as if their actions had been good all the time. But we think it worth asking, when they are to pay for all their thefts in which individuals suffered hardship and for their violent robberies, since Ambrose testifies that 'sin is not forgiven unless the object stolen is restored'.

But, to say nothing of the lost money, which in comparison is trivial, though strict account of it ought to be given, how, or when, will such wretched, indeed, most wretched, prelates restore the waste of so many souls, lost because of pastoral neglect, for whom Christ laid down his life and for whose ransom he shed his most precious blood, when they themselves expose both their own souls, and the souls of their underlings to eternal damnation and perdition? What account will they give for their stewardship on that day of dreadful judgement, when the angels

the *Speculum Ecclesie*, 3, 2 (*Op.* iv, p. 145, 27–8). The immediate source is Gratian, c. 1, C. XIV, q. 6: *non remittetur peccatum nisi restituatur ablatum*, but the idea comes from Augustine (not Ambrose, see note on 437), *Ep.* 153, 20 (*CSEL*, 44, 1904, pp. 419–20); cf. *Verbum Abbreviatum*, 144B.

495–6. rationem villicationis sue] Luke xvi, 2: *Redde rationem vilicationis tuae.*

columpne celi pavebunt, ubi tunc miserabiles illi comparebunt? Qualiter in conspectu tanti iudicis assistere tunc ausi erunt, cuius tamen
iudicium declinare non poterunt? Meticulosa quippe res est forum
500 illud adire, maxime ubi meritorum exigentia iudex graviter offensus,
et exili ⌜in⌝ causa et valde invalida cum consciencia nimirum undique
cauteriata stabunt miseri et tremuli, in tanta audiencia et a tanto iudice
iudicandi, quos etenim rodere non cessat in terris consciencie proprie
vermis, qui deo et hominibus odibiles fiunt, dum et deum et proximum
505 irreverenter et incessanter offendunt, qui tum demum a malo desistunt,
cum alios amplius ledere non possunt, qui de commissis aut omissis
minime satisfaciunt, dum nec oppressis et vim passis aut eorundem
proximis vel etiam ecclesie consilio sublata vel extorta restituunt.
Sed sub ⌜forma⌝ tali et tam inperfecte discedunt nec aliter in fine vel
510 ante se corrigunt, sed et ewangelica scripta sacreque scripture dogmata
f.94ᵛᵇ et divina | statuta tanquam frivola et solum ad terrorem emissa dam-
pnabili temeritate contempnunt. Nonne ex fidei defectu maximo miseris
et obstinatis et precitis ad mortem ac reprobatis hec cuncta proveniunt?

Ut autem post digressionem longam, nec preter rem tamen aut
515 inutiliter factam, stilus noster ad vos denuo convertatur ac revertatur
et verbis ad hec autenticis confidenter utatur: si recte egistis nobiscum,
recte sit vobis, sin autem perverse, iudicet ille, cui datum est a patre
iudicium omne. Nobis vero sufficiat rem gestam literis et scriptis per-
petua⌜re et⌝ innocenciam nostram preter spem et meritum oppressam
520 presentibus et posteris quasi querulo carmine propalare, poeticum illud
sepius ⌜ad⌝ animum revocando: *Non expectato vulnus ab hoste tuli*,
et illud eiusdem: *Que venit indigne pena, dolenda venit*. Item et illud
Gregorii pacienciam nobis adicere potest, quoniam *apud christianos*
miserabilior est qui infert iniuriam quam qui suffert.

525 Verumtamen si inermis hec ulcio, mitis et mansueta, non profecerit,
facere poterit indignatio sola quod forte sequetur armata et talioni
magis obnoxia, quamquam tamen graviora sint vulnera stilo inflicta
quam telo: ista nimirum beneficio temporis atque medele plerumque

---

504 odibiles *ex* hodibiles *corr. V*   509 discedunt *scripsi*] descendunt (*pr.* n
expunctum) *V*   520 querulo] *alt.* u eras. *V*   527 graviora] *pr.* a *ss. V*

512–13. This is perhaps a reference to Giraldus' lost work *De fidei fructu fideique*
defectu. Cf. 453, Ep. 7, 316–7, and *supra*, part ii, 415.
517–18. Cf. John v, 22: *Neque enim pater iudicat quemquam, sed omne iudicium dedit*
filio.   520 (and 3). See note on Ep. 2, 79–80.
521. Ovid, *Heroides* vi, 82; *supra*, part i, 73.
522 (and Ep. 4, 95). Ovid, *Heroides* v, 8; *supra*, part i, 75.
522–4. illud Gregorii] The same quotation in *De Principis Instructione*, I, 5, (*Op.*
viii, p. 18, 5–7): *Gregorius: Apud christianos non qui patitur, sed qui facit iniuriam miser*
est (not identified).

will tremble, when the doves of heaven will be afraid, and they will appear in wretchedness? How will they then have the courage to stand in the sight of such a mighty judge, whose judgement they will not be able to avert? Indeed, it is a fearful matter to approach that court, especially when the judge is very angry at their lack of merit, and they stand, wretched and trembling, with a case that is thin and very weak, and the knowledge branded on all sides, to be judged in such a great audience by such a great judge; when the worm of their own knowledge never ceases to gnaw at them on earth, when they become hateful both to God and men, since they are unceasingly disrespectful to God and his son: when they at long last cease their wrongdoings, because they cannot harm others any further; when they get very little satisfaction from their deeds or omission, since they restore nothing of what they have deliberately taken or extorted either to those they oppressed and who suffered violence, or their relatives or even to the Church. But they die with such imperfect ideals, and they do not repent either at the end or before, but with damnable rashness treat evangelical writings, the teachings of Holy Writ, and divine statutes with contempt, as if they were trifles only to scare them. Are not all these the results of a very great lack of faith on the part of the wretched, the obstinate, the damned, and the reprobate?

However, let us return once more to you personally after our long digression, though it was not beside the point nor made without purpose, and with confidence use the following authoritative words: if you have acted in a straightforward manner towards us, may things be straightforward with you; if, however, you have acted in an underhand manner, may he, to whom all judgement was given by his father, judge you. But we would be content with keeping the affair alive in our writings and letters, and proclaiming our innocence, which was unexpectedly and undeservedly oppressed, to the present and future generations with a sort of song of complaint, frequently bringing to mind that phrase of the poet: 'I have suffered a wound from an unexpected enemy'; and, again, 'the pain that is undeserved is grievous'. In the same way, that phrase of Gregory can inspire us with patience: 'In the eyes of Christians the man who inflicts injury is more pitiful than he that suffers it.'

But, if this harmless, soft and tame punishment is of no avail, indignation alone will be able to bring it about that punishment will follow armed and liable to punishment in kind, though wounds inflicted by the pen are mightier than those by the sword. Sword wounds

f. 95ra cicatricem | obducunt, illa vero perpetuis literarum vinculis quasi cum
530 eternitate contendunt.

Utinam diu et bene valere possitis et parentali filios affectu diligere
precipueque bonis ac bene meritis benignus et gratus esse velitis et
virtute perfecta iuxta doctrinam apostolicam nec malum etiam pro malo
reddere, nedum pro bono, nec caritatem extinguere neque vinci a malo,
535 sed vincere magis in bono malum modis omnibus satagatis.

531. See note on Ep. 1, 40.   533–5. See note on Ep. 2, 56–7.

generally scar with the healing influence of time, but those of the pen have to contend with immortality in the eternal chains of literature.

It is our prayer that you are able to enjoy long and good health, and love your sons with fatherly affection and especially that it is your desire to be kind and pleasant to good and worthy men, and that according to the teaching of the apostles with perfect virtue you render neither evil for evil, let alone evil for good, nor quench your charity, nor be overcome by evil, but rather with all your efforts endeavour to overcome the evil in the good.

7

Priori de Lantonei

SICUT amicis communicanda sunt gaudia ut congaudeant, sic et eisdem interdum propalanda sunt tristia, si contingat, quatinus consilio simul et prudentia remedium aliquod, si fieri potest, adhibeant aut saltem
5 premuniti exemplo et perterriti, similia caveant et maliciosos hominum mores plenius agnoscant.

Scire vos itaque volumus quia quamdiu spem habuimus aliquam quod episcopus noster nepotem nostrum erroneum, impium, ingratum et iniquum ab errore suo, quin immo furore, pontificali potentia pariter
10 et diligentia revocare vellet, sicut deceret, dissimulatione quadam ex industria usi fuimus, que nobis et aliis liquido constabant iuxta comicum
f. 95ʳᵇ illud: *Ego | autem quod scio nescio,* tanquam incognita pretereuntes. Sed postquam ab hac spe decidimus, illum quippe, qui tam turpia totis nisibus extinguere deberet, sicut ab inicio suggestor eorum fuerat,
15 auctor et instigator, sic continue, quamquam occulte, fotorem eorundem et fultorem certissimis indiciis comperientes, non amplius locum esse dissimulationi vel utile censuimus vel honestum. Probis igitur et discretis per Angliam et Walliam viris et presertim amicis ac benivolis sunt hec decetero propalanda, quatinus, si nos commotos quandoque
20 per hec agnoverint, iuxta poeticum illud: *Qui me commorit, melius non tangere, clamo,* minus admirentur, dum tante commocionis et perturbationis nostre causas urgentissimas non ignoraverint.

Discretionem itaque vestram latere non debet, quod illo nepote nostro a nostro consilio tam lubrice dilapso, statim ad episcopum
25 nostrum, de cuius amicicia plenam adhuc non inmerito fiduciam habuimus, nuncios et litteras misimus, rogantes et supplicantes quatinus, si nepos ille noster administrationem nostram pravo consilio turbare
f. 95ᵛᵃ presumeret,| ipse pontificaliter obviaret et pueriles ineptias eius indulta sibi potentia pariter et iusticia refrenaret et, nisi via ad hoc incedendum
30 commodiore videret, tam eius institutionem quam nostram administrationem (quoniam ab ipso utramque et per ipsum habitam), ne congesta prudenter pueriliter dissolverentur interim in manu sua sequestraret. Ipse vero apud Herefordiam inventus, ubi pro arbitrio quodam

---

1. priori] probably Gilbert, see *supra,* p. lvi n. 154.
5. Cf. *supra,* part i, 96.   7. See note on Ep. 2, 64.
8-10. See note on 49-50.   12. Plautus, *Bacchides* 791 (iv, 6, 21).
20-1. Horace, *Serm.* ii, 1, 45.

[7.] *To the Prior of Lanthony*

JUST as joyful news should be given to friends so that they may share it, so, too, sorrows should be divulged to them on occasions, if such should be the case, so that their counsel and wisdom may offer some remedy, if one can be found, or that they may avoid similar circumstances, and recognize more clearly the wicked ways of mankind, with our example serving at least as a warning and deterrent.

We want you therefore to know that as long as we had some hope that our bishop would be willing to bring our erring, impious, ungrateful, wicked nephew back from his sin, or rather madness, as he should with his episcopal power as well as his diligence, we purposely pretended that we were ignorant of those facts which were as clear as crystal to us and others: rather as the comic poet says: 'I do not know, however, what I do know.' But after we had given up this hope, and had discovered with positive proof that the man who ought to have exerted all his powers to suppress such criminal enterprises, had from the beginning been their promoter, originator, and instigator, and even had continually, though secretly, been their supporter and fomenter, we considered that there was no further point, usefulness, or credit in our pretence. So, in future these facts are to be revealed to all honest and understanding men in England and Wales, especially to friends and well-wishers, so that, if they hear that we have been occasionally upset by these actions (as in the poet: 'I declare, it is better for the man who upsets me not to touch me') they may be less amazed, when they realize the very serious reasons for our being upset and disturbed.

Therefore, it should not be concealed from your discerning gaze, that when that nephew of ours so craftily withdrew from our company, we immediately sent messengers and letters to our bishop, in whose friendship we fully trusted so far with good reason: we begged and requested that, if that nephew of ours should dare to upset our administration with his wicked plans, he should intervene pontifically, and, using his powers of justice, curb the nephew's childish follies, and, unless he saw him proceed in a more acceptable way in this matter, he should meanwhile sequestrate personally both his installation and our administration (since both appointments stem from him) so that what has been gathered together wisely should not be dissipated childishly. But he turned out to be at Hereford, where a number of ecclesiastics

28. pontificaliter] Cf. 132; Ep. 5, 40, and *supra*, part i, 230–1: episcopaliter agens.

faciendo simul cum decano Herefordensi et precentore plures ec-
35 clesiastici viri parcium illarum tunc simul cum ipso convenerant, non
solum id non fecit, verum etiam nepotem nostrum ibidem in publica
audientia contra nos appellantem pacienter admisit nec in aliquo cor-
ripuit nec verbum aliquod castigationis ammisit, et cum decanus, ex
uno episcopi latere sedens, secreto quereret ab ipso, contra quem
40 appellaret et utrum contra patruum suum, respondit episcopus se
nescire, contra conscientiam scilicet et mentem loquens, cum ipse
totum utique sciret reique totius auctor existeret. Decanus autem ab
eo, qui pro nepote nostro loquebatur, quoniam ut prolocutorem habeat
f. 95ᵛᵇ opus est elingui, quesivit coram omnibus, contra | quem appellaret
45 archidiaconus ille et utrum contra patruum suum; respondit ille, contra
gravamina cuncta et contra ipsum quoque vel alium quemlibet ipsum
gravare volentem. Respondit decanus: 'Contra eum igitur appellat, qui
totum, quod habet, ei contulit ipsumque nutrivit et tanquam ex nichilo
creavit: pravo proculdubio fungitur consilio.' Episcopus autem, quasi
50 clausis oculis et conniventibus sub silentio cuncta preteriens, appellationem emissam ipsa taciturnitate non inprobavit.

Hiis autem apud Herefordiam sic patratis, immo et perperam actis,
statim nepos ille et magister suus Capre Willelmus sive Capelle usque
Brechene accelerantes, convocatis capitulis appellationem contra nos
55 in singulis et ibi fecerunt et fidelitates clericorum de novo ceperunt
et nos domibus nostris de Landu, quas fecimus, et terris etiam laicis
nec non et ecclesia cum archidiaconatus administratione tota, sicut
et paulo post prebende, Meneviam transeundo ibique contra nos appellando seque per appellationes has tam crebras apud probos viros et
60 discretos longe diffamando magis quam iuvando, destituerunt, episcopo
nimirum in remotis valde de Lanthon' in Ewias vallibus imis interim
f. 103ʳᵃ existente et, propter obiectos undique montes excelsos | rumoribus ad
ipsum pervenire non valentibus, omnia nimirum hec ignorante, set
longe verius cuncta dissimulante et per tacitum consensum approbante
65 et ratum pariter ac gratum habente. Putabat autem nos forte regulam illam iuris ignorare: *Ratihabitio mandato comparatur*, et canonem
illum Ignacii pape: *Error, cui non resistitur, approbatur et veritas cum
minime defensatur, obprimitur*, et illum Innocencii: *Negligere cum possis*

---

34 plures *scripsi coll. 35*, tunc] pluries (*cf. 117*) *V*   42 utique totum *trans-*
posuit V   64 tacidum *V*

---

44. elingui] Cf. 233, and Ep. 6, 299.   47-9 (233-4, 284). See note on Ep. 2, 91
49-50 (cf. 8-10). = Ep. 5, 42-3.
53. Cf. *supra*, part ii, 2 and *passim*.   59-60. See note on Ep. 2, 24-5.
61. in remotis valde de Lanthon' in Ewias vallibus imis] Cf. *Itinerarium Kambriae*,
I, 3 (*Op.* vi, p. 37): *De Ewias et Lanthonei.*

of those parts as well as the dean and the precentor of Hereford had congregated with him to judge some case or other. Not only did he not carry out our request, but he patiently allowed our nephew to appeal against us there in public, without rebuking him in any way, and without uttering any word of reproof. When the dean, who was sitting on one side of the bishop, secretly asked him against whom he was appealing and whether it was against his uncle, the bishop replied that he did not know, though he was speaking contrary to his cognizance and knowledge, since he in fact knew all and was the instigator of the whole affair. However, in front of everyone the dean asked the man who was speaking on our nephew's behalf (since the inarticulate man needs somebody to speak on his behalf) against whom that archdeacon was appealing, and whether it was against his uncle. He replied that it was against all grievances, as well as against him or anyone else who would try to oppress him. The dean replied: 'He is appealing against the man who has given him everything he has and has reared him and almost created him from naught; without doubt this is a wicked plot he is executing.' However, the bishop, passing over everything in silence, as if he had his eyes closed in connivance, sitting mute did not refute the launching of the appeal.

When this business had been concluded, indeed erroneously executed, at Hereford, our nephew and his tutor, William the whoreson de Capella, immediately hastened to Brecon and convened the chapters. They made their appeal against us there item by item, and took the oath of the priests again. They deprived us of our houses we had built at Llanddew, and even our secular estates, together with the church and the whole administration of the archdeaconry, just as shortly afterwards they did with the prebend, when going to St. David's and appealing against us there (by their frequent appeals ruining their own reputation, rather than aiding it, in the eyes of just and prudent men). The bishop, who was buried away deep in the remote valleys of Llanthony in Ewias, nevertheless ignored all this completely, since the rumours could not reach him because of the barrier of high mountains on all sides; but it is nearer the truth to say that he turned a blind eye to everything, and approved everything with his tacit consent, and considered the whole affair as signed and sealed. However, he perhaps thought that we were ignorant of the law that 'Approbation comes close to authorization'; and of the canon of Pope Ignatius: 'To fail to correct an error is to approve it, and to fail to defend truth is to repress it'; and that of Innocent: 'Not to correct when possible those who have gone

66–71. See note on Ep. 5, 44–9.

perturbare perversos, nichil est aliud quam fovere nec caret scrupulo socie-
70 *tatis occulte, qui manifesto facinori desinit obviare,* presertim etiam cum
ad hoc ex officio teneatur.

Nos igitur tam manifestum diocesiani defectum attendentes nec non
et archiepiscopi presentia carentes, ad ultimum refugium atque remedium in terris Romam statim semel et iterum impigre misimus, ea ibi
75 perquirentes, per que deo opitulante et sole sereniore lucente nobis
ablata restituentur et iniuriarum acciones, iam diu sopite nimis atque
sepulte, iure denuo urgente resurgent et reviviscent.

Ceterum ad remociora respiciamus: cum ultimo in Hibernia fuimus,
idem episcopus noster ad instantiam Osberti archidiaconi de Ker-
80 merthin, qui tanquam individuus ei tunc temporis comes adherebat
f. 103rb et propter aggerem avene, que sicut avide crescit (unde et | nomen
accepit), sic et avidos facit, nuper ob hoc datum, gratiam eiusdem
plenius optinuerat, quandam prebende nostre de Martru porcionem
diucius a nobis ⌐iuste⌐ possessam simul cum decimis autumpni illius
85 subito sequestravit, cum tamen neque nos neque procuratores nostri
unquam in ius super hoc vocati fuerimus aut citati, longe quidem
promptior ad hanc faciendam sequestrationem iniustam, quam ad illam,
pro qua supplicavimus ei, sicut iam diximus, quam potuit facere et
debuit iuri per omnia consentaneam.

90 Sicut ergo tam promptulus tunc et preceps fuit ad sequestrationes
contra nos faciendas et non pro nobis, sic, iuxta suorum iactitationem,
et in eadem adhuc erga nos benignitate persistit: aiunt enim sui et
asseverant, quod duabus ecclesiis nostris vel tribus in Menevie partibus
et Penbrochie iam nos destituit easque nobis nec vocatis nec citatis more
95 suo sequestravit. Novit autem deus quia non solum duabus vel tribus,
verum etiam omnibus per diocesim suam ecclesiis nostris simili modo
per ipsum nos destitutos esse vellemus, quatinus et nos iustissime
motos et ad ultionem provocatos cuncti viderent et, quoniam ante
ruinam exaltabitur cor, tam multiplicate iniurie et tam manifeste con-
100 fusionem eius et deiectionem prompcius et expedicius accelerarent.

f. 103va Ad | hec etiam, cum transactis annis V vel VI Lincolniam studii
causa profecturi et nepotem nostrum nobiscum ducturi, capitula de
Eleveyn et Melenit et Buel tanquam in discessu coram nobis apud
Locheis haberemus, testimonio clericorum et officialium parcium

91 sicut (*cf. 90*) *V*   103 (et Ep. 8, 170) dicessu *V*

---

75 (278). See note on Ep. 6, 202.
81–2. For this etymology cf. Bede, *De orthographia* (Keil, *Grammatici latini*, vii
(1880), p. 264, 18–19): *Avenae sterile germen, habenae retinacula iumentorum, hoc de
habendi potestate, illud de occupandi aviditate dictum.*

astray is tantamount to encouraging them; nor is the man who fails to take action against a patent crime free of the suspicion of being secretly in league with it', especially when he is held to this by his office.

Since we were aware of the obvious defection of the diocesan bishop, and since there was no archbishop, we sent eagerly once and twice to the last refuge and remedy on earth, Rome, asking for the means whereby with God's aid and under sunnier skies that which had been stolen from us might be restored, and the actions against injustice which have been buried and dormant for ages might be resurrected and revived with fresh force of law.

But let us look at more distant affairs: when we were last in Ireland, that same bishop of ours suddenly sequestrated part of our prebend of Mathry which we had long justly held as well as the tithes of that harvest, though neither we nor our proctors had ever been summoned or called to law over this matter. It was done at the instigation of Osbert, archdeacon of Carmarthen, who at that time was his inseparable companion and had gained more of his favour because of the amount of payment of oats (which increases as avidly—the word is derived from the Latin, oats—as it makes men avid) which he had recently given for this purpose. Indeed, he was more ready to make this unjust sequestration than to make the one we had begged him to make, as we just said, which he could and ought to have done, since it was in complete accordance with the law.

Therefore, just as he was so keen and eager to make sequestrations against us, and not on behalf of us, at that time, so, according to the boast of his men, he is still just as well disposed to us: for they declare positively that he has already deprived us of two or three of our churches in the St. David's and Pembroke areas, and he has sequestrated them in his usual manner without summoning or calling us before the courts. However, God knows that it would be our desire to be deprived by him in a similar fashion not only of two or three, but of all the churches throughout his diocese, so that everyone might see that we were very justly enraged and provoked into taking revenge and, since the heart will be lifted up before a fall, the manifold and manifest damages will hasten more swiftly and quickly his overthrow and downfall.

In addition, when, after five or six years had elapsed, we were about to leave for Lincoln to study and to take our nephew with us, we had the chapters of Elfael, Maelienydd, and Builth in our presence at Llowes on our departure. We heard the sworn testimony of the

88. iam diximus] 31–3.
98–9. Cf. Prov. xvi, 18: *Ante ruinam exaltatur spiritus.*

105 illarum iuratorum accepimus episcopum, dum nos paulo ante Romam
ultimo profecti fuimus, de hiis, que ad archidiaconi portionem absque
dubio pertinebant, marcas V vel VI preocupasse. Unde cum Lincolnie
constituti scripsimus ei, quod dicta pecunia nobis refunderetur, rescri-
psit nobis se neque scire neque credere quod quicquam ad nos spectans
110 accepisset, set mandavit et monuit quod archidiaconum nepotem
nostrum ad certam rerum istarum indaginem simul cum ipso faciendam
ei remitteremus; ad quod rescripsimus nec nepoti nostro nec nobis id
profuturum, ipsum de tam remotis partibus cum tribus equis vel
quatuor in Walliam propter hoc mittere: posset enim peccuniam vel
115 maiorem eundo expendere et redeundo, preter corporis vexationem et
temporis etiam amissionem, nec debere tantillo lucro tantum dampnum
conpensari. Cum autem pluries ei super hoc scriberemus, dedecore
quidem rei ipsius longe plus quam dampno commoti, instante ad hoc
f. 103vb quoque nepote nostro, quoniam res eius agere videbatur | et dignitas
120 periclitari, necnon et magistro suo (utroque in dolo tamen id totum
agente, sicut ex post facto patuit, cum litteras ipsas nobis furtive sub-
reptas postmodum episcopo detulerint, ut ipsum erga nos exasperarent
sibique propicium redderent), nichil aliud ad litteras nostras tociens
missas respondit, nisi ut archidiaconum ei modis omnibus remittere-
125 mus, tanquam administratoris generalis et perpetui super hiis sollicitari
nichil interesse, sed tantum proprietarii per hoc innuere volens: maluit
enim cum archidiacono novello super hiis agere quam cum antiquo,
sciens quippe quia iocundius cum catulo luditur quam cum cane
vetusto. Nos autem econtra rescripsimus, sacius et longe sacius necnon
130 et honestius fore, canonicos alios et archidiaconos ecclesie sue, vino
venerique et ocio passim indulgentes, ut scolas peterent studiisque
vacarent compellere pontificaliter et artare, quam in scole gignasio
sudantes et laborantes preter causas urgentissimas abinde revocare.
Unum est autem quod pro episcopis huiusmodi facere forte videri pot-
135 est: sciunt enim archidiaconos et clericos subditos tales habere fatuos,
illitteratos, viciosos et ignavos, qui capud contra ipsos erigere non
audeant, magis quam probos viros, validos et eruditos, expediens fore.
f. 96ra Vi|dentes itaque res nostras in absentia nostra per ambicionem et
avariciam talem direptioni datas, cautelam aliquam adhibere volentes
140 scripsimus episcopo nos Thomam personam de Haia generalem officialem

118 ipsius] ipsi vel V

---

120. magistro] Cf. 53.
128–9 (154–5). Cf. *supra*, part ii, 496, 652–3, 1125.   132. pontificaliter] Cf. 28.
137. See note on Ep. 2, 24–5.   140. Cf. *supra*, part ii, 357–8.

clergy and the officials of those parts that while we had set out for Rome for the last time shortly before, the bishop had taken five or six marks of that income which certainly belonged to the archdeacon's share. Thus, when we were settled in Lincoln, we wrote to him to refund us the money. He wrote back to us that he neither knew nor believed that he had received anything belonging to us, but he commanded and advised us that we should send back our nephew, the archdeacon, to make a strict examination of the matter in question with him. We wrote back that it would be no use either for our nephew or us to send him to Wales from such distant parts with three or four horses for this purpose: for he would have to spend that money or even more going and coming back, to say nothing of the physical exertion and waste of time, and such a great expense ought not to be paid out for such a trifling sum. Though, however, we wrote to him several times about this, angered much more by the disgraceful nature of the affair than the loss, and our nephew, to say nothing of his tutor, insisted that it seemed to be his business to act, and his dignity was at stake (though both were doing all this fraudulently, as became clear from the subsequent action, since they carried off to the bishop those letters which they had secretly stolen from us, to stir up his anger against us and to curry favour for themselves), the bishop made no other reply to the letters we sent so frequently, than that we should send the archdeacon to him by every means, as if by doing so he wished to intimate that it was not the concern of the general and permanent administrator to be troubled over this, only the owner: for he preferred to conduct his business with the new archdeacon rather than the old, since he knew that it is better to play with a pup than an old hound. However, we wrote back to say that it would be better, far better, and far more decent for him to use his episcopal powers to compel and constrain other canons and archdeacons of his church, who were generally given over to wine, women, and idleness, to go to school and devote their attention to studying, rather than recall (unless for the most urgent reasons) those sweating and toiling in the school gymnasium. This, however, is one thing which perhaps could obviously be done for the sake of the bishops of this kind: for they know that it would be advantageous to have archdeacons and priests under them that are stupid, illiterate, immoral, and idle, who would not dare to raise their heads against them, rather than honest, stout, and educated ones. Therefore, seeing our property given over in our absence to depredation because of ambition and avarice, and wishing to use some caution, we wrote to the bishop that we had appointed Thomas, parson of Hay, as our general

nostrum per archidiaconatum de Brechene, dum in scolis essemus,
constituisse; qui cum litteras audisset, respondit se litteras et sigillum
magistri Giraldi ibi videre, non autem archidiaconi Giraldi, tanquam
per hoc iterum innuere volens non ad magistrum Giraldum, sed ad
145 archidiaconum Giraldum super officiali statuendo pertinere, sic erga
nos animum suum et hic denudans, quoniam Symaco testante *nichil
simulatum valet esse diuturnum*, et Seneca: *nemo diu fictam facere personam
potest*. Sed scire debuit, quoniam administrator publicus et perpetuus
officialem suum propria auctoritate constituere et negotia sub se tan-
150 quam coadiutori, maxime in absentia sua, gerenda committere potest.
Ut etiam ex laicis administrationibus id tanquam exemplo doceatur,
vicecomites, qui quasi momentanei sunt et non perpetui, officiales suos
et subvicecomites constituere solent. Nichil igitur hic aliud, nisi quod
sepius in hoc casu dicere consuevimus, quia iocundius cum catulo ludi-
155 tur quam cum cane vetusto.

Preterea quam cito littere nostre de curia Romana venerunt, cum
citationibus binis, nepoti nostro scilicet et magistro suo, in Walliam
venimus; qualiter in primo episcopus adventu nostro, tanquam paterno
nobis compaciens affectu, tam veritati testimonium coram iudicibus
160 nostris perhibendo, cum locus affuerit, quam et negocia nostra pro
posse promovendo se nobis propicium fore promiserit, et cum secundo |
f. 96rb aut tercio ad ipsum venimus qualiter hec promissio semper in peius
evanuerit, satis viva voce vobis indicavimus.

Ad hec etiam cum in finibus de Brechene, scilicet apud Landu, nos
165 prior de Pembroch ad ecclesiam de Tinebeh per monacum suum et
litteras suas presentaverit, ubi et inductione sua, ne seductione dicamus,
nepotem nostrum ecclesie illius personam fieri consensimus, vicaria
⌐tantum⌐ nobis retenta, nondum tamen reconciliatum, sed sicut pro-
missum nobis et suasum fuerat cicius ob hoc reconciliandum, qualiter
170 et quam lubrice de puncto in punctum erga nos in possessionem vicarie
illius inducendos actum fuit et responsum, ut biennales iam fructus
⌐nobis per eius avariciam⌐ auferrentur, cuilibet auditori probo et discreto
viro pudorem pariter et stuporem incutere potest, ⌐sicut in epistola
priore, que sic incipit: *Inter varias querimoniarum causas*, de utraque
175 duplicitate expresse poterit inveniri.⌐ Item cum, facta institutione de
iam dicta ecclesia nepoti nostro et nobis vicaria per pensiunculam

161 promovendo *e* proponendo *corr. V*   175 instututione *V*

146-7. See note on Ep. 2, 19-20.
147-8. *De clementia* i, 1, 6: *Nemo . . . potest personam diu ferre: ficta cito in naturam
suam recidunt.*
154-5 = 128-9.

official for the archdeaconry of Brecon, while we were at school. When the letters were read to him, he replied that he saw the letters and the seal of Master Giraldus, not Giraldus the archdeacon, there, as if he wished to imply once more that it was not Master Giraldus', but Giraldus the archdeacon's business to appoint an official, thus revealing here also his attitude to us. As Symmachus says: 'Nothing false can last long'; and Seneca: 'No one can keep up a pose for long.' But he knew very well that a public, permanent administrator can appoint his own official with proper authority, and allow business to be conducted by him as a kind of fellow auditor, especially in his absence. To give you an example from secular administration, sheriffs, who are temporary and not permanent, usually appoint their own officials and vice-sheriffs. The case here is no different, except that in this case we usually said, it is better to play with a pup than an old hound.

Furthermore, as soon as our letters had come from the curia at Rome, we came to Wales with two summonses, one for our nephew and one for his tutor. We have given you sufficient oral evidence of how on the first occasion on our arrival the bishop commiserated with us with a sort of fatherly love, promising to bear witness to the truth before our judges, should it come to that, to promote our business as much as possible, and to help us, and how, when we came on the second and third occasion, this promise became more and more airy.

In addition to this, when at Llanddew near Brecon the prior of Pembroke presented us to the church of Tenby by a monk of his and his own letters, and there at his suggestion, not to say at his seduction, we consented to our nephew's becoming parson of that church, while we retained only the vicarage, although a reconciliation had not yet taken place, because we had been promised and persuaded that the reconciliation should take place more quickly for this. The nature and manner of the crafty and punctilious way he acted and responded to our induction to the office of vicar, to rob us of the biennial returns because of his greed, can strike shame and astonishment into the heart of any good and upright man who hears of it. (A detailed description of the duplicity of both can be found in our preceding letter which starts: 'Among our various reasons for complaint . . .') The installation of our nephew in the aforementioned church was made, and the post of vicar with a small

---

159–60. veritati testimonium . . . perhibendo] Cf. John v, 33 and xviii, 37.
166 (and 175–7). Cf. Ep. 6, 59–64.   169–71. See note on Ep. 6, 59–62.
170. Cf. *Symbolum Electorum*, 1, 24 (*Op*. i, p. 287, 8–9): *Itaque cum breve sit tempus, cum punctum et etiam minus puncto sit quo vivimus* . . .
172–3. See note on Ep. 2, 24–5.   174. See Ep. 6, 2.
175–7 (and 166). Cf. Ep. 6, 59–64.

assignata et ibidem die concordie apud Penbrochiam inter nos prefixo,
coram episcopo scilicet et Willelmo de Barri nepote nostro primevo et
precipuo, in Quadragesima sequente et utraque parte ad hoc ab episcopo
180 per fidem astricta, cum de remotis Lincolnie finibus, ob hoc interrupto
studio in tempore tam ydoneo, apud Lanwadein ad episcopum venimus, ilico in procinctu itineris eundi in Angliam fore se finxit et cum
nullatenus retineri posset, sic spe concordie promisse nos fraudavit et
laborem nostrum tam longinquum ex toto frustravit.

185 　　Ad iniuriarum quoque cumulum et qualem erga nos animum gerat
probacionem apertam id nuper accessit, quod in hac Quadragesima
f. 96ᵛᵃ proxima cum archidiaconus nepos noster ad | ipsum accederet, statim
eum in possessionem dicte ecclesie tanquam personam induxit, qui
nos a simili beneficio, nobis revera debito, qui totum perquisivimus et
190 longe plus meruimus, si merita tamen digne pensari possent, iam fere
per triennium perfunctorie quidem et frustratorie nimis elongavit.

　　Sane mirari quis potest et secum querere, cum ceteros promotionis
sue fautores iuxta facultatis modulum ample remuneravit, filium magistri Martini Menevensis puerum canonicaverit, Iohanni de Landu
195 canonicam contulerit et postmodum archidiaconatus honorem, Osberto
archidiacono de Kermerthin manerium suum de Landewi, scilicet
apud Goer, Reginaldo Foliot ecclesiam de Landestephan, cur nobis,
qui finalem, ut nostis, promotioni sue cum effectu calculum adiecimus,
ecclesie, quam ipsi perquisivimus, vicariam invidet et possessionem
200 conferre detractat: causam assignare non possumus, nisi quoniam
graves ei sumus ad videndum, graviores etiam ad vivendum; vivere
tamen aliquamdiu per dei gratiam adhuc, si permitteret ipse, et ultimis diebus his nostris ignorantias nostras et delicta nostra ⌐in pace et
quiete⌐ deflere vellemus.

205 　　Porro si ⌐ad⌐ prescriptos beneficiandum, quos archiadversarius
noster contra nos allexerat, quibus tenebatur conventione prehabita
obligatus extitit et artatus, item si causam status et dignitatis ecclesie
Menevensis contra Cantuariensem ecclesiam se nunquam moturum,
papa id litteris suis, quas perquisivimus, districte prohibente, vel in
210 secreto, quod absit, cautionem emisit, totus in trenos ire valebit.

　　181 venimus ad episcopum *transposuit* V

---

180. cum (= 175, cum): pleonastic.　　　　　　192–3. Cf. Ep. 6, 291–3.
200–4 (and 248–50). Cf. Ep. 5, 172–6.
205–6. archiadversarius] Cf. notes on Ep. 2, 65 and on Ep. 5, 16.
209. papa . . . prohibente] Cf. Innocent III's letter of 25 May, 1203, to the bishops
of Ely and Worcester (Migne, *P.L.* 215, col. 70; also *De Invectionibus*, iv, 4, ed. W. S.

pension was assigned to us. A day in the following Lent was there and then set aside for a reconciliation between us at Pembroke, in the presence of the bishop and our eldest and distinguished nephew, William de Barri, and both sides were bound by oath to this by the bishop. Then, when we came to the bishop at Llawhaden, from distant Lincoln, specifically interrupting our studies at an opportune time, he pretended that he was on the point of leaving there for England, and, since he could not be stopped by any means, he thus tricked us of our hope of the promised reconciliation and completely frustrated our protracted efforts.

During this last Lent, when our nephew, the archdeacon, came to him, he immediately inducted him as parson into the possession of the aforementioned church—and this man for almost three years prevented us from getting a similar benefice, which we truly deserved, since we acquired it all and deserved it far more, if indeed what is deserved could be required; this new incident adds to the list of our injustices, and gives visible proof of his feelings towards us.

Indeed one could wonder and ask oneself, since he has amply rewarded the rest of those who urged his promotion according to his powers (he appointed the young son of Master Martin of St. David's a canon, he granted John of Llanddew a canonry and later an archdeaconry, he gave Osbert, archdeacon of Carmarthen, his manor at Llanddewi in Gower, and he gave Reginald Foliot the church of Llansteffan), why he is prejudiced against giving us the post of vicar at the church we ourselves have acquired, and why he is reluctant to induct us, since, as you know, we cast the final and effective vote for his promotion. We cannot give a reason, unless it is that it annoys him to see us and it annoys him even more that we are alive. Still, by God's grace, we should like to live for a short while, if he would let us, and, in peace and quietness, in these last days of ours lament our oversights and transgressions.

Moreover, if he has also been bound to reward those aforementioned characters, whom our arch-enemy had stirred up against us, and to whom he was held obliged by previous agreement, and if he has secretly— God forbid!—given a bond that he would never stir up against the church of Canterbury the case of the status and dignity of the church of St. David's, which the pope expressly forbade in his letters, which we acquired, he will regret it bitterly.

Davies, p. 172). On the dispute between Canterbury and St. David's concerning the metropolitan dignity cf. M. Richter, *Giraldus Cambrensis*, pp. 87–133, at 122–4.
210. Cf. 299–300 and *De Iure et Statu*, etc., 7 (*Op.* iii, p. 347, 31–2): *Totus igitur in threnos ire potuit dictus prior ille* . . . Also *supra*, part ii, 1289.

Preter hec etiam, sicut a vobis et aliis accepimus, conqueritur de |

f. 96ᵛᵇ nobis quod litteras quasi famosas ei et de eo scripsimus. Ad quod respondemus quod facit ut equus, qui mordet et ferit et statim quasi graviter lesus clamat et hinnit. Delicati sunt enim nimis et deliciosi,

215 qui delinquere graviter et crebro presumunt et tamen ea ruminari a populo et publicari valde moleste ferunt, cum tamen poeticum illud non ignoretur: *Taceant homines, iumenta loquentur*, necnon et comicum illud: *Qui pergit dicere que vult*, nedum facere, *audiet que non vult*. Sumus ergo quasi puer male verberatus et tamen flere non ausus.

220 Litteras autem nullas vel episcopo vel de episcopo scripsimus aut scribemus, quas deo pacem ecclesie restituente coram maioribus Anglie viris ecclesiasticis warantizare et ea que in eis continentur probare loco et tempore parati non simus. Conqueritur ergo quod conquerimur, quod per quinquennii spacium afflicti graviter et molestati

225 nunc demum in fletum erumpimus, paciencer autem tanto tempore sustinuimus et paternam de die in diem consolationem inaniter expectavimus, dum graviores de die in diem iniurias nobis inferri iugiter experti sumus.

Si moti nunc ergo sumus, si nunc demum in lacrimas et lamenta

230 prorumpimus, nemo miretur: nondum enim tante perfectionis iter arripuimus, ut possimus tantis iniuriis tam manifestis et tam diuturnis non moveri. *Certo* nimirum *certius* id esse constat, quod nunquam nepos ille noster, tam lingua fere quam litteratura carens et quem

234 creavimus, tantum erga nos scelus aggressus fuisset, nisi magnis

f. 97ʳᵃ suggestionibus ad hoc inpulsus eiusque precipue, qui non instiga|tor talium et tam turpium, sed pocius extinctor, non fultor quidem, sed ultor esse deberet. Quod si forte iuvenilis etatis impetu et inconsulto calore per se proprioque motu scelus hoc aggressus fuisset, potuisset eum episcopus suus absque dubio per minus quam quinquennii

240 spacium ab hoc errore, si voluisset, ad viam equitatis et honestatis revocasse, sicut Nicholaum Meilerii filium Menevensis canonici, qui nepotis nostri exemplo prebenda, quam ei similiter cesserat, patrem destituit, statim compescuit et ad patris redire consilium pontificali potestate coegit, cum tamen ille nec administrationem in cessione sibi

---

211 vobis] nobis *V*   219 verberatus male *transposuit V*

214. See note on Ep. 2, 36.
217. Juvenal, 9, 103: *Servi ut taceant, iumenta loquentur.*
218. Terence, *Andria*, 920; quoted also Ep. 2, 54.   223–4. Cf. 273.
230–2 (cf. 329–30). See note on Ep. 2, 55 ff.
232. Plautus, *Captivi*, 644 (iii, 4, 111).   233 (cf. 44). Cf. Ep. 6, 298–300.
233–4 (47–9, 284). See note on Ep. 2, 91.   241. Cf. Ep. 6, 48–9

Furthermore, according to what we have heard from you and others, he complains that we have written defamatory letters to him and about him. Our rejoinder is that he is like the horse that bites and rages, and then immediately neighs and whinnies as if badly hurt. Those who dare to commit serious and frequent transgressions, and yet are upset when they are discussed by the public and publicized are thin-skinned and namby-pamby, though they should not be unaware of what the poet says: 'Let men be silent, and the beasts speak', and what the comic poet says: 'Let the man who persists in saying what he wants'—let alone doing what he wants—'listen to what he does not want to hear.' We are, then, like a badly beaten child who does not dare to cry.

We have, however, never written and will never write any letters to or about the bishop, which we are not prepared to guarantee before the church dignitaries of England, when God restores peace to the Church, and whose contents we are not prepared to prove at the time and place. He therefore complains that we are complaining that, after suffering terrible tribulation and pain for five years, we have now at last burst into tears, yet we have borne it for all this time and we have vainly expected from day to day fatherly comfort, while we continually found greater injustices being inflicted on us day in day out.

If, therefore, we are now distracted, if we have now at last burst into tears of lamentation, no one should be surprised: for we have not so far set out on the road of such great perfection, that we cannot be distressed by such great, such obvious, such continual injustice. Everyone would agree that it is surer than sure that that nephew of ours, who is almost as inarticulate as he is illiterate, and whom we made, would never have entered on such a criminal enterprise against us, had he not been incited to it by the powerful promptings especially of the man who should not have been the instigator but the suppressor, not the promoter, but the punisher of such evil crimes. Had he entered upon this road of crime through his own youthful impetuosity, the unexpected heat of his madness, and his own promptings, his bishop could certainly have brought him back from the error of his ways to the path of justice and honesty in less than five years, had he wished. He did this in the case of Nicholas fitzMeiler, son of the canon of St. David's. When that man followed our nephew's example and destituted his father of the prebend which he had ceded to him in a similar way, the bishop immediately restrained him and using his episcopal authority forced him to return to his father's flock, though in the transaction the father had neither retained the administration for himself, nor relied

245 retinuisset nec aliquo repetendi iure, nisi de antiqua ecclesie Menevensis
consuetudine, qua communiter et nos uti deberemus, fultus ad hoc
fuisset. Sed cur ergo illi ⌜propicius⌝ et non nobis extitit? Vel pocius:
cur illi propicius et nobis adversarius fuit? Causam superius assi-
gnavimus nec aliam assignare valemus, nisi quia graves ei sumus
250 ad videndum, graviores etiam ad vivendum. Aut igitur antiquam et
autenticam Menevensis ecclesie consuetudinem illam, hactenus apro-
batam nec etiam ab ipso papa, cum coram illo recoleretur, inprobatam,
occasione nostri nunc dampnet et deleat, ut sibi decetero quisque
precaveat, aut si ratam ipsam esse permiserit, eadem nos in nostros qua
255 ceteros in suos faciat libertate gaudere.

Qualiter etiam in minoribus negociis nostris, veluti de terra de Landu
petenda ceterisque similibus sicut et maioribus nobis et forsan contra
promissa totis ibique nisibus incomodaverit, qualiter etiam litteras
f 97ʳᵇ nostras et nuncios recipi per | diocesim suam interdixerit necnon et
260 nos ipsos hospitio suscipi et karitative tractari publice prohibuerit et,
quod auditu longe horribilius et actu periculosius, nos verbum domini
seminare et sicienti populo pocula salutis monitaque salubria propinare
non permiserit, qualiter et hoc, quod longe gravius tulimus, nos in
presentia sua conviciis quandoque lacerari turpibus et in domo sua,
265 qualiter etiam et ibidem nos minis acerrimis affici quasi sub silentio
preterivit nec conviciantes aut comminantes pontificali ullatenus
auctoritate repressit nec ea, que audiebat, sibi displicere gestibus ullis
aut verbis ostendit, nimis est notum, tanquam infamie nostre deni-
gracione sue plurimum adiectum esse fame coniectans. Superciliose
270 nimirum iactancie notam esse Seneca testante noveritis, culpando illustres
viros suo nomini famam querere.

Qui hactenus ergo nobis adversarius erat occultus, occasiones iam
querit, conquerendo scilicet quod conquerimur, ut amodo fiat manifestus. Sed esto nunc etiam, esto, quoniam occulta gravius vulnerant
275 iacula quam manifesta, iuxta poeticum illud: *Nam levius ledit quicquid
previdimus ante*, unde gravissime semper ille sunt inimicicie, que sub
specie et fuco amicicie latent.

Latitandum est igitur in hac tempestate et contra dies sereniores
sibi cum effectu prospiciendum. Accidit enim peccatis urgentibus, ut
280 qui decetero quiescere viteque statum per dei gratiam in melius emen-
f. 97ᵛᵃ dare parati fuimus,| iam graves ad labores et bella tanquam intestina

---

248–50 (200–4). See note on Ep. 5, 172–6.   256–68. See note on Ep. 6, 59–62.
261–2. Cf. Mark iv, 14; Jer. xxv, 15–17.
269–71. Seneca testante] Cf. Martin of Braga, ed. Barlow (see note on Ep. 5, 193–5),
Formula Vitae Honestae, p. 245, 60–1: *famae bonae neque tuae seminator neque alienae
invidus.* Cf. Ep. 8, 124.   273. Cf. 223–4.

on any law of redress, save the old tradition of the church of St. David's, which we too should have used. But why, then, did he show kindness to him and not to us? Or rather, why did he show kindness to him and enmity to us? We gave the reason above, and cannot give any other: it annoys him to see us, and annoys him even more that we are alive. He should in our case now either annul and get rid of this old and formal tradition of the church of St. David's, which has hitherto been respected, and was not disapproved by the pope himself, when it was mentioned in his presence, so that in future every man may take take care for himself, or, if he considers it right, he should see that we enjoy the same freedom to deal with our own people as others do with theirs.

It is all too well known how even in our lesser affairs (e.g. the claim on the estate at Llanddew and other similar cases) just as in our more important affairs, he has exerted all his efforts to be a trouble-maker, despite his promises. It is all too clear how he has banned our letters and messages from being received throughout his diocese, and, moreover, has publicly prohibited us from being received as a guest, and, what is more dreadful to hear of, and more perilous to do, he has refused permission for us to spread the word of the Lord, and to offer the cup of salvation, and the saving words to the people that thirst. It is all too clear that he has even allowed us to be disgracefully reviled in his presence, and even in his own home (a matter which we take far more to heart) and has even allowed us to be threatened viciously there, without crushing the revilers or threateners in any way with his pontifical authority and without indicating by word or gesture that what he heard displeased him, as if he thought that denigrating us added to his reputation. You will realize that it is a mark of disdainful arrogance, as Seneca testifies, to seek fame for oneself by accusing famous men.

Since, then, he was our secret enemy, he is now looking for a chance to become our open enemy, by complaining that we are complaining, as will still become obvious. But let him be, let him be now, since secret weapons wound more seriously than open ones: as the poet says: 'The weapon we foresee only grazes.' Thus, those enmities that lurk in the guise of friendship are always the most harmful.

We must keep under cover in this storm, and wait effectively for brighter days. The result of the weight of sins has been that we, who were prepared to enjoy retirement and improve the state of our life by God's grace, are provoked to hard work and, as it were, internecine

275–6. *Disticha Catonis*, ii, 24, 2.   277. fuco] See note on Ep. 1, 12.
278 (75). See note on Ep. 6, 202.   281–4. See Ep. 5, 234.

provocamur: quod enim magis intestinum, quod magis detestabile
bellum, quam inter nepotem et patruum, quin immo inter patrem et
filius? Nepotem etiam, quem educavit et tanquam ex nichilo creavit
285 patruus et patrem quoque, cuius promocioni finalem effectum adiecit
filius. Hanc autem mutationem pravam maliciosus ille hostis antiquus,
bonis semper iniciis invidens et intentionibus ac zizania seminans est
machinatus, dum ingratitudinis vitio venenosissimo res undique intoxi-
cante inter tam coniunctos caritate prorsus extincta, spirituale iam gau-
290 dium et fraterne dilectionis vinculum, saluti tam necessarium, in odium
inexorabile convertit et vix placabile. Magna vis igitur mali et magna
nimis in humanam miseriam maligni illius malicia viget, dum illos, quos
karitas antea Christo copulavit, fraternum iam odium ab eodem dissociavit et de membris Christi membra diaboli fecit. O quanta cano-
295 nici, quanta presbiteri, quanta et episcopi religio, qui tantas inter suos
seminando discordias et fovendo, quas ex officii debito totis extinguere
nisibus tenebatur, tantis undique malis et animarum periculis ob
avariciam solam et diabolicam invidiam causas et occasiones dedit!
Sed nonne qui hec et similia perpetravit totus in trenos, sicut iam
300 diximus, ire valebit? Nonne sacius ei vel alii fuisset et longe salubrius
in monasterio pulcro et honesto et sufficienter opimo gregi, cui preerat,
pastorali cura prodesse quam in episcopatu, modis predictis et utinam
per omnia bonis adepto, tot subditorum suorum milibus, quorum nec
f. 97ᵛᵇ linguam nec mores agnovit, incestus creberrimos et adulteria, | cedes
305 in locis sacris et incendia ceteraque nimis enormia dissimulando et,
quod omnium est gravissimum, bona ecclesiastica dilapidando et
gieziticis actibus pravis passim insistendo miserumque clerum tirannicis
exactionibus iugiter affligendo, laicis quoque direptionibus indefensum
exponendo et institutiones novas cartasque recentes in veterum preiudi-
310 cia ⌐favore curialium seu timore⌐ conficiendo, tam inutiliter tantoque
defectu, quin immo et cum adeo manifesta dampnatione, preesse?
⌐O quam duro commercio pontificalis hec in terris tam desiderata
pompositas tam male quesita peiusque ministrata et baculi illius mitre-
que minacitas (quoniam *cornu ferit ille, caveto!*), et tamen hec tota tam
315 parum duratura potestas sibi tragedicum exitum cum gehennali pena

284 (47–9, 233–4). See note on Ep. 2, 91.
285. patrem] the bishop, cf. 198.
287. See note on Ep. 5, 177–9.
294. membris Christi] Cf. 1 Cor. vi, 15. Cf. Ep. 8, 90.
299–300. See note on 210.
301. in monasterio . . . cui preerat] Before his election to the see of St. David's
Bishop Geoffrey had been prior of Lanthony Secunda (by Gloucester).
304–5. Cf. Ep. 6, 464–6.
307. See note on Ep. 6, 450.

strife: for what strife could be more internecine, what strife could be more hateful than that betweeen nephew and uncle, apart from that between father and son? Even when it is a nephew whom the uncle has educated and created from nothing, and a father for whose promotion the son had cast the final vote. However, that old, malignant enemy, who is always hostile to good beginnings and intentions, and sows tares of discord, brought about this wicked change, until, with the festering vice of ingratitude infecting the whole world, and the extinction of love between those so close, he has converted spiritual joy and the bond of brotherly love, which is so necessary to salvation, to inexorable and implacable hatred. The force of evil, and the malice of that malignity is so powerful over human misery, since those whom love previously joined with Christ, brotherly hatred has separated from Christ and made followers of the devil out of followers of Christ. Oh, what piety the canon has! what piety the priest has! what piety the bishop has, when solely because of avarice and diabolical malice he has given reason and opportunities for such great wickedness and peril of souls by fostering and sowing among his flock the discord which he is by duty bound to exert all his efforts to stamp out! Should not the man who did these and similar things repent, as we said above? Would it not have been better and far more wholesome for him and any other if he looked after the flock which was in his charge with his pastoral care in that beautiful, respectable, and sufficiently rich monastery, than to be in charge of so many subordinates whose language and customs he does not understand, in a diocese he had obtained in the ways described above (we wish they had been good) so uselessly, with such detriment, and with such obvious damage, when he turns a blind eye to incests and adulteries, murder and arson in holy places, and a whole lot of other scandals, when, what is most serious of all, he dilapidates church property, when here and there he presses on with wicked, simoniac transactions, when he continually afflicts the poor clergy with tyrannical demands, when he exposes them defenceless to secular plundering, when he draws up new institutions and charters in prejudice of the old, with the approval or rather fear of the officials, how useless he is in his prominent place, or rather how positively harmful! With what hard bargaining is this pontifical pomp, which is so desired on earth, and the threatening aspect of that crosier and mitre ('look out, for it has a horn!') are wickedly sought and administered in a worse way! Yet all this power, which is so short-lived, will have its tragic outcome with

309–10. See note on Ep. 6, 335–7.
314. Virgil, *Buc.* ix, 25 (on the *caper*! Cf. Ep. 6, 248, note).

fine carente comparabit. Set, ut alibi diximus, ex fidei defectu maximo hec et similia cuncta proveniunt.⌐

Sane cum suo in tempore coram magnis viris ad hoc deputatis horum districtius inquisitio fiet, ad tot iniuriarum talionem reddendam vindicis
320 animi studio totis absque dubio nisibus elaborabitur, quoniam, ut ait Aristotiles, *omnino protervienti omnino est adversandum*, iuxta illud etiam in iure scriptum: *expedit peccata nocentum publice nota esse.* Unde nec actione iniuriarum tenetur quis nec infamare quemquam dici debet, qui contra eum probanda defert et emendanda proponit.

325 Utinam autem vindictam omnino nullam appeteremus, sed equanimiter omnia sustinere possemus, adeo ut in una maxilla percussi et alteram incontinenti preberemus, nulli malum pro malo reddentes neque vinci a malo, sed vincere magis in bono malum per omnia satagentes! Hanc autem doctrinam apostolicam sepius ⌐quidem⌐ audivi-
330 mus, sed ad eius revera perfectionem nondum pervenire prevaluimus: veterem enim imperfectionem adhuc imitantes et qui nostra tollit pro inimico reputantes, et amicos diligimus et inimicos nostros ⌐presertim vero pertinaciter et irrevocabiliter in nos grassantes⌐ exosos habemus.

Valeat in domino cara nobis fraternitas vestra.

320 studio *correxi* (vicio *V*) coll. *De Iure et Statu Menev. Eccl. 7 (Op. iii, p. 373, 3)*: (simul cum . . .) Duorum Speculo, vindicis animi digestis studio; *Itinerarium Kambriae I, II (Op. vi, p. 84, 2)*: animo vindice.

316–17. See note on Ep. 6, 512–13.
320. See app. crit., and *supra*, part ii, 296-7.
321. Not identified.
322. in iure] Dig. 47, 10, 18: *Eum qui nocentem infamavit, non esse bonum aequum ob eam rem condemnari: peccata enim nocentium nota esse et oportere et expedire.*
326–7. Matt. v, 39; Luke vi, 29.
327–8. See note on Ep. 2, 55, 56–7. Cf. also Petrus Alphonsus (whom Giraldus apparently refers to in part ii, 752), *Disciplina Clericalis*, Exemplum IV, ed. Hilka–Söderhjelm, Heidelberg, 1911, p. 11, 37–9: *Ne reddas malum ne similis sis malo, sed redde bonum ut melior sis malo* (cf. Migne, *P.L.* 157, col. 679B).
329–30. Cf. 230–2.

the ceaseless punishment of Gehenna. But, as we have said elsewhere, all this and things like it are the result of a very great lack of faith.

Indeed, when in its own time a stricter inquiry is made before great men chosen for this purpose, certainly no effort will be spared, and it will be the judge's intention that these numerous injustices be paid for; as Aristotle says, 'the man who is a complete wanton must suffer a complete reverse'; and, as it says in law: 'it is appropriate that the sins of the guilty be censured in public.' Thus no one is bound by an action for damages, and no one should be called a slanderer when he lays charges that can be proved and puts forward things that can be reformed.

But we wish we were not seeking revenge but could bear it all calmly to such an extent that when we were smitten on one cheek, we would immediately turn the other, not returning evil for evil, and endeavouring not to be overcome by evil, but rather to overcome evil by good. However, we have heard this teaching of the apostle quite often, but we have not had the strength to reach this absolute perfection; for we cling to our old imperfection and anyone who has robbed us we consider an enemy. We still love our friends, and hate our enemies, especially when they have plundered us incessantly and irrevocably.

We pray that your brotherly love, which is dear to us, may grow strong in the Lord.

8

Galfrido Menevensi episcopo

PATRI in Christo dilecto et utinam per omnia digne diligendo Galfrido
dei gratia Menevensi episcopo magister Giraldus de Barri simul cum
clero Menevensi etsi nondum nominatim expresso, suo tamen in
5 tempore ⌐cum locus et opus fuerit⌐ palam per dei gratiam perdituro,
salutem et morum emendacionem.

Quoniam patrem enormiter exorbitantem filii karitative corripere
tenentur, super enormibus excessibus vestris, publicis quidem et fere
notoriis, vos iam tercio premonere et karitatis intuitu ad correctionem
10 denunciare dignum duximus et non indebitum.

In primis igitur super rerum ecclesiasticarum dilapidacionibus variis
et auditu horrendis vos corripimus et premonemus, veluti de terra de
Landegof, militaribus scilicet feodis duobus vel tribus Nicholao Avenel
minus licite et nimis cupide distractis. Item super feodo prebende de
15 Brewidi in militare et laicale obsequium nota satis et inhonesta causa
converso. Item super manerio de Landewi in Goer et ecclesia sancti
David de Langavelach, Menevensium antistitum ecclesia propria et
tanquam eorundem sede secunda, filio vestro carnali collatis. Item
19 super villis de Lancadoch et Landegewith, presulum Menevensium
usque ad dies vestros propriis, quas | alienastis, necnon et terris aliis
de Stratdewi cunctis non infructuosis, quas post promocionem vestram
nunquam intrastis aut visitastis, per incuriam vestram et negligenciam
amissis. Item super manerio de Tralan iuxta Aberhothenei et Landu
in terra pacifica constituto, Owelo filio Trahern pro bobus et vaccis
25 fere dimidiato. Set nonne lapidacione digni forent tales rerum ecclesiasticarum dilapidatores? Num etiam stercore bovino, ut ad duriora
prorumpat indignacio et veritati non parcat, lapidari deberent et de-
honestari, qui terras ecclesiasticas fertiles et utiles, sibi commendatas
tantum et non appropriatas, pro bobus et vaccis venundare et in per-
30 petuum alienare nec verecundantur nec verentur?

2. Cf. Ep. 1, 2.
11–12. Cf. *De Iure et Statu*, etc., 7 (*Op.* iii, p. 349, 30–1): *et dilapidationibus rerum ac
terrarum ecclesie sue crebris et auditu horrendis ac miserandis.* See note on 11–30.

[8.] *To Geoffrey, bishop of St. David's*

GIRALDUS de Barri, together with the clergy of St. David's, who, though not yet named individually, will come into the open in due course, as the situation and need arises, sends his greetings and hopes for the mending of his ways to Geoffrey, beloved father in Christ (Oh that he were in all things worthy of that love!), by God's grace bishop of St. David's.

Since sons are bound by duty to reprove a father lovingly when he has gone far astray, we think it right and proper to give you a third warning over your gross excesses, which have become public and almost notorious, and prompted by charity denounce you so that you may correct your ways.

First of all, then, we rebuke and admonish you for the various dilapidations of Church property, which make dreadful hearing; for example the two or three knights' fees of the manor of Landegof taken from Nicholas Avenel without legality but with excessive greed. Again the dishonest reason for the conversion of the fee of the prebend of Brawdy into a knight's and lay fee is sufficiently well known. Again you conferred the manor of Llanddewi in Gower and the church of St. David of Llangyfelach, which is the property of the bishop of St. David's and virtually his second episcopal church, to your carnal son. Again, by your indifference and negligence you lost the vills of Llangatwg and Llangewydd, the property of the bishops of St. David's until your time—you alienated them—and other estates of Ystradyw, all of which were not barren—you neither set foot into them nor made a visitation to them at any time after your promotion. Again, you halved the manor of Trallong near Brecon and Llanddew, sited in pacified country, to Hywel fitzTrahern for oxen and cattle. Do not such dilapidations deserve a flogging? If indignation calls for harsher penalties and does not spare the truth, should not those who have no fear or hesitation in bringing up for sale fertile, useful Church property, which is entrusted to their care and not appropriated, and parting with them permanently in exchange for bulls and cows, be pelted with cattle-dropping and disgraced?

11–30. The same account is given almost verbatim (the prices are mentioned!) in the *De Iure et Statu*, etc., 7 (*Op.* iii, p. 349, 32– p. 350, 26); see also note on 11–12.

26–7. Cf. Ecclus. xxii, 2: *De stercore boum lapidatus est piger.*

28–9. sibi commendatas tantum et non appropriatas] Cf. Gratian, C. XII, q. 2 c. 52, *Sine exceptione*, as quoted in *Symbolum Electorum* i, 7 (*Op.* i, p. 220, 8–10).

Item super sequestracionibus crebris et illegitimis et preterquam in casibus iure expressis omnino illicitis et prohibitis, in gieziticos demum actus conversis et pecunie interventu relaxatis, sicut de Philippo filio Wetheleu per V librarum extorsionem. Item et de Kenewec clerico
35 de Luel sequestracionem ecclesie sue per pecuniam redimente et sicut de Eustacio clerico de Stakepole sequestracionem ecclesie sue parcium

f. 98ᵛᵃ illarum, in qua canonice fuerat insti|tutus, illegitime factam per X marcas extortas redimente, ⌐Osberto nimirum canonico vestro, immo verius demoniaco, opera prava concinnante et Gyezi secundo non
40 solum munera Naaman illicita cum lepra eiusdem, interiore quidem tantoque graviore passim et absque delectu, set non absque delicto maximo suscipiente, verum etiam non verum Eliseum, set subornatum, fictum et fucatum ad scandala similia deformante.

Item super institucionibus novis et cartis in veterum preiudicium
45 emissis, sicut anno preterito de Lanpaer Maur. Item super negligenciis et pastoralibus officiis omissis, veluti apud locum eundem venerabilem et sanctum sagrilegiis hoc anno perpetratis nec per vos correctis aut per ullam iusticiam ecclesiasticam emendatis.

Item super appellancium tam ad domnum papam quam ad archiepi-
50 scopum oppressione et nulla prorsus appellacionibus legitime interpositis reverencia exibita, vel dilacione.

Item et apud Buelth, non specie indirecta aut sequestracionis nomine subornata vel alieno quovis fuco discolorata, set pocius directa specie, ubi publice quidem ut fiat datur, a monacho de Cumhir pro fratre suo
55 clerico, quatinus in ecclesia quadam parcium illarum vacante instituere-tur, marca argenti coram capitulo toto est numerata.

Item qualiter in finibus de Melenith et Elevein plerosque tam clericos
f. 98ᵛᵇ quam laicos qui religionis habitum sumpserant et | aliquandiu por-taverant, ad laicales tam habitus quam ⟨mores⟩ redire seu pastorali
60 negligencia seu etiam quavis turpi et indecenti causa permisistis.

Item et de tallagiis vestris enormibus reticeri non debet, qualiter non longe scilicet a promocione vestra, set statim anno primo, clericos diocesis vestre ⟨convocatos⟩ quasi salutando set non letificando, auxilium

51 dilacione, cf. Ep. 5. 145] delacione V   63 convocatos (cf. 72) De Iure et
Statu, etc. Op. iii, p. 141, 22.

31-2. Cf. De Iure et Statu 7 (Op. iii, p. 348, 29): preterquam in casibus iure expres-sis ...

32 and 39-40. See note on Ep. 6, 450.   43 and 53. See note on Ep. 1, 12.
44-5. See note on Ep. 6, 335-7.

61-88 The same passage in De Iure et Statu, etc., 1 (Op. iii, p. 141, 21-p. 142, 27), where between pp. 141 and 147 many phrases are more or less identical with lines 61-249 of the present letter.

Again there is the matter of your frequent illegal sequestrations which are completely illicit and banned and, moreover, explicitly mentioned in law; you involved them in simoniacal business deals, and exempted them after the intervention of a bribe, as you did in the case of Philip fitzWetherly from whom you extorted five pounds. There is the case of Kenwec, priest of Builth, who redeemed his church after its sequestration by paying a sum of money, just as there is the case of Eustace, priest of Stackpole, who redeemed his church in that area, in which he had been instituted canonically, after an illegal sequestration, with the ten marks that were extorted from him. Indeed, Osbert, your canon, or more correctly your demon, was in concert with these criminal activities, and like another Gehazi not only took over the illegal duties of Naaman as well as his leprosy, which was altogether more serious because it was internal, without delight, but not without the greatest dereliction, but also twisted the truth, which was not of Elisha, but faked, feigned, and coloured, for similar scandals.

Again there is the matter of the new institutions, and the issue of new charters to the disadvantage of the old ones, as in the case of Llanbadarn Fawr last year. Again there is the matter of negligence and neglect of pastoral duties, as in the case of the sacrileges committed at that venerable and sacred spot last year, which were neither reproved by you nor put right by ecclesiastical litigation.

Again there is the matter of oppressing those who appealed to the Lord Pope as well as to the archbishop, and your total lack of respect or regard shown to those further appeals raised legitimately.

Again at Builth there was that incident, not disguised or dignified with the title of sequestration or masked in any other way, but rather openly, as one gives in public when things are done in their proper way: in front of the whole chapter, a monk from Cwm Hir paid one mark of silver in order that his brother, a priest, might be installed in a vacant church in that area.

Again there is the way in which you allowed a great many regular and lay brothers in the area of Maelienydd and Elfael, who had taken the habit of religion and worn it for some time, to return to wearing secular clothes, either by your pastoral neglect or some sort of other wicked and ungodly reason.

Again, one ought not to hold one's peace over your gross tallages: there is the way in which not long after your promotion, in fact immediately in the first year, as if greeting the priests of your diocese in convocation, but not gladdening them, you requested their aid, which,

ab eis, quod tamen versum est in tallagium inmoderatum, postulastis.

65 Qui cum inposicionis inmoderanciam communiter recusassent, promisistis eis quod si ad voluntatem vestram se tunc gravarent, vos decetero, nisi necessitas ecclesie vel utilitas evidens exposceret, auxilium ab eis non petiturum, set de hoc ipsorum auxilio vos terras vestras instaurare et inde quidem non de exaccionibus aut extorsionibus vivere

70 velle dixistis. Cum autem hoc denique concesso clerici, promissis episcopi fidem habentes, pacifice et quiete se postea diu degere posse sperarent, protinus anno proximo sequente convocatis clericis auxilium

f. 99ra de ovibus ad terras vestras instaurandum ab eis pe|tistis. Qui plurimum admirantes promissionem anni preteriti et convencionem vos ad animum

75 revocare velle nil proficiendo suplicarunt. Respondistis enim et assessores vestri, qui ad miserorum gravamen linguas suas acuerant sicut serpentes, quod illa anni preteriti promissio de denariis facta fuit, non de ovibus vel de rebus aliis aut possessionibus, et sic a miseris et indefensis ad nutum suum denuo tallagium extorserunt. Qui enim

80 oves habebat, oves dabat ad equiperacionem datorum anno preterito denariorum: scriptum enim de singulis anno preterito datis vel pocius violenter, ne dicam fraudulenter, ablatis secum pre manibus habebant et pretendebant et ad formulam illam, quamquam informem nimis et enormem, cursum intencionis sue dirigebant. Qui autem agnos

85 habebat et non oves, ad valenciam ovium agnos dabat, qui vero nec oves nec agnos habebat, sive vicarius seu persona, nec ob hoc potuit excusari: denarios enim ad oves emendum, iuxta quod anno preterito

f. 99rb dederat, dare nunc ite|rum modis omnibus oportebat. Mirum autem, quod anno tercio de vaccis auxilium non petistis!

90 O quam religio magna, o quanta karitatis vel pocius cupiditatis indicia manifestissima, ubi tanta et tam excogitata pastoris ad gregem spoliandum versatur et tam exquisita versucia! Hoc ergo secure dicere possumus, quod numquam clerus Menevensis de monasterio Anglicano prelatum amplius habere vellet, sicut duos hos ultimos sinistris abinde

95 casibus et principum violenciis ab eisdem constat assumptos. Qui duo quidem omnes predecessores suos rapinis et extorsionibus superaverunt et ultimus quoque longe penultimum: antepenultimus enim non de monasterio, sed de clero assumptus et de archidiacono Menevensis ecclesie presul eiusdem effectus. Cum autem XXVII et amplius annis

---

91 manifessima *V*

73. See note on Ep. 5, 16.
76–7. Ps. cxxxix, 4: *Acuerunt linguas suas sicut serpentis (serpentes).*
78–9. Apparently copying in haste, Giraldus forgot to change the word *suum* [= *De Iure et Statu*, etc., i (*Op.* iii, p. 142, 12)] into *vestrum*. See also note on Ep. 6, 391.

however, turned out to be a gross tallage. When they unanimously refused the excessive terms of the imposition, you promised them that if they acceded to your wishes on that occasion, you would make no further demands for their help in future, unless some need or obvious necessity of the Church demanded it, but you said you wished to stock your estates with their aid and had no intention of living in future on levies and extortions. However, when this was eventually agreed upon, and the clergy, believing the bishop's promises, hoped that they could live in peace and quiet for a long time, the very next year you convened them and asked their aid in form of sheep to restock your estates. In utter amazement they begged that you would recall the promises and agreement of the previous year, but to no avail. For you and your assessors, who had 'sharpened their tongues like serpents' to trouble the wretched, replied that that promise of the previous year had been concerned with money, not sheep, or any other thing or property, and thus extorted a second tallage from the poor, defenceless wretches as you liked. For anyone who had sheep, gave sheep equivalent to the money given in the previous year. For they had with them a receipt of what they had given, or rather, of what had been forcibly, not to say fraudulently, stolen the previous year; they produced these forms and showed that they had been co-operative, although scandalously much had been demanded. Those, however, who had lambs—and not sheep—gave lambs to the value of the sheep, but if anyone, whether vicar or parson, had neither sheep nor lambs, he was not excused for this: he had to give money once again to the same amount as in the previous year, so that lambs could be bought. It is amazing that in the third year you did not request aid in the form of cows!

What a great religion! What manifest signs of charity, or rather greed, when such great, such studied, such refined ingenuity is employed by the shepherd to plunder his flock. We can, then, say with absolute certainty that the clergy of St. David's would not wish to have in future a prelate from an English monastery like these last two, who, as is well known, were taken on by them in grave circumstances and with acts of violence of the princes. Indeed, these last two surpassed all their predecessors in their rapine and extortions, the last, too, far surpassing the one before him, for the antepenultimate prelate had come, not from a monastery, but from the clergy, and become bishop of St. David's after being archdeacon there. Though he was bishop for more than

---

87. See note on Ep. 5, 16.   90. Cf. Ep. 7, 294.
94. duos hos ultimos] Geoffrey de Henlaw and Peter de Leia.
97. antepenultimus] David fitzGerald (bp. 1148–76).

100 sedisset, tantum semel a clericis suis auxilium peciit et tunc ob causam
adeo iustam et honestam, quod a papa Alexandro tercio ad Turonense
concilium vocatus fuerat. Et tunc quidem non per palpones presulum
f. 99va et assessores ad pecuniam augendam | proterviter et inmisericorditer
insistentes, set quod quisque primo verbo et sponte offerre volebat,
105 eo presul cum gratiarum actione contentus erat', nec clericorum hic
hospicia dignabatur adire, archidiaconis quippe singulisque canonicis
et clericis suis integre sua iura relinquens. Unde vix semel in anno vel
etiam biennio ad clericum quempiam et tunc ad multas eiusdem in-
stancias et suplicaciones plurimas divertebat, modestiam per omnia
110 servans et parsimoniam. Sic itaque semper augmentatur aviditas et
iuxta poeticum illud *sic omnia fato | in peius ruere et retro sublapsa
referri.*

⌐Novit autem ille, qui omnia novit, quod si nunquam intraturus
amodo Walliam essem aut etiam eam decetero visurus, misere tamen
115 Menevensi ecclesie non mediocriter condolerem, que adeo per iam
dictos choritas de Anglia in Walliam nec naturaliter nec adoptive nec
legitime vel canonice, set violenter, ut dictum est, transplantatos usque
ad extremam fere inopiam atque penuriam apporiata est pariter et
depilata. Hec est enim Anglorum opinio et quasi sentencia rata, quod
120 vilis et abiectus in Anglia validus et acceptus est in Wallia et iuxta
Augustini de talibus irrisionem, sicut malus choraula bonus symphoniacus est, ita et malus monachus bonus clericus, sic quoque malus
in Anglia bonus in Wallia.⌐

Non igitur monachi, non canonici de religionis habitu superciliosi
125 existant: multos enim in habitu et non in actu vidimus. Da michi, queso,
cucullatum Nicholao similem, da Martino et, ut etiam exemplum
propius sumamus, da Thome Cantuariensi in sanctitatis et iusticie

---

115 iam per *transposuit* V

101–2. Turonense concilium] Council of Tours (1163).
102–10. Cf. the legislation of the Third Lateran Council (1179), *Decret. Greg. IX,*
III, 39, 6.
111–12. Virgil, *Georg.* i, 199–200; the same quotation in the *Gemma Ecclesiastica,*
2, 33 and 37 (*Op.* ii, p. 325, 27–8, and p. 356, 31–2); *Speculum Ecclesie,* 4, 12 (*Op.* iv,
p. 286, 14–15); and *Itinerarium Kambriae,* pref. 1 (*Op.* vi, p. 4, 18–19).
113. See note on Ep. 1, 33–4.
119–23. Cf. *De Iure et Statu,* etc., 1 (*Op.* iii, p. 121, 15–23): *Hec etenim Anglorum
opinio est et quasi sententia rata, quod vilis et abiectus in Anglia validus et acceptus in
Wallia. Unde iuxta Augustini de talibus irrisionem: . . . 'Sicut', inquit, 'malus choraula
bonus simphoniacus est, ita et malus monachus bonus clericus', sic quoque malus Anglicus
bonus Wallicus, hoc est malus in Anglia bonus in Wallia; also in the Symbolum Electorum,*
1, 28 (*Op.* i, p. 301, 29–35): *Illud autem Augustini in monachos similes istis malitiosos*

twenty-seven years, he only once asked for money from his clergy, and then it was for an altogether honest and just reason, since he had been summoned to the Council of Tours by Pope Alexander III. Then the collection was not carried out by the bishop's toadies and assessors, wickedly and pitilessly trying to get more money, but with grateful thanks the bishop was content with what each wished to offer on his own initiative and without prompting. Nor did he burden the guest-houses of his clergy, but left untouched the rights of the archdeacons, as well as those of each canon and priest. Thus he used to visit each priest scarcely once a year, or even every two years only, and even then only at the repeated insistence and supplication of the priest. Through-out he observed modesty and frugality. Thus, then, greed has always been on the increase. As the poet says: 'Thus everything is fated to deteriorate and relapse and be degenerate.'

However, he who knows all knows that if we were never to enter Wales again, or even see it again, we would be extremely sorry for the poor church of St. David's which has been plundered and robbed to the extremes of penury and poverty by the aforementioned monks who were transferred from England to Wales, neither spontaneously nor by way of adoption, neither legitimately nor canonically, but violently, as has been said. For Englishmen believe and accept almost unqualified that whosoever is vile and cheap for England is good and acceptable for Wales, and, like that satirical remark of Augustine about such men, 'a bad flautist is a good accompanist', so a bad monk is a good priest, and thus, someone bad for England is good enough for Wales.

Arrogant men should not become monks or priests by wearing the proper dress: for we see a great many in the dress but not practising their belief. I beg you, show me a monk like Nicholas, show me a monk like Martin, or, to take an example nearer home, show me a man equal to Thomas of Canterbury, in holiness and justice: for true religion

---

pariter et ambitiosos ironice et irrisorie dictum et hic adaptari potest: '*Sicut malus choraula bonus symphoniacus est, sic forte malus monachus bonus clericus*', *sic quoque malus Anglicus bonus Wallicus, sic vilis et abiectus in Anglia . . . cathedra digni in Wallia.* The quotation is from Augustine, *Ep.* 60, 1, *CSEL*, 34, 1895, p. 221, 16–19: . . . *nisi forte, sicut vulgares dicunt, malus choraula bonus symphoniacus est; ita idem ipsi vulgares de nobis iocabuntur, dicentes:* '*Malus monachus bonus clericus est*', but the words have been taken from Gratian, c. 36, C. XVI, q. 1. The quotation is also found in the *Symbolum Electorum*, 1, 7 (*Op.* i, p. 224, 12–14 and 25–7) and in the *Speculum Ecclesie*, 2, 26 (*Op.* iv, p. 84, 4–7) and, with the opposition *Anglici/Wallici*, etc., in the *De Invectionibus*, 5, 6 (*Op.* i, p. 13ː, 12–16; ed. Davies, p. 187, c. vi, 12–17).

124. superciliosi] Cf. Ep. 7, 269.

125–8. The same comparison with St. Nicholas, St. Martin, and St. Thomas Becket is found, also preceded by *ut propius exempla sumamus*, in the *De Invectionibus*, 6, 27 (*Op.* i, p. 191, 24–8; ed. Davies, pp. 233–4), the *Gemma Ecclesiastica*, 2, 38 (*Op.* ii, p. 359, 21–4), and the *Speculum Ecclesie*, 4, 39 (*Op.* iv, pp. 349–50).

constancia parem: non enim in cuculla, non in veste pulla, sed magis
in medulla et consciencia pura latet religio vera.

130   Item, ut ad priora revertamur, quasi quarto vel quinto vestre pro-
f. 99ᵛᵇ mocionis anno coac|tis in unum clericis, quatinus vel semel iustam
petendi auxilii causam pretendere possetis, coram omnibus assertive
proposuistis vos ob dignitatem ecclesie vestre metropoliticam Romam
iturum et in brevi quidem iter arepturum; propter quod auxilium
135   vobis tunc libenter et cum gravamine fecerunt, nec tamen vos a curia
Romana reversum aut iter etiam illuc aggressum adhuc viderunt.

Item eadem vice vel alia generale tallagium per episcopatum faciens,
decanatui de Elevein V libras vobis reddendas et ad terminum brevem
inposuistis. Quod gravamen cum se ferre nec velle nec posse com-
140   muniter asseverassent, dicentes nunquam decessorem vestrum, qui
valde tamen honerosus in exaccionibus huiusmodi fuit, ultra III
marcas aut quatuor ad plus in uno auxilio ab eis sumpsisse, et cum
in hoc persisterent et ad voluntatem vestram talem inclinari non possent,
officiis simul et beneficiis omnes suspendistis. Set cum et hoc diucius
145   pertulissent, adeo ut provincia de Elevein tota non absque laicorum,
f. 100ʳᵃ qui nichil in hoc deliquerant, querimonia mag|na per dimidium annum
et amplius divinis caruisset, tandem quatinus etsi non recte, quocumque
tamen modo vincere possetis et cupiditati magis quam karitati morem
gerere, clericorum familiam et precipue concubinas patronis ecclesia-
150   rum et potentibus patrie viris ad diripiendum exposuistis. Quo facto
cum propter suas redimendas et earum pacem, sine quibus miserrimi
esse, quamquam non absque utroque, tam corporis scilicet quam anime
dampno non modico, vel nolunt vel nesciunt, honus inpositum ad-
misissent, statim revocato mandato et focarie ad focum, auctore non
155   dico pontifice set pretore, et concubine ad cubiculum sunt reverse.
Set ecce prelati opera sancti, ecce sub religionis habitu non ficta quidem
set vera religio.

Item preter iam dicta talliarum incommoda tanta, cupiditas crescens
et mala semper augmentans multiplex diebus vestris misero Menevensi
160   clero preter solitum gravamen adiecit. Maximum autem omnium
f. 100ʳᵇ gravaminum et urgentissimum | esse constat in crebra per episcopos
hospiciorum visitacione, que verius quidem ad archidiaconorum

---

128 parem constancia *transposuit V*

133–4. Giraldus records in the *De Invectionibus*, 5, 22 (ed. Davies, p. 202) that King
John actually encouraged *him* to take up once again the metropolitan controversy
between St. David's and Canterbury to embarrass Archbishop Stephen Langton.

137–57. *De Iure et Statu*, etc., 1 (*Op.* iii, p. 142, 28–p. 143, 17).

154–5. Cf. *Speculum Ecclesie*, 3, 8 (*Op.* iv, p. 170, 25): *in foco focariam et in cubiculo
concubinam.*   156–7. Cf. 2 Cor. vi, 6; 1 Tim. i, 5.

does not lurk in a cowl, or in a dark vestment, but in the heart and the clear conscience.

Let us turn once again to things not long past: four or five years after your promotion you called the clergy together, pretending to ask for their support at least once for a good cause: in the presence of all of them you suggested plainly that you would be going to Rome for the sake of the metropolitan dignity of your church, and would be setting out in a short while: for this purpose, then, they gave you aid freely, though with hardship; however, to date they have neither seen you return from the curia at Rome, nor even set out there.

Again, on the same occasion, or on another, while making a general tallage throughout your diocese, you imposed a levy of five pounds on the deanery of Elfael, to be paid to you in a short time. When the clergy swore that they neither would nor could bear such an imposition, saying that your predecessor, who had been exceedingly oppressive in exactions of this kind, had never taken more than three marks, or four at most, from them in one levy, and when they persisted in this and would not bend to your will, you at once suspended them all from their offices and benefices. But when they held out further, so much so that the area of Elfael was without pastoral guidance for six months or even longer, not without considerable protestation from the laity who had not committed any offence in this matter, at length, in order to defeat them by any means whatsoever, and to cloak with morality your cupidity rather than your charity, though for the wrong reasons, you exposed for plunder to the patrons of the churches and those in power the households and especially the concubines of the priests. When this was done, and they admitted the imposition to get their women back, and for their peace (since the wretches either do not wish or else do not know how to live without them, though the physical as well as the spiritual damage is considerable) you immediately revoked your mandate and under political rather than spiritual aegis, the housekeepers went back to the kitchen, and the concubines to the bedroom. Behold such work of a holy prelate! and try to find true, not false, religion in such guise!

Again, over and above the excessive burden of the tallages already mentioned, growing greed and ever increasing variety of evil have added an unusual imposition on the wretched clergy of St. David's in your days. The greatest and most burdensome of all impositions is certainly how frequently the bishops visit the hospices, something which, in fact, is recognized to be the duty of the archdeacon, unless

158-78. *De Iure et Statu*, etc., 1 (*Op.* iii, p. 144, 1-29).

officium spectare dinoscitur, nisi quoniam niti in vetitum aviditas solet
et sorte sua minime contenta ardencius ad aliena semper hanelat.
165 Fautores tamen episcoporum sic forte distingunt, ut clericorum casas
visitent episcopi, ecclesias autem archidiaconi. Set utinam et has et illas
magister et minister cum effectu visitent et ab omni macula, maxime
mortali, plenarie purgent! Porro si lauta et splendida fuerit episcopi
mensa et ferculis ac pigmentis plene referta, precipueque si munera
170 sibi in discessu pulcra totique fere familie more cardinalium et trans-
missorum a curia Romana legatorum fuerint donaria data, quod revera
novelle adinvencionis in Wallia certum est esse (non dicimus tamen,
quod vestre: dicant qui conscii sunt et experti), si hec, inquam, hoc
174 ordine provenerint, tunc nulla prorsus macula vel menda, tunc nec in
f. 100ᵛᵃ hospiciis nec in ecclesiis discon|veniencia notabitur ulla.

Nec ad remota solum a terris et maneriis suis clericorum tecta diver-
tunt, per que transire forte necessitas urget, set etiam ad propinqua
valde, quia per unum miliare tantum vel duo distancia, veluti a ⌐manerio
de Launtefei ex uno latere Stakepole et ex altero Kairreu seu etiam
180 Tinebech, sicut et apud Brechene a manerio de Landu, Lanbiliauc,
Brenleis et Mara⌐ cumque familia nimia nec solum propria, set undecumque collecta. Unde pauper ille vicarius de Tinebech, pauperis ecclesie illius quarta solum porcione contentus, cum poeta dicere poterit:
Mantua ve misere nimium vicina Cremone—et non solum vicarius, verum
185 etiam rector ecclesie precipuus, si iusticia locum haberet, illud idem
dicere posset. Set deo annuente et sole serenius illucente, piscibus tam
ibi voratis quam avide nimis et avare iam per triennium et amplius
cum ceteris fructibus inde sublatis et asportatis, condigna debent suo
in tempore salsamenta parari. In hiis autem hospiciis sic usurpatis et
190 tanquam ad nutum debitis, ⌐ubi tamen dicere presumit ambicio:
f. 100ᵛᵇ 'Eamus accipere hospicia nostra',⌐ nichil pontificale prorsus | exercent,
set crapule solum et castrimargie minus honeste minusque modeste
quam deceret indulgentes, tanquam *inmunes resident aliena ad pabula
fuci.* ⌐Alibi namque in episcopos archidiaconi ascendere ⟨solent, hic⟩
195 ediverso episcopos in archidiaconos aviditas de⟨scendere fa⟩cit et avaricia.⌐

165 distringunt *De Iure et Statu, etc. Op. iii, p. 144, 11*   170 (*et Ep. 7, 103*) dicessu *V*
178 *post* veluti a *expunctum est* Launtefei Tinebech *V*   194–5 *quae supplevi coll.*
De Iure et Statu, etc. Op. iii, p. 145, 4–7, in V iam non legi possunt

163. Cf. Ovid, *Amores*, iii, 4, 17: *Nitimur in vetitum (semper cupimusque negata)*;
the same quotation in *De Rebus a se Gestis*, i, 3 (*Op.* i, p. 25, 18).

164. Horace, *Serm.* i, 1, 1–3: *Qui fit, Maecenas, ut nemo quam sibi sortem | seu ratio
dederit seu fors obiecerit, illa | contentus vivat?*

greed tends to try the forbidden, and discontented with its own fortune always desires someone else's the more eagerly. The supporters of the bishops chance to make this distinction: the bishops are to visit the priests' houses, and the archdeacons the churches. But would it were that the master and servant visited both effectively, and completely purged them of all, especially mortal, sin. Moreover, if the table of the bishop is famous and splendid and completely filled with dishes and spices, and especially if the gifts offered to him on his departure are beautiful and given to almost the whole household, after the manner of the cardinals and legates sent from the curia at Rome—that would indeed be a great innovation in Wales (we do not say that it would be for you: let those who know and have tasted it, speak!)—if, we say, these things happen in this way, then there will be absolutely no sin or fault, and no inconvenience will be noticed in the hospices and churches.

Not only do they resort to the houses of the priests far from their estates and manors, through which necessity happens to compel them to pass, but even those very close, when the distance is a matter of a mile or two, like the distance from the manor of Lamphey to Stackpole on one side and Caerau or even Tenby on the other, or, as in Brecon, from the manor of Llanddew to Llanfilo, Bronllys, and Mara. And they turn up with a huge entourage, not only their own household, but with a crowd collected from all over the place. Thus that poor vicar of Tenby, enjoying not more than a quarter of that poor church, could cry with the poet: 'Mantua, too close a neighbour of poor Cremona'. Not only the vicar, but also the distinguished rector of the church, if justice were to have its due, could express the same sentiments. But, God willing, once the sun shines more brightly again, a worthy meal will be prepared in due course from the fish and all the other fruit and vegetables which were carried off and stolen all too eagerly and greedily. In hospices thus usurped and bound to obey a whim, where ambition has the audacity to say: 'let us accept our hospitality', they carry out absolutely no pontifical duty, but they indulge in boozing and gormandizing with less honesty and less moderation than is fitting, and, as it were, settle like privileged drones on others' food. Whereas elsewhere archdeacons sometimes rise to become bishops, there, on the contrary, greed and avarice cause bishops to drop back to the level of archdeacons.

170-1. Cf. *Speculum Ecclesie*, 4, 18 (*Op.* iv, pp. 300-1).
184. Virgil, *Buc.* ix, 28, also quoted in the *Speculum Ecclesie*, 3, 8 and 12 (*Op.* iv, p. 168, 8 and p. 206, 8, cf. p. 203, 22).
189-96. *De Iure et Statu*, etc., 1 (*Op.* iii, p. 144, 30-p. 145, 7).
193-4. Virgil, *Georg.* iv, 244: *immunisque sedens aliena ad pabula fucus.*

Advertant autem tonsores ovium tales, ne dicam excoriatores, quot
mala quondam in tonsionibus ovium contigerunt, sicut de Nabal viro
stulto, negante exenia David in ovium suarum tonsione: unde post
200 X dies Nabal percussus interiit. Item cum iret Laban ad tondendas
oves, Rachel furata est ydola patris sui. In tonsione ovium unus filiorum
David regis ⌐Absalon⌐ ob sororis iniuriam fratrem suum ⌐Amon⌐
interemit. Item cum iret Iudas ad tonsores ovium suarum, invenit
obiter Thamar nurum suam, cum qua fornicatus est putans meretricem
205 esse. Porro si tales leguntur eventus tonsorum animaliumque brutorum,
solum in signum et tipum ad nostram doctrinam et castigacionem dati,
quam graviores erunt casus excoriatorum rei rationalis reique sub celo
f. 101ra dignissime et ad ymaginem dei plasmate, sive | temporaliter hic inchoati
sive ira vindice longe duriore usque in gehennam protelati!

210 Item legitur in Luca de puplicanis venientibus ad Iohannem ut
baptizarentur ab eo et interrogantibus: *Magister, quid faciemus* ne
excidamur et in ignem mittamur? Quibus responsum est: *Nichil
amplius quam quod statutum ⟨est⟩ vobis faciatis* (aut iuxta translacionem
aliam: *Nichil ultra prescriptum exigatis*) *et neminem concuciatis.* Quid
215 ergo dicetur de illis, qui longe ultra statutum sibique de iure concessum
exigunt et extorqunt? Nonne *securi iam ad radicem posita excidentur et
in ignem mittentur?* ⌐Unde Ieremias: *Ve pastoribus, qui dispergunt et
dilacerant gregem pascue mee, dicit dominus.*⌐

Ceterum prelati tales et predones pocius quam pastores et gregis
220 excoriatores, nonne Moysi, nonne Samueli, nonne et Paulo longe
dissimiles? Legitur enim in libro Numeri: Moyse increpante Dathan
et Abiron murmurantes contra Aaron, responderunt ei, dicentes:
'*Numquid parum est tibi quod eduxisti nos de terra lacte et melle manante,*
224 *nisi occideres nos in deserto, nisi et dominatus fueris nostri? An et oculos*
f. 101rb *nostros vis eruere?' Iratusque Moyses valde* | *ait ad dominum: 'Ne respicias
sacrificia eorum: tu scis quod nec asellum quidem unquam acceperim ab eis
nec afflixerim quempiam illorum.'* Item et in libro Regum: *Dixit Samuel
ad universum Israel: 'Audivi vocem vestram iuxta omnia que locuti estis*

---

213 est *textus biblicus et De Iure et Statu, etc. Op. iii, p. 147, 33*   219 predones
dicendi potius De Iure et Statu, etc. Op. iii, p. 148, 5

197–249. *De Iure et Statu*, etc., 1 (*Op.* iii, p. 147, 10–p. 149, 9), cf. *Gemma Ecclesiastica*,
2, 34 (*Op.* ii, pp. 329–30). Lines 197–205 are adapted from Petrus Cantor, *Verbum
Abbreviatum*, Migne, *PL*, 205, 83B–84B: *tonsores, excoriatores . . . lac et lanam in ovibus
querentes, lucro inhiantes potius quam saluti animarum intendentes* (cf. 248–9, and Ep. 6,
468–70), etc.
    198–200. Nabal] 1 Sam. xxv, 2–38.   200–1. Gen. xxxi, 19; cf. Ep. 6, 184.
    201–3. 2 Sam. xiii (1–22 and) 23–9.
    203–5. Gen. xxxviii (6–12 and) 13–20.   210–14. Luke iii, 12–14.
    213–14. translacionem aliam] No version is nearer to Giraldus' text than Ambrose,

Such sheep-shearers—let us not say fleecers—should know the erst-while dangers in sheep-shearing, as in the case of the stupid Nabal who refused David gifts while shearing his sheep: as a result after ten days Nabal was stabbed and killed. Again when Laban came to shear sheep Rachel stole her father's idols. During a sheep-shearing Absalom, one of the sons of King David, killed his brother Amnon for assaulting his sister. Similarly, when Judah was going to see his sheep-shearers, he met Tamar, his daughter-in-law, on the way, and slept with her, thinking she was a whore. If such are the ends we read of shearers and brute animals, given only as an outward sign and allegory for our in-struction and chastisement, how much graver will be the fall of the ideal essence, the most noble essence on earth, the raw material for the image of God, of the fleecers, whether it is begun here on earth, or carried on with vindictive and far greater wrath to Gehenna!

In Luke we read of the publicans coming to John to be baptized by him, and asking, 'Master, what shall we do? lest we be cut down, and cast into the fire.' He replied: 'Do nothing more than that which is appointed to you' (or, in another translation: 'Exact no more than the agreed sum') 'and do violence to no man.' What then is to be said of those who exact far more than the agreed sum, and the sum allowed them by law? Is not 'the axe laid to the root of the trees, and they shall be cut down and cast into the fire'? Thus, according to Jeremiah, 'Woe to the pastors that scatter and tear the sheep of my pasture, saith the Lord.'

But are not such prelates and pirates (rather than pastors) who flay whole herds, completely different from Moses, Samuel, and Paul? We read in the Book of Numbers, when Moses was rebuking Dathan and Abiram for muttering against Aaron, they said in reply to him, 'Is it a small matter to thee that thou hast brought us out of a land that flowed with milk and honey, to kill us in the desert, except thou rule also like a lord over us? Wilt thou also pluck out our eyes?' Moses therefore being very angry, said to the Lord: 'Respect not their sacrifices. Thou knowest that I have not taken of them so much as a young ass at any time; nor have I injured any of them.' And again we read in the Book of Samuel: 'Samuel said to all Israel: "Behold, I have hearkened to your voice in all that you have said to me, and have made a king over

In Lucam, CC, 14, p. 64, 1027:... *publicanis, ne* ultra praescriptum exigant (= Bede, *In Lucam*, CC, 120, I, p. 79, 2366). Giraldus probably uses again Petrus Cantor, *Verbum Abbreviatum*, Migne, *PL*, 205, 145C: *Ambrosius et Beda aliam legunt translationem, scilicet hanc: Nihil . . . exigatis* (the same version in 279A).

216–17. Matt. iii, 10 = Luke iii, 9.   217–18. Jer. xxiii, 1 (*disperdunt*).
221–7. Num. xvi, 1–15 (13–15).   227–34. 1 Sam. xii, 1–3.

ad me, et constitui super vos regem, qui graditur ante vos, et nunc senui
230 *conversatus coram vobis ab adolescencia mea usque in diem hanc. Ecce*
presto sum: loquimini de me coram domino et coram christo eius, Saule
scilicet, *utrum bovem cuiusquam vestrum tulerim aut asinum, si quempiam*
calumpniatus sum, si oppressi aliquem, si de manu cuiusquam munus accepi;
et contempnam illud hodie vobisque restituam.' Item et Paulus in Actibus
235 Apostolorum: *Vos scitis, a prima die qua ingressus sum in Asiam, qualiter*
vobiscum per omne tempus fuerim conversatus, serviens domino in omni
humilitate et lacrimis, et texens sermonem moralissimum ultimo an-
nectit de officio prelatorum, docens eos cavere avariciam exemplo sui,
f. 101va cum ait: *Argen|tum et aurum aut vestem ullius non concupivi: ipsi scitis*
240 *quoniam ad ea, que michi opus erant et hiis, qui mecum sunt, ministraverunt*
manus mee. Similiter in epistola secunda ad Corinthios: *Quid est enim*
quod minus habuistis pre ceteris ecclesiis, nisi quod ego ipse non gravavi vos?
Donate michi hanc iniuriam. Ecce tercio iam paratus sum venire ad vos et
non ero gravis vobis: non enim quero que vestra sunt, set vos: nec enim
245 *debent filii parentibus thesaurizare, set parentes filiis.* O quam pauci
sunt hodie episcopi, qui hoc cum Paulo in veritate dicere possint:
'Non querimus que vestra sunt, set querimus vos': cupiditati namque ⌜plerique⌝ per omnia dediti et caritate vacui pecuniarum lucrum
ardentissime siciunt, non animarum. ⌝

250 Item, cum clericorum familia sub ecclesiastica protectione esse
consueverit, qualiter in Menevie partibus eam laicali direpcioni et
f. 101vb gravissime redempcioni nuper | exposuistis, lucri tam inhonesti, sicut
patria publice clamat, particeps esse non abhorrens, adeo ut more
inaudito clerici miserrimi suos vel suas a carcere tenebroso per pecuniam
255 oblatam nullatenus eripere possent, nisi et unam quoque ecclesiarum
suarum, si duas aut plures haberent, resignarent et fratribus aut filiis
predonum, tirannicorum clericis, cederent et quietam omnino remit-
terent.

Item haut dissimiliter in partibus de Brechene nuper facte sunt
260 cessiones huiusmodi et instituciones per inpressiones et violentas
curialium extorsiones, que modis omnibus, sicut et alie, pastorali
rigore reprimi debuissent, sicut in prioris scilicet de Brechene et
aliorum quorundam de partibus illis dampnum maximum et gravamen
evidenter apparet: nullus quippe tergiversandi locus in hiis et predictis
265 aut excusandi datur, ⌜nulla quidem hic vulpina dolositate, nullo falsitatis
fuco solito se fraus defendere potest:⌝ *error enim,* ut ait Ignacius papa,

234–7. Acts xx, 18–19.   239–41. Acts xx, 33–4.   241–5. 2 Cor. xii, 13–14.
249. See note on 197(–249).   265. Cf. *supra,* part ii, 528.
266. fuco] See note on Ep. 1, 12.   266–72. See note on Ep. 5, 44–9.

you. And now the king goeth before you. But I am old and having then conversed with you from my youth unto this day, behold, here I am. Speak of me before the Lord and before his anointed' (i.e. Saul) 'whether I have taken any man's ox, or ass: if I have wronged any man, if I have oppressed any man, if I have taken a bribe at any man's hand. And I will despise it this day, and will restore it to you."' Similarly, Paul says in the Acts of the Apostles: 'You know from the first day that I came into Asia, in what manner I have been with you, for all the time serving the Lord with all humility and with tears.' As he weaves his most moral sermon, he finally works in a passage on the duty of the prelates, instructing them to avoid avarice, following his example; he says: 'I have not coveted any man's silver, gold, or apparel, as you yourselves know. For such things as were needful for me and them that are with me, these hands have furnished.' Similarly, he writes in his second Epistle to the Corinthians: 'For what is there that you have had less than the other churches but that I myself was not burthensome to you? Pardon me this injury. Behold now the third time I am ready to come to you and I will not be burthensome unto you. For I seek not the things that are yours, but you. For neither ought the children to lay up for the parents, but the parents for the children.' Alas, how few bishops are there today who can say in all truth with Paul: 'We seek not the things that are yours, but we seek you.' For most of them are completely given to avarice and lack charity: they thirst most eagerly for money, not souls.

Similarly, though normally the family of priests is under the protection of the church, how much have you recently exposed them to the depredations of the laity and to the very heavy ransoms in the diocese without a qualm, as the country shouts out in public, about sharing dishonest profit, so much so that in a way unheard of the wretched priests could not rescue their men and womenfolk from the darkness of the dungeon by offering bribes, unless they resigned and ceded one of their churches (if they had two or more) to the brothers or sons of the pirates, the tyrants of the priesthood, and paid quit rent.

In a similar manner transactions of this kind occurred in the Brecon area and institutions by bringing pressure to bear, and violent extortion on the part of the courts, which, like others, ought to have been absolutely suppressed by every means with pastoral sternness, as it clearly appears to the detriment and inconvenience of the prior of Brecon and certain others in that diocese. There is no room for evasion or excuse in this and the affairs previously mentioned: there is no fox-like cunning, there is none of the usual deceitful colouring that can defend this fraud.

f. 102ra *cui non resistitur, approbatur et veri|tas cum minime defensatur, opprimitur.*
Cui et Innocencii canon ille concordat: *Negligere cum possis perturbare*
perversos, nichil est aliud quam fovere nec caret scrupulo societatis occulte,
270 *qui manifesto facinori desinit obviare,* presertim etiam cum ad hoc ex
officio teneatur, et in iure quoque scriptum est: *Ratihabicio mandato*
comparatur. Item et super illud Ieremie: *Nolite tacere super iniquitatem*
eius, dicit expositor: *Qui enim tacendo consentit, particeps est culpe*
simul et pene.

275 Set nonne miseri prelati tales et meticulosi, qui ad nutum curialium
parati sunt in hunc modum et promtuli ad fas omne nefasque (cum
tamen scriptum sit quia *episcopus si timet, actum est de eo*) propter hos
solum excessus, et si ceterorum criminum enormium non tot turbe con-
currerent, a cathedris, quas inutiliter et cum scandalo tenent, deici
280 cum dedecore deberent et deponi?

Preter hec etiam hostilitatis tempore gravius urgente cum uterque
populus, tam advene scilicet quam indigene, loca sacra non solum
f. 102rb depre|dando et spoliando, verum etiam cedibus et incendiis prophan-
ando per diocesim vestram debacari more paganico non cessarunt,
285 statim fugiens a patria, per abacias Anglie remotas circueundo quatinus
ad vos querimonie pervenire non possent, unde iusticia sequi deberet,
per dimidium et amplius annum delituistis, ubi pocius pastor bonus
pro domo domini se tanquam murum opponeret et pro ovibus etiam si
opus ingrueret, animam suam poneret. Set iuxta ewangelicum illud,
290 *mercenarius fugit, quia mercenarius est et non pertinet ad ipsum de ovibus*
et lupus rapit et dispergit, immo et lupi multi, sicut est hodie in Wallia
videre. Ibi ergo nimirum grex omnino periclitatur et perit, ubi lupi
innumeri et pastores rarissimi, et hii mercenarii tantum et fugitivi.

Item et super hoc quoque correpcio addenda est et correccio, quod
295 ordini Cisterciensi, tam favorabili per orbem tanteque ecclesie colum-
f. 102va pne, tociens in diocesi vestra et diebus | vestris spoliate tociensque a
membris diaboli predis abductis graviter apporiate, nullam ecclesiasticam
iusticiam nisi precio pretaxato et pregustato, equo videlicet ad minus

272-3. Jer. li, 6.
273-4. expositor] (Cf. Ep. 4, 66) Rabanus Maurus, *Exp. super Ieremiam,* 17, 51,
Migne, *P.L.* 111, 1160B: *Qui enim tacendo consentit perversa voluntate aut prava actione*
iniquitati Babylonis et non magis reprehenderit eam, particeps est delicti eius et consors
vindictae, quoted in the form given to them by the *Glossa Ordinaria.* Cf. *supra,* part ii,
342-3.   277. See note on Ep. 6, 338.
287-9. John x, 14: *Ego sum pastor bonus . . .* (15) *et animam meam pono pro ovibus*
meis; Ezek. xiii, 5: *neque opposuistis murum pro domo Israel.*

'For', as Pope Ignatius says, 'to fail to correct an error is to approve it, and to fail to defend truth is to repress it.' That canon of Innocent is in agreement with this: 'Not to correct when possible those who have gone astray is tantamount to encouraging them; nor is the man who fails to take action against a patent crime free of the suspicion of being secretly in league with it', especially when he is held to this by his office. It is also written in the law: 'Ratification comes close to authorization.' In addition, on this passage from Jeremiah, 'be not silent upon her iniquity', the commentator says: 'the man who gives his tacit consent shares the sin as well as the punishment.'

But ought not such miserable, timid prelates, who are so ready to obey their courts in this way, and so quick to any violent act or crime (though there is a saying, 'if the bishop is afraid, he is done for') to be thrown out and deposed from office which they hold to no purpose and to the general scandal, in disgrace even if there were not so many hosts of all the others outrageous offences, just because of these excesses?

In addition to this, when the time of hostilities was more pressing, since both the alien and native population were not only pillaging and despoiling sanctuaries, but also profaning them with murder and arson, and had not stopped their pagan orgies throughout your diocese, you promptly left the country and made a tour of far-away abbeys in England, so that complaints could not reach you which otherwise would have to be followed up by legal action, and you went into hiding for six months or more, when the good shepherd should have set himself up as a wall for the house of the Lord, or even, if need arose, laid down his life for his sheep. But according to the Gospel, 'the hireling fleeth, because he is a hireling; and he hath no care for the sheep, and the wolf catcheth and scattereth the sheep' especially when there are many wolves, as is the case in Wales today. Indeed the flock is in grave danger and perishes when there are innumerable wolves, the shepherds are few and far between, and hirelings and runaways at that.

Again in addition to this a word of reproof and chastisement must be added as well: you have never been willing to show any ecclesiastical justice to the Cistercian Order, which is such a favourite throughout the world, and such a strong pillar of the Church, but which has so often been despoiled in your diocese in your time, and has so often been beggared by the depredations of the associates of the Devil, unless you were given a previously agreed and proven bribe—e.g. a horse which is

290–1. John x, 13 and 12.
295–6. This favourable opinion contrasts singularly with Giraldus' usual attitude towards the Cistercians, cf. *Speculum Ecclesie*, 3, 6 (*Op.* iv, p. 160, 8–9): *A monachorum malitia, maxime vero Cisterciensium, libera nos, domine* . . .

egregio de totis equiciis ad hoc electo, exibere voluistis. Unde et abas
300 de Cumhir R(irid) litteris et nunciis hunc vestrum defectum et ordinis
gravamen abati Cisterciensi significavit et ille statim, iniuriam ordinis
non facilem reputans, a curia Romana litteras gravis in personam
vestram, si sic inveniretur, animadversionis inpetrare et dicto abati
remittere non tardavit; verum interveniente favore nonnullo seu prece
305 seu precio suppressum est rescriptum et non comparuit.

Item et super hoc quoque, quod nec etiam pacis tempore parochianis
vestris, doctrina bona tantum indigentibus, vel per vos, ubi linguam
vestram noverunt, vel per interpretem ubi non noverunt, vite pabulum
f. 102ᵛᵇ seminare curastis, set lac et | lanam, ut diximus, avide nimis et cupide
310 consumere debitamque saluti gregis curam prorsus omittere non
erubuistis. Vidimus autem virum venerabilem et sanctum Baldewinum
Cantuariensem archiepiscopum Walliam ob crucis obsequium intrare
devotoque labore penitimas eiusdem partes circuire pariter et penetrare,
qui Walensibus linguam eius ignorantibus cotidie fere verba salutis ore
315 proprio seminare non cessabat et postmodum etiam per fideles inter-
pretes eadem illis diligenter exponi faciebat. Unde magnam ipsis de-
vocionem incuciebat et ad crucis signacionem, propter quod venerat,
multitudinem magnam inducebat. Exemplum quoque abatis Bernardi
predicantis Theutonicis laicis et ad lacrimas ac fletum eos commoventis,
320 quem tamen non intelligebant, hic apponere preter rem non putavi:
cuius sermonem retexuit post eum interpres optimus, monachus scilicet,
f. 104ʳᵃ quo loquente | nichil moti sunt, ex quo patet quia qui non ardet, non
incendit. In sacra namque scriptura res, non verba loquuntur, iuxta
poeticum illud : *Res age, tutus eris.* In ea nimirum res pocius quam verba
325 perorant et persuadent: voces enim exterius pulsant nec penetrant,
spiritus autem est, qui intus agit et operatur. Unde et super epistolam
Iohannis primam dicit expositor : *Nemo doctori attribuat quod ex ore*
docentis intelligit: nisi enim intus sit qui doceat, in vanum exterius doctoris
lingua laborat. Effectus itaque doctrine celestis in duobus consistit,

299–300. abas de Cumhir] Abbey-Cwmhir, Cistercian house, Radnorshire, daughter
of Whitland (Carmarthens.), founded in 1143, refounded in 1176, cf. Knowles and
Hadcock, *Religious Houses* (1971 edition), pp. 112, 115. For the identity of the abbot see
S. W. Williams, 'The Cistercian Abbey of Cwmhir, Radnorshire', *Cym. Trans.* 1894–5,
p. 72. He is given as Rind in Knowles, Brooke, London, *Heads of Religious Houses* (1972),
p. 126.   301. abati] Guido II or Arnaldus I, cf. *Gallia Christiana* iv, 990–1.
304–5. prece seu precio] See note on Ep. 6, 337.
309. lac et lanam] Ezek. xxxiv, 3.   ut diximus] in Ep. 6, 469 (addressed also to
Bishop Geoffrey de Henlaw).
311–13. Cf. *De Rebus a se Gestis*, 2, 18 (*Op.* i, pp. 74–6): *De Baldwino Cantuariensi*
archiepiscopo crucem per Walliam predicante . . . , and the *Speculum Ecclesie*, 3, 1 (*Op.* iv,
pp. 142, 31–3): *viri boni et sancti Cantuarie archiepiscopi Baldwini per Wallie fines in*
crucis obsequium itinerantis olim et devote laborantis . . . Cf. *supra*, part i, 863 ff.
318–23 and 323–4. The anecdote is also told in the passage quoted in the note on

at least outstanding and the pick of the whole stable. So Ririd, abbot of
Cwm Hir, denounced this vice of yours and the imposition of the Order
in letters and messages to the abbot of Cîteaux, and he, considering the
slight to the Order no trivial matter, immediately hastened to get letters
of serious censure from Rome against your parson, if he was to be found,
and send them to Abbot Ririd. However, some favourable intervention
occurred, whether an entreaty or a private treaty, and the mandate was
lost and not found.

In addition to this there is the fact that in time of peace you did not
even bother to administer communion to your parishioners, who only
lacked good instruction, either personally, when they knew your language, or through an interpreter, when they did not, but you had no
qualms at consuming the 'milk and wool', as we have said, with un-
toward greed and cupidity, while completely neglecting the proper care
for the salvation of your flock. However, we saw that venerable and holy
man, Baldwin, archbishop of Canterbury, enter Wales to preach the crusade, and with the labour of love go round and penetrate the inmost
regions. Though the Welsh could not understand his language, almost
every day he was continually preaching the word of salvation with his
own lips, and afterwards had it expounded to them through faithful inter-
preters. And so he filled them with great devotion, and induced a great
number of them to take the cross—the purpose of his visit. I think it is
not beside the point to draw a parallel with the example of Abbot Bernard,
who preached to the Germans and moved them to tears and weeping,
though they did not understand him. His sermon was translated after
him by his interpreter, a monk, and when that man spoke, they were
unmoved. It is clear from this that a man who is not on fire does not
inflame his audience. In Sacred Scripture it is deeds, not words, which
speak; as the poet says: 'Fight on. You will be safe.' In this matter it is
the deeds rather than the words that plead and persuade; for voices
will beat on the outside and not penetrate, while it is the spirit that acts
and works within. Thus the commentator on the first Epistle of John
says: 'No one should attribute to the teacher what he has heard from
the lips of the teacher; for unless he who teaches is within, the tongue
of the teacher toils in vain without.' Thus the effective teaching of

311–13 (2, 18, p. 76, 6–14) and in the *Gemma Ecclesiastica*, 1, 51 (*Op.* ii, p. 152, 15–22).
It has been taken, mostly verbatim, and together with the lines 321–3 and the quotation
from Ovid, *Rem. Am.* 144 (see note on Ep. 6, 243) from Petrus Cantor, *Verbum Ab-*
breviatum, 37 c–d (see note on lines 213–14). The words *quia qui non ardet, non accendit*
(sic), also ibid. 38c (VII). On Bernard of Clairvaux preaching the crusade to the
Germans see *Vita Prima*, Lib. III, ch. 3 (Migne, *P.L.* 185, col. 307b).

327. expositor] (see notes on 273–4 and on Ep. 4, 66) Alulfus, *Exp. super Ep. 1*
Iohannis (2, 27) (Migne, *P.L.* 79, 1392d), quoted from the *Glossa Ordinaria*.

330 in vita scilicet et sanctitate docentis meritisque bonis verbum devote
suscipientis.

Mirum autem, quomodo tam temere tamque tirannice subditorum
suorum episcopi tales temporalia metunt et trans metam omnem atque
modestiam diripere et asportare contendunt, qui per se vel per alios
335 nec eis spiritualia spergunt nec verba salutis ulla proponunt. O, quam
f. 104rb illud Isaie ad prelatos parum | attendunt: *Clama, ne cesses, tanquam*
tuba exalta vocem tuam. Item et illud: *Si non annunciaveris populo meo*
scelera eorum, sanguinem ipsius de manu tua requiram. Ibi enim pastorali
clamore opus esset valde assiduo et pervalido, ubi ex doctrine defectu,
340 quia nec verbo nec vite grex informatur exemplo, et nimis habundant
vicia et scelera ab antiquo sunt radicata.

Super hiis igitur omnibus et singulis et longe pluribus, quia criminum
enormium cotidie crescit exercitus, forsan etiam in iure vel alibi
quandoque vobis ⌐si necesse fuerit⌐ exprimendis, vos utinam in brevi
345 corrigere velitis et a similibus decetero excessibus abstinere.

Set quoniam interdum cautela non nocet habundans contra precipites
prelatorum sentencias, ira vindice zeloque magis amaritudinis quam
rectitudinis ⌐emissas, nuper in capitulo⌐ de Pembroch et Ros per
f. 104va clericos nostros et litteras nostras | patentes, item et tam coram priore
350 de Brechene et loci eiusdem decano apud Aberhothenei quam etiam
apud Lantonei in Ewias coram loci eiusdem priore et subpriore et aliis
canonicis quam plurimis ⌐sicut et quandoque in presencia vestra⌐ nos
clipeum appellationis opposuisse noveritis.

Utinam bene valere et a vilibus huiusmodi iam hic ex parte conscriptis,
355 que scandala per Walliam pariunt, tanta dextere Excelsi mutacione
viriliter resurgere velitis et exemplo Petri negantis set statim penitentis
et Pauli persequentis set postea predicantis, demum hostie vel caudam
immolans feliciter et cum effectu resipiscere valeatis.

336–8. Ezek. iii, 18: *Si (dicente me ad ipsum: Morte morieris) non adnuntiaveris (ei*
neque locutus fueris, ut avertatur a via sua impia et vivat, ipse impius in iniquitate sua
morietur), sanguinem autem eius de manu tua requiram, and Isa. lviii, 1: *Clama, ne cesses,*
quasi tuba exalta vocem tuam et adnuntia populo meo scelera eorum . . . ; cf. Ep. 6, 466–7.
351. Cf. Ep. 6, 98.   354 ff. See note on Ep. 1, 40.
355. Ps. lxxvi, 11: *Haec mutatio dexterae Excelsi.*
356. Petri negantis] Mark xiv, 66–72.
357. Pauli persequentis] Acts ix, 1–22.
357. hostie vel caudam] Cf. R. B. C. Huygens, 'Deux commentaires sur la séquence
"Ave, praeclara maris stella" ', *Cîteaux, Commentarii Cistercienses,* 20, 1969, p. 127
n. 285: *finis bonus in cauda hostie designatur.*

heaven consists of two things: the life and sanctity of the teacher, and the merits of those who listen devoutly.

It is, however, remarkable how rashly and tyrannically such bishops harvest the temporal powers of their subordinates, and strive to pass and go beyond all bounds of moderation, while they never spread spiritual matters, or preach the word of salvation to them, either themselves, or through others. What scant attention they give to Isaiah's words to prelates: 'Cry, cease not, lift up thy voice like a trumpet'; or 'If thou declare not to my people their wicked doings, I will require its blood at thy hand.' Thus there should be a continual, loud pastoral outcry, where, as a result of lack of teaching (the flock is taught neither by the word, nor by example from life), wickedness abounds and crime is long-established and deep-rooted.

As far as all these crimes are concerned, each individual one and a great many others (since the legion of outrageous offences is on the increase daily) which you ought to stamp out, either by law, or in some other way, if it is necessary, we wish that you would improve yourself, and keep yourself from similar excesses in future.

But, since there is no harm in the meantime in a strong warning against the rash utterances of the prelates, published out of vindictive rage and a zeal more from bitterness than justice, and recently revealed by our priests and our letters at the chapters of Pembroke and Rhos, you should know that we have put up the shield of our appeal before the prior of Brecon and the dean at Brecon, and at Llanthony in Ewias before the prior and sub-prior of that area, and as many other canons as possible, just as we once did before you.

It is our prayer that you enjoy good health, and desire to rise manfully from offences as described in part here, which are causing scandals in Wales, by the great conversion of the right hand of the most high and take the example of Peter who denied and then repented, and Paul, who persecuted and then preached, and that finally, sacrificing the tail of the victim, you may happily and effectively repent.

APPENDIX

Notes on the letters

I. *Ep. 6, 345–417*

THE lines 345–417 are found, either verbatim or with slight variants, in so many other works of Giraldus that it is impossible to note all parallels under the text of Ep. 6. Lines 345–51, *utatur*, also occur in the *De Iure et Statu Menevensis Ecclesie*, 1 (*Op.* iii, p. 147, 1–9, cf. 7, p. 343, 14–24), 345–64 (but without the addition *Unde . . . declarans*), in the *Symbolum Electorum*, 1, 7 (*Op.* i, p. 220, 4–35), and 345–57 (with the same omission), and 357–64 in the *Speculum Ecclesie*, 4, 20 (*Op.* iv, p. 307, 2–17 and 24–34). The addition *Plus valet meum quam nostrum* (351–4) may also be found in the same, but differently told, anecdote, *De Iure et Statu*, etc., 7 (*Op.* iii, p. 343, 4–8). Lines 365–6, 366–71, and 371–3 are also in *De Iure et Statu*, etc., 1 and 7 (*Op.* iii, p. 140, 23–5, p. 140, 32–p. 141, 5, and (dist. 7) p. 367, 1–7), and p. 140, 25–9; lines 366–71 and 371–3 also in the *Speculum Ecclesie*, 4, 17 (*Op.* iv, p. 296 (ch. 17), 3–10, and p. 297, 1–3), lines 373–8 and 373–81 in the same chapters of the *Speculum Ecclesie* and the *De Iure*, etc., *Op.* iv, p. 296 (ch. 17), 10–17, and *Op.* iii, p. 141, 5–16 (lines 366–73 and 366–79 respectively, also in the *Symbolum Electorum*, 1, 28, and 1, 7 (*Op.* i, p. 304, 14–23, and p. 218, 27–p. 219, 16); lines 379–81 are not only found in *De Iure*, etc., 1 (*Op.* iii, p. 141, 13–16), but also in 7 (*Op.* iii, p. 337, 18–22) and in the *Symbolum Electorum*, 1, 31 (*Op.* i, p. 320, 35–6). In this last work can also be found lines 382–94, 396–416, and 416–17, *Op.* i, p. 221, 1–19, p. 222, 1–29 (this passage also in the *Speculum Ecclesie*, 4, 21 (*Op.* iv, p. 308, 1–19), and p. 221, 19–20 respectively. In the *Speculum Ecclesie* are also found lines 402–16, and 406–8, in chapters 4, 21, and 4, 18 (*Op.* iv, p. 309, 5–24, and p. 300, 28–30) respectively.

II. *Ep. 6, 418–60*

The lines 418–60 (with the exception of the additional ones 423–7) are also found in *De Iure et Statu Menevensis Ecclesie*, 1 (*Op.* iii, p. 149, 10–p. 150, 26). The quotations 420–2, 427–8, and 428–9 also occur together in *De Invectionibus*, 6, 27 (*Op.* i, p. 190, 27–9, 11–13, and 13–15 = ed. Davies, p. 233, 17–19, 4–5, and 5–7), where they have been taken from the *Gemma Ecclesiastica*, 2, 38 (*Op.* ii, p. 358, 20–3, 5–7, and 8–9), and reappear in the *Speculum Ecclesie*, 4, 20 and 39 (*Op.* iv, p. 310, 28–31, p. 311, 3–5 and 5–7, and p. 349, 9–12, p. 348 (ch. 39), 11–12 and 13–15; the lines 428–9 also in the *Symbolum Electorum*, 1, 21 (*Op.* i, p. 259, 1–2). The words *Sciant episcopi* (420) and

(*exempla*) *prava* (421) are also attributed to Ambrose in the passage quoted from *De Iure*, etc. (*Op.* iii, p. 149, 16–17), at the beginning of this appendix. Elsewhere, they always begin with the words *Scire prelati debent*, attributed not to Ambrose but to Jerome; from all these instances, the word *prava* is read only in the *Speculum Ecclesie*, 4, 20 (but not in 4, 39!) (*Op.* iv, p. 310, 31). As for lines 427–8, they represent a summary of a quotation which, in the works quoted above, is always given in full, e.g. *De Invectionibus*, 6, 27 (*Op.* i, p. 190, 11–13 = ed. Davies, p. 233, 4–5): *Episcopus nisi verbo et exemplo subditos edificet, canis impudicus dicendus est, non episcopus*. Finally, the lines 433–4, *ostendit*, are also read in the *Symbolum Electorum*, 1, 24 (*Op.* i, p. 280, 26–9): *Item Ieronimus super Mattheum: Non . . . ostendit*.

It is thus apparent that, when writing this Ep. 6, Giraldus used extensively (sometimes more than once) sections from his own earlier works, e.g. *Symbolum Electorum, Gemma Ecclesiastica, De Invectionibus*. He would use the same material again in later works, the *De Iure et Statu Menevensis Ecclesie* and *Speculum Ecclesie*. In parts I and II of this appendix, I have given the references with the lines of the letter published in the present volume as a starting-point. Below a similar analysis will be given, this time based on the other works of Giraldus. As for the *Symbolum Electorum*, it should be noted that Letter No. 7 is addressed to Bishop Peter de Leia of St. David's, the predecessor of Geoffrey de Henlaw, to whom Epp. 6 and 8 in the present collection are addressed.

1. *De Iure et Statu Menevensis Ecclesie*, 1, *Op.* iii, p. 140, 23–5, 25–9, 32— p. 141, 5, and p. 141, 5–16 = Ep. 6, 365–6, 371–3, 366–71, and 373–81; p. 147, 1–9 = Ep. 6, 345–51 (p. 147, 10–p. 149, 9 = Ep. 8, 197–249); p. 149, 10– p. 150, 26 = Ep. 6, 418–60; Dist. vii, *Op.* iii, p. 337, 18–22 = Ep. 6, 379–81; p. 343, 4–8 = Ep. 6, 351–4 (addition), and p. 367, 1–7 = Ep. 6, 366–71.

2. *Symbolum Electorum*, Letter No. vii, *Op.* i, p. 218, 14–p. 219, 16 = Ep. 6, 366–79; p. 220, 4—p. 221, 20 = Ep. 6, 345–64, 382–94, and 416–17; p. 222, 1–29 = Ep. 6, 396–416; some lines also in Letter No. xxi, p. 259, 1–2 = Ep. 6, 428–9; Letter No. xxiv, p. 280, 26–9 = Ep. 6, 433–4; Letter No. xxviii, p. 304, 14–23 = Ep. 6, 366–73; and Letter No. xxxi, p. 320, 35–6 = Ep. 6, 379–81.

3. *Speculum Ecclesie*, Dist. 4, *Op.* iv, p. 296, 3–10 and 10–17 = Ep. 6, 366–71 and 373–8; p. 297, 1–3 = Ep. 6, 371–3; p. 300, 28–30 = Ep. 6, 406–8; p. 307, 2–17 and 24—p. 308, 19 = Ep. 6, 345–57, 357–64, and 396–416; p. 309, 5–24 = Ep. 6, 402–16; p. 310, 28–31 = Ep. 6, 420–2; p. 311, 3–7 = Ep. 6, 427–9; p. 348, 11–15 = Ep. 6, 427–9, and p. 349, 9–12 = Ep. 6, 420–2.

4. *Gemma Ecclesiastica*, 2, 38 (*Op.* ii, p. 358, 5–9 and 20–3) = Ep. 6, 427–9 and 420–2, repeated from this chapter in the *De Invectionibus*, 6, 27 (*Op.* i, p. 190, 11–15 and 27–9 = ed. Davies, p. 233, 4–7 and 17–19).

5. *De Invectionibus*. See under 4.

III. *Peculiarities of spelling*

In the Latin text of the Letters, the following orthographical peculiarities are found, mostly cases of haplography or dittography of consonants or vowels (apart from the usual medieval forms):

b abas, abacia Ep. 8, 285, 299, 301, 303, 318; see also *p*.

c acusare 6, 415; ocultus 5, 48; preocupare 7, 107; sagrilegium 8, 47; peccunia 7, 114.

g agressus 5, 120, 216, 221; 6, 300; aumentare 6, 330; see also *c*.

h abstraere 6, 19; distraere 6, 334, 442; hanelare 8, 164.

m comodum 6, 324 (very frequent); incomodum, incomodare 4, 17, 160; 7, 258; comuniter 6, 386.

n anunciare 6, 466.

p apellare 6, 103; aprobare 7, 251; puplicus 6, 377, 411, 440, 465; puplicanus 8, 210; suplicare, suplicacio 8, 75, 109; suplicium 6, 435, 457; dupplicitas 6, 154.

qu extorqunt 8, 216; iniqus 5, 265; 6, 33, 298; antiqus 5, 275.

r aripere 8, 134; corigere 5, 259; corumpere 4, 28; 5, 276.

LIST OF QUOTATIONS AND ALLUSIONS

(The references are to *pages* of this book)

A. BIBLICAL

Genesis iv: 140
  viii, 22: 42
  ix: 34
  xvi: 140
  xix, 1–11: 168
  xix, 24–5: 168
  xxv: 140
  xxxi, 19: 218, 274
  xxxi, 27, 30: 218
  xxxviii, 13–20: 274
  xlii–xliv: 24
  xliv, 1–13: 182
Exodus iv, 16: 76
  xv, 18: 178
  xx, 12: 72
  xx, 15: 36
Leviticus xviii, 23: 168
Numbers xvi, 1–15: 274
  xxiii: 36
Deuteronomy xxxii, 7: 54
  xxxiii, 9: 148
Judges viii, 7: 34
1 Samuel iv, 5–6: 22
  viii: 130
  xii, 1–3: 274
  xxv, 2–38: 274
2 Samuel xiii, 23–9: 274
2 Kings ii, 23–4: 34
  v, 20: 234
  xxiii: 130
2 Chronicles xxii–xxiv: 118
Job xii, 12: 54
Psalms i, 1: 34
  vii, 16: 16
  x, 5: 14
  xi, 3: 36, 156
  xvii, 26: 50
  xxx, 5: 6
  xxx, 19: 156
  xxxii, 5: 180
  xxxv, 5: 108
  xxxvii, 21: 22
  xl, 10: 4, 218
  xlviii, 13: 128
  xlix, 17: 34
  xlix, 18: 96
  xlix, 18–19: 90
  xlix, 19: 190
  liv, 13–14: 6

liv, 22: 86, 112
liv, 24: 38
lxi, 5: 36
lxv, 12: 234
lxxii, 9: 36
lxxii, 14: 42
lxxii, 18: 216
lxxvi, 11: 282
lxxvii, 3: 54
lxxvii, 36–7: 36
xci, 13: 220
xciii, 11: 178
cviii, 3: 22
cviii, 5: 22
cviii, 18: 62
cix, 5: 102
cxviii, 66: 42
cxix, 2: 116
cxxvi, 1: 46
cxxxix, 2: 116
cxxxix, 4: 266
cxxxix, 12: 38
cxl, 4: 20, 190
cxl, 9: 6
cxlii, 4: 182
cxlvii, 21–2: 54
Proverbs i, 7: 32
  i, 8–9: 44
  i, 17: 160
  i, 24–5: 46
  iii, 29: 6
  iv, 24–5: 76
  v, 11–14: 150
  ix, 7: 30, 32
  x, 9: 142
  xi, 9: 86
  xii, 1: 32
  xiii, 20: 50
  xiii, 24: 22
  xv, 12: 32
  xvi, 18: 246
  xvii, 24: 132
  xix, 29: 34
  xx, 21: 66, 124
  xxii, 6: 42
  xxii, 10: 62
  xxvi, 8: 128
  xxvi, 25: 112
  xxvi, 27: 16

Alleged Biblical, unidentified:

B. PATRISTIC AND BIBLICAL COMMENTARY

Jerome (*cont.*):
In Ezechielem i, 4: 28
In Nahum: 180
Praefatio in Ezram: 48, 166
Prologus in librum Isaie: 166
Martin of Braga, *Formula Vitae Honestae*: 200, 256
Rabanus Maurus, *Expositio super Ieremiam* xvii: 46, 96, 278

Patristic, unidentified:

Ambrose: Sciant episcopi quia tot mortibus digni sunt, quot perdicionis ad subditos exempla prava transmittunt. (232)

Anselm: Ille difficile vitatur, qui in labiis bona portat et in corde mala occultat. (88)

Augustine: Ex quo semel aperti sunt rivuli seminis, intolerabilis est molestia carnis. (102)

Bede: Qui veneni poculum porrigit, labium calicis melle tangit, ut quod dulce est presenciatur, ne quod mortiferum est timeatur. (88)

Boethius: Res quidem puerilibus auribus accommodatas senior philosophie tractatus eliminat. (138)

Gregory: Apud Christianos miserabilior est qui infert iniuriam quam qui suffert. (238)

Jerome: Librum epistola redolere debeat. (152)

Non prodest cause, set nec honestati competens est neque modestie maledicentibus maledicere et adversarium talione mordere. (98–100)

Illum habeas comitem cuius sermo, habitus et incessus sint doctrina virtutum. (52)

Plus terram diligimus que post spinas exaratas fructus uberes producit quam que nullas spinas habuit, set tamen exculta fertilem segetem gignit. (48)

Grandis miseria ubi, quia desperatur emendacio, non adhibetur correctio. (48)

Frustra laborat doctor nisi Deus faciat ut proficiat. (46)

Multociens enim bona parantur invitis, dum eorum pocius utilitati consulitur quam voluntati. (24)

Qualis quisque est talium consorcio delectatur. (52)

Non sciencia scripturarum notum Deo facit, quem operum iniquitas indignum ostendit, quin immo quanto sciencius peccat, tanto gravius et damnabilius in Gehenne suplicia se precipitat. (234)

Biblical commentary, unidentified:

Glosa (on Gen. xlii–xliv) Verba pro verberibus irrogat fratribus, ne remaneant ipsorum vel commissa vel inpunita delicta. (24)

(on Gen. xlii–xliv) Multa erat in verbis severitas, multa in corde tranquillitas, ut hinc doceatur quantam hiis benevolentiam ostendamus quos interdum zelo correctionis et impulsu dilectionis aspere corripimus. (24)

(on Prov. xxvi, 8) Per acervum Mercurii intellige idolatriam, et honorem suple scilicet ecclesiasticum. Suggillantur enim qui dignitates ecclesiasticas carnaliter distribuunt. (128)

(on John viii, 44) Non est maledictio vel obiurgacio, quia correctio. (22)

C. CLASSICAL

Aulus Gellius, 13, 8, 3: 50
Cato
    Disticha 2, 15, 2: 164
        2, 24, 2: 256
        3, 4: 26
        4, 28: 88
    Monosticha: 186
Cicero
    De Amicitia xxvi, 97: 86
    De Inventione i, 32, 54: 214
    De Oratore ii, 9, 36: 170
    De Senectute v, 13: 64
        x, 34: 64
        xi, 35–6: 62
        xi, 37: 62

Fragmenta E ix, 1: 58
Invectiva i, 1: 162
Post Reditum ad Quirites 21: 114, 116
Tusculanarum Disputationum i, 22–3: 216
Claudian, *In Rufinum* i, 22–3: 216
Horace
    Ars Poetica 138: 30
        141–2: 54
        159: 52
        181: 188
    Epistularum i, 1, 66: 94
        i, 2, 42–3: 102
        i, 2, 68: 50
        i, 6, 45–6: 104
        i, 10, 24: 40

Classical, unidentified:

Aristoteles: Omnino protervienti omnino est adversandum. (260)

Aulus Gellius: Sine culpa mole sarcine vincitur, qui ad portandum onus, etsi impar, tamen devotus occurrit. (202)

Cicero: Plurimus mihi sermo est cum libris meis. (138)

Democritus: Iustum est nimirum ut ridentes rideantur. (32)

Martial: Virus adulator dulci sermone refundit, / Irretire volens quem facit absque metu: / Set, dum blanditur

Martial (cont.):
    vox blesa et dulcia verba / Supra
    oleum mollit, tunc tibi tu caveas. (88)
Poeta: Quo stetit equatur campo col-
    lataque nescit / Maiestatem acies;
    minuit presencia famam. (104)
Seneca: Odibilem facit hominem risus
    aut superbus et clarus aut furtivus

et malignus aut alienis malis evo-
    catus. (34)
Omnis enim amicitia vera provenit ex
    morum concordia. (34)
Vaticinium Sibille: Veniet dies et ve illis,
    quibus leges oblitterabunt scienciam
    litterarum. (122; but cf. *Op.* iv, p. 7)

D. LEGAL

Corpus Iuris Civilis
  Cod. 9, 36, 1: 160
  Dig. 7, 62, 10: 204
    14, 2, 8: 74
    26, 10, 6: 116
    36, 1, 22: 184
    47, 10, 18: 260
    50, 17, 152: 192, 214, 222, 244, 278
  Inst. 3, 25, 9: 114
Gratian, *Decretum*
  D. LXXXIII, c. 3: 22, 192, 222, 244,
    276–8
  D. LXXXVI, c. 2: 22
  D. XCIII, c. 23: 232
  D. XCIII, c. 24: 230
  D. XCIV, c. 3: 228
  D. XCV, c. 7: 228

C. I, q. 1, c. 45: 232
C. II, q. 7, c. 29: 232
C. II, q. 7, c. 32: 232
C. II, q. 7, c. 47: 230
C. II, q. 7, c. 55: 192, 222, 244–6, 278
C. II, q. 7, c. 57: 230
C. XII, q. 1, c. 21: 228
C. XII, q. 2, c. 52: 228, 262
C. XII, q. 5, c. 4: 228
C. XIV, q. 6, c. 1: 236
C. XVI, q. 1, c. 36: 268
C. XXII, q. 1, c. 17: 100
C. XXII, q. 5, c. 4: 102
Decret. Greg. IX
  i, 31, 4: 214
  iii, 39, 6: 268

E. MEDIEVAL, PROVERBIAL, FLORILEGIA
(Often unacknowledged)

'Caecilius Balbus' (see p. 86, note on
  175–6)
  xv, 6: 108
  xv, 11: 116
  xv, 12: 88
  xxiii, 3: 116
  xxiv, 3: 114
John of Salisbury, *Policraticus*: 50, 52, 100
  Epp. 177, 254: 94
Marcialis Cocus (Godfrey of Winchester):
  24
Petrus Alphonsus, *Disciplina Clericalis*:
  260
Petrus Cantor, *Verbum Abbreviatum* ch. 2:
  170, 184
  6: 280
  7: 232
  46: 274
  47: 148–50
  70: 50, 52, 90, 96
  71: 148
  123: 226
  139: 124, 224
Peter of Blois, *Canon episcopalis*: 192,
  234

Sapiens (? Giraldus): 40, 102, 122, 180
Serlon de Wilton 76, 1: 136
  76, 2: 122
Walter Map, *De Nugis Curialium*: 46, 52,
  94, 136, 140, 198, 246, 248
H. Walther, *Lateinische Sprichwörter* no.
  141: 136
  1257a: 140
  2710: 32
  3597: 52
  8952: 18, 146
  10077a: 102
  21550a: 102
  21709b: 40

Medieval, unidentified:

Episcopus papae: Ubi non delinquimus,
  pares sumus. (230)
Eugenius: Fili, vacasti iuventute; sterilem
  habebis senectutem; nunquam in
  vita mea promoveberis. (44)
Poeta: Detestor morum crimina, corpus
  amo. (22)
Tunc prima est inculpabilis etas, / Cum
  ludis ponunt tempora metas. (138)

INDEX

References are to *pages* of this book. The following abbreviations are used: abp. = archbishop; bp. = bishop; Mr. = magister. Persons are generally indexed under their family name, not their Christian name. Giraldus, uncle and nephew, are indexed under 'Barri'; in cross-references they are referred to as 'Mr. Giraldus' and 'the young Giraldus' respectively